W9-AMP-840

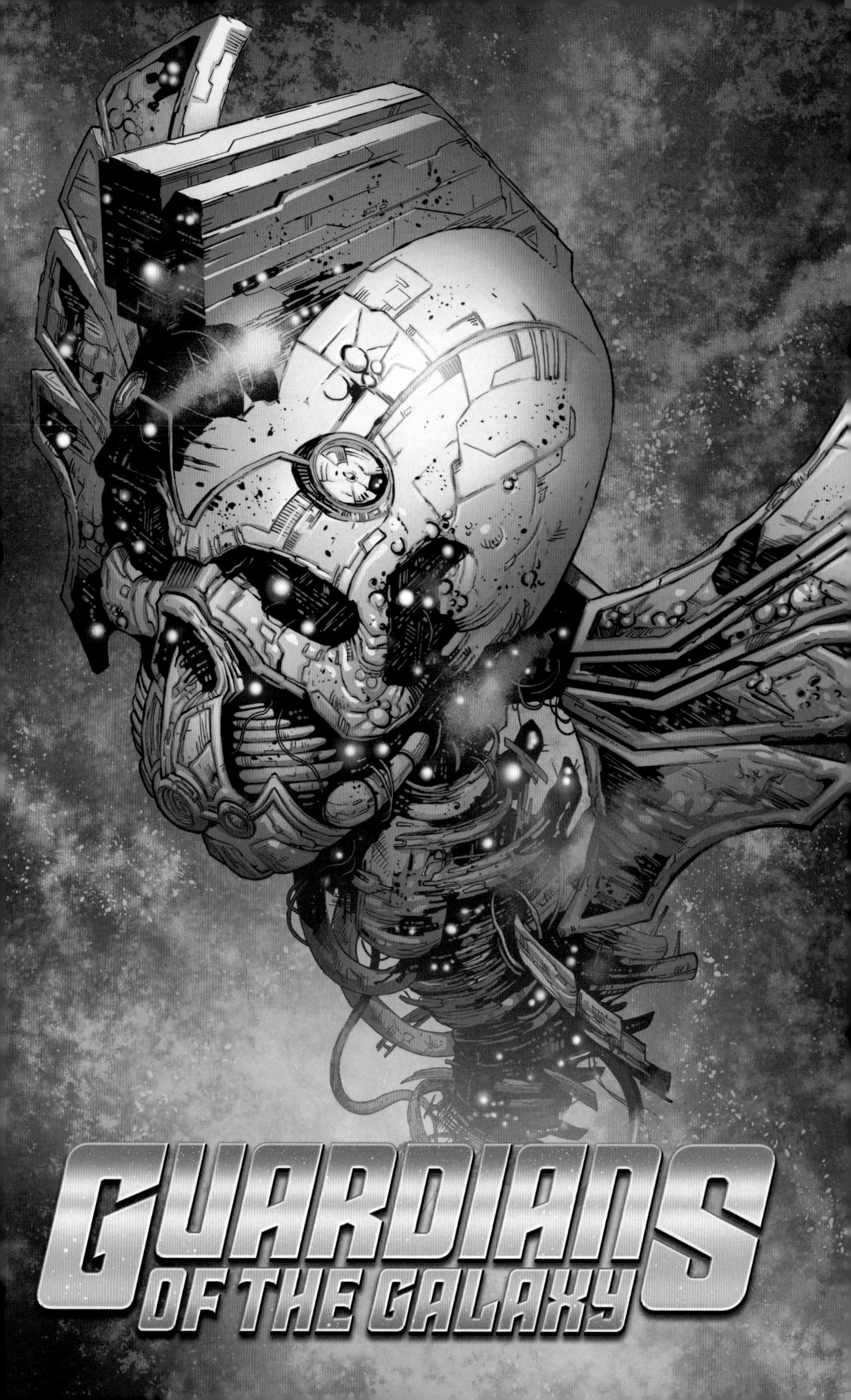
GUARDIANS
OF THE GALAXY

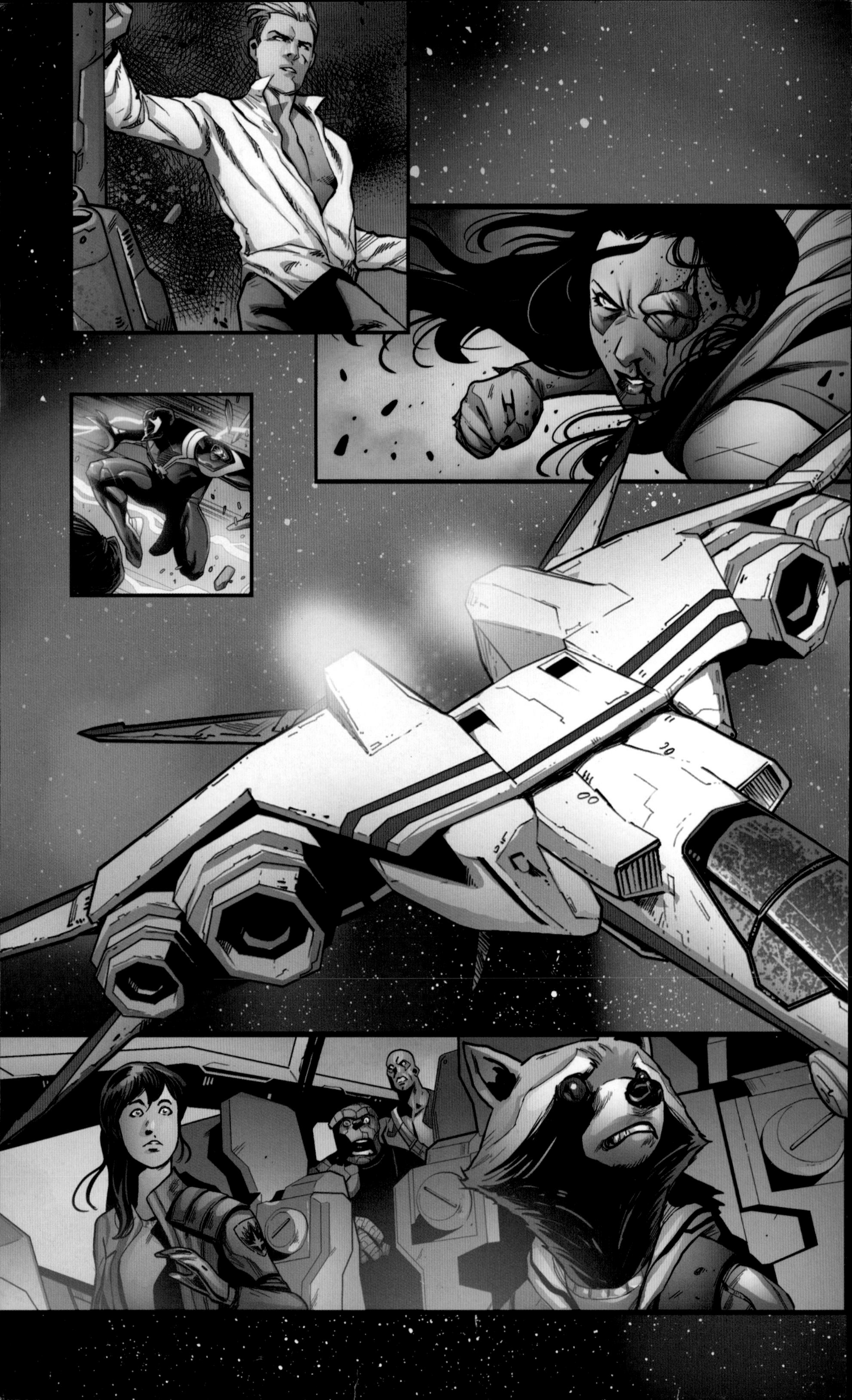

GUARDIANS OF THE GALAXY

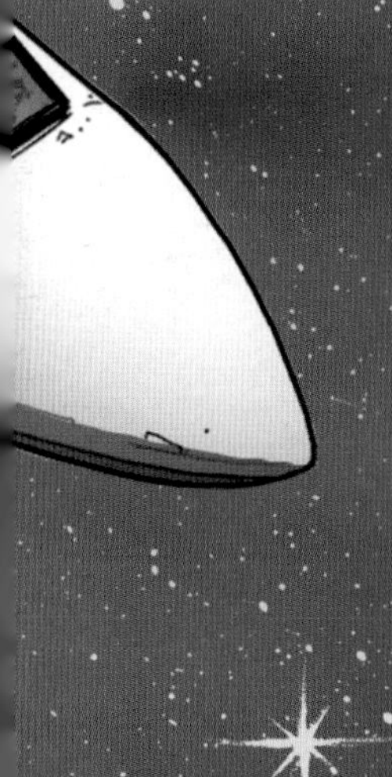

BRIAN MICHAEL BENDIS
WRITER

VALERIO SCHITI
ARTIST

RICHARD ISANOVE
COLOR ARTIST

VC'S CORY PETIT
LETTERER

ART ADAMS COVER ARTIST

DAVE STEWART (#1), **JASON KEITH** (#2, #4-10) & **PETER STEIGERWALD** (#3)
COVER COLORISTS

KATHLEEN WISNESKI
ASSISTANT EDITOR

JAKE THOMAS
ASSOCIATE EDITOR

NICK LOWE
EDITOR

COLLECTION EDITOR: *JENNIFER GRÜNWALD*
ASSISTANT EDITOR: *CAITLIN O'CONNELL*
ASSOCIATE MANAGING EDITOR: *KATERI WOODY*
EDITOR, SPECIAL PROJECTS: *MARK D. BEAZLEY*
VP PRODUCTION & SPECIAL PROJECTS: *JEFF YOUNGQUIST*
SVP PRINT, SALES & MARKETING: *DAVID GABRIEL*
BOOK DESIGNER: *JAY BOWEN*

EDITOR IN CHIEF: *AXEL ALONSO*
CHIEF CREATIVE OFFICER: *JOE QUESADA*
PRESIDENT: *DAN BUCKLEY*
EXECUTIVE PRODUCER: *ALAN FINE*

[GU]ARDIANS OF THE GALAXY VOL. 4. Contains material originally published in magazine form as GUARDIANS OF THE GALAXY #1-10. First printing 2017. ISBN# 978-1-302-90437-1. Published by MARVEL WORLDWIDE, INC., a subsidiary of [MA]RVEL ENTERTAINMENT, LLC. OFFICE OF PUBLICATION: 135 West 50th Street, New York, NY 10020. Copyright © 2017 MARVEL No similarity between any of the names, characters, persons, and/or institutions in this magazine with those [of a]ny living or dead person or institution is intended, and any such similarity which may exist is purely coincidental. **Printed in China.** DAN BUCKLEY, President, Marvel Entertainment; JOE QUESADA, Chief Creative Officer; TOM BREVOORT, [SVP] of Publishing; DAVID BOGART, SVP of Business Affairs & Operations, Publishing & Partnership; C.B. CEBULSKI, VP of Brand Management & Development, Asia; DAVID GABRIEL, SVP of Sales & Marketing, Publishing; JEFF YOUNGQUIST, [VP o]f Production & Special Projects; DAN CARR, Executive Director of Publishing Technology; ALEX MORALES, Director of Publishing Operations; SUSAN CRESPI, Production Manager; STAN LEE, Chairman Emeritus. For information regarding [adv]ertising in Marvel Comics or on Marvel.com, please contact Vit DeBellis, Integrated Sales Manager, at vdebellis@marvel.com. For Marvel subscription inquiries, please call 888-511-5480. **Manufactured between 8/11/2017 and [9/]23/2017 by R.R. DONNELLEY ASIA PRINTING SOLUTIONS, CHINA.**

[10] 9 8 7 6 5 4 3 2 1

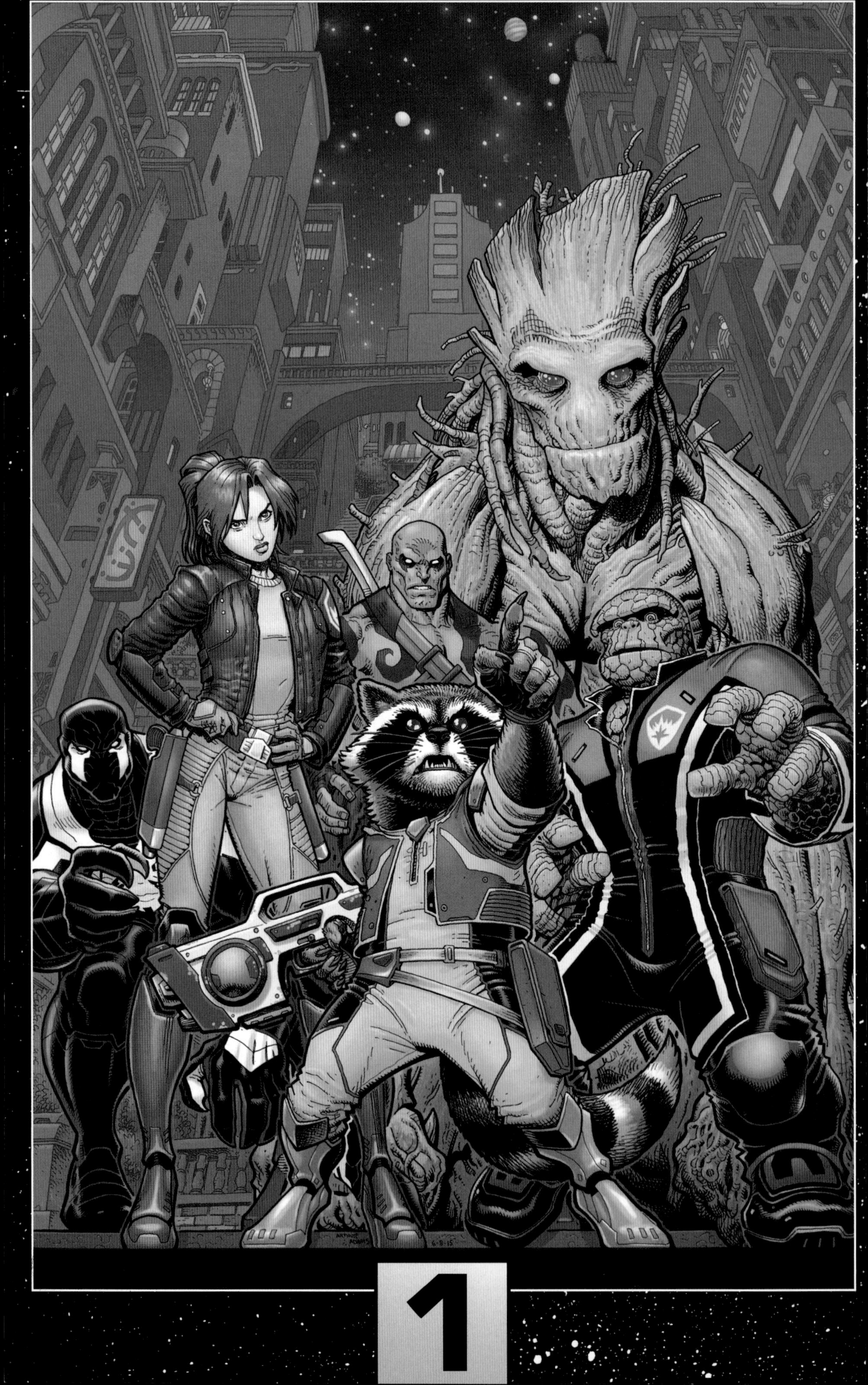

1

The entire galaxy is a mess. Warring empires and cosmic terrorists plague every corner. Someone has to rise above it all and fight for those who have no one to fight for them. Against their natures, a group of misanthropes and misfits came together to serve a higher cause. **Drax the Destroyer**, **Gamora**, the most dangerous woman in the universe, **Rocket Raccoon**, **Groot**, and **Flash Thompson**, a.k.a. **Venom** all joined together under the leadership of **Peter Quill, Star-Lord** to be the saviors of the spaceways, the conservators of the cosmos, the…

But things have changed.

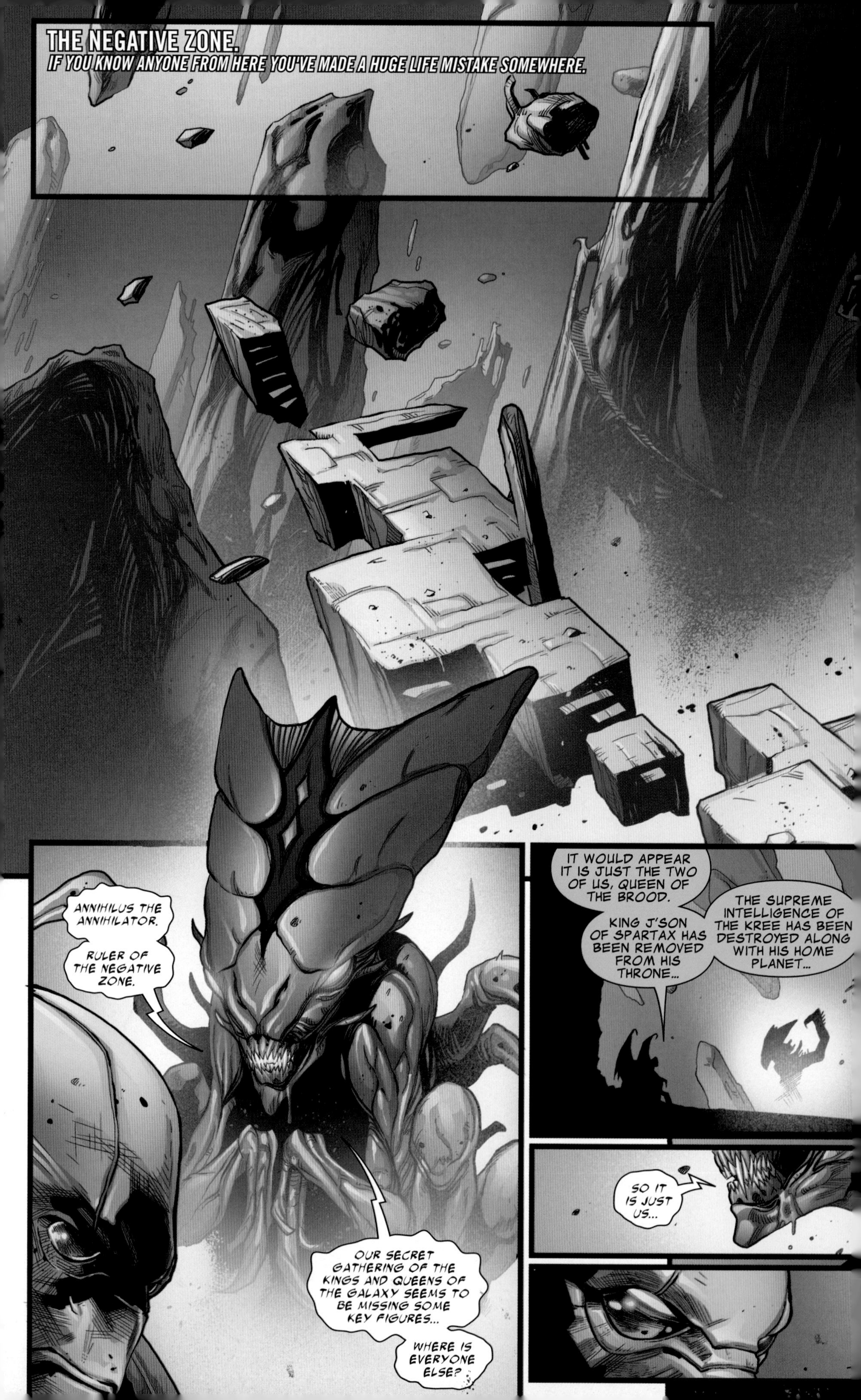
THE NEGATIVE ZONE.
IF YOU KNOW ANYONE FROM HERE YOU'VE MADE A HUGE LIFE MISTAKE SOMEWHERE.
ANNIHILUS THE ANNIHILATOR.
RULER OF THE NEGATIVE ZONE.
OUR SECRET GATHERING OF THE KINGS AND QUEENS OF THE GALAXY SEEMS TO BE MISSING SOME KEY FIGURES...
WHERE IS EVERYONE ELSE?
IT WOULD APPEAR IT IS JUST THE TWO OF US, QUEEN OF THE BROOD.
KING J'SON OF SPARTAX HAS BEEN REMOVED FROM HIS THRONE...
THE SUPREME INTELLIGENCE OF THE KREE HAS BEEN DESTROYED ALONG WITH HIS HOME PLANET...
SO IT IS JUST US...

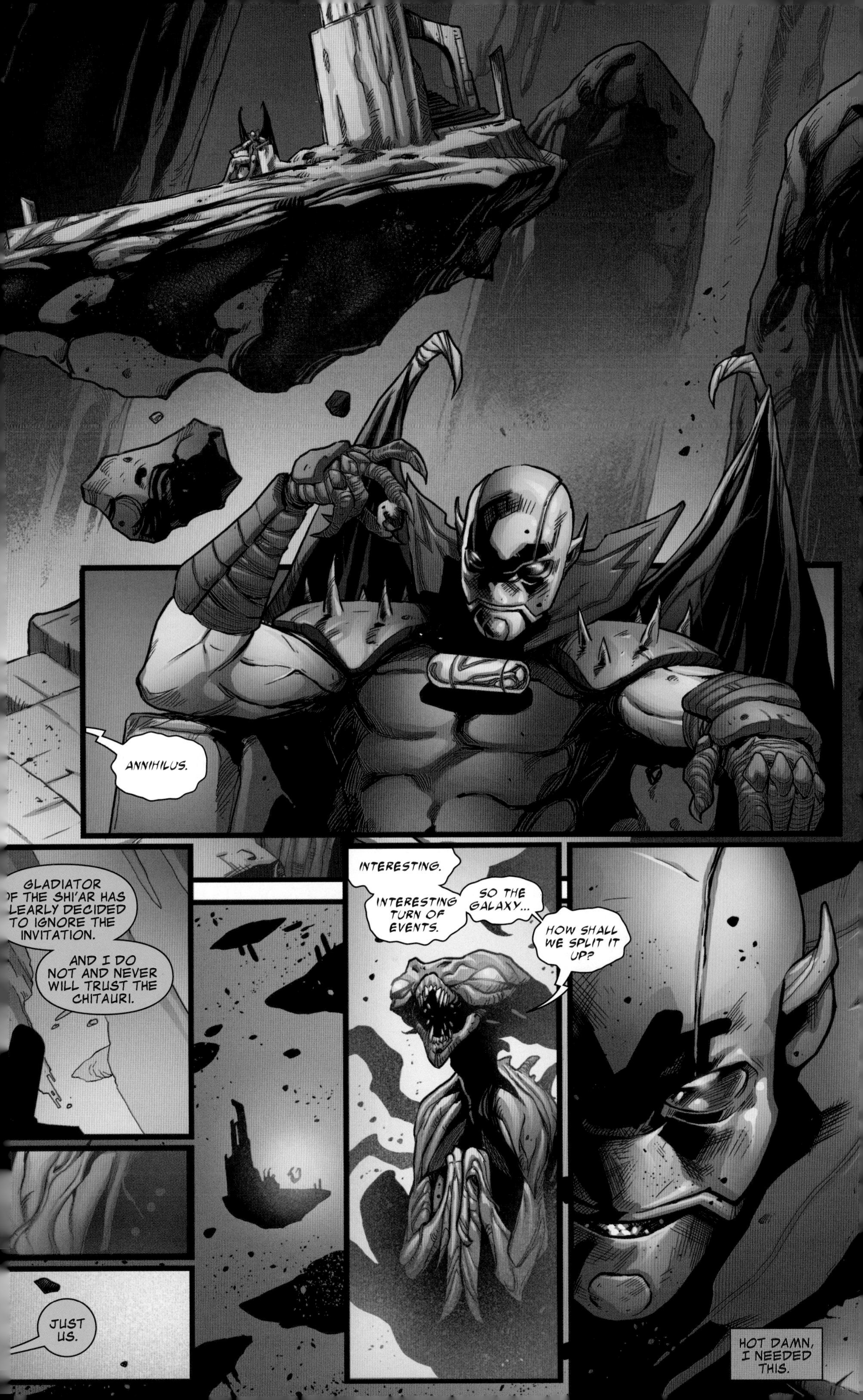
ANNIHILUS.
GLADIATOR OF THE SHI'AR HAS CLEARLY DECIDED TO IGNORE THE INVITATION.
AND I DO NOT AND NEVER WILL TRUST THE CHITAURI.
JUST US.
INTERESTING.
INTERESTING TURN OF EVENTS.
SO THE GALAXY...
HOW SHALL WE SPLIT IT UP?
HOT DAMN, I NEEDED THIS.

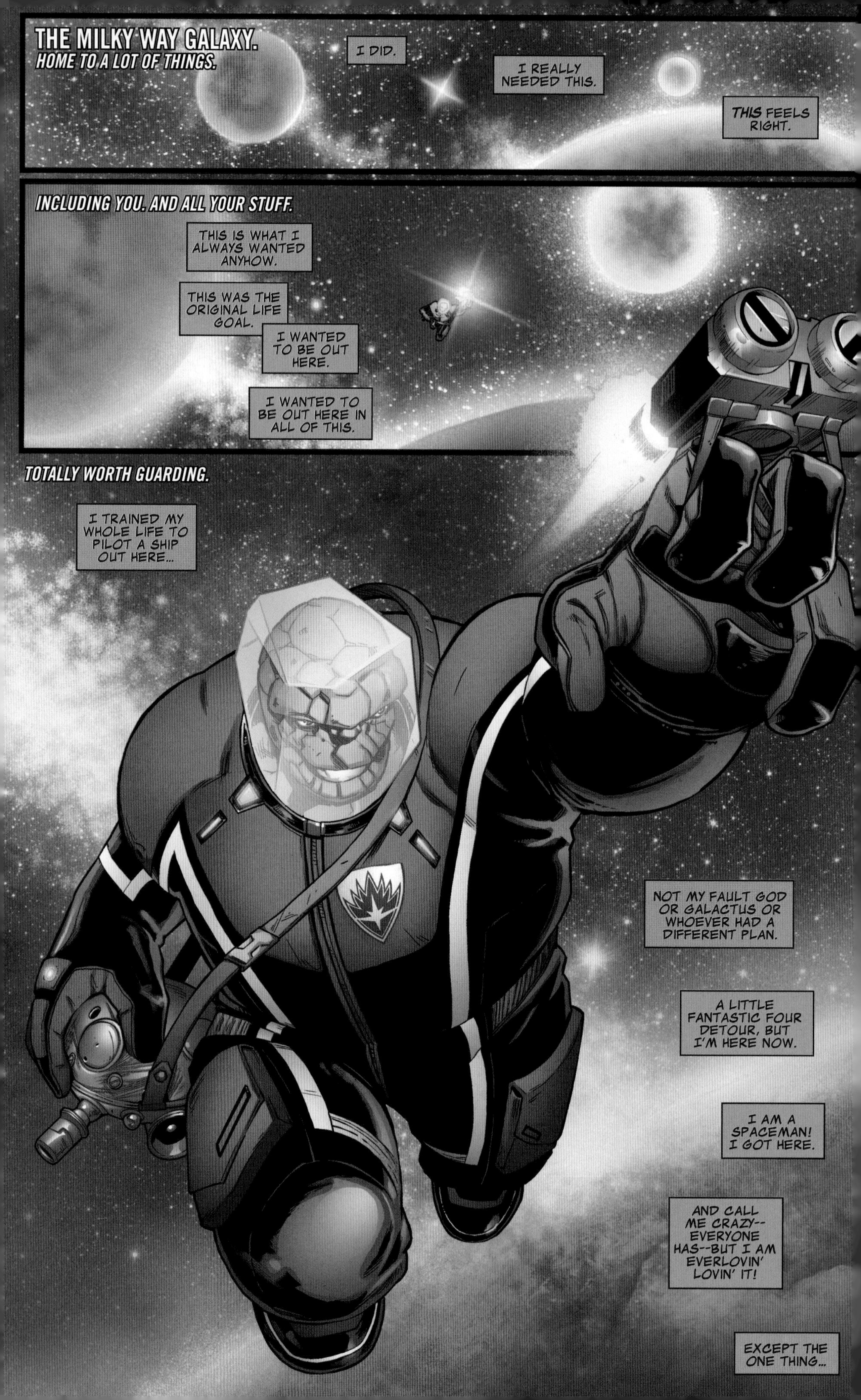
THE MILKY WAY GALAXY.
HOME TO A LOT OF THINGS.
I DID.
I REALLY NEEDED THIS.
THIS FEELS RIGHT.
INCLUDING YOU. AND ALL YOUR STUFF.
THIS IS WHAT I ALWAYS WANTED ANYHOW.
THIS WAS THE ORIGINAL LIFE GOAL.
I WANTED TO BE OUT HERE.
I WANTED TO BE OUT HERE IN ALL OF THIS.
TOTALLY WORTH GUARDING.
I TRAINED MY WHOLE LIFE TO PILOT A SHIP OUT HERE...
NOT MY FAULT GOD OR GALACTUS OR WHOEVER HAD A DIFFERENT PLAN.
A LITTLE FANTASTIC FOUR DETOUR, BUT I'M HERE NOW.
I AM A SPACEMAN! I GOT HERE.
AND CALL ME CRAZY--EVERYONE HAS--BUT I AM EVERLOVIN' LOVIN' IT!
EXCEPT THE ONE THING...

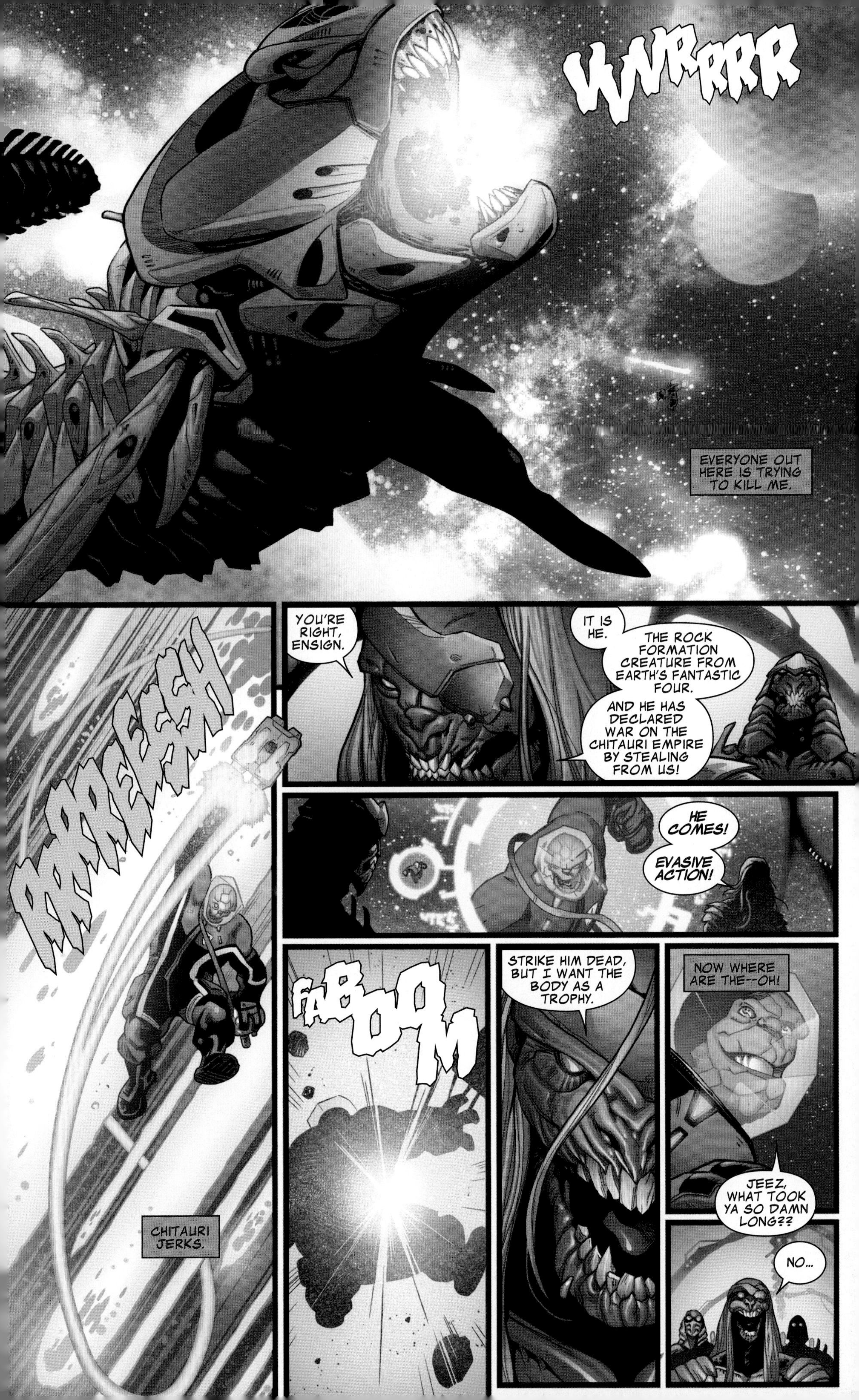
WWRRRR
EVERYONE OUT HERE IS TRYING TO KILL ME.
RRRREEESH
CHITAURI JERKS.
YOU'RE RIGHT, ENSIGN.
IT IS HE.
THE ROCK FORMATION CREATURE FROM EARTH'S FANTASTIC FOUR.
AND HE HAS DECLARED WAR ON THE CHITAURI EMPIRE BY STEALING FROM US!
HE COMES!
EVASIVE ACTION!
FABOOOM
STRIKE HIM DEAD, BUT I WANT THE BODY AS A TROPHY.
NOW WHERE ARE THE--OH!
JEEZ, WHAT TOOK YA SO DAMN LONG??
NO...

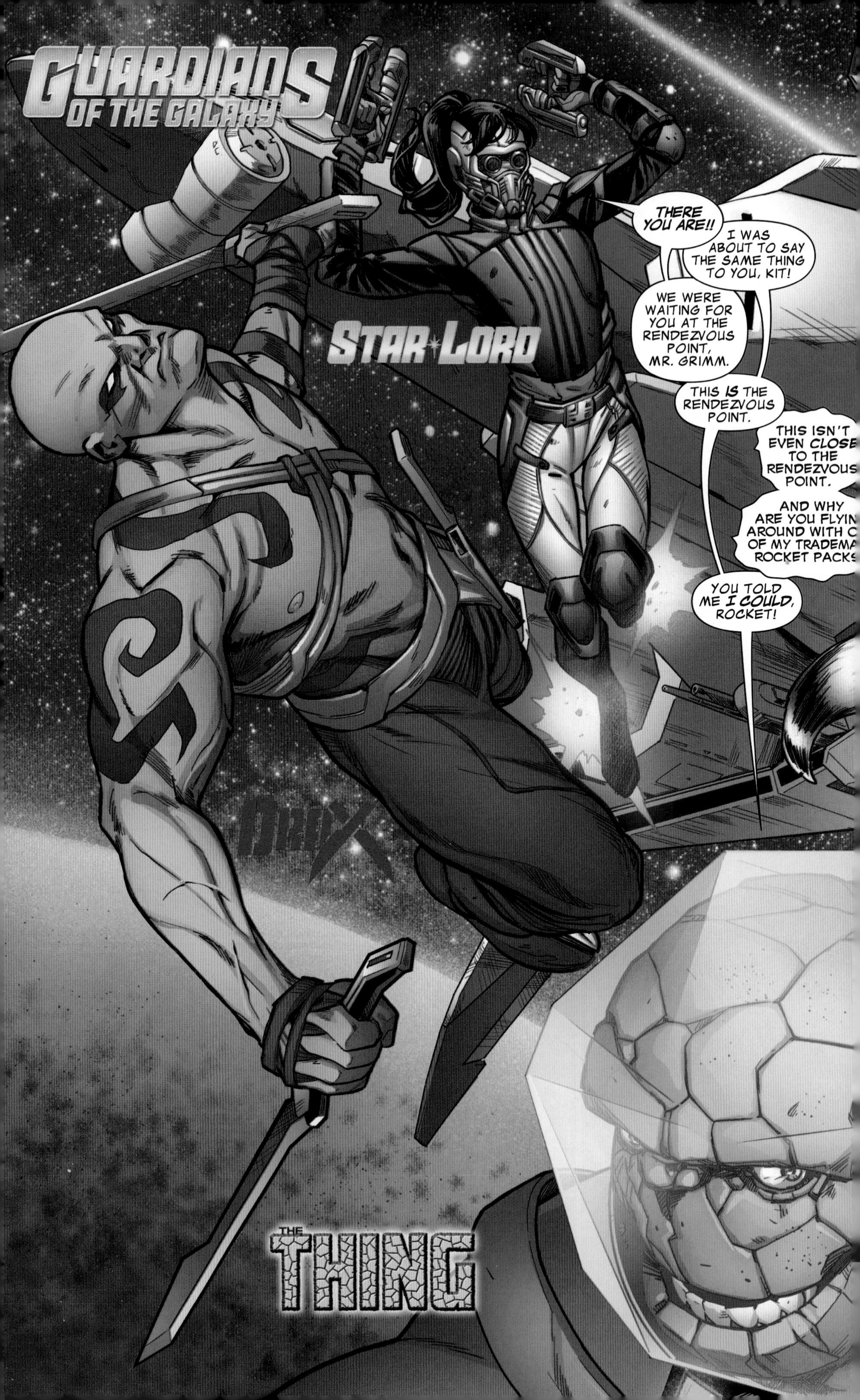
GUARDIANS OF THE GALAXY
STAR-LORD
THERE YOU ARE!!
I WAS ABOUT TO SAY THE SAME THING TO YOU, KIT!
WE WERE WAITING FOR YOU AT THE RENDEZVOUS POINT, MR. GRIMM.
THIS IS THE RENDEZVOUS POINT.
THIS ISN'T EVEN CLOSE TO THE RENDEZVOUS POINT.
YOU TOLD ME I COULD, ROCKET!
THE THING

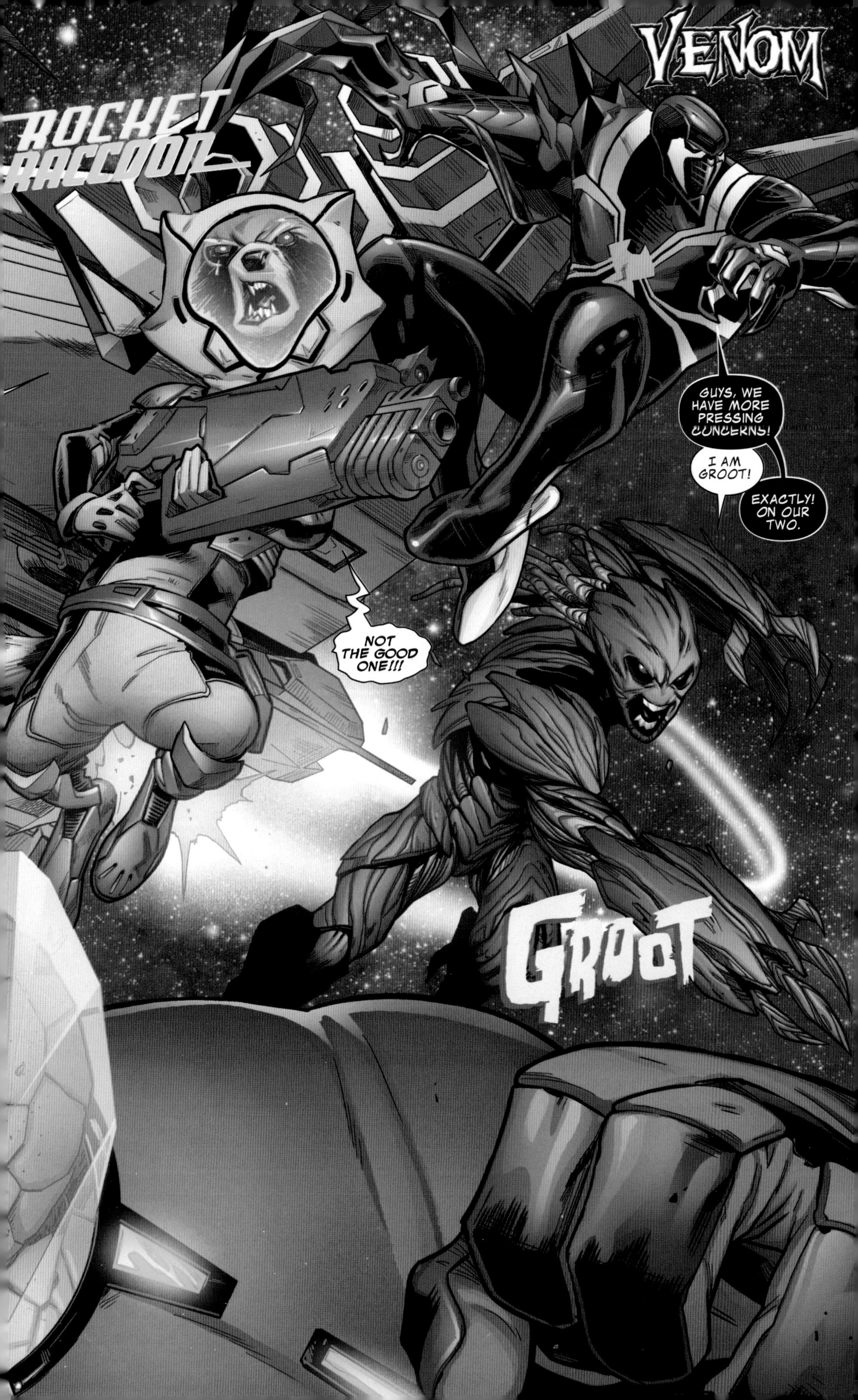
VENOM
ROCKET RACCOON
GUYS, WE HAVE MORE PRESSING CONCERNS!
I AM GROOT!
EXACTLY! ON OUR TWO.
NOT THE GOOD ONE!!!
GROOT

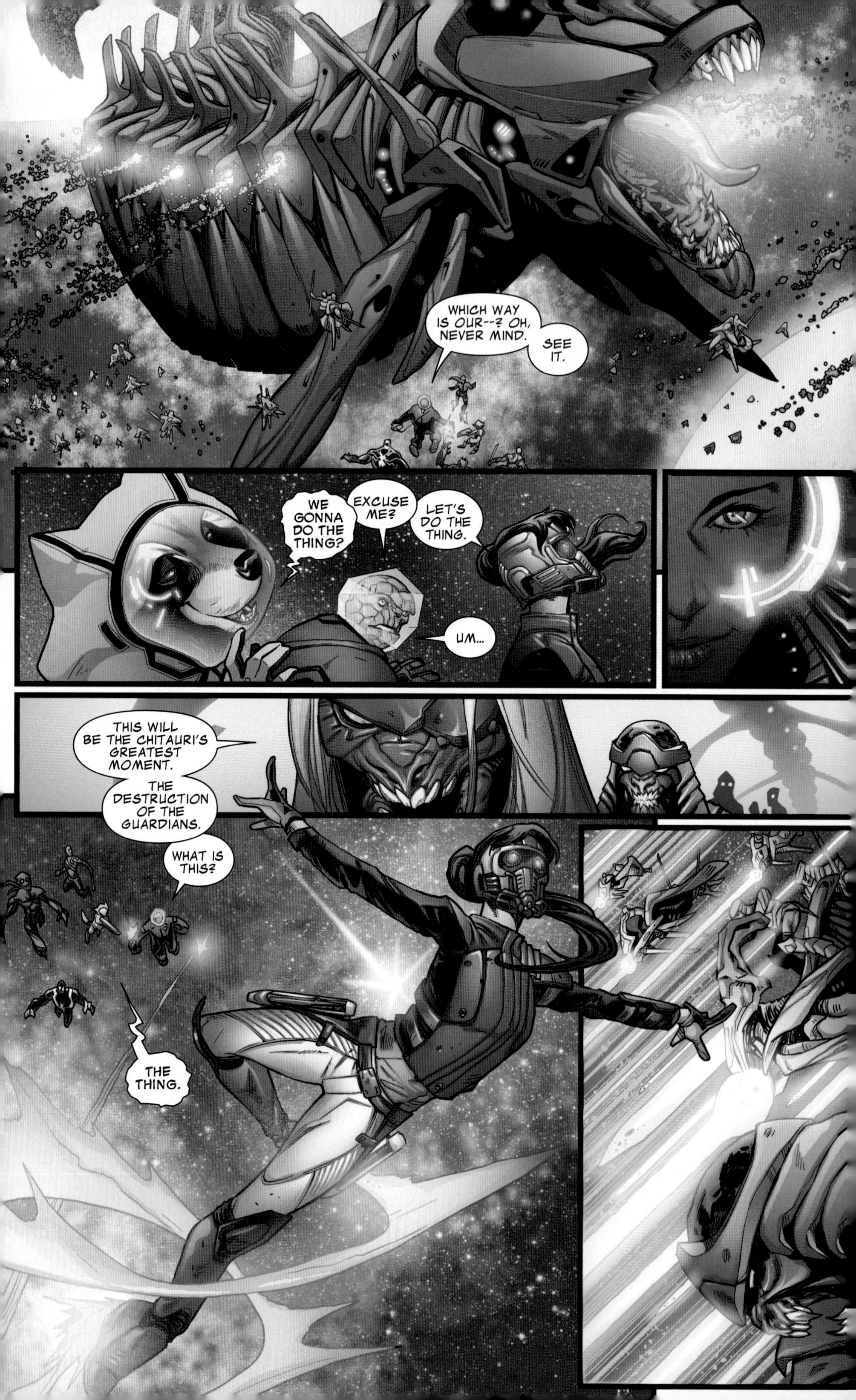
WHICH WAY IS OUR--? OH, NEVER MIND.
SEE IT.
WE GONNA DO THE THING?
EXCUSE ME?
LET'S DO THE THING.
UM...
THIS WILL BE THE CHITAURI'S GREATEST MOMENT.
THE DESTRUCTION OF THE GUARDIANS.
WHAT IS THIS?
THE THING.

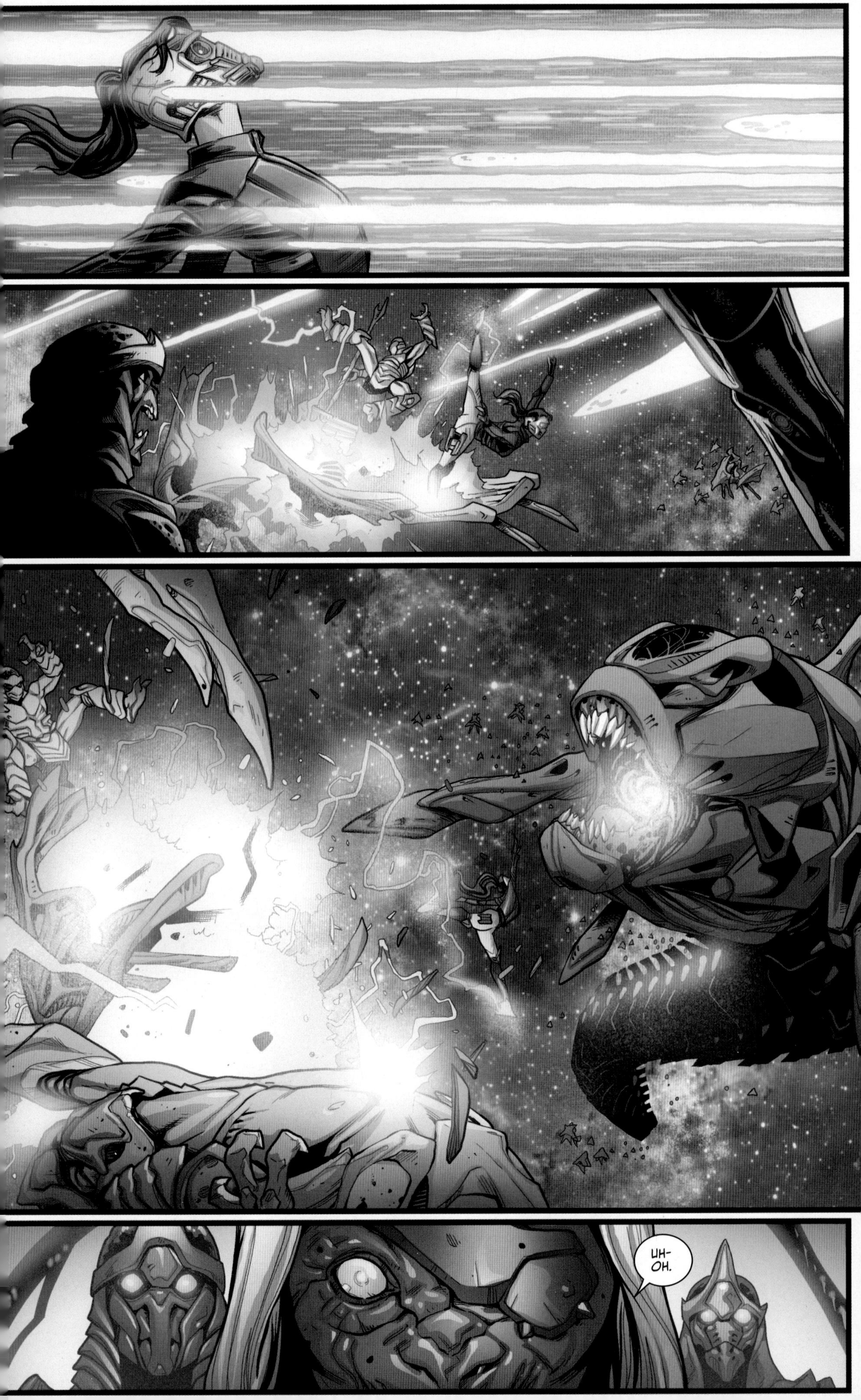
UH-OH.

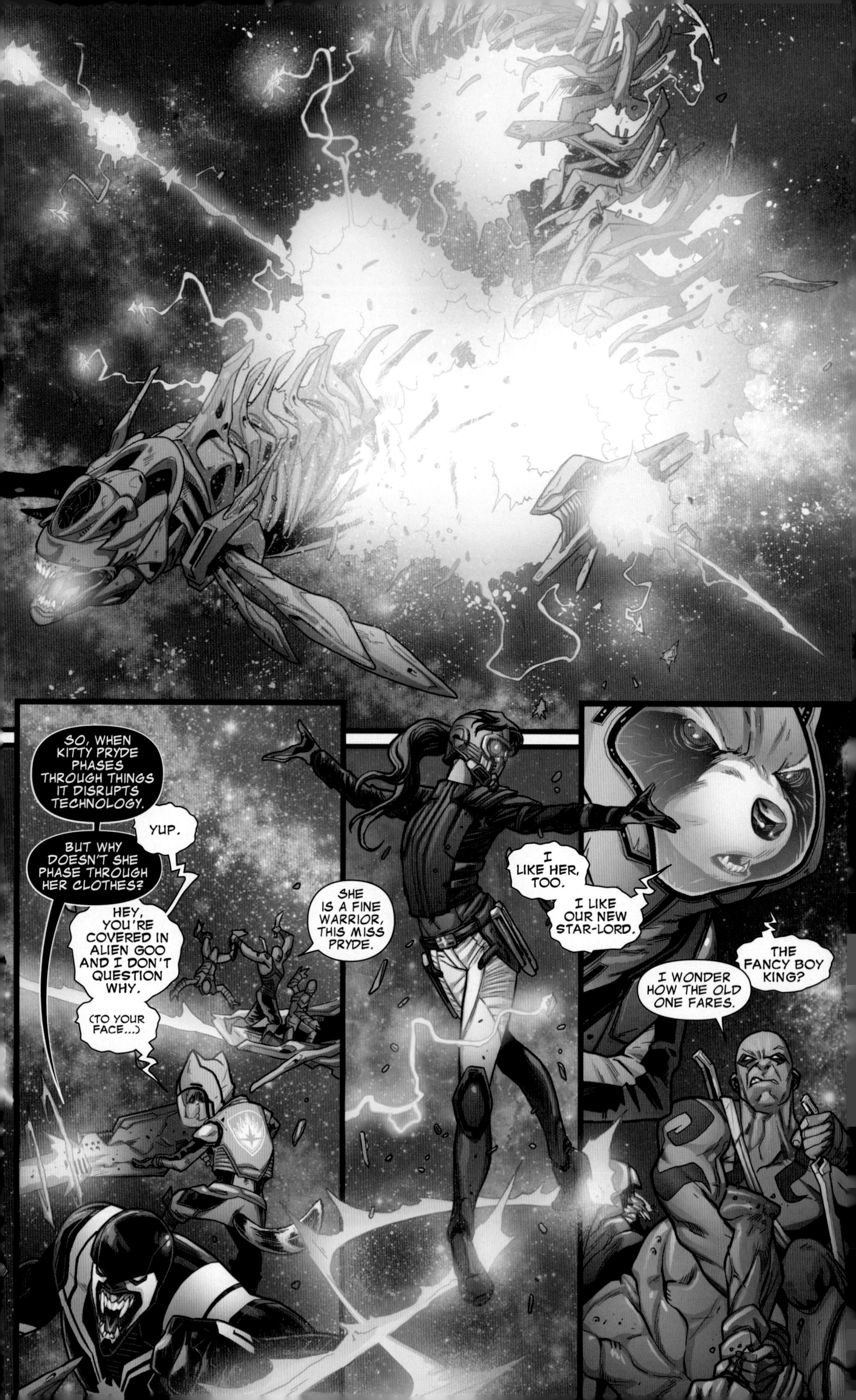
SO, WHEN KITTY PRYDE PHASES THROUGH THINGS IT DISRUPTS TECHNOLOGY.
YUP.
BUT WHY DOESN'T SHE PHASE THROUGH HER CLOTHES?
HEY, YOU'RE COVERED IN ALIEN GOO AND I DON'T QUESTION WHY.
(TO YOUR FACE...)
SHE IS A FINE WARRIOR, THIS MISS PRYDE.
I LIKE HER, TOO.
I LIKE OUR NEW STAR-LORD.
I WONDER HOW THE OLD ONE FARES.
THE FANCY BOY KING?

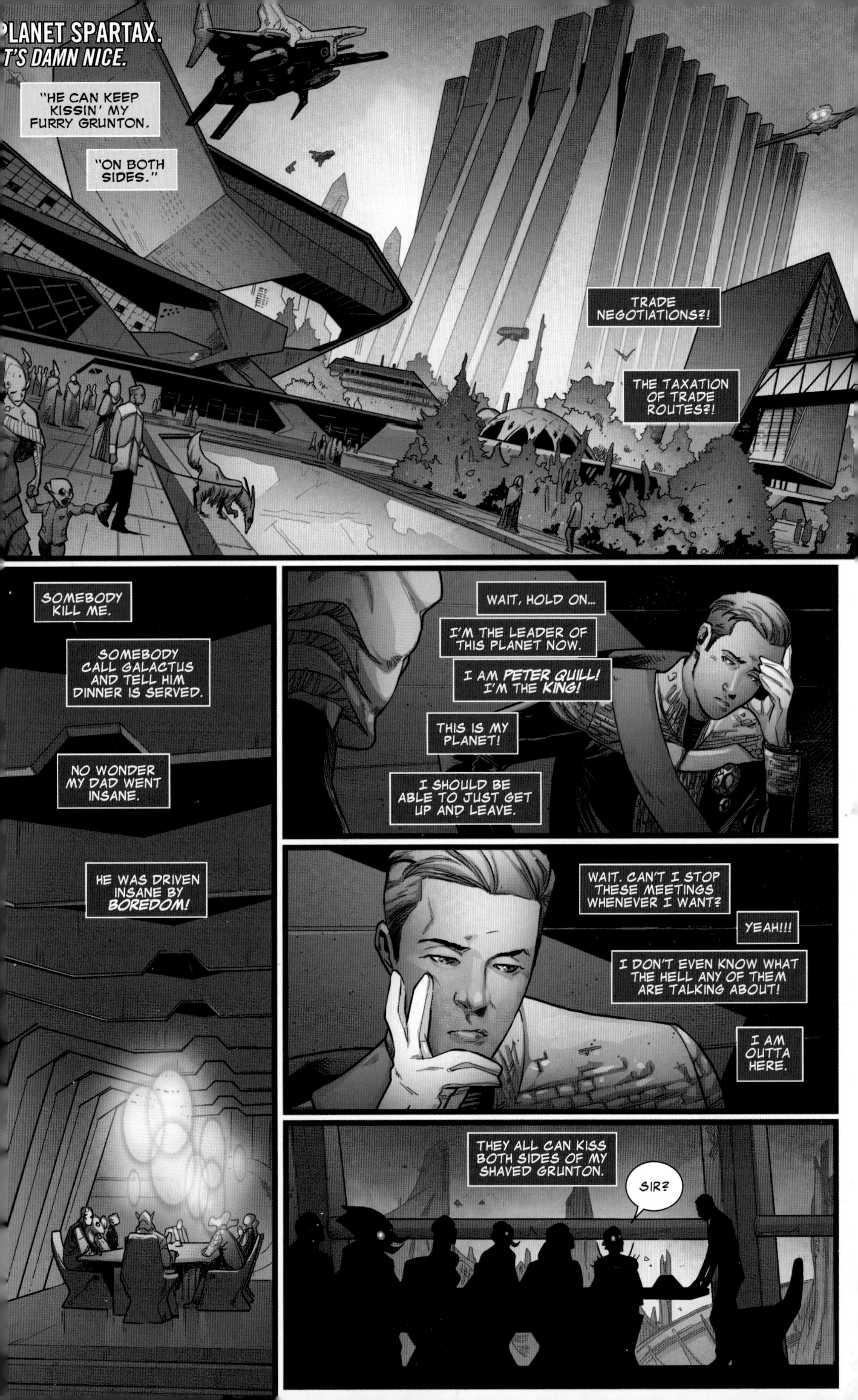

PLANET SPARTAX.
T'S DAMN NICE.
"HE CAN KEEP KISSIN' MY FURRY GRUNTON.
"ON BOTH SIDES."
TRADE NEGOTIATIONS?!
THE TAXATION OF TRADE ROUTES?!
SOMEBODY KILL ME.
SOMEBODY CALL GALACTUS AND TELL HIM DINNER IS SERVED.
NO WONDER MY DAD WENT INSANE.
HE WAS DRIVEN INSANE BY BOREDOM!
WAIT, HOLD ON...
I'M THE LEADER OF THIS PLANET NOW.
I AM PETER QUILL! I'M THE KING!
THIS IS MY PLANET!
I SHOULD BE ABLE TO JUST GET UP AND LEAVE.
WAIT. CAN'T I STOP THESE MEETINGS WHENEVER I WANT?
YEAH!!!
I DON'T EVEN KNOW WHAT THE HELL ANY OF THEM ARE TALKING ABOUT!
I AM OUTTA HERE.
THEY ALL CAN KISS BOTH SIDES OF MY SHAVED GRUNTON.
SIR?

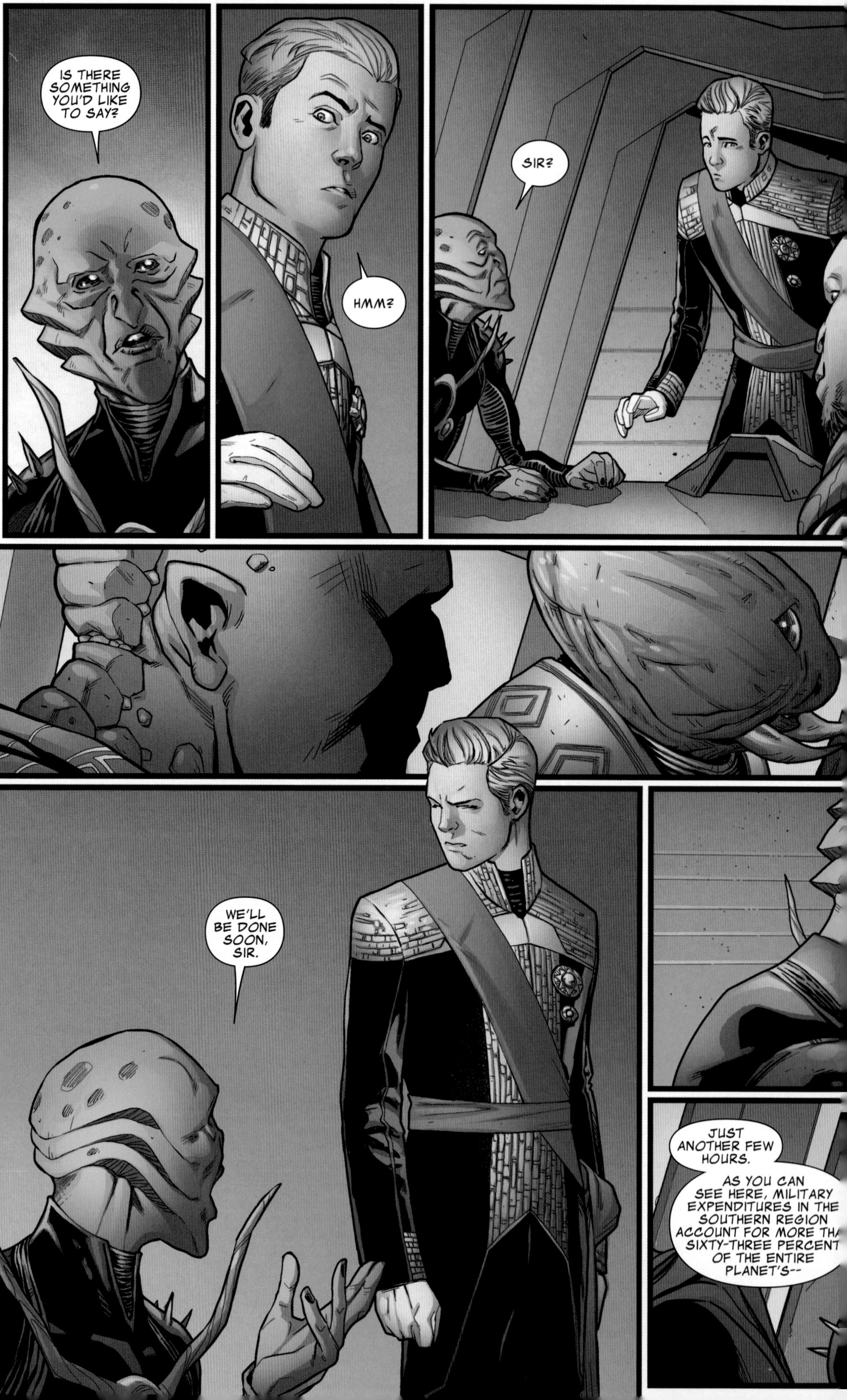
IS THERE SOMETHING YOU'D LIKE TO SAY?
HMM?
SIR?
WE'LL BE DONE SOON, SIR.
JUST ANOTHER FEW HOURS.
AS YOU CAN SEE HERE, MILITARY EXPENDITURES IN THE SOUTHERN REGION ACCOUNT FOR MORE THA SIXTY-THREE PERCENT OF THE ENTIRE PLANET'S--

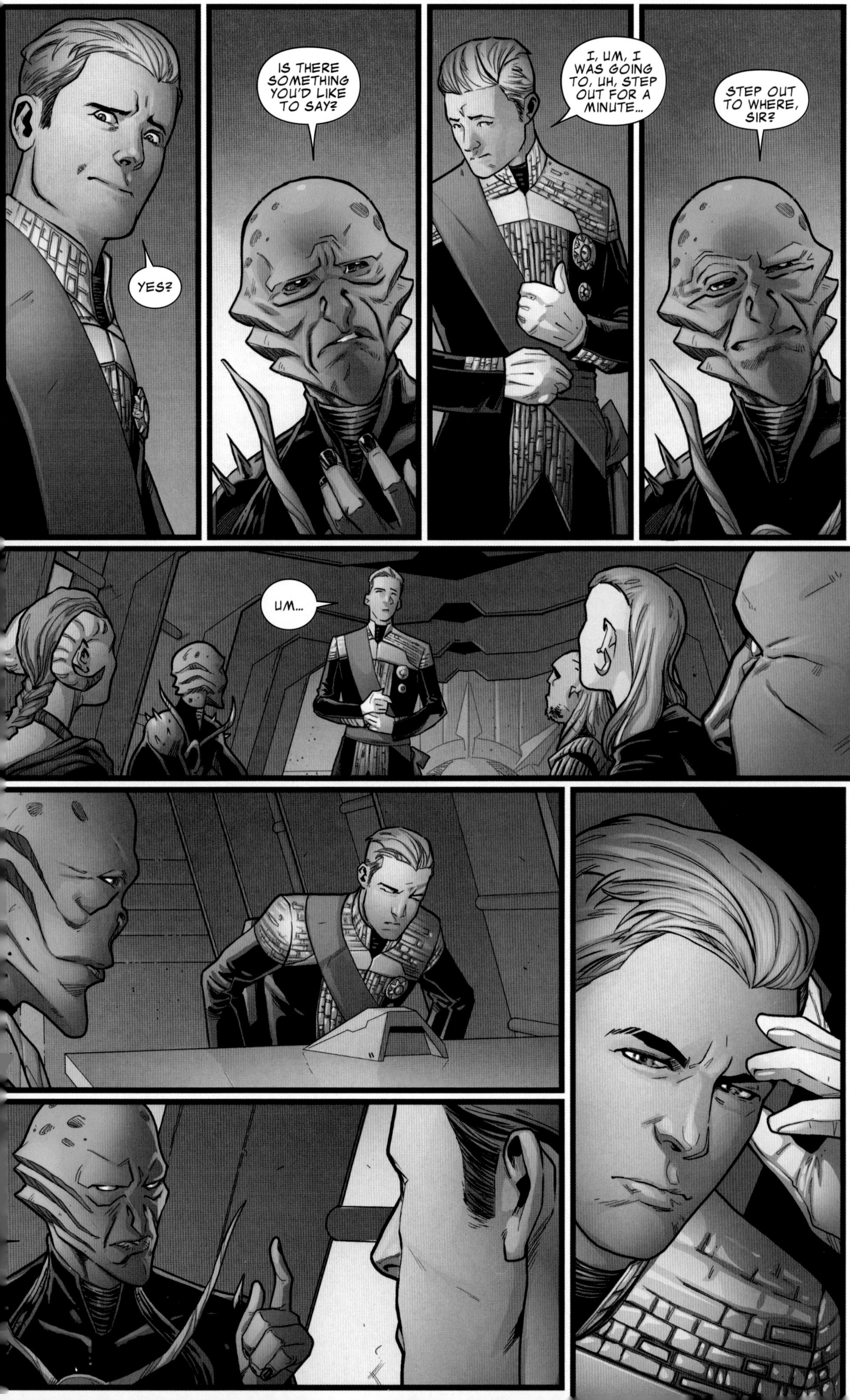
YES?
IS THERE SOMETHING YOU'D LIKE TO SAY?
I, UM, I WAS GOING TO, UH, STEP OUT FOR A MINUTE...
STEP OUT TO WHERE, SIR?
UM...

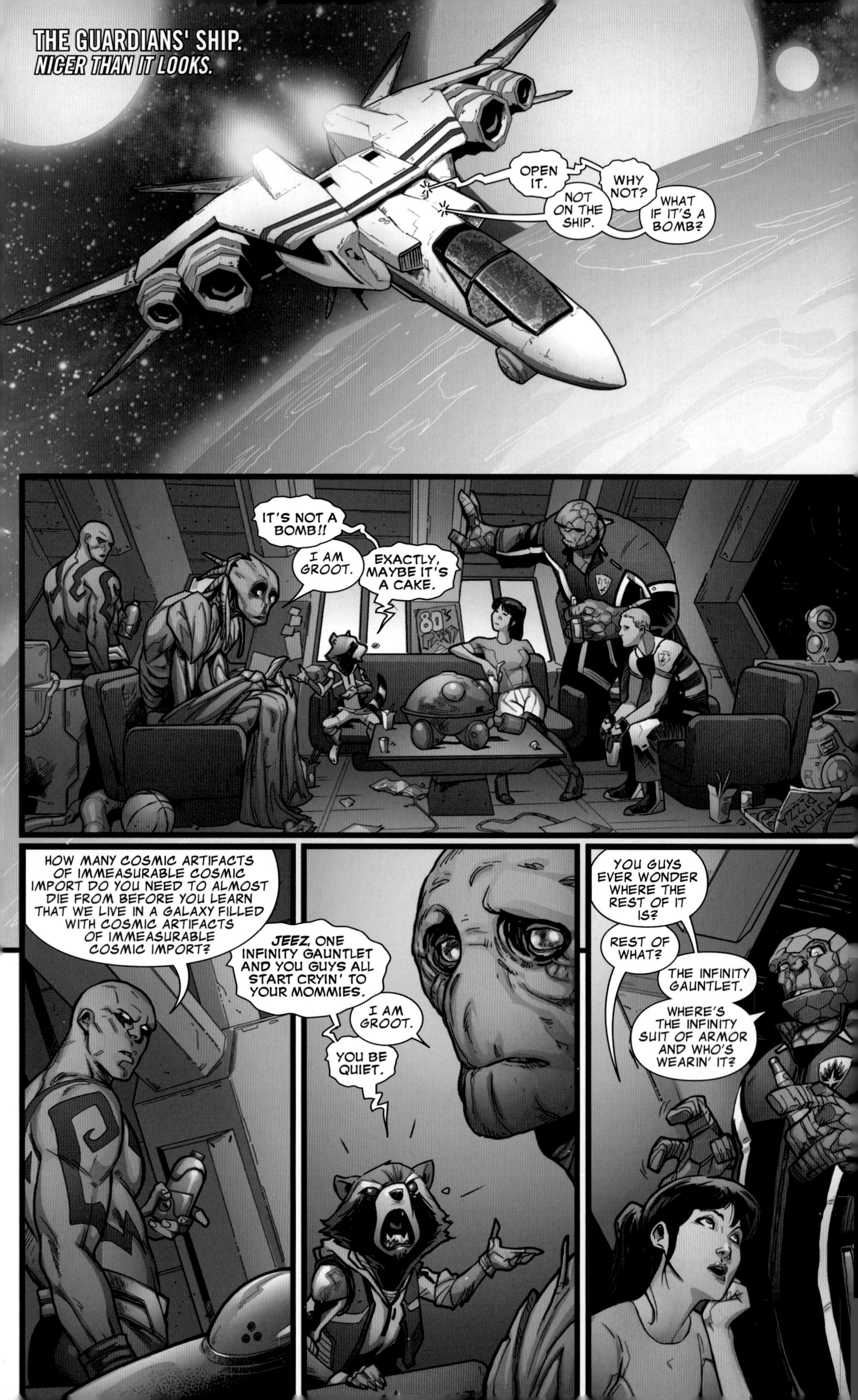
THE GUARDIANS' SHIP.
NICER THAN IT LOOKS.
OPEN IT.
WHY NOT?
NOT ON THE SHIP.
WHAT IF IT'S A BOMB?
IT'S NOT A BOMB!!
I AM GROOT.
EXACTLY, MAYBE IT'S A CAKE.
HOW MANY COSMIC ARTIFACTS OF IMMEASURABLE COSMIC IMPORT DO YOU NEED TO ALMOST DIE FROM BEFORE YOU LEARN THAT WE LIVE IN A GALAXY FILLED WITH COSMIC ARTIFACTS OF IMMEASURABLE COSMIC IMPORT?
JEEZ, ONE INFINITY GAUNTLET AND YOU GUYS ALL START CRYIN' TO YOUR MOMMIES.
I AM GROOT.
YOU BE QUIET.
YOU GUYS EVER WONDER WHERE THE REST OF IT IS?
REST OF WHAT?
THE INFINITY GAUNTLET.
WHERE'S THE INFINITY SUIT OF ARMOR AND WHO'S WEARIN' IT?

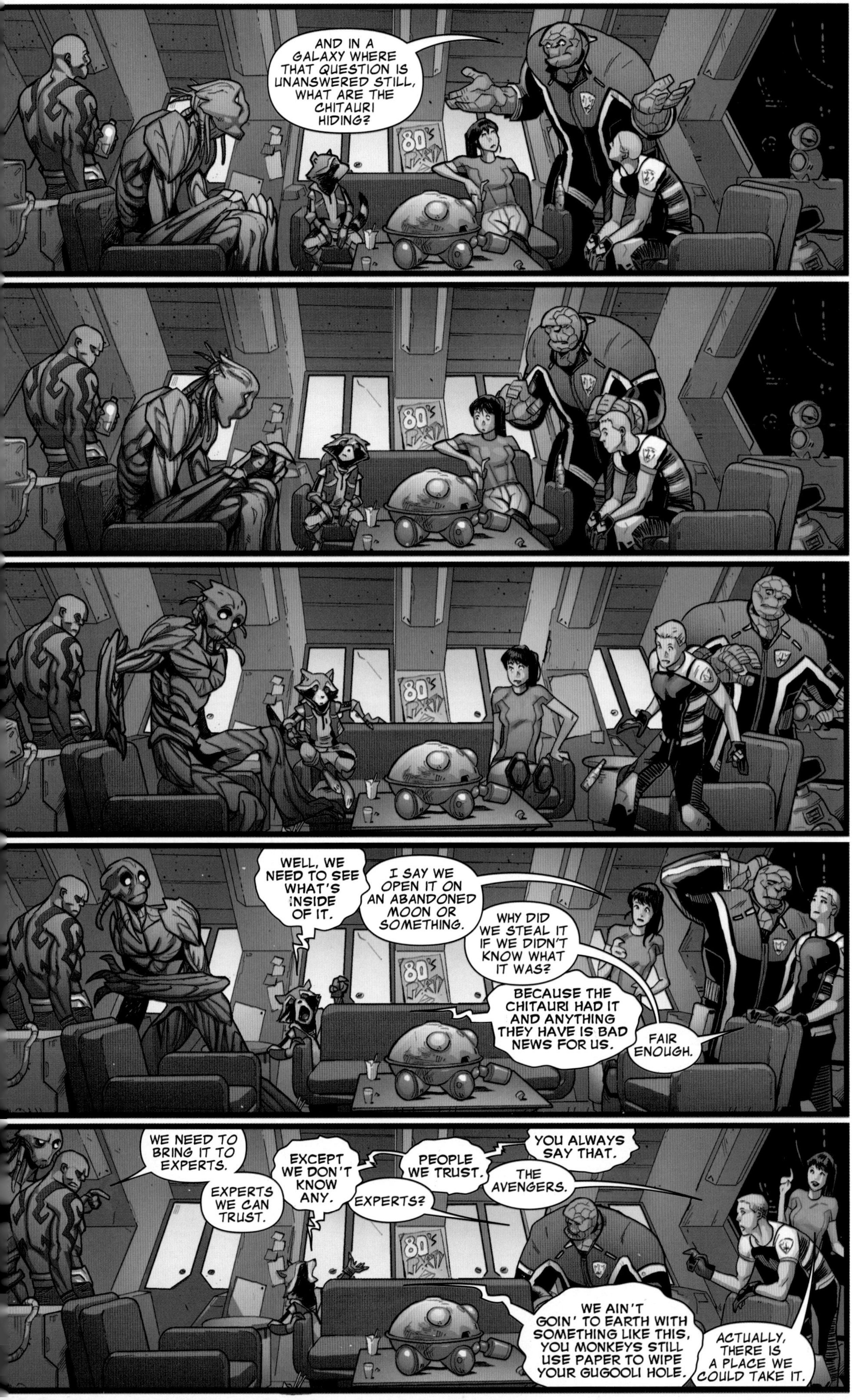
AND IN A GALAXY WHERE THAT QUESTION IS UNANSWERED STILL, WHAT ARE THE CHITAURI HIDING?
80's
80's
80's
WELL, WE NEED TO SEE WHAT'S INSIDE OF IT.
I SAY WE OPEN IT ON AN ABANDONED MOON OR SOMETHING.
WHY DID WE STEAL IT IF WE DIDN'T KNOW WHAT IT WAS?
BECAUSE THE CHITAURI HAD IT AND ANYTHING THEY HAVE IS BAD NEWS FOR US.
FAIR ENOUGH.
80's
WE NEED TO BRING IT TO EXPERTS.
EXPERTS WE CAN TRUST.
EXCEPT WE DON'T KNOW ANY.
EXPERTS?
PEOPLE WE TRUST.
YOU ALWAYS SAY THAT.
THE AVENGERS.
80's
WE AIN'T GOIN' TO EARTH WITH SOMETHING LIKE THIS, YOU MONKEYS STILL USE PAPER TO WIPE YOUR GUGOOLI HOLE.
ACTUALLY, THERE IS A PLACE WE COULD TAKE IT.

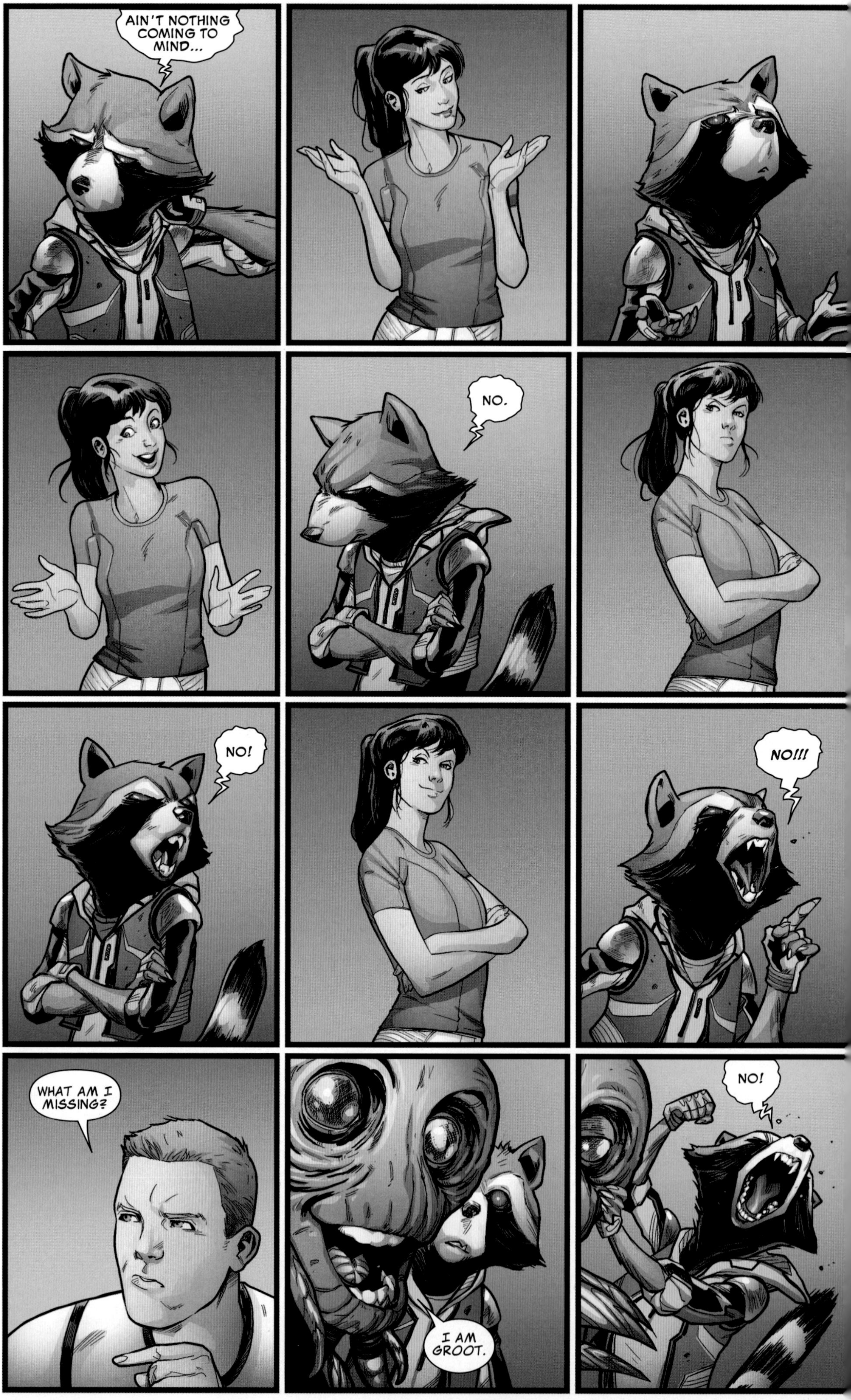
AIN'T NOTHING COMING TO MIND...
NO.
NO!
NO!!!
WHAT AM I MISSING?
I AM GROOT.
NO!

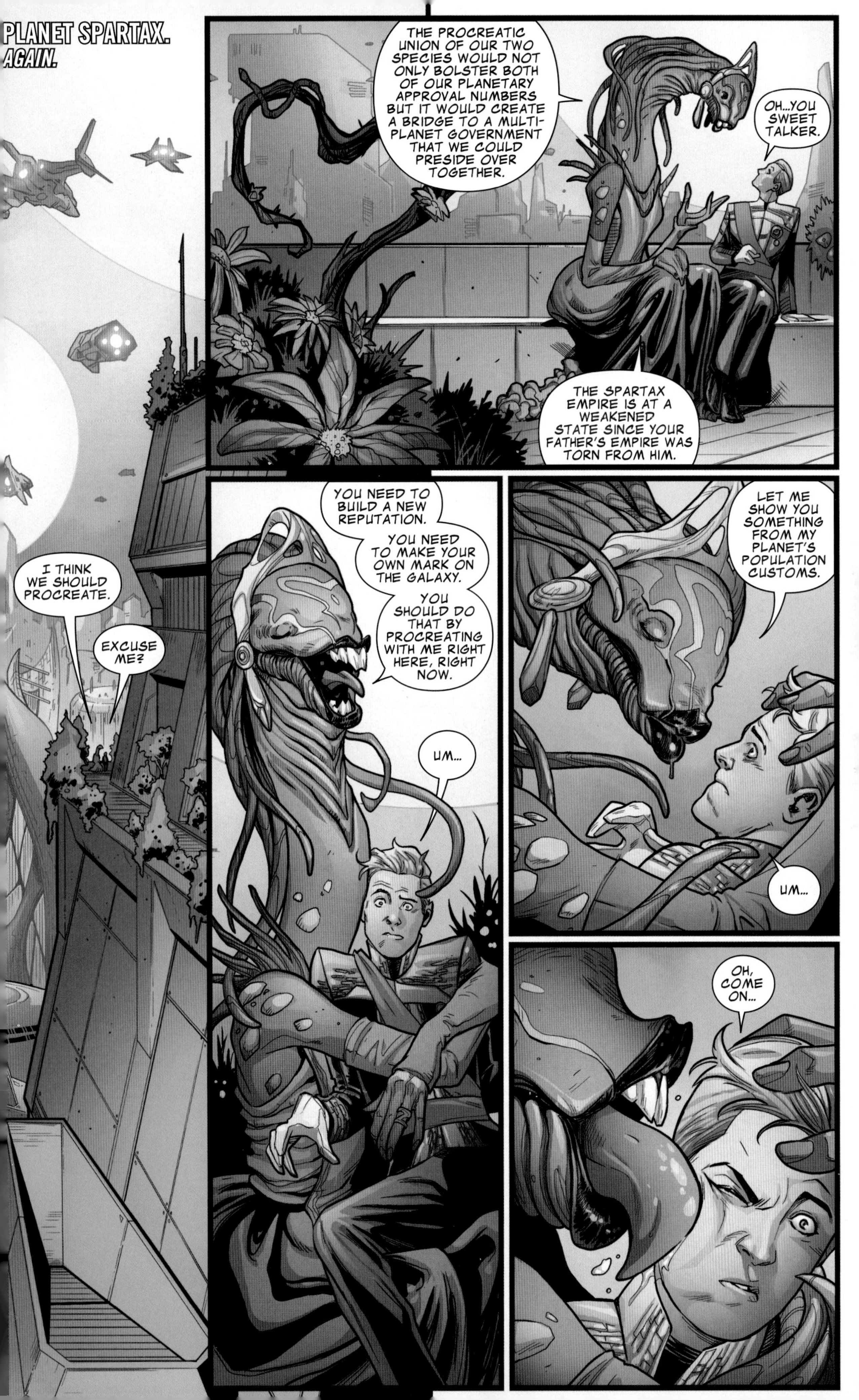
PLANET SPARTAX. AGAIN.
THE PROCREATIC UNION OF OUR TWO SPECIES WOULD NOT ONLY BOLSTER BOTH OF OUR PLANETARY APPROVAL NUMBERS BUT IT WOULD CREATE A BRIDGE TO A MULTI-PLANET GOVERNMENT THAT WE COULD PRESIDE OVER TOGETHER.
OH...YOU SWEET TALKER.
THE SPARTAX EMPIRE IS AT A WEAKENED STATE SINCE YOUR FATHER'S EMPIRE WAS TORN FROM HIM.
I THINK WE SHOULD PROCREATE.
EXCUSE ME?
YOU NEED TO BUILD A NEW REPUTATION.
YOU NEED TO MAKE YOUR OWN MARK ON THE GALAXY.
YOU SHOULD DO THAT BY PROCREATING WITH ME RIGHT HERE, RIGHT NOW.
UM...
LET ME SHOW YOU SOMETHING FROM MY PLANET'S POPULATION CUSTOMS.
UM...
OH, COME ON...

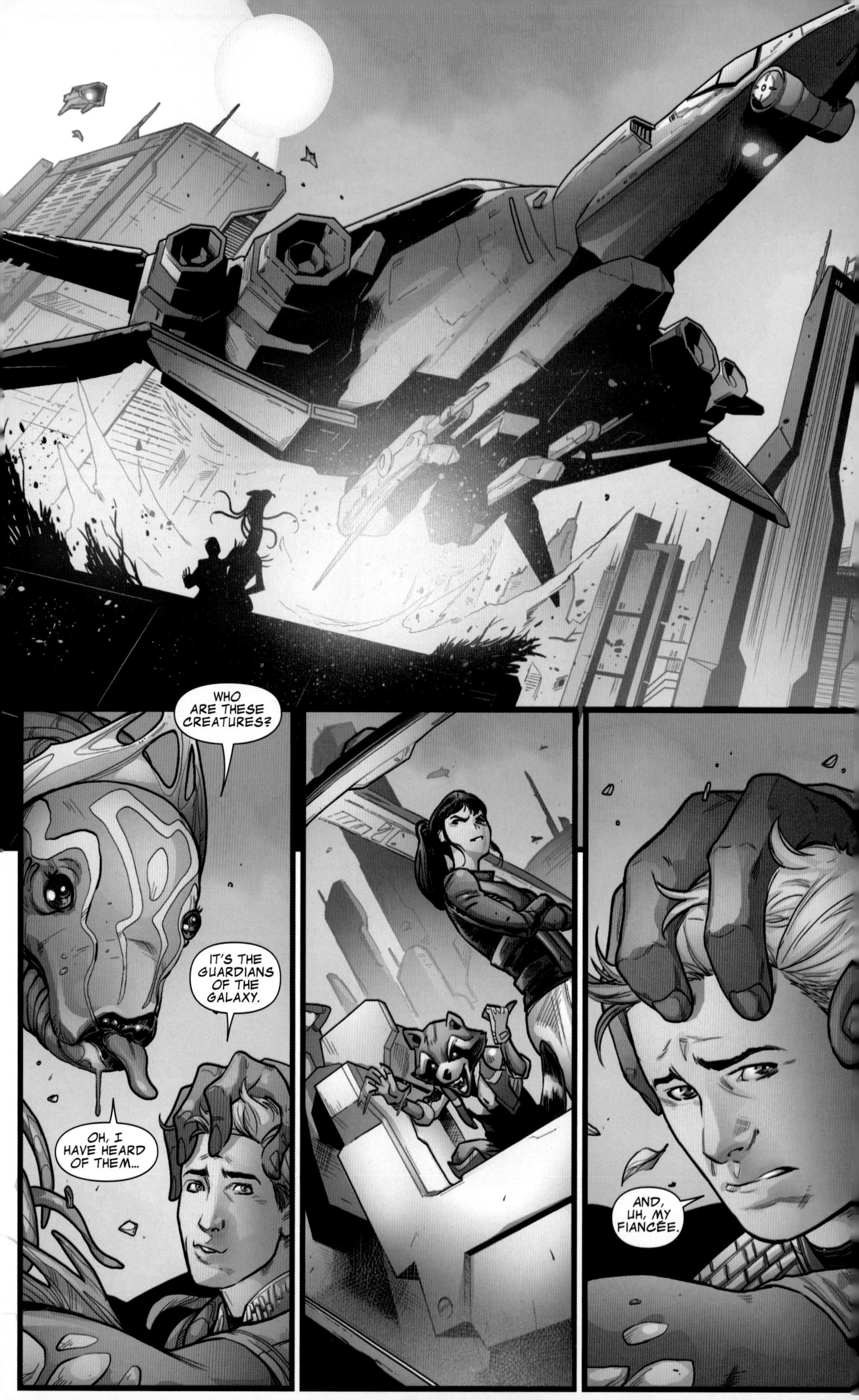
WHO ARE THESE CREATURES?
IT'S THE GUARDIANS OF THE GALAXY.
OH, I HAVE HEARD OF THEM...
AND, UH, MY FIANCÉE.

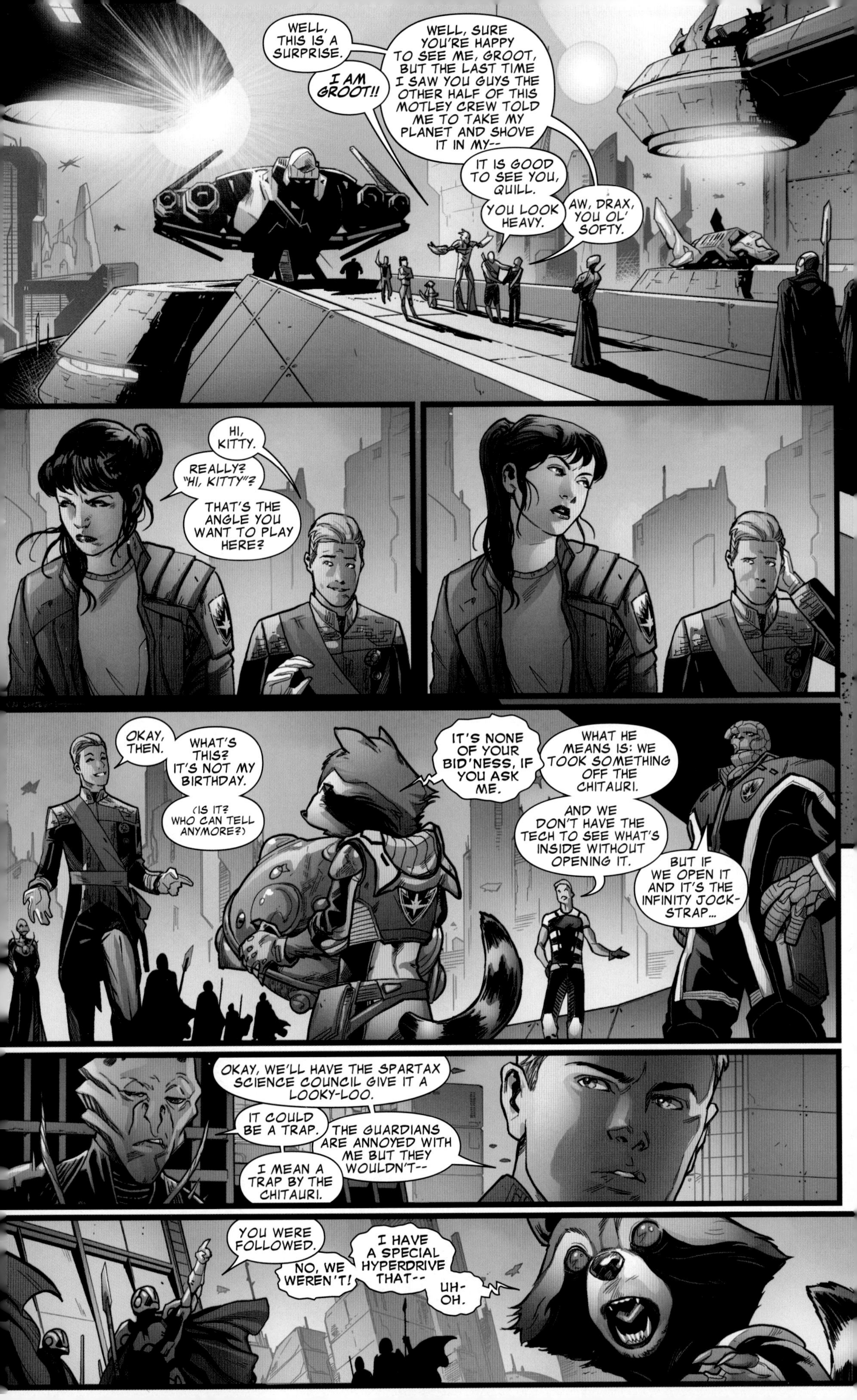

WELL, THIS IS A SURPRISE.
I AM GROOT!!
WELL, SURE YOU'RE HAPPY TO SEE ME, GROOT, BUT THE LAST TIME I SAW YOU GUYS THE OTHER HALF OF THIS MOTLEY CREW TOLD ME TO TAKE MY PLANET AND SHOVE IT IN MY--
IT IS GOOD TO SEE YOU, QUILL.
YOU LOOK HEAVY.
AW, DRAX, YOU OL' SOFTY.
HI, KITTY.
REALLY? "HI, KITTY"?
THAT'S THE ANGLE YOU WANT TO PLAY HERE?
OKAY, THEN.
WHAT'S THIS? IT'S NOT MY BIRTHDAY.
(IS IT? WHO CAN TELL ANYMORE?)
IT'S NONE OF YOUR BID'NESS, IF YOU ASK ME.
WHAT HE MEANS IS: WE TOOK SOMETHING OFF THE CHITAURI.
AND WE DON'T HAVE THE TECH TO SEE WHAT'S INSIDE WITHOUT OPENING IT.
BUT IF WE OPEN IT AND IT'S THE INFINITY JOCK-STRAP...
OKAY, WE'LL HAVE THE SPARTAX SCIENCE COUNCIL GIVE IT A LOOKY-LOO.
IT COULD BE A TRAP.
THE GUARDIANS ARE ANNOYED WITH ME BUT THEY WOULDN'T--
I MEAN A TRAP BY THE CHITAURI.
YOU WERE FOLLOWED.
NO, WE WEREN'T!
I HAVE A SPECIAL HYPERDRIVE THAT--
UH-OH.

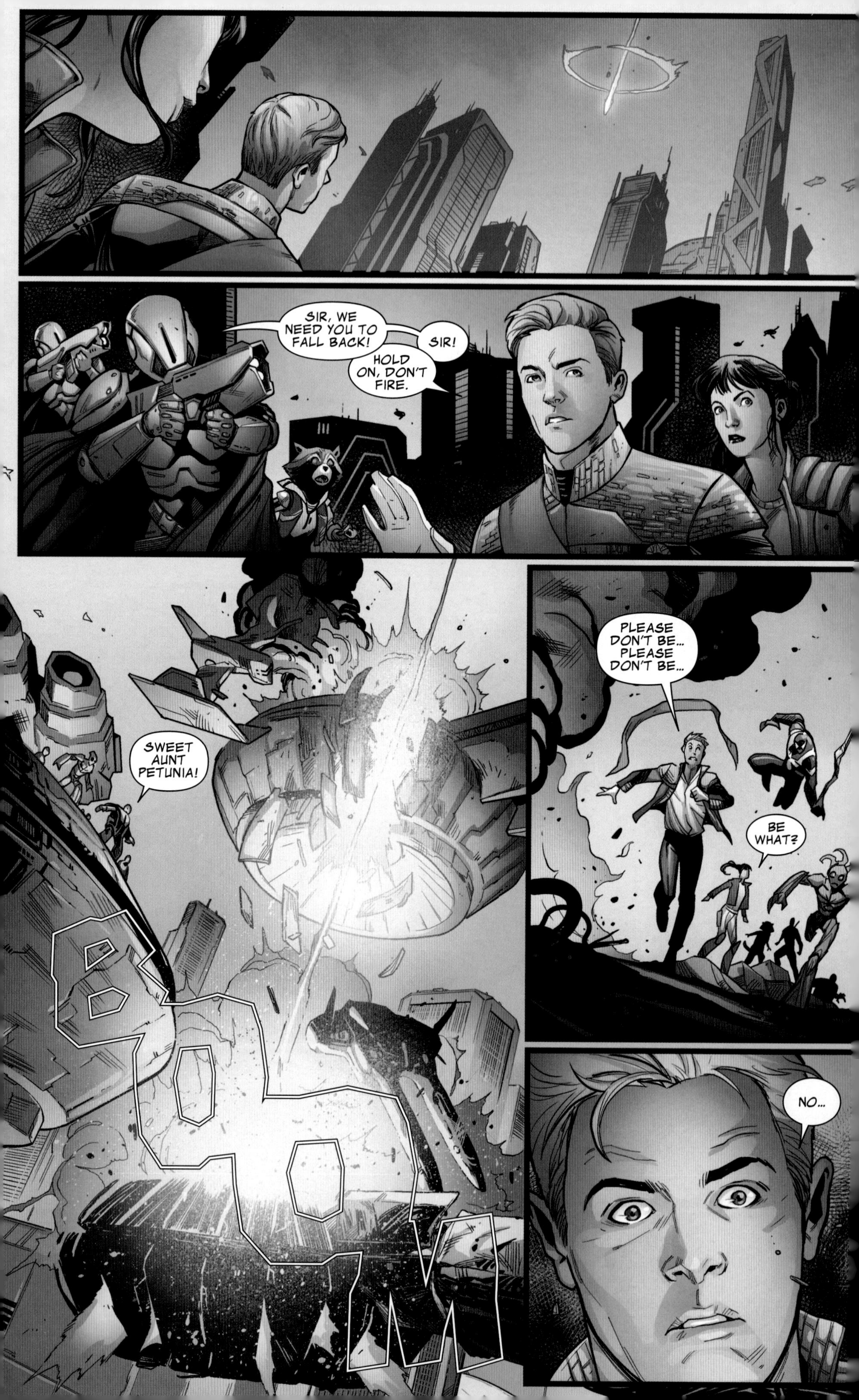
SIR, WE NEED YOU TO FALL BACK!
SIR!
HOLD ON, DON'T FIRE.
SWEET AUNT PETUNIA!
BOOM
PLEASE DON'T BE... PLEASE DON'T BE...
BE WHAT?
NO...

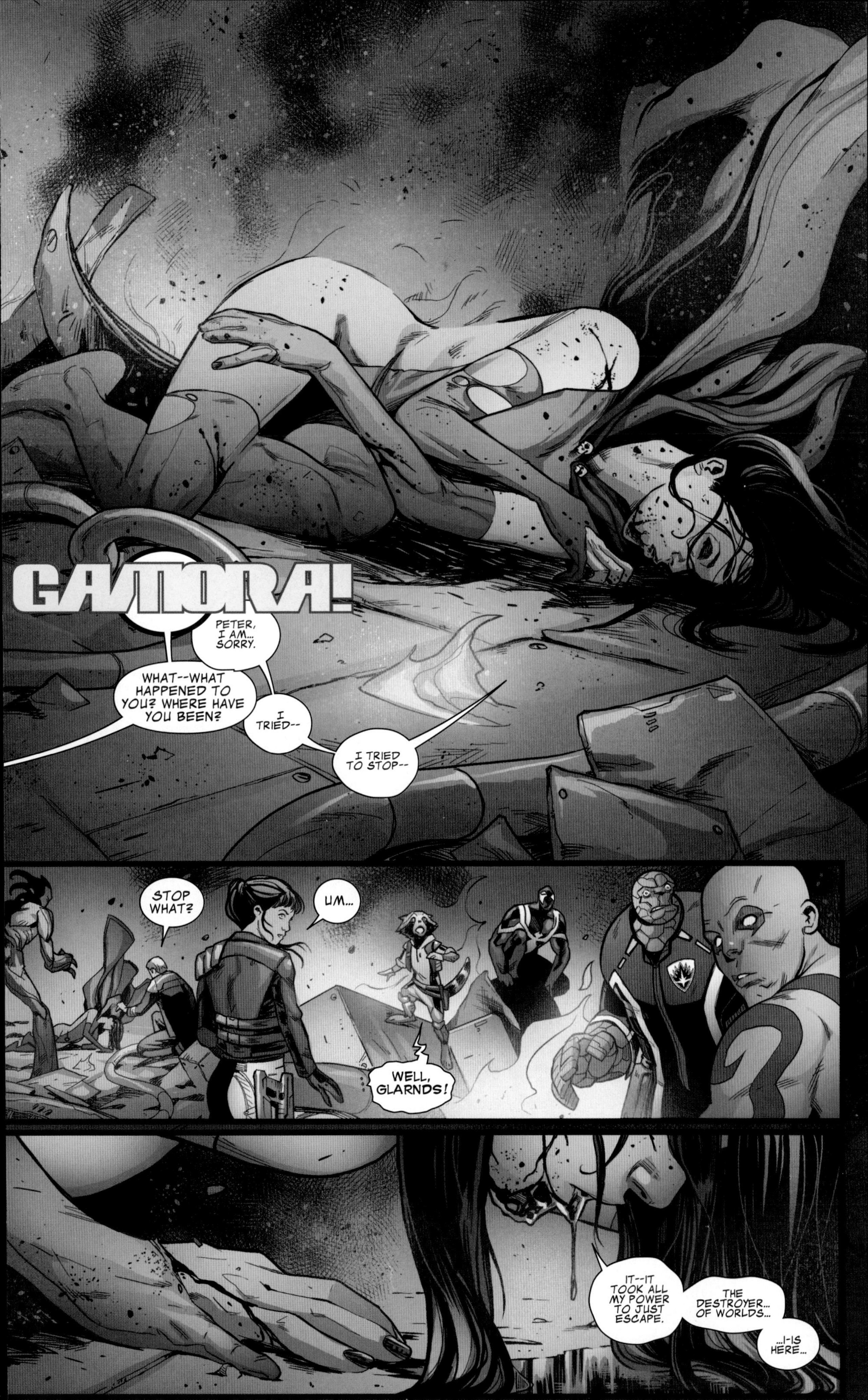
GAMORA!
WHAT--WHAT HAPPENED TO YOU? WHERE HAVE YOU BEEN?
PETER, I AM... SORRY.
I TRIED--
I TRIED TO STOP--
STOP WHAT?
UM...
WELL, GLARNDS!
IT--IT TOOK ALL MY POWER TO JUST ESCAPE.
THE DESTROYER... OF WORLDS...
...I-IS HERE...

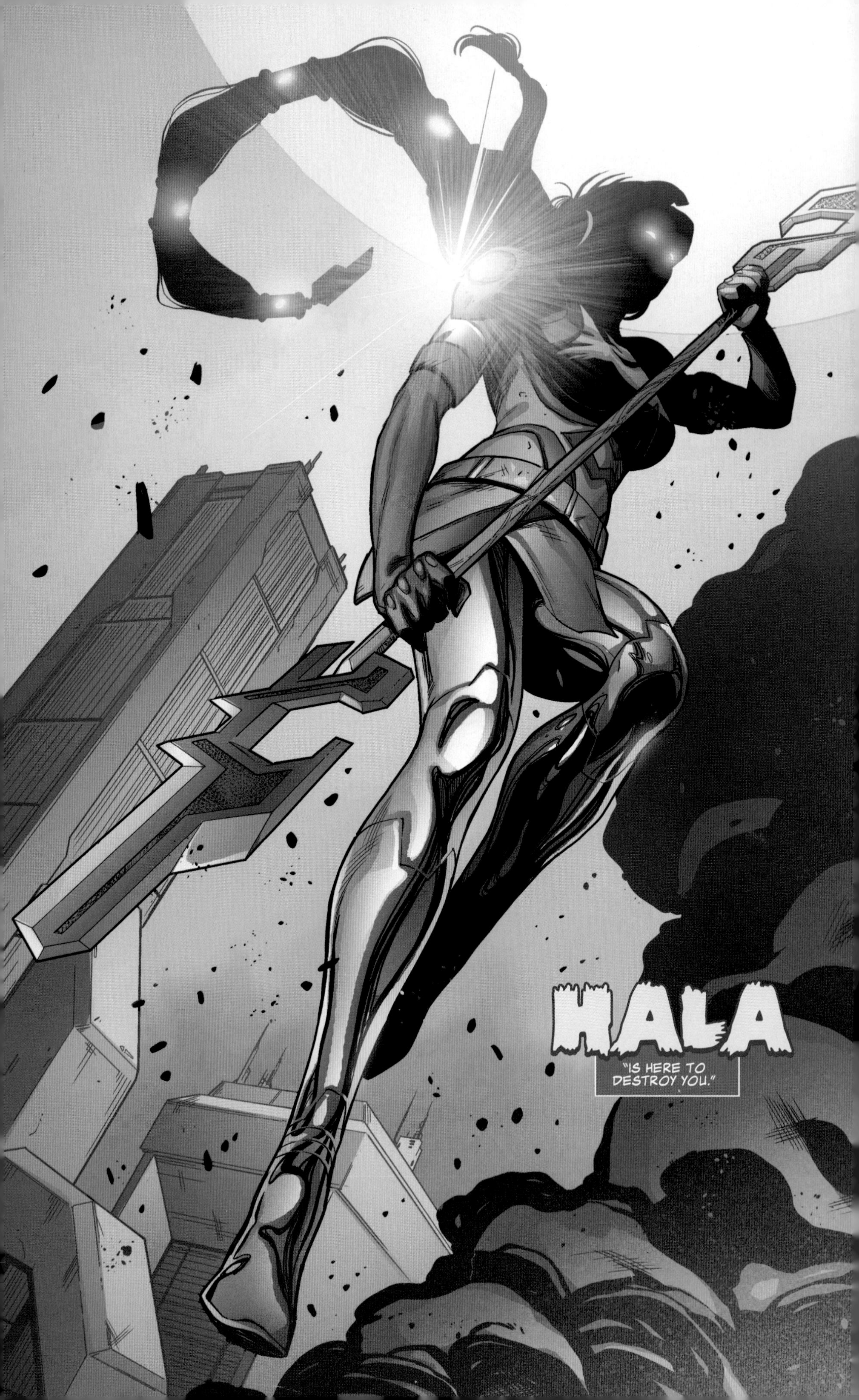
HALA
"IS HERE TO DESTROY YOU."

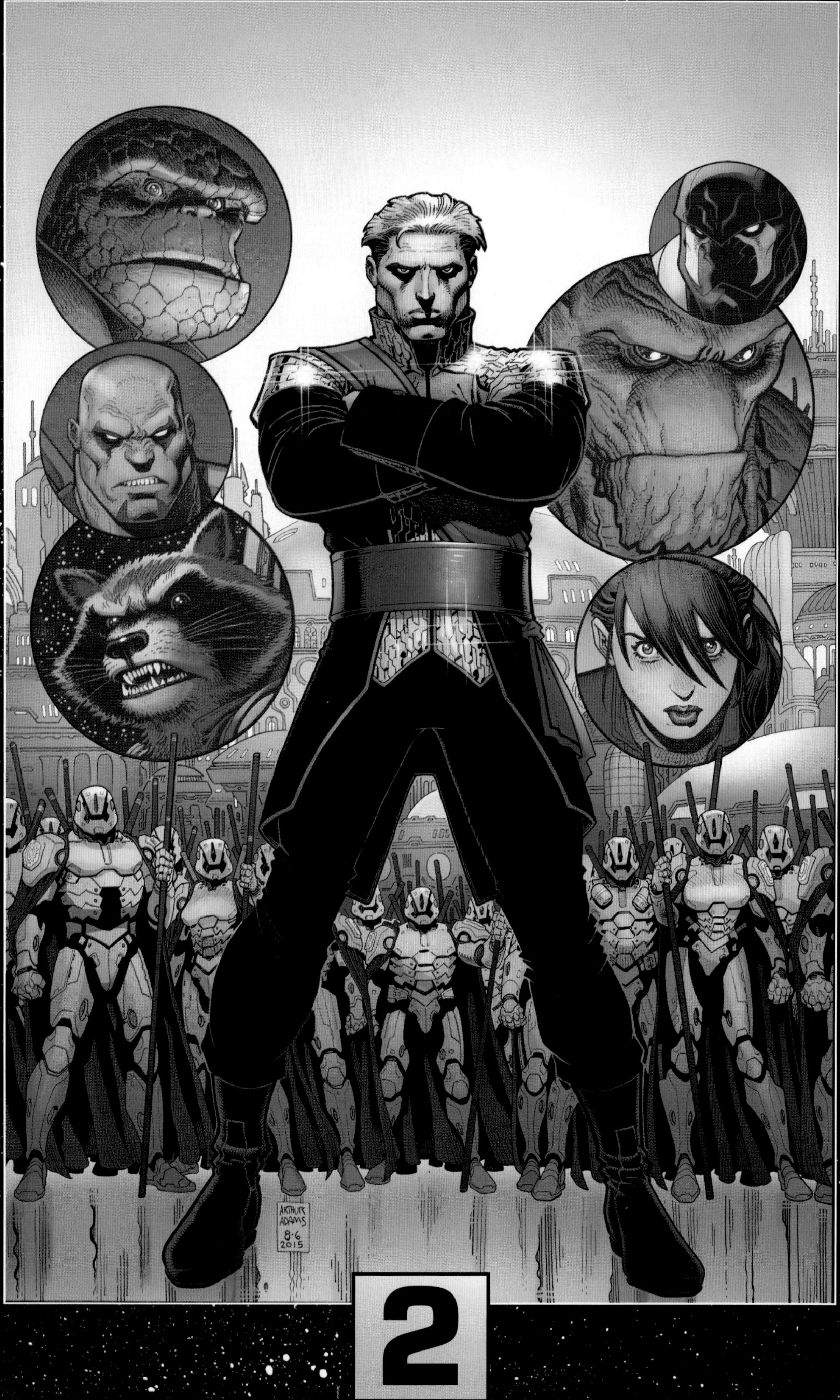
ARTHUR ADAMS
8·6
2015
2

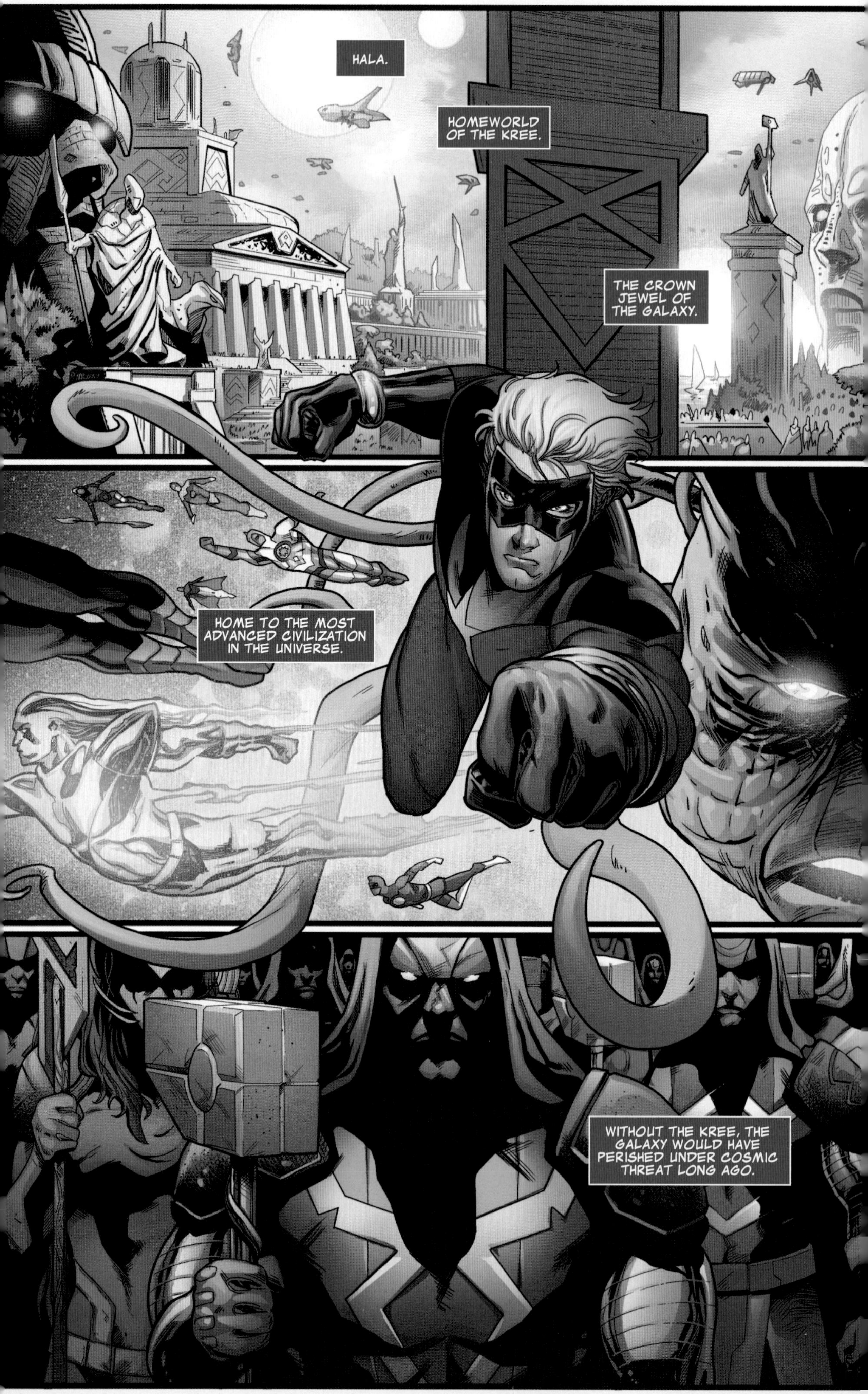
HALA.
HOMEWORLD OF THE KREE.
THE CROWN JEWEL OF THE GALAXY.
HOME TO THE MOST ADVANCED CIVILIZATION IN THE UNIVERSE.
WITHOUT THE KREE, THE GALAXY WOULD HAVE PERISHED UNDER COSMIC THREAT LONG AGO.

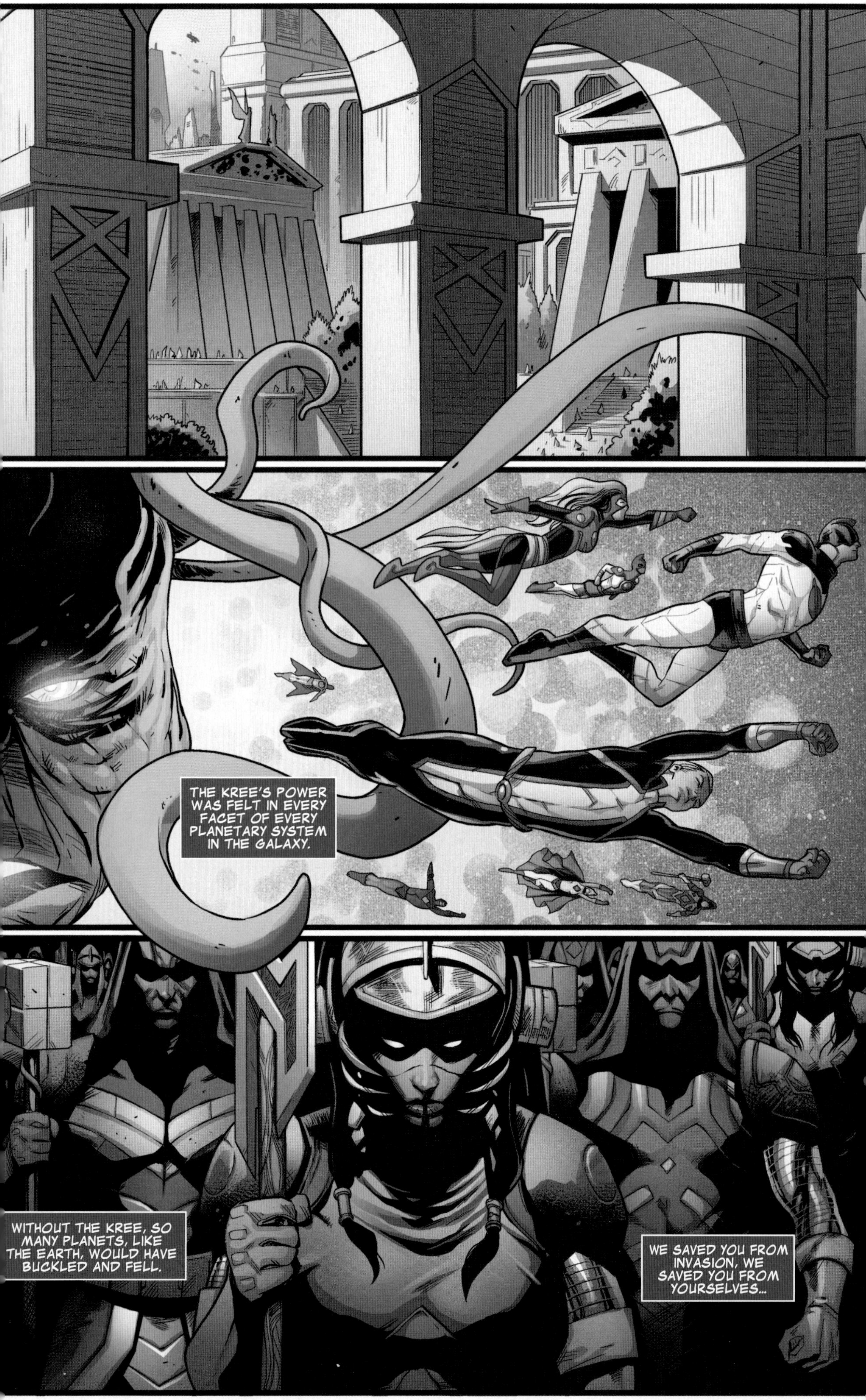
THE KREE'S POWER WAS FELT IN EVERY FACET OF EVERY PLANETARY SYSTEM IN THE GALAXY.
WITHOUT THE KREE, SO MANY PLANETS, LIKE THE EARTH, WOULD HAVE BUCKLED AND FELL.
WE SAVED YOU FROM INVASION, WE SAVED YOU FROM YOURSELVES...

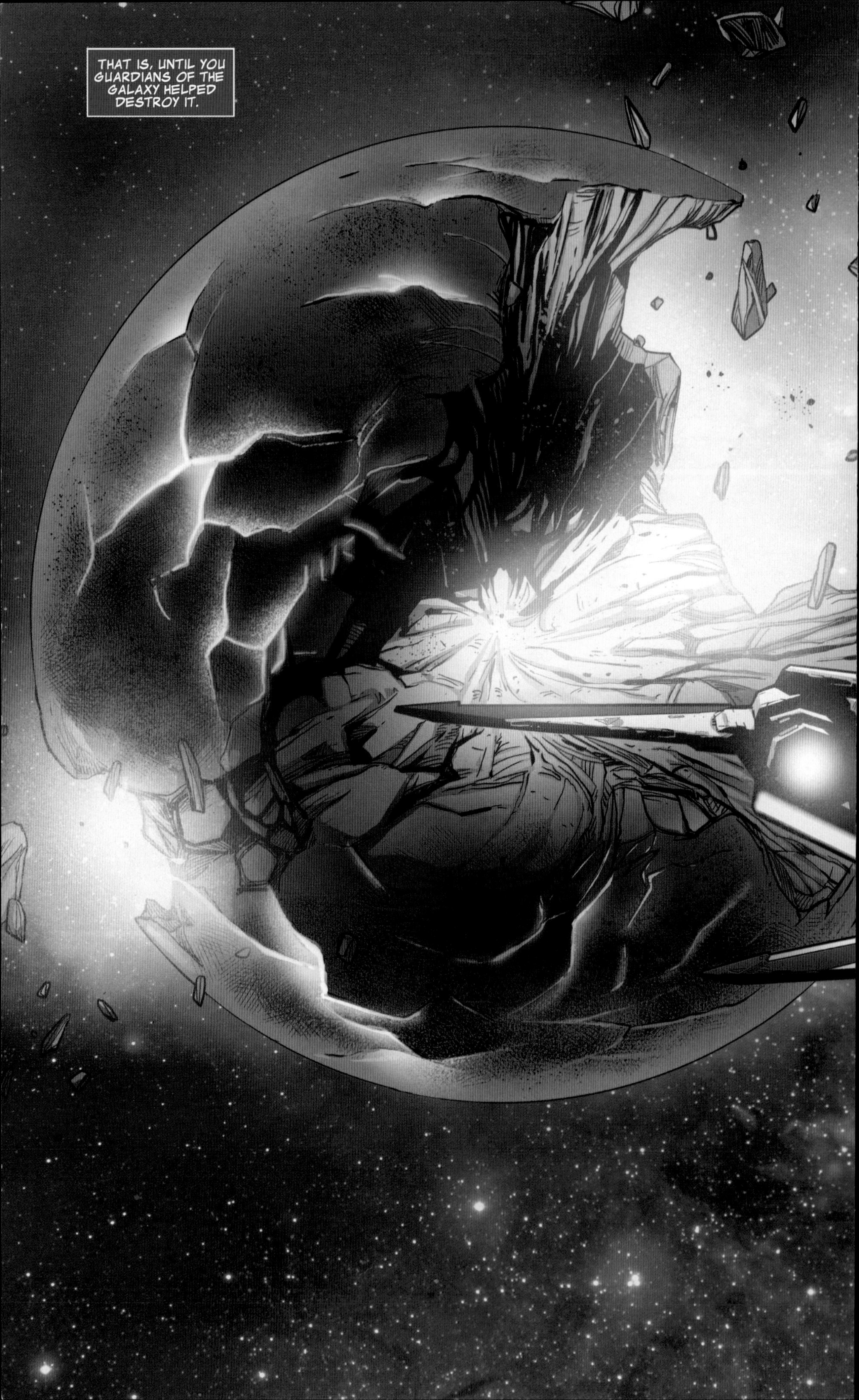
THAT IS, UNTIL YOU GUARDIANS OF THE GALAXY HELPED DESTROY IT.

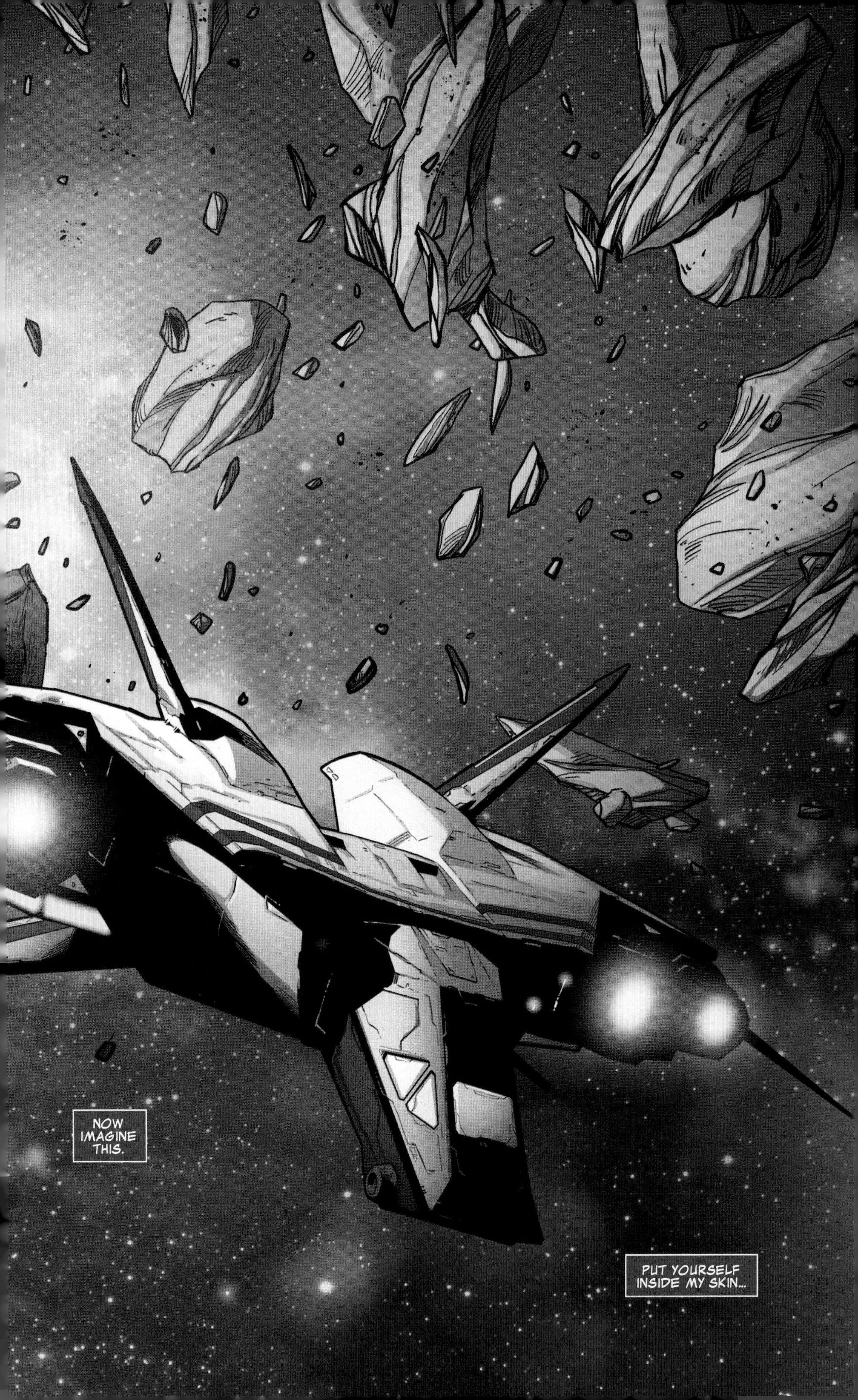
NOW IMAGINE THIS.
PUT YOURSELF INSIDE MY SKIN...

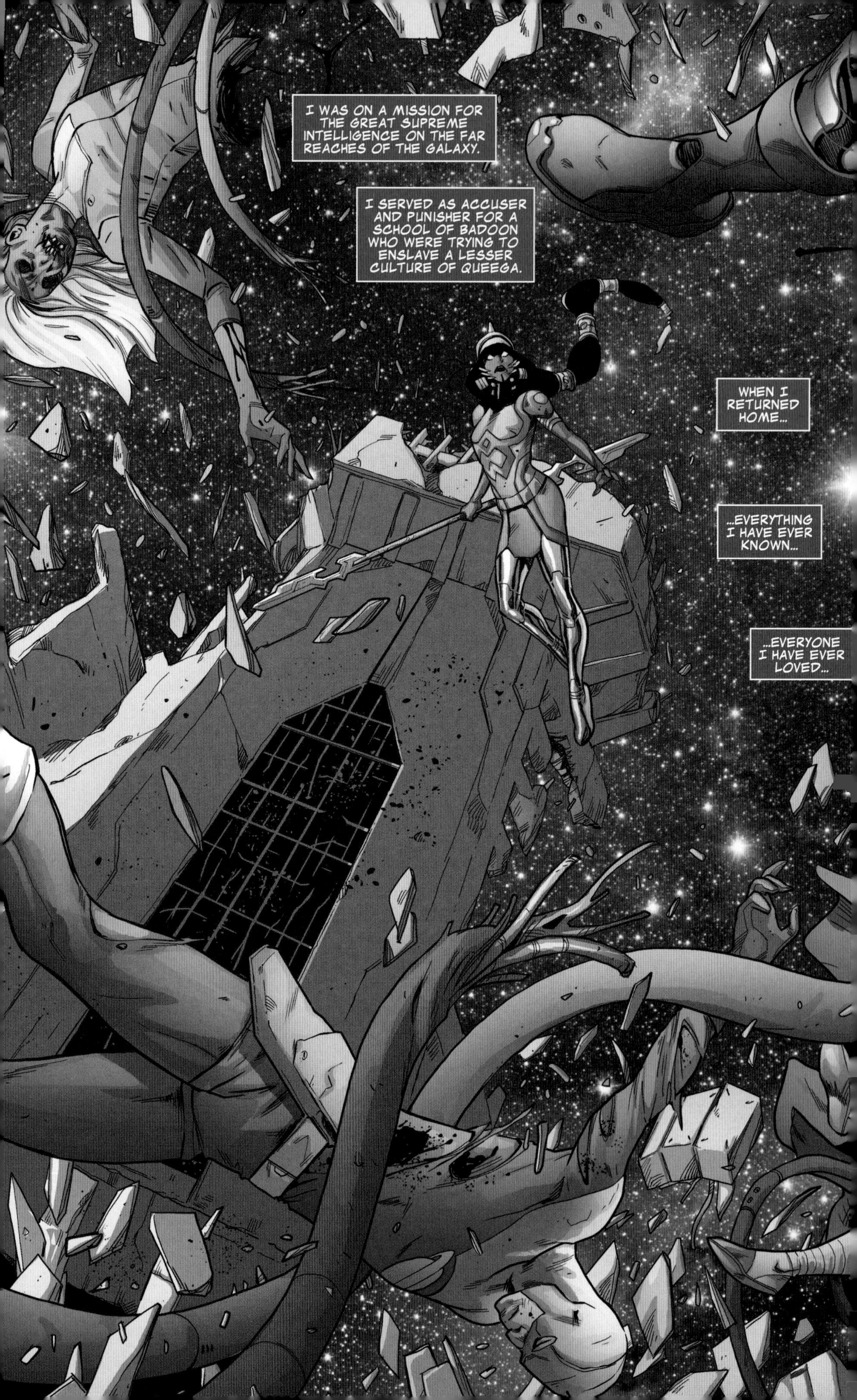
I WAS ON A MISSION FOR THE GREAT SUPREME INTELLIGENCE ON THE FAR REACHES OF THE GALAXY.
I SERVED AS ACCUSER AND PUNISHER FOR A SCHOOL OF BADOON WHO WERE TRYING TO ENSLAVE A LESSER CULTURE OF QUEEGA.
WHEN I RETURNED HOME...
...EVERYTHING I HAVE EVER KNOWN...
...EVERYONE I HAVE EVER LOVED...

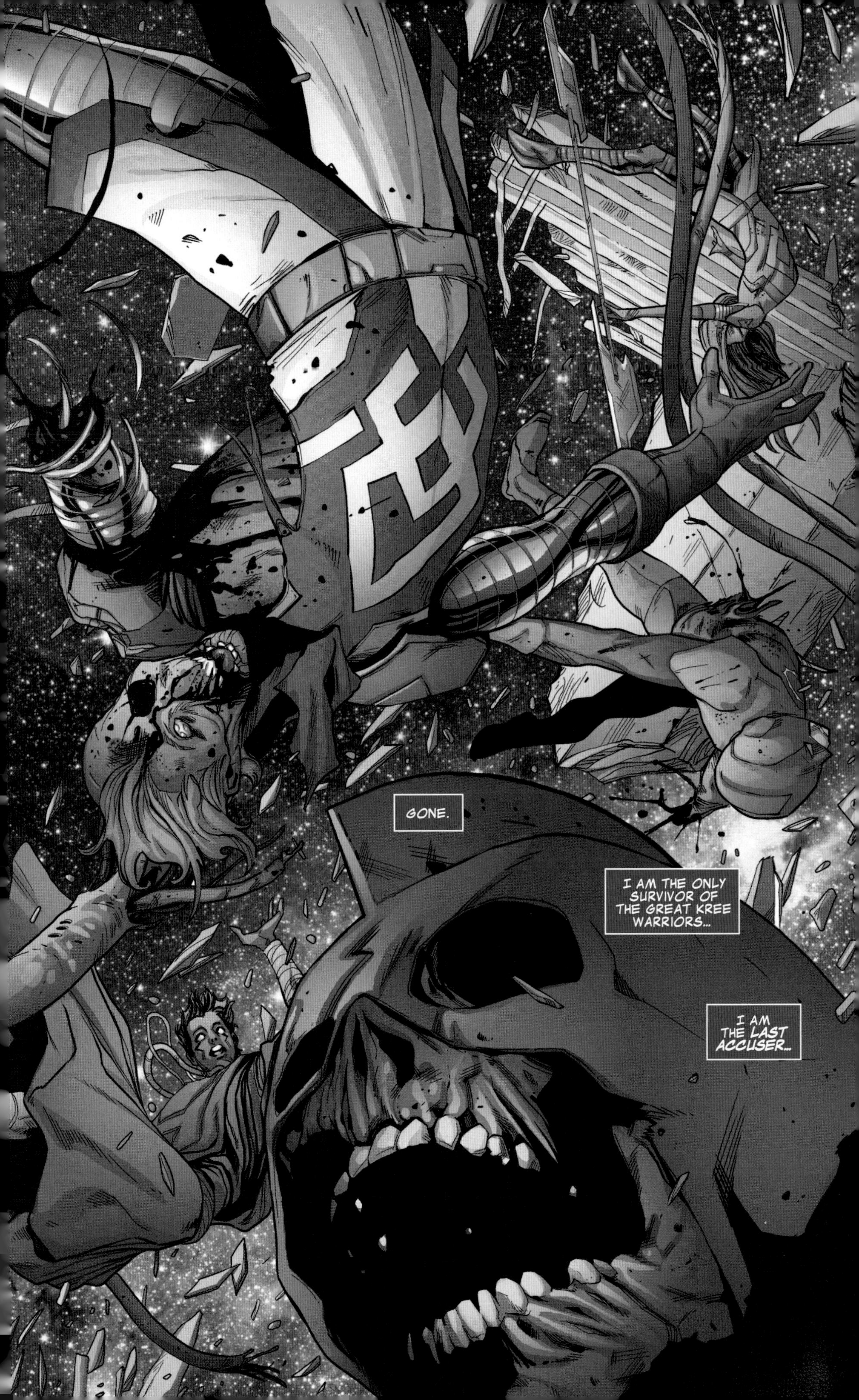
GONE.
I AM THE ONLY SURVIVOR OF THE GREAT KREE WARRIORS...
I AM THE LAST ACCUSER...

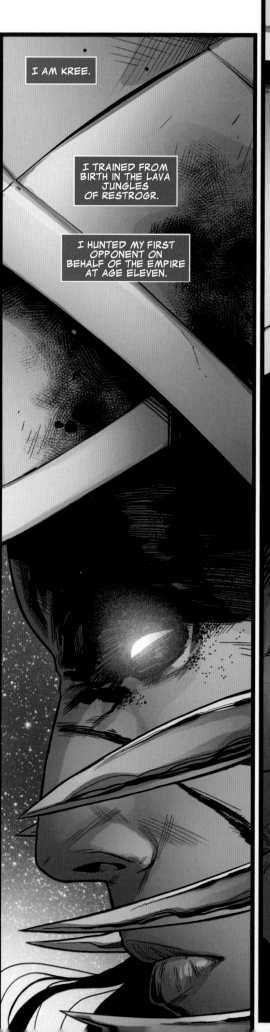

I AM KREE.

I TRAINED FROM BIRTH IN THE LAVA JUNGLES OF RESTROGR.

I HUNTED MY FIRST OPPONENT ON BEHALF OF THE EMPIRE AT AGE ELEVEN.

I JOINED THE HONORED RANKS OF THE ACCUSERS BY PASSING A TEST OF BLOOD AND COURAGE HANDED DOWN FROM THREE THOUSAND GENERATIONS OF KREE.

I PROTECTED THE GALAXY ON BEHALF OF THE SUPREME INTELLIGENCE IN EVERY WAY I WAS ASKED TO.

I AM KREE.

AND BECAUSE OF YOU THE KREE ARE NO MORE.

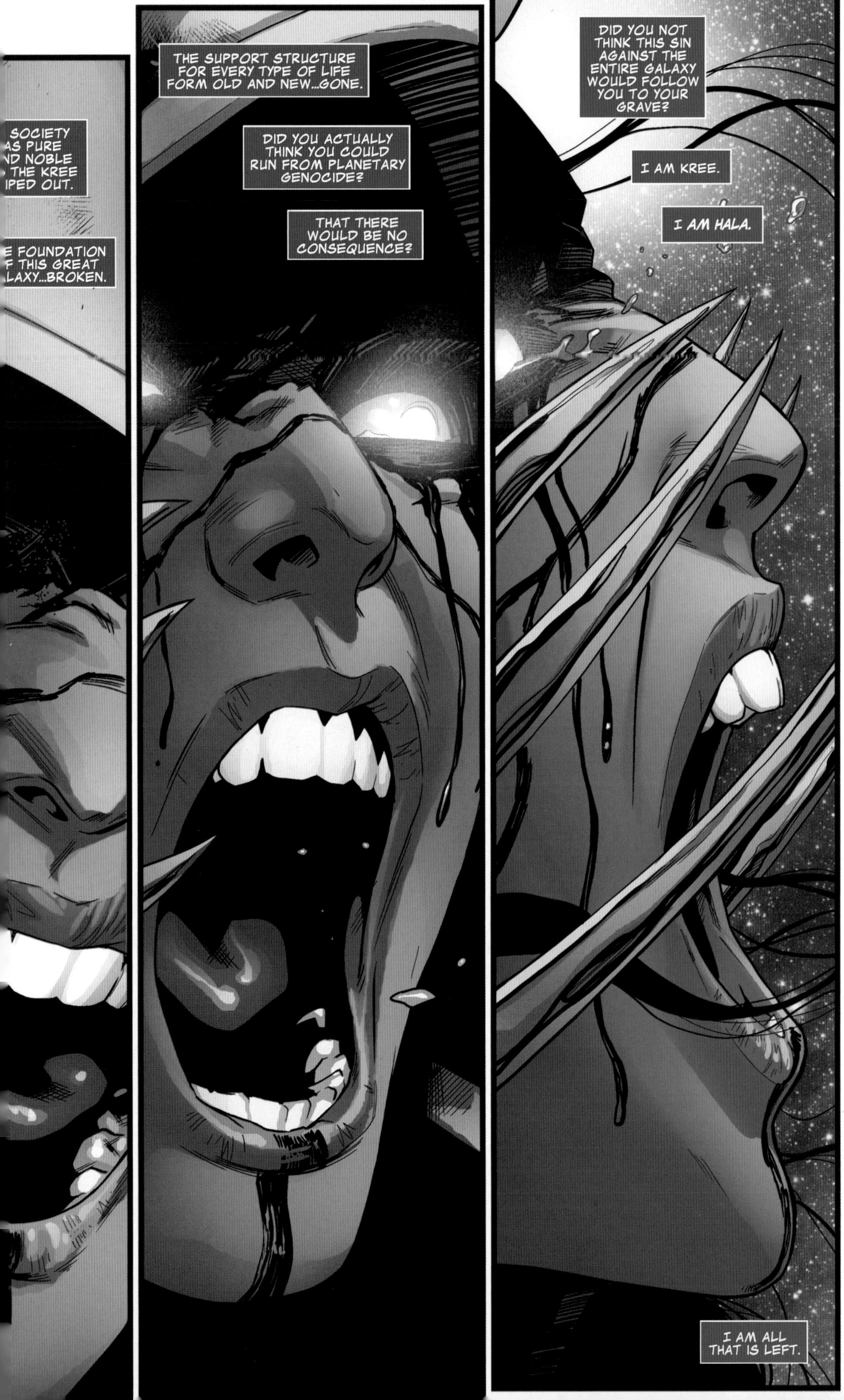
SOCIETY
AS PURE
ND NOBLE
THE KREE
IPED OUT.
E FOUNDATION
F THIS GREAT
ALAXY...BROKEN.
THE SUPPORT STRUCTURE FOR EVERY TYPE OF LIFE FORM OLD AND NEW...GONE.
DID YOU ACTUALLY THINK YOU COULD RUN FROM PLANETARY GENOCIDE?
THAT THERE WOULD BE NO CONSEQUENCE?
DID YOU NOT THINK THIS SIN AGAINST THE ENTIRE GALAXY WOULD FOLLOW YOU TO YOUR GRAVE?
I AM KREE.
I AM HALA.
I AM ALL THAT IS LEFT.

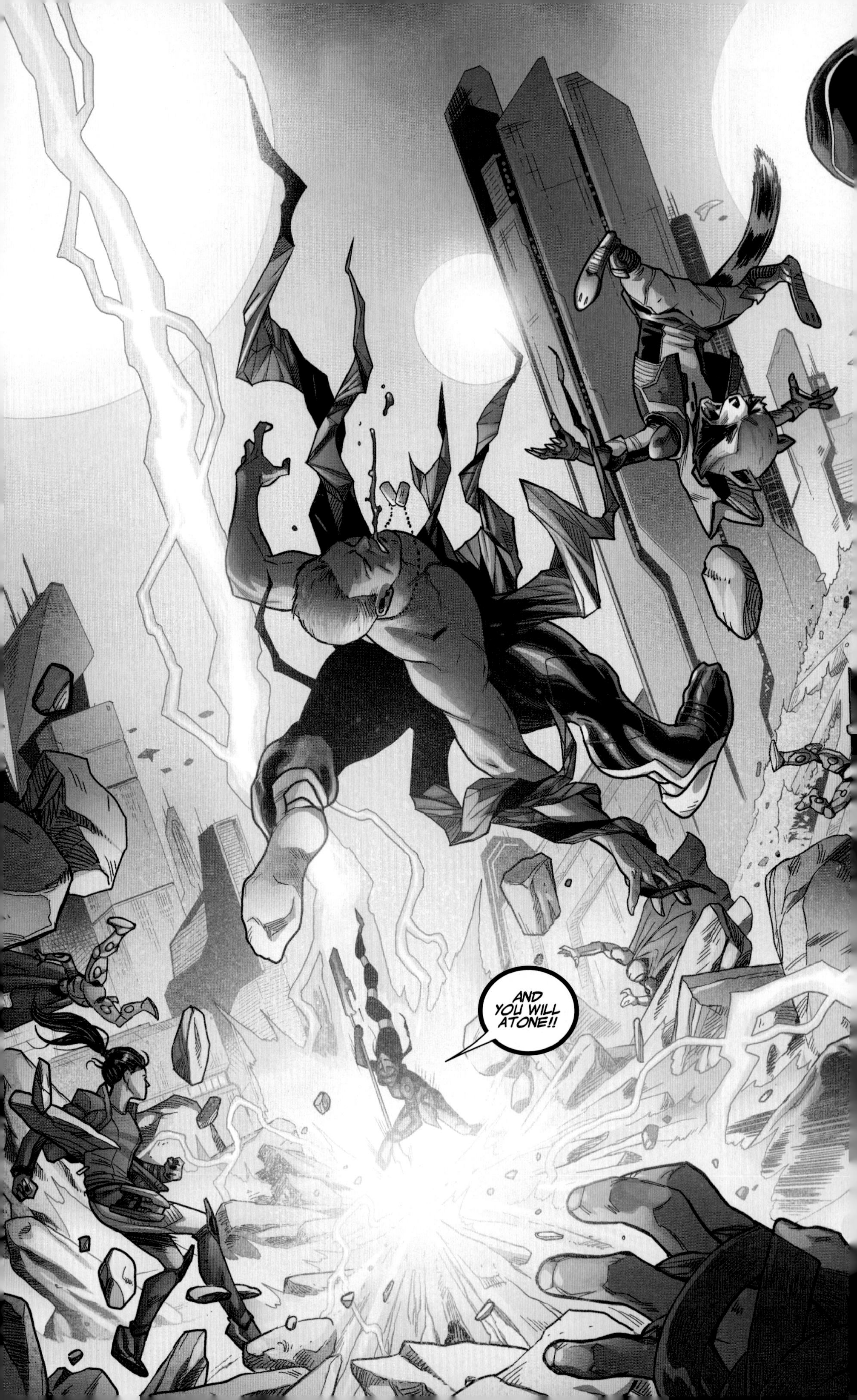
AND YOU WILL ATONE!!

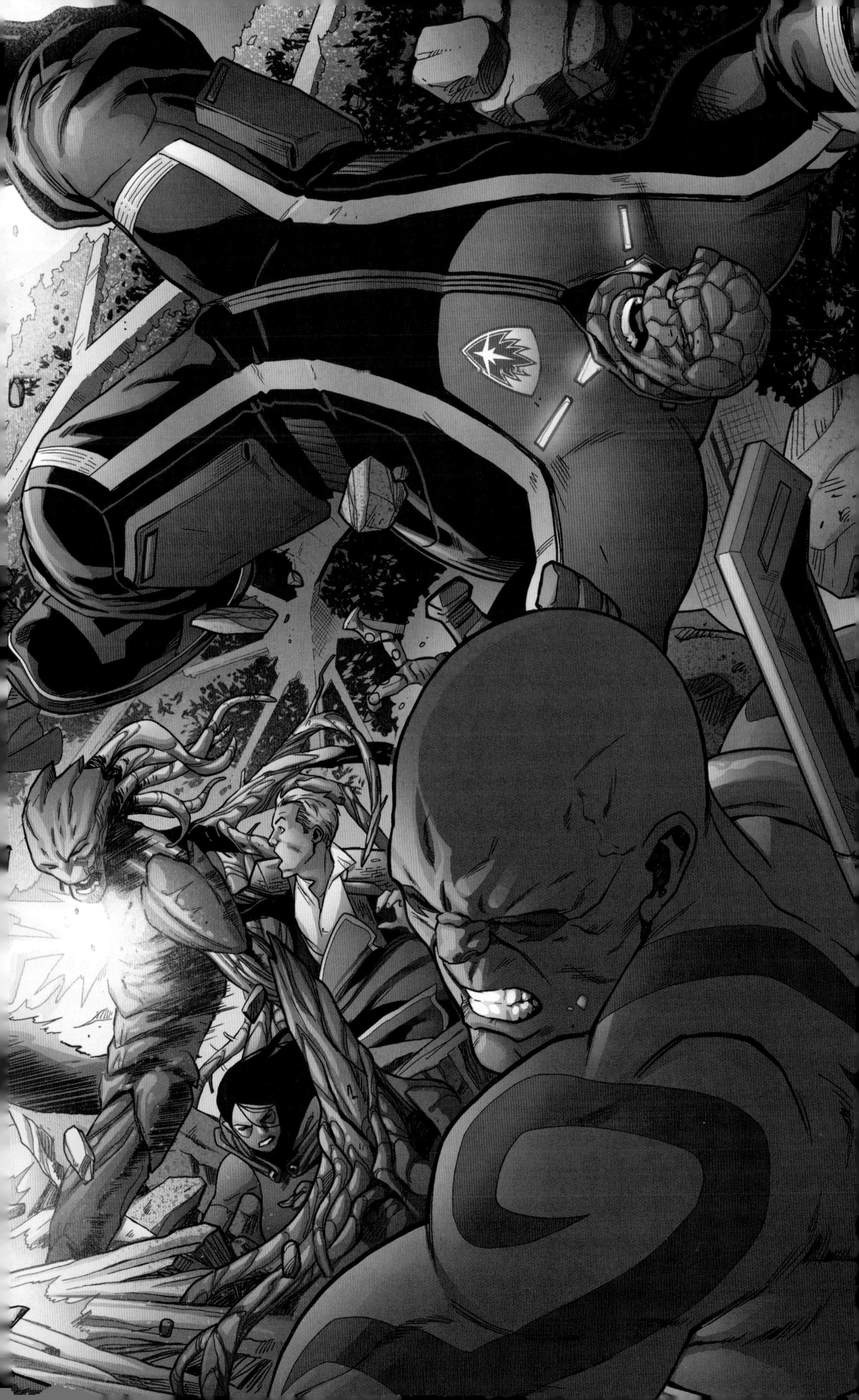

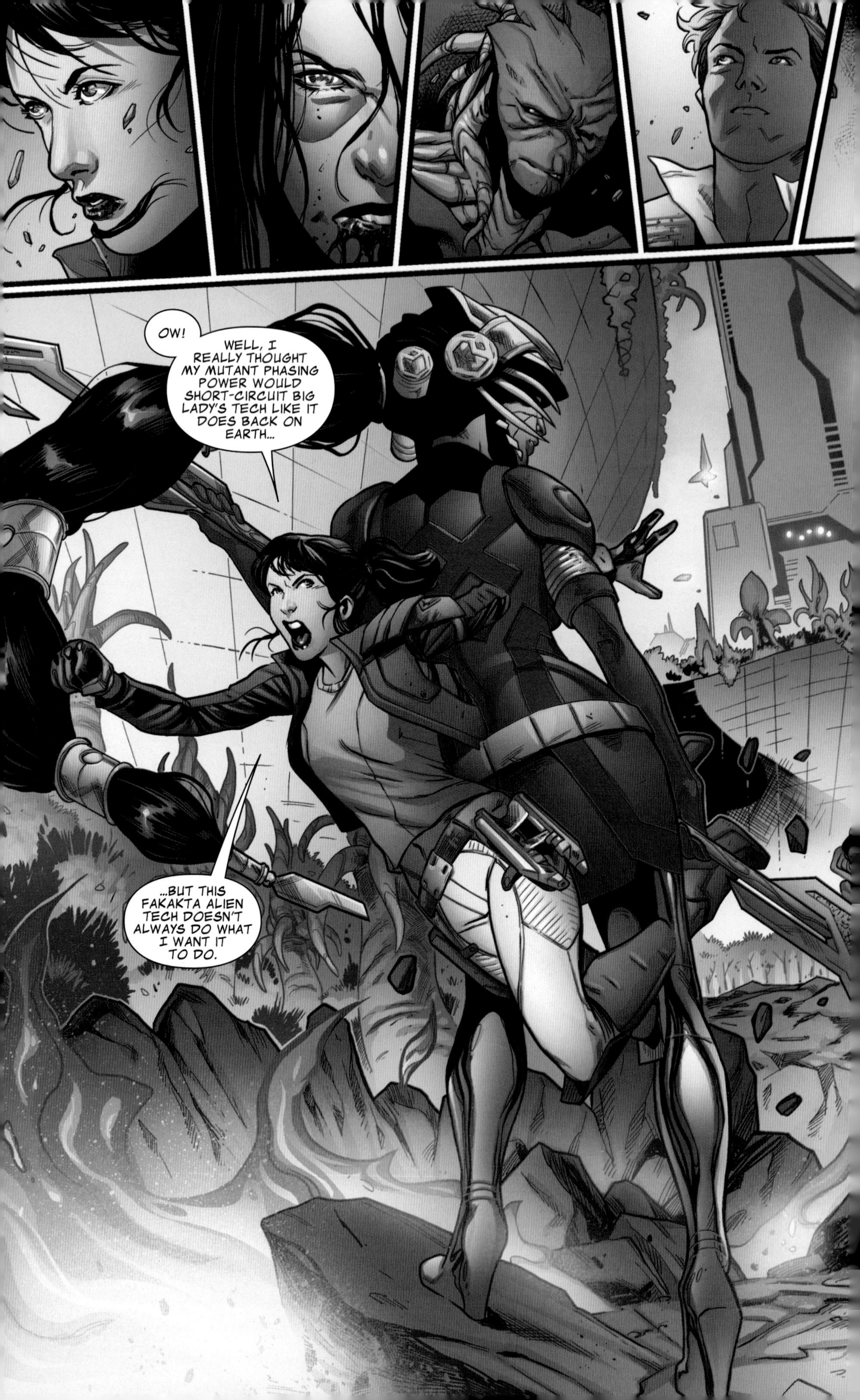
OW!
WELL, I REALLY THOUGHT MY MUTANT PHASING POWER WOULD SHORT-CIRCUIT BIG LADY'S TECH LIKE IT DOES BACK ON EARTH...
...BUT THIS FAKAKTA ALIEN TECH DOESN'T ALWAYS DO WHAT I WANT IT TO DO.

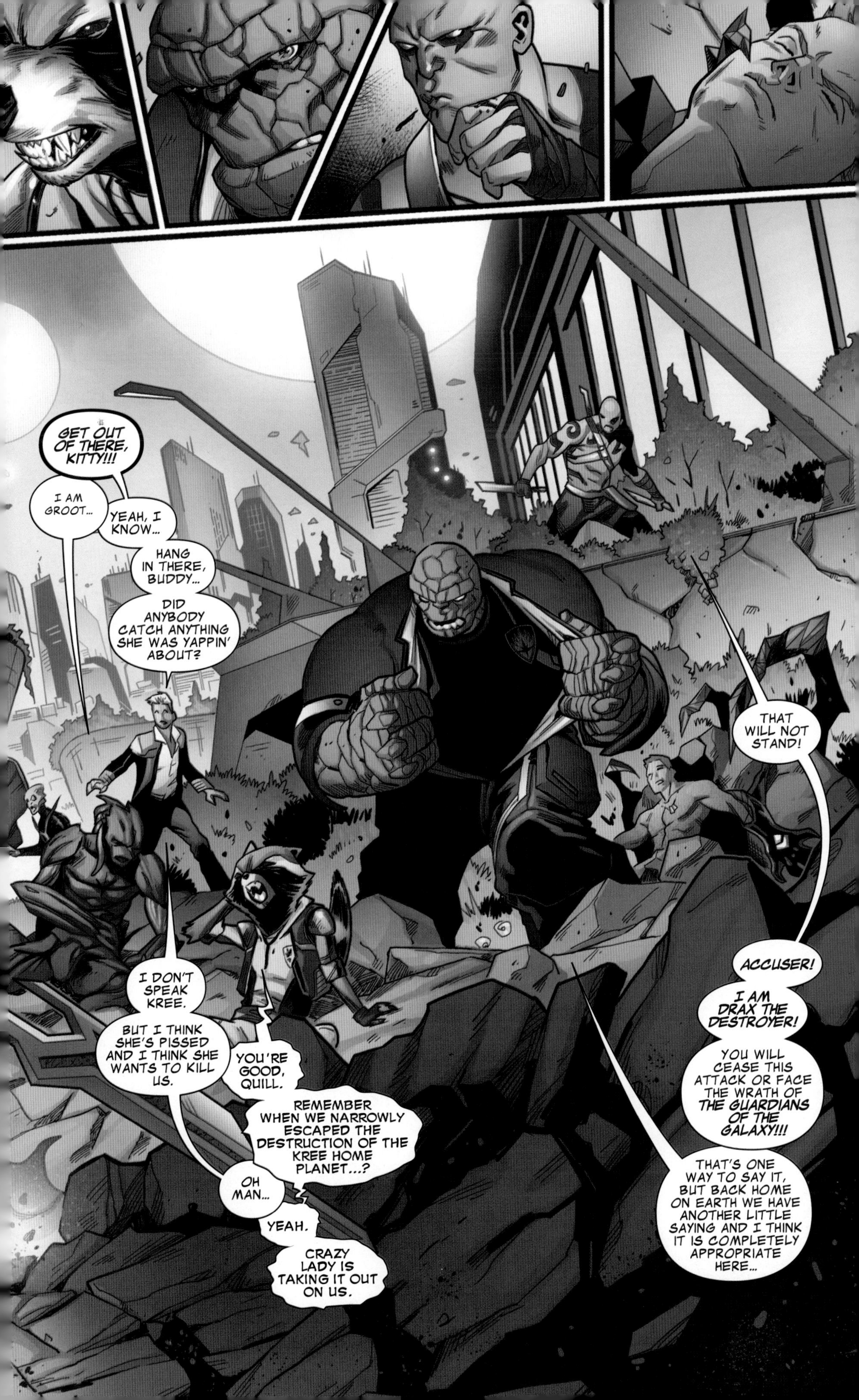
GET OUT OF THERE, KITTY!!!
I AM GROOT...
YEAH, I KNOW...
HANG IN THERE, BUDDY...
DID ANYBODY CATCH ANYTHING SHE WAS YAPPIN' ABOUT?
THAT WILL NOT STAND!
ACCUSER!
I AM DRAX THE DESTROYER!
YOU WILL CEASE THIS ATTACK OR FACE THE WRATH OF THE GUARDIANS OF THE GALAXY!!!
I DON'T SPEAK KREE.
BUT I THINK SHE'S PISSED AND I THINK SHE WANTS TO KILL US.
YOU'RE GOOD, QUILL.
REMEMBER WHEN WE NARROWLY ESCAPED THE DESTRUCTION OF THE KREE HOME PLANET...?
OH MAN...
YEAH.
CRAZY LADY IS TAKING IT OUT ON US.
THAT'S ONE WAY TO SAY IT, BUT BACK HOME ON EARTH WE HAVE ANOTHER LITTLE SAYING AND I THINK IT IS COMPLETELY APPROPRIATE HERE...

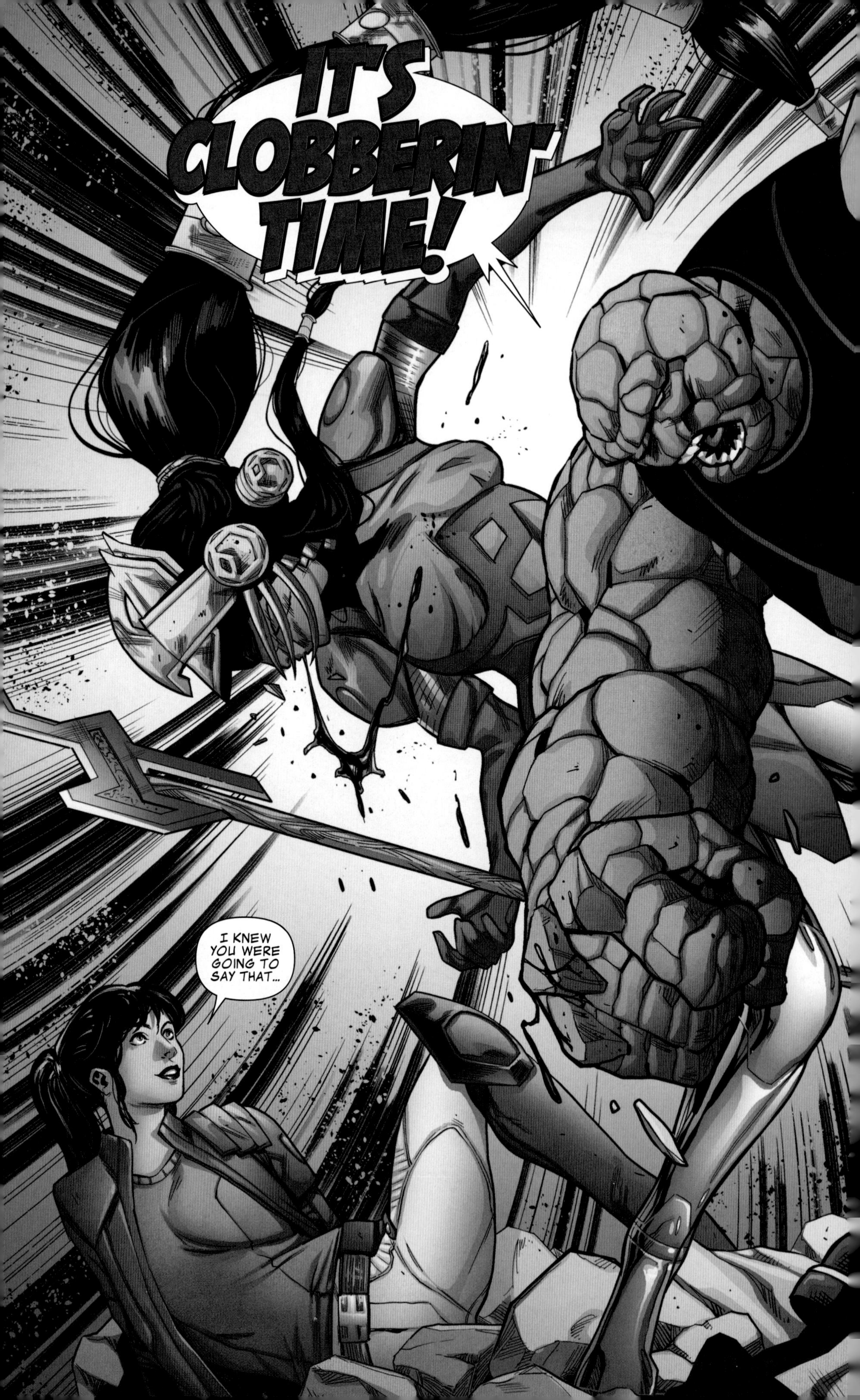
IT'S CLOBBERIN' TIME!
I KNEW YOU WERE GOING TO SAY THAT...

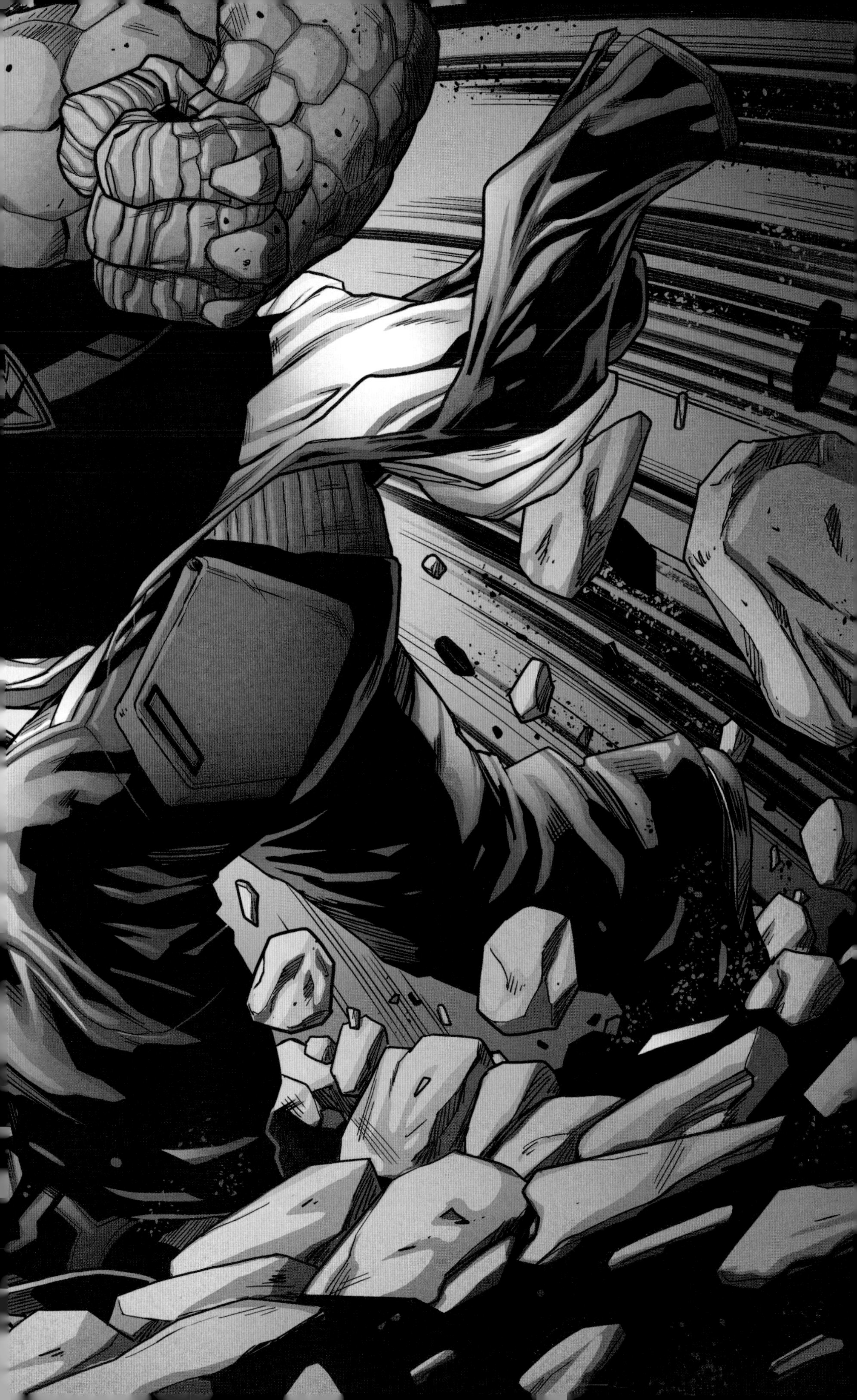

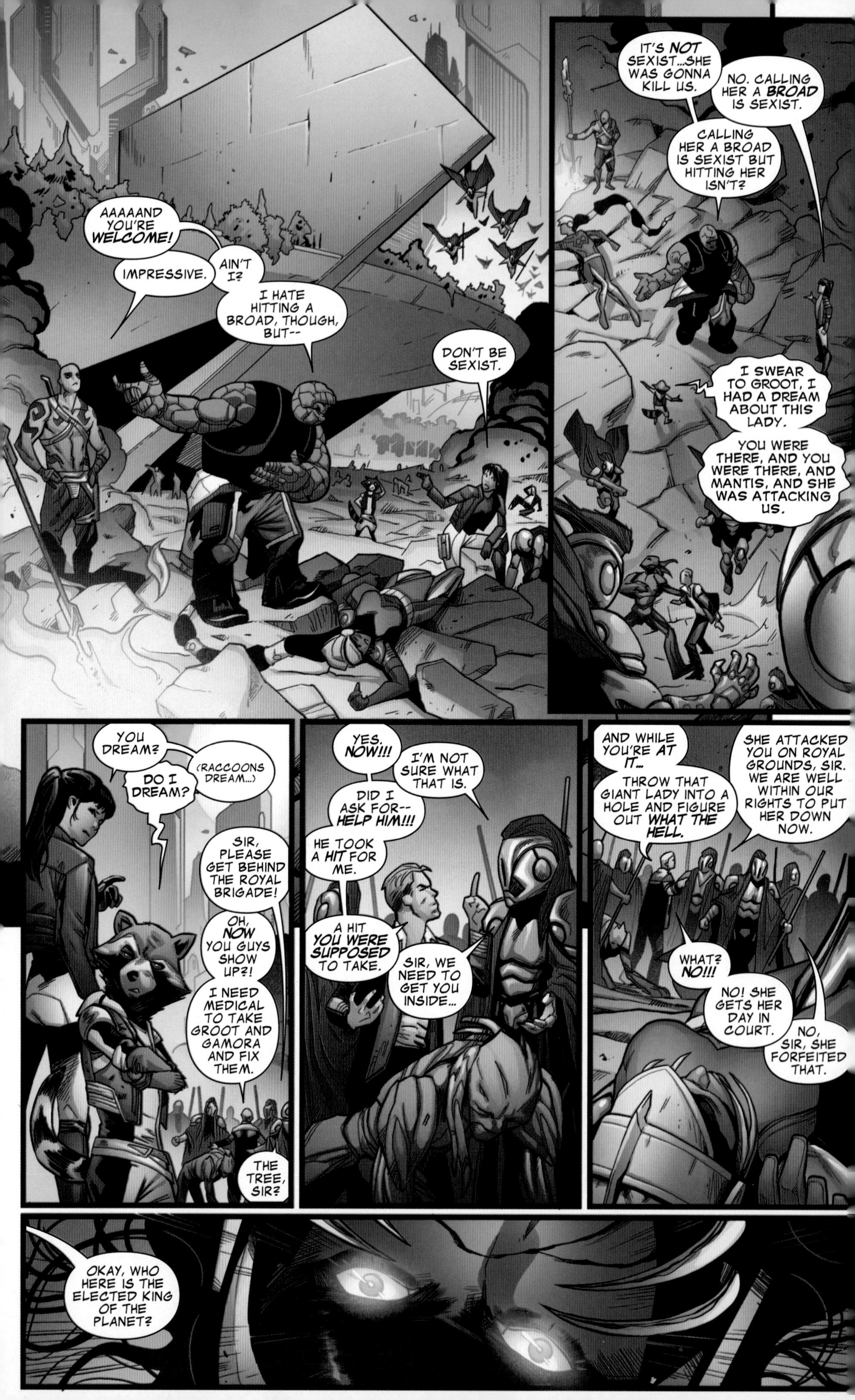

AAAAAND YOU'RE WELCOME!
IMPRESSIVE.
AIN'T I?
I HATE HITTING A BROAD, THOUGH, BUT--
DON'T BE SEXIST.
IT'S NOT SEXIST...SHE WAS GONNA KILL US.
NO. CALLING HER A BROAD IS SEXIST.
CALLING HER A BROAD IS SEXIST BUT HITTING HER ISN'T?
I SWEAR TO GROOT, I HAD A DREAM ABOUT THIS LADY.
YOU WERE THERE, AND YOU WERE THERE, AND MANTIS, AND SHE WAS ATTACKING US.
YOU DREAM?
(RACCOONS DREAM...)
DO I DREAM?
SIR, PLEASE GET BEHIND THE ROYAL BRIGADE!
OH, NOW YOU GUYS SHOW UP?!
I NEED MEDICAL TO TAKE GROOT AND GAMORA AND FIX THEM.
THE TREE, SIR?
YES. NOW!!!
I'M NOT SURE WHAT THAT IS.
DID I ASK FOR-- HELP HIM!!!
HE TOOK A HIT FOR ME.
A HIT YOU WERE SUPPOSED TO TAKE.
SIR, WE NEED TO GET YOU INSIDE...
AND WHILE YOU'RE AT IT...
THROW THAT GIANT LADY INTO A HOLE AND FIGURE OUT WHAT THE HELL.
SHE ATTACKED YOU ON ROYAL GROUNDS, SIR. WE ARE WELL WITHIN OUR RIGHTS TO PUT HER DOWN NOW.
WHAT? NO!!!
NO! SHE GETS HER DAY IN COURT.
NO, SIR, SHE FORFEITED THAT.
OKAY, WHO HERE IS THE ELECTED KING OF THE PLANET?

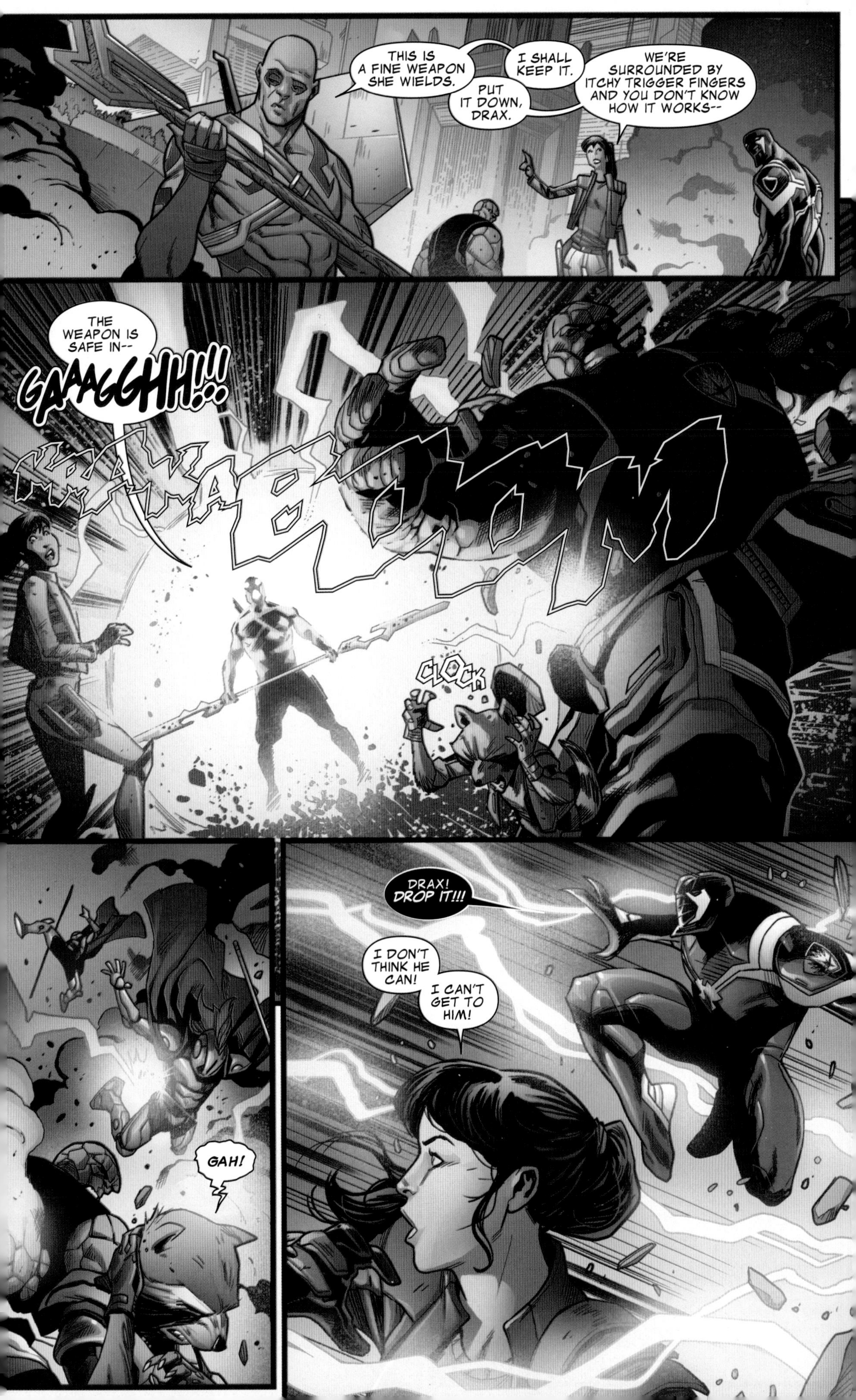

THIS IS A FINE WEAPON SHE WIELDS.
I SHALL KEEP IT.
PUT IT DOWN, DRAX.
WE'RE SURROUNDED BY ITCHY TRIGGER FINGERS AND YOU DON'T KNOW HOW IT WORKS--
THE WEAPON IS SAFE IN--
GAAAGGHH!!!
KKAKABOOM
CLOCK
DRAX! DROP IT!!!
I DON'T THINK HE CAN!
I CAN'T GET TO HIM!
GAH!

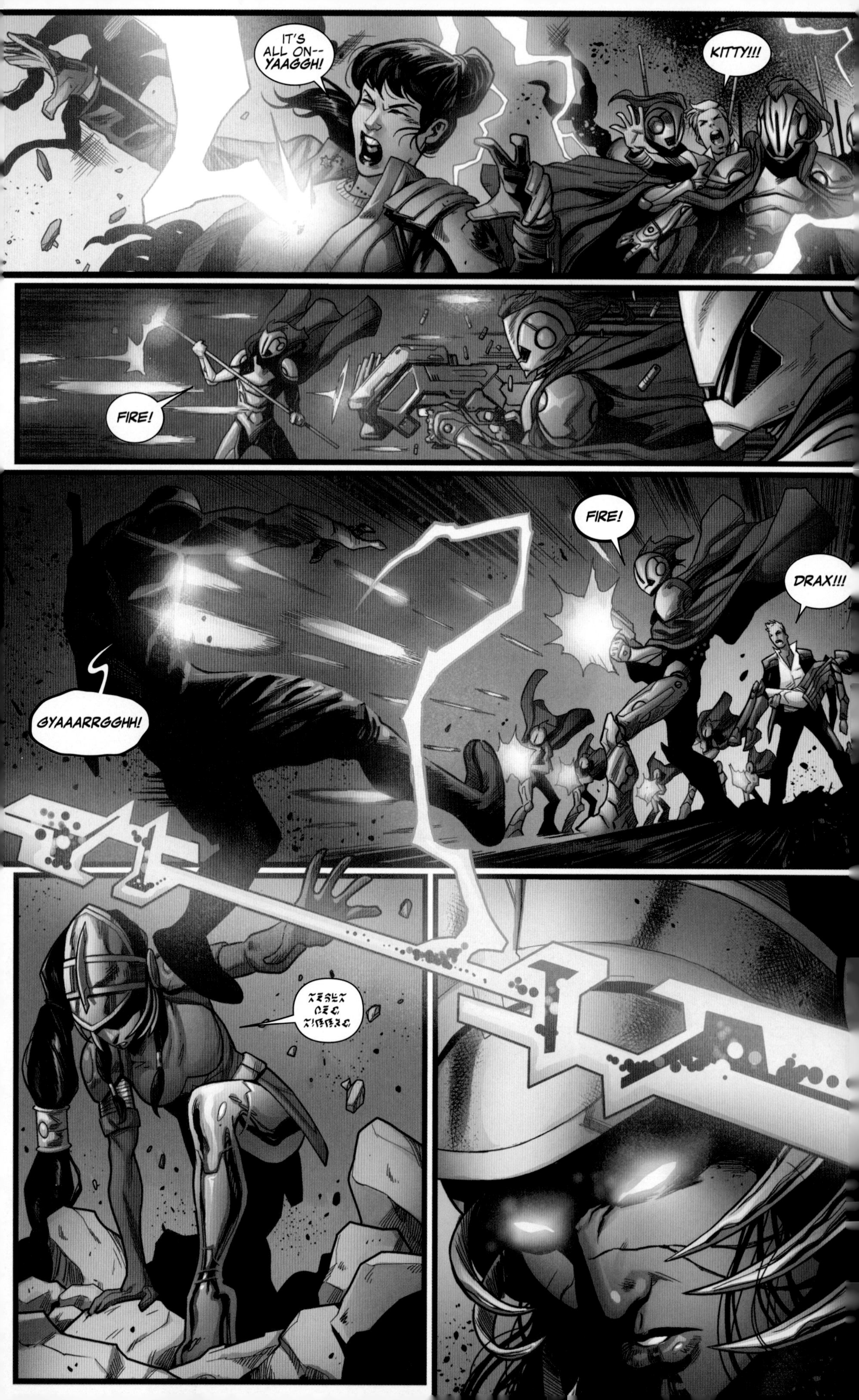
IT'S ALL ON-- YAAGGH!
KITTY!!!
FIRE!
FIRE!
DRAX!!!
GYAAARRGGHH!

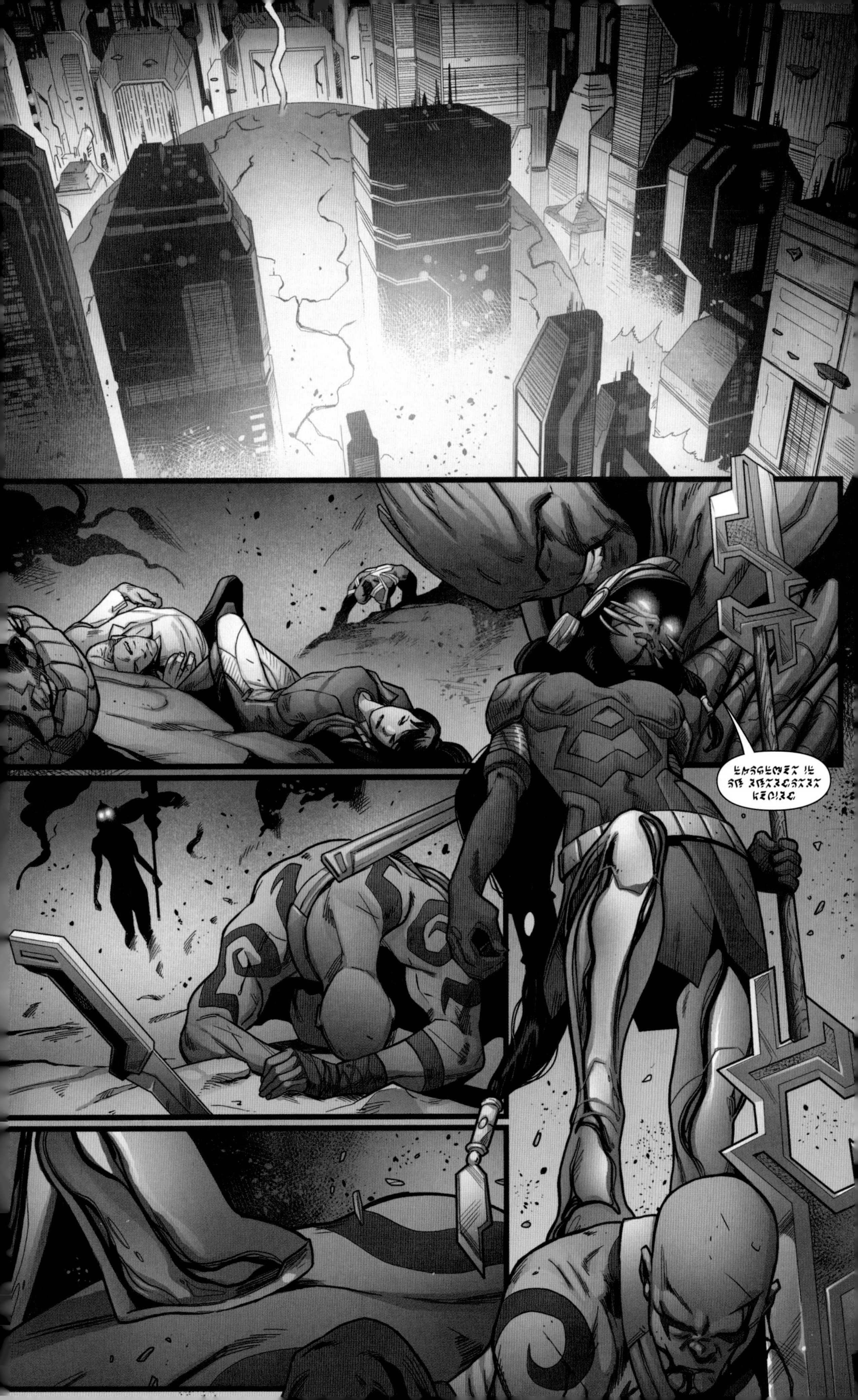

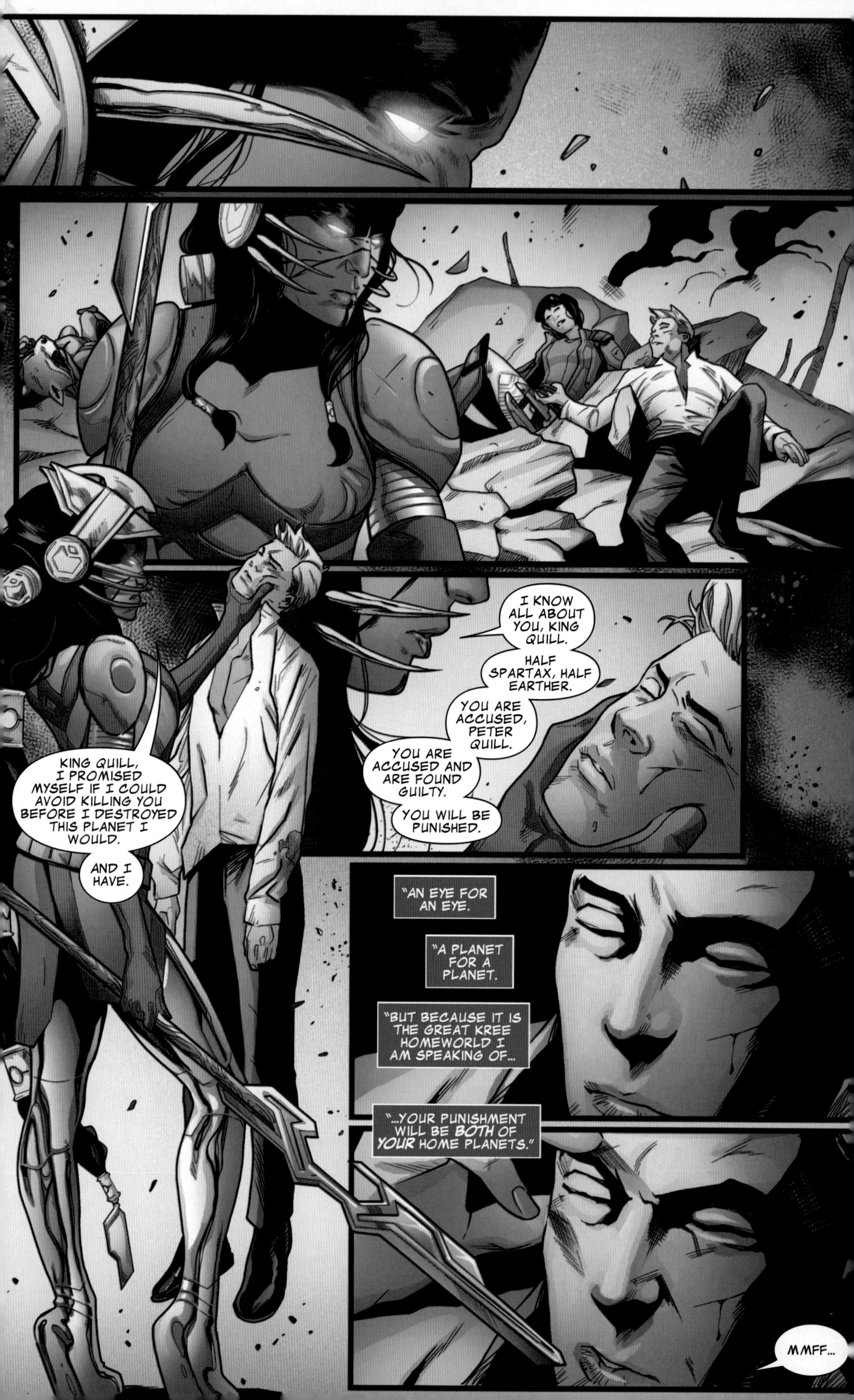
I KNOW ALL ABOUT YOU, KING QUILL.
HALF SPARTAX, HALF EARTHER.
YOU ARE ACCUSED, PETER QUILL.
YOU ARE ACCUSED AND ARE FOUND GUILTY.
YOU WILL BE PUNISHED.
KING QUILL, I PROMISED MYSELF IF I COULD AVOID KILLING YOU BEFORE I DESTROYED THIS PLANET I WOULD.
AND I HAVE.
"AN EYE FOR AN EYE.
"A PLANET FOR A PLANET.
"BUT BECAUSE IT IS THE GREAT KREE HOMEWORLD I AM SPEAKING OF...
"...YOUR PUNISHMENT WILL BE BOTH OF YOUR HOME PLANETS."
MMFF...

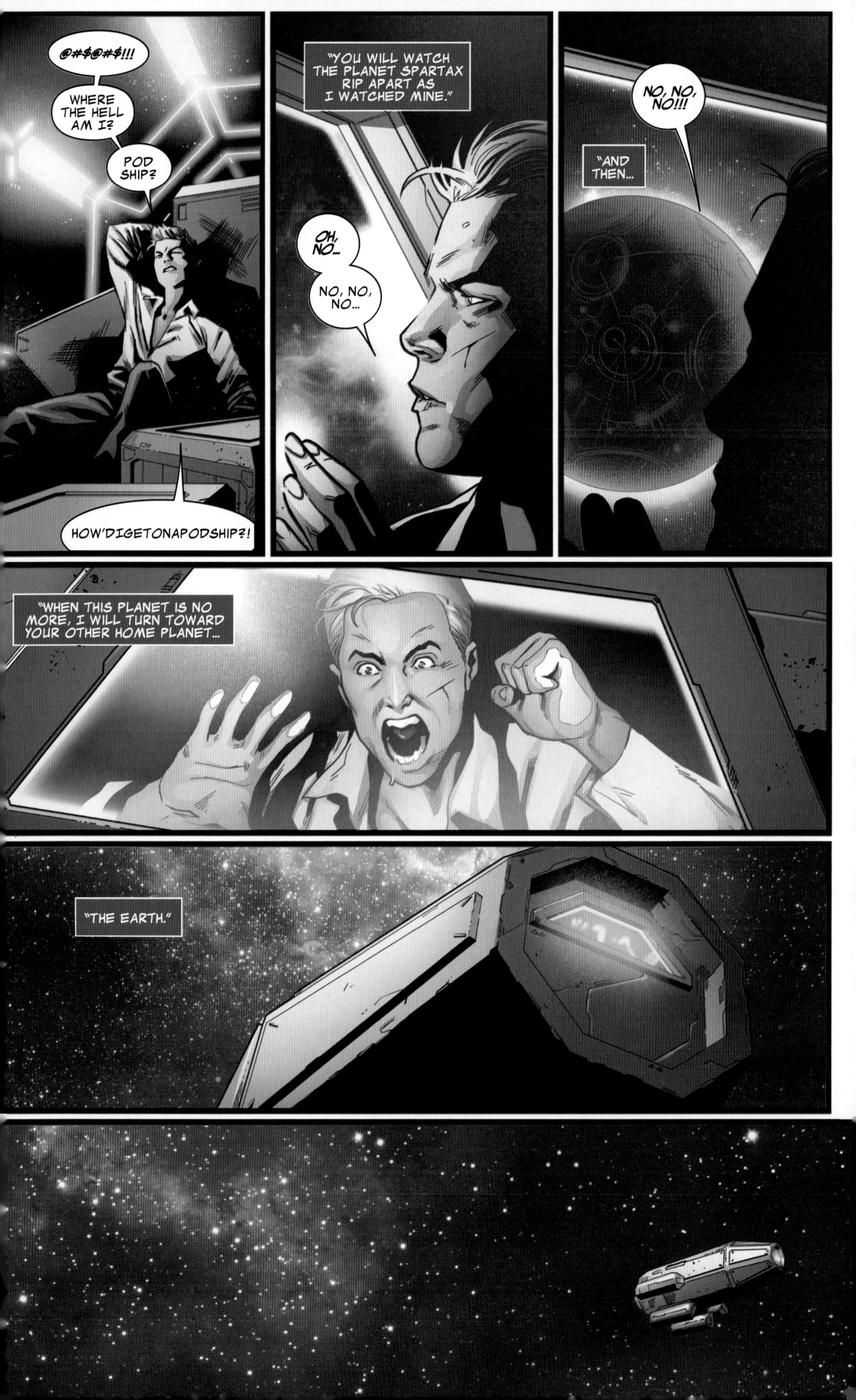
@#$@#$!!!
WHERE THE HELL AM I?
POD SHIP?
HOW'DIGETONAPODSHIP?!
"YOU WILL WATCH THE PLANET SPARTAX RIP APART AS I WATCHED MINE."
OH, NO...
NO, NO, NO...
NO, NO, NO!!!
"AND THEN...
"WHEN THIS PLANET IS NO MORE, I WILL TURN TOWARD YOUR OTHER HOME PLANET...
"THE EARTH."

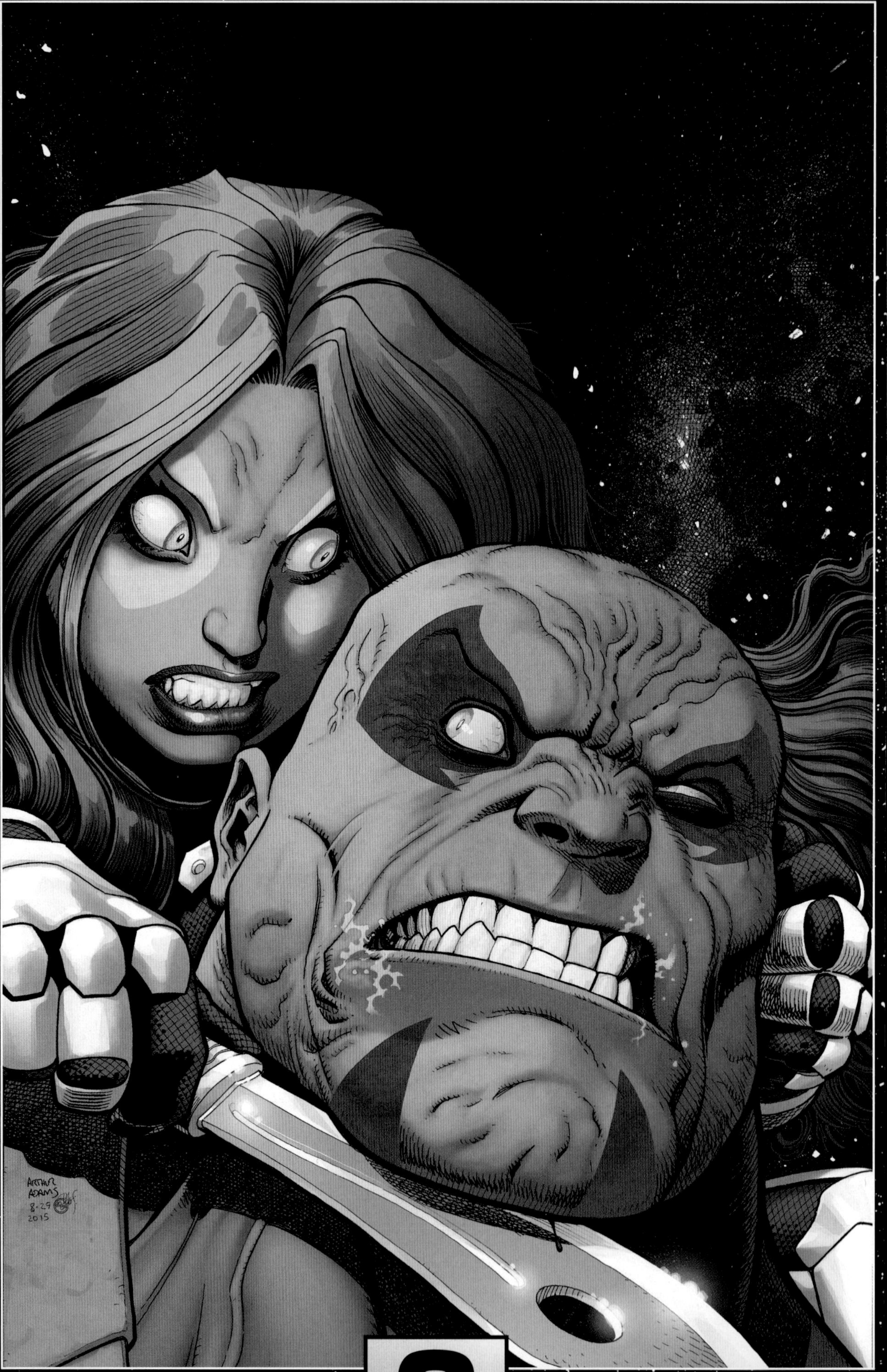
ARTHUR ADAMS
8-27
2015

3

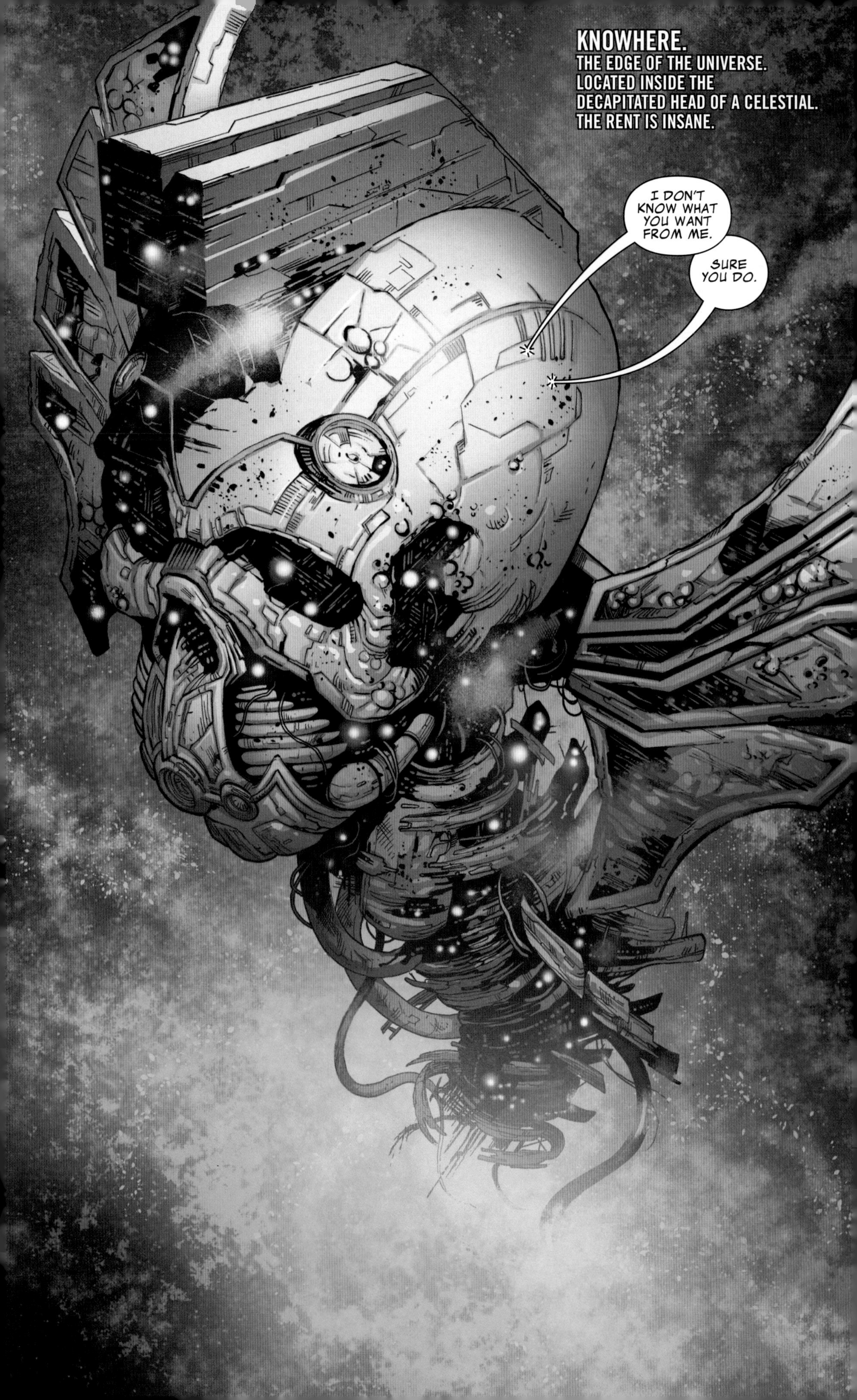
KNOWHERE.
THE EDGE OF THE UNIVERSE. LOCATED INSIDE THE DECAPITATED HEAD OF A CELESTIAL. THE RENT IS INSANE.
I DON'T KNOW WHAT YOU WANT FROM ME.
SURE YOU DO.

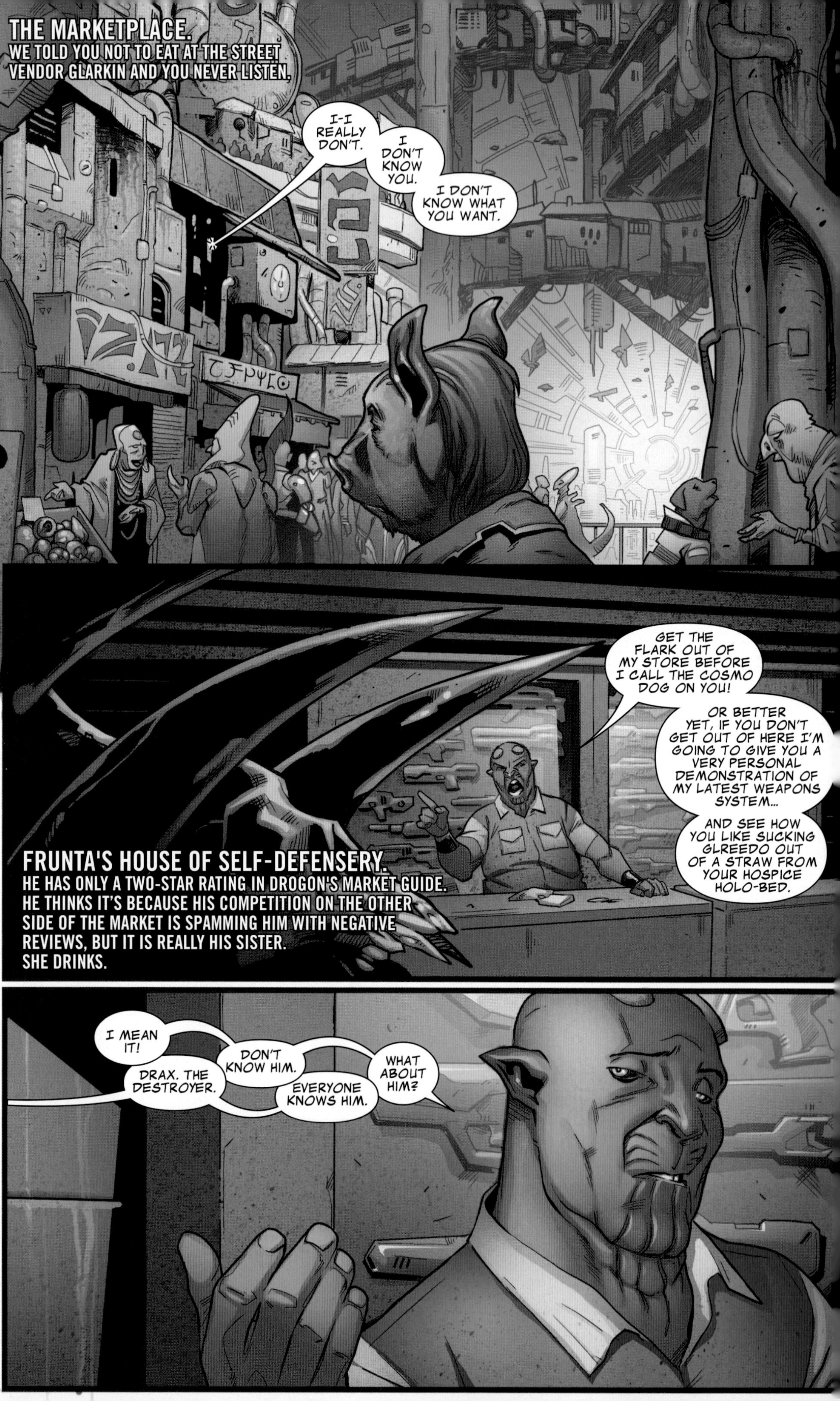
THE MARKETPLACE.
WE TOLD YOU NOT TO EAT AT THE STREET VENDOR GLARKIN AND YOU NEVER LISTEN.
I-I REALLY DON'T.
I DON'T KNOW YOU.
I DON'T KNOW WHAT YOU WANT.
GET THE FLARK OUT OF MY STORE BEFORE I CALL THE COSMO DOG ON YOU!
OR BETTER YET, IF YOU DON'T GET OUT OF HERE I'M GOING TO GIVE YOU A VERY PERSONAL DEMONSTRATION OF MY LATEST WEAPONS SYSTEM...
AND SEE HOW YOU LIKE SUCKING GLREEDO OUT OF A STRAW FROM YOUR HOSPICE HOLO-BED.
FRUNTA'S HOUSE OF SELF-DEFENSERY.
HE HAS ONLY A TWO-STAR RATING IN DROGON'S MARKET GUIDE. HE THINKS IT'S BECAUSE HIS COMPETITION ON THE OTHER SIDE OF THE MARKET IS SPAMMING HIM WITH NEGATIVE REVIEWS, BUT IT IS REALLY HIS SISTER. SHE DRINKS.
I MEAN IT!
DRAX. THE DESTROYER.
DON'T KNOW HIM.
EVERYONE KNOWS HIM.
WHAT ABOUT HIM?

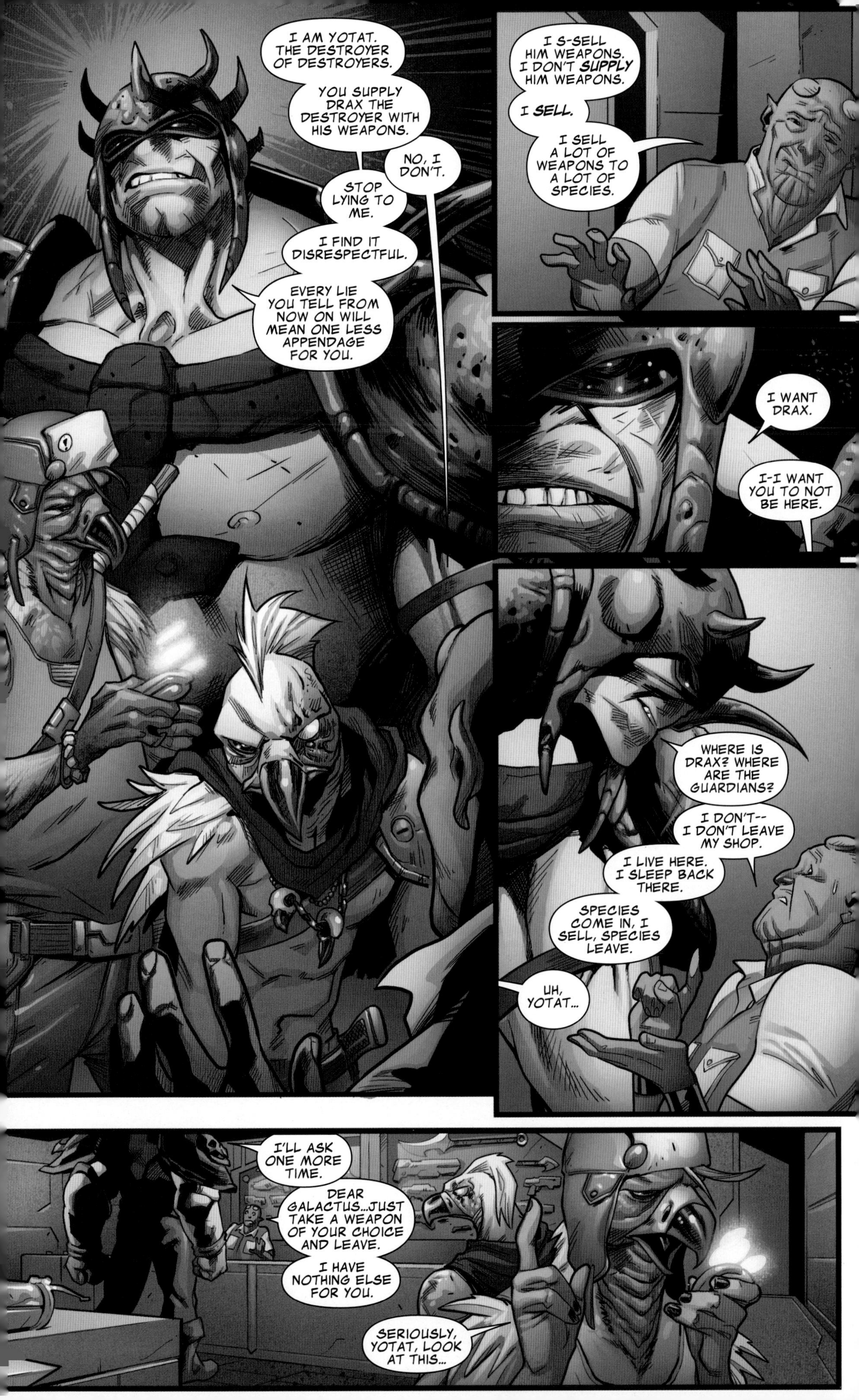

I AM YOTAT. THE DESTROYER OF DESTROYERS.
YOU SUPPLY DRAX THE DESTROYER WITH HIS WEAPONS.
NO, I DON'T.
STOP LYING TO ME.
I FIND IT DISRESPECTFUL.
EVERY LIE YOU TELL FROM NOW ON WILL MEAN ONE LESS APPENDAGE FOR YOU.
I S-SELL HIM WEAPONS. I DON'T **SUPPLY** HIM WEAPONS.
I **SELL.**
I SELL A LOT OF WEAPONS TO A LOT OF SPECIES.
I WANT DRAX.
I-I WANT YOU TO NOT BE HERE.
WHERE IS DRAX? WHERE ARE THE GUARDIANS?
I DON'T-- I DON'T LEAVE MY SHOP.
I LIVE HERE. I SLEEP BACK THERE.
SPECIES COME IN, I SELL, SPECIES LEAVE.
UH, YOTAT...
I'LL ASK ONE MORE TIME.
DEAR GALACTUS...JUST TAKE A WEAPON OF YOUR CHOICE AND LEAVE.
I HAVE NOTHING ELSE FOR YOU.
SERIOUSLY, YOTAT, LOOK AT THIS...

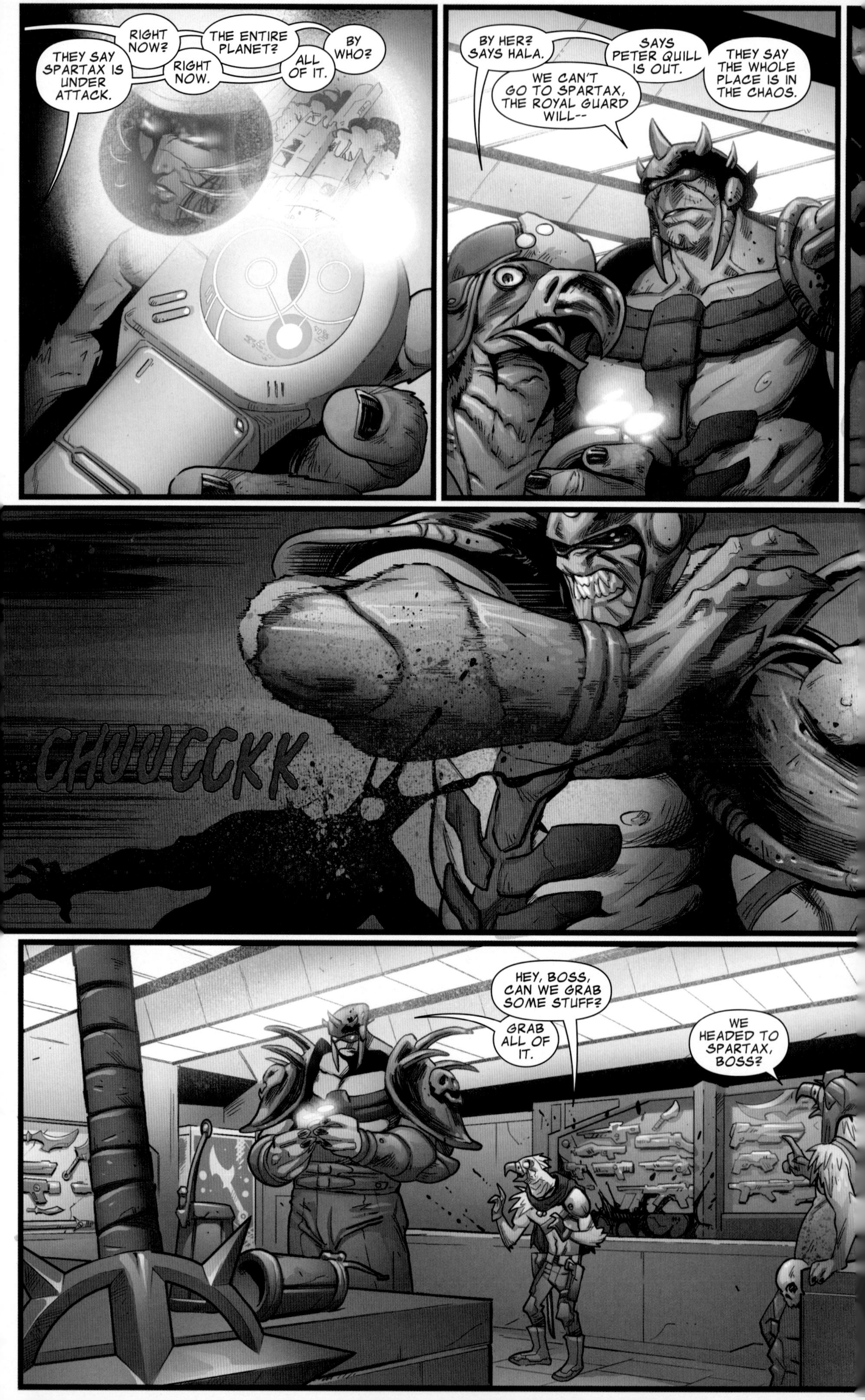
THEY SAY SPARTAX IS UNDER ATTACK.
RIGHT NOW?
RIGHT NOW.
THE ENTIRE PLANET?
ALL OF IT.
BY WHO?
BY HER? SAYS HALA.
SAYS PETER QUILL IS OUT.
WE CAN'T GO TO SPARTAX, THE ROYAL GUARD WILL--
THEY SAY THE WHOLE PLACE IS IN THE CHAOS.
CHUUCCKK
HEY, BOSS, CAN WE GRAB SOME STUFF?
GRAB ALL OF IT.
WE HEADED TO SPARTAX, BOSS?

GOOD.

GO--GO THERE.

THERE'S YOUR GUARDIANS.

GO. GO.

YOU'VE BEEN NO HELP AT ALL.

I TOLD YOU I DIDN'T KNOW ANY--

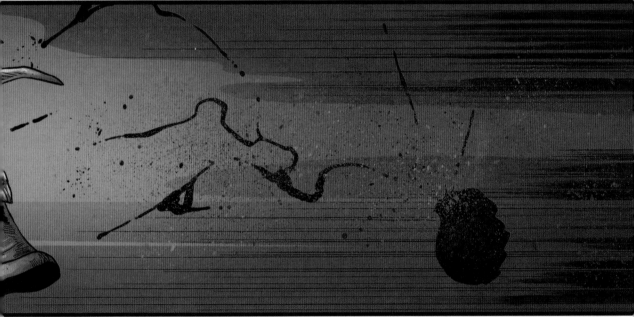

YER DAMN RIGHT WE ARE. AND IF THAT TALL-TREE WARRIOR IS THE ONE RIPPING SPARTAX IN HALF, I MIGHT HAVE FOUND MY LIFE MATE.

BEFORE DO...

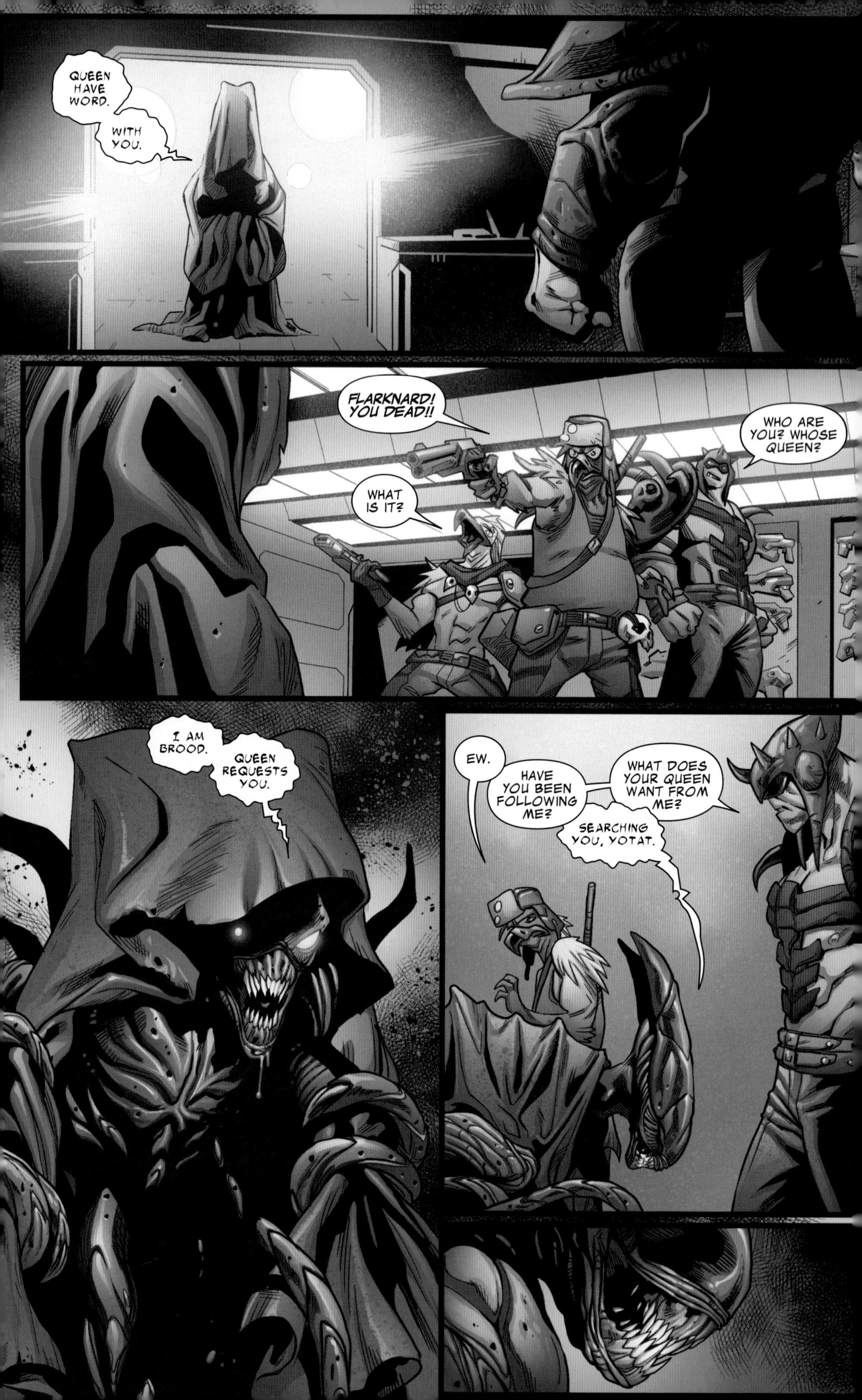
QUEEN HAVE WORD.
WITH YOU.
FLARKNARD! YOU DEAD!!
WHAT IS IT?
WHO ARE YOU? WHOSE QUEEN?
I AM BROOD.
QUEEN REQUESTS YOU.
EW.
HAVE YOU BEEN FOLLOWING ME?
WHAT DOES YOUR QUEEN WANT FROM ME?
SEARCHING YOU, YOTAT.

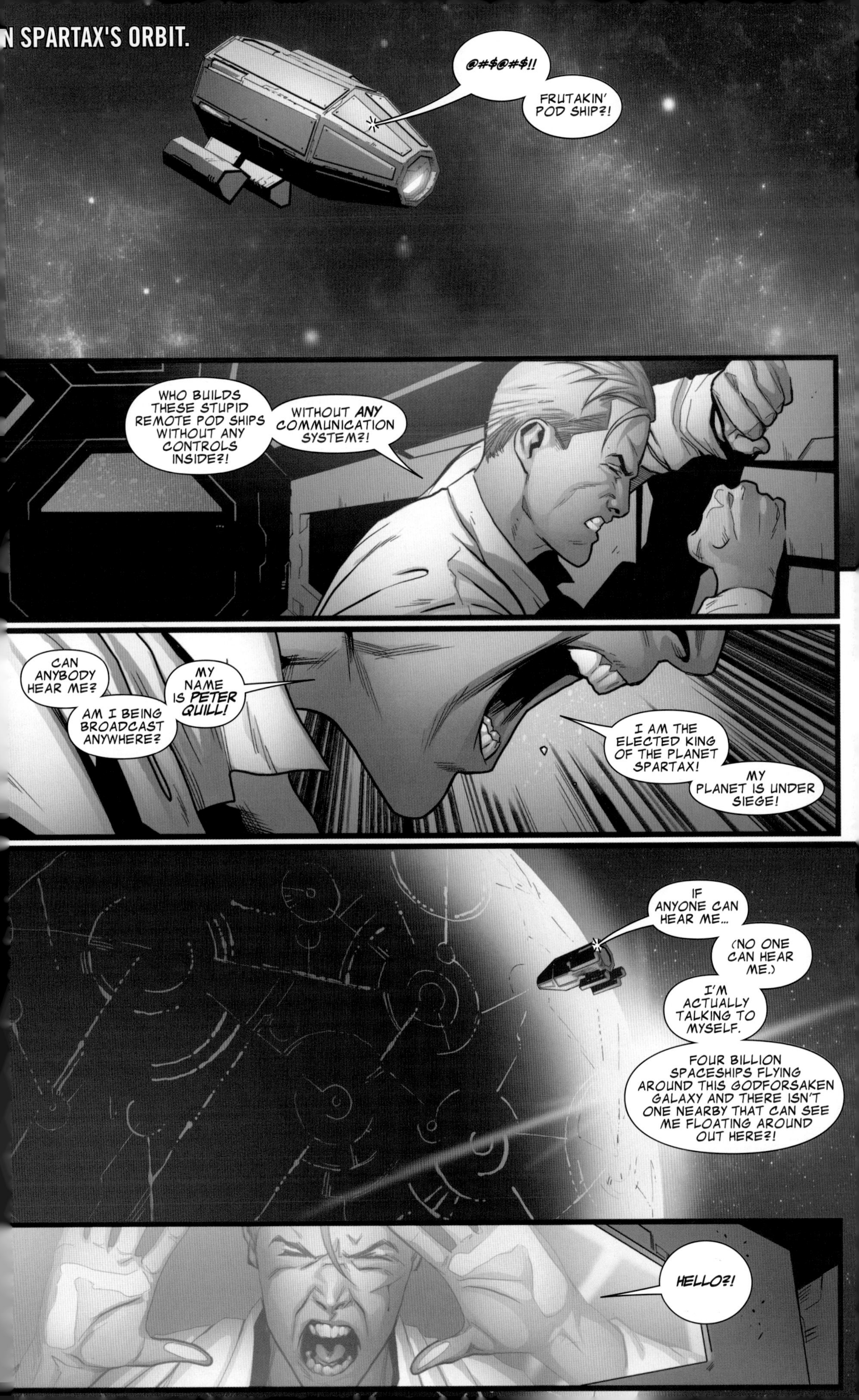
N SPARTAX'S ORBIT.
@#$@#$!!
FRUTAKIN' POD SHIP?!
WHO BUILDS THESE STUPID REMOTE POD SHIPS WITHOUT ANY CONTROLS INSIDE?!
WITHOUT ANY COMMUNICATION SYSTEM?!
CAN ANYBODY HEAR ME?
AM I BEING BROADCAST ANYWHERE?
MY NAME IS PETER QUILL!
I AM THE ELECTED KING OF THE PLANET SPARTAX!
MY PLANET IS UNDER SIEGE!
IF ANYONE CAN HEAR ME...
(NO ONE CAN HEAR ME.)
I'M ACTUALLY TALKING TO MYSELF.
FOUR BILLION SPACESHIPS FLYING AROUND THIS GODFORSAKEN GALAXY AND THERE ISN'T ONE NEARBY THAT CAN SEE ME FLOATING AROUND OUT HERE?!
HELLO?!

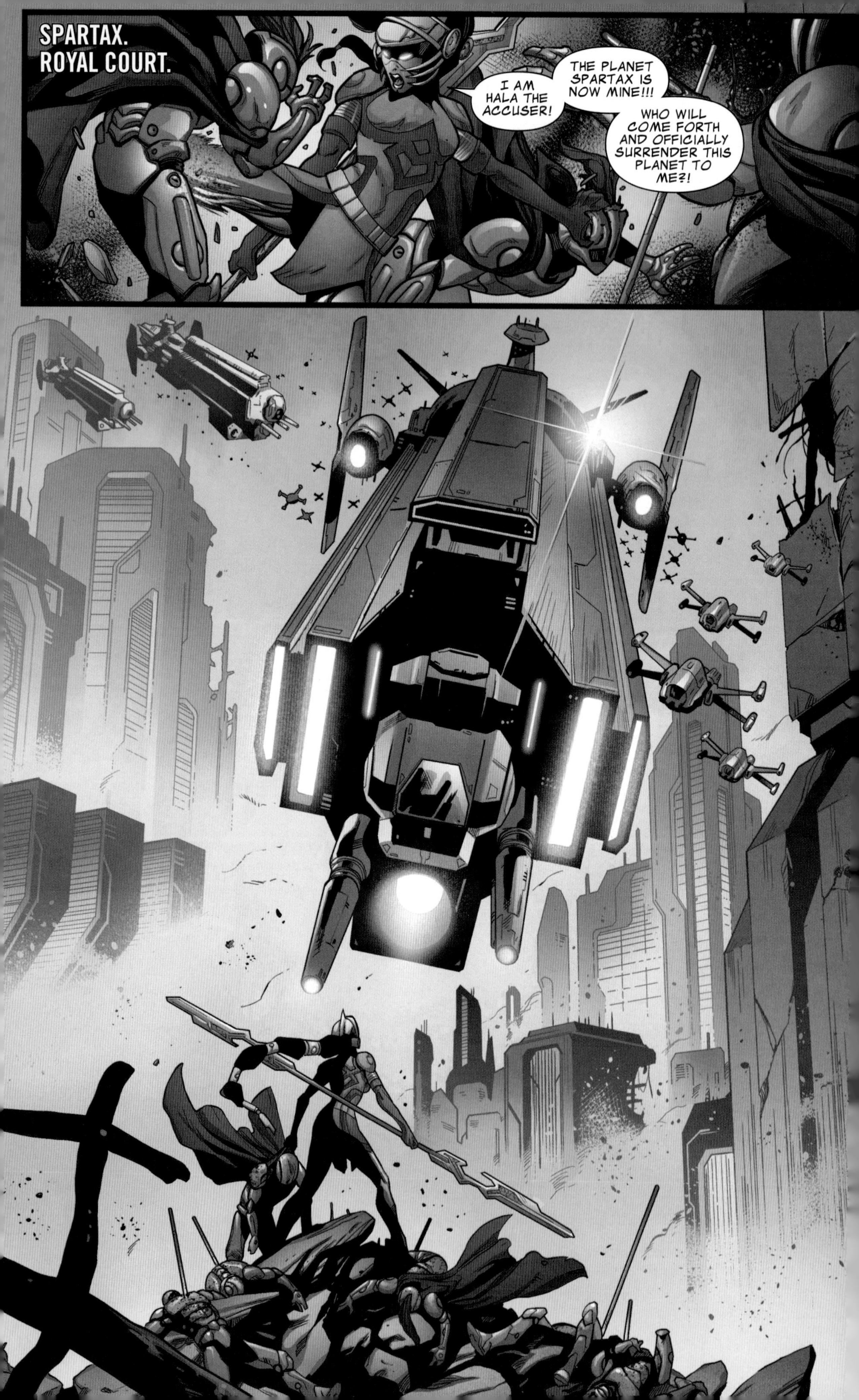
SPARTAX.
ROYAL COURT.
I AM HALA THE ACCUSER!
THE PLANET SPARTAX IS NOW MINE!!!
WHO WILL COME FORTH AND OFFICIALLY SURRENDER THIS PLANET TO ME?!

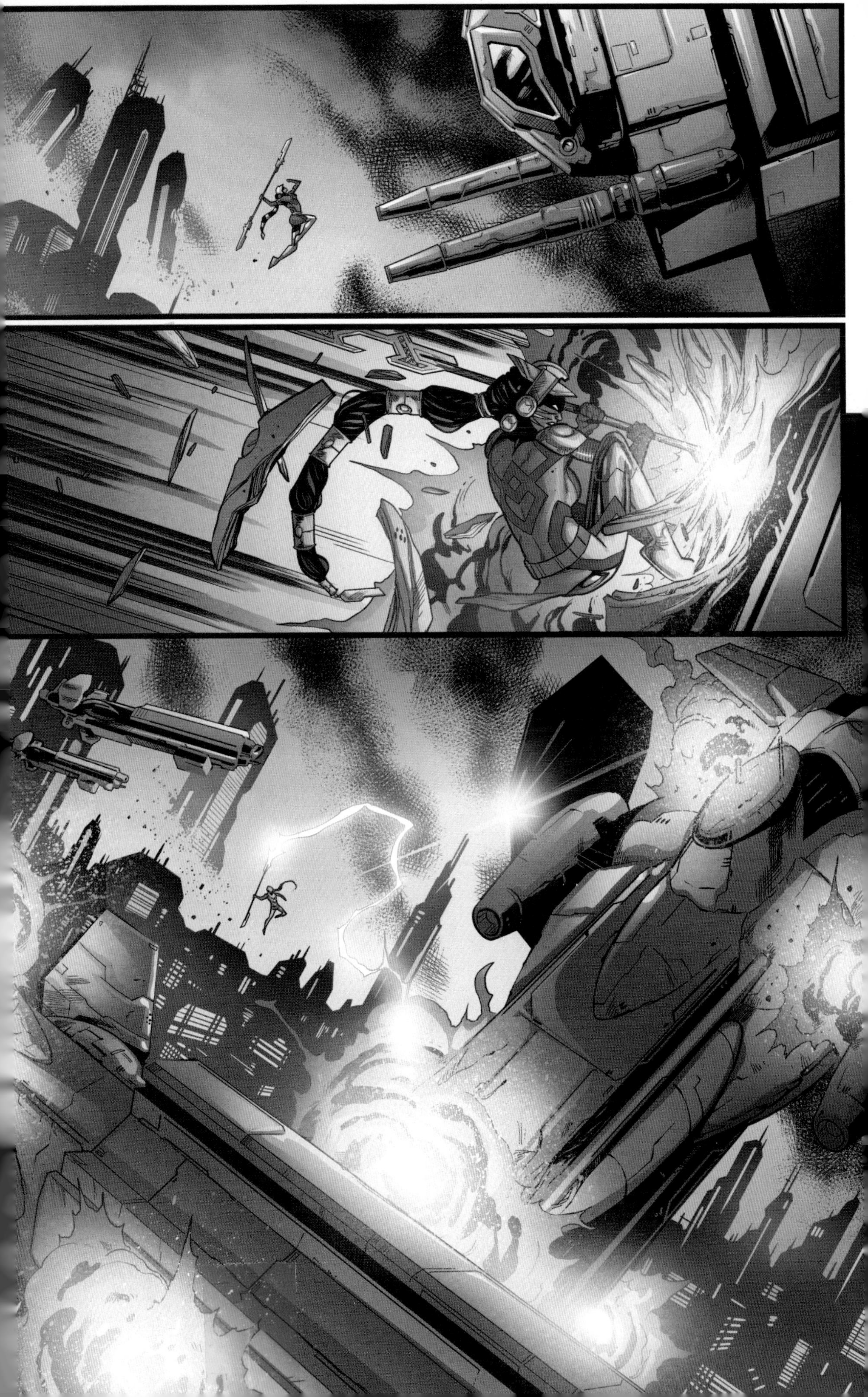

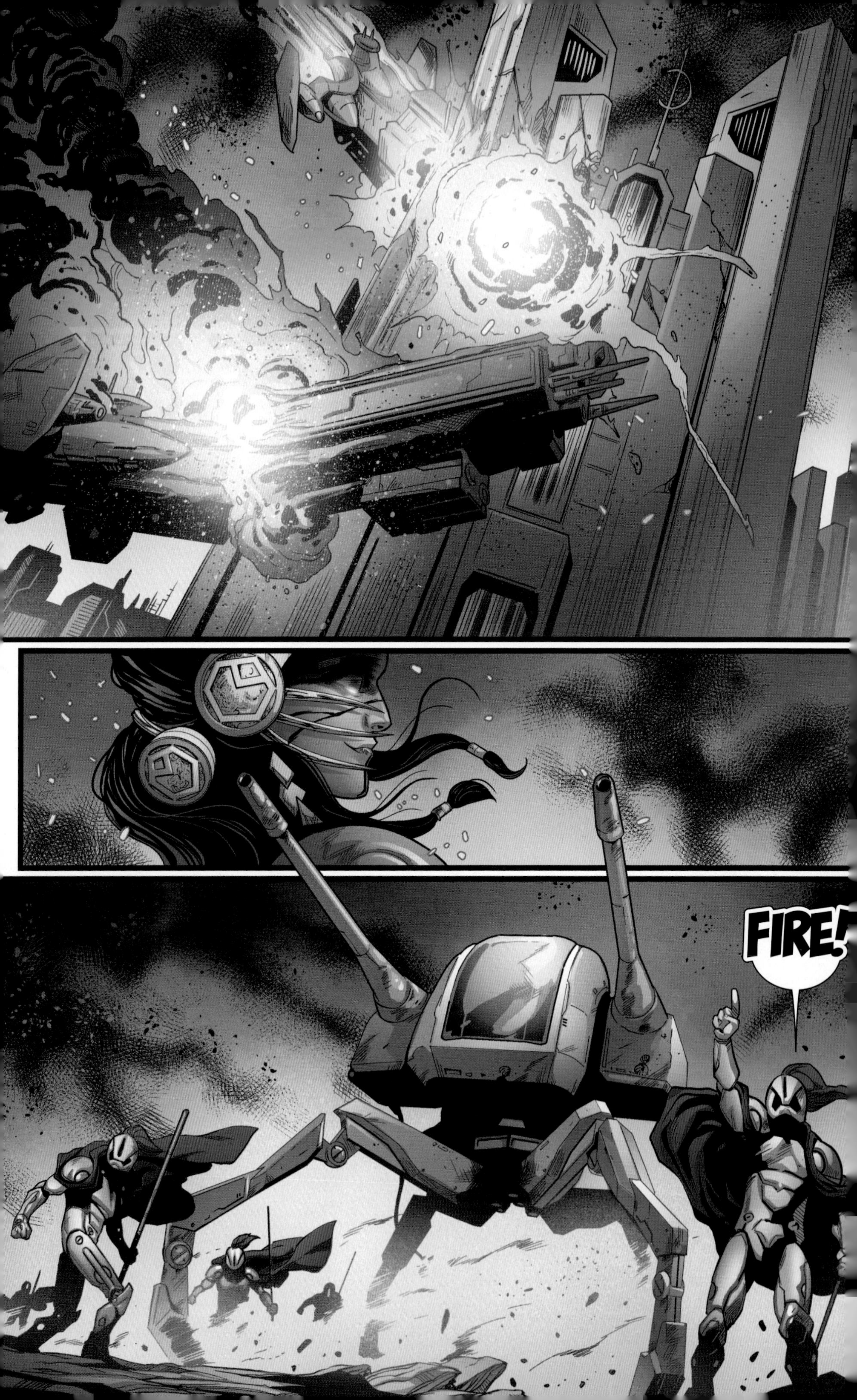
FIRE!

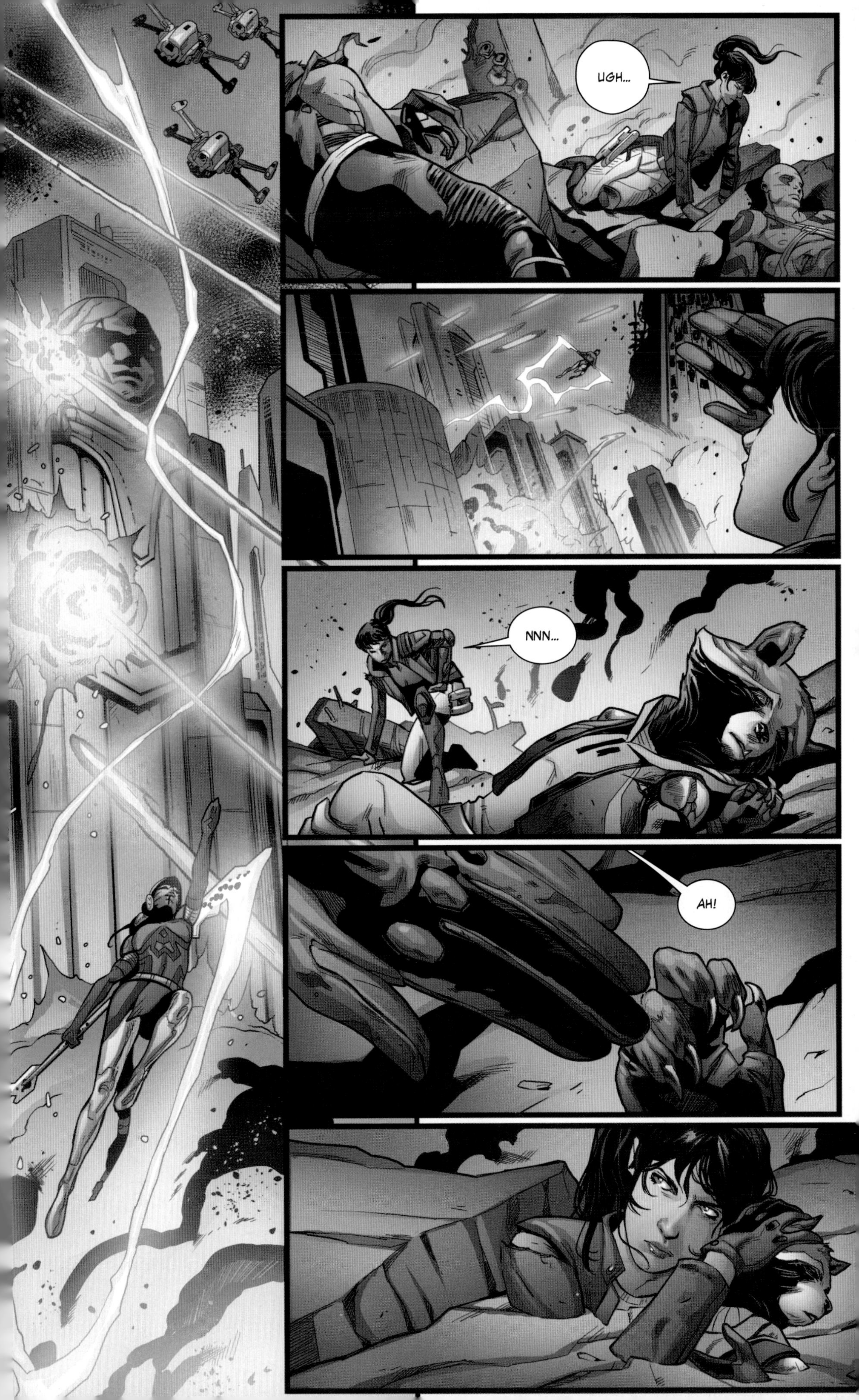
UGH...
NNN...
AH!

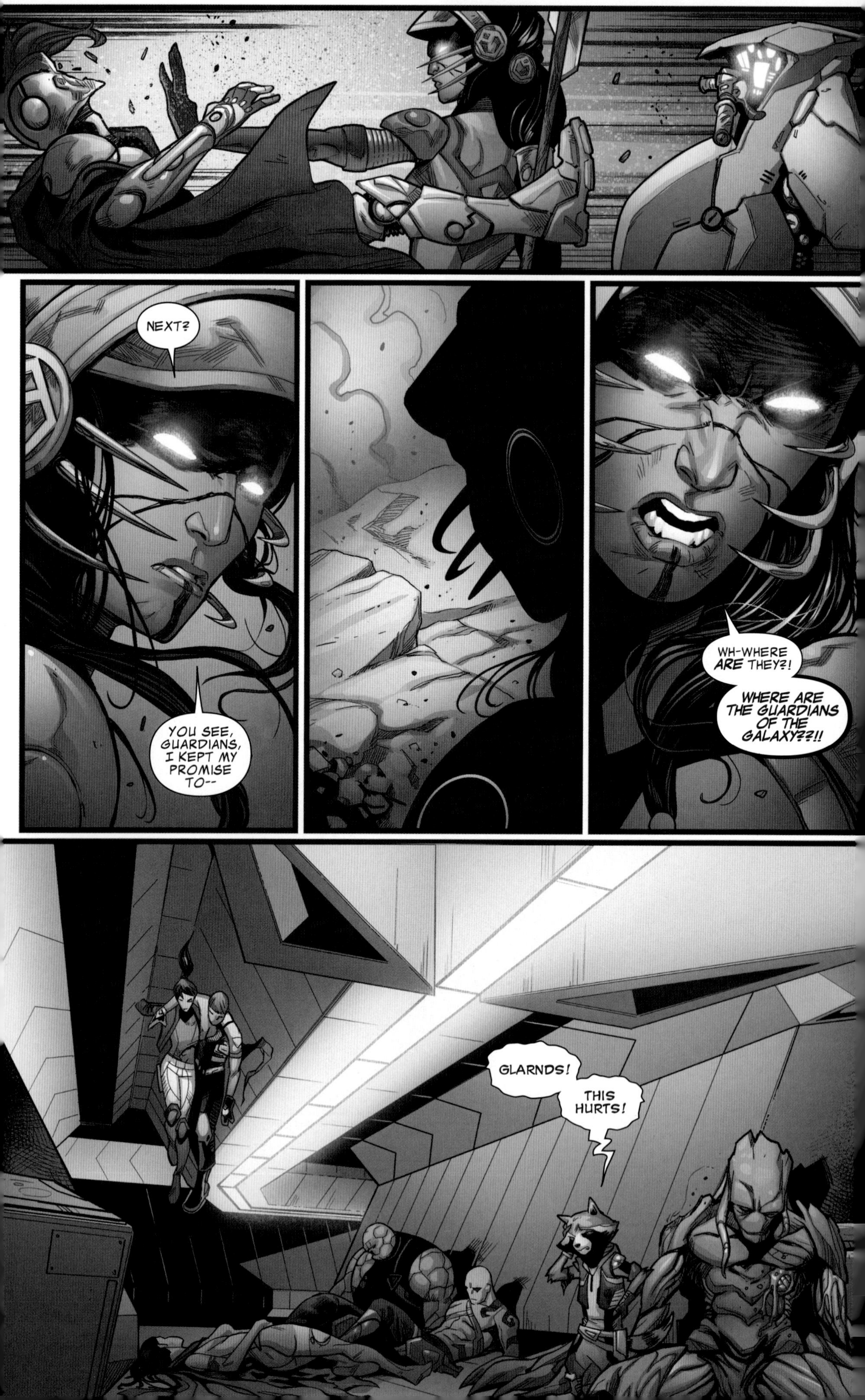
NEXT?
YOU SEE, GUARDIANS, I KEPT MY PROMISE TO--
WH-WHERE ARE THEY?!
WHERE ARE THE GUARDIANS OF THE GALAXY??!!
GLARNDS!
THIS HURTS!

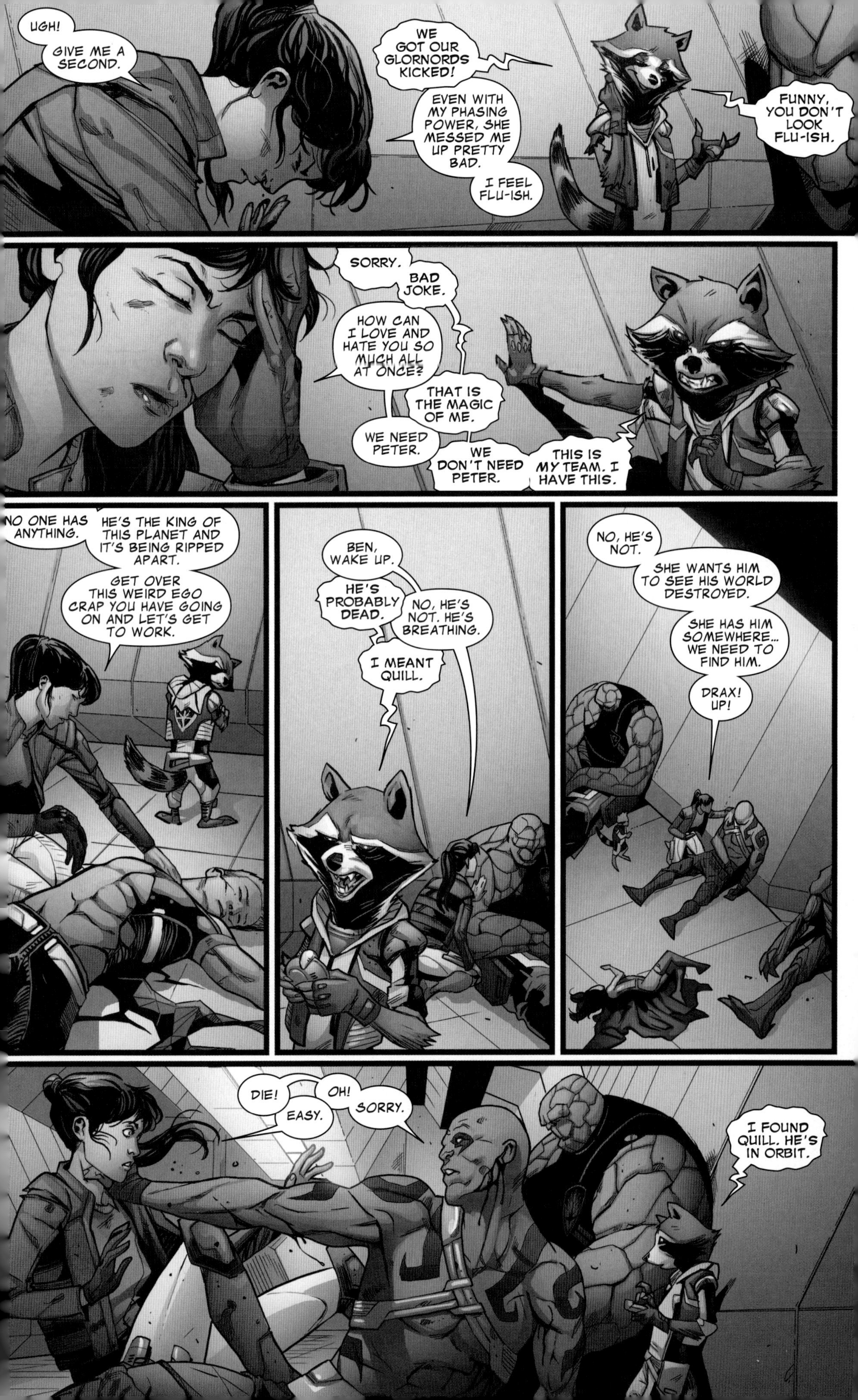
UGH!
GIVE ME A SECOND.
WE GOT OUR GLORNORDS KICKED!
EVEN WITH MY PHASING POWER, SHE MESSED ME UP PRETTY BAD.
I FEEL FLU-ISH.
FUNNY, YOU DON'T LOOK FLU-ISH.
SORRY.
BAD JOKE.
HOW CAN I LOVE AND HATE YOU SO MUCH ALL AT ONCE?
THAT IS THE MAGIC OF ME.
WE NEED PETER.
WE DON'T NEED PETER.
THIS IS MY TEAM. I HAVE THIS.
NO ONE HAS ANYTHING.
HE'S THE KING OF THIS PLANET AND IT'S BEING RIPPED APART.
GET OVER THIS WEIRD EGO CRAP YOU HAVE GOING ON AND LET'S GET TO WORK.
BEN, WAKE UP.
HE'S PROBABLY DEAD.
NO, HE'S NOT. HE'S BREATHING.
I MEANT QUILL.
NO, HE'S NOT.
SHE WANTS HIM TO SEE HIS WORLD DESTROYED.
SHE HAS HIM SOMEWHERE... WE NEED TO FIND HIM.
DRAX! UP!
DIE!
EASY.
OH!
SORRY.
I FOUND QUILL. HE'S IN ORBIT.

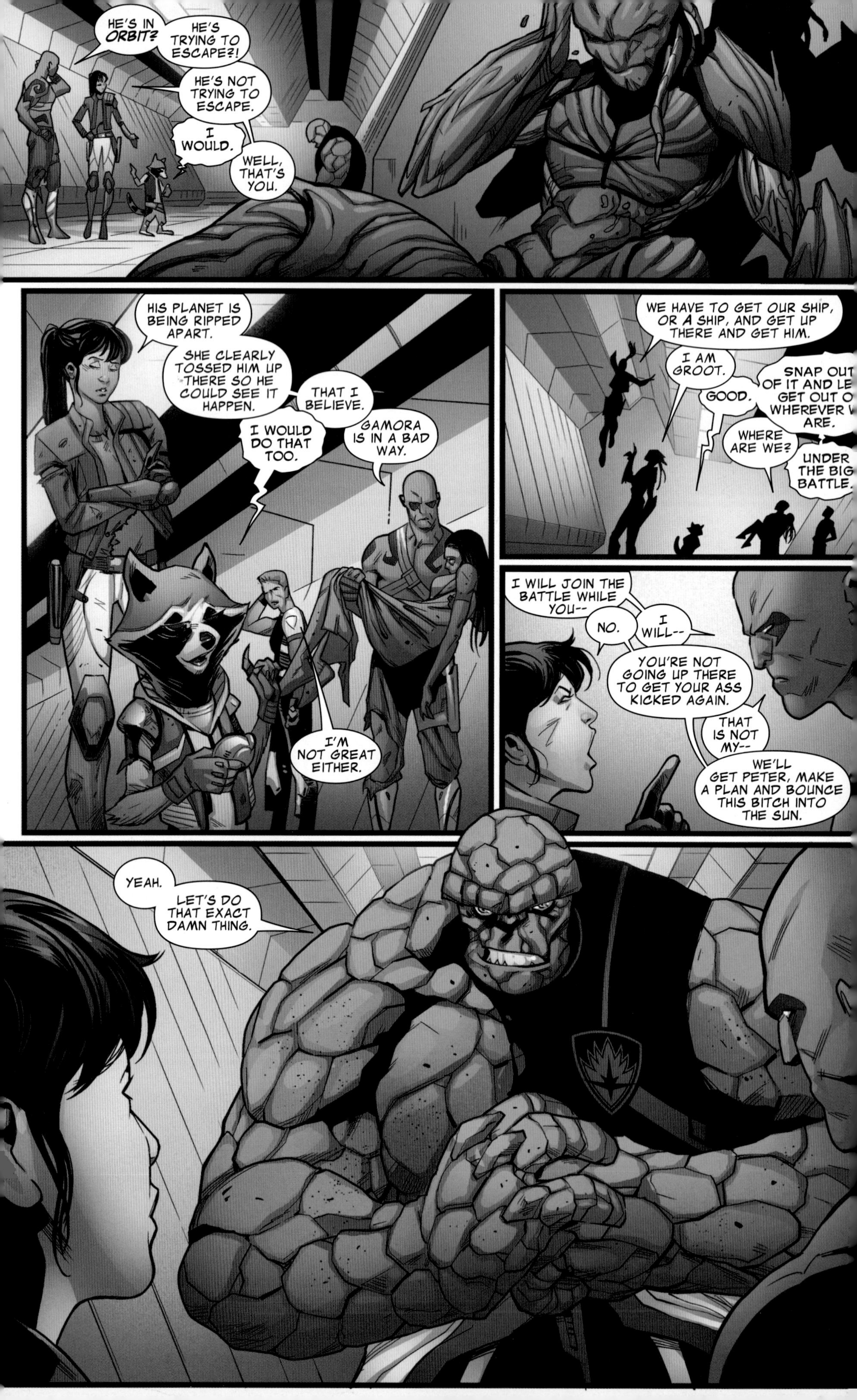

HE'S IN ORBIT?
HE'S TRYING TO ESCAPE?!
HE'S NOT TRYING TO ESCAPE.
I WOULD.
WELL, THAT'S YOU.
HIS PLANET IS BEING RIPPED APART.
SHE CLEARLY TOSSED HIM UP THERE SO HE COULD SEE IT HAPPEN.
THAT I BELIEVE.
I WOULD DO THAT TOO.
GAMORA IS IN A BAD WAY.
I'M NOT GREAT EITHER.
WE HAVE TO GET OUR SHIP, OR A SHIP, AND GET UP THERE AND GET HIM.
I AM GROOT.
GOOD.
WHERE ARE WE?
I WILL JOIN THE BATTLE WHILE YOU--
NO.
I WILL--
YOU'RE NOT GOING UP THERE TO GET YOUR ASS KICKED AGAIN.
THAT IS NOT MY--
WE'LL GET PETER, MAKE A PLAN AND BOUNCE THIS BITCH INTO THE SUN.
YEAH.
LET'S DO THAT EXACT DAMN THING.

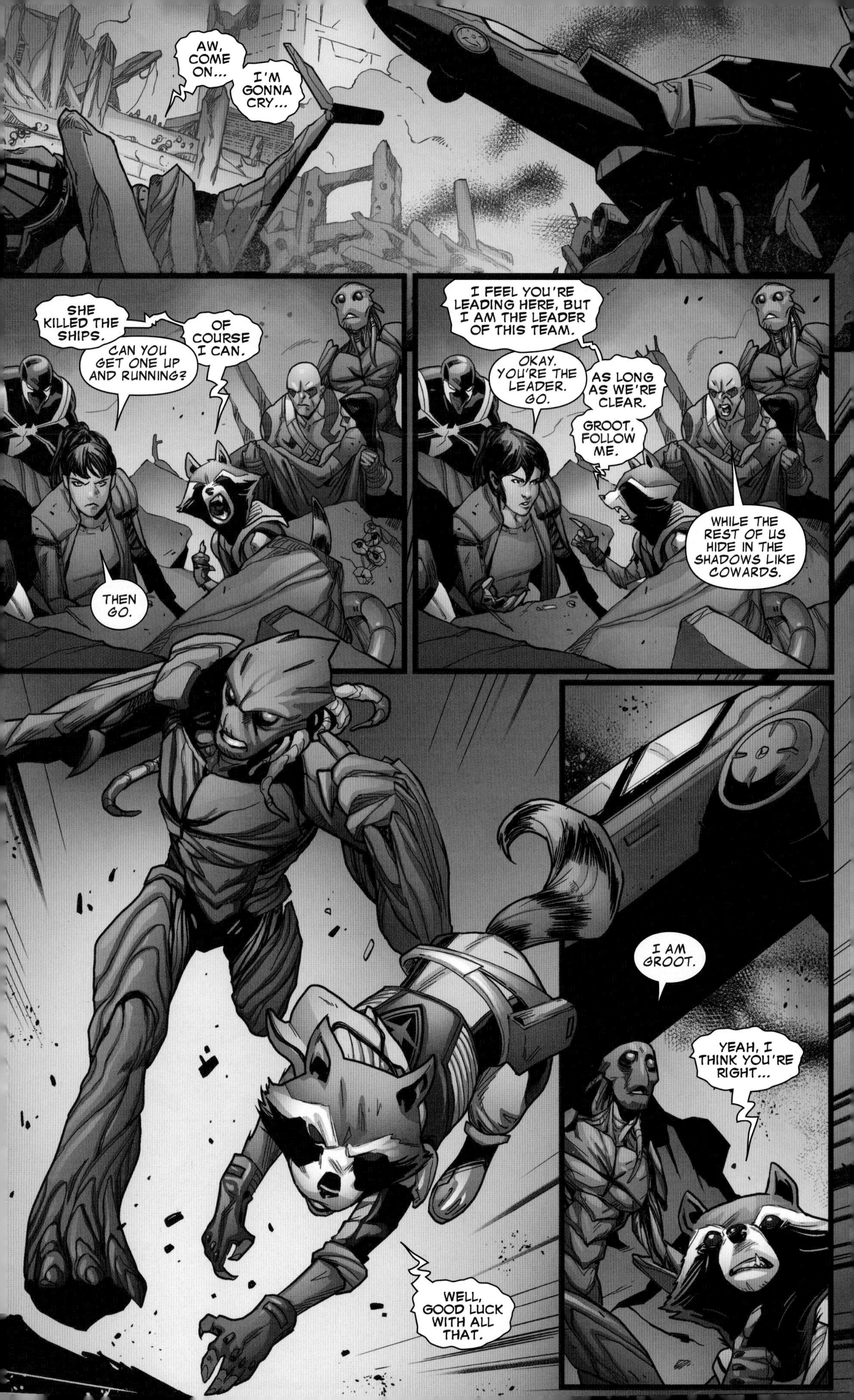
AW, COME ON...
I'M GONNA CRY...
SHE KILLED THE SHIPS.
CAN YOU GET ONE UP AND RUNNING?
OF COURSE I CAN.
THEN GO.
I FEEL YOU'RE LEADING HERE, BUT I AM THE LEADER OF THIS TEAM.
OKAY. YOU'RE THE LEADER. GO.
AS LONG AS WE'RE CLEAR.
GROOT, FOLLOW ME.
WHILE THE REST OF US HIDE IN THE SHADOWS LIKE COWARDS.
WELL, GOOD LUCK WITH ALL THAT.
I AM GROOT.
YEAH, I THINK YOU'RE RIGHT...

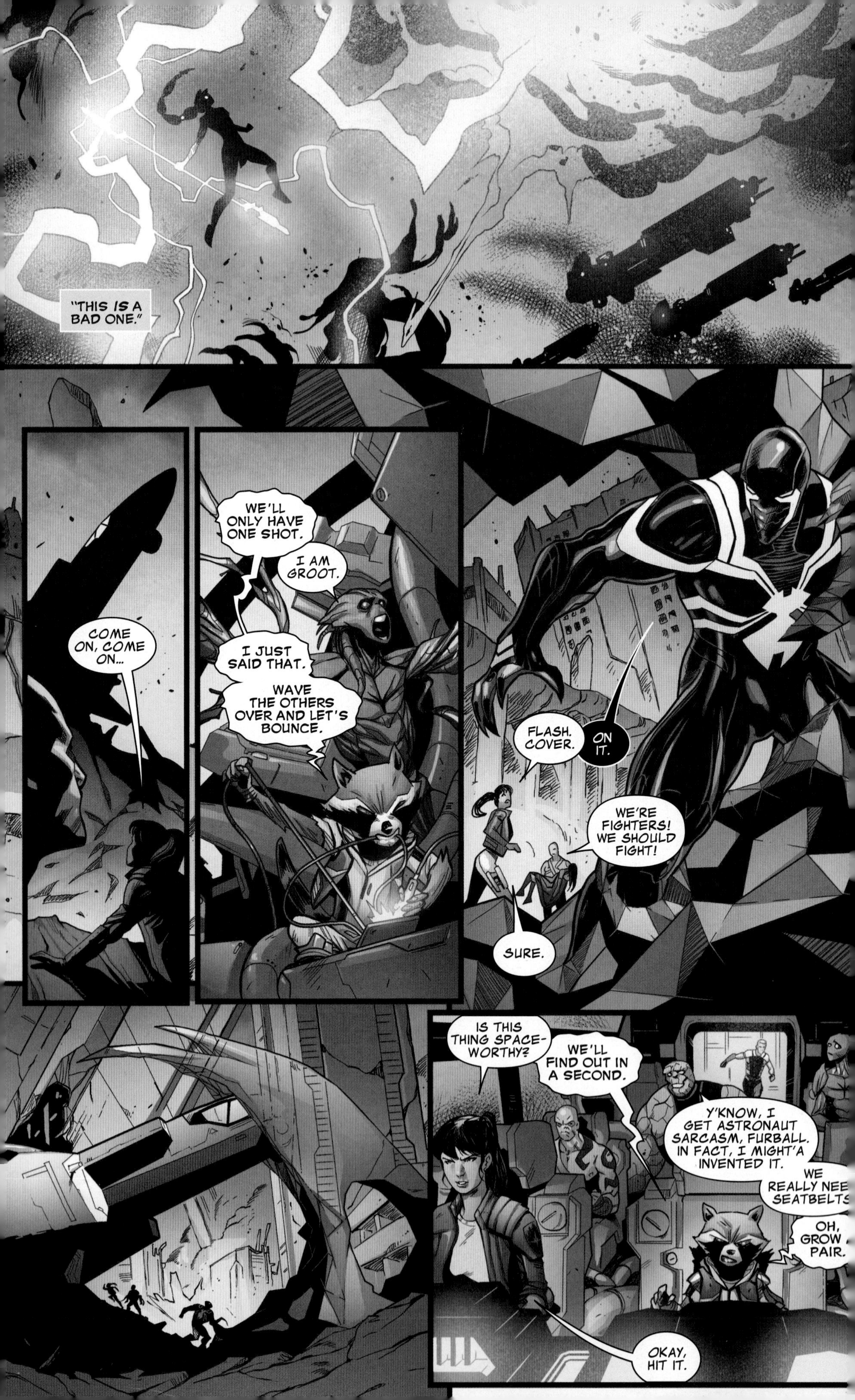
"THIS IS A BAD ONE."
COME ON, COME ON...
WE'LL ONLY HAVE ONE SHOT.
I AM GROOT.
I JUST SAID THAT.
WAVE THE OTHERS OVER AND LET'S BOUNCE.
FLASH. COVER.
ON IT.
WE'RE FIGHTERS! WE SHOULD FIGHT!
SURE.
IS THIS THING SPACE-WORTHY?
WE'LL FIND OUT IN A SECOND.
Y'KNOW, I GET ASTRONAUT SARCASM, FURBALL. IN FACT, I MIGHT'A INVENTED IT.
WE REALLY NEE SEATBELTS
OH, GROW PAIR.
OKAY, HIT IT.

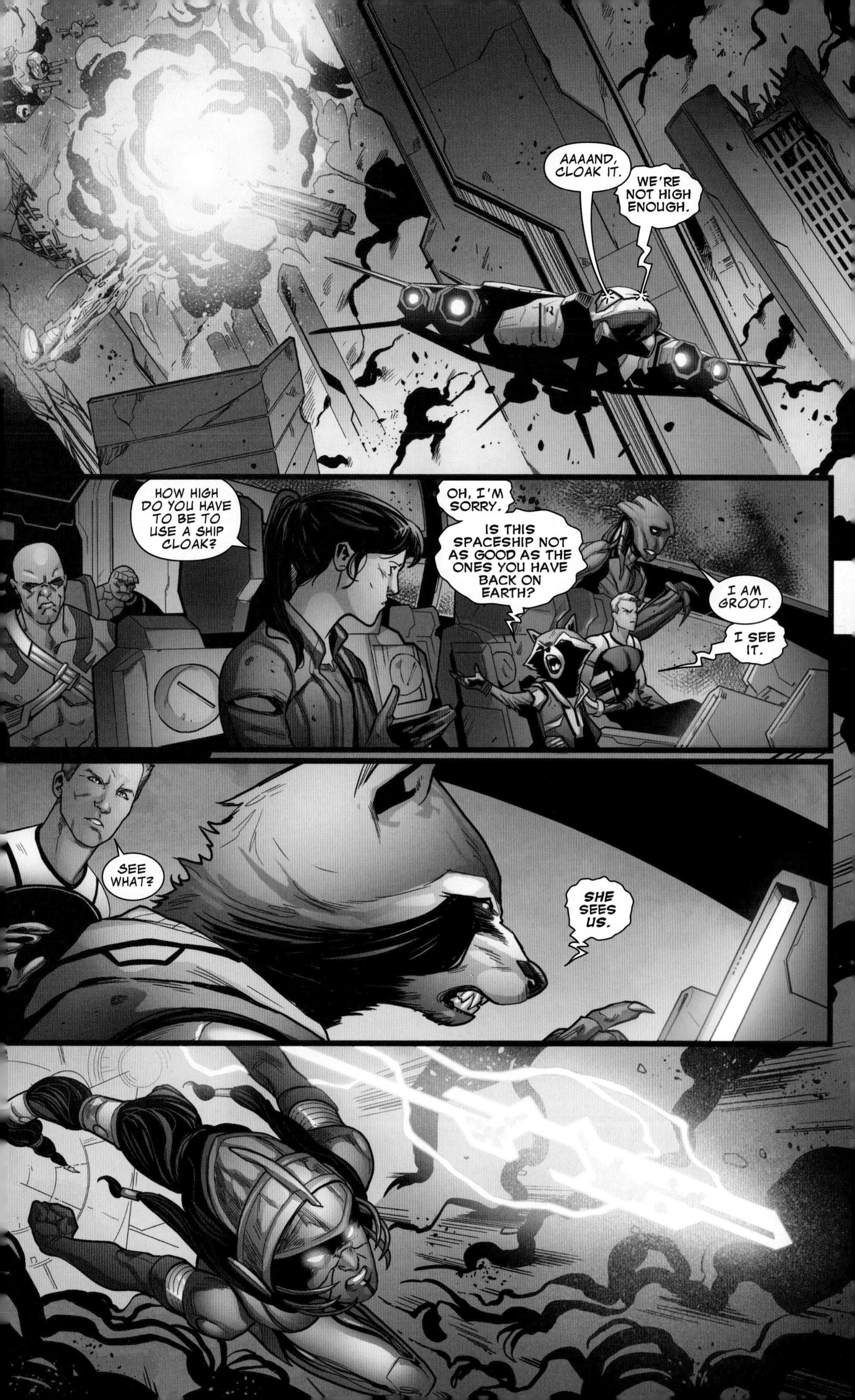
AAAAND, CLOAK IT.
WE'RE NOT HIGH ENOUGH.
HOW HIGH DO YOU HAVE TO BE TO USE A SHIP CLOAK?
OH, I'M SORRY.
IS THIS SPACESHIP NOT AS GOOD AS THE ONES YOU HAVE BACK ON EARTH?
I AM GROOT.
I SEE IT.
SEE WHAT?
SHE SEES US.

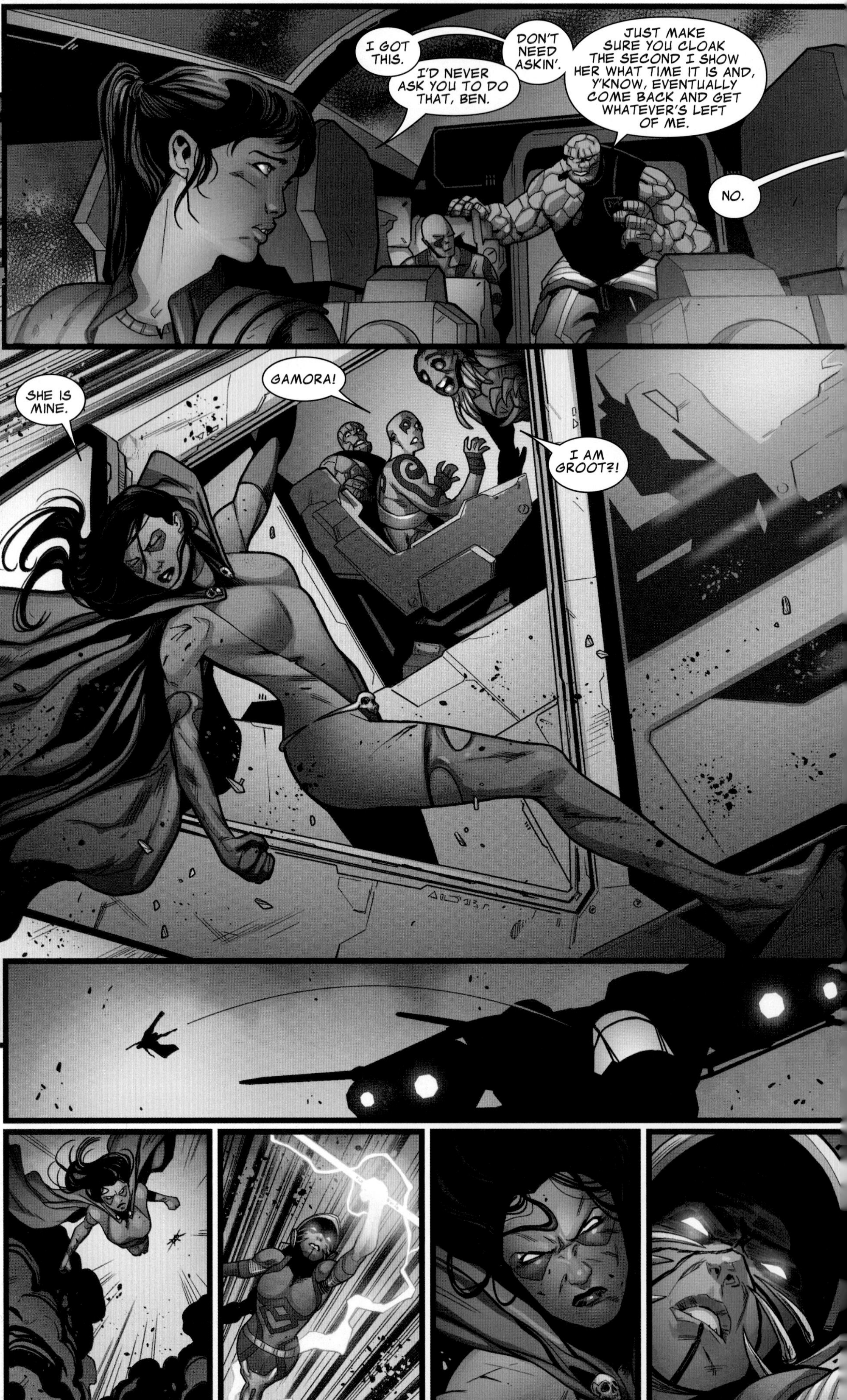
I GOT THIS.
DON'T NEED ASKIN'.
I'D NEVER ASK YOU TO DO THAT, BEN.
JUST MAKE SURE YOU CLOAK THE SECOND I SHOW HER WHAT TIME IT IS AND, Y'KNOW, EVENTUALLY COME BACK AND GET WHATEVER'S LEFT OF ME.
NO.
SHE IS MINE.
GAMORA!
I AM GROOT?!

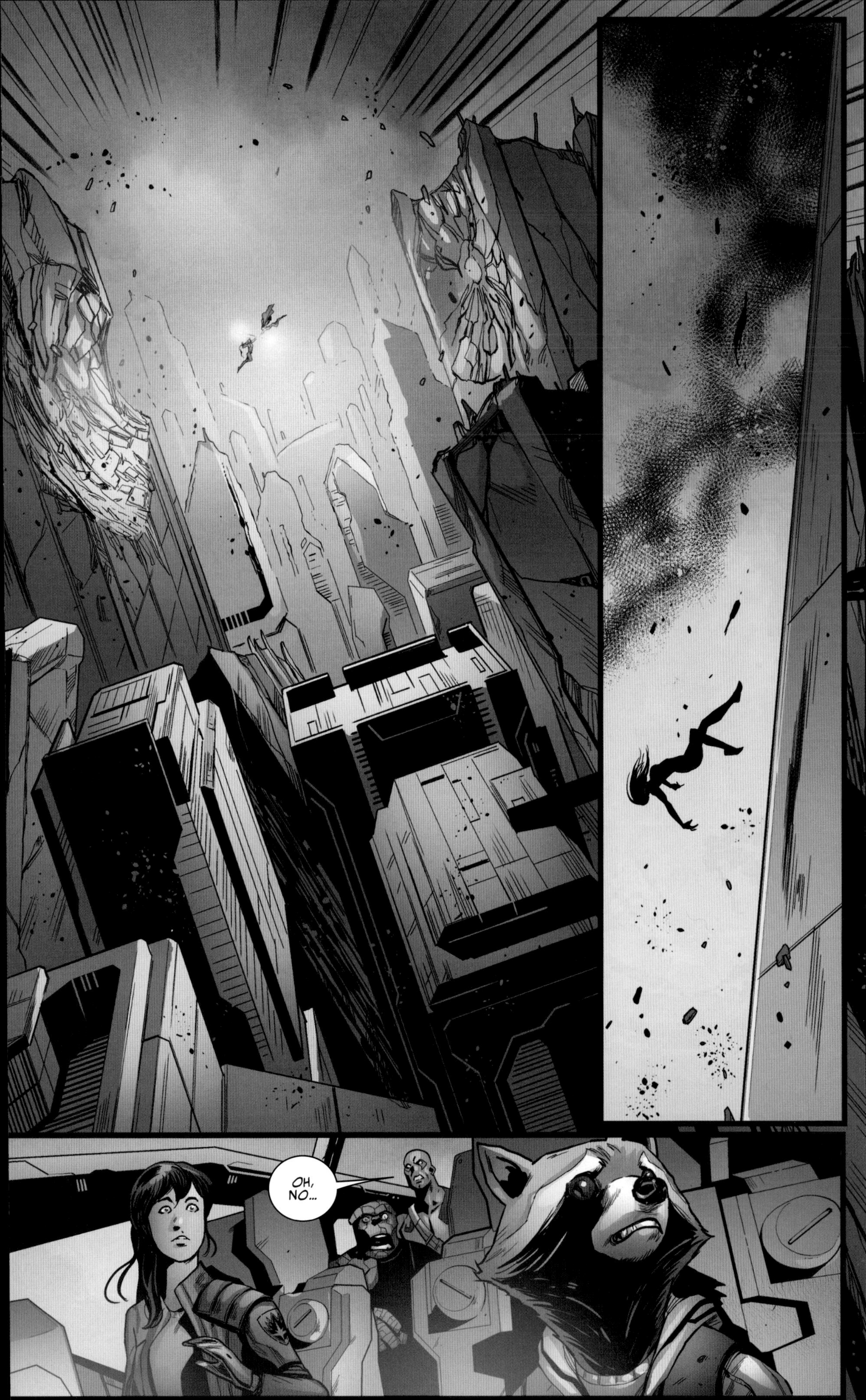
OH, NO...

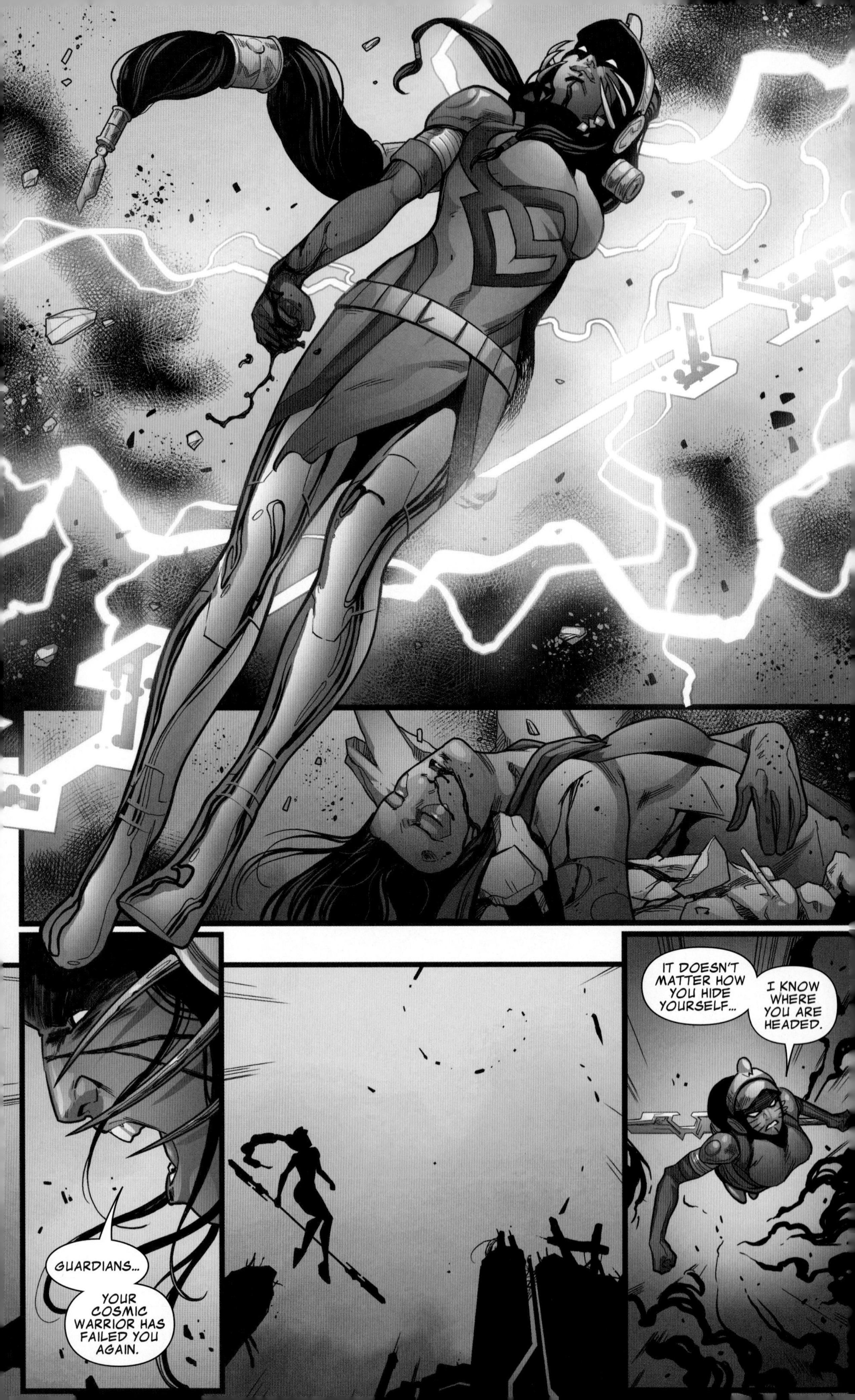
GUARDIANS...
YOUR COSMIC WARRIOR HAS FAILED YOU AGAIN.
IT DOESN'T MATTER HOW YOU HIDE YOURSELF...
I KNOW WHERE YOU ARE HEADED.

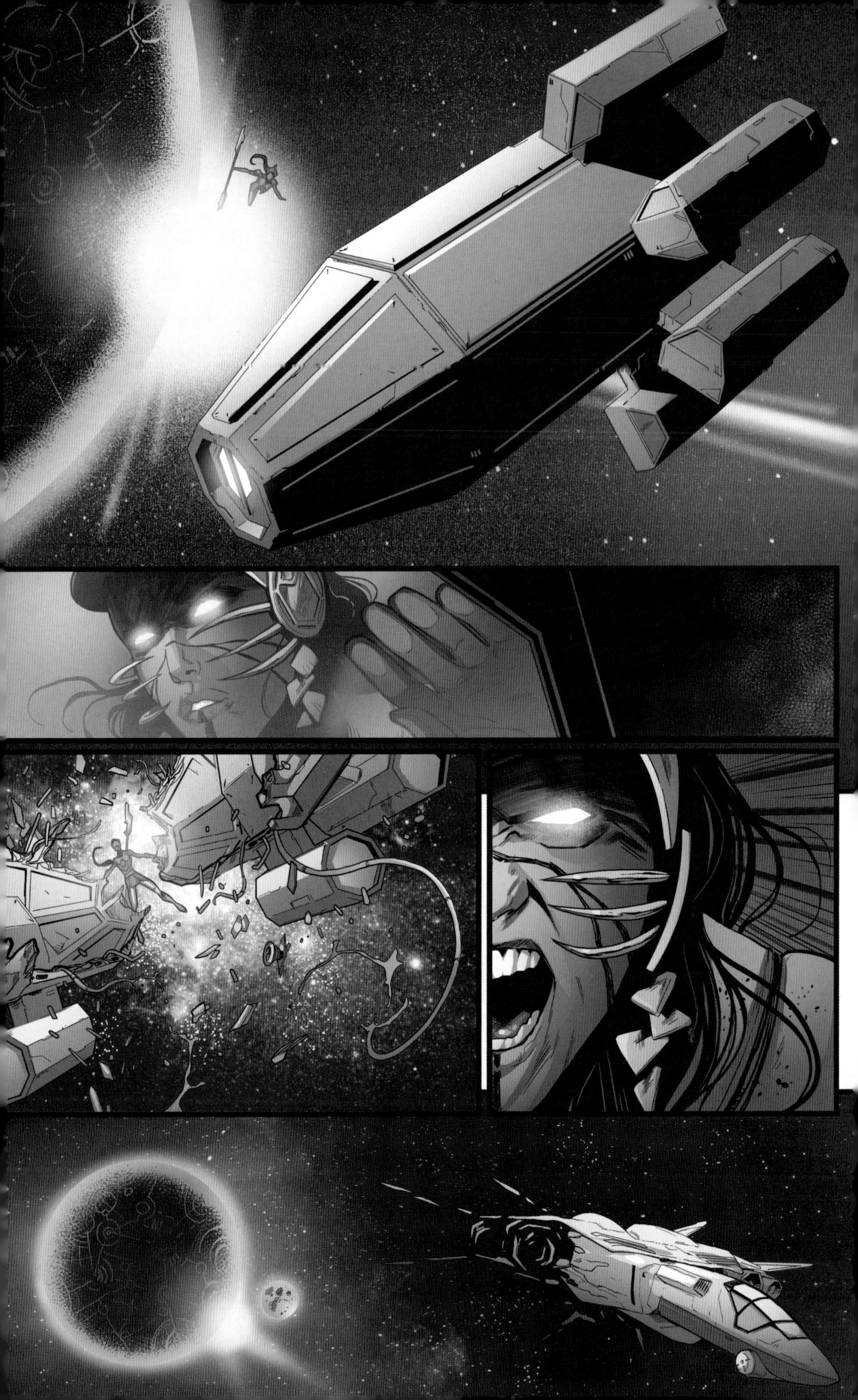

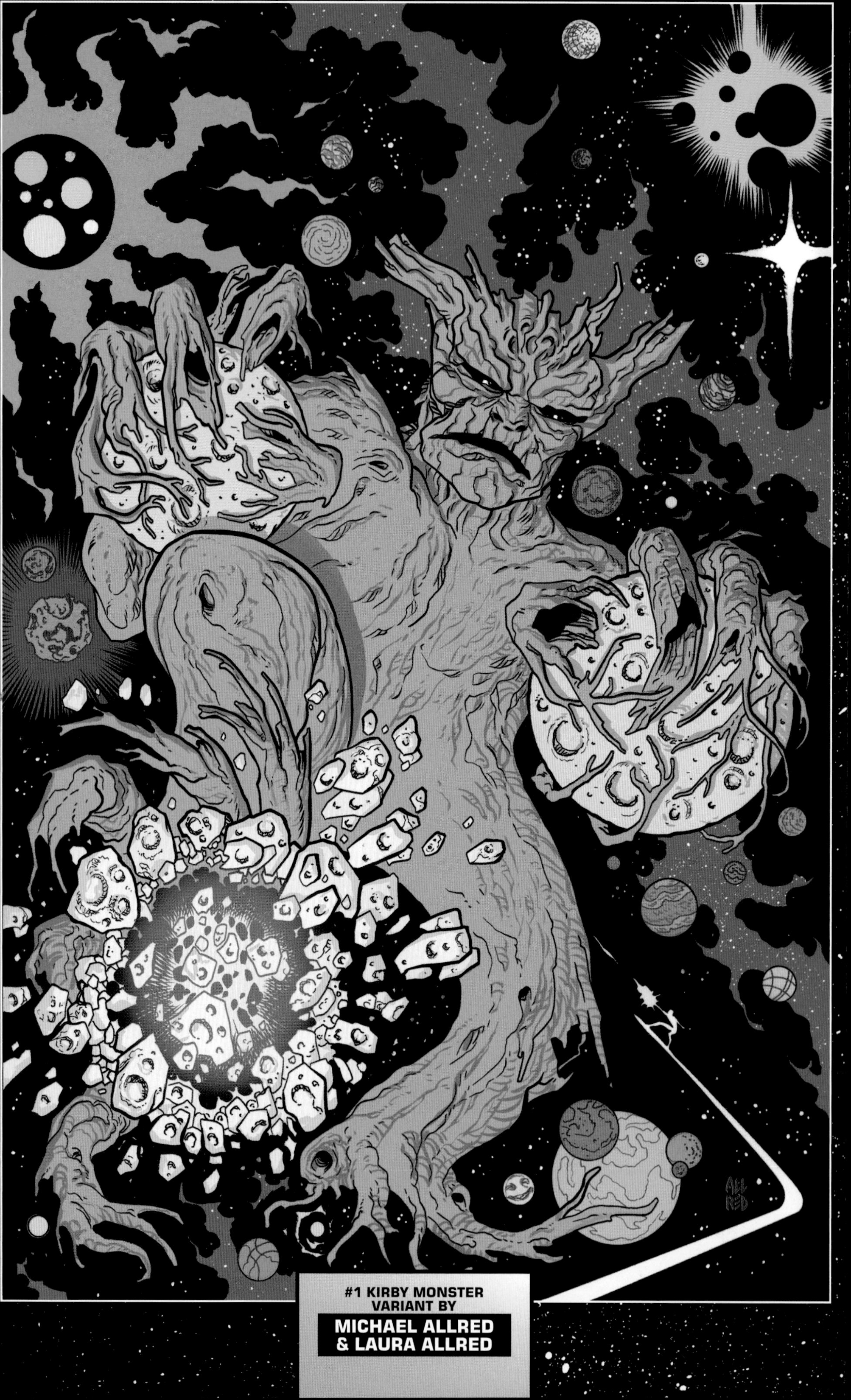

#1 KIRBY MONSTER VARIANT BY

MICHAEL ALLRED & LAURA ALLRED

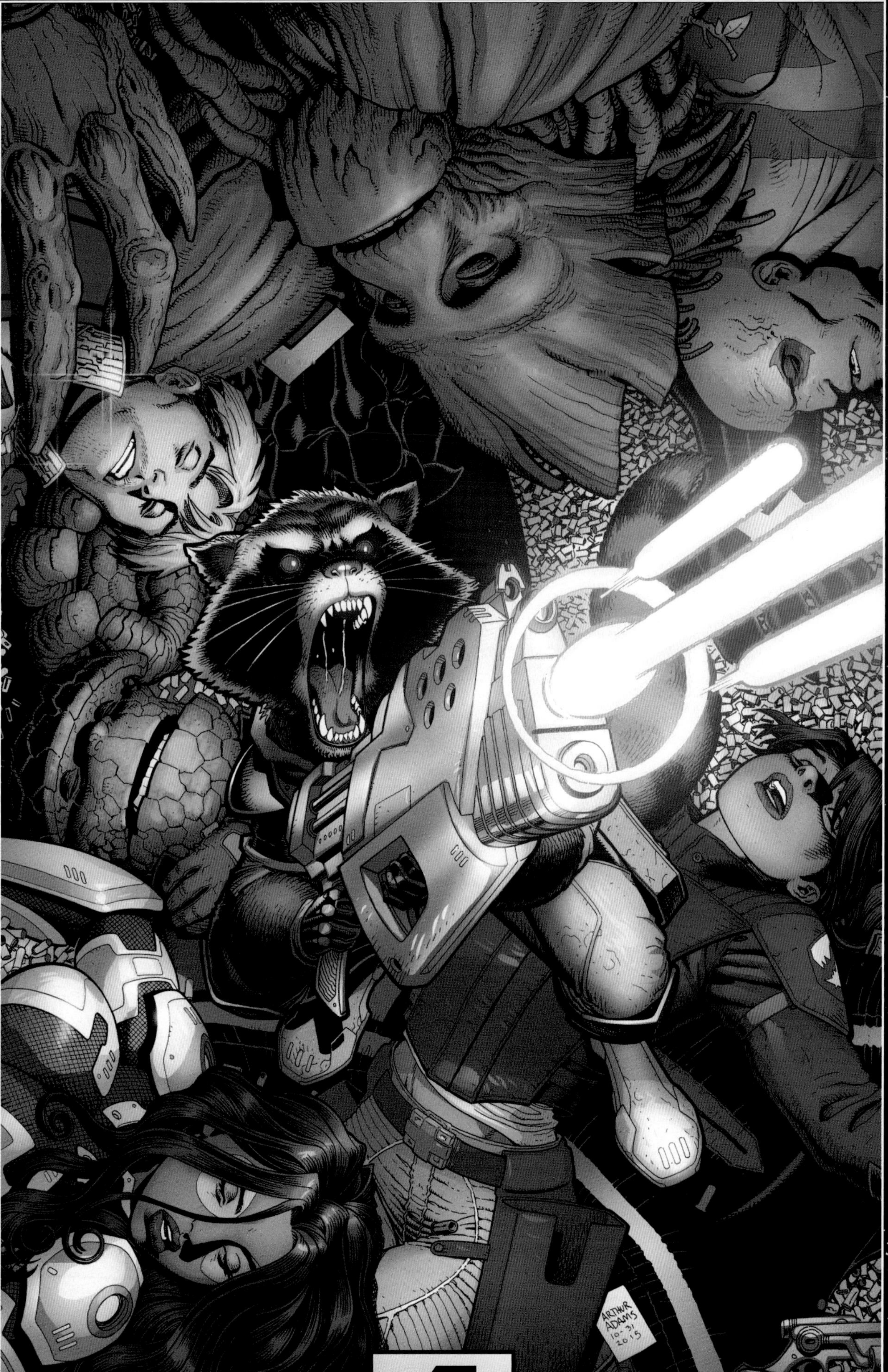
ARTHUR ADAMS 10-31 2015

4

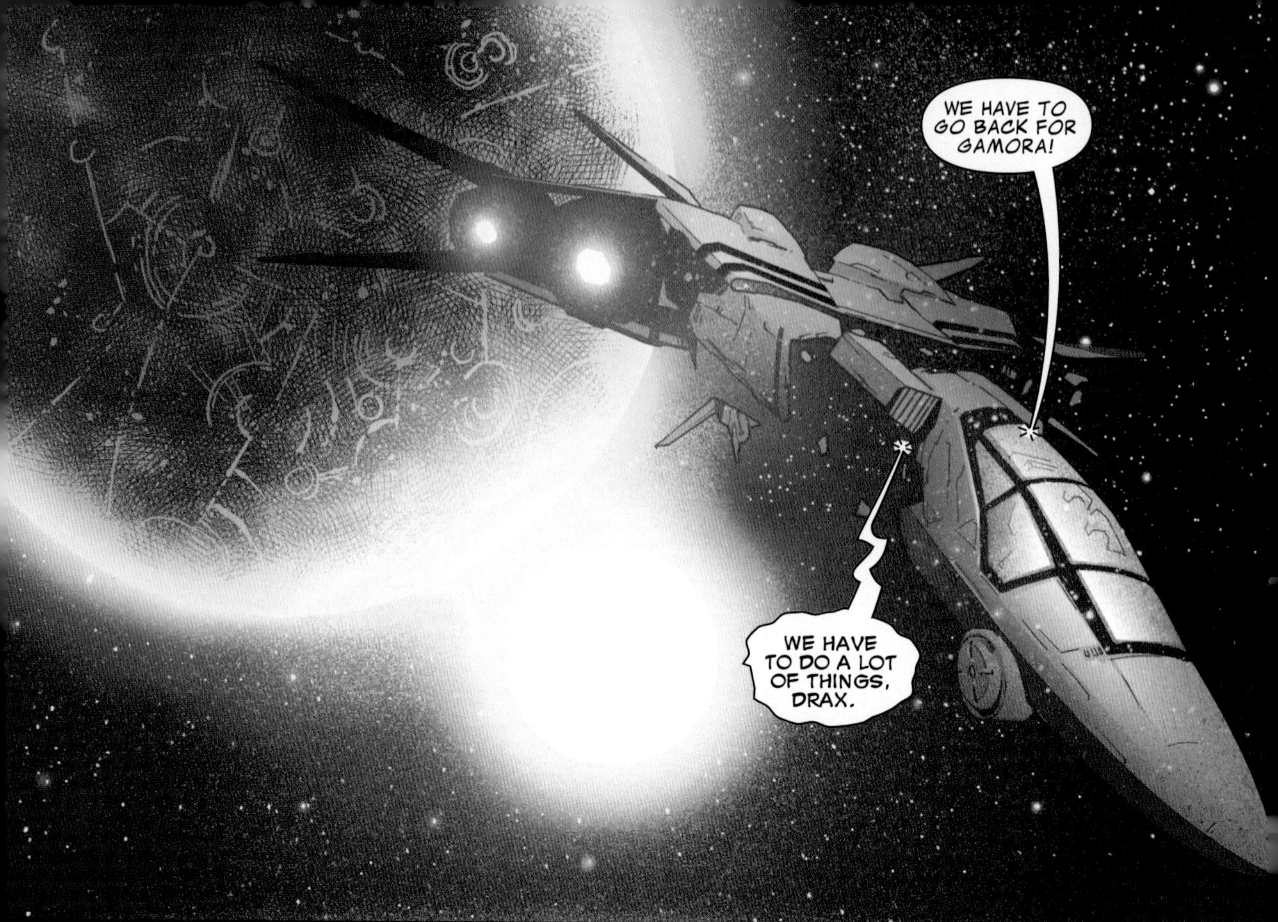

WE HAVE TO GO BACK FOR GAMORA!
WE HAVE TO DO A LOT OF THINGS, DRAX.

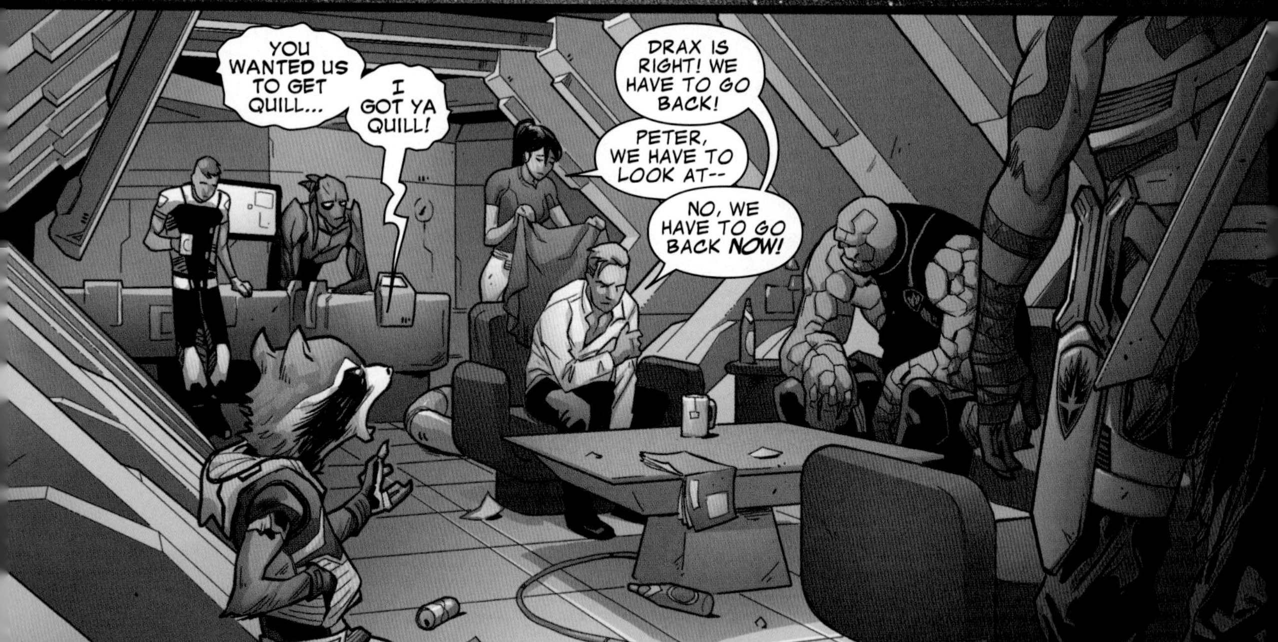

YOU WANTED US TO GET QUILL...
I GOT YA QUILL!
DRAX IS RIGHT! WE HAVE TO GO BACK!
PETER, WE HAVE TO LOOK AT--
NO, WE HAVE TO GO BACK NOW!

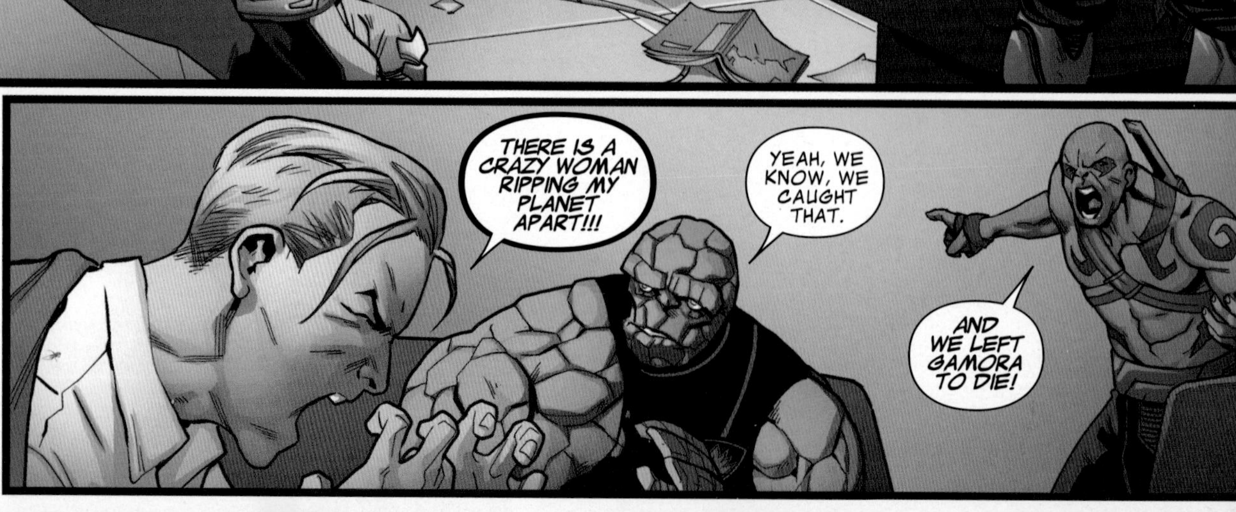

THERE IS A CRAZY WOMAN RIPPING MY PLANET APART!!!
YEAH, WE KNOW, WE CAUGHT THAT.
AND WE LEFT GAMORA TO DIE!

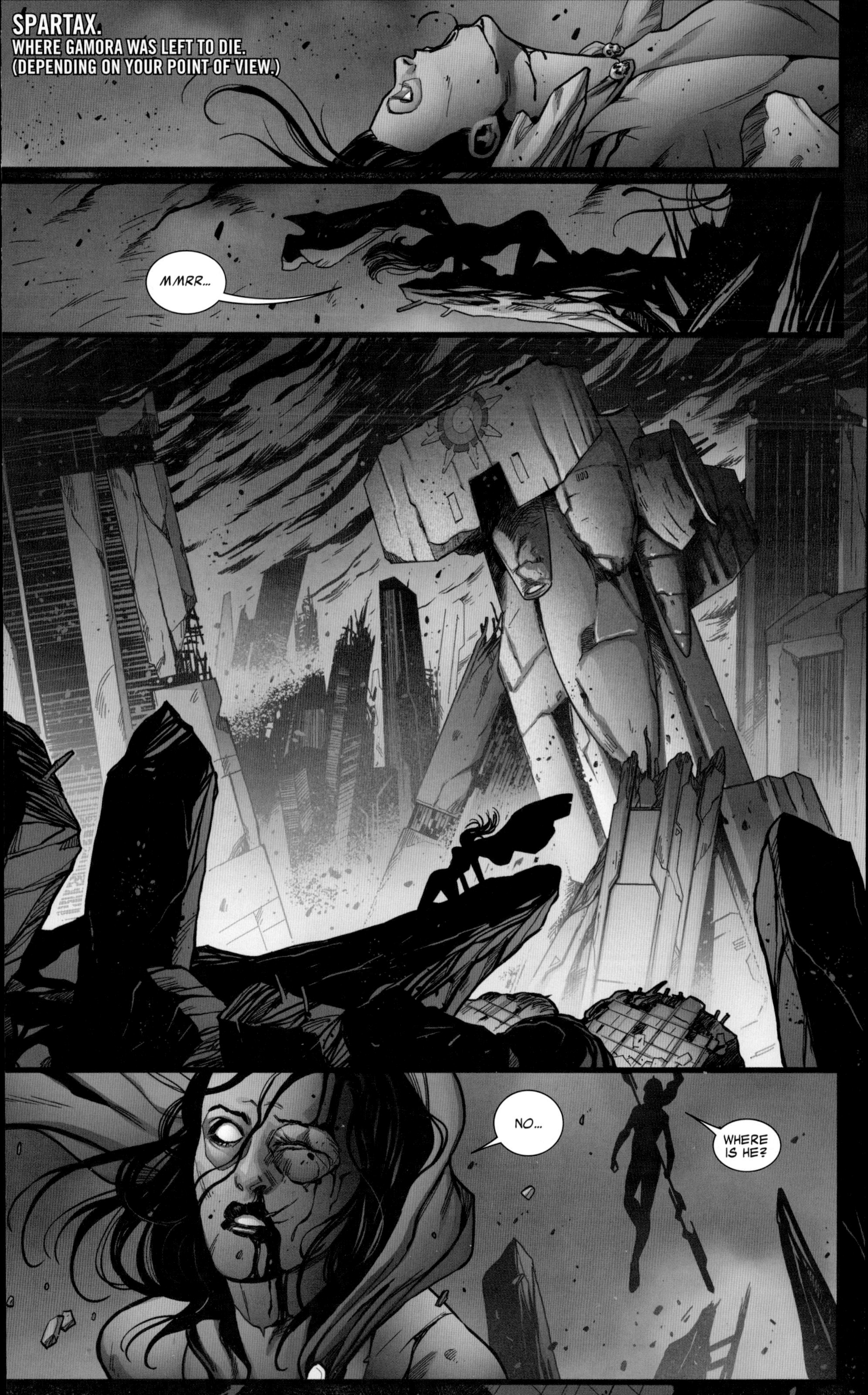
SPARTAX.
WHERE GAMORA WAS LEFT TO DIE.
(DEPENDING ON YOUR POINT OF VIEW.)
MMRR...
NO...
WHERE IS HE?

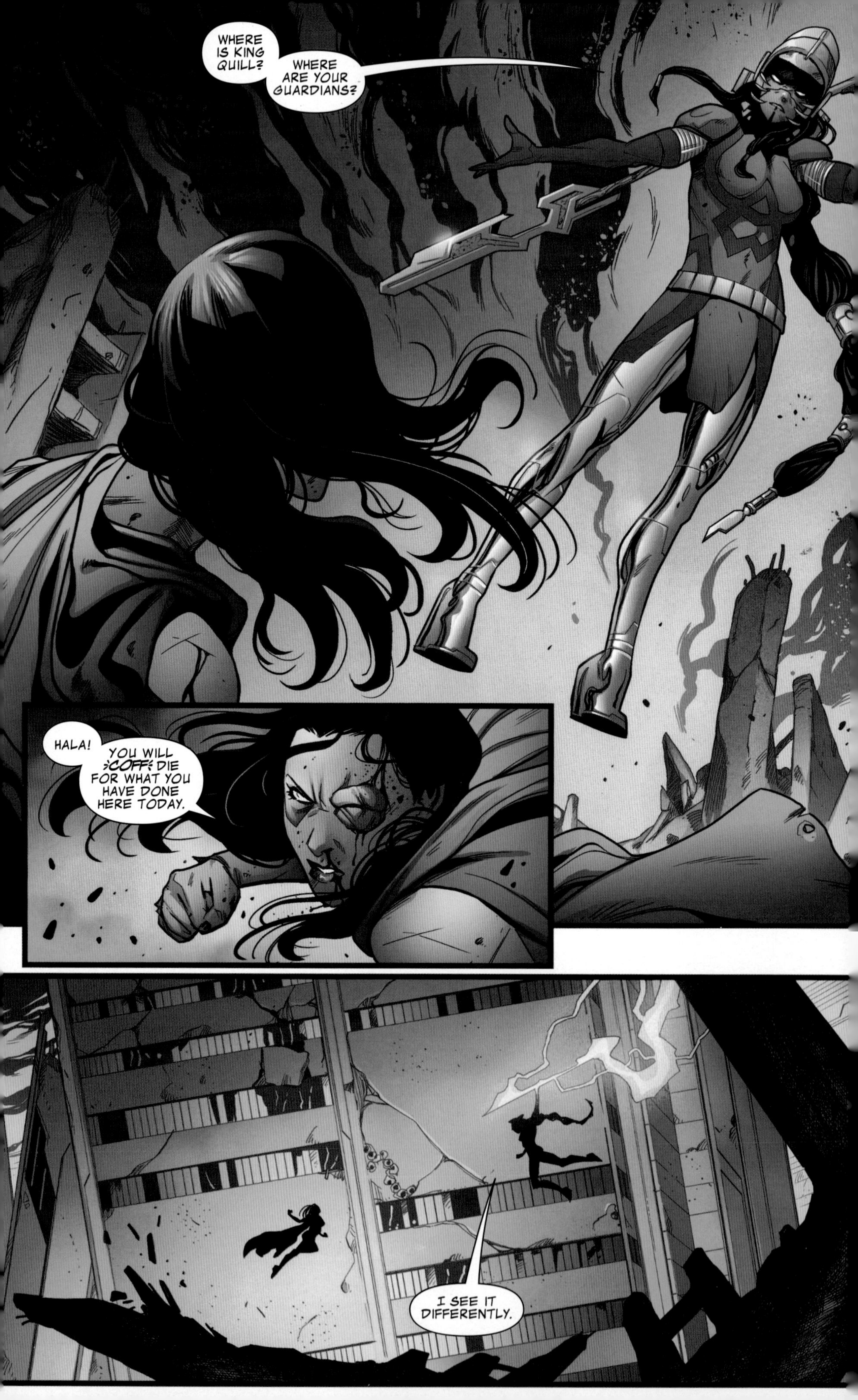
WHERE IS KING QUILL?
WHERE ARE YOUR GUARDIANS?
HALA!
YOU WILL *COFF* DIE FOR WHAT YOU HAVE DONE HERE TODAY.
I SEE IT DIFFERENTLY.

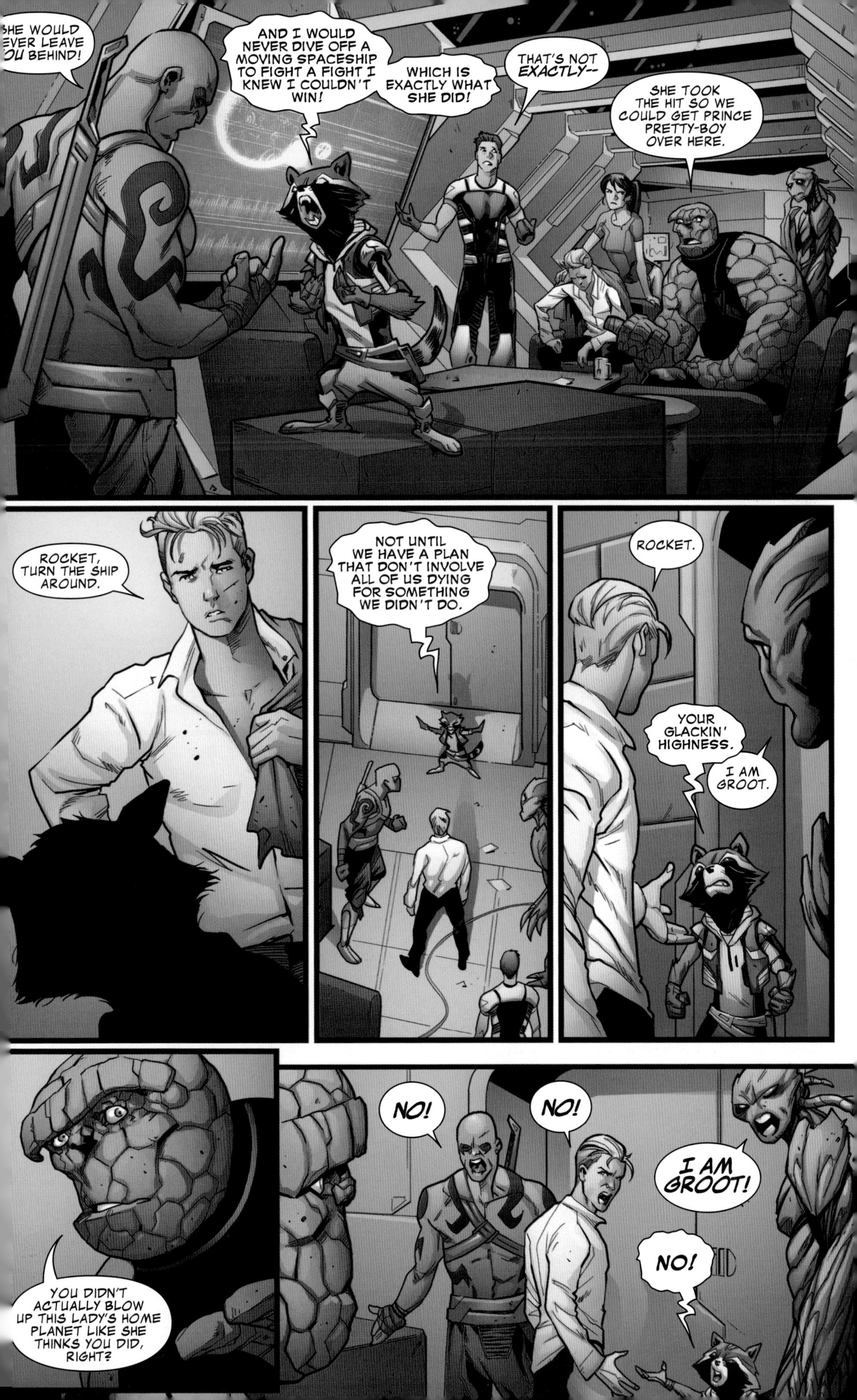
SHE WOULD NEVER LEAVE YOU BEHIND!
AND I WOULD NEVER DIVE OFF A MOVING SPACESHIP TO FIGHT A FIGHT I KNEW I COULDN'T WIN!
WHICH IS EXACTLY WHAT SHE DID!
THAT'S NOT EXACTLY--
SHE TOOK THE HIT SO WE COULD GET PRINCE PRETTY-BOY OVER HERE.
ROCKET, TURN THE SHIP AROUND.
NOT UNTIL WE HAVE A PLAN THAT DON'T INVOLVE ALL OF US DYING FOR SOMETHING WE DIDN'T DO.
ROCKET.
YOUR GLACKIN' HIGHNESS.
I AM GROOT.
YOU DIDN'T ACTUALLY BLOW UP THIS LADY'S HOME PLANET LIKE SHE THINKS YOU DID, RIGHT?
NO!
NO!
I AM GROOT!
NO!

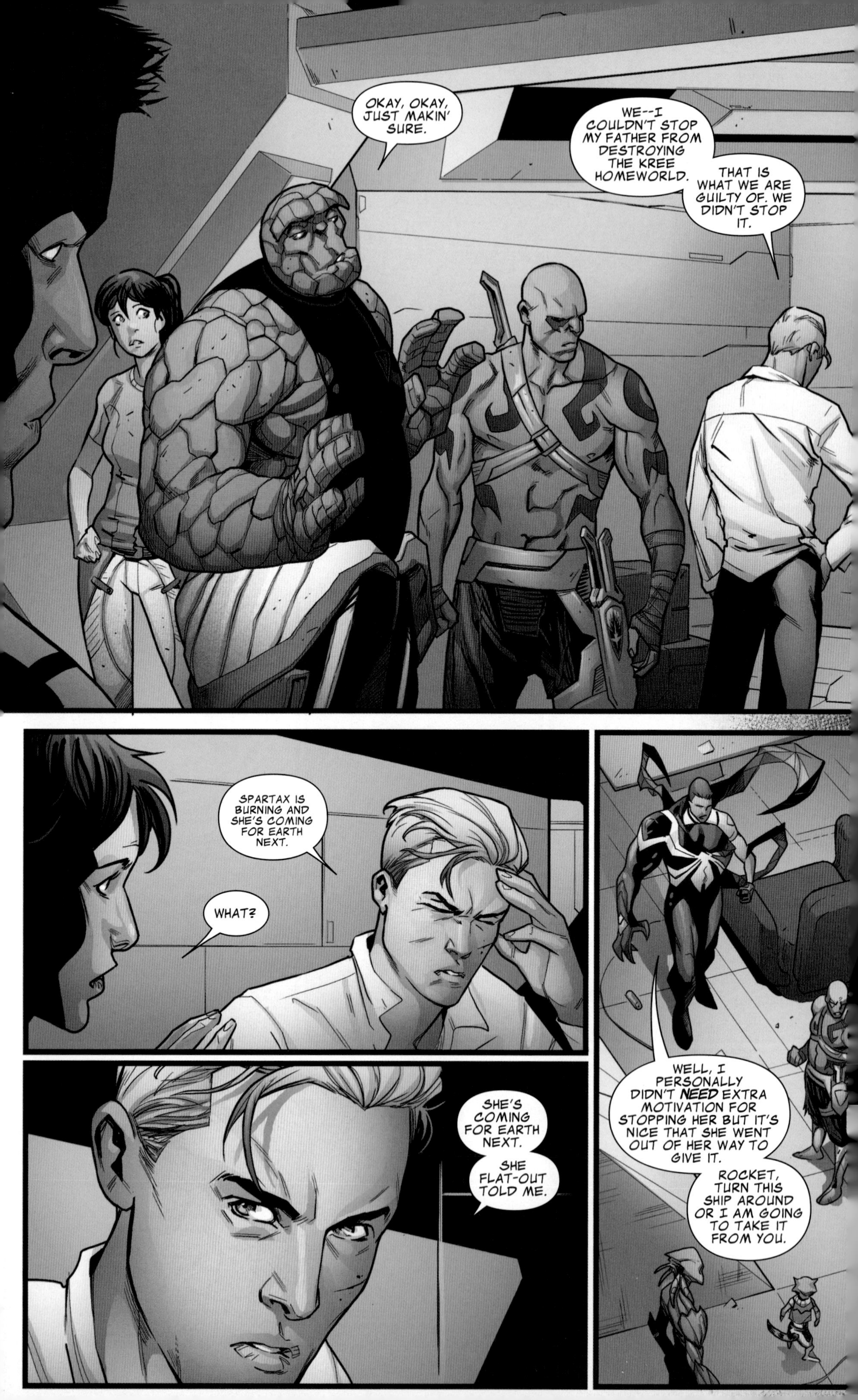
OKAY, OKAY, JUST MAKIN' SURE.
WE--I COULDN'T STOP MY FATHER FROM DESTROYING THE KREE HOMEWORLD.
THAT IS WHAT WE ARE GUILTY OF. WE DIDN'T STOP IT.
SPARTAX IS BURNING AND SHE'S COMING FOR EARTH NEXT.
WHAT?
SHE'S COMING FOR EARTH NEXT.
SHE FLAT-OUT TOLD ME.
WELL, I PERSONALLY DIDN'T **NEED** EXTRA MOTIVATION FOR STOPPING HER BUT IT'S NICE THAT SHE WENT OUT OF HER WAY TO GIVE IT.
ROCKET, TURN THIS SHIP AROUND OR I AM GOING TO TAKE IT FROM YOU.

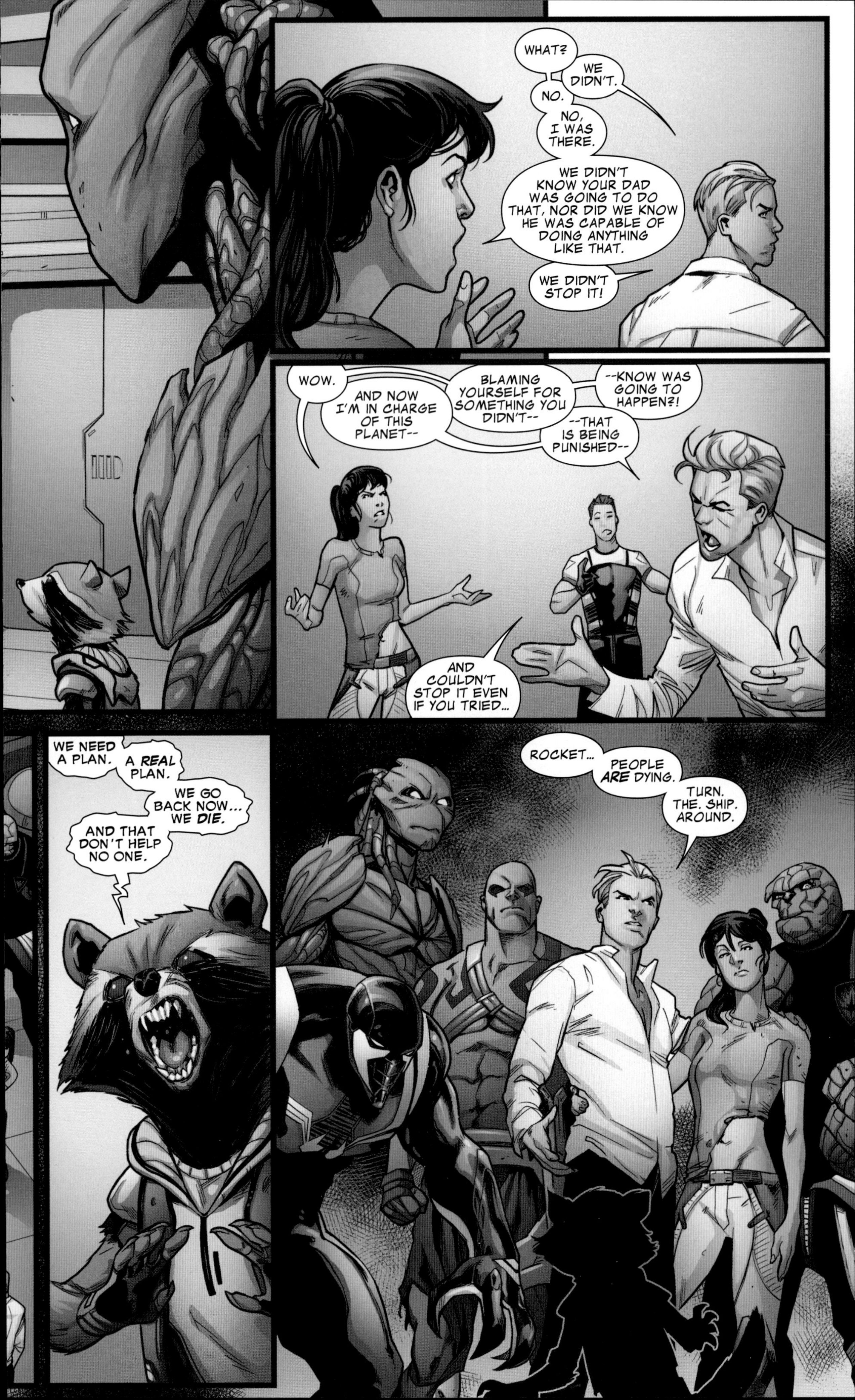

WHAT?
WE DIDN'T.
NO.
NO, I WAS THERE.
WE DIDN'T KNOW YOUR DAD WAS GOING TO DO THAT, NOR DID WE KNOW HE WAS CAPABLE OF DOING ANYTHING LIKE THAT.
WE DIDN'T STOP IT!
WOW.
AND NOW I'M IN CHARGE OF THIS PLANET--
BLAMING YOURSELF FOR SOMETHING YOU DIDN'T--
--KNOW WAS GOING TO HAPPEN?!
--THAT IS BEING PUNISHED--
AND COULDN'T STOP IT EVEN IF YOU TRIED...
WE NEED A PLAN.
A REAL PLAN.
WE GO BACK NOW... WE DIE.
AND THAT DON'T HELP NO ONE.
ROCKET...
PEOPLE ARE DYING.
TURN. THE. SHIP. AROUND.

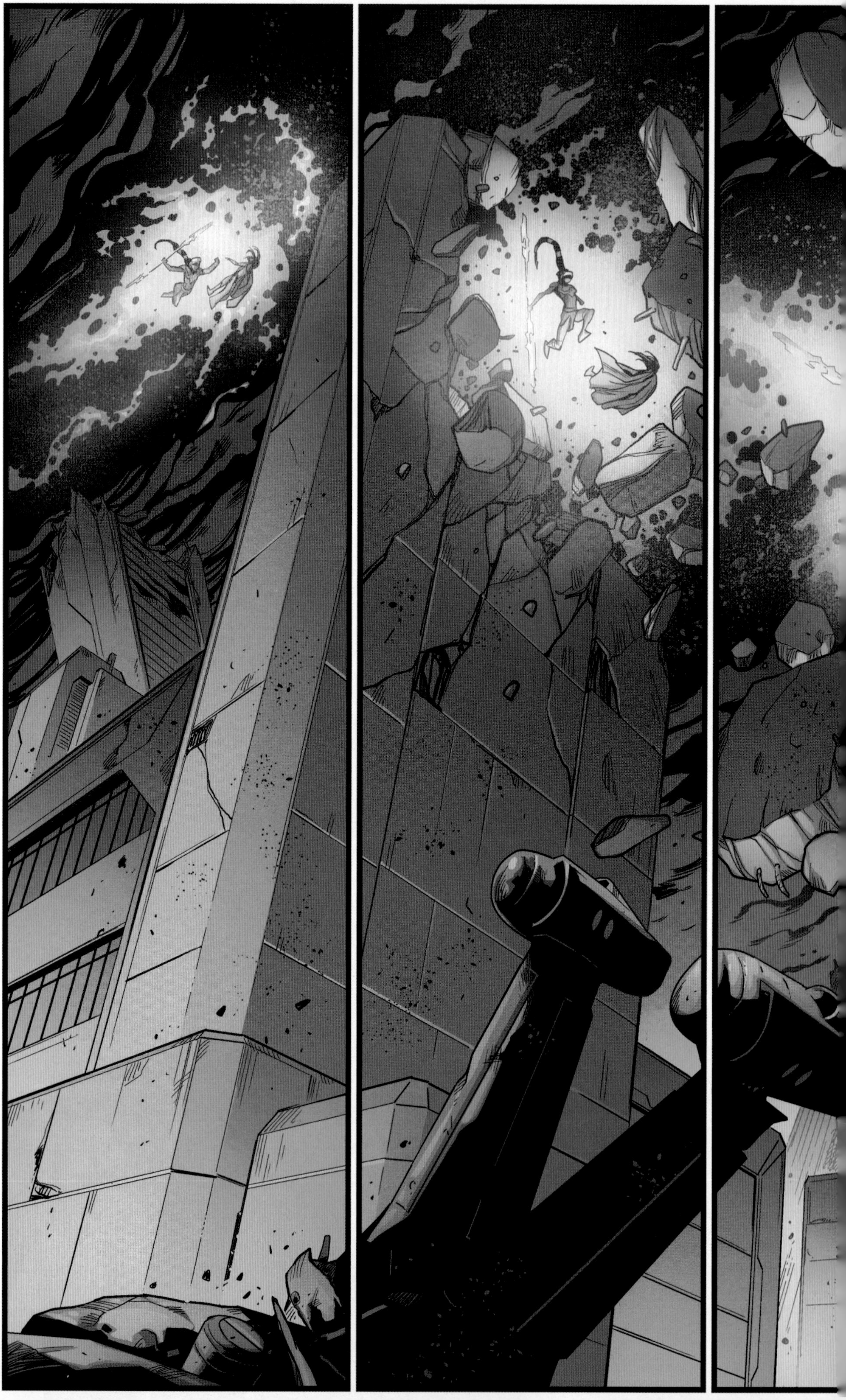

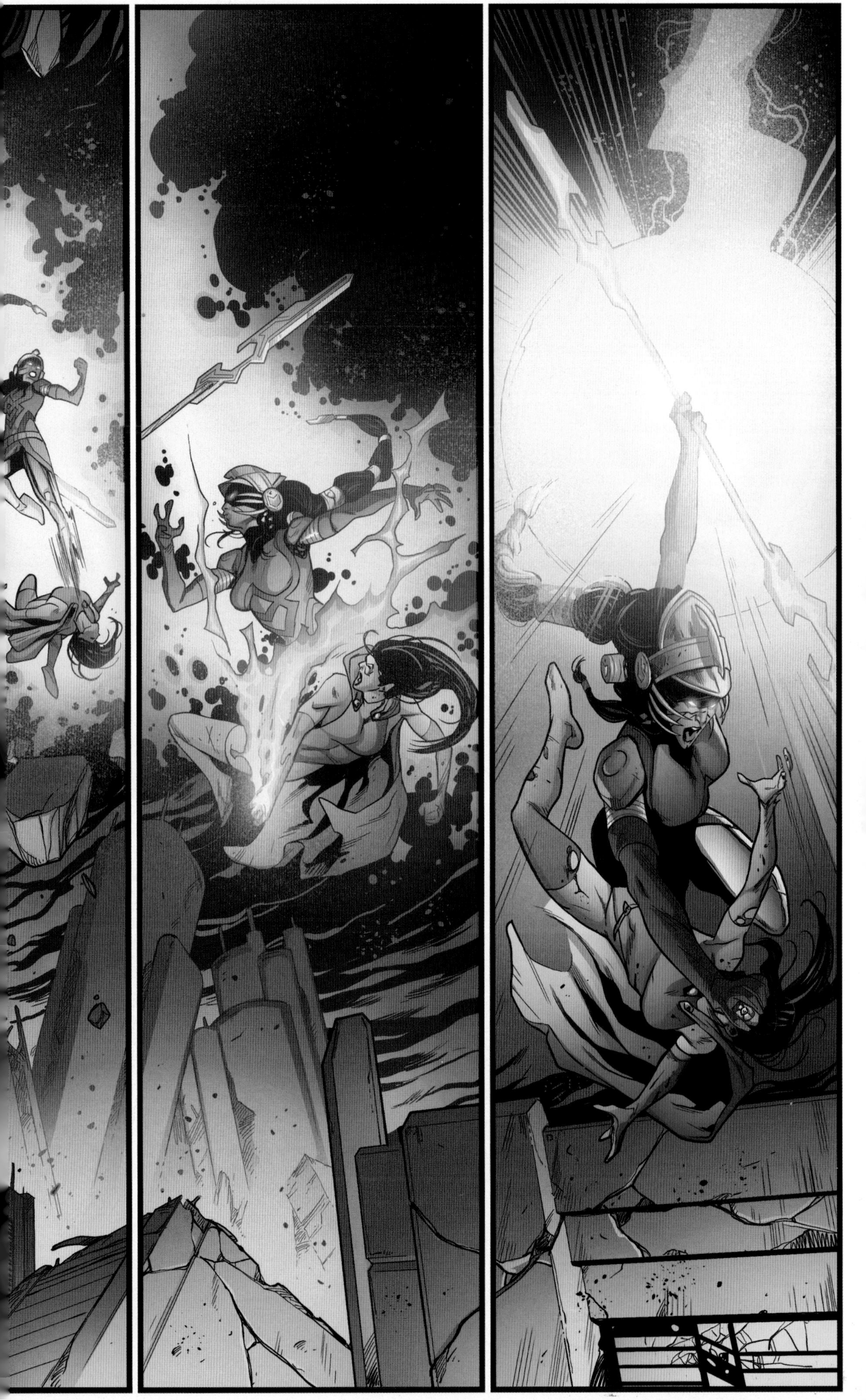

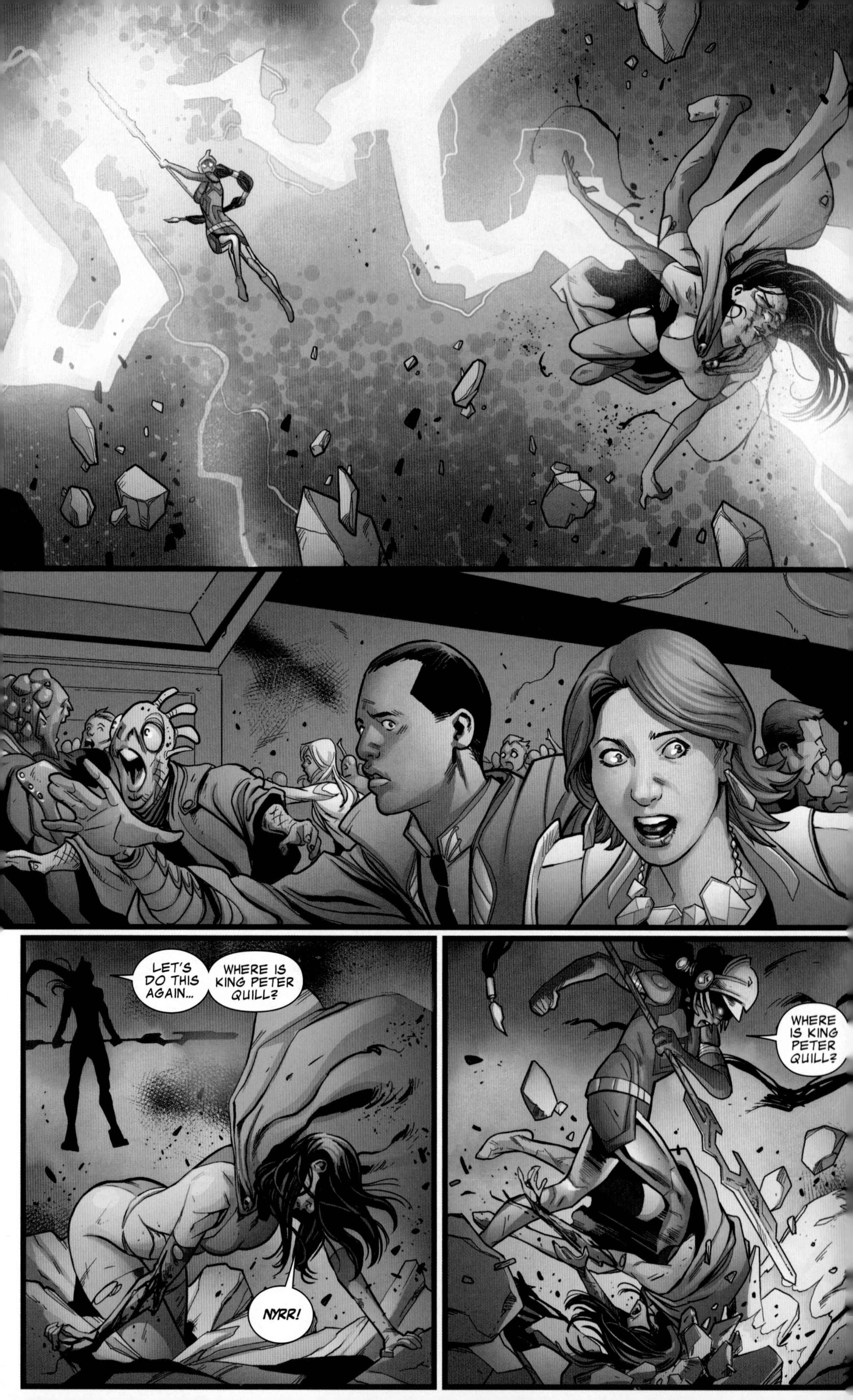
LET'S DO THIS AGAIN...
WHERE IS KING PETER QUILL?
NYRR!
WHERE IS KING PETER QUILL?

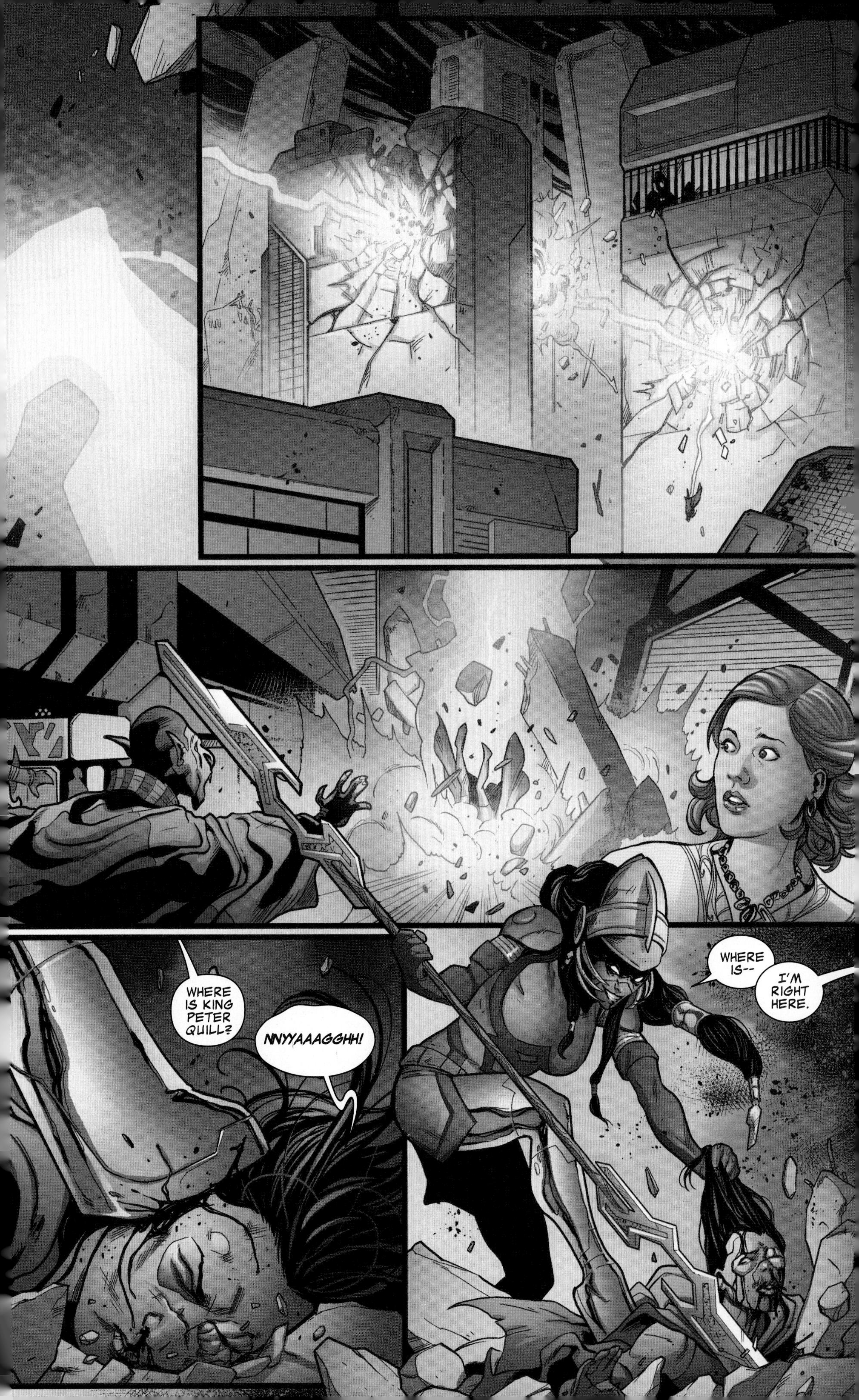
WHERE IS KING PETER QUILL?
NNYYAAAGGHH!
WHERE IS--
I'M RIGHT HERE.

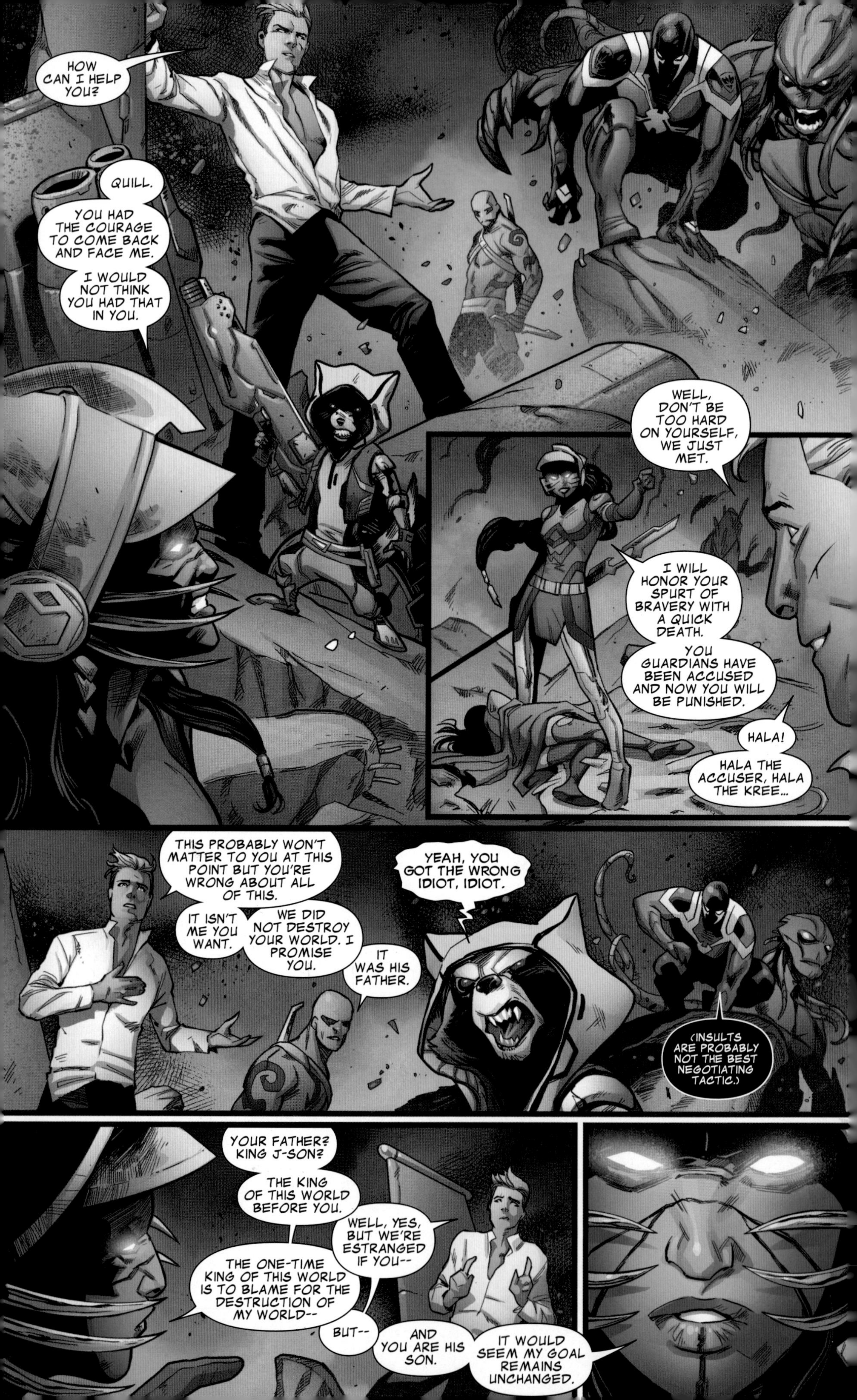
HOW CAN I HELP YOU?
QUILL.
YOU HAD THE COURAGE TO COME BACK AND FACE ME.
I WOULD NOT THINK YOU HAD THAT IN YOU.
WELL, DON'T BE TOO HARD ON YOURSELF, WE JUST MET.
I WILL HONOR YOUR SPURT OF BRAVERY WITH A QUICK DEATH.
YOU GUARDIANS HAVE BEEN ACCUSED AND NOW YOU WILL BE PUNISHED.
HALA!
HALA THE ACCUSER, HALA THE KREE...
THIS PROBABLY WON'T MATTER TO YOU AT THIS POINT BUT YOU'RE WRONG ABOUT ALL OF THIS.
IT ISN'T ME YOU WANT.
WE DID NOT DESTROY YOUR WORLD. I PROMISE YOU.
IT WAS HIS FATHER.
YEAH, YOU GOT THE WRONG IDIOT, IDIOT.
(INSULTS ARE PROBABLY NOT THE BEST NEGOTIATING TACTIC.)
YOUR FATHER? KING J-SON?
THE KING OF THIS WORLD BEFORE YOU.
WELL, YES, BUT WE'RE ESTRANGED IF YOU--
THE ONE-TIME KING OF THIS WORLD IS TO BLAME FOR THE DESTRUCTION OF MY WORLD--
BUT--
AND YOU ARE HIS SON.
IT WOULD SEEM MY GOAL REMAINS UNCHANGED.

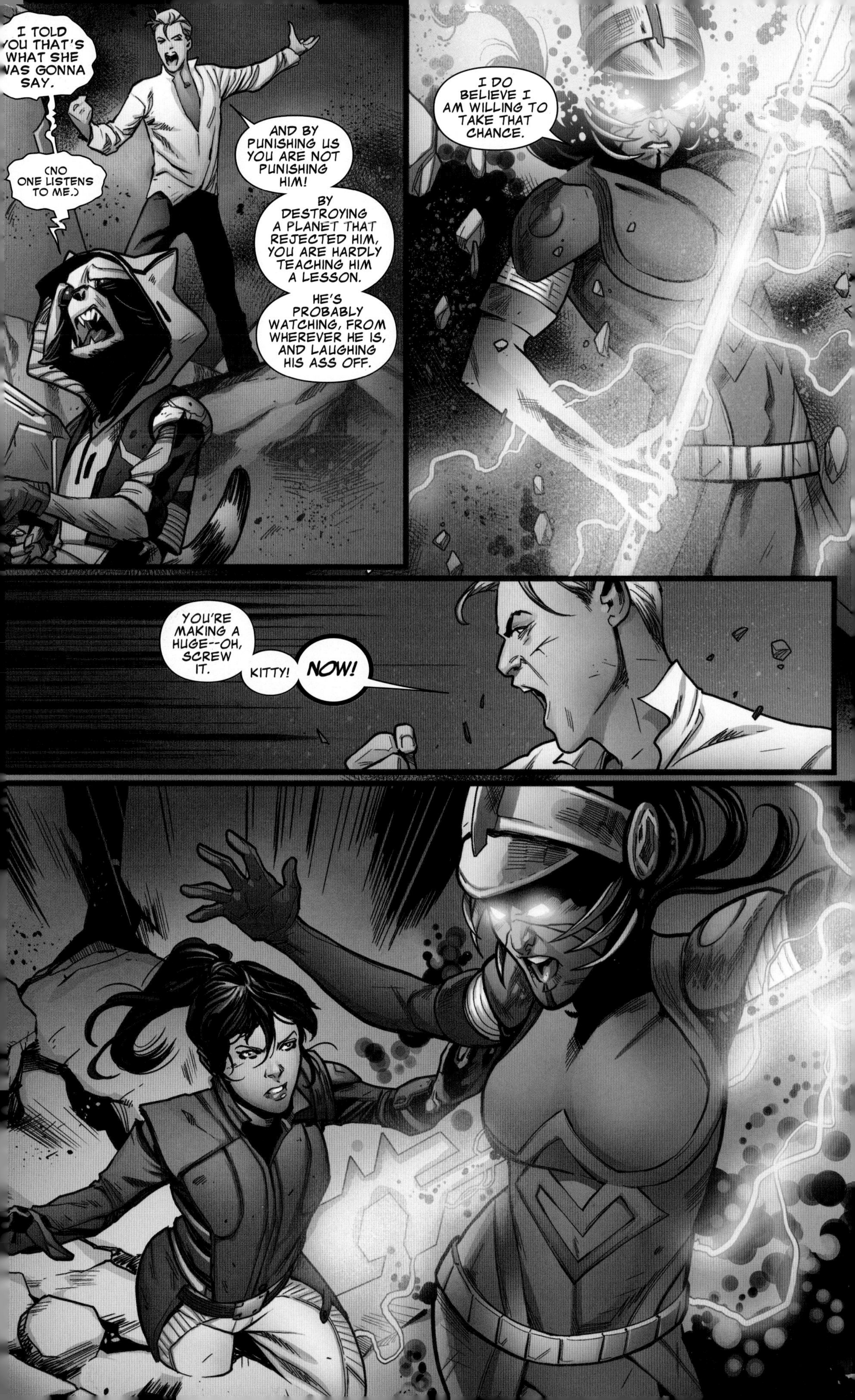

I TOLD YOU THAT'S WHAT SHE WAS GONNA SAY.
(NO ONE LISTENS TO ME.)
AND BY PUNISHING US YOU ARE NOT PUNISHING HIM!
BY DESTROYING A PLANET THAT REJECTED HIM, YOU ARE HARDLY TEACHING HIM A LESSON.
HE'S PROBABLY WATCHING, FROM WHEREVER HE IS, AND LAUGHING HIS ASS OFF.
I DO BELIEVE I AM WILLING TO TAKE THAT CHANCE.
YOU'RE MAKING A HUGE--OH, SCREW IT.
KITTY!
NOW!

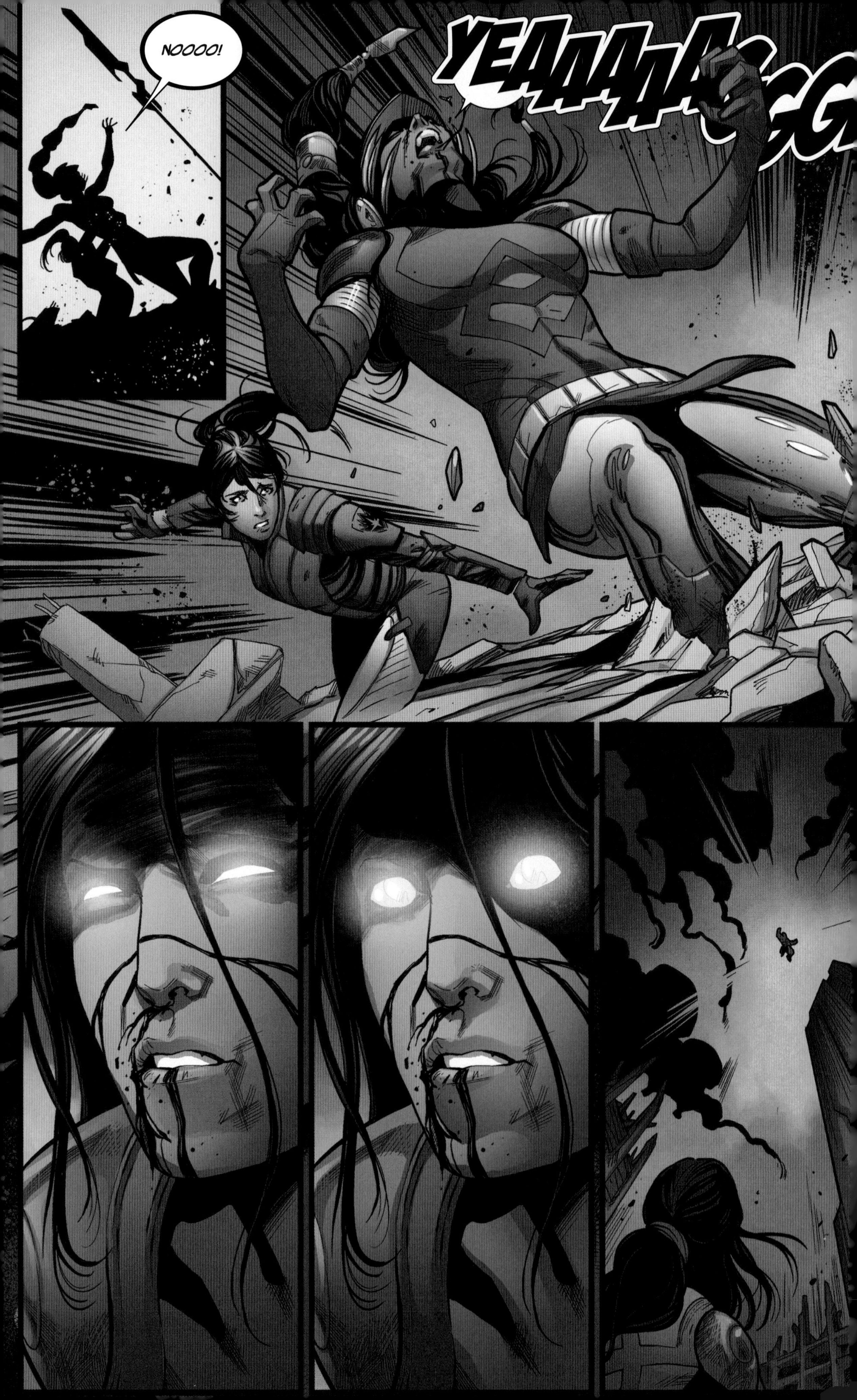
NOOOO!
YEAAAAAAGGG

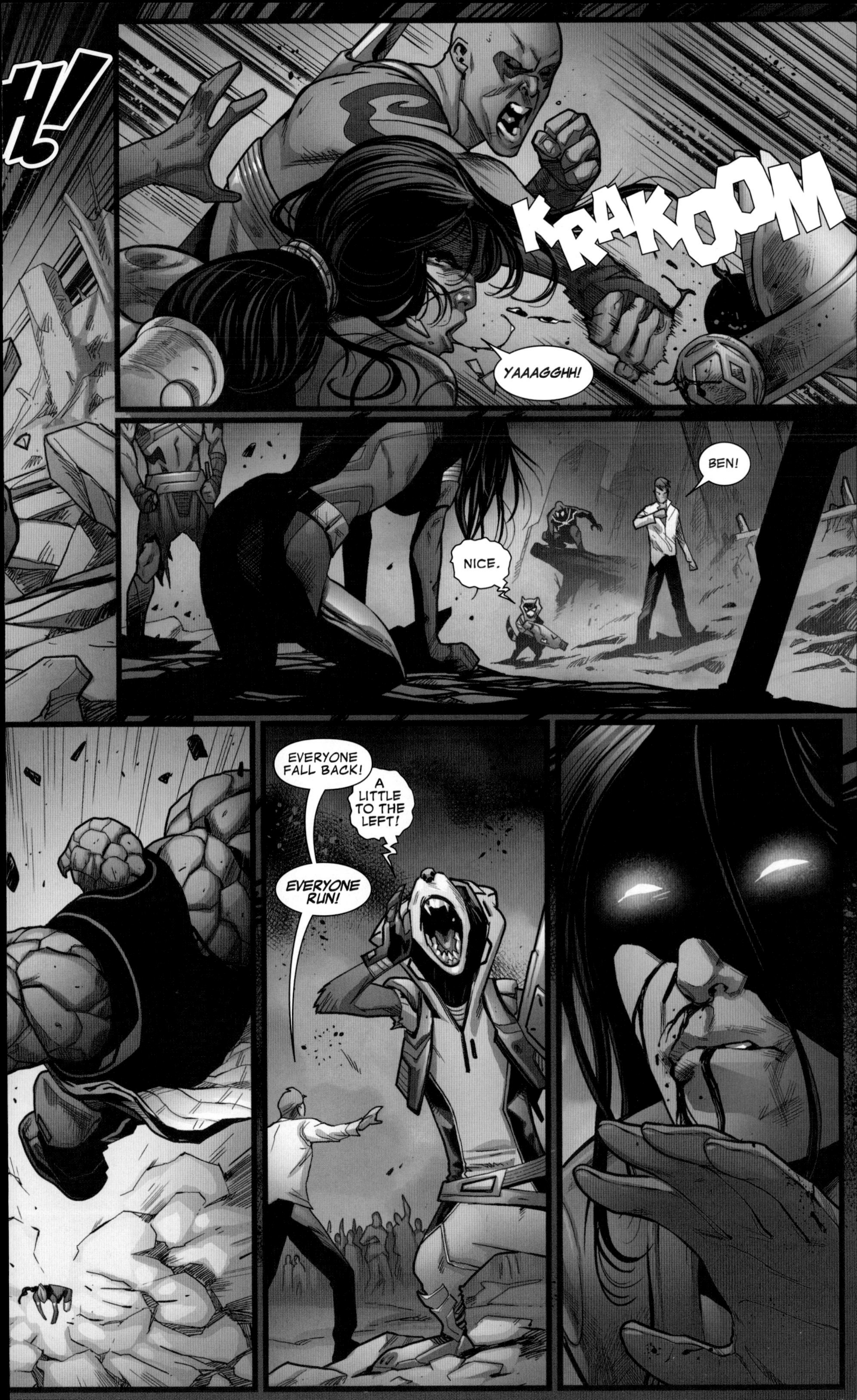

H!
KRAKOOM
YAAAGGHH!
BEN!
NICE.
EVERYONE FALL BACK!
A LITTLE TO THE LEFT!
EVERYONE RUN!

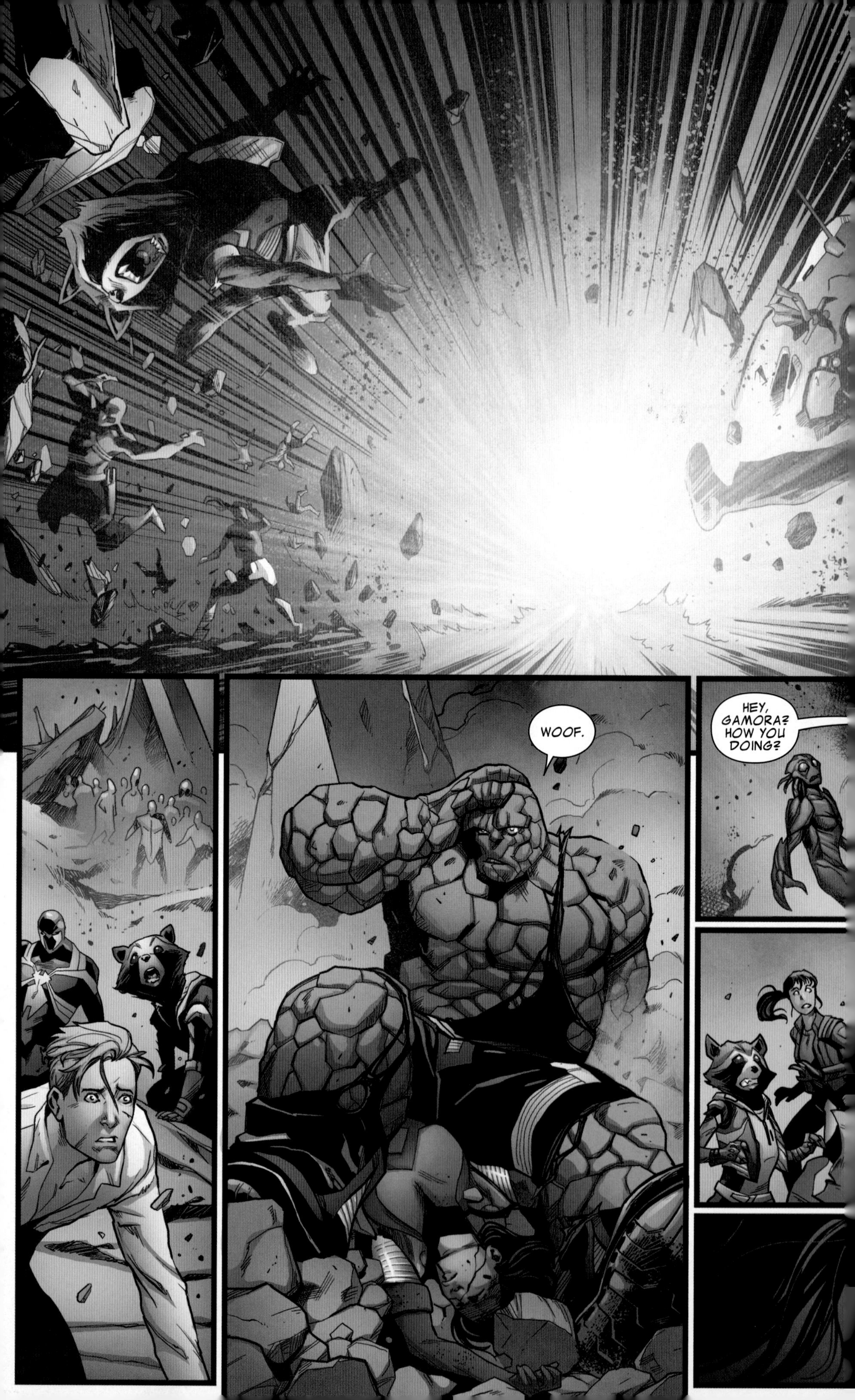
WOOF.
HEY, GAMORA? HOW YOU DOING?

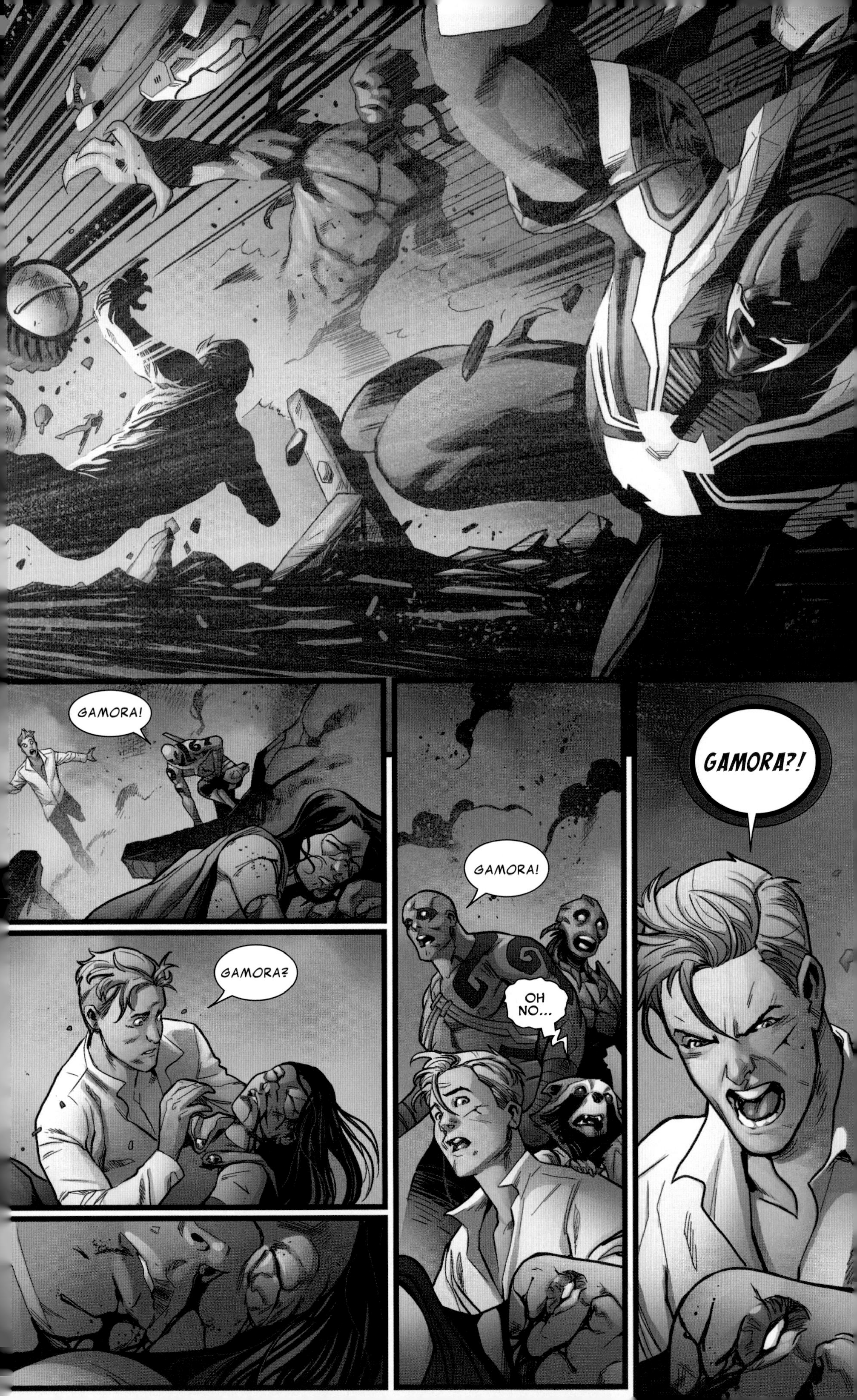
GAMORA!
GAMORA?
GAMORA!
OH NO...
GAMORA?!

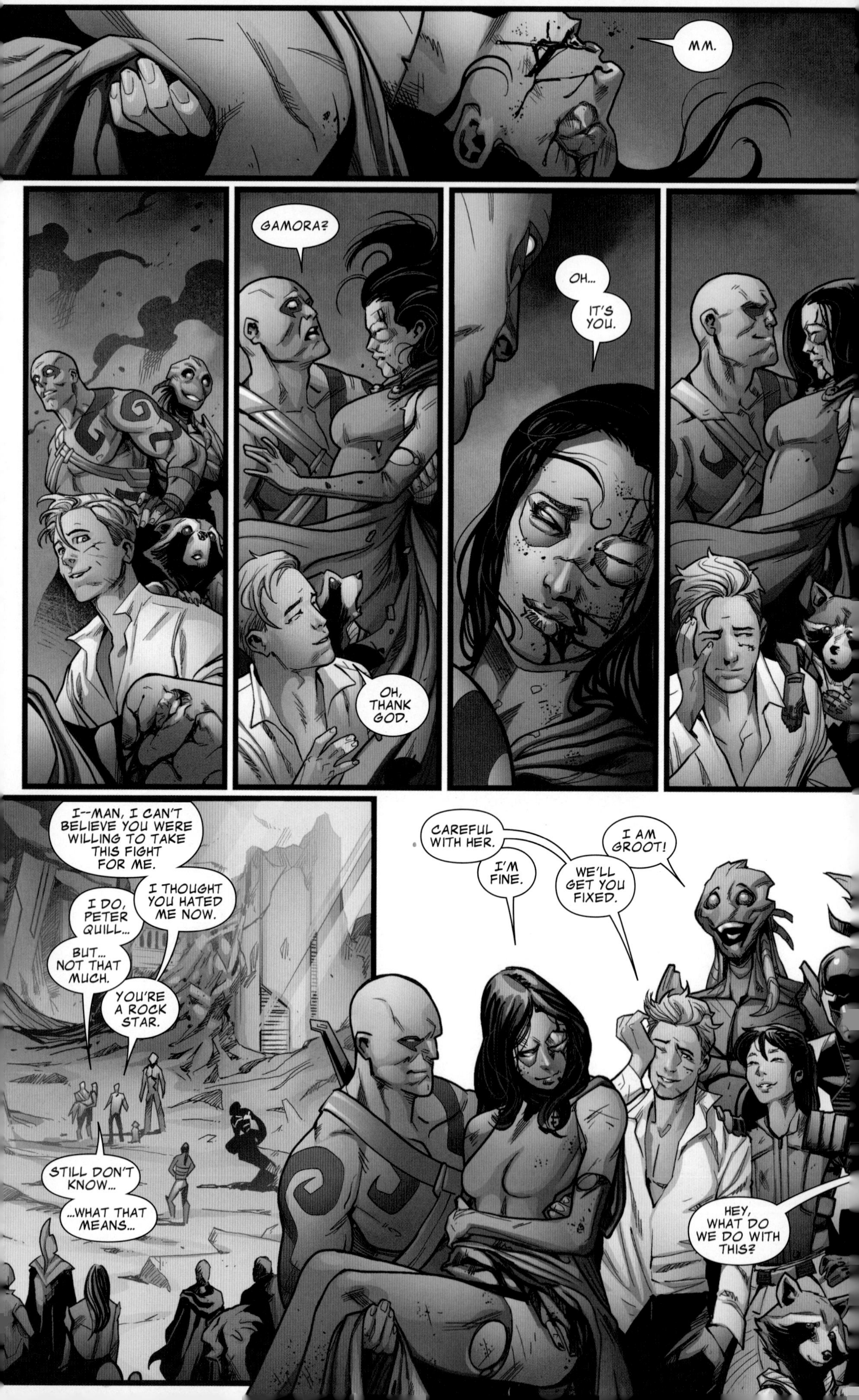
MM.
GAMORA?
OH, THANK GOD.
OH...
IT'S YOU.
I--MAN, I CAN'T BELIEVE YOU WERE WILLING TO TAKE THIS FIGHT FOR ME.
I THOUGHT YOU HATED ME NOW.
I DO, PETER QUILL...
BUT... NOT THAT MUCH.
YOU'RE A ROCK STAR.
STILL DON'T KNOW...
...WHAT THAT MEANS...
CAREFUL WITH HER.
I'M FINE.
WE'LL GET YOU FIXED.
I AM GROOT!
HEY, WHAT DO WE DO WITH THIS?

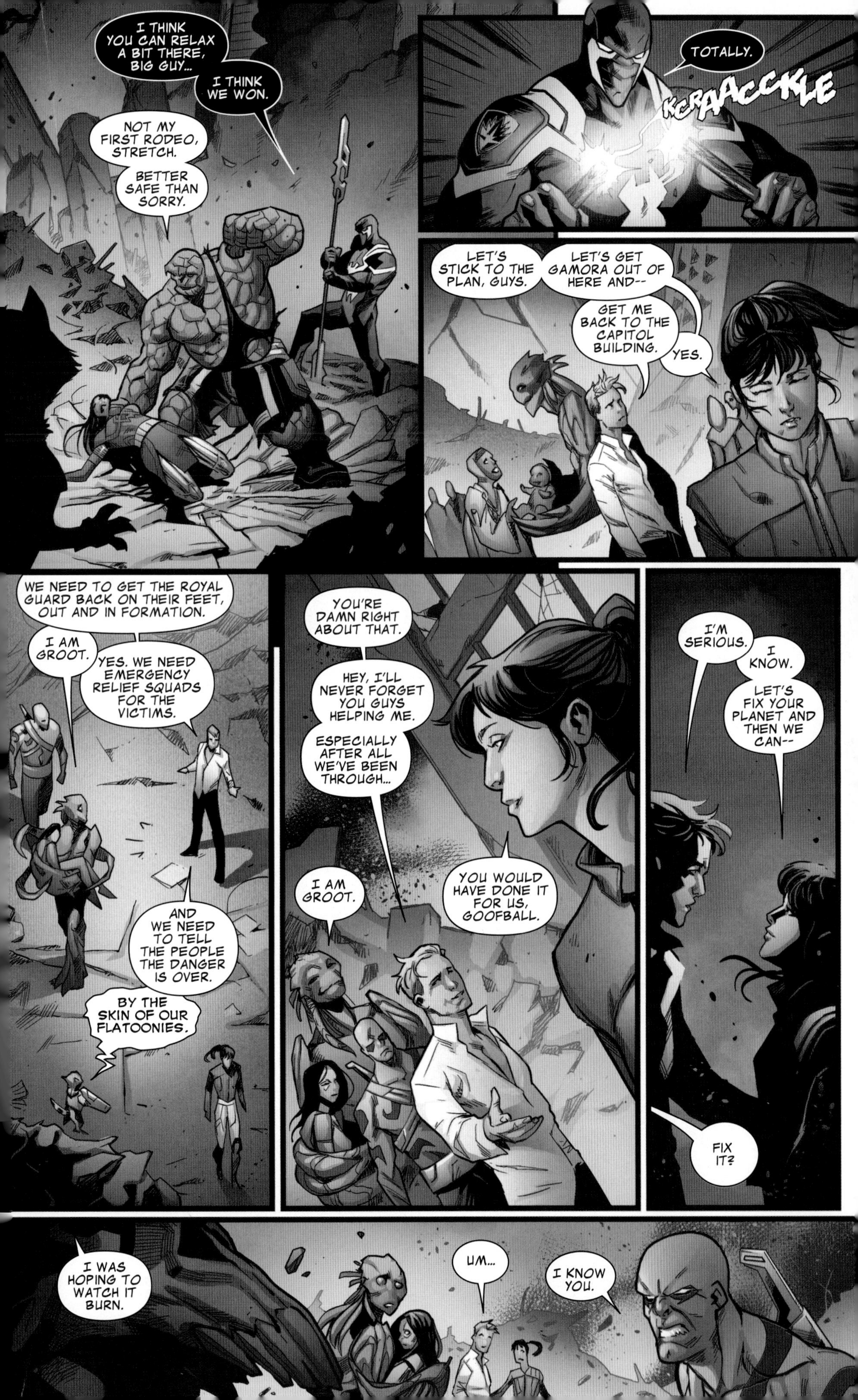
I THINK YOU CAN RELAX A BIT THERE, BIG GUY...
I THINK WE WON.
NOT MY FIRST RODEO, STRETCH.
BETTER SAFE THAN SORRY.
TOTALLY.
KCRAACCKKLE
LET'S STICK TO THE PLAN, GUYS.
LET'S GET GAMORA OUT OF HERE AND--
GET ME BACK TO THE CAPITOL BUILDING.
YES.
WE NEED TO GET THE ROYAL GUARD BACK ON THEIR FEET, OUT AND IN FORMATION.
I AM GROOT.
YES. WE NEED EMERGENCY RELIEF SQUADS FOR THE VICTIMS.
AND WE NEED TO TELL THE PEOPLE THE DANGER IS OVER.
BY THE SKIN OF OUR FLATOONIES.
YOU'RE DAMN RIGHT ABOUT THAT.
HEY, I'LL NEVER FORGET YOU GUYS HELPING ME.
ESPECIALLY AFTER ALL WE'VE BEEN THROUGH...
I AM GROOT.
YOU WOULD HAVE DONE IT FOR US, GOOFBALL.
I'M SERIOUS.
I KNOW.
LET'S FIX YOUR PLANET AND THEN WE CAN--
FIX IT?
I WAS HOPING TO WATCH IT BURN.
UM...
I KNOW YOU.

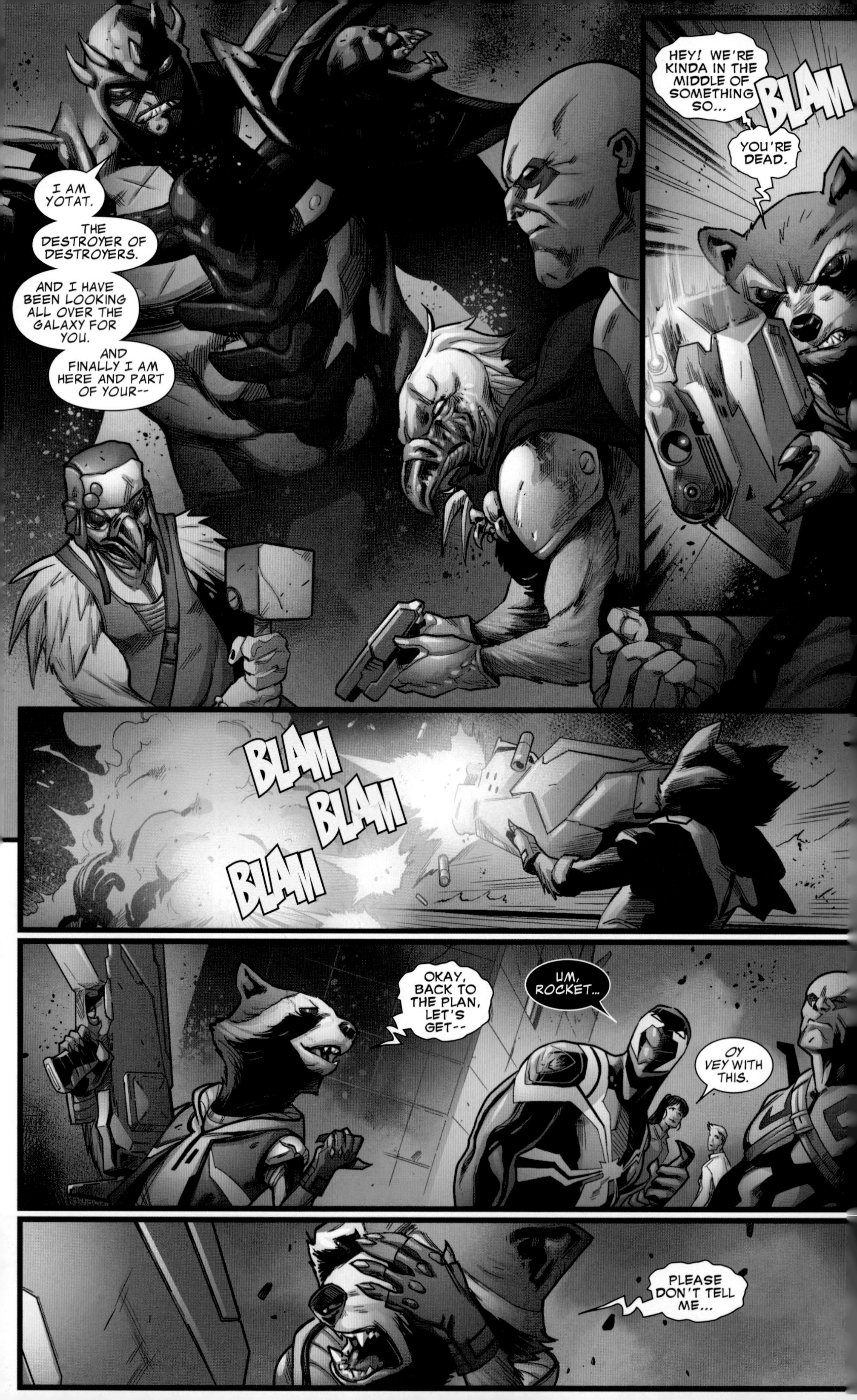
I AM YOTAT.
THE DESTROYER OF DESTROYERS.
AND I HAVE BEEN LOOKING ALL OVER THE GALAXY FOR YOU.
AND FINALLY I AM HERE AND PART OF YOUR--
HEY! WE'RE KINDA IN THE MIDDLE OF SOMETHING SO...
BLAM
YOU'RE DEAD.
BLAM
BLAM
BLAM
OKAY, BACK TO THE PLAN, LET'S GET--
UM, ROCKET...
OY VEY WITH THIS.
PLEASE DON'T TELL ME...

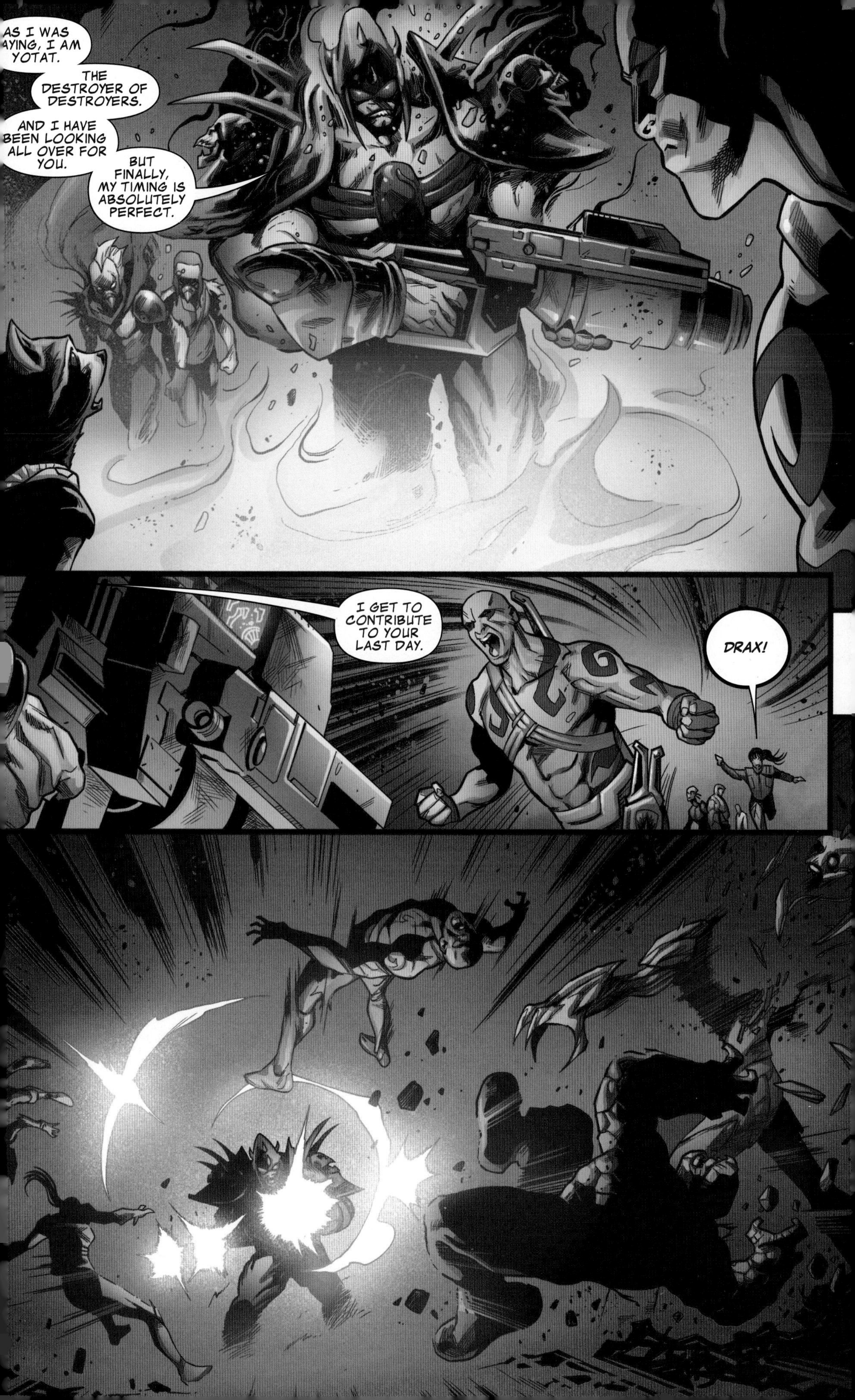
AS I WAS
AYING, I AM
YOTAT.
THE DESTROYER OF DESTROYERS.
AND I HAVE BEEN LOOKING ALL OVER FOR YOU.
BUT FINALLY, MY TIMING IS ABSOLUTELY PERFECT.
I GET TO CONTRIBUTE TO YOUR LAST DAY.
DRAX!

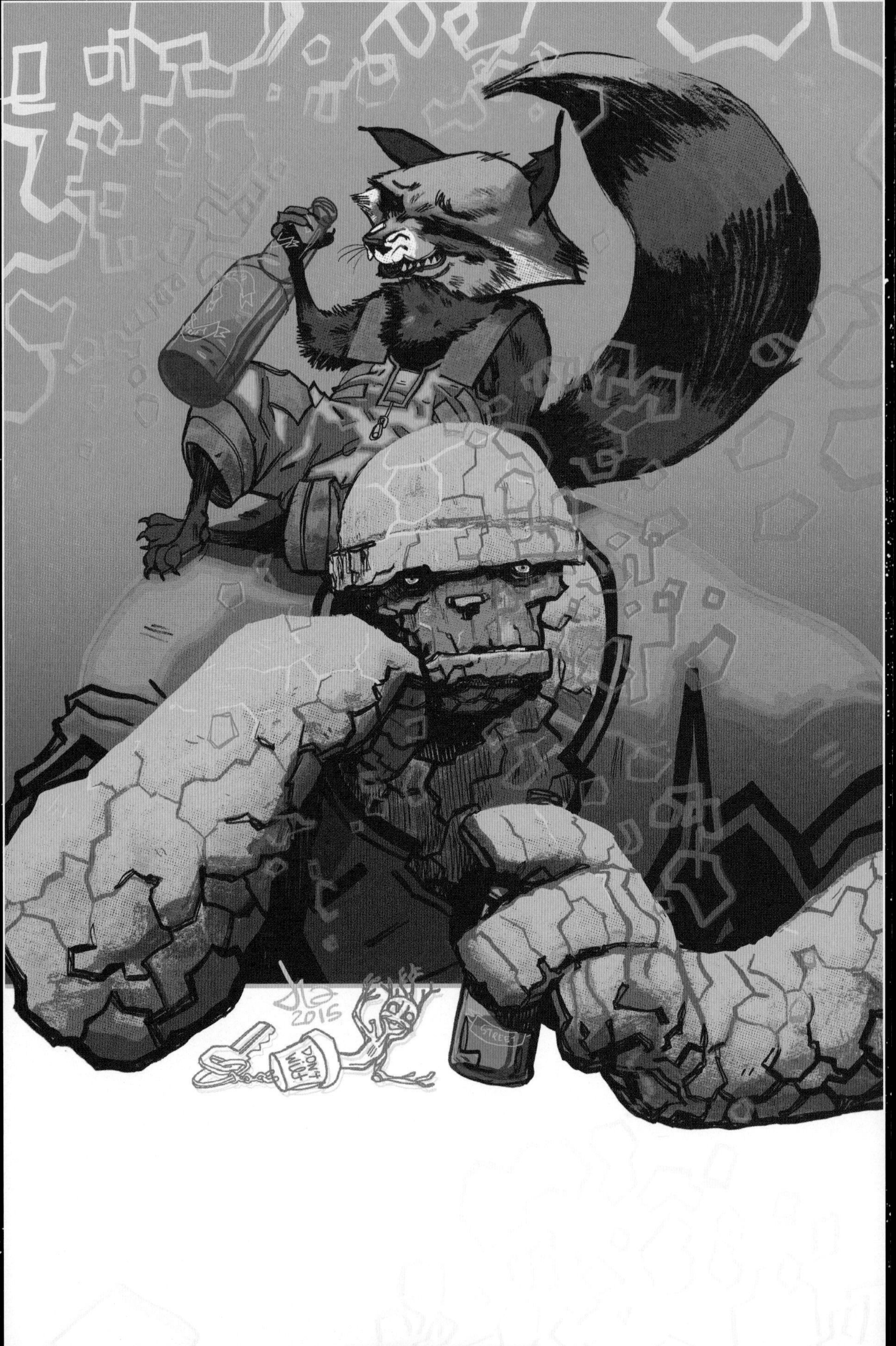
2015
STREET

#1 VARIANT BY
JASON LATOUR

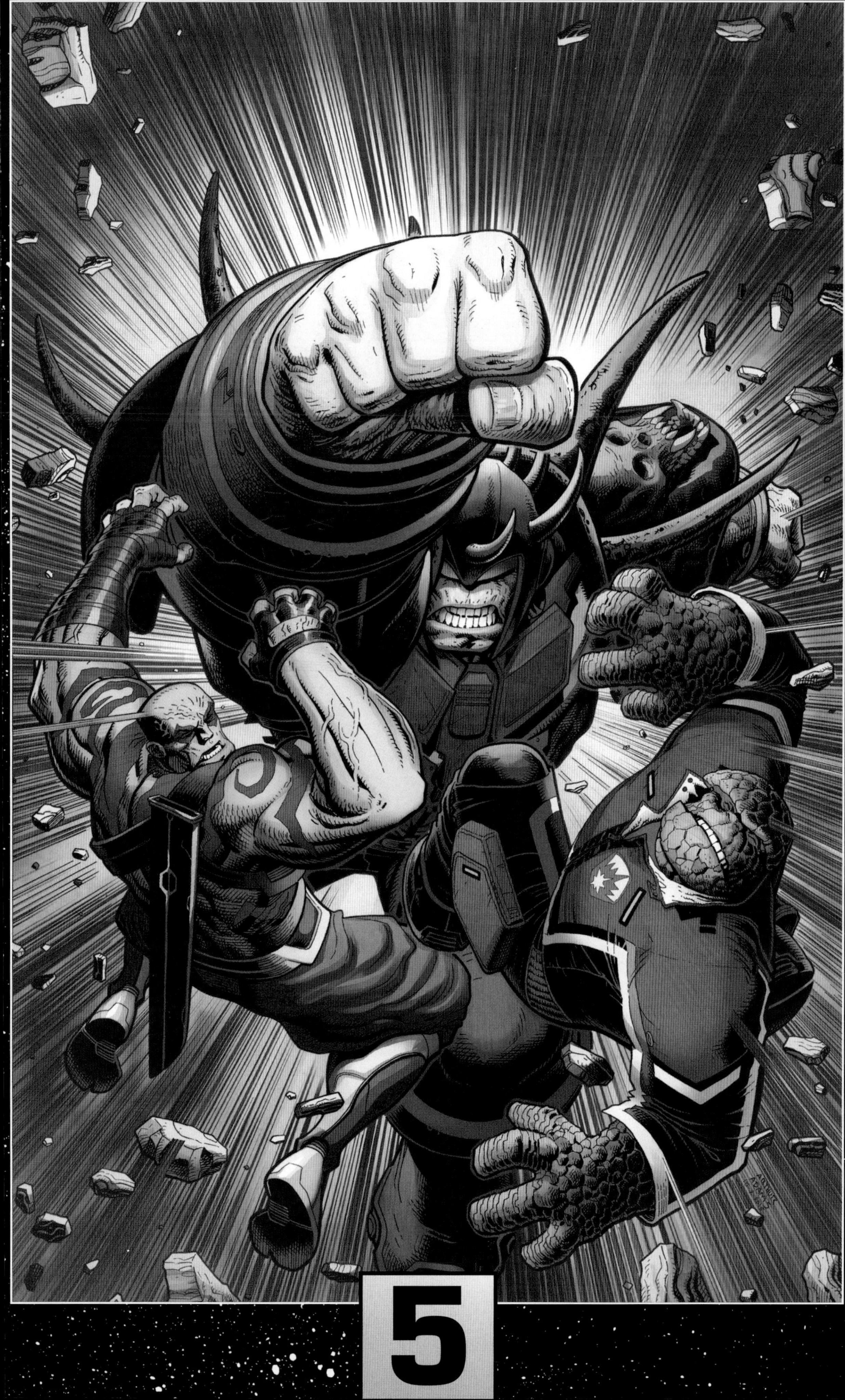
5

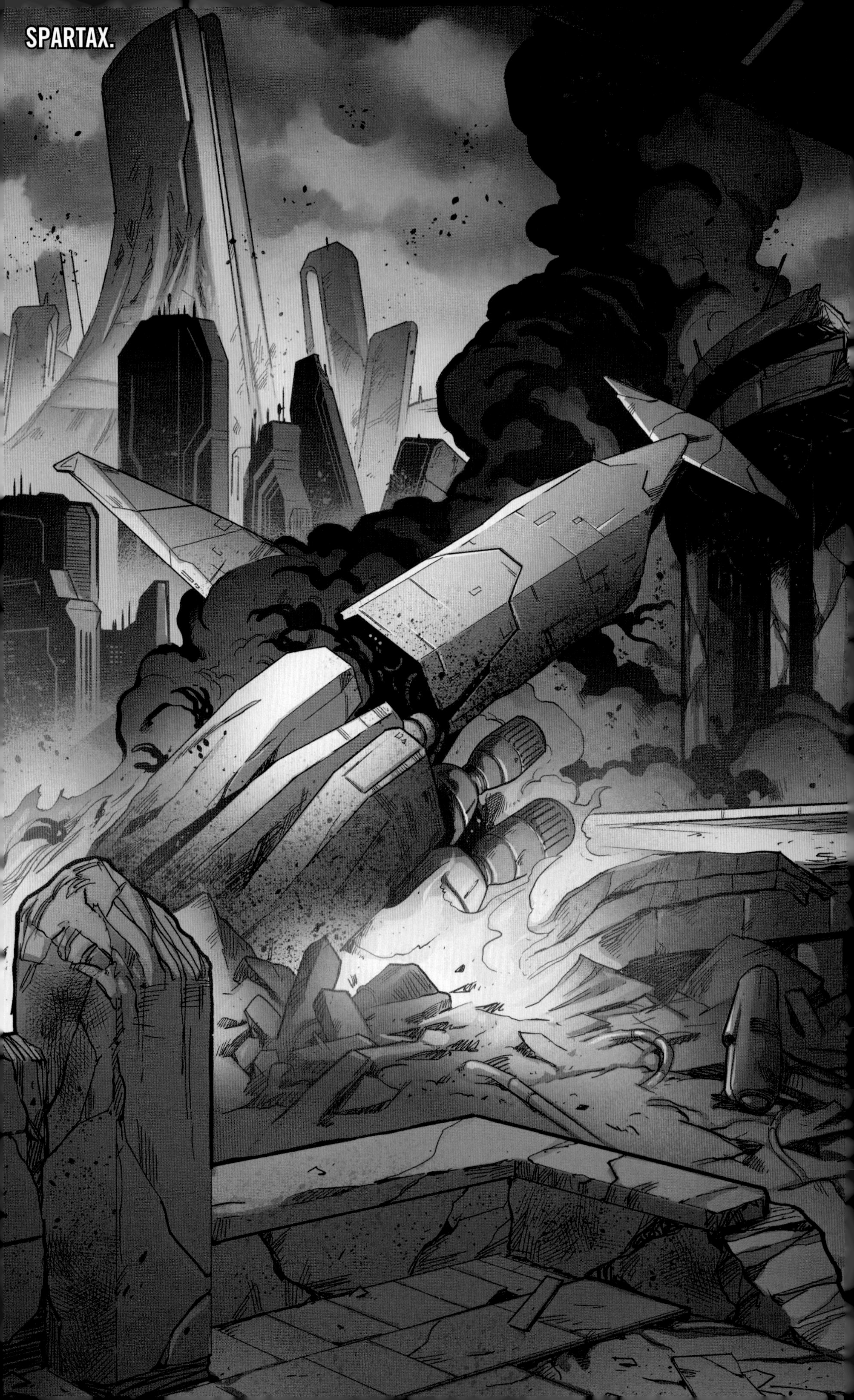
SPARTAX.

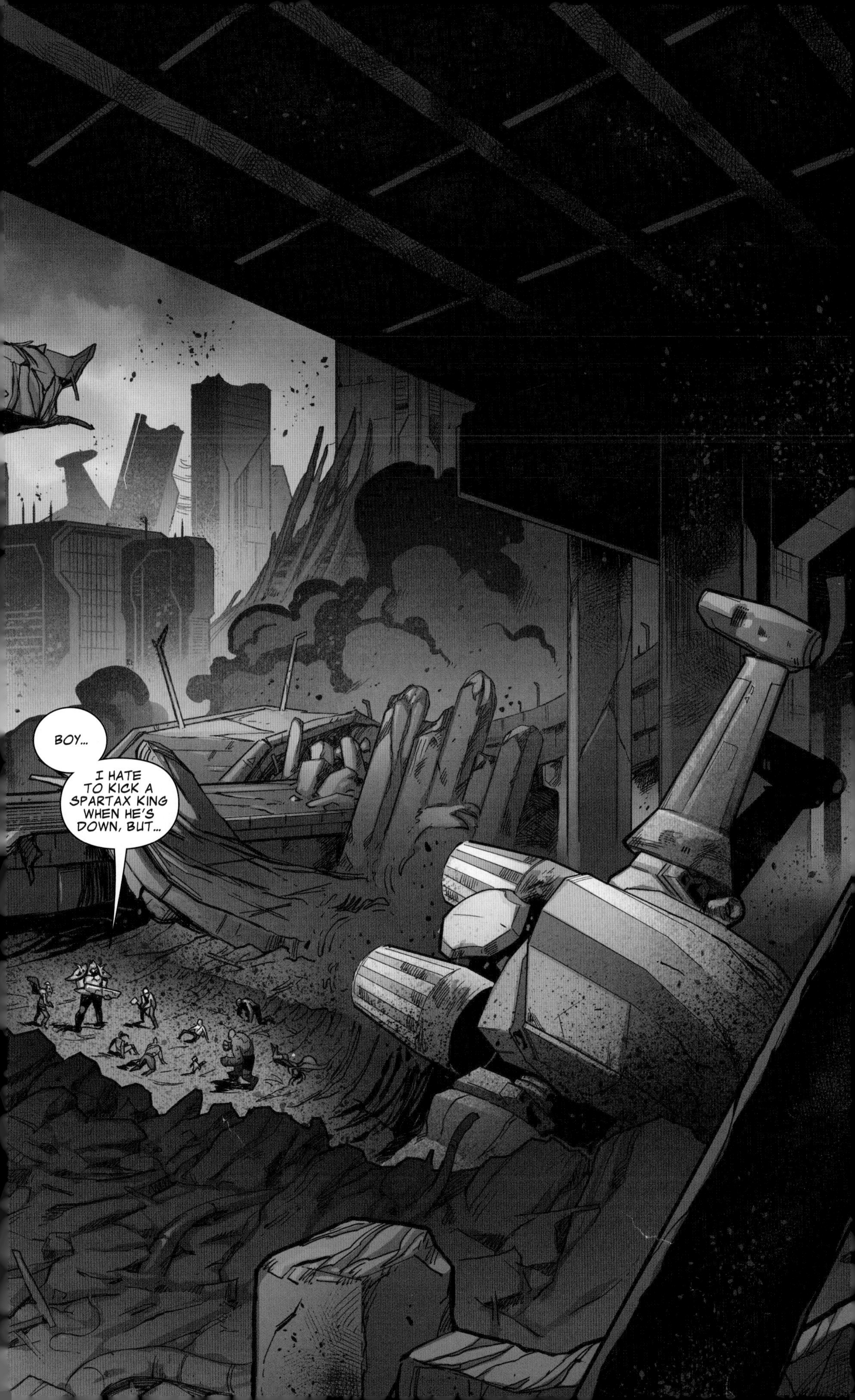
BOY...
I HATE TO KICK A SPARTAX KING WHEN HE'S DOWN, BUT...

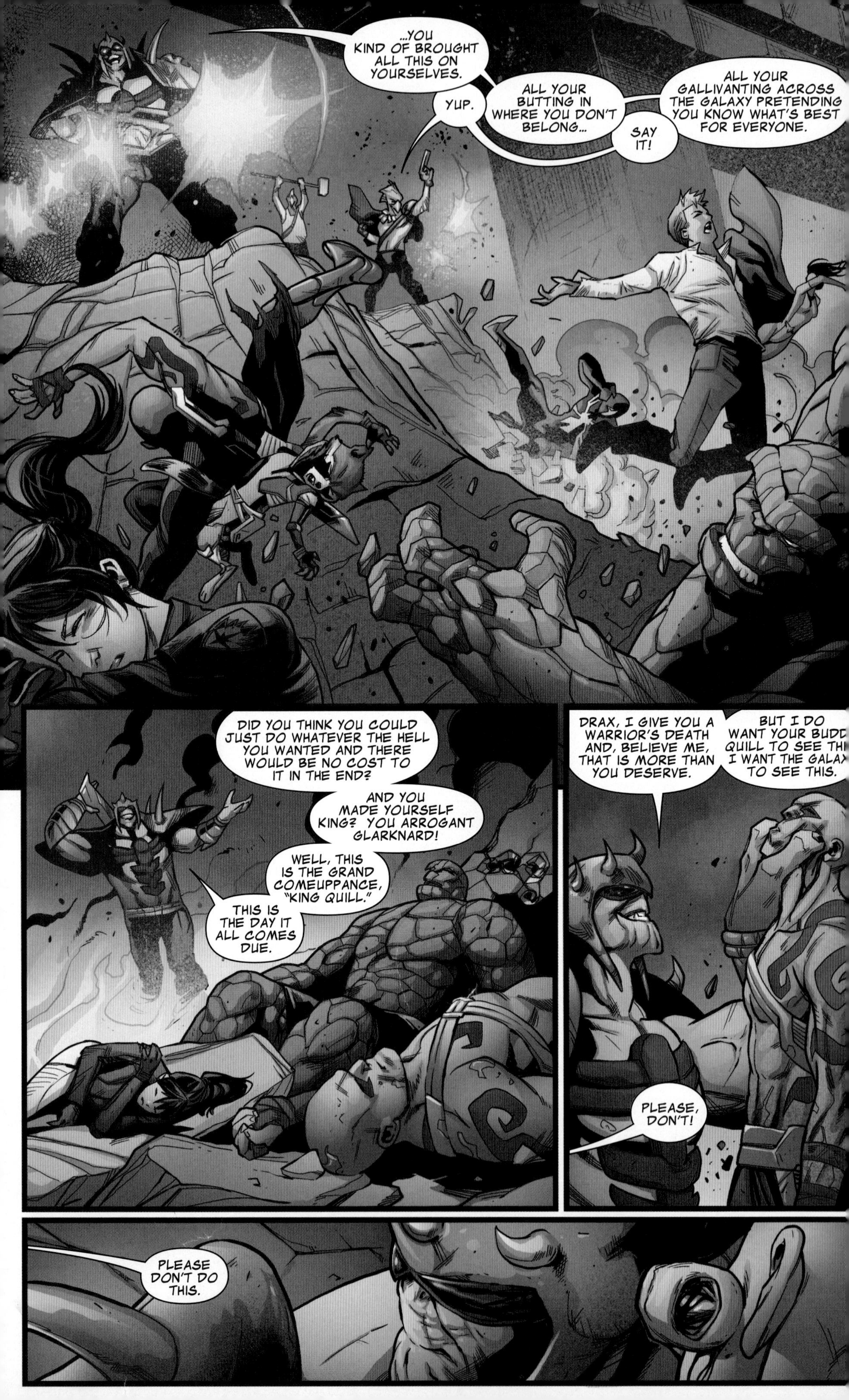
...YOU KIND OF BROUGHT ALL THIS ON YOURSELVES.
YUP.
ALL YOUR BUTTING IN WHERE YOU DON'T BELONG...
SAY IT!
ALL YOUR GALLIVANTING ACROSS THE GALAXY PRETENDING YOU KNOW WHAT'S BEST FOR EVERYONE.
DID YOU THINK YOU COULD JUST DO WHATEVER THE HELL YOU WANTED AND THERE WOULD BE NO COST TO IT IN THE END?
AND YOU MADE YOURSELF KING? YOU ARROGANT GLARKNARD!
WELL, THIS IS THE GRAND COMEUPPANCE, "KING QUILL."
THIS IS THE DAY IT ALL COMES DUE.
DRAX, I GIVE YOU A WARRIOR'S DEATH AND, BELIEVE ME, THAT IS MORE THAN YOU DESERVE.
BUT I DO WANT YOUR BUDD QUILL TO SEE THI I WANT THE GALAX TO SEE THIS.
PLEASE, DON'T!
PLEASE DON'T DO THIS.

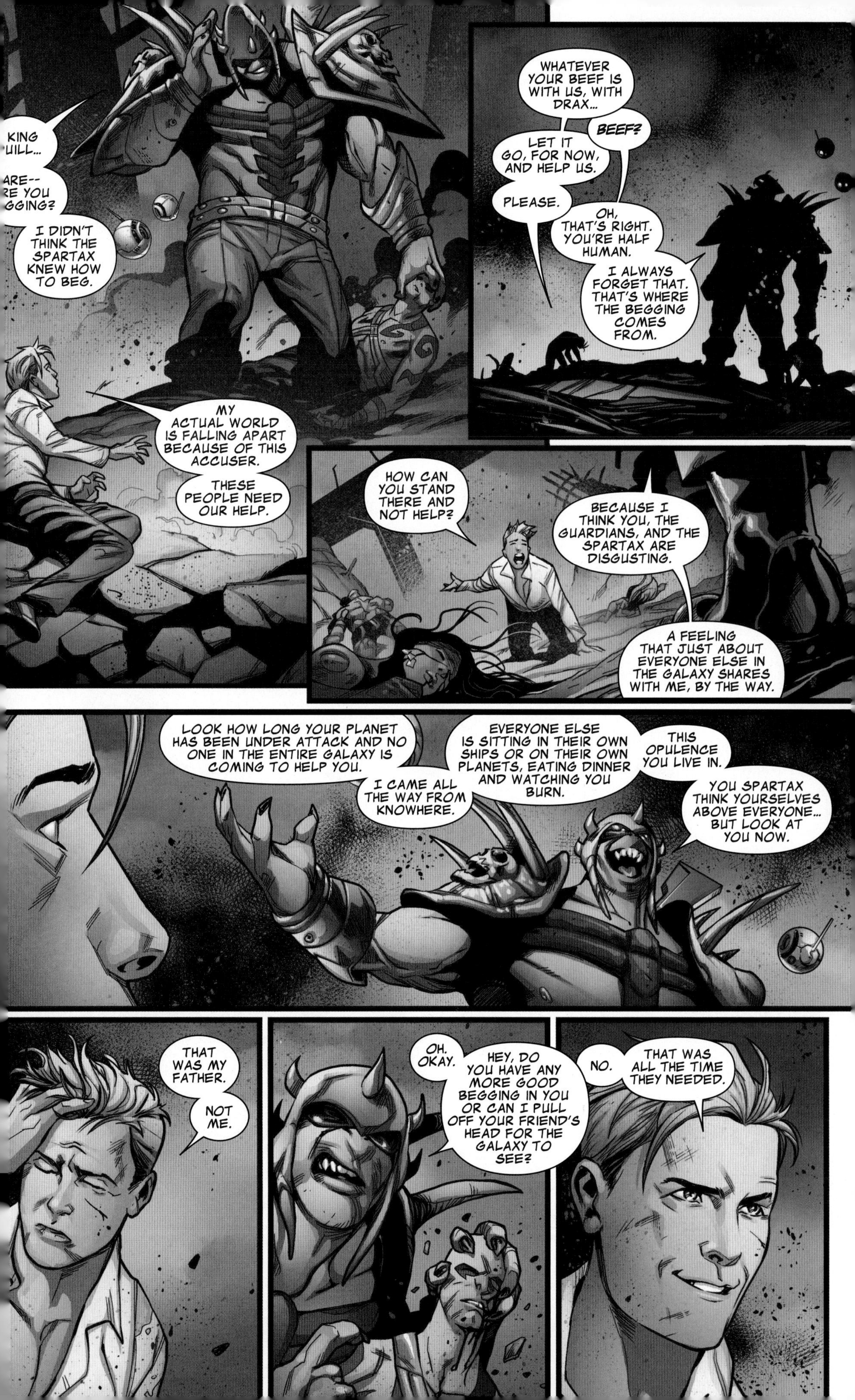

KING
QUILL...
ARE--
ARE YOU
BEGGING?
I DIDN'T
THINK THE
SPARTAX
KNEW HOW
TO BEG.
WHATEVER
YOUR BEEF IS
WITH US, WITH
DRAX...
BEEF?
LET IT
GO, FOR NOW,
AND HELP US.
PLEASE.
OH,
THAT'S RIGHT.
YOU'RE HALF
HUMAN.
I ALWAYS
FORGET THAT.
THAT'S WHERE
THE BEGGING
COMES
FROM.
MY
ACTUAL WORLD
IS FALLING APART
BECAUSE OF THIS
ACCUSER.
THESE
PEOPLE NEED
OUR HELP.
HOW CAN
YOU STAND
THERE AND
NOT HELP?
BECAUSE I
THINK YOU, THE
GUARDIANS, AND THE
SPARTAX ARE
DISGUSTING.
A FEELING
THAT JUST ABOUT
EVERYONE ELSE IN
THE GALAXY SHARES
WITH ME, BY THE WAY.
LOOK HOW LONG YOUR PLANET
HAS BEEN UNDER ATTACK AND NO
ONE IN THE ENTIRE GALAXY IS
COMING TO HELP YOU.
I CAME ALL
THE WAY FROM
KNOWHERE.
EVERYONE ELSE
IS SITTING IN THEIR OWN
SHIPS OR ON THEIR OWN
PLANETS, EATING DINNER
AND WATCHING YOU
BURN.
THIS
OPULENCE
YOU LIVE IN.
YOU SPARTAX
THINK YOURSELVES
ABOVE EVERYONE...
BUT LOOK AT
YOU NOW.
THAT
WAS MY
FATHER.
NOT
ME.
OH.
OKAY.
HEY, DO
YOU HAVE ANY
MORE GOOD
BEGGING IN YOU
OR CAN I PULL
OFF YOUR FRIEND'S
HEAD FOR THE
GALAXY TO
SEE?
NO.
THAT WAS
ALL THE TIME
THEY NEEDED.

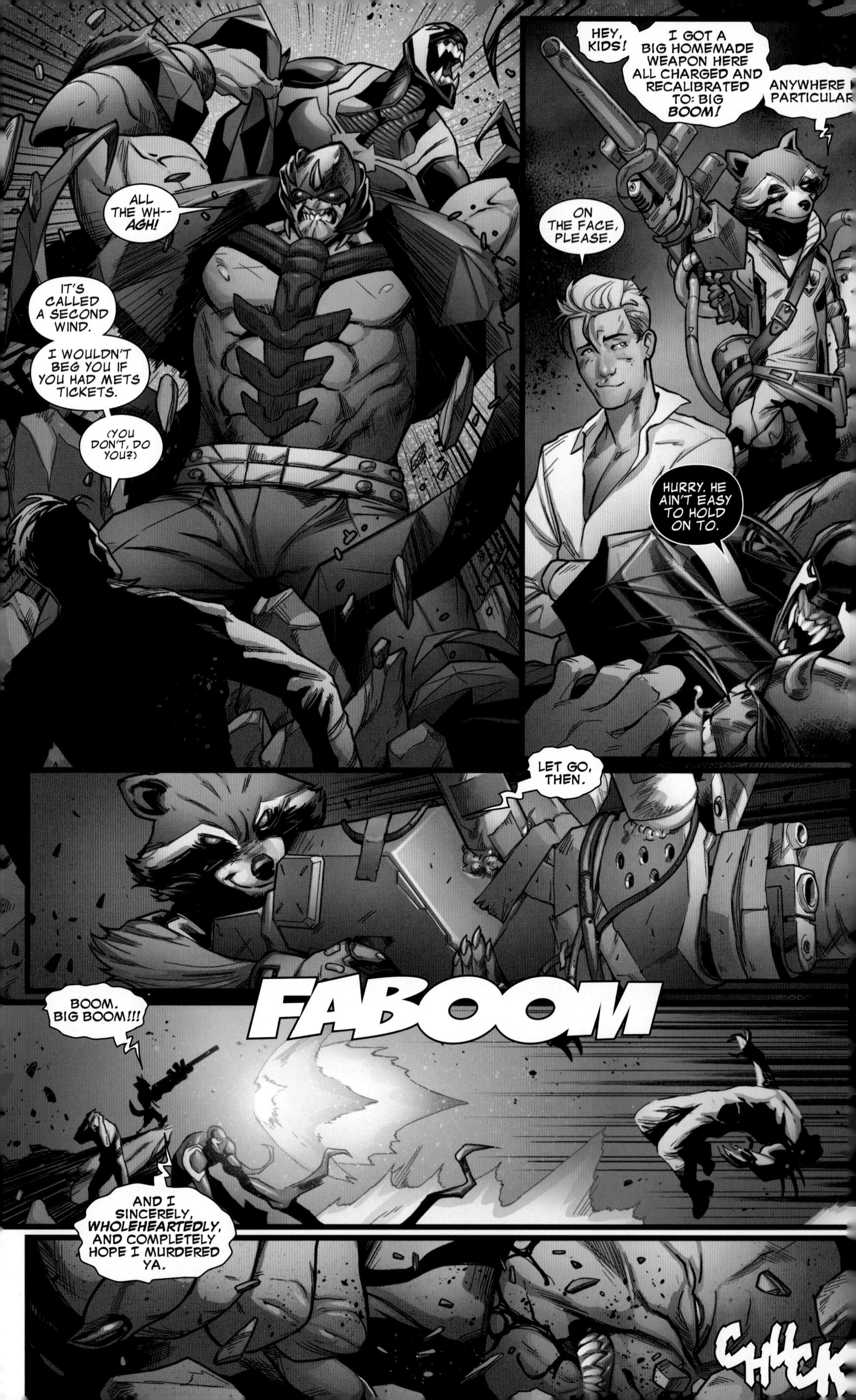

ALL THE WH-- *AGH!*
IT'S CALLED A SECOND WIND.
I WOULDN'T BEG YOU IF YOU HAD METS TICKETS.
(YOU DON'T, DO YOU?)
HEY, KIDS!
I GOT A BIG HOMEMADE WEAPON HERE ALL CHARGED AND RECALIBRATED TO: BIG *BOOM!*
ANYWHERE
PARTICULAR
ON THE FACE, PLEASE.
HURRY. HE AIN'T EASY TO HOLD ON TO.
LET GO, THEN.
FABOOM
BOOM. BIG BOOM!!!
AND I SINCERELY, *WHOLEHEARTEDLY*, AND COMPLETELY HOPE I MURDERED YA.
CHUCK

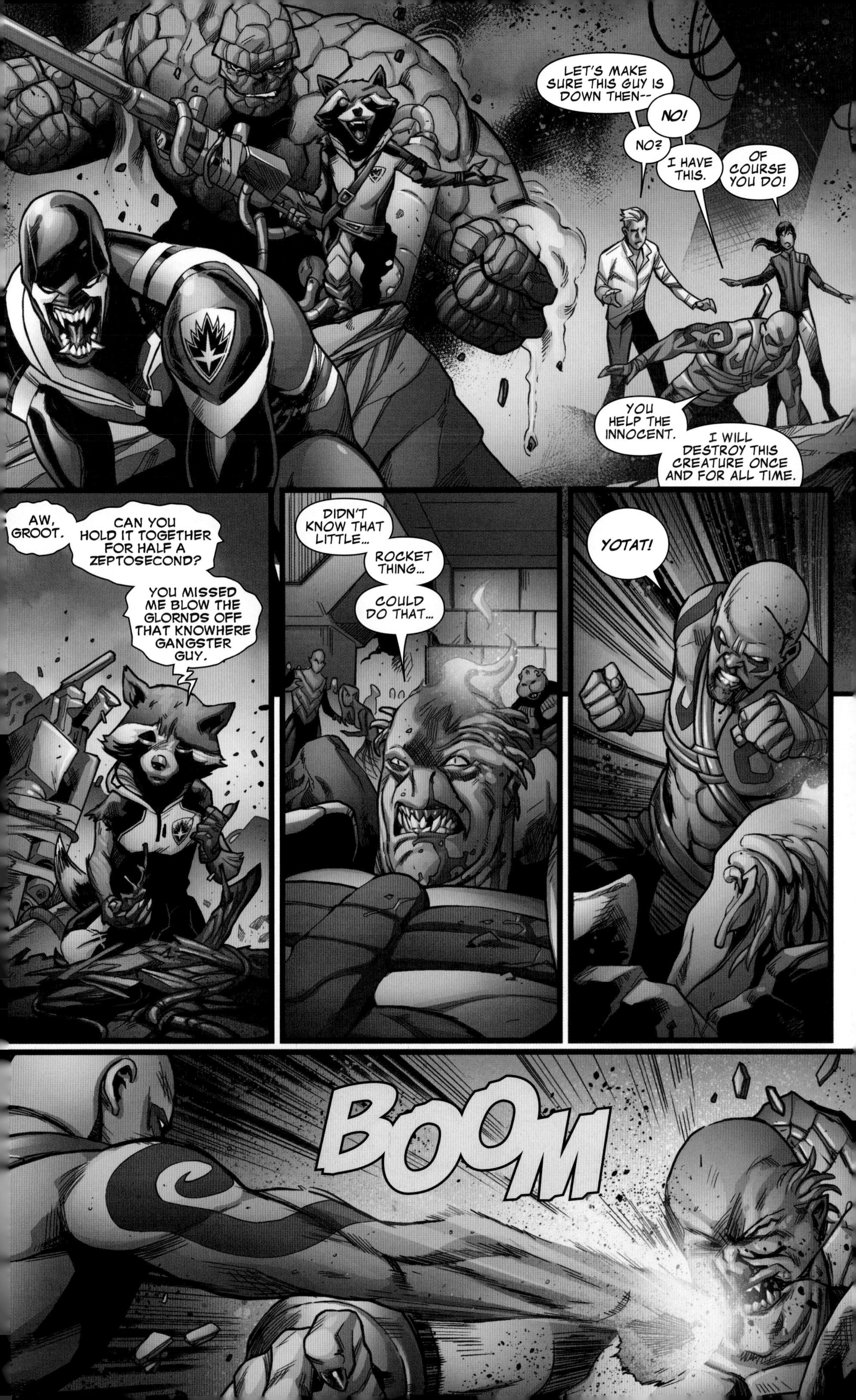
LET'S MAKE SURE THIS GUY IS DOWN THEN--
NO!
NO?
I HAVE THIS.
OF COURSE YOU DO!
YOU HELP THE INNOCENT.
I WILL DESTROY THIS CREATURE ONCE AND FOR ALL TIME.
AW, GROOT.
CAN YOU HOLD IT TOGETHER FOR HALF A ZEPTOSECOND?
YOU MISSED ME BLOW THE GLORNDS OFF THAT KNOWHERE GANGSTER GUY.
DIDN'T KNOW THAT LITTLE...
ROCKET THING...
COULD DO THAT...
YOTAT!
BOOM

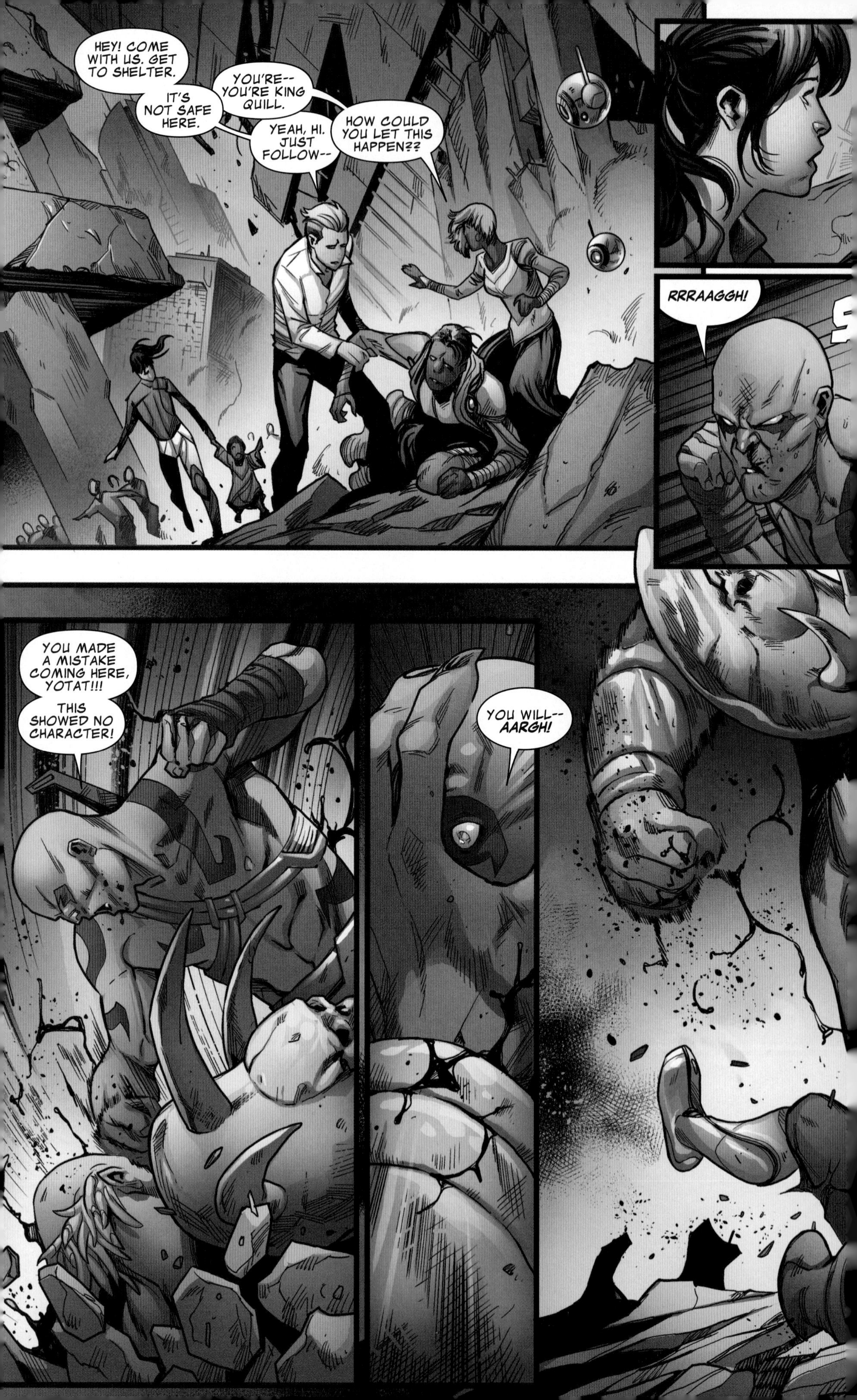
HEY! COME WITH US. GET TO SHELTER.
IT'S NOT SAFE HERE.
YOU'RE-- YOU'RE KING QUILL.
YEAH, HI. JUST FOLLOW--
HOW COULD YOU LET THIS HAPPEN??
RRRAAGGH!
YOU MADE A MISTAKE COMING HERE, YOTAT!!!
THIS SHOWED NO CHARACTER!
YOU WILL-- AARGH!

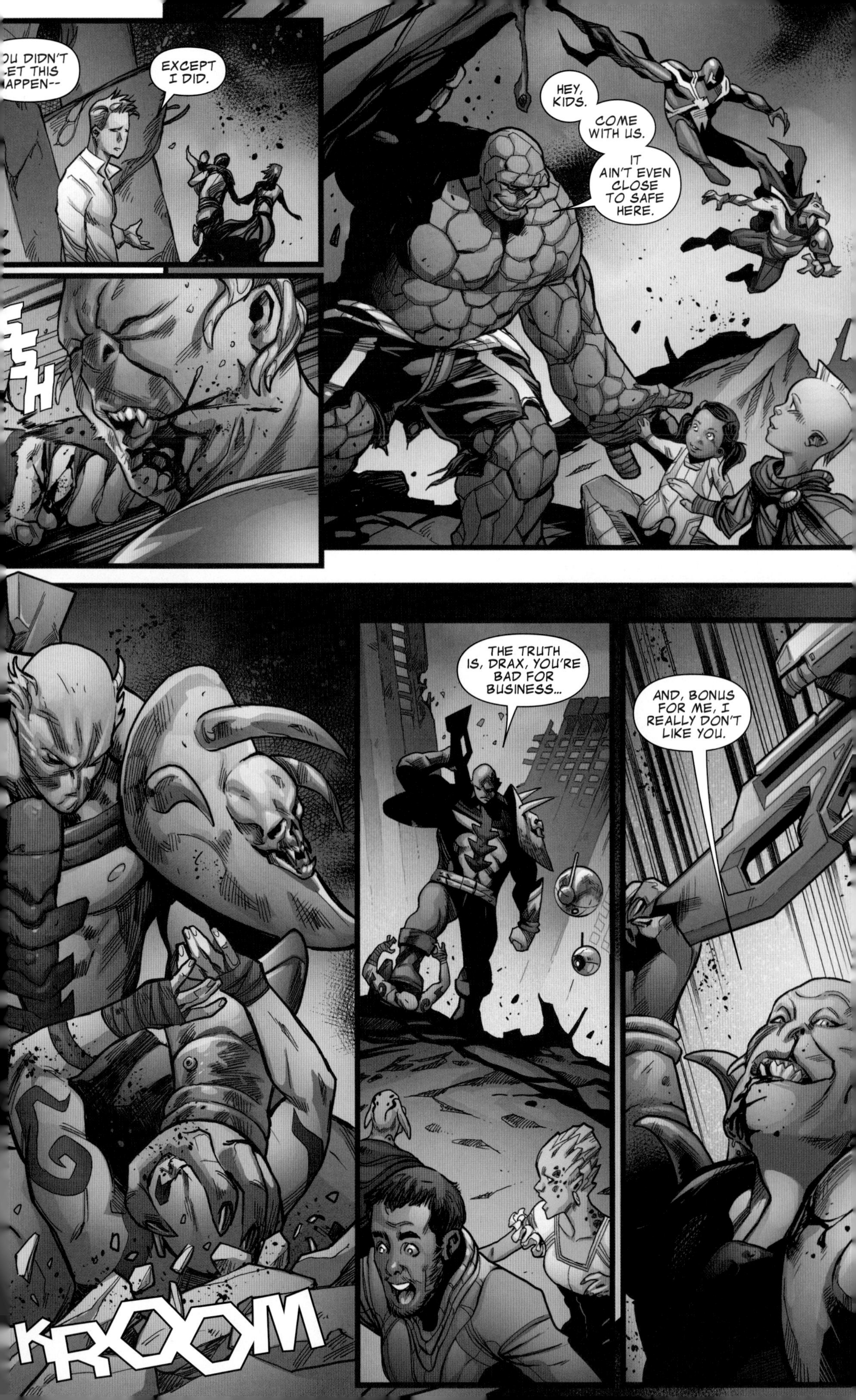
OU DIDN'T
ET THIS
APPEN--
EXCEPT I DID.
HEY, KIDS.
COME WITH US.
IT AIN'T EVEN CLOSE TO SAFE HERE.
KROOM
THE TRUTH IS, DRAX, YOU'RE BAD FOR BUSINESS...
AND, BONUS FOR ME, I REALLY DON'T LIKE YOU.

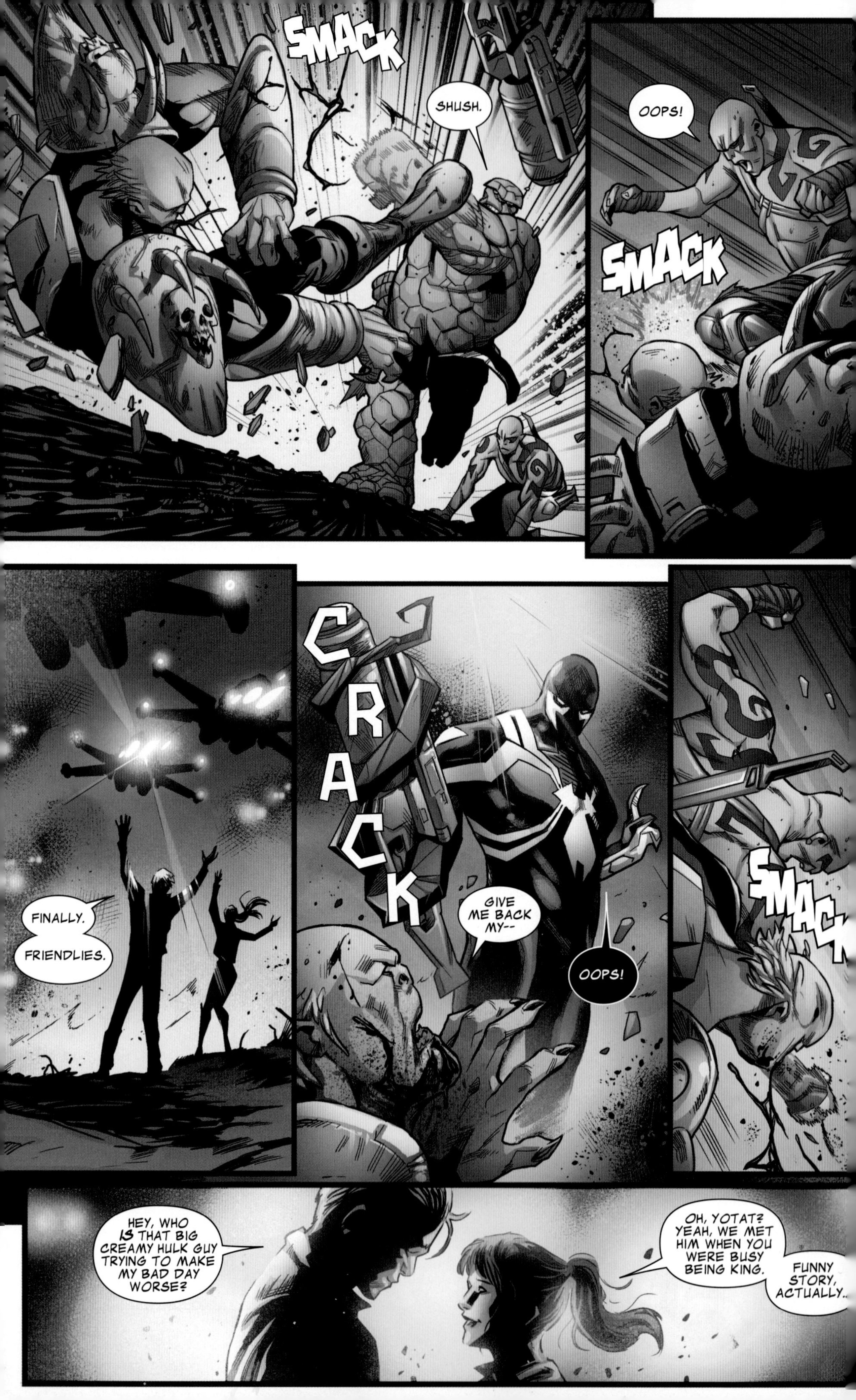
SMACK
SHUSH.
OOPS!
SMACK
FINALLY.
FRIENDLIES.
CRACK
GIVE ME BACK MY--
OOPS!
SMACK
HEY, WHO IS THAT BIG CREAMY HULK GUY TRYING TO MAKE MY BAD DAY WORSE?
OH, YOTAT? YEAH, WE MET HIM WHEN YOU WERE BUSY BEING KING.
FUNNY STORY, ACTUALLY...

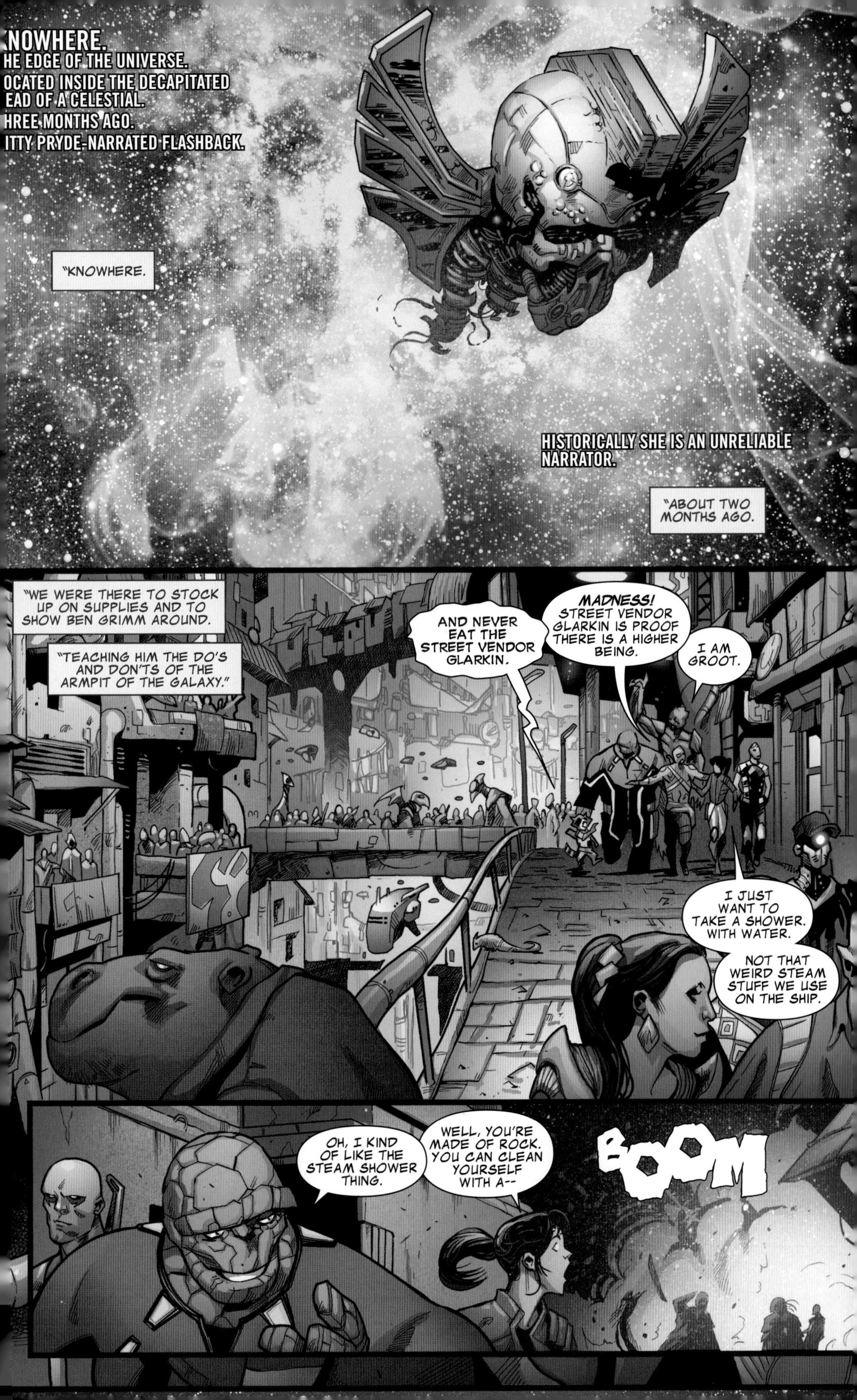
NOWHERE.
HE EDGE OF THE UNIVERSE.
OCATED INSIDE THE DECAPITATED EAD OF A CELESTIAL.
HREE MONTHS AGO.
ITTY PRYDE-NARRATED FLASHBACK.
"KNOWHERE.
HISTORICALLY SHE IS AN UNRELIABLE NARRATOR.
"ABOUT TWO MONTHS AGO.
"WE WERE THERE TO STOCK UP ON SUPPLIES AND TO SHOW BEN GRIMM AROUND.
"TEACHING HIM THE DO'S AND DON'TS OF THE ARMPIT OF THE GALAXY."
AND NEVER EAT THE STREET VENDOR GLARKIN.
MADNESS! STREET VENDOR GLARKIN IS PROOF THERE IS A HIGHER BEING.
I AM GROOT.
I JUST WANT TO TAKE A SHOWER. WITH WATER.
NOT THAT WEIRD STEAM STUFF WE USE ON THE SHIP.
OH, I KIND OF LIKE THE STEAM SHOWER THING.
WELL, YOU'RE MADE OF ROCK. YOU CAN CLEAN YOURSELF WITH A--
BOOM

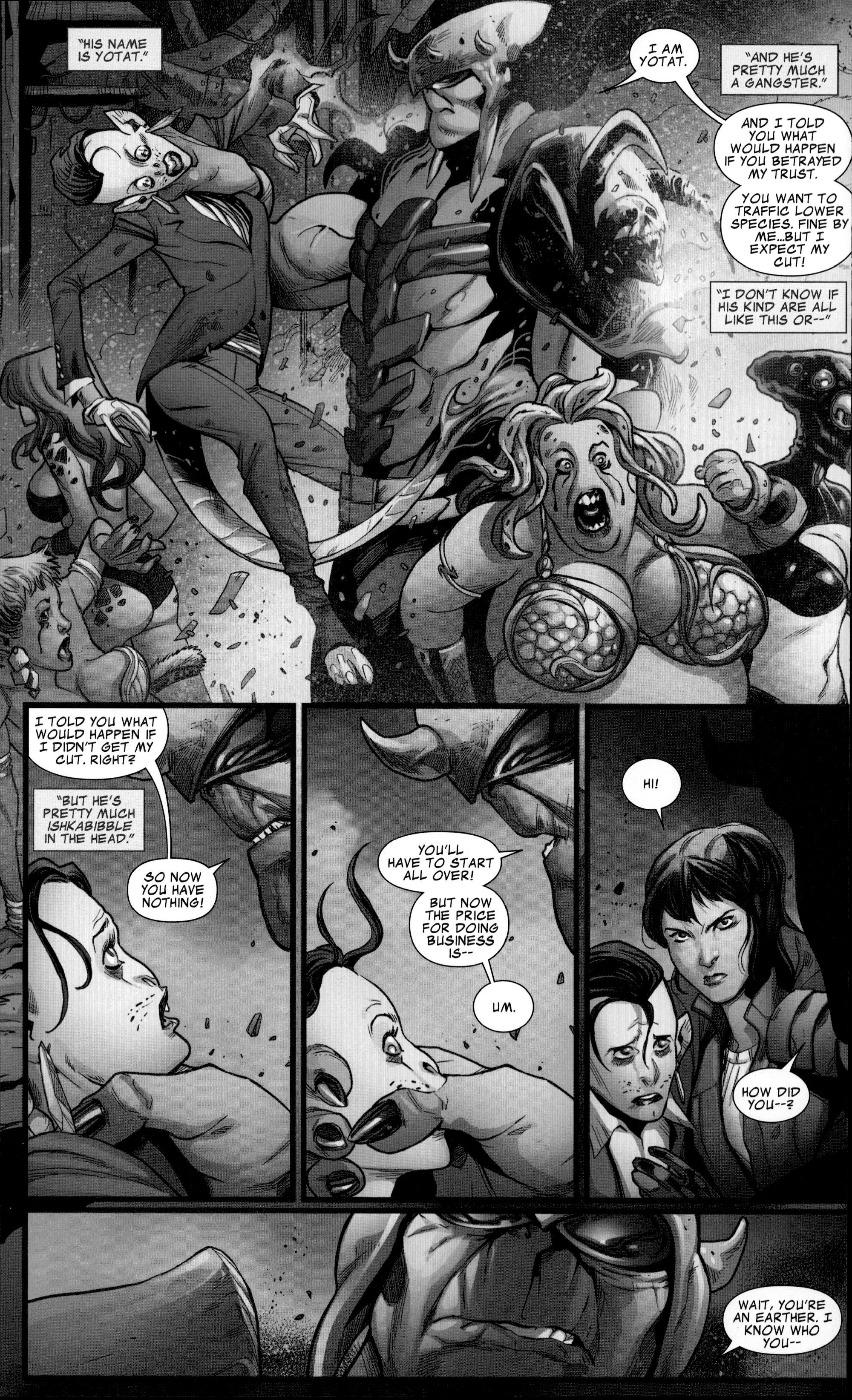
"HIS NAME IS YOTAT."
I AM YOTAT.
"AND HE'S PRETTY MUCH A GANGSTER."
AND I TOLD YOU WHAT WOULD HAPPEN IF YOU BETRAYED MY TRUST.
YOU WANT TO TRAFFIC LOWER SPECIES. FINE BY ME...BUT I EXPECT MY CUT!
"I DON'T KNOW IF HIS KIND ARE ALL LIKE THIS OR--"
I TOLD YOU WHAT WOULD HAPPEN IF I DIDN'T GET MY CUT. RIGHT?
"BUT HE'S PRETTY MUCH ISHKABIBBLE IN THE HEAD."
SO NOW YOU HAVE NOTHING!
YOU'LL HAVE TO START ALL OVER!
BUT NOW THE PRICE FOR DOING BUSINESS IS--
UM.
HI!
HOW DID YOU--?
WAIT, YOU'RE AN EARTHER. I KNOW WHO YOU--

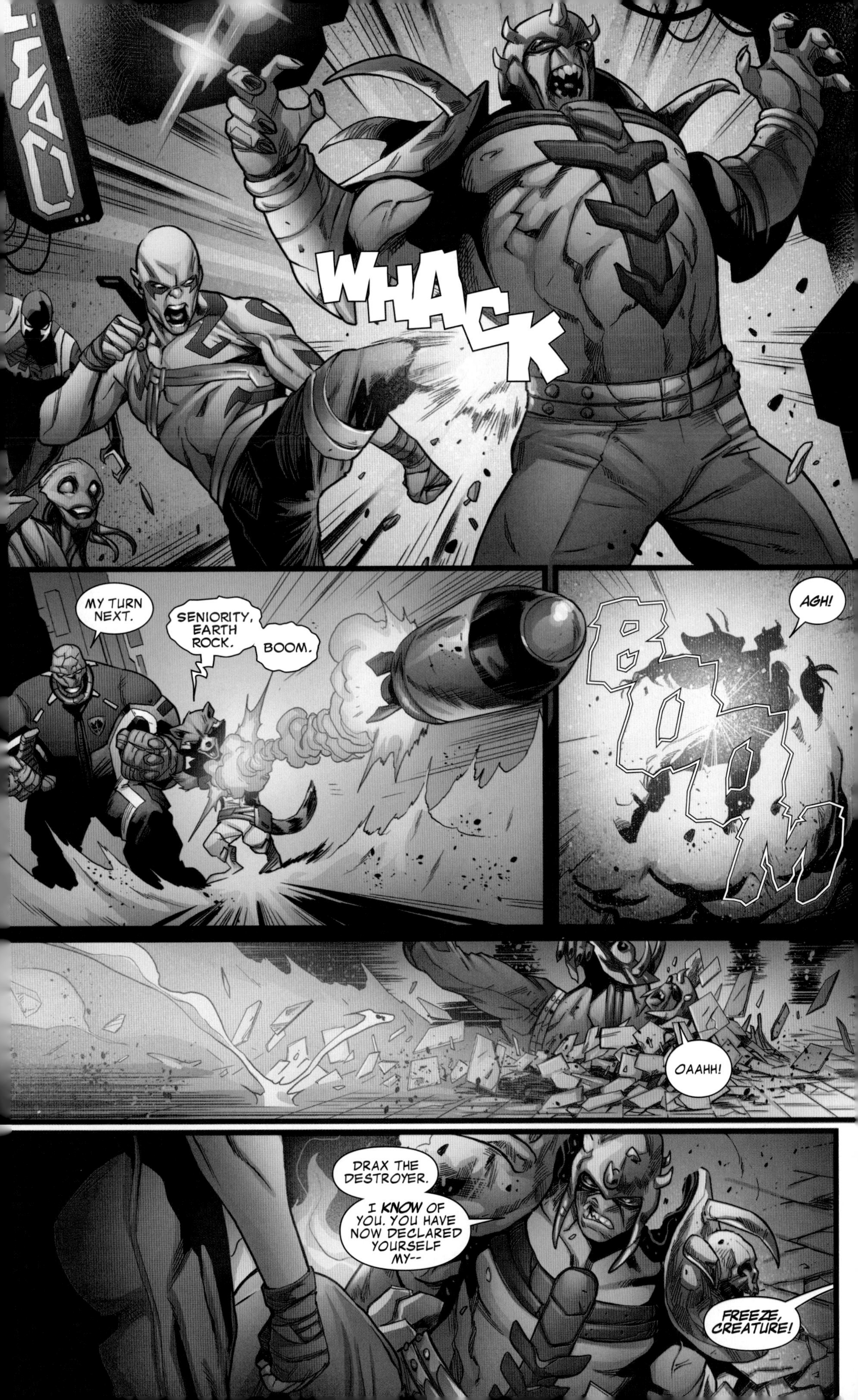

WHACK
MY TURN NEXT.
SENIORITY, EARTH ROCK.
BOOM.
BOOM
AGH!
OAAHH!
DRAX THE DESTROYER.
I KNOW OF YOU. YOU HAVE NOW DECLARED YOURSELF MY--
FREEZE, CREATURE!

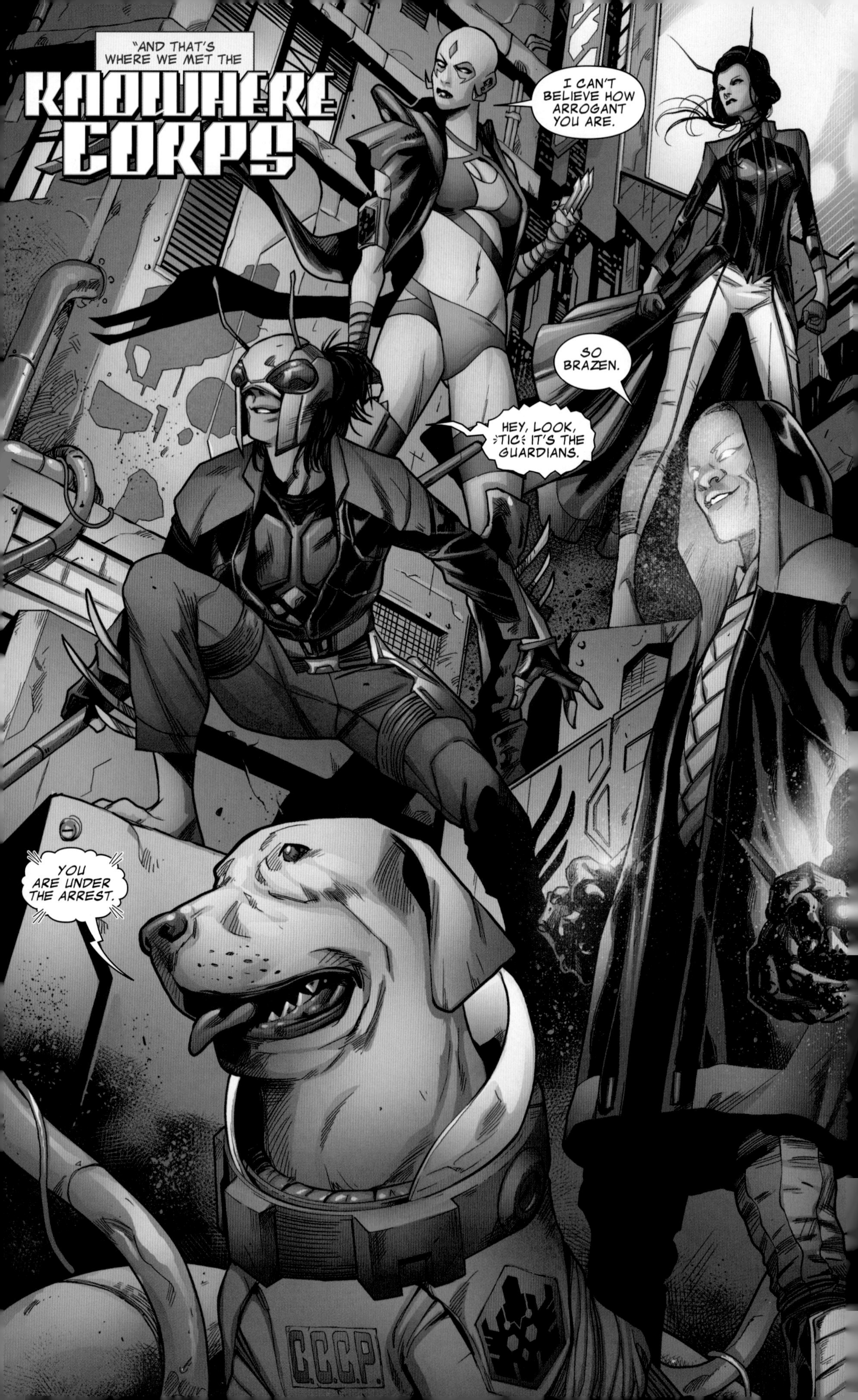
"AND THAT'S WHERE WE MET THE
KNOWHERE CORPS
I CAN'T BELIEVE HOW ARROGANT YOU ARE.
SO BRAZEN.
HEY, LOOK, TIC IT'S THE GUARDIANS.
YOU ARE UNDER THE ARREST.
C.C.C.P.

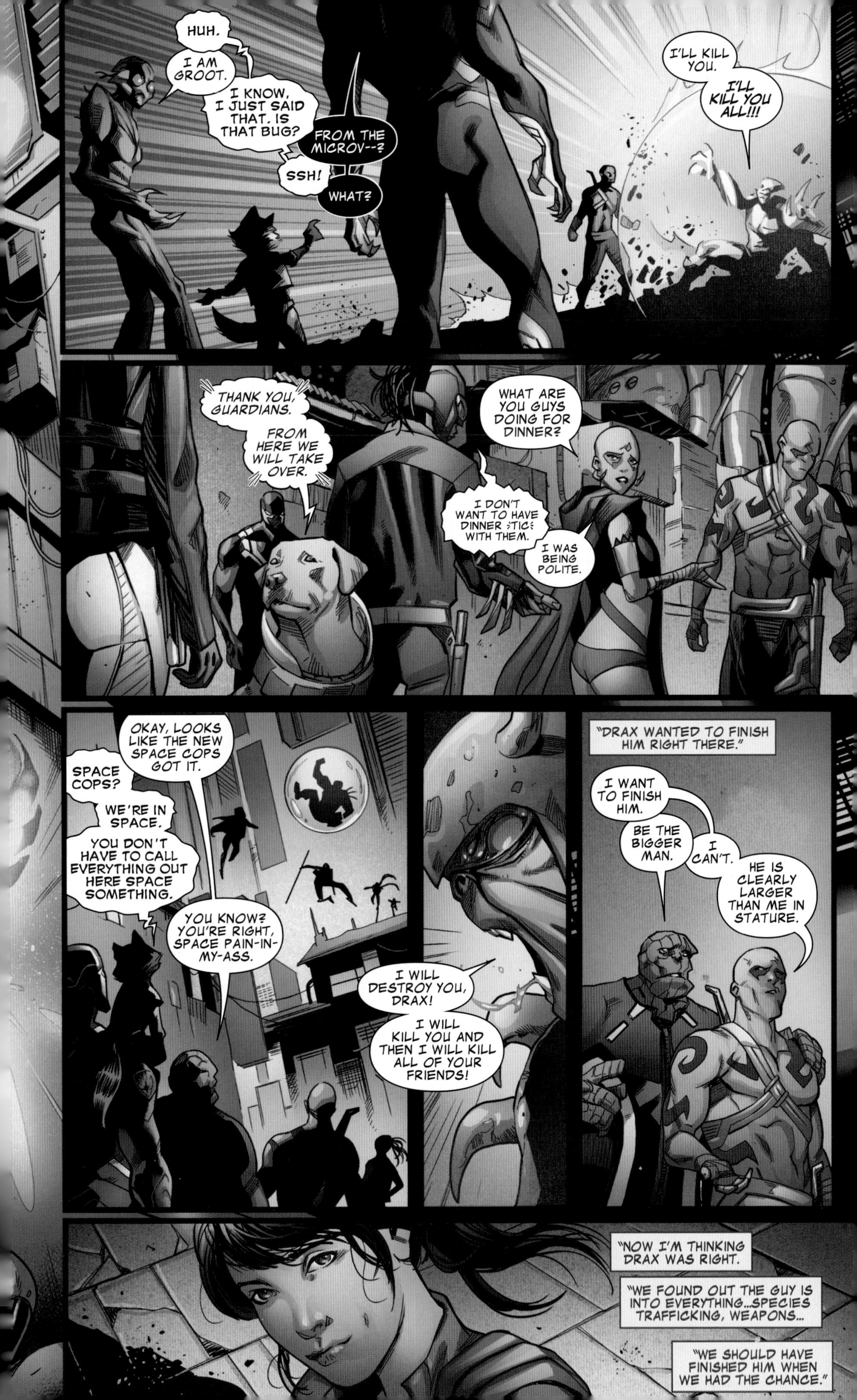
HUH.
I AM GROOT.
I KNOW, I JUST SAID THAT. IS THAT BUG?
FROM THE MICROV--?
SSH!
WHAT?
I'LL KILL YOU.
I'LL KILL YOU ALL!!!
THANK YOU, GUARDIANS.
FROM HERE WE WILL TAKE OVER.
WHAT ARE YOU GUYS DOING FOR DINNER?
I DON'T WANT TO HAVE DINNER *TIC* WITH THEM.
I WAS BEING POLITE.
OKAY, LOOKS LIKE THE NEW SPACE COPS GOT IT.
SPACE COPS?
WE'RE IN SPACE.
YOU DON'T HAVE TO CALL EVERYTHING OUT HERE SPACE SOMETHING.
YOU KNOW? YOU'RE RIGHT, SPACE PAIN-IN-MY-ASS.
I WILL DESTROY YOU, DRAX!
I WILL KILL YOU AND THEN I WILL KILL ALL OF YOUR FRIENDS!
"DRAX WANTED TO FINISH HIM RIGHT THERE."
I WANT TO FINISH HIM.
BE THE BIGGER MAN.
I CAN'T.
HE IS CLEARLY LARGER THAN ME IN STATURE.
"NOW I'M THINKING DRAX WAS RIGHT.
"WE FOUND OUT THE GUY IS INTO EVERYTHING...SPECIES TRAFFICKING, WEAPONS...
"WE SHOULD HAVE FINISHED HIM WHEN WE HAD THE CHANCE."

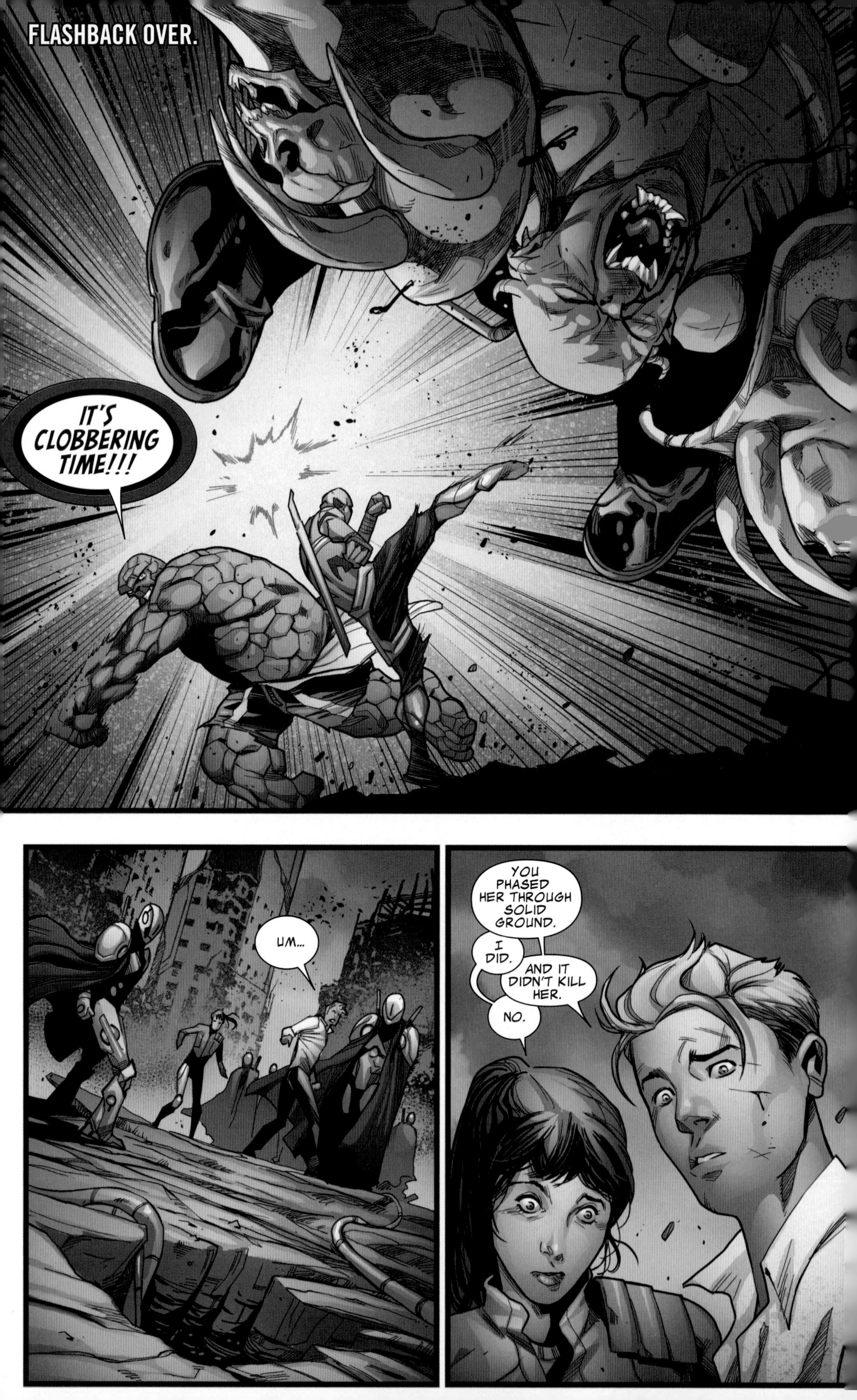
FLASHBACK OVER.
IT'S CLOBBERING TIME!!!
UM...
YOU PHASED HER THROUGH SOLID GROUND.
I DID.
AND IT DIDN'T KILL HER.
NO.

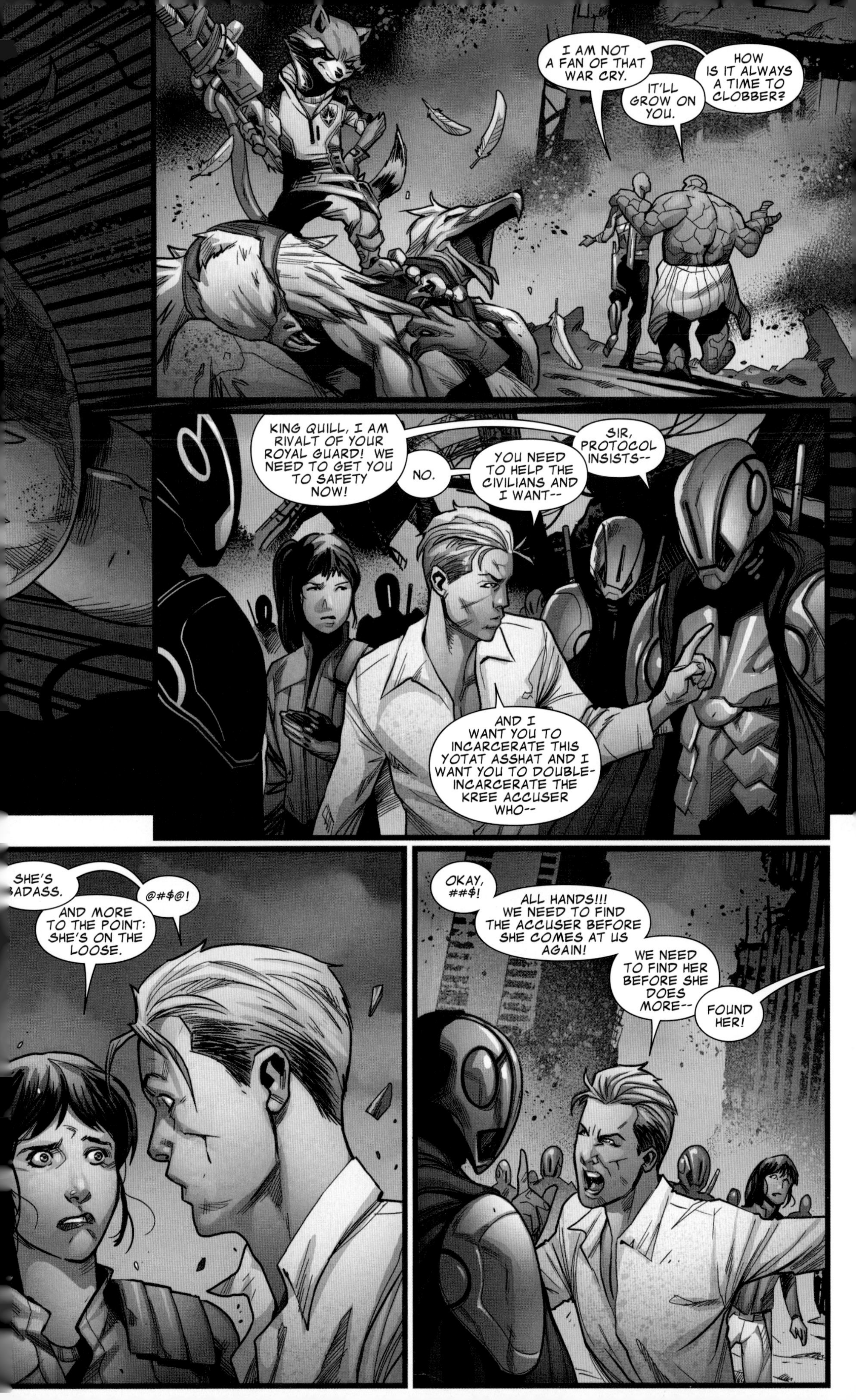
I AM NOT A FAN OF THAT WAR CRY.
HOW IS IT ALWAYS A TIME TO CLOBBER?
IT'LL GROW ON YOU.
KING QUILL, I AM RIVALT OF YOUR ROYAL GUARD! WE NEED TO GET YOU TO SAFETY NOW!
NO.
SIR, PROTOCOL INSISTS--
YOU NEED TO HELP THE CIVILIANS AND I WANT--
AND I WANT YOU TO INCARCERATE THIS YOTAT ASSHAT AND I WANT YOU TO DOUBLE-INCARCERATE THE KREE ACCUSER WHO--
SHE'S BADASS.
@#$@!
AND MORE TO THE POINT: SHE'S ON THE LOOSE.
OKAY, ##$!
ALL HANDS!!! WE NEED TO FIND THE ACCUSER BEFORE SHE COMES AT US AGAIN!
WE NEED TO FIND HER BEFORE SHE DOES MORE--
FOUND HER!

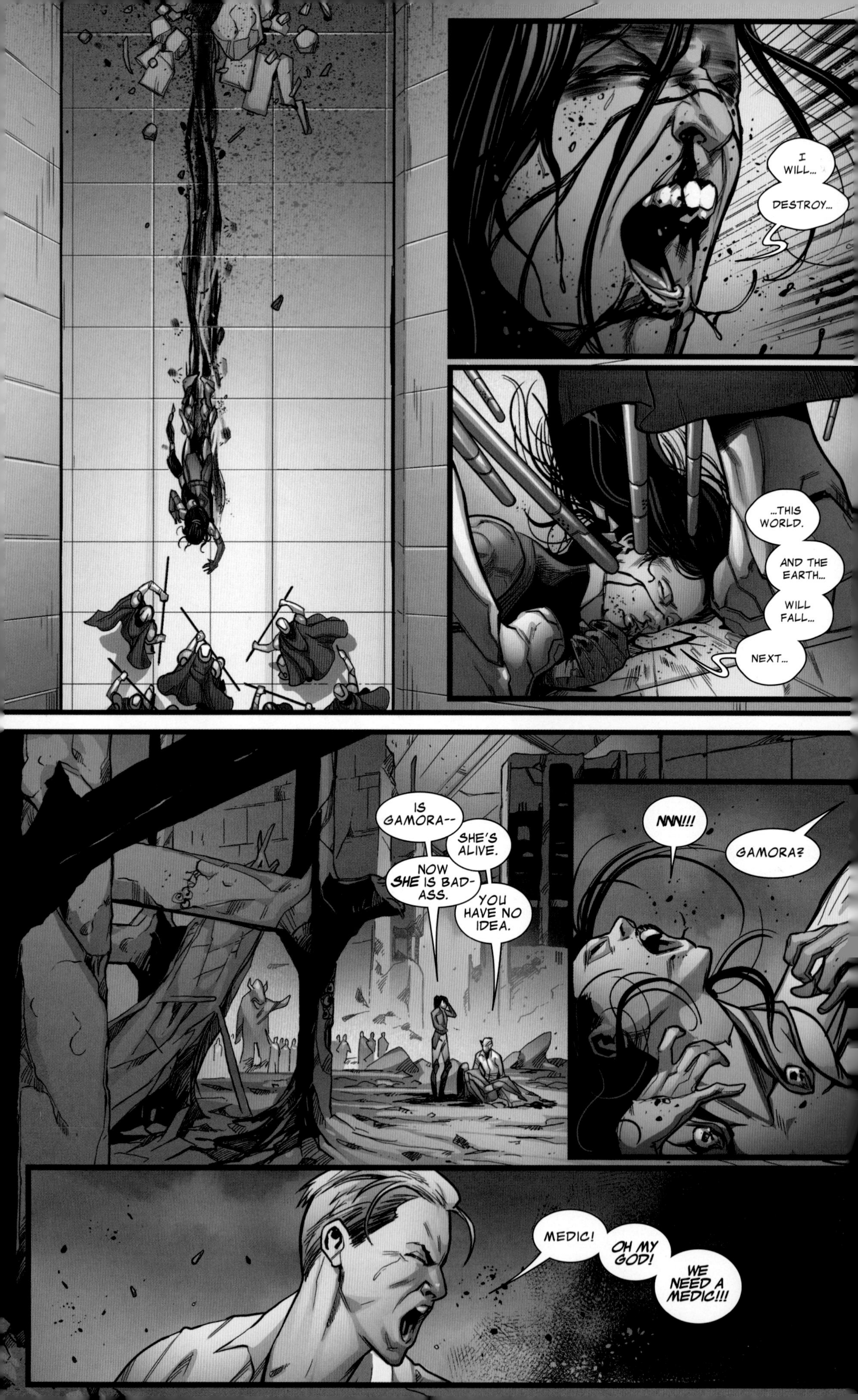
I WILL...
DESTROY...
...THIS WORLD.
AND THE EARTH...
WILL FALL...
NEXT...
IS GAMORA--
SHE'S ALIVE.
NOW SHE IS BAD-ASS.
YOU HAVE NO IDEA.
NNN!!!
GAMORA?
MEDIC!
OH MY GOD!
WE NEED A MEDIC!!!

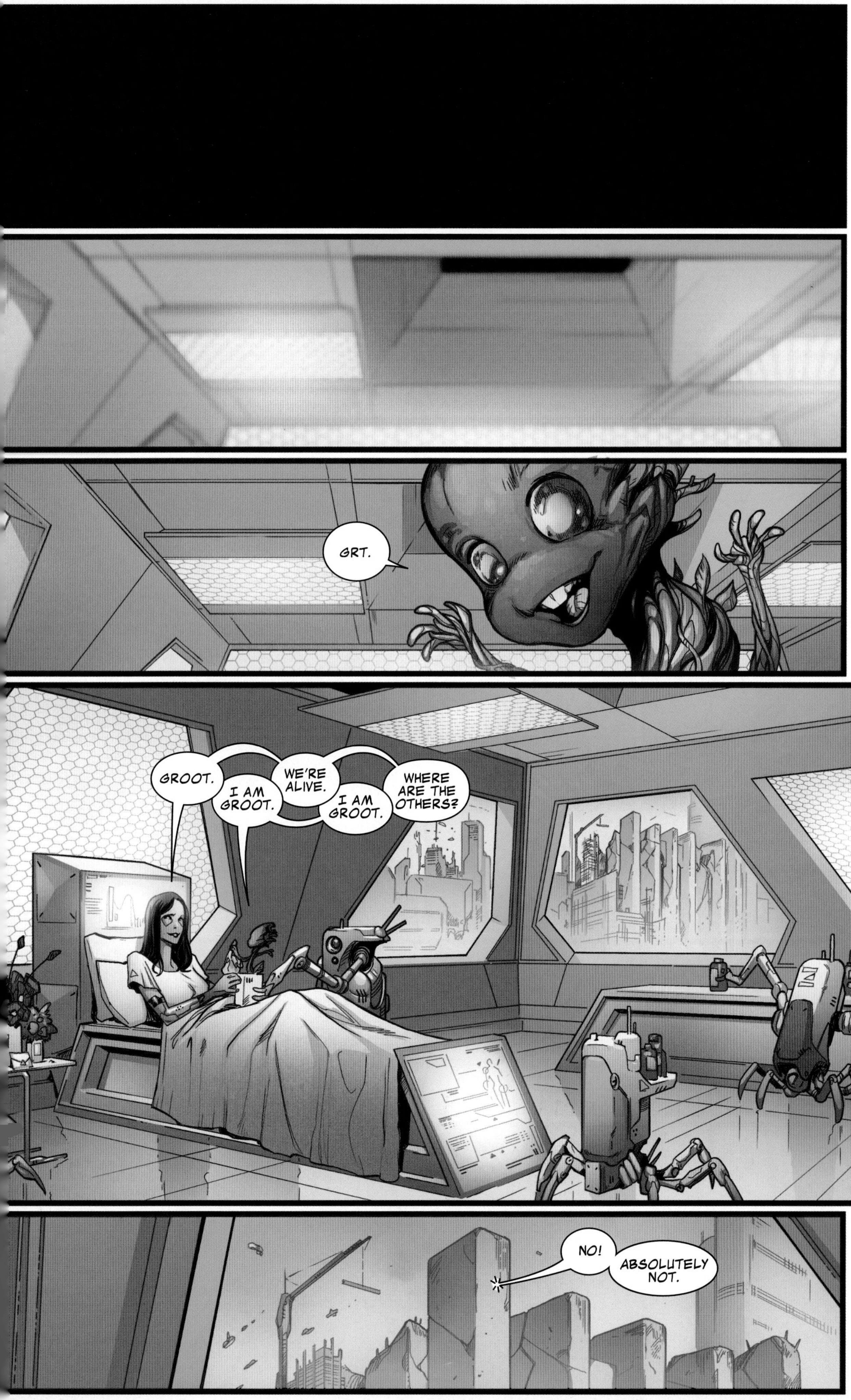
GRT.
GROOT.
I AM GROOT.
WE'RE ALIVE.
I AM GROOT.
WHERE ARE THE OTHERS?
NO!
ABSOLUTELY NOT.

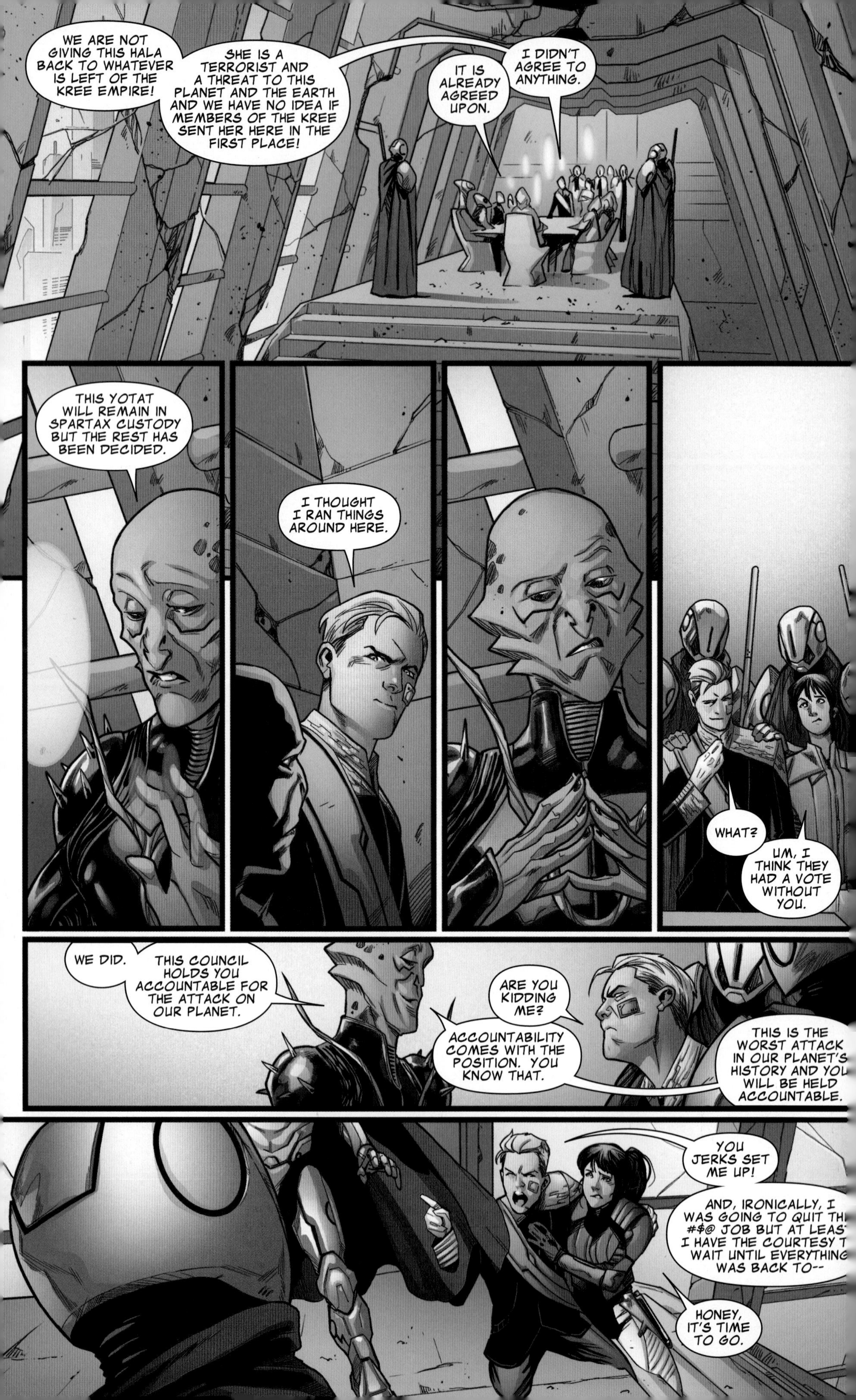
WE ARE NOT GIVING THIS HALA BACK TO WHATEVER IS LEFT OF THE KREE EMPIRE!
SHE IS A TERRORIST AND A THREAT TO THIS PLANET AND THE EARTH AND WE HAVE NO IDEA IF MEMBERS OF THE KREE SENT HER HERE IN THE FIRST PLACE!
IT IS ALREADY AGREED UPON.
I DIDN'T AGREE TO ANYTHING.
THIS YOTAT WILL REMAIN IN SPARTAX CUSTODY BUT THE REST HAS BEEN DECIDED.
I THOUGHT I RAN THINGS AROUND HERE.
WHAT?
UM, I THINK THEY HAD A VOTE WITHOUT YOU.
WE DID.
THIS COUNCIL HOLDS YOU ACCOUNTABLE FOR THE ATTACK ON OUR PLANET.
ARE YOU KIDDING ME?
ACCOUNTABILITY COMES WITH THE POSITION. YOU KNOW THAT.
THIS IS THE WORST ATTACK IN OUR PLANET'S HISTORY AND YOU WILL BE HELD ACCOUNTABLE.
YOU JERKS SET ME UP!
AND, IRONICALLY, I WAS GOING TO QUIT THE #$@ JOB BUT AT LEAST I HAVE THE COURTESY TO WAIT UNTIL EVERYTHING WAS BACK TO--
HONEY, IT'S TIME TO GO.

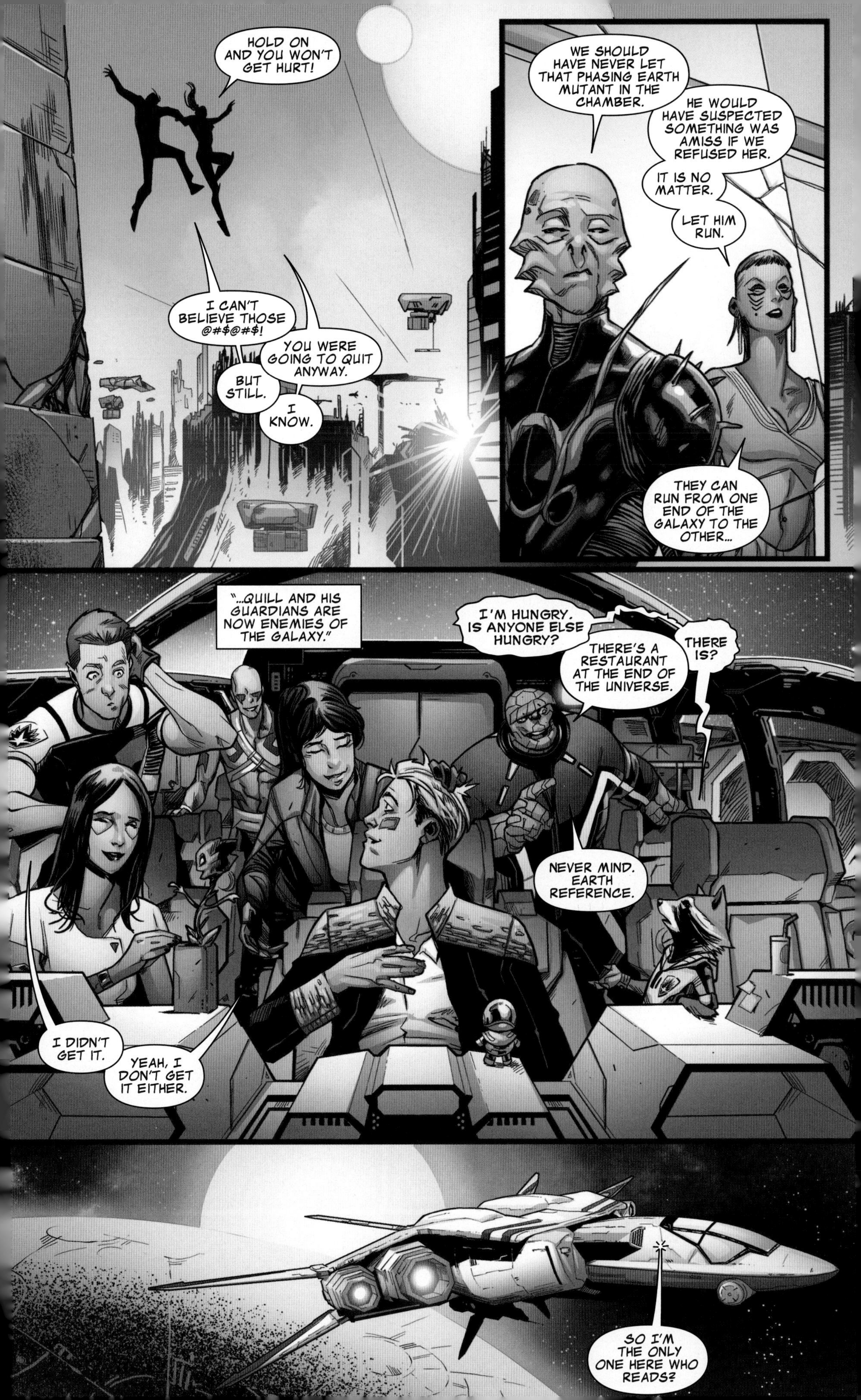
HOLD ON AND YOU WON'T GET HURT!
I CAN'T BELIEVE THOSE @#$@#$!
YOU WERE GOING TO QUIT ANYWAY.
BUT STILL.
I KNOW.
WE SHOULD HAVE NEVER LET THAT PHASING EARTH MUTANT IN THE CHAMBER.
HE WOULD HAVE SUSPECTED SOMETHING WAS AMISS IF WE REFUSED HER.
IT IS NO MATTER.
LET HIM RUN.
THEY CAN RUN FROM ONE END OF THE GALAXY TO THE OTHER...
"...QUILL AND HIS GUARDIANS ARE NOW ENEMIES OF THE GALAXY."
I'M HUNGRY. IS ANYONE ELSE HUNGRY?
THERE'S A RESTAURANT AT THE END OF THE UNIVERSE.
THERE IS?
NEVER MIND. EARTH REFERENCE.
I DIDN'T GET IT.
YEAH, I DON'T GET IT EITHER.
SO I'M THE ONLY ONE HERE WHO READS?

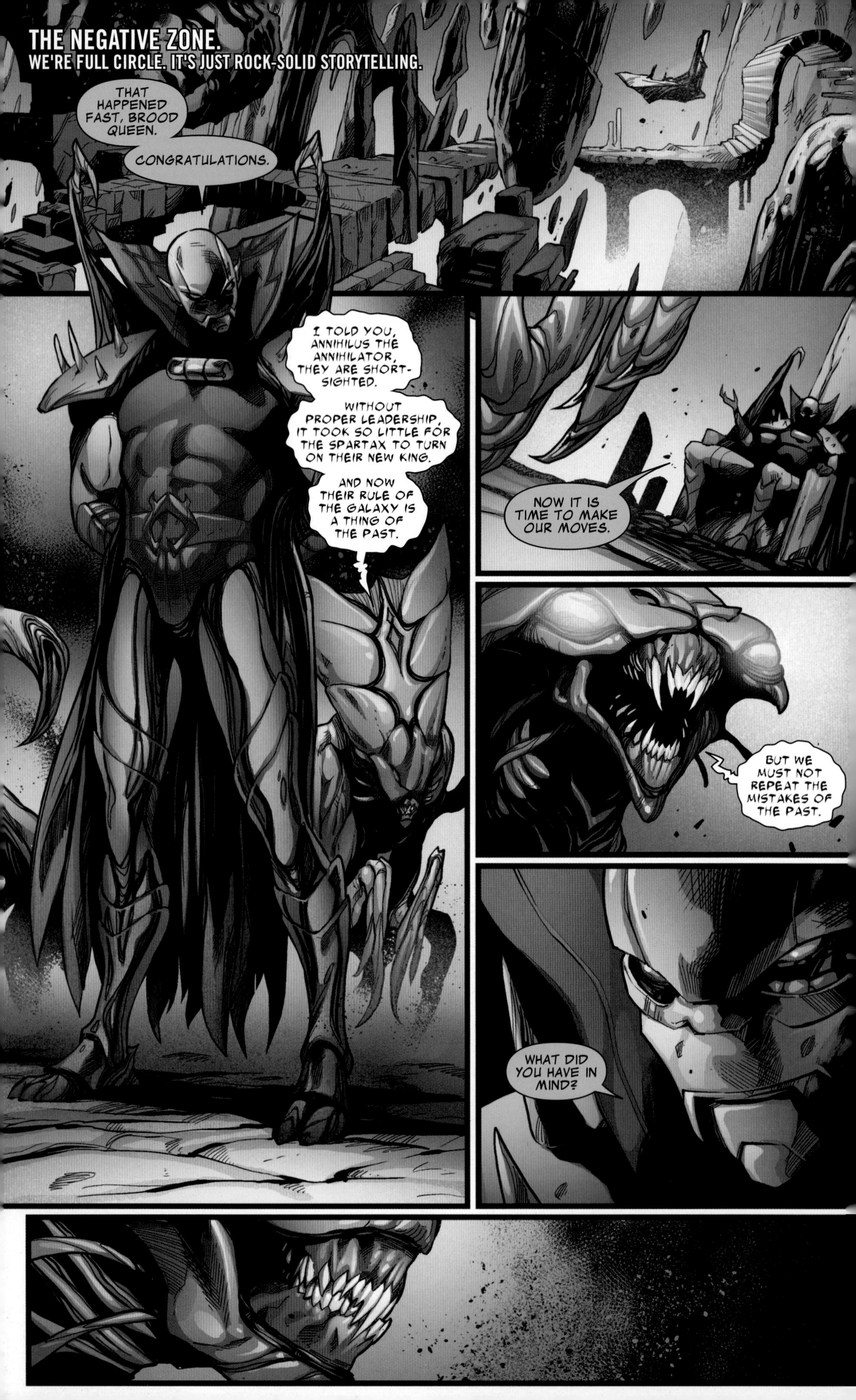
THE NEGATIVE ZONE.
WE'RE FULL CIRCLE. IT'S JUST ROCK-SOLID STORYTELLING.
THAT HAPPENED FAST, BROOD QUEEN.
CONGRATULATIONS.
I TOLD YOU, ANNIHILUS THE ANNIHILATOR, THEY ARE SHORT-SIGHTED.
WITHOUT PROPER LEADERSHIP, IT TOOK SO LITTLE FOR THE SPARTAX TO TURN ON THEIR NEW KING.
AND NOW THEIR RULE OF THE GALAXY IS A THING OF THE PAST.
NOW IT IS TIME TO MAKE OUR MOVES.
BUT WE MUST NOT REPEAT THE MISTAKES OF THE PAST.
WHAT DID YOU HAVE IN MIND?

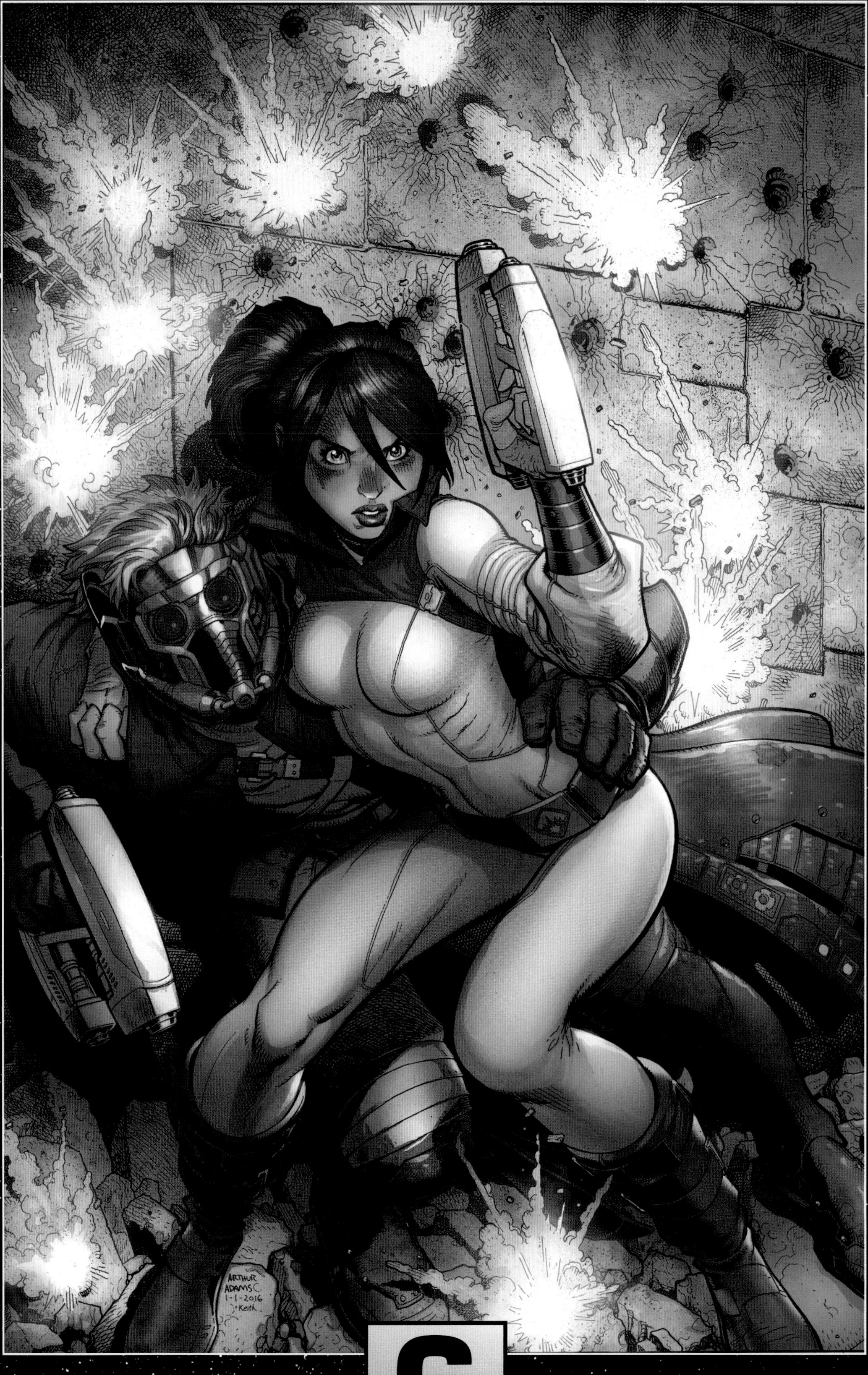
ARTHUR
ADAMS©
1-1-2016
+Keith

6

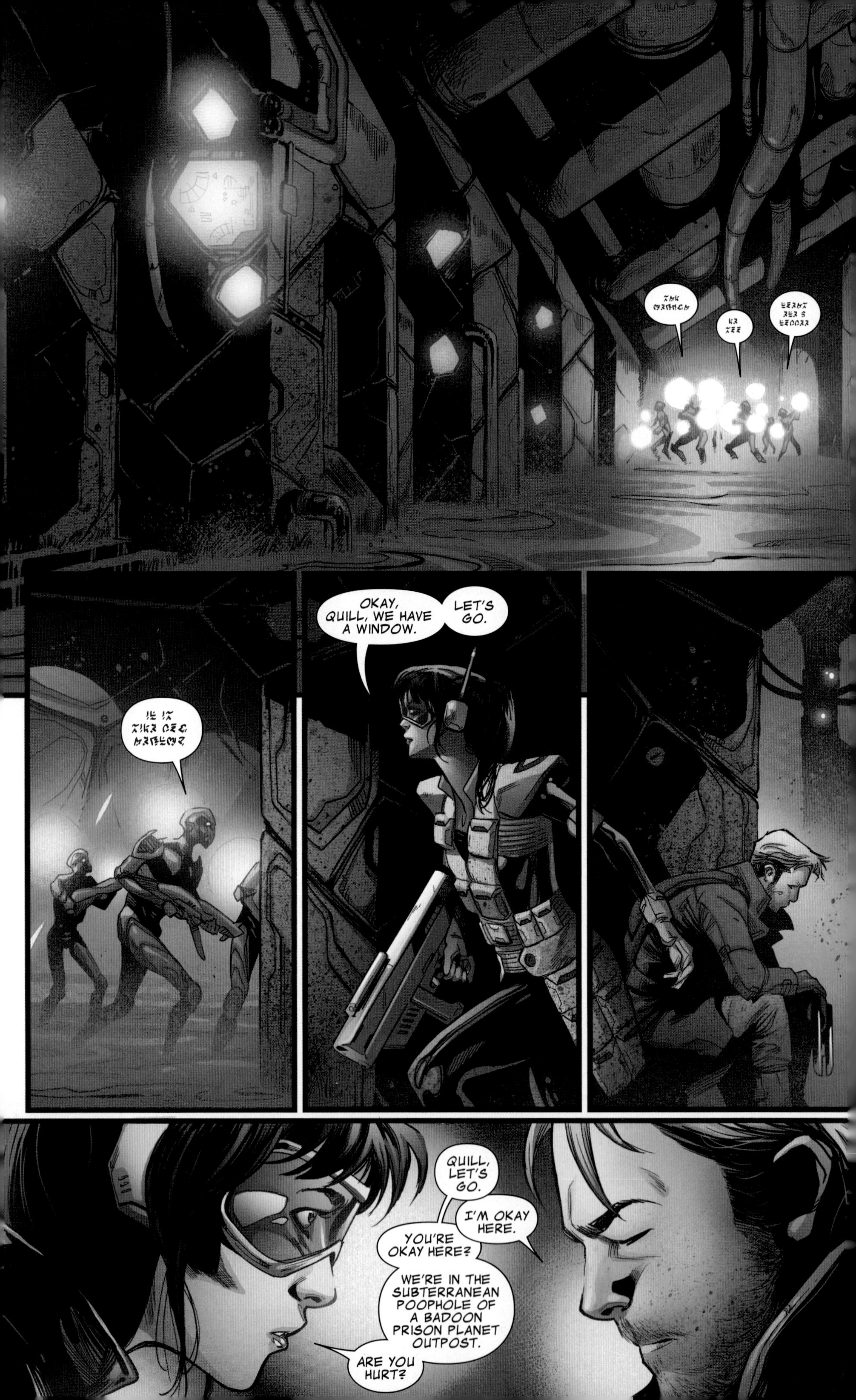
OKAY, QUILL, WE HAVE A WINDOW.
LET'S GO.
QUILL, LET'S GO.
I'M OKAY HERE.
YOU'RE OKAY HERE?
WE'RE IN THE SUBTERRANEAN POOPHOLE OF A BADOON PRISON PLANET OUTPOST.
ARE YOU HURT?

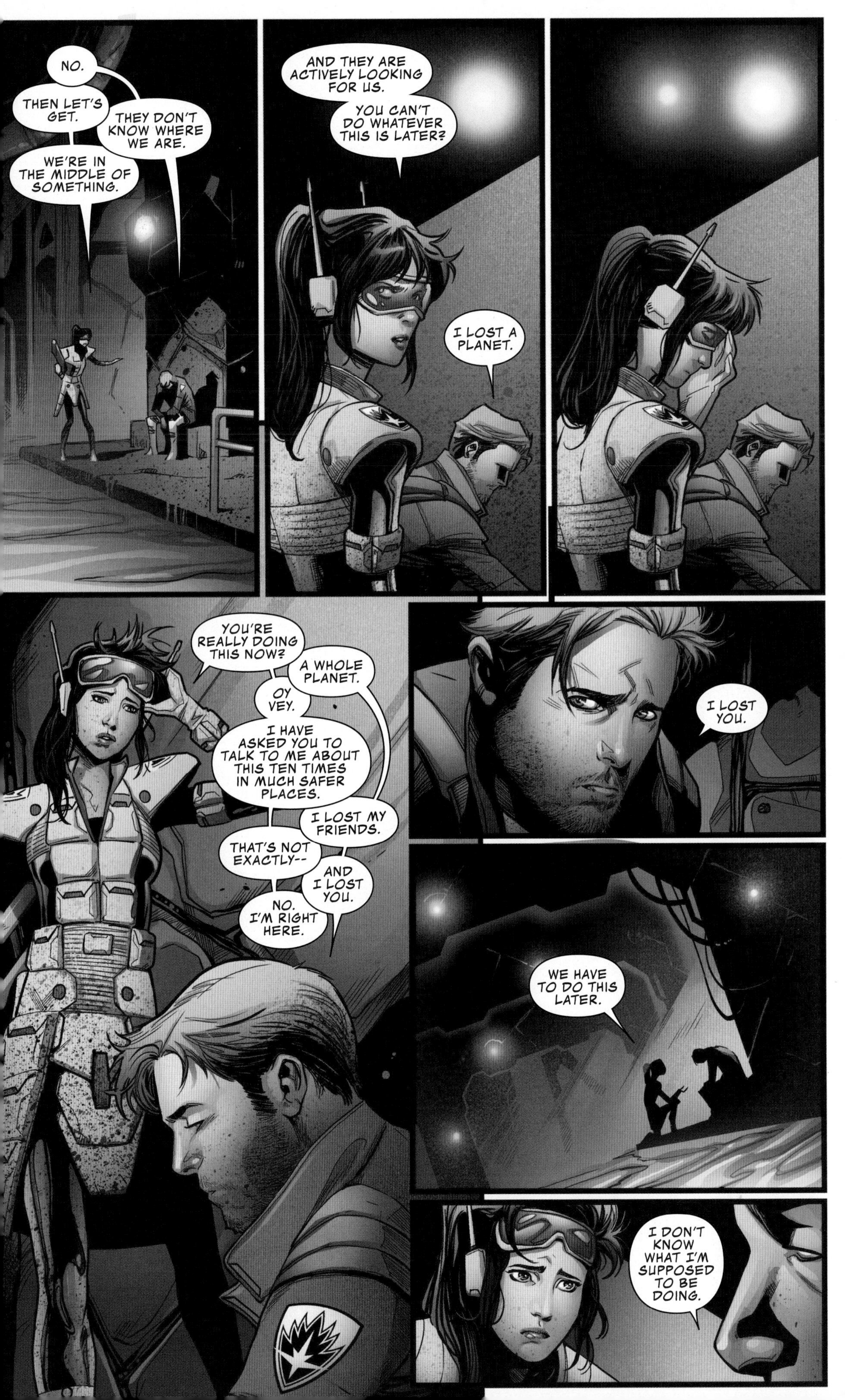
NO.
THEN LET'S GET.
THEY DON'T KNOW WHERE WE ARE.
WE'RE IN THE MIDDLE OF SOMETHING.
AND THEY ARE ACTIVELY LOOKING FOR US.
YOU CAN'T DO WHATEVER THIS IS LATER?
I LOST A PLANET.
YOU'RE REALLY DOING THIS NOW?
A WHOLE PLANET.
OY VEY.
I HAVE ASKED YOU TO TALK TO ME ABOUT THIS TEN TIMES IN MUCH SAFER PLACES.
I LOST MY FRIENDS.
THAT'S NOT EXACTLY--
AND I LOST YOU.
NO. I'M RIGHT HERE.
I LOST YOU.
WE HAVE TO DO THIS LATER.
I DON'T KNOW WHAT I'M SUPPOSED TO BE DOING.

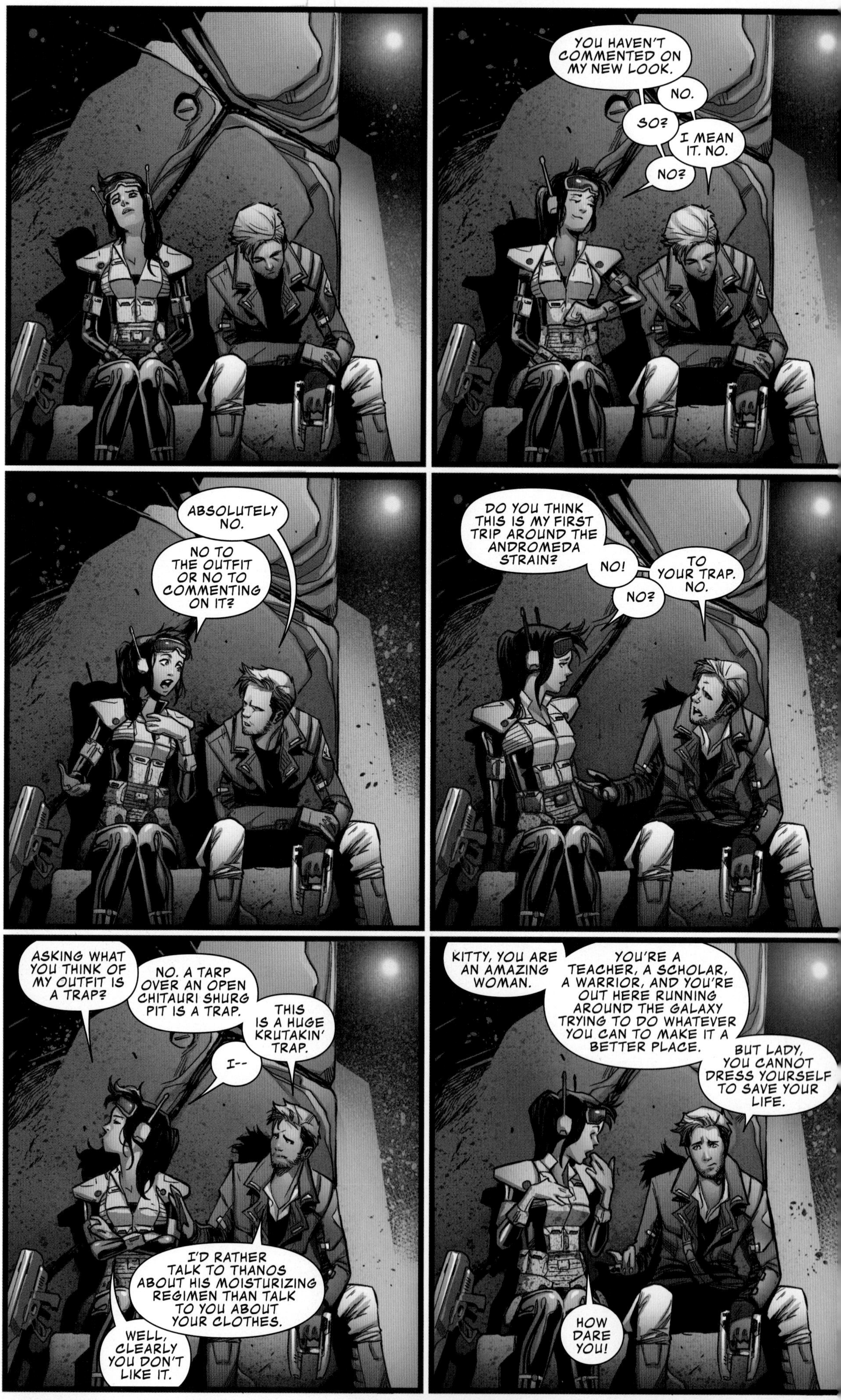

YOU HAVEN'T COMMENTED ON MY NEW LOOK.
NO.
SO?
I MEAN IT. NO.
NO?
ABSOLUTELY NO.
NO TO THE OUTFIT OR NO TO COMMENTING ON IT?
DO YOU THINK THIS IS MY FIRST TRIP AROUND THE ANDROMEDA STRAIN?
NO!
NO?
TO YOUR TRAP. NO.
ASKING WHAT YOU THINK OF MY OUTFIT IS A TRAP?
NO. A TARP OVER AN OPEN CHITAURI SHURG PIT IS A TRAP.
THIS IS A HUGE KRUTAKIN' TRAP.
I--
I'D RATHER TALK TO THANOS ABOUT HIS MOISTURIZING REGIMEN THAN TALK TO YOU ABOUT YOUR CLOTHES.
WELL, CLEARLY YOU DON'T LIKE IT.
KITTY, YOU ARE AN AMAZING WOMAN.
YOU'RE A TEACHER, A SCHOLAR, A WARRIOR, AND YOU'RE OUT HERE RUNNING AROUND THE GALAXY TRYING TO DO WHATEVER YOU CAN TO MAKE IT A BETTER PLACE.
BUT LADY, YOU CANNOT DRESS YOURSELF TO SAVE YOUR LIFE.
HOW DARE YOU!

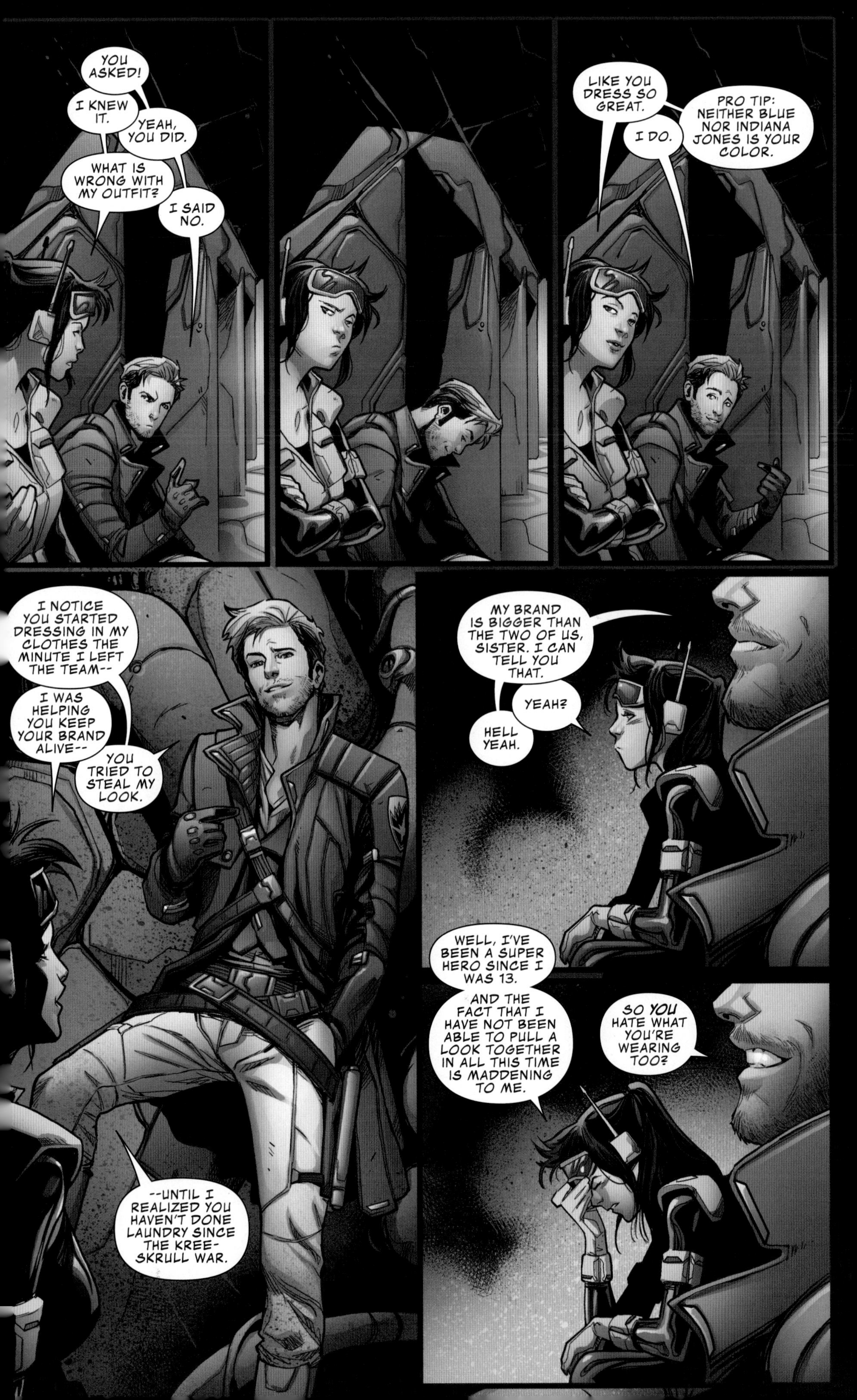
YOU ASKED!
I KNEW IT.
YEAH, YOU DID.
WHAT IS WRONG WITH MY OUTFIT?
I SAID NO.
LIKE YOU DRESS SO GREAT.
I DO.
PRO TIP: NEITHER BLUE NOR INDIANA JONES IS YOUR COLOR.
I NOTICE YOU STARTED DRESSING IN MY CLOTHES THE MINUTE I LEFT THE TEAM--
I WAS HELPING YOU KEEP YOUR BRAND ALIVE--
YOU TRIED TO STEAL MY LOOK.
--UNTIL I REALIZED YOU HAVEN'T DONE LAUNDRY SINCE THE KREE-SKRULL WAR.
MY BRAND IS BIGGER THAN THE TWO OF US, SISTER. I CAN TELL YOU THAT.
YEAH?
HELL YEAH.
WELL, I'VE BEEN A SUPER HERO SINCE I WAS 13.
AND THE FACT THAT I HAVE NOT BEEN ABLE TO PULL A LOOK TOGETHER IN ALL THIS TIME IS MADDENING TO ME.
SO YOU HATE WHAT YOU'RE WEARING TOO?

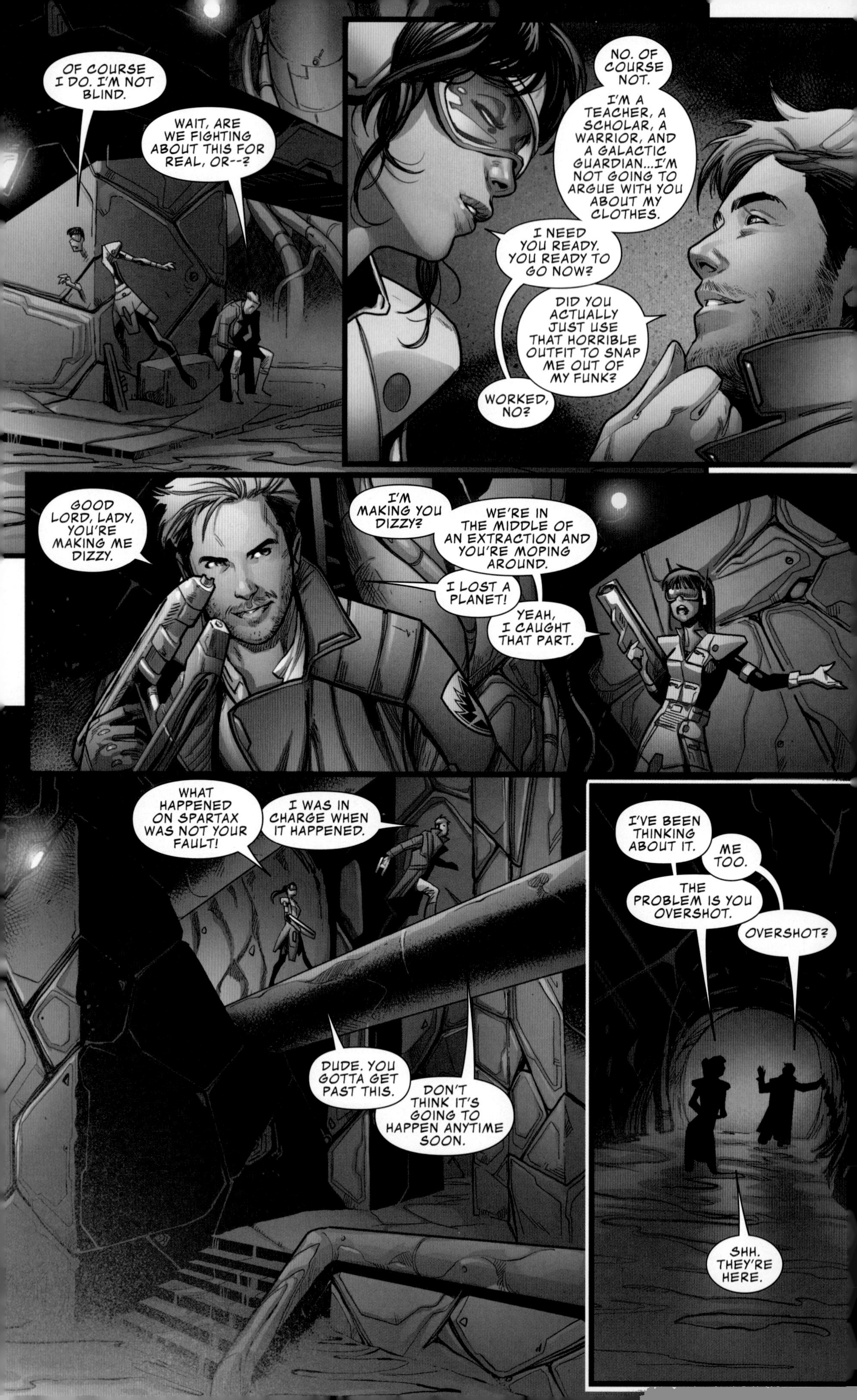

OF COURSE I DO. I'M NOT BLIND.
WAIT, ARE WE FIGHTING ABOUT THIS FOR REAL, OR--?
NO. OF COURSE NOT.
I'M A TEACHER, A SCHOLAR, A WARRIOR, AND A GALACTIC GUARDIAN...I'M NOT GOING TO ARGUE WITH YOU ABOUT MY CLOTHES.
I NEED YOU READY. YOU READY TO GO NOW?
DID YOU ACTUALLY JUST USE THAT HORRIBLE OUTFIT TO SNAP ME OUT OF MY FUNK?
WORKED, NO?
GOOD LORD, LADY, YOU'RE MAKING ME DIZZY.
I'M MAKING YOU DIZZY?
WE'RE IN THE MIDDLE OF AN EXTRACTION AND YOU'RE MOPING AROUND.
I LOST A PLANET!
YEAH, I CAUGHT THAT PART.
WHAT HAPPENED ON SPARTAX WAS NOT YOUR FAULT!
I WAS IN CHARGE WHEN IT HAPPENED.
DUDE. YOU GOTTA GET PAST THIS.
DON'T THINK IT'S GOING TO HAPPEN ANYTIME SOON.
I'VE BEEN THINKING ABOUT IT.
ME TOO.
THE PROBLEM IS YOU OVERSHOT.
OVERSHOT?
SHH. THEY'RE HERE.

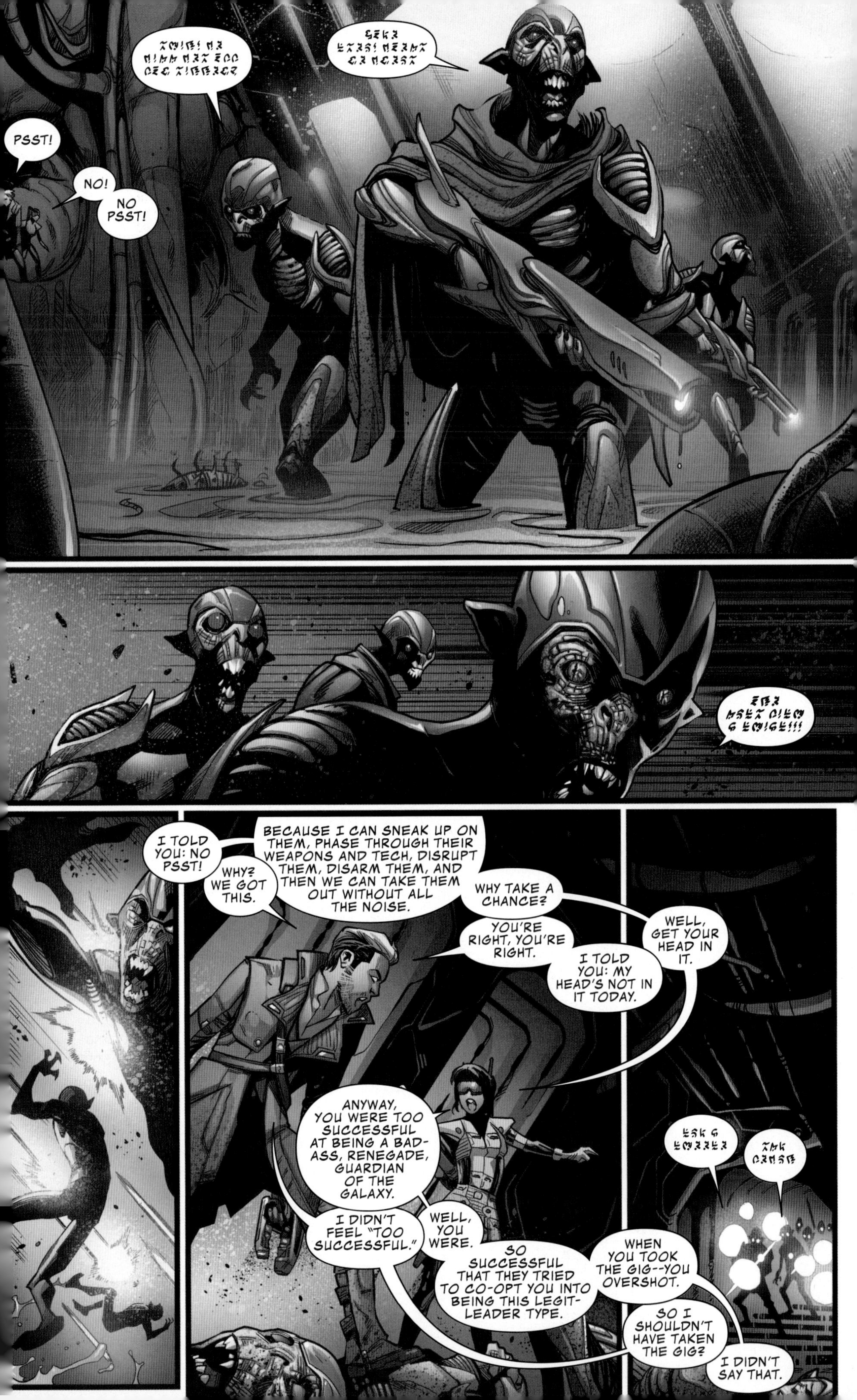
PSST!
NO!
NO PSST!
I TOLD YOU: NO PSST!
WHY? WE GOT THIS.
BECAUSE I CAN SNEAK UP ON THEM, PHASE THROUGH THEIR WEAPONS AND TECH, DISRUPT THEM, DISARM THEM, AND THEN WE CAN TAKE THEM OUT WITHOUT ALL THE NOISE.
WHY TAKE A CHANCE?
YOU'RE RIGHT, YOU'RE RIGHT.
WELL, GET YOUR HEAD IN IT.
I TOLD YOU: MY HEAD'S NOT IN IT TODAY.
ANYWAY, YOU WERE TOO SUCCESSFUL AT BEING A BAD-ASS, RENEGADE, GUARDIAN OF THE GALAXY.
I DIDN'T FEEL "TOO SUCCESSFUL."
WELL, YOU WERE.
SO SUCCESSFUL THAT THEY TRIED TO CO-OPT YOU INTO BEING THIS LEGIT-LEADER TYPE.
WHEN YOU TOOK THE GIG--YOU OVERSHOT.
SO I SHOULDN'T HAVE TAKEN THE GIG?
I DIDN'T SAY THAT.

SEE, I THOUGHT YOU WERE DISAPPOINTED IN ME FOR TAKING THE GIG.

I KNOW YOU THOUGHT THAT.

I WASN'T. IN FACT, I SAID AT THE TIME I SUPPORTED YOU.

YEAH, BUT TO BE FAIR A LOT OF PEOPLE SAY A LOT OF THINGS.

I WAS DISAPPOINTED IN YOU FOR NOT USING THE SAME BAD-ASS, RENEGADE, GUARDIANS OF THE GALAXY KICK-ASSERY WHEN YOU OVERSHOT.

YOU WERE LETTING THEM PUPPET YOU, AND IT WAS FRANKLY HARD TO WATCH.

I WASN'T LETTING THEM PUPPET ME.

I WAS TRYING TO BEHAVE LIKE AN ADULT FOR ONCE.

I WAS TRYING TO SHUT UP, LISTEN, AND LEARN.

WELL, IT WAS HARD TO WATCH.

I CAN SEE THAT.

YOU SHOULD HAVE COME IN THERE SWAGGER FIRST.

THAT'S WHAT THE PLANET NEEDED.

THAT'S WHO YOU ARE. INSTEAD YOU... OVERSHOT... AND MISSED.

SO, NOW... IT'S TIME TO GET BACK TO BASICS.

YOUR BASICS.

BASICS?

SPACE-PIRATE GALACTIC GUARDIAN THAT ANSWERS TO NO ONE BUT HIS OWN CONSCIENCE. LIKE, RIGHT NOW. RIGHT HERE.

YOU DO THAT AND--

ᴚᴇᴚ ᴛᴏᴠᴉᴇᴚ ᴛᴏᴚᴚ ᴏᴚᴏᴚ ᴇᴚᴇᴛᴚ ᴚᴏᴠᴉᴇᴏᴚᴇᴚ

UH-OH.

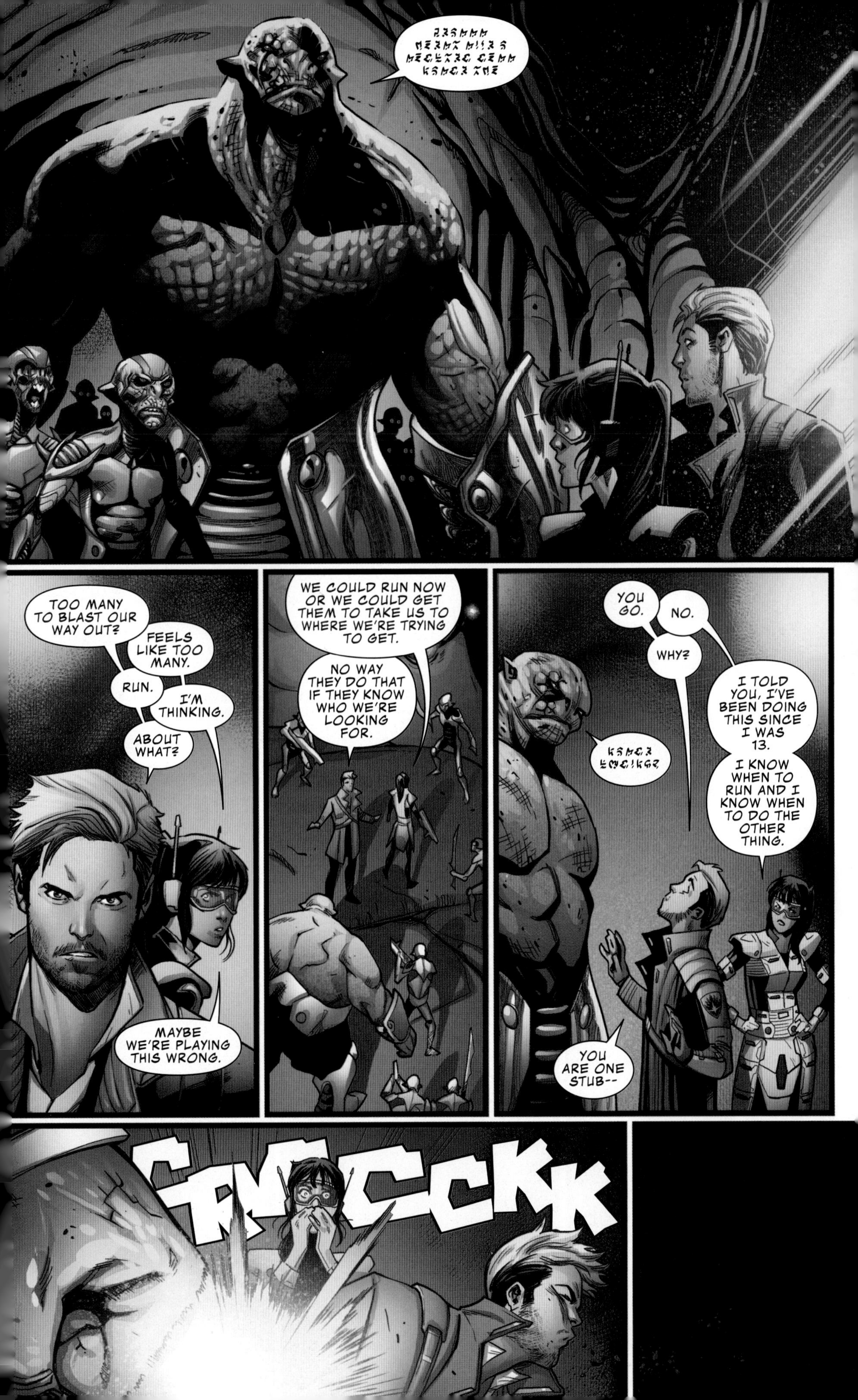

TOO MANY TO BLAST OUR WAY OUT?
FEELS LIKE TOO MANY.
RUN.
I'M THINKING.
ABOUT WHAT?
MAYBE WE'RE PLAYING THIS WRONG.
WE COULD RUN NOW OR WE COULD GET THEM TO TAKE US TO WHERE WE'RE TRYING TO GET.
NO WAY THEY DO THAT IF THEY KNOW WHO WE'RE LOOKING FOR.
YOU GO.
NO.
WHY?
I TOLD YOU, I'VE BEEN DOING THIS SINCE I WAS 13.
I KNOW WHEN TO RUN AND I KNOW WHEN TO DO THE OTHER THING.
YOU ARE ONE STUB--

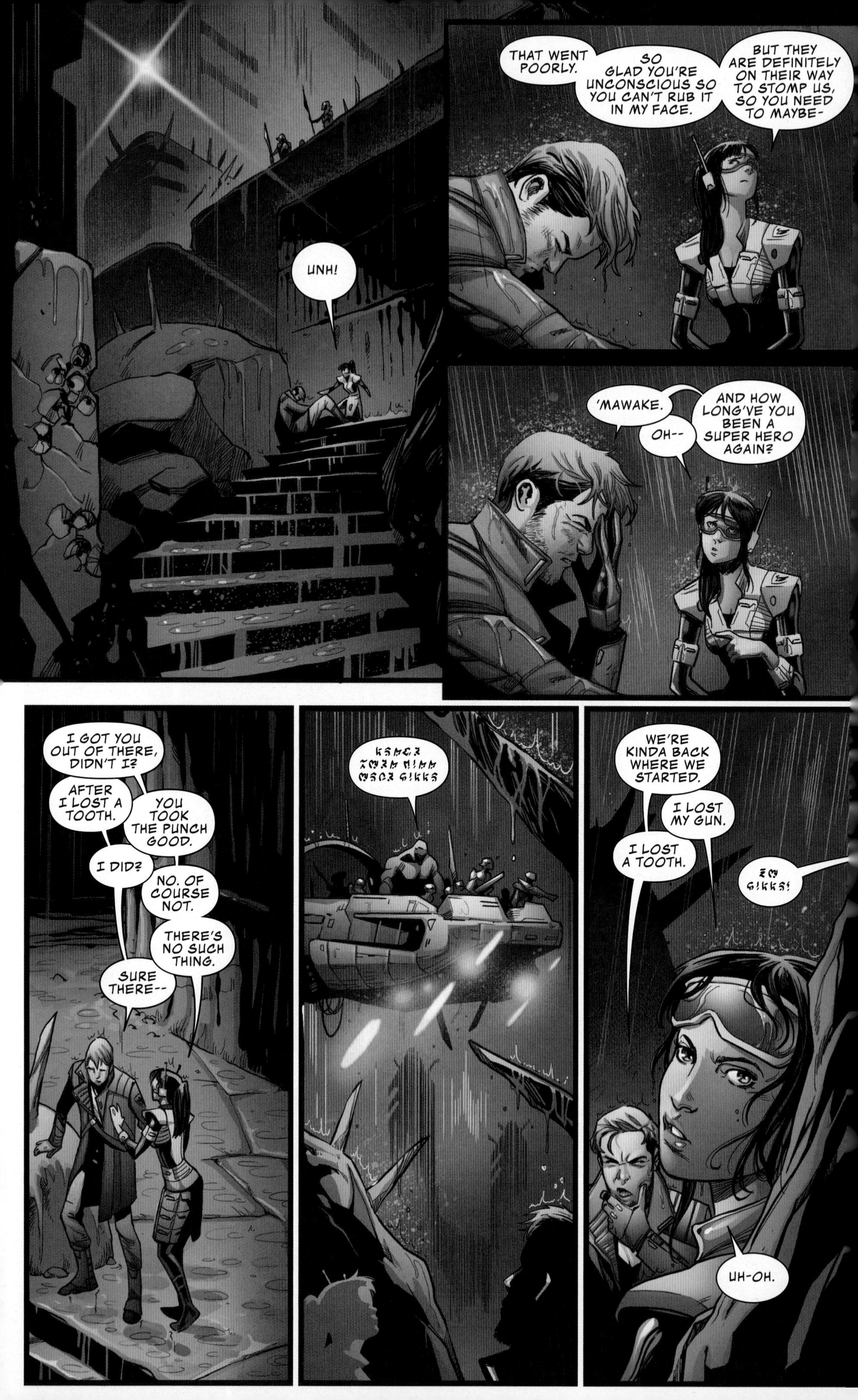
UNH!
THAT WENT POORLY.
SO GLAD YOU'RE UNCONSCIOUS SO YOU CAN'T RUB IT IN MY FACE.
BUT THEY ARE DEFINITELY ON THEIR WAY TO STOMP US, SO YOU NEED TO MAYBE-
'MAWAKE.
OH--
AND HOW LONG'VE YOU BEEN A SUPER HERO AGAIN?
I GOT YOU OUT OF THERE, DIDN'T I?
AFTER I LOST A TOOTH.
YOU TOOK THE PUNCH GOOD.
I DID?
NO. OF COURSE NOT.
THERE'S NO SUCH THING.
SURE THERE--
WE'RE KINDA BACK WHERE WE STARTED.
I LOST MY GUN.
I LOST A TOOTH.
UH-OH.

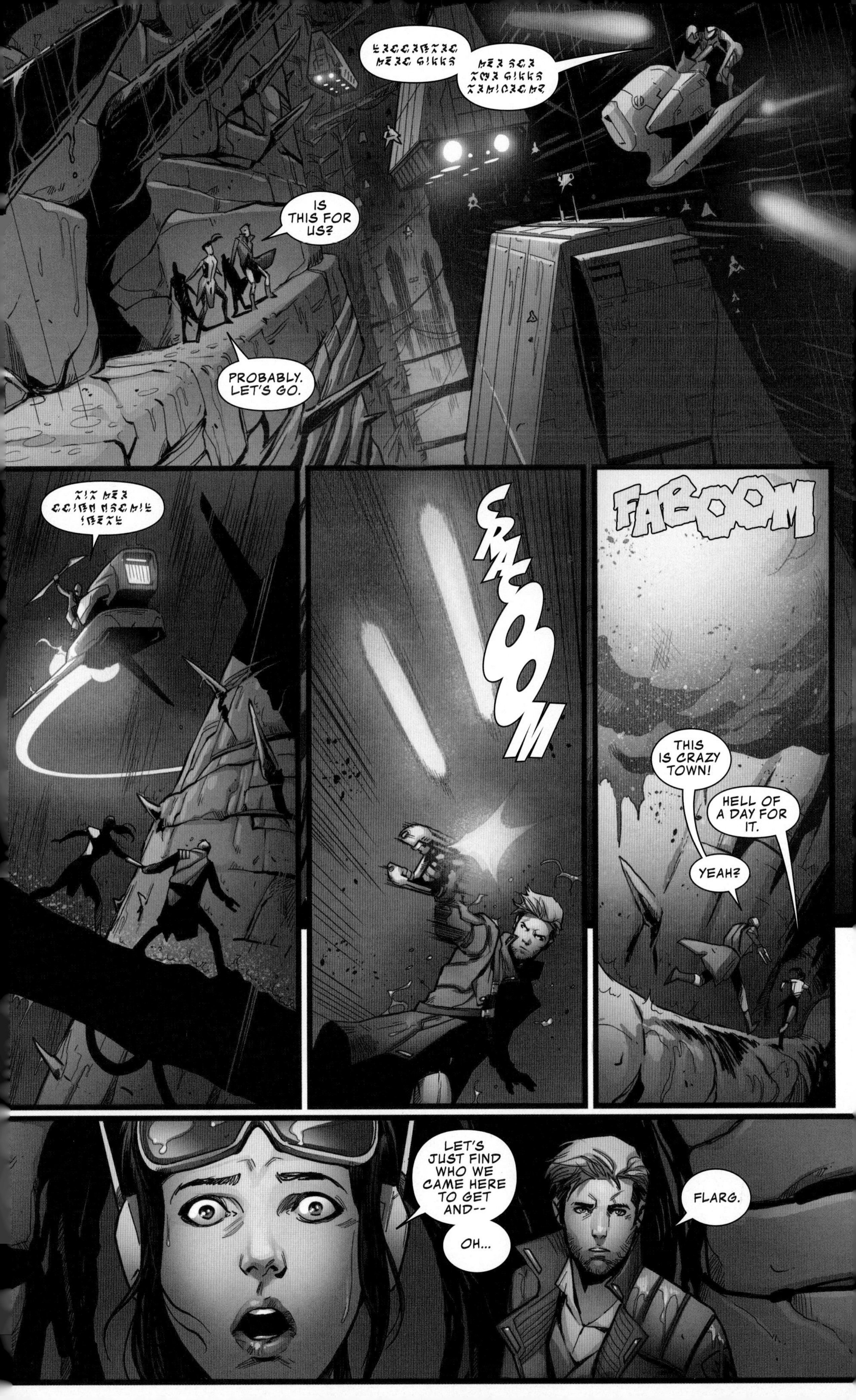
IS THIS FOR US?
PROBABLY. LET'S GO.
CRACOOM
FABOOM
THIS IS CRAZY TOWN!
HELL OF A DAY FOR IT.
YEAH?
LET'S JUST FIND WHO WE CAME HERE TO GET AND--
OH...
FLARG.

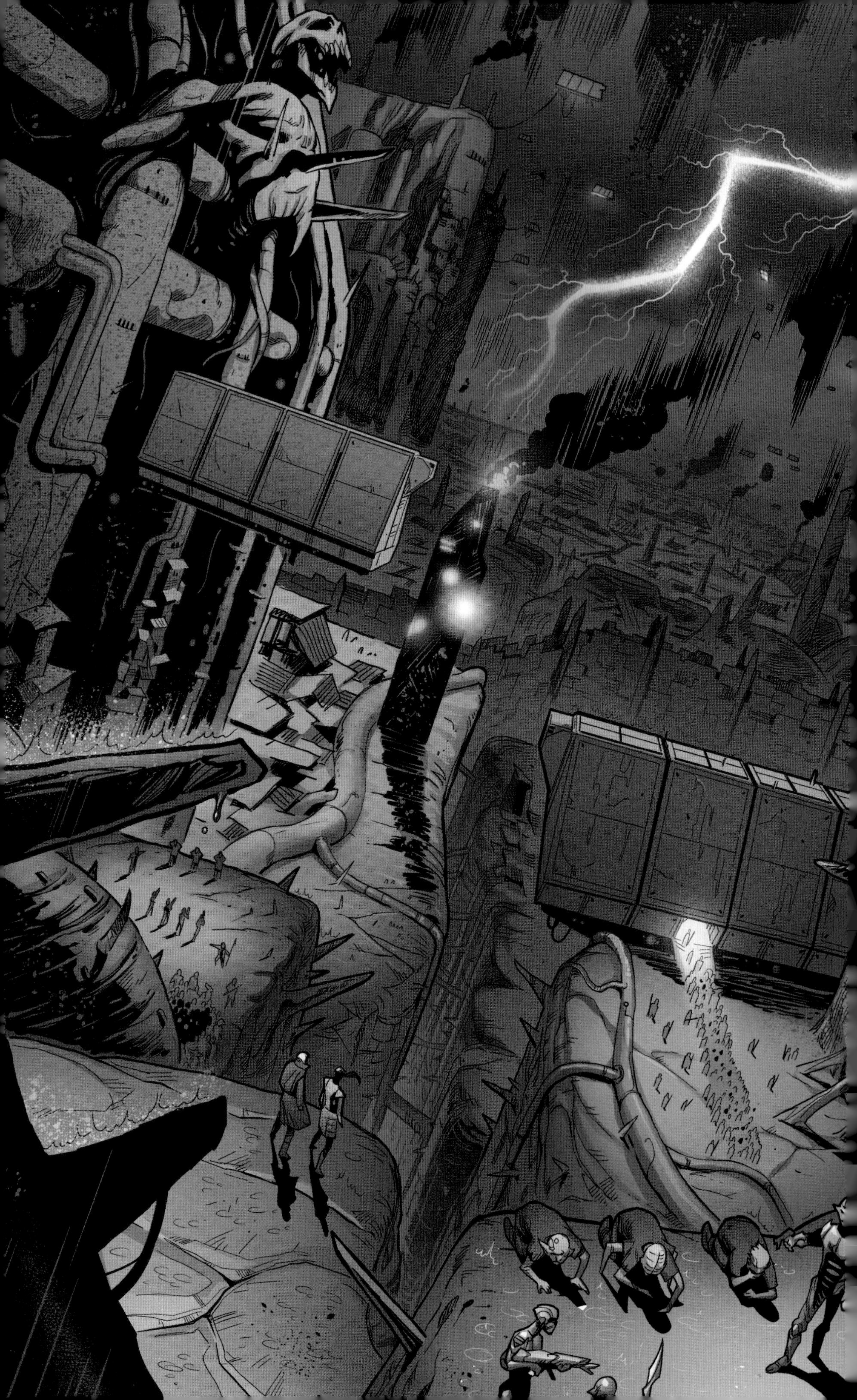

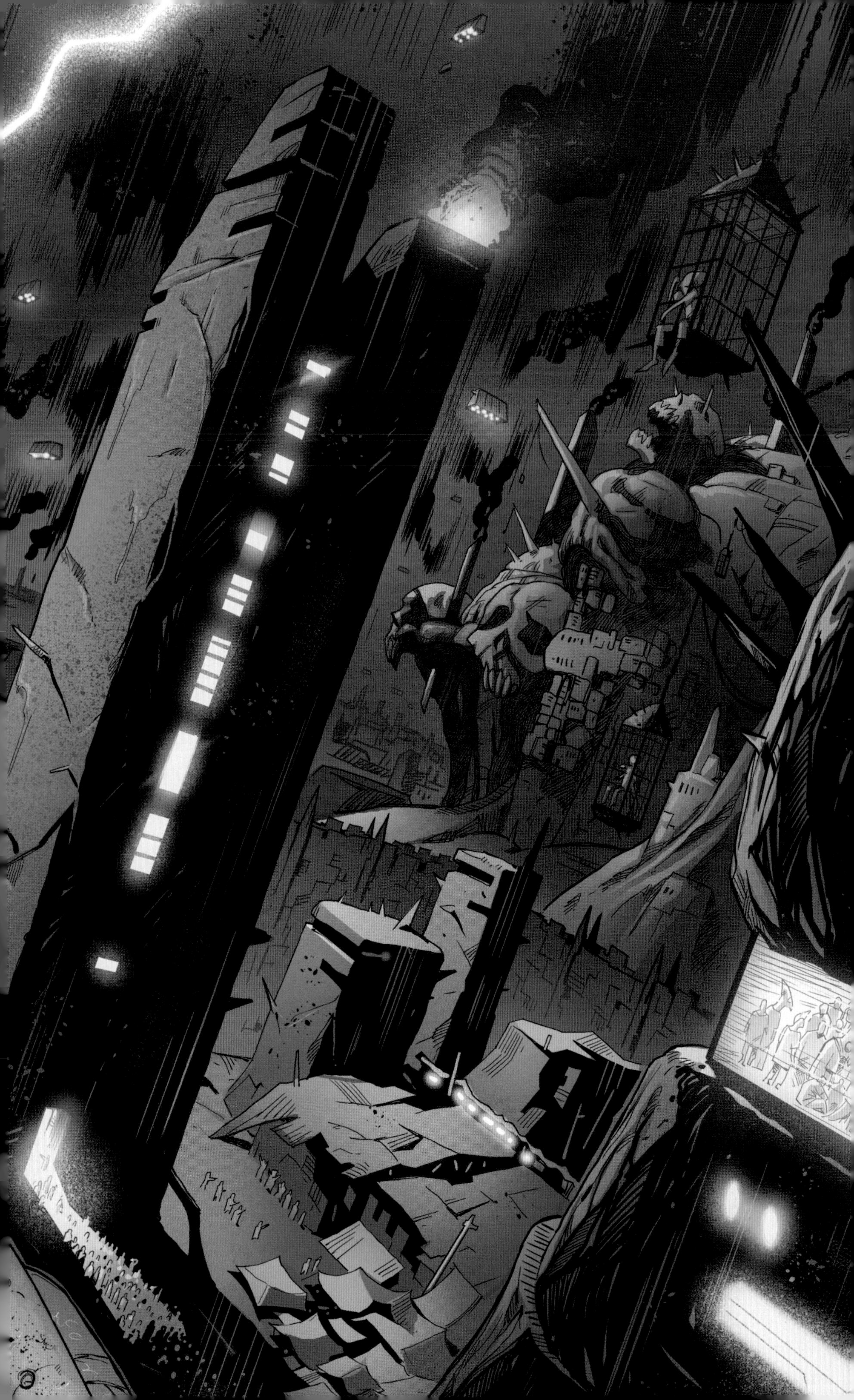

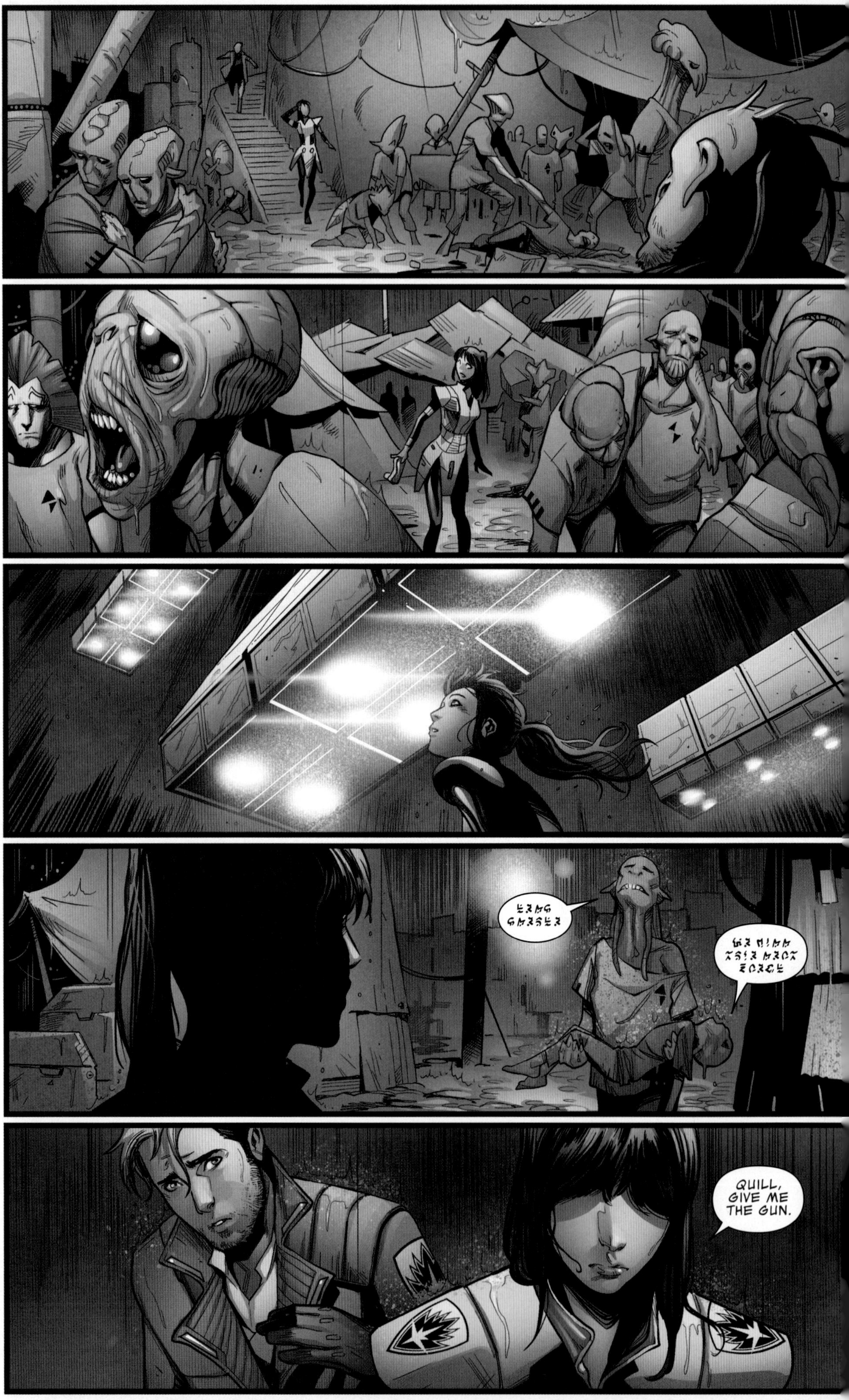
QUILL, GIVE ME THE GUN.

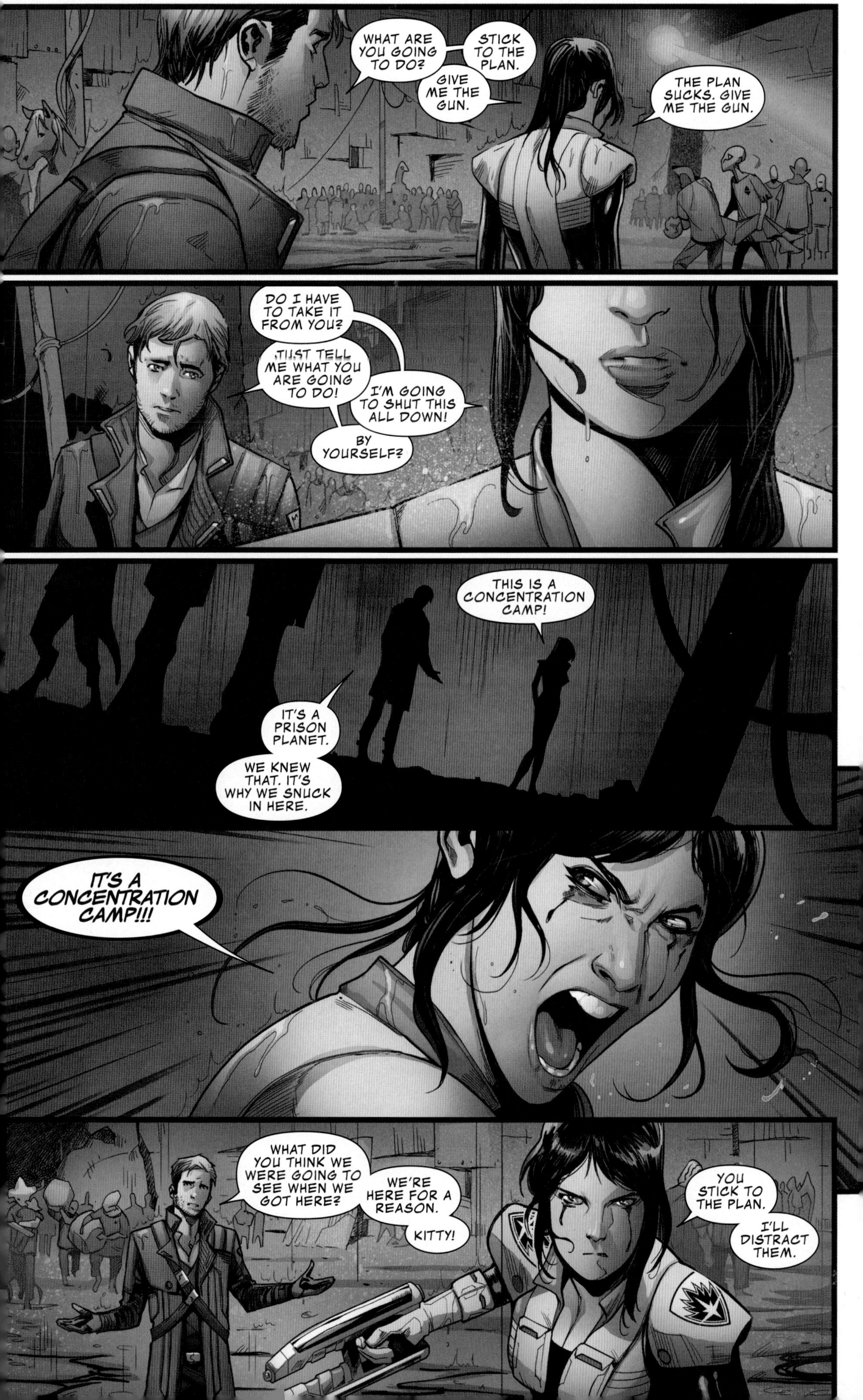
WHAT ARE YOU GOING TO DO?
STICK TO THE PLAN.
GIVE ME THE GUN.
THE PLAN SUCKS. GIVE ME THE GUN.
DO I HAVE TO TAKE IT FROM YOU?
JUST TELL ME WHAT YOU ARE GOING TO DO!
I'M GOING TO SHUT THIS ALL DOWN!
BY YOURSELF?
THIS IS A CONCENTRATION CAMP!
IT'S A PRISON PLANET.
WE KNEW THAT. IT'S WHY WE SNUCK IN HERE.
IT'S A CONCENTRATION CAMP!!!
WHAT DID YOU THINK WE WERE GOING TO SEE WHEN WE GOT HERE?
WE'RE HERE FOR A REASON.
KITTY!
YOU STICK TO THE PLAN.
I'LL DISTRACT THEM.

OH, YOO-HOO!

KITTY!

SKRAAA

M!Z!

RUN! 라고 도시를 부셔라! 빨리 뛰어 도망쳐라

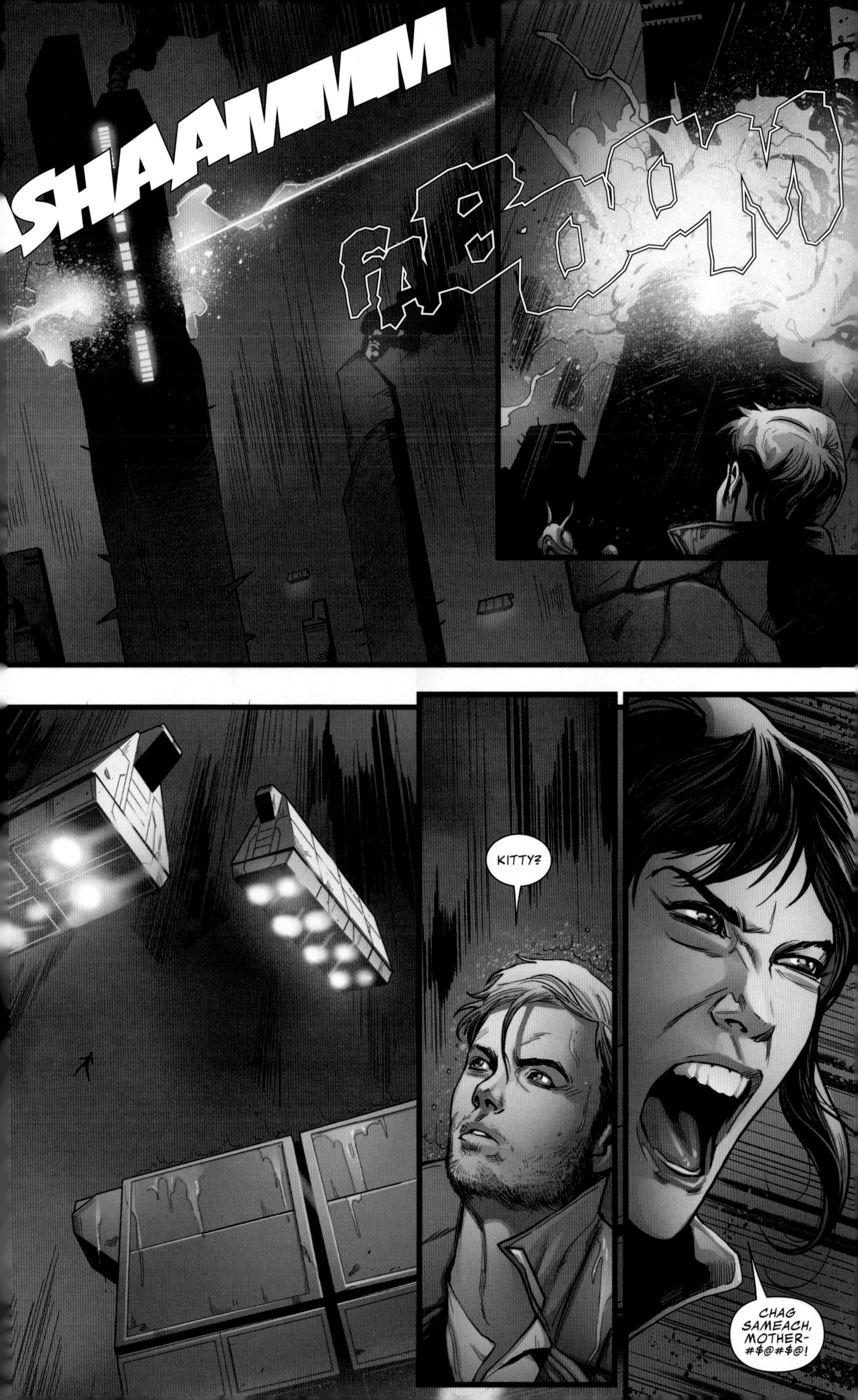
SHAAMMM
FABOOOM
KITTY?
CHAG SAMEACH, MOTHER-#$@#$@!

FSSHAAAMM

OOPS.

BBAA BOOOM

SCCMM

THAT'LL DO.

ᎬᏃᎻᏂ ᎢᎾᎷᎻᎡ!!

ᏳᎬᏃ ᎶᏬᏃᎶᎻᎬᎡᎻ ᎷᎬ ᎴᎬ ᎰᏬᎡ ᏚᎥᎶᎥᏂᎬᎷᎥ!

ᏳᏳᎶᏟ ᏃᎷᎥᎶᏟ ᏟᎽᎶᎥᏟᎬ ᏚᏴᎽ ᎷᎬᎢ*

*HEY, HEY!!
UH, EVERYONE GO TO THE AIRFIELD!
GRAB THEIR SHIPS AND GO!

YOU SAVED OUR LIVES, KING QUILL.

I'M NOT--

YOU ARE A HERO TO THESE PEOPLE.

DO YOU KNOW WHERE THEY KEEP THE HIGH-RISK POLITICAL PRISONERS?

IT IS AN HONOR TO HAVE MET YOU.

OKAY, THANKS, BUT THAT DOESN'T REALLY--

--HELP ME...

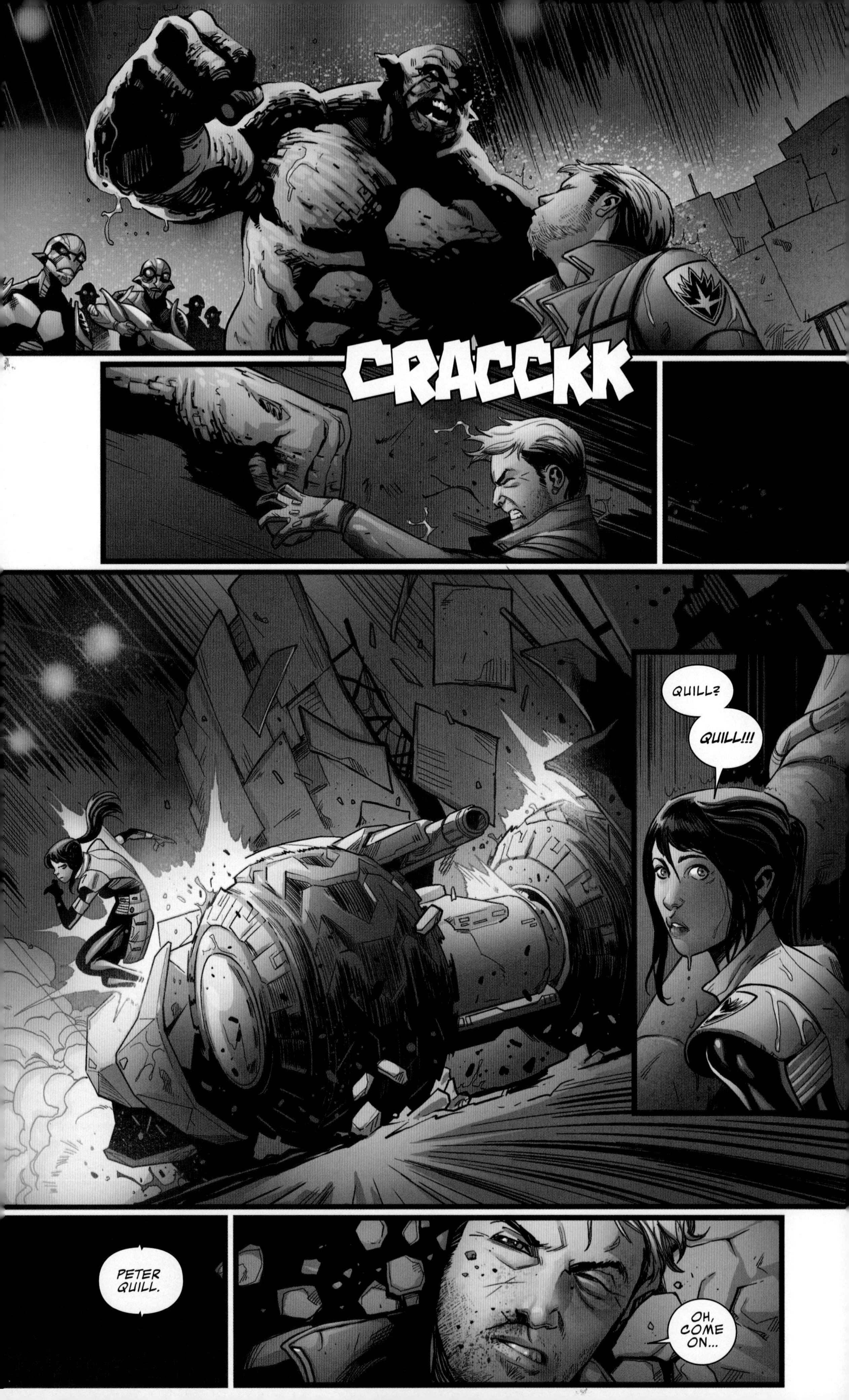
CRACCKK
QUILL?
QUILL!!!
PETER QUILL.
OH, COME ON...

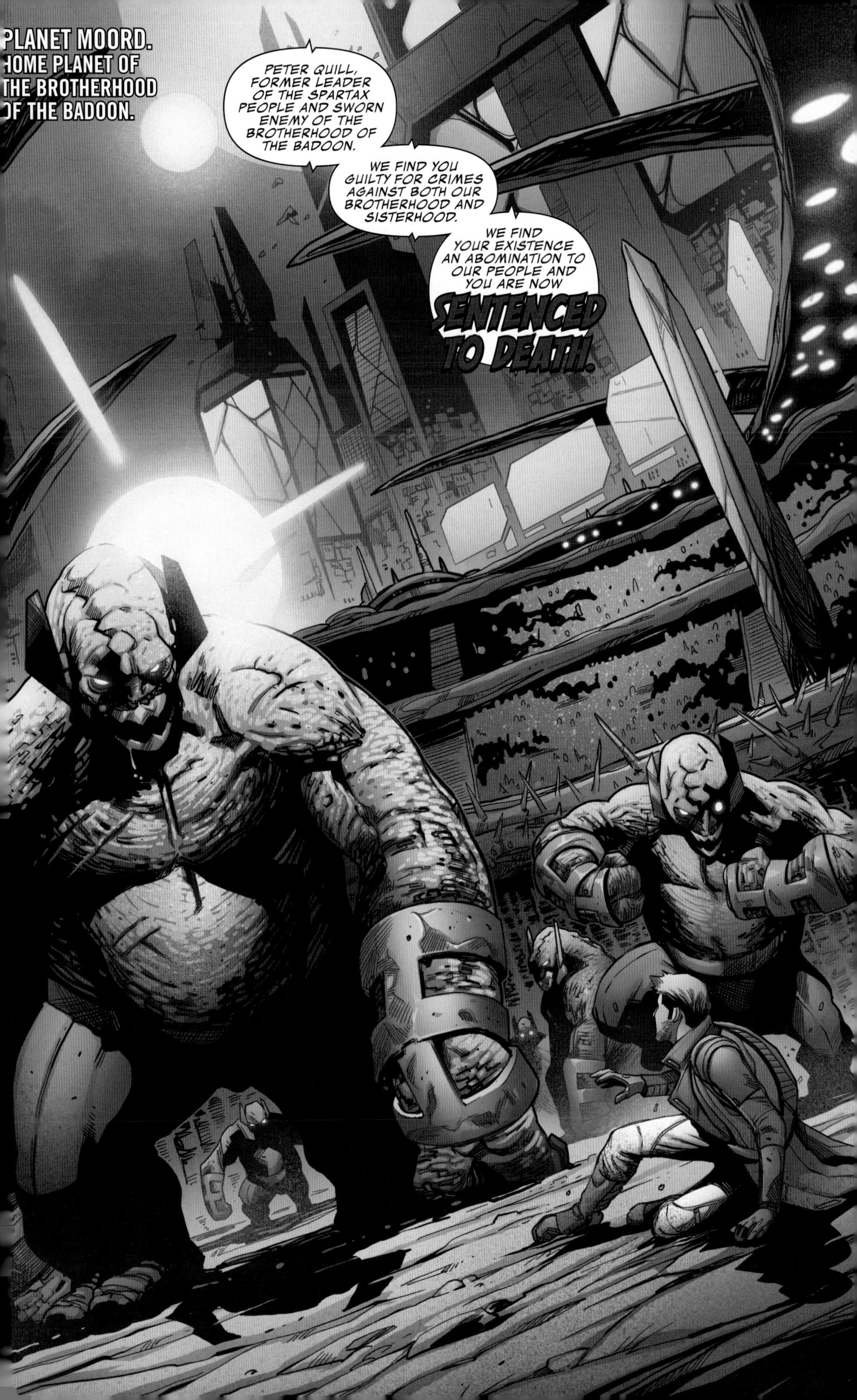
PLANET MOORD. HOME PLANET OF THE BROTHERHOOD OF THE BADOON.
PETER QUILL, FORMER LEADER OF THE SPARTAX PEOPLE AND SWORN ENEMY OF THE BROTHERHOOD OF THE BADOON.
WE FIND YOU GUILTY FOR CRIMES AGAINST BOTH OUR BROTHERHOOD AND SISTERHOOD.
WE FIND YOUR EXISTENCE AN ABOMINATION TO OUR PEOPLE AND YOU ARE NOW SENTENCED TO DEATH.

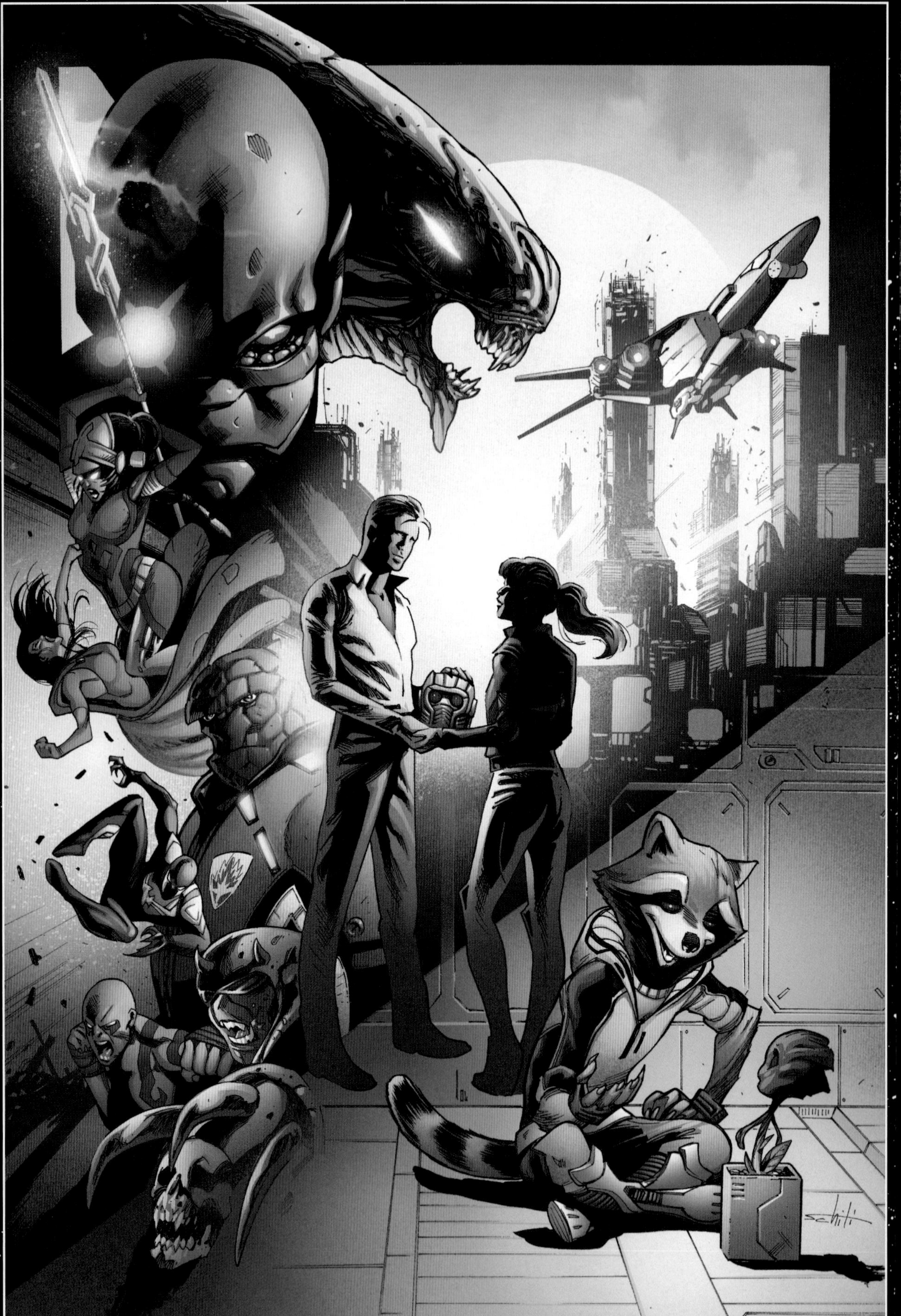
schiti

#6 STORY THUS FAR VARIANT BY

VALERIO SCHITI & RICHARD ISANOVE

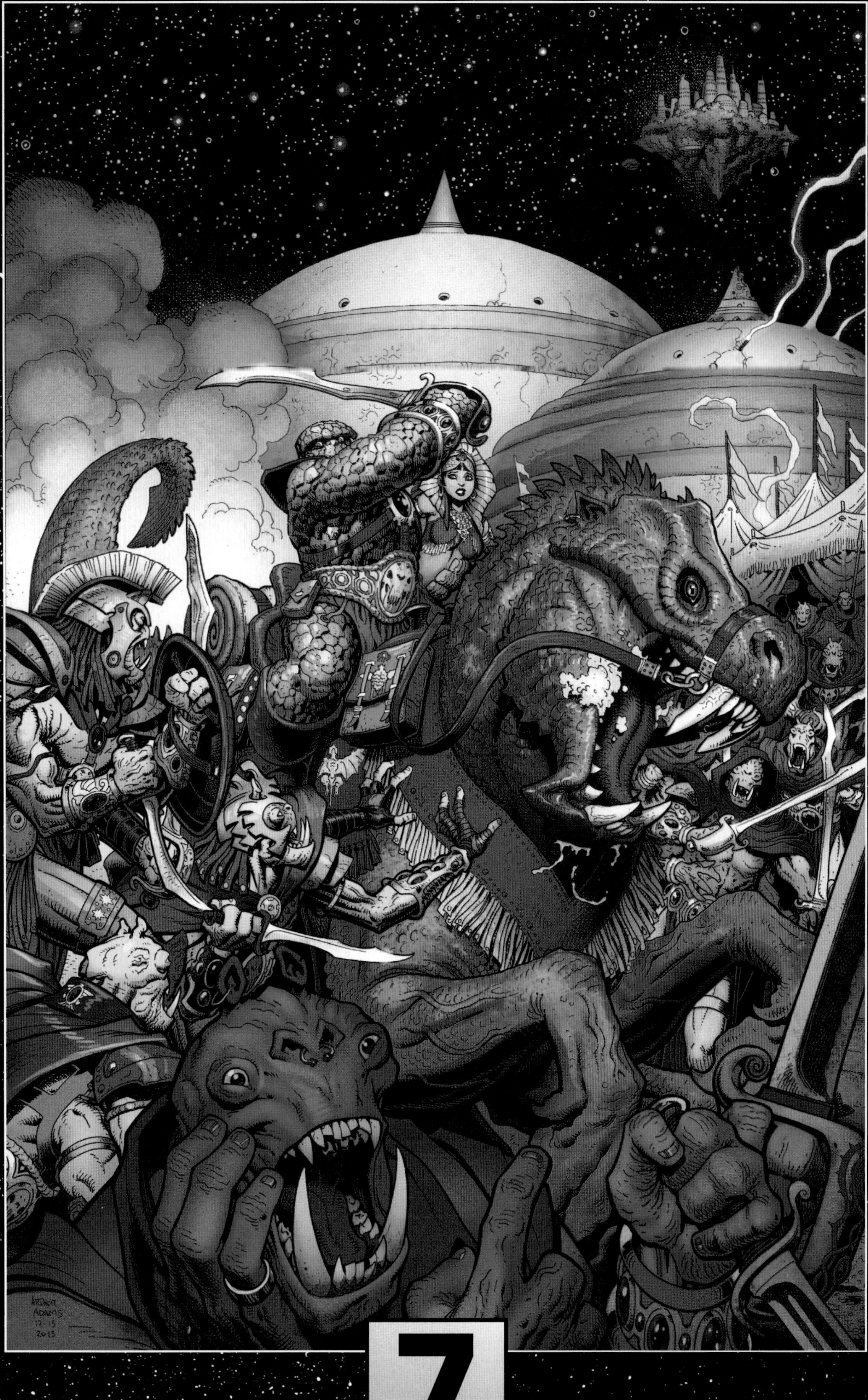
ARTHUR ADAMS
12-15
2013

7

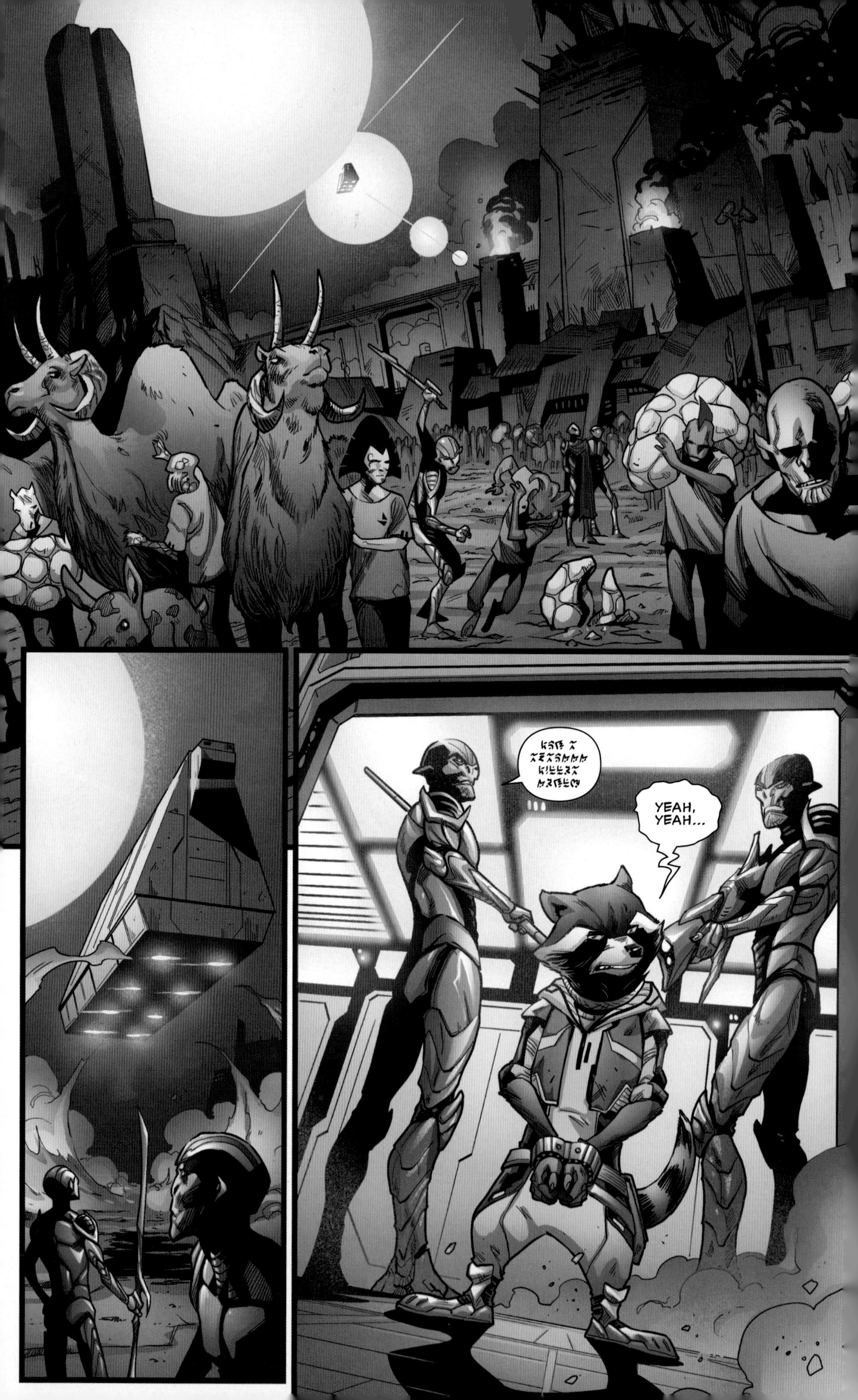
YEAH, YEAH...

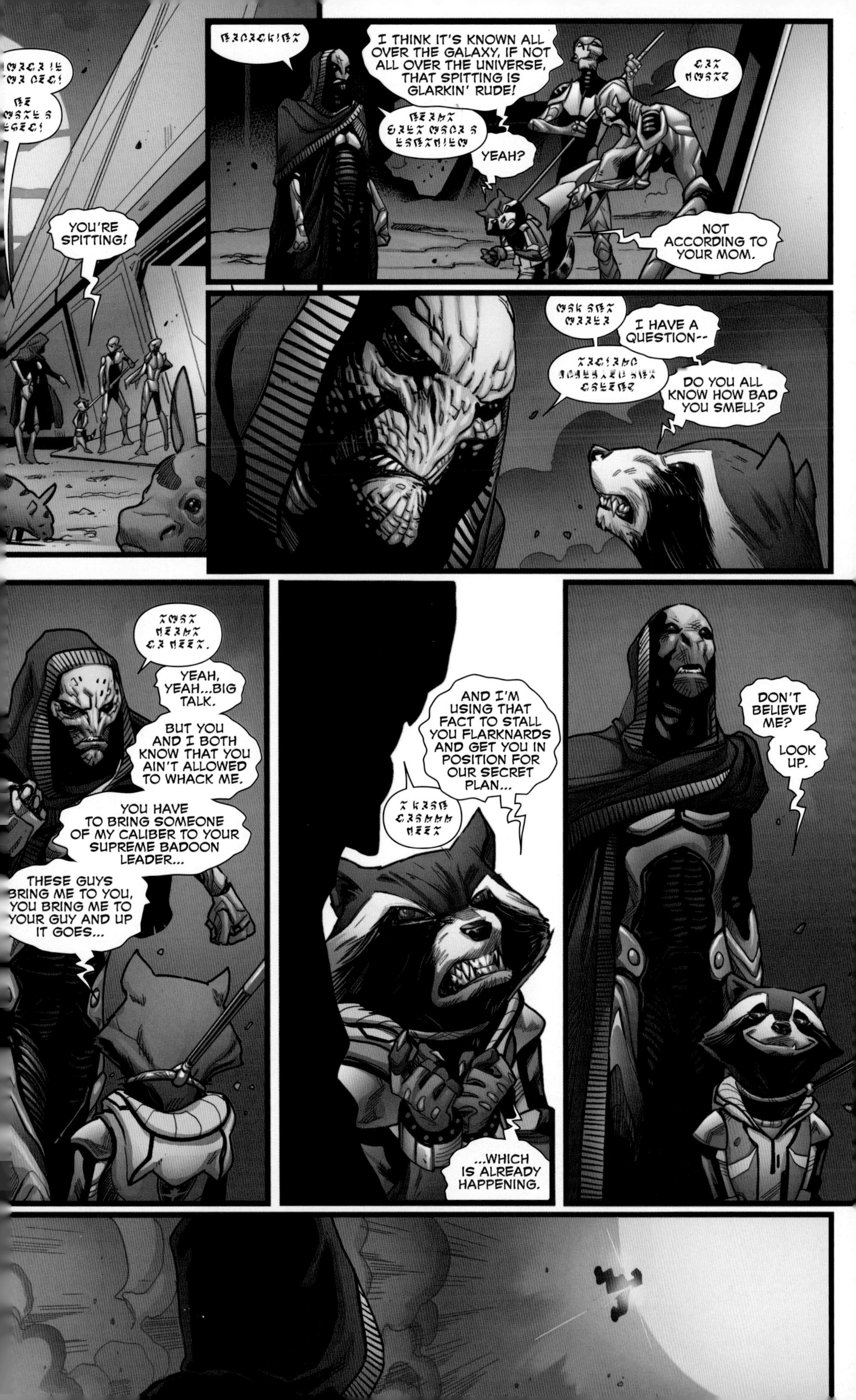

YOU'RE SPITTING!
I THINK IT'S KNOWN ALL OVER THE GALAXY, IF NOT ALL OVER THE UNIVERSE, THAT SPITTING IS GLARKIN' RUDE!
YEAH?
NOT ACCORDING TO YOUR MOM.
I HAVE A QUESTION--
DO YOU ALL KNOW HOW BAD YOU SMELL?
YEAH, YEAH...BIG TALK.
BUT YOU AND I BOTH KNOW THAT YOU AIN'T ALLOWED TO WHACK ME.
YOU HAVE TO BRING SOMEONE OF MY CALIBER TO YOUR SUPREME BADOON LEADER...
THESE GUYS BRING ME TO YOU, YOU BRING ME TO YOUR GUY AND UP IT GOES...
AND I'M USING THAT FACT TO STALL YOU FLARKNARDS AND GET YOU IN POSITION FOR OUR SECRET PLAN...
...WHICH IS ALREADY HAPPENING.
DON'T BELIEVE ME?
LOOK UP.

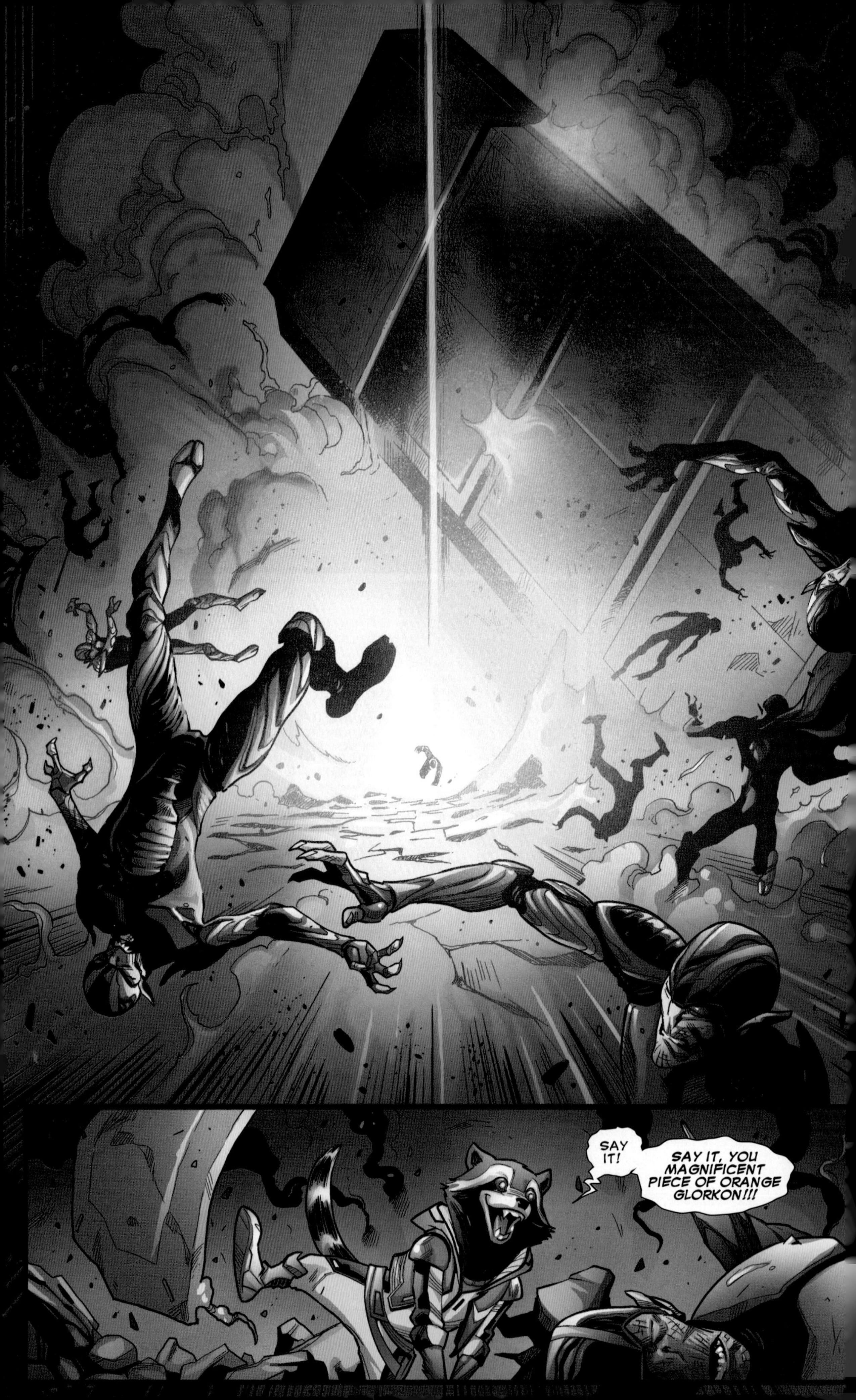
SAY IT!
SAY IT, YOU MAGNIFICENT PIECE OF ORANGE GLORKON!!!

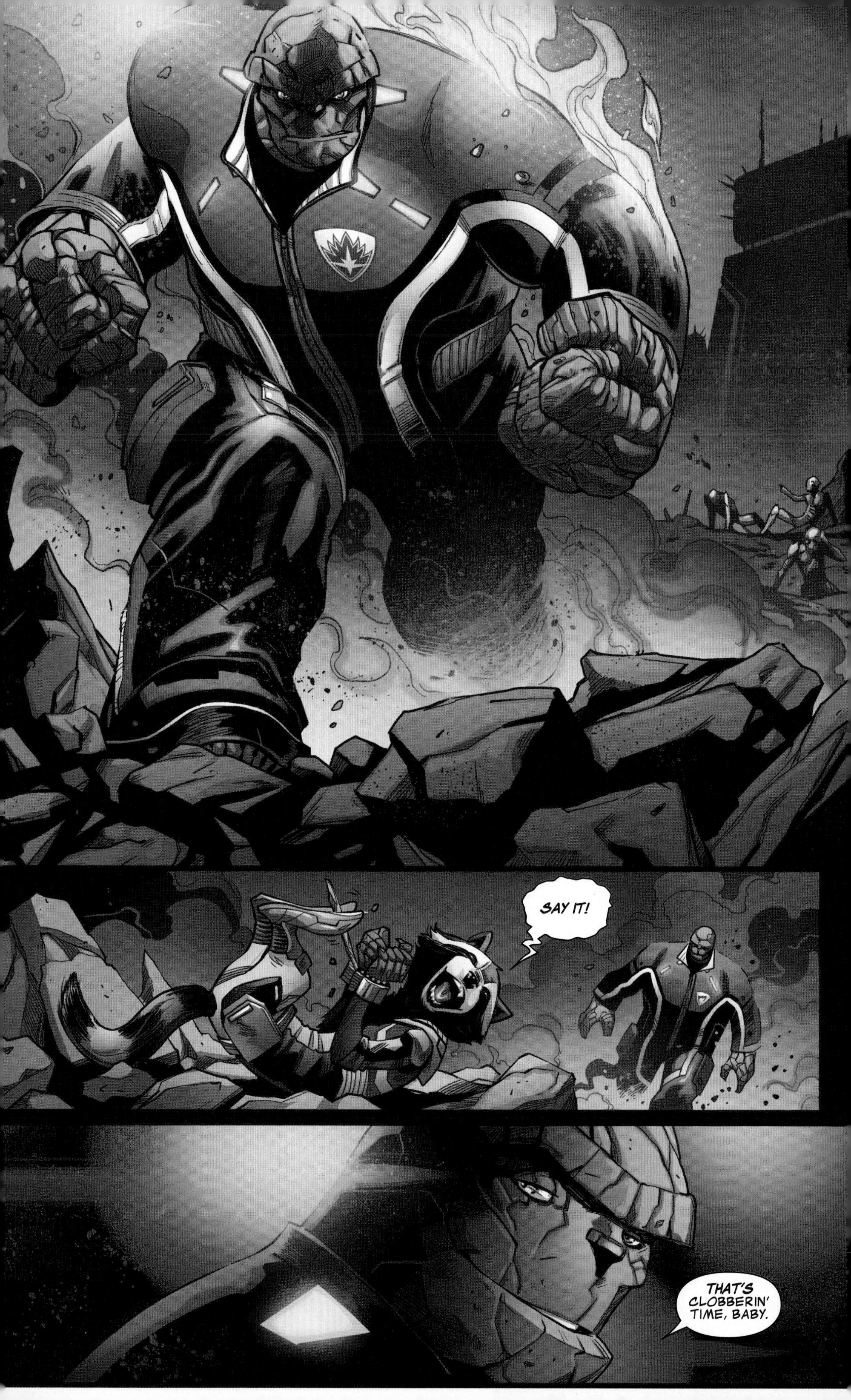
SAY IT!
THAT'S CLOBBERIN' TIME, BABY.

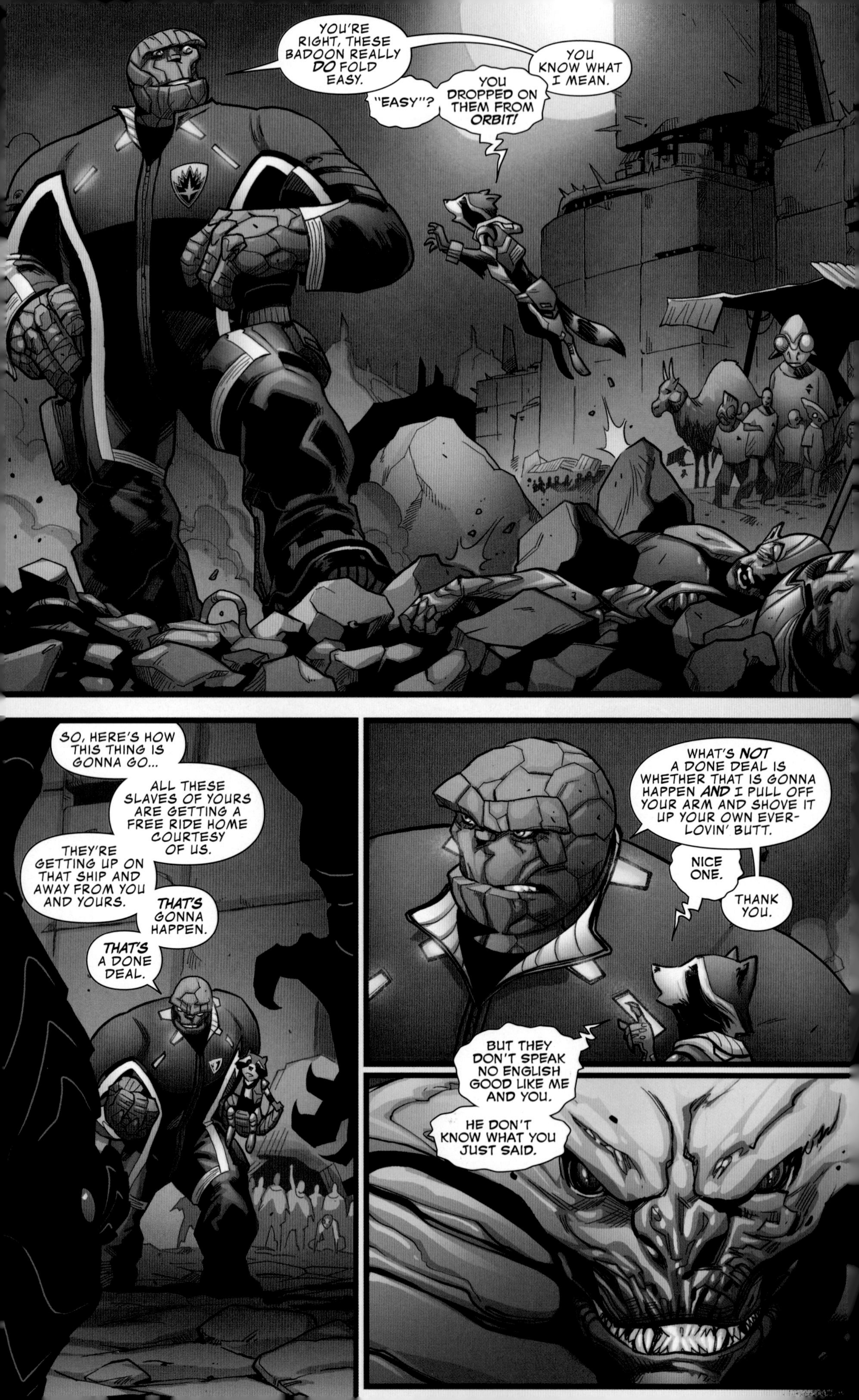
YOU'RE RIGHT, THESE BADOON REALLY *DO* FOLD EASY.
"EASY"?
YOU DROPPED ON THEM FROM *ORBIT!*
YOU KNOW WHAT I MEAN.
SO, HERE'S HOW THIS THING IS GONNA GO...
ALL THESE SLAVES OF YOURS ARE GETTING A FREE RIDE HOME COURTESY OF US.
THEY'RE GETTING UP ON THAT SHIP AND AWAY FROM YOU AND YOURS.
THAT'S GONNA HAPPEN.
THAT'S A DONE DEAL.
WHAT'S *NOT* A DONE DEAL IS WHETHER THAT IS GONNA HAPPEN *AND* I PULL OFF YOUR ARM AND SHOVE IT UP YOUR OWN EVER-LOVIN' BUTT.
NICE ONE.
THANK YOU.
BUT THEY DON'T SPEAK NO ENGLISH GOOD LIKE ME AND YOU.
HE DON'T KNOW WHAT YOU JUST SAID.

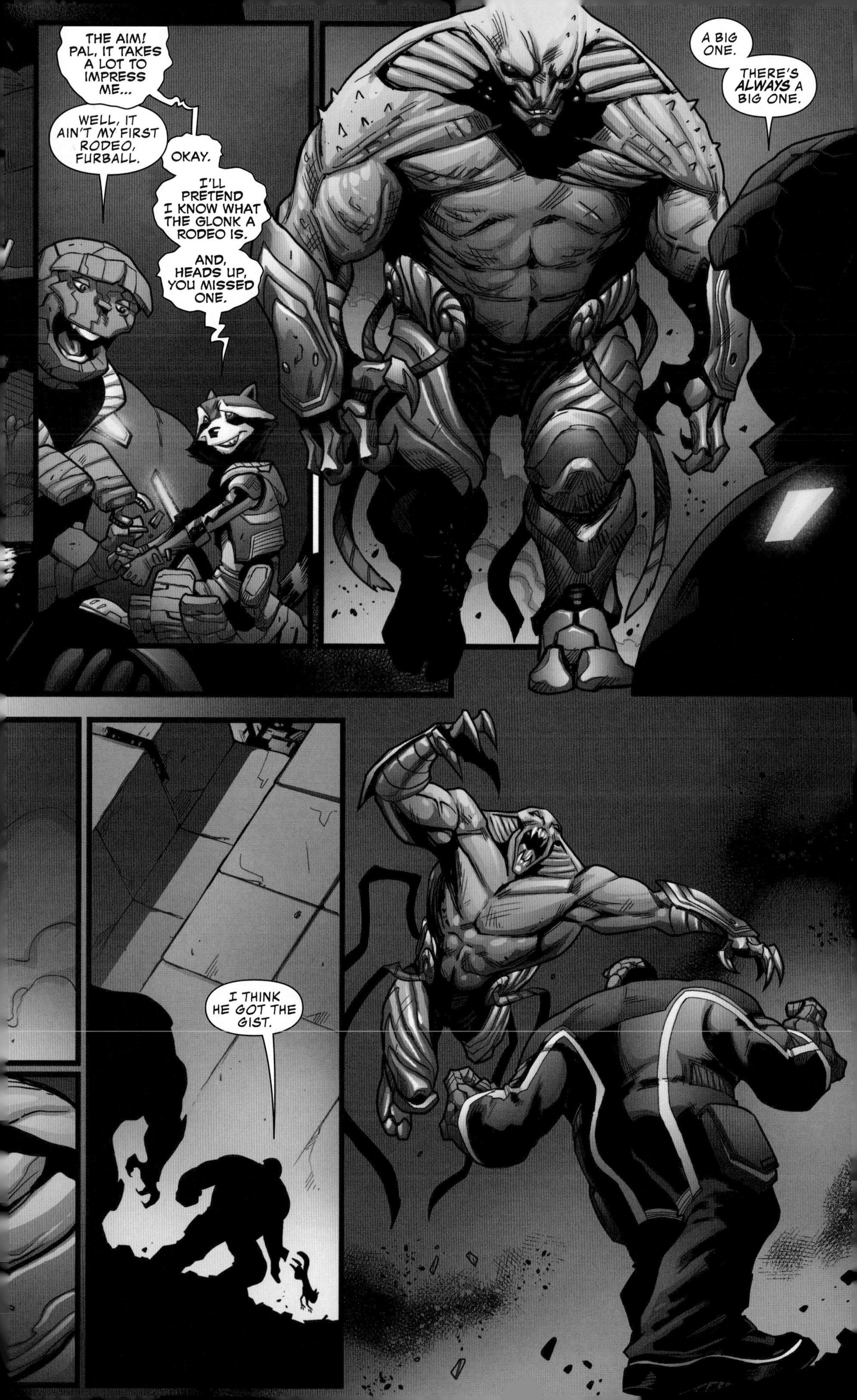
THE AIM! PAL, IT TAKES A LOT TO IMPRESS ME...
WELL, IT AIN'T MY FIRST RODEO, FURBALL.
OKAY.
I'LL PRETEND I KNOW WHAT THE GLONK A RODEO IS.
AND, HEADS UP, YOU MISSED ONE.
A BIG ONE.
THERE'S *ALWAYS* A BIG ONE.
I THINK HE GOT THE GIST.

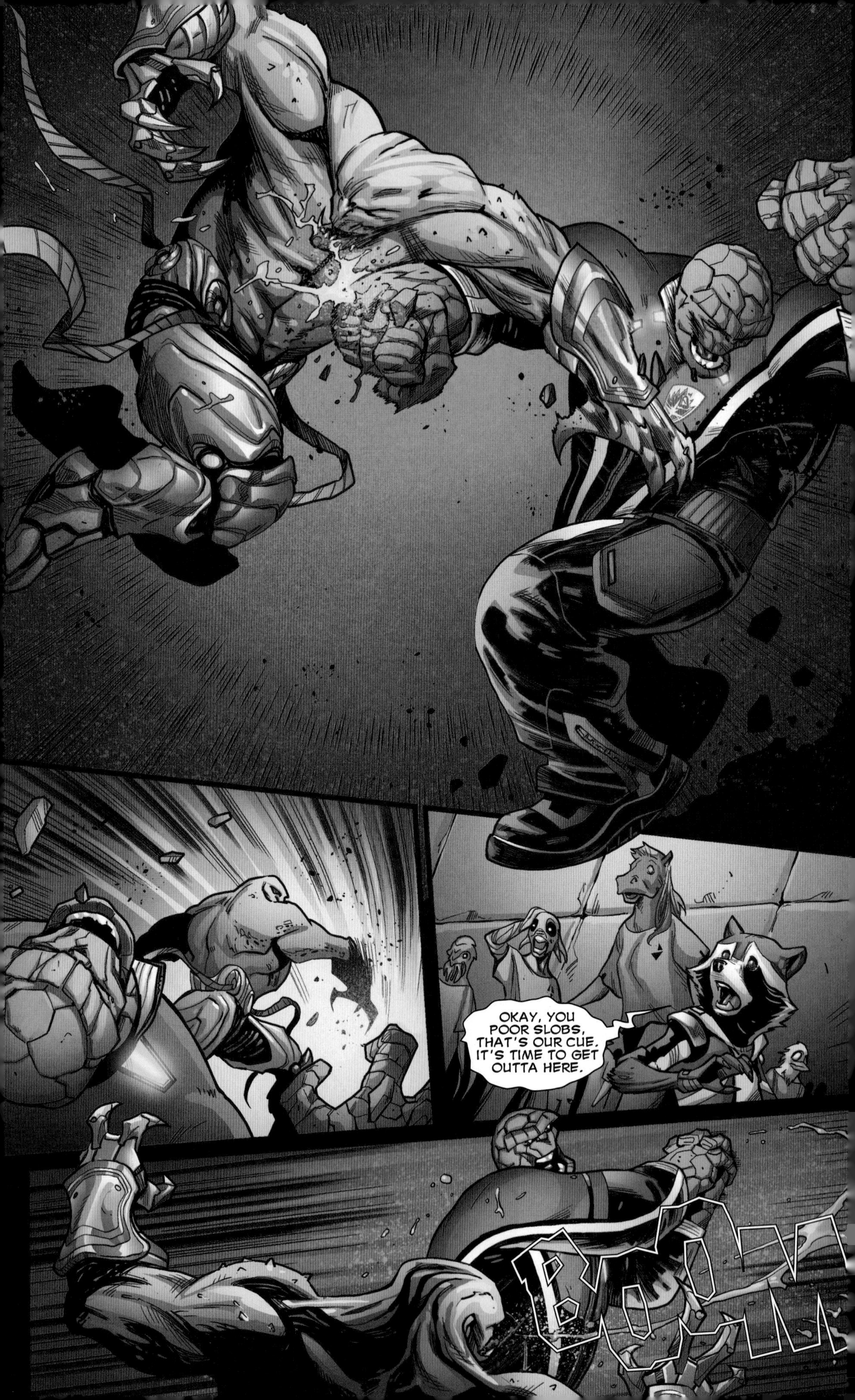
OKAY, YOU POOR SLOBS, THAT'S OUR CUE. IT'S TIME TO GET OUTTA HERE.
BOOM

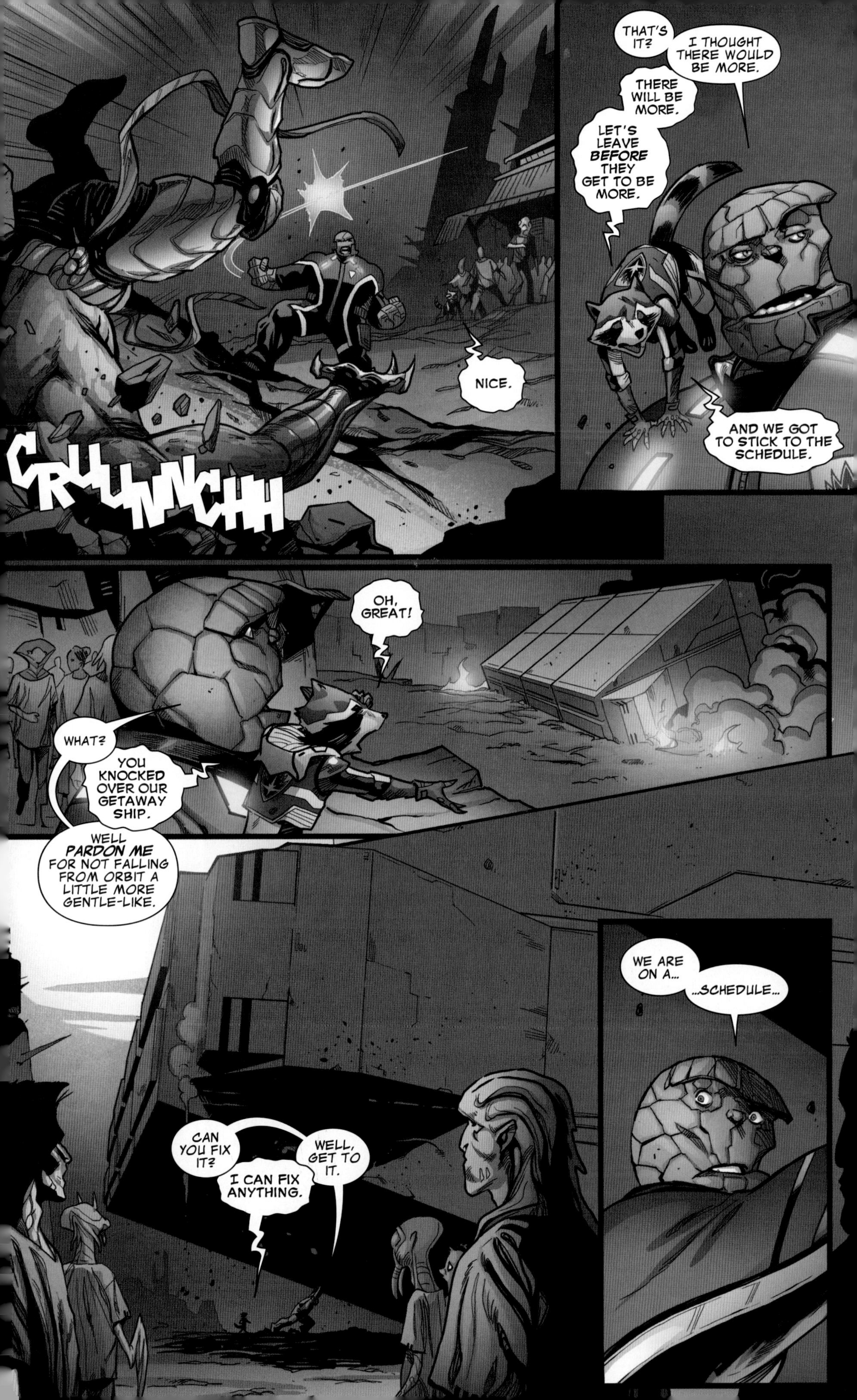
NICE.
CRUUNNCHH
THAT'S IT?
I THOUGHT THERE WOULD BE MORE.
THERE WILL BE MORE.
LET'S LEAVE BEFORE THEY GET TO BE MORE.
AND WE GOT TO STICK TO THE SCHEDULE.
OH, GREAT!
WHAT?
YOU KNOCKED OVER OUR GETAWAY SHIP.
WELL PARDON ME FOR NOT FALLING FROM ORBIT A LITTLE MORE GENTLE-LIKE.
WE ARE ON A...
...SCHEDULE...
CAN YOU FIX IT?
I CAN FIX ANYTHING.
WELL, GET TO IT.

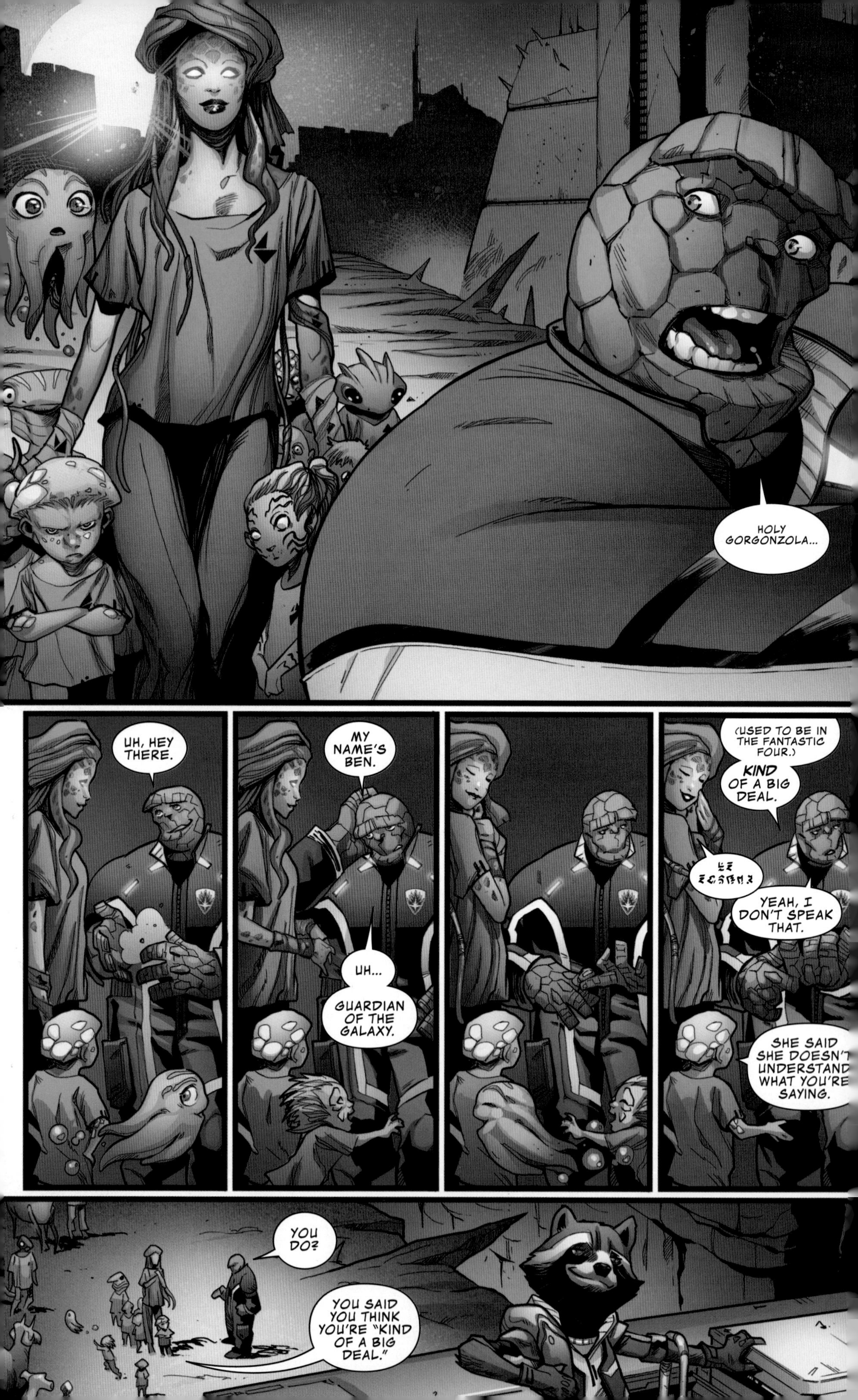
HOLY GORGONZOLA...
UH, HEY THERE.
MY NAME'S BEN.
UH...
GUARDIAN OF THE GALAXY.
(USED TO BE IN THE FANTASTIC FOUR.)
KIND OF A BIG DEAL.
YEAH, I DON'T SPEAK THAT.
SHE SAID SHE DOESN'T UNDERSTAND WHAT YOU'RE SAYING.
YOU DO?
YOU SAID YOU THINK YOU'RE "KIND OF A BIG DEAL."

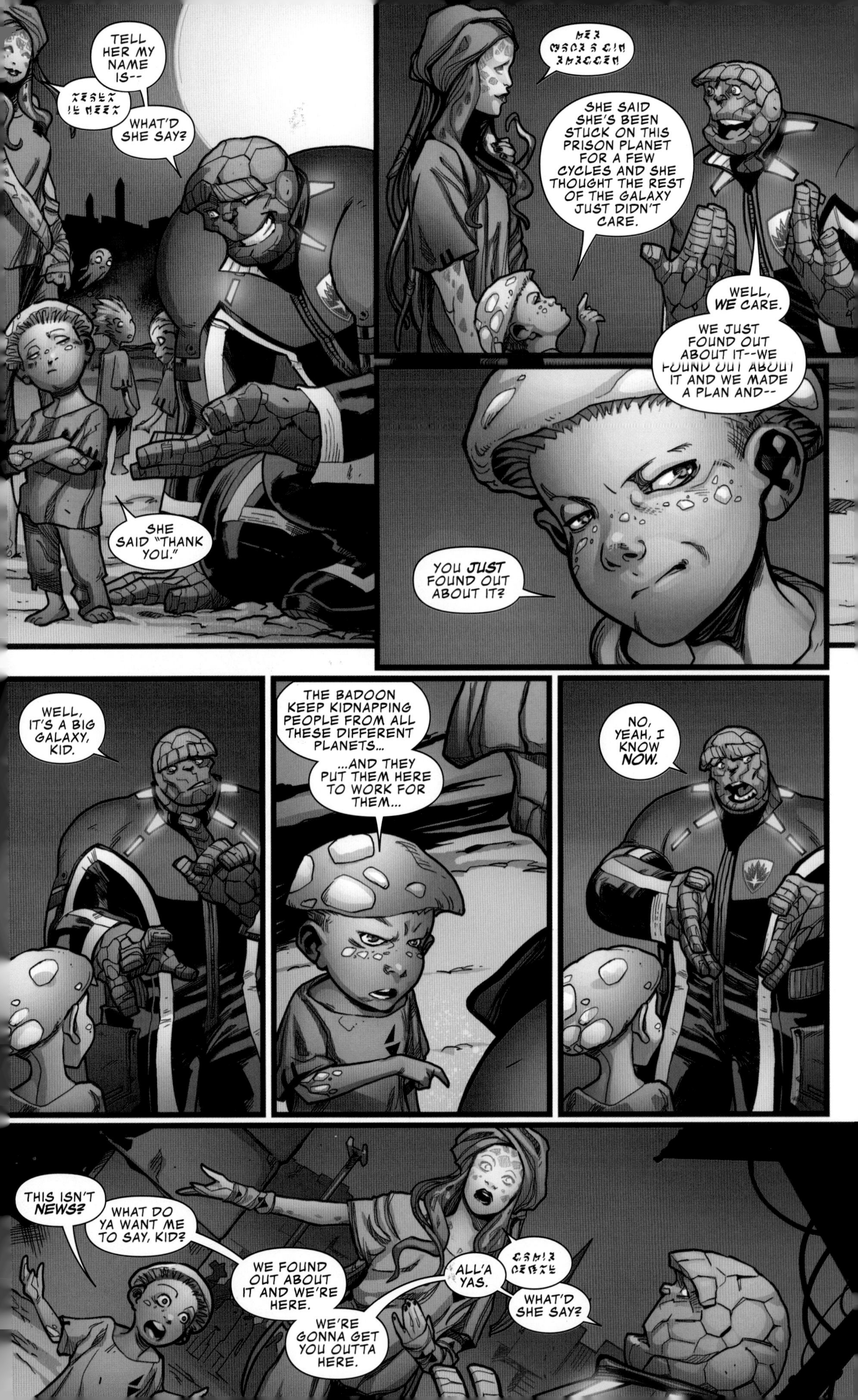
TELL HER MY NAME IS--
WHAT'D SHE SAY?
SHE SAID "THANK YOU."
SHE SAID SHE'S BEEN STUCK ON THIS PRISON PLANET FOR A FEW CYCLES AND SHE THOUGHT THE REST OF THE GALAXY JUST DIDN'T CARE.
WELL, WE CARE.
WE JUST FOUND OUT ABOUT IT--WE FOUND OUT ABOUT IT AND WE MADE A PLAN AND--
YOU JUST FOUND OUT ABOUT IT?
WELL, IT'S A BIG GALAXY, KID.
THE BADOON KEEP KIDNAPPING PEOPLE FROM ALL THESE DIFFERENT PLANETS...
...AND THEY PUT THEM HERE TO WORK FOR THEM...
NO, YEAH, I KNOW NOW.
THIS ISN'T NEWS?
WHAT DO YA WANT ME TO SAY, KID?
WE FOUND OUT ABOUT IT AND WE'RE HERE.
WE'RE GONNA GET YOU OUTTA HERE.
ALL'A YAS.
WHAT'D SHE SAY?

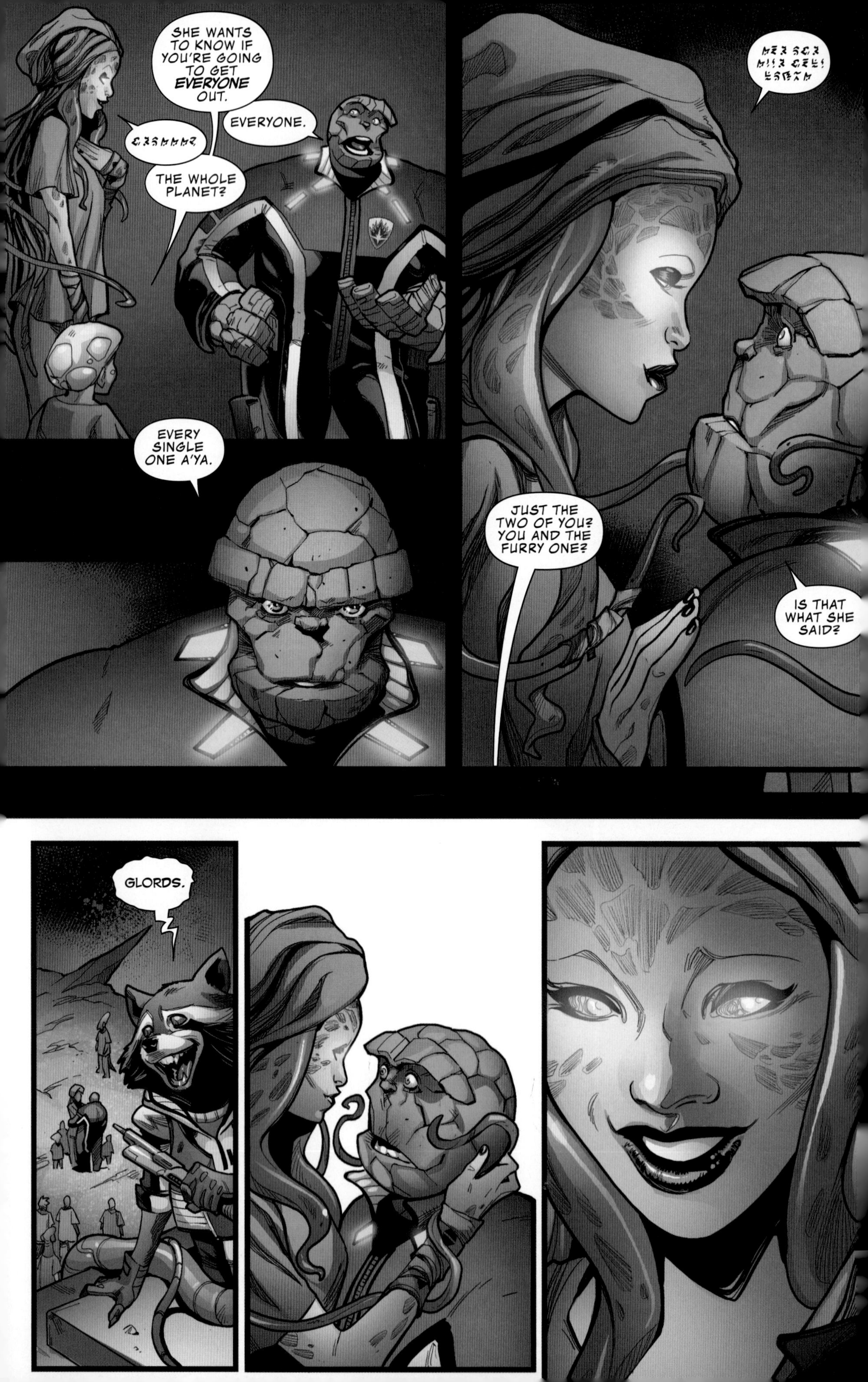
SHE WANTS TO KNOW IF YOU'RE GOING TO GET **EVERYONE** OUT.
EVERYONE.
THE WHOLE PLANET?
EVERY SINGLE ONE A'YA.
JUST THE TWO OF YOU? YOU AND THE FURRY ONE?
IS THAT WHAT SHE SAID?
GLORDS.

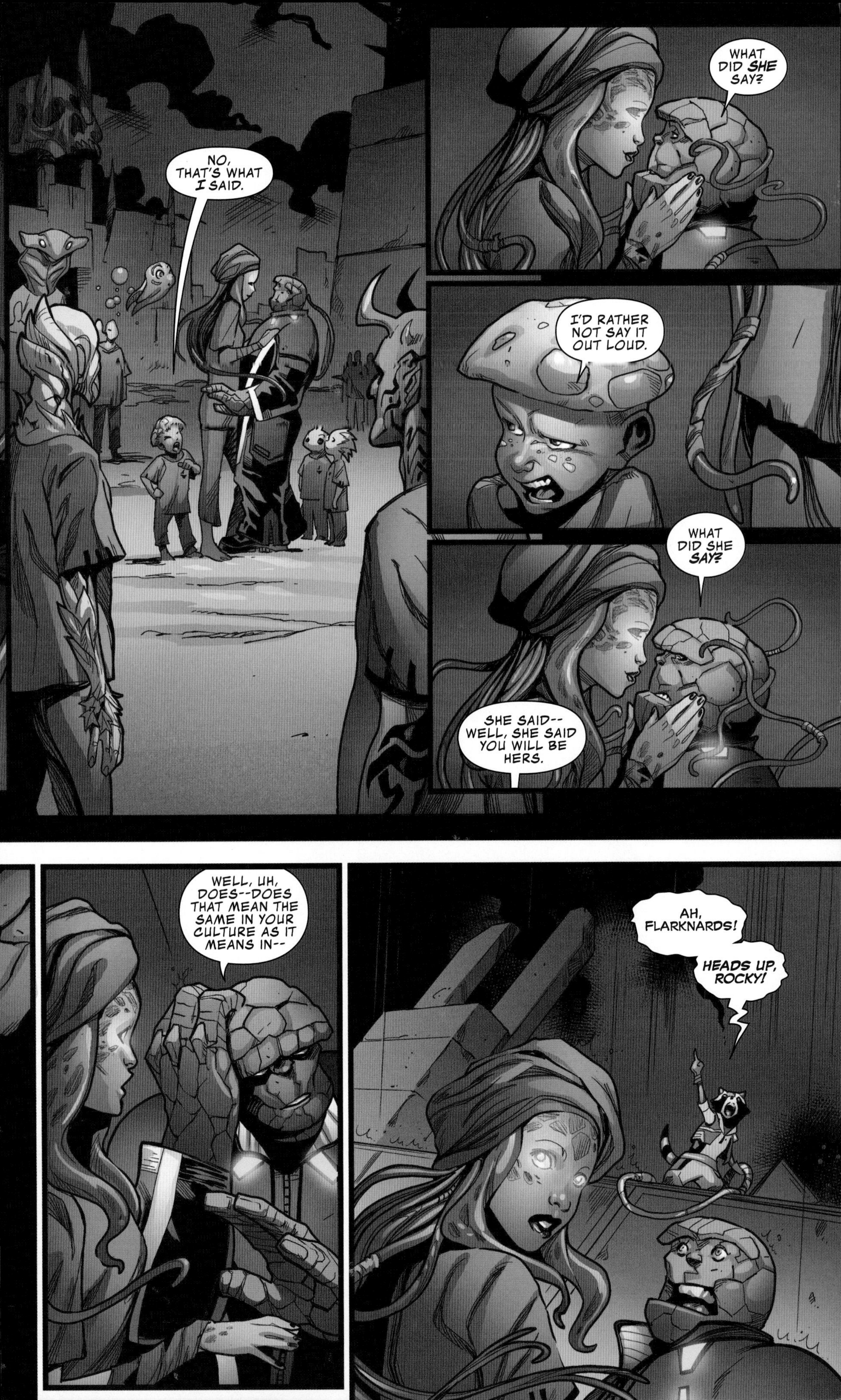
NO, THAT'S WHAT I SAID.
WHAT DID SHE SAY?
I'D RATHER NOT SAY IT OUT LOUD.
WHAT DID SHE SAY?
SHE SAID-- WELL, SHE SAID YOU WILL BE HERS.
WELL, UH, DOES--DOES THAT MEAN THE SAME IN YOUR CULTURE AS IT MEANS IN--
AH, FLARKNARDS!
HEADS UP, ROCKY!

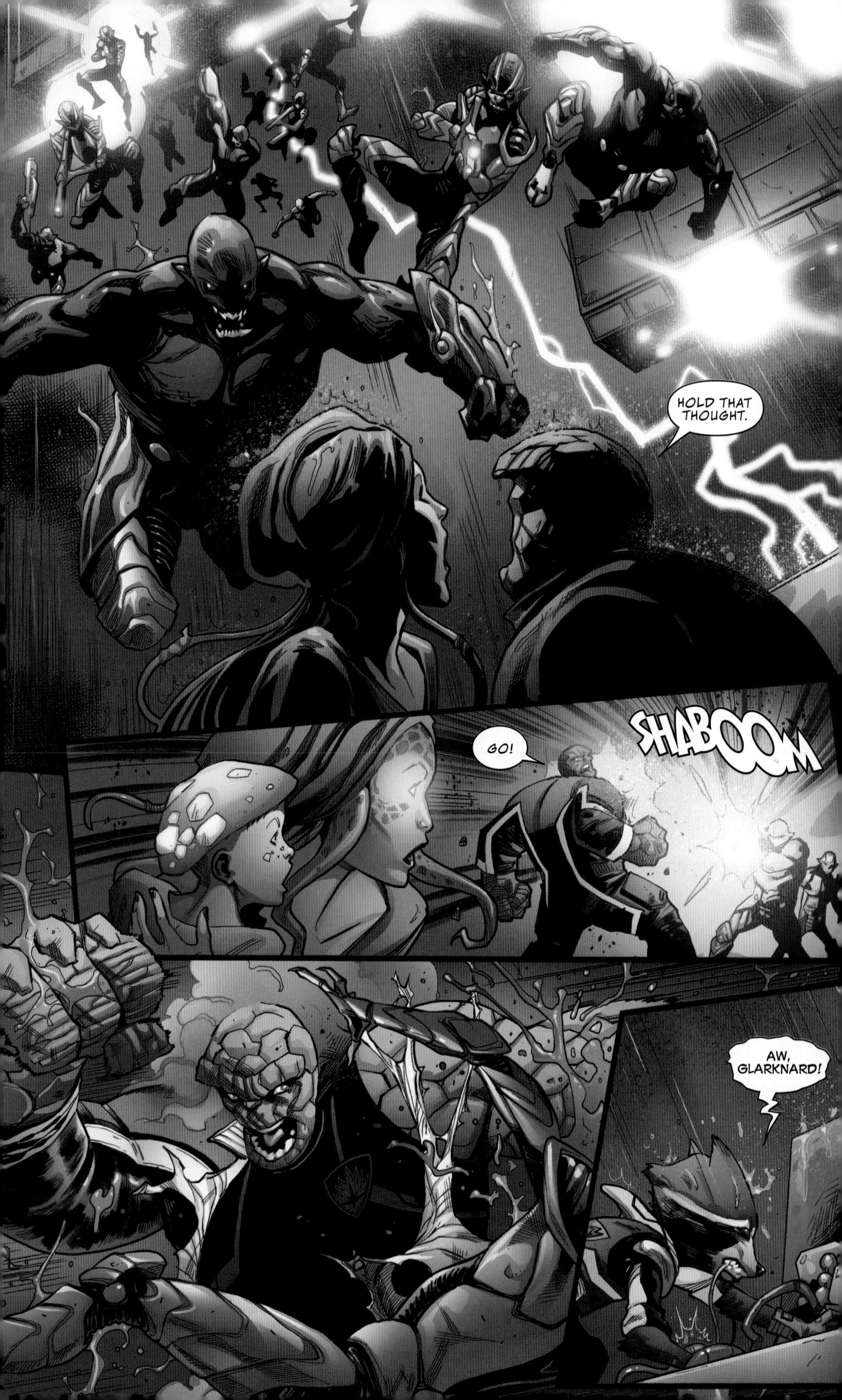
HOLD THAT THOUGHT.
SHABOOM
GO!
AW, GLARKNARD!

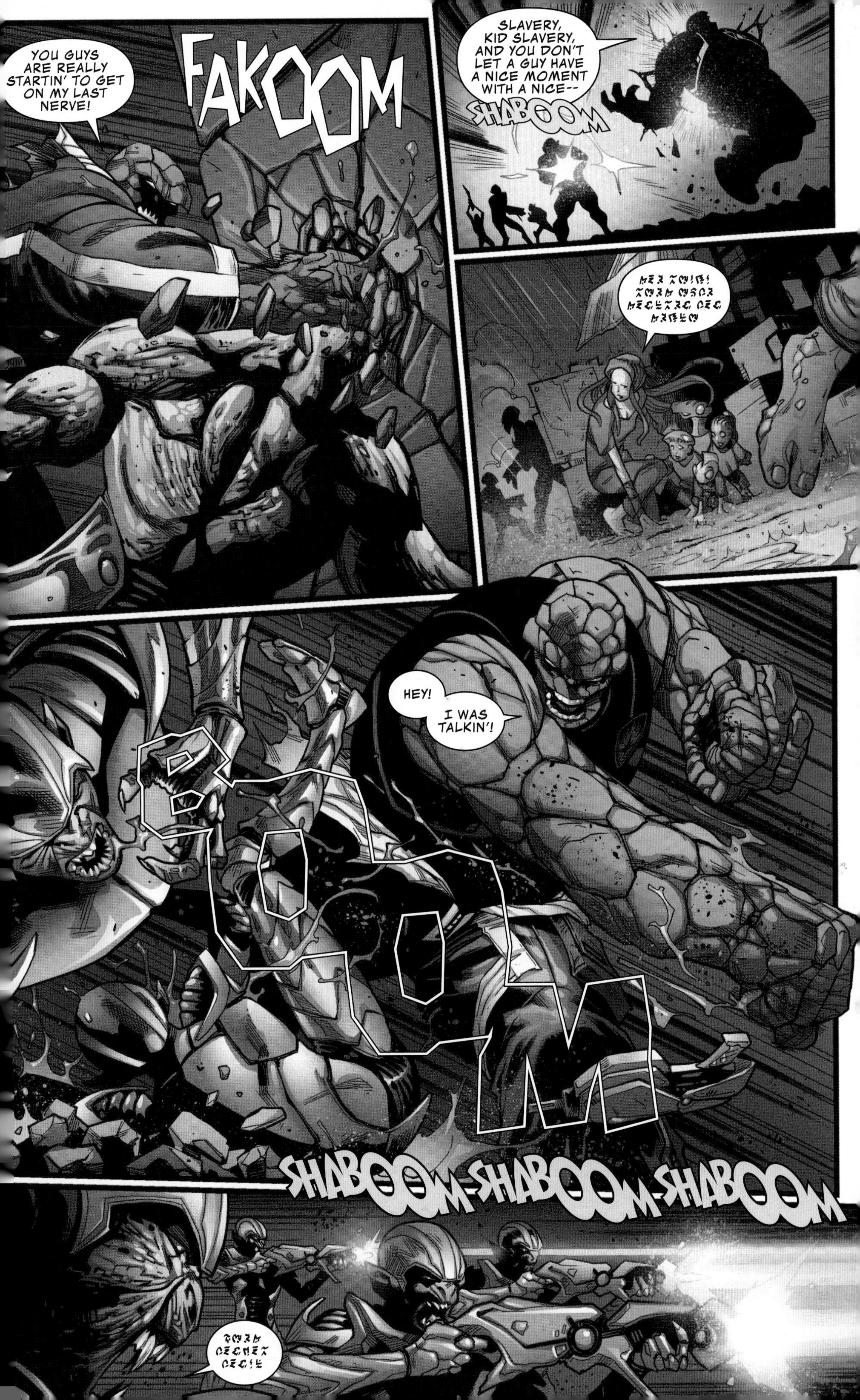
YOU GUYS ARE REALLY STARTIN' TO GET ON MY LAST NERVE!
FAKOOM
SLAVERY, KID SLAVERY, AND YOU DON'T LET A GUY HAVE A NICE MOMENT WITH A NICE--
SHABOOM
HEY!
I WAS TALKIN'!
BOOM
SHABOOM SHABOOM SHABOOM

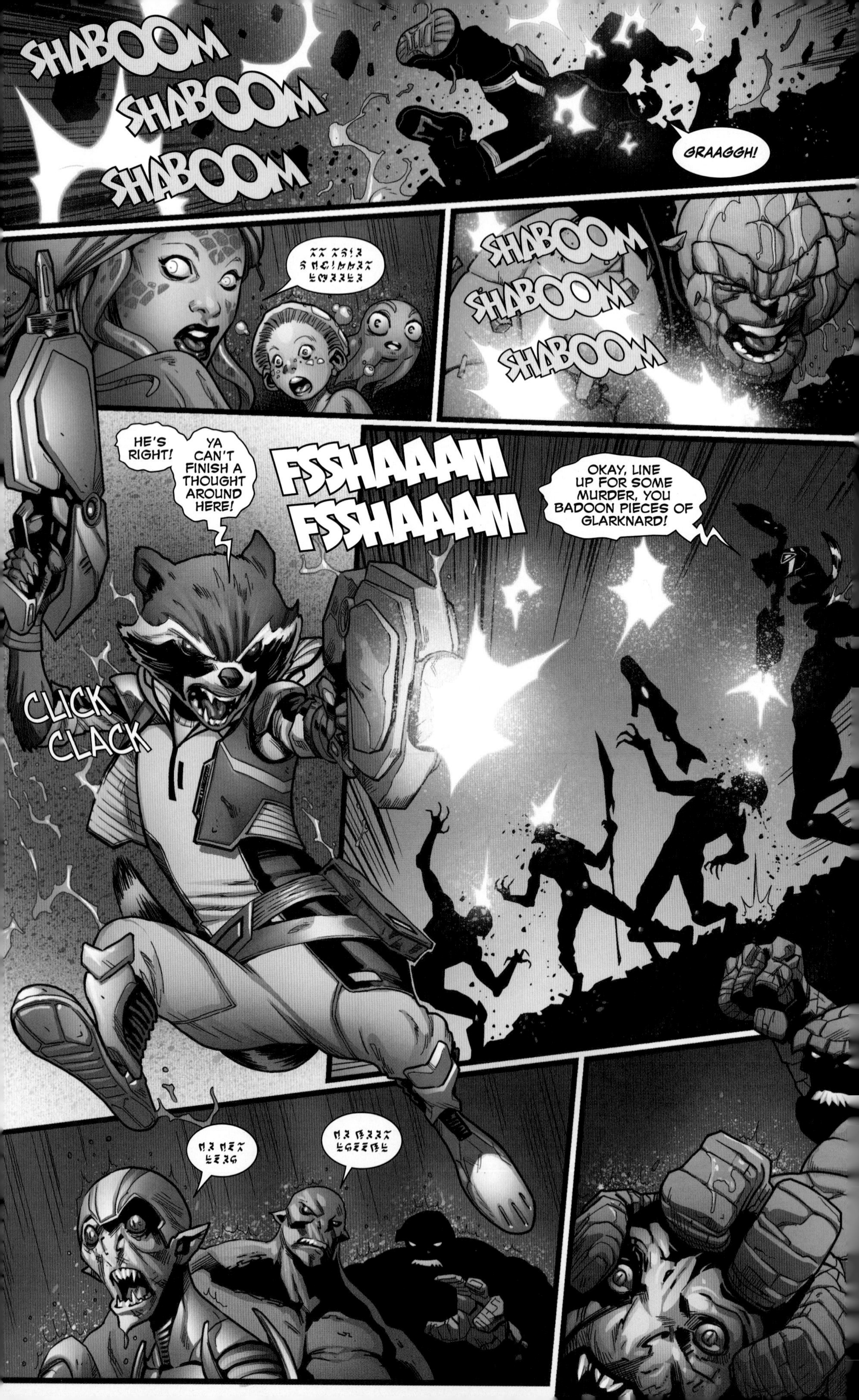
SHABOOM
SHABOOM
SHABOOM
GRAAGGH!
SHABOOM
SHABOOM
SHABOOM
HE'S RIGHT!
YA CAN'T FINISH A THOUGHT AROUND HERE!
FSSHAAAM
FSSHAAAM
OKAY, LINE UP FOR SOME MURDER, YOU BADOON PIECES OF GLARKNARD!
CLICK CLACK

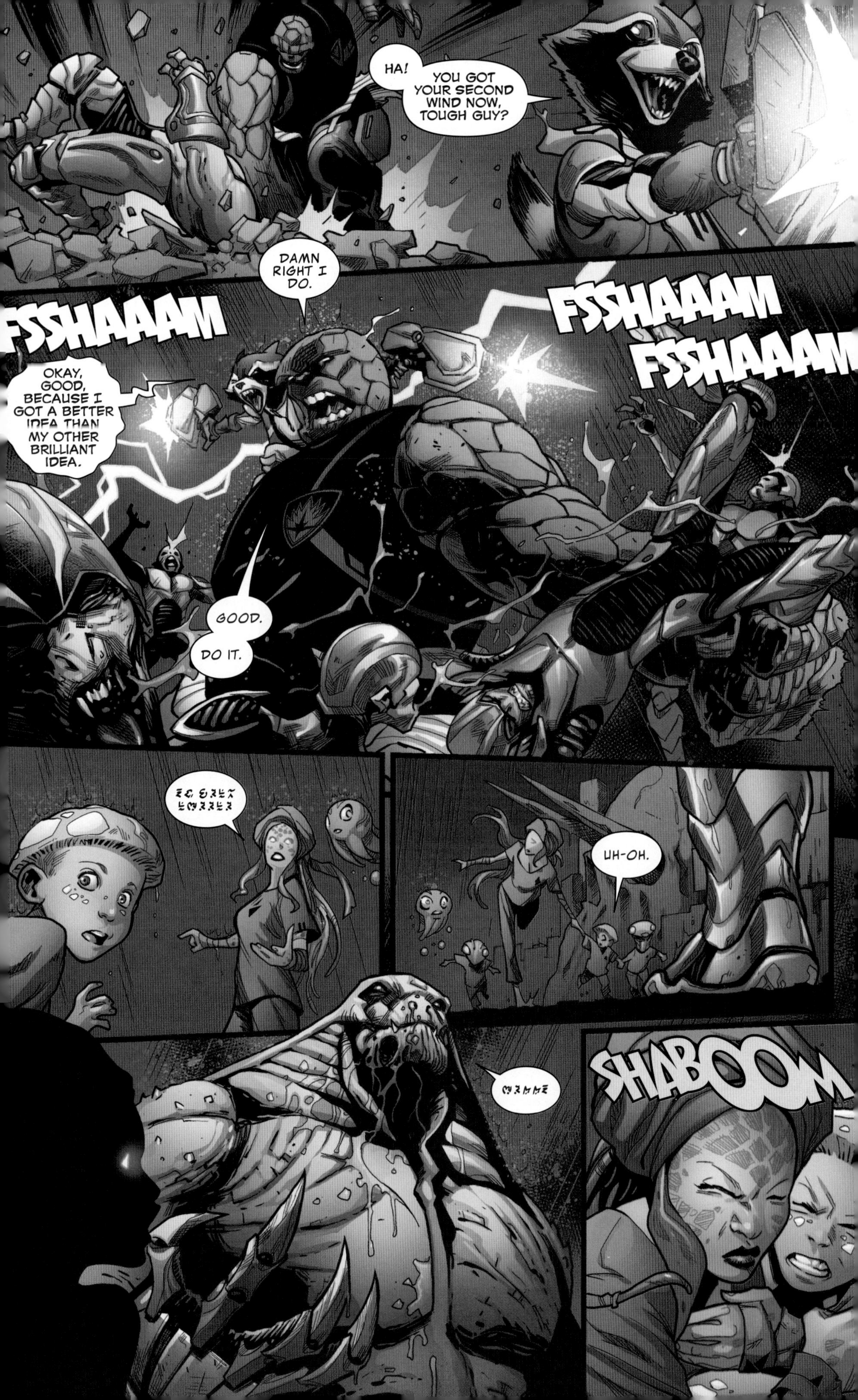
HA!
YOU GOT YOUR SECOND WIND NOW, TOUGH GUY?
DAMN RIGHT I DO.
FSSHAAAM
OKAY, GOOD, BECAUSE I GOT A BETTER IDEA THAN MY OTHER BRILLIANT IDEA.
FSSHAAAM
FSSHAAAM
GOOD.
DO IT.
UH-OH.
SHABOOM

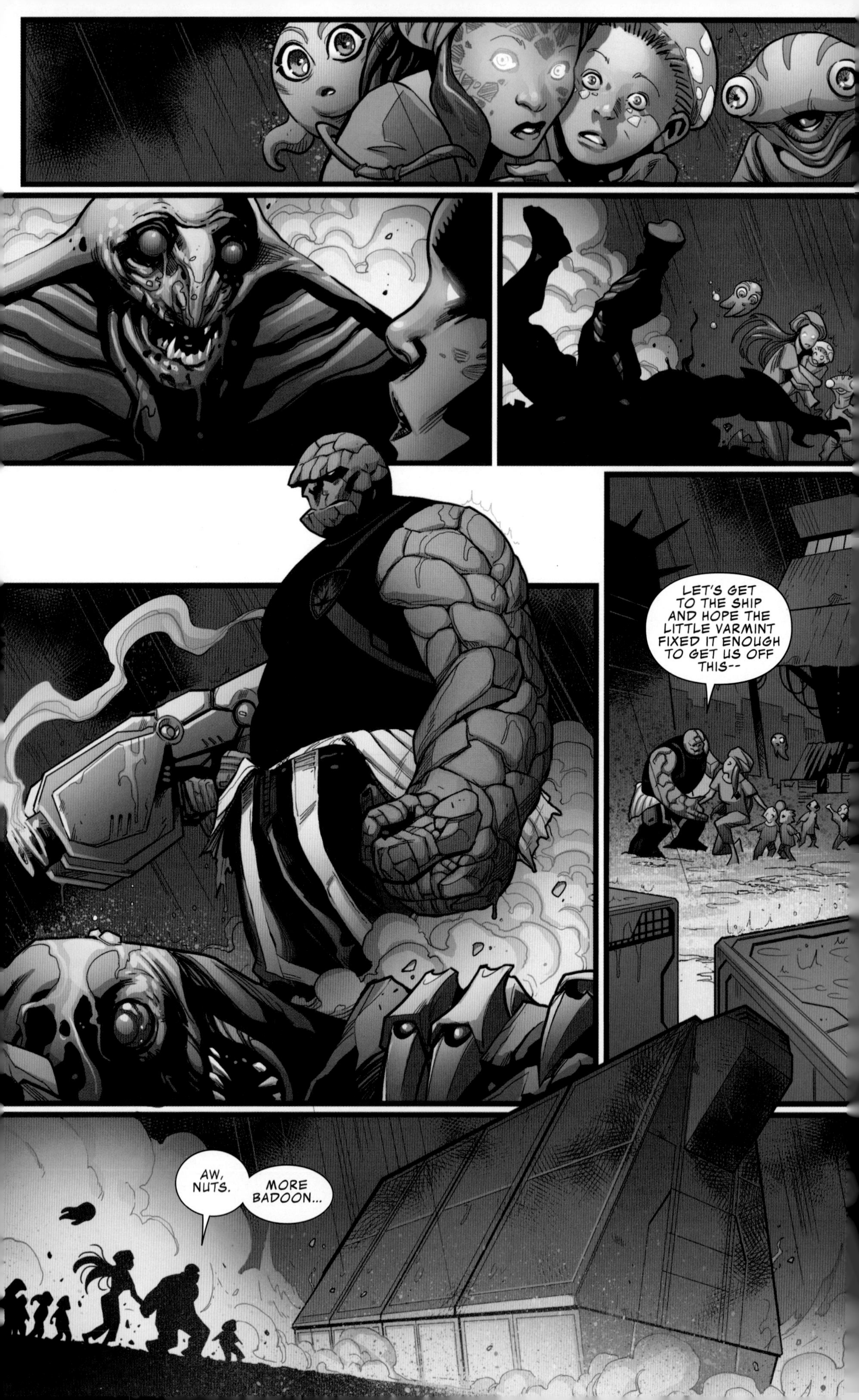
LET'S GET TO THE SHIP AND HOPE THE LITTLE VARMINT FIXED IT ENOUGH TO GET US OFF THIS--
AW, NUTS.
MORE BADOON...

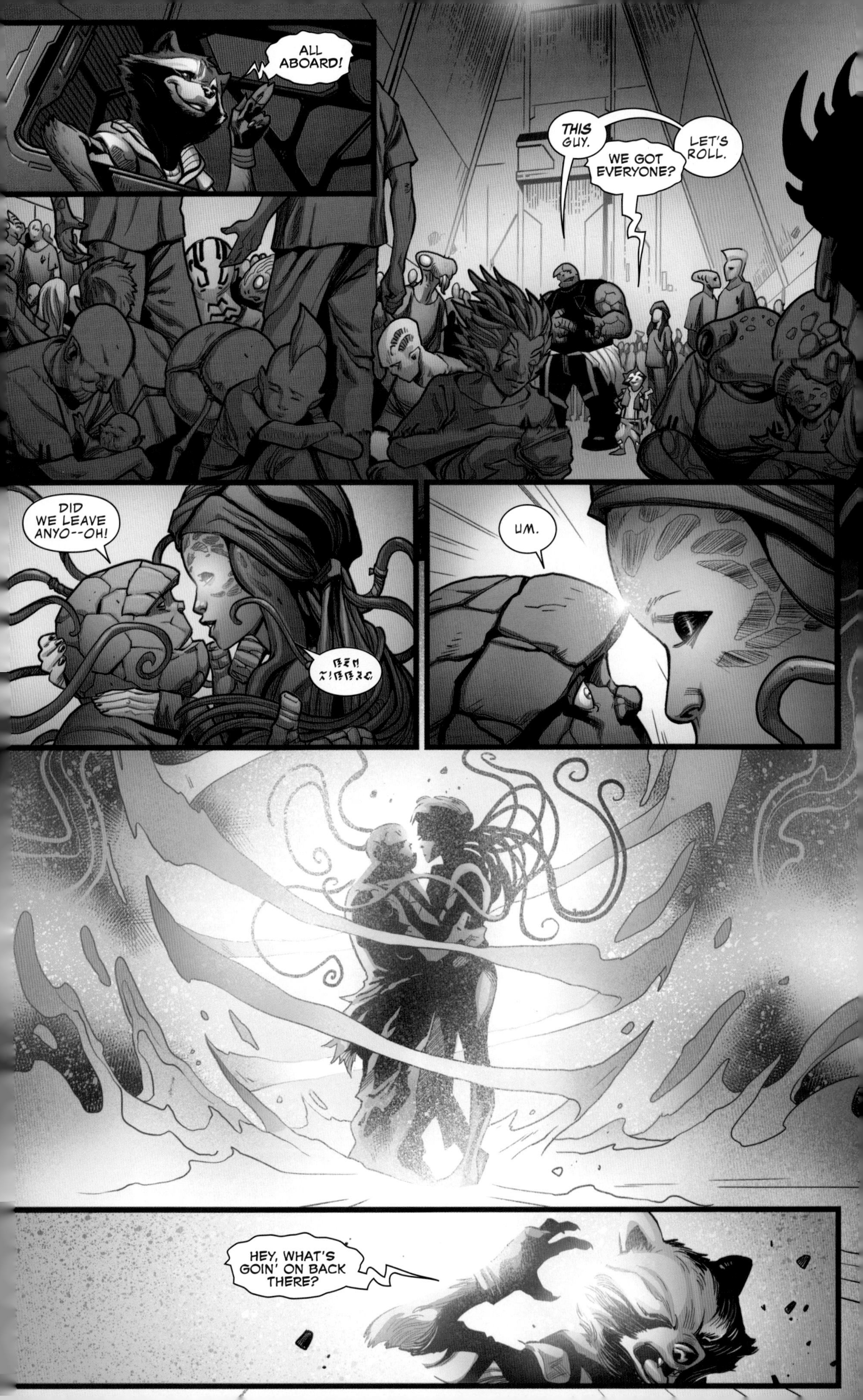
ALL ABOARD!
THIS GUY.
WE GOT EVERYONE?
LET'S ROLL.
DID WE LEAVE ANYO--OH!
UM.
HEY, WHAT'S GOIN' ON BACK THERE?

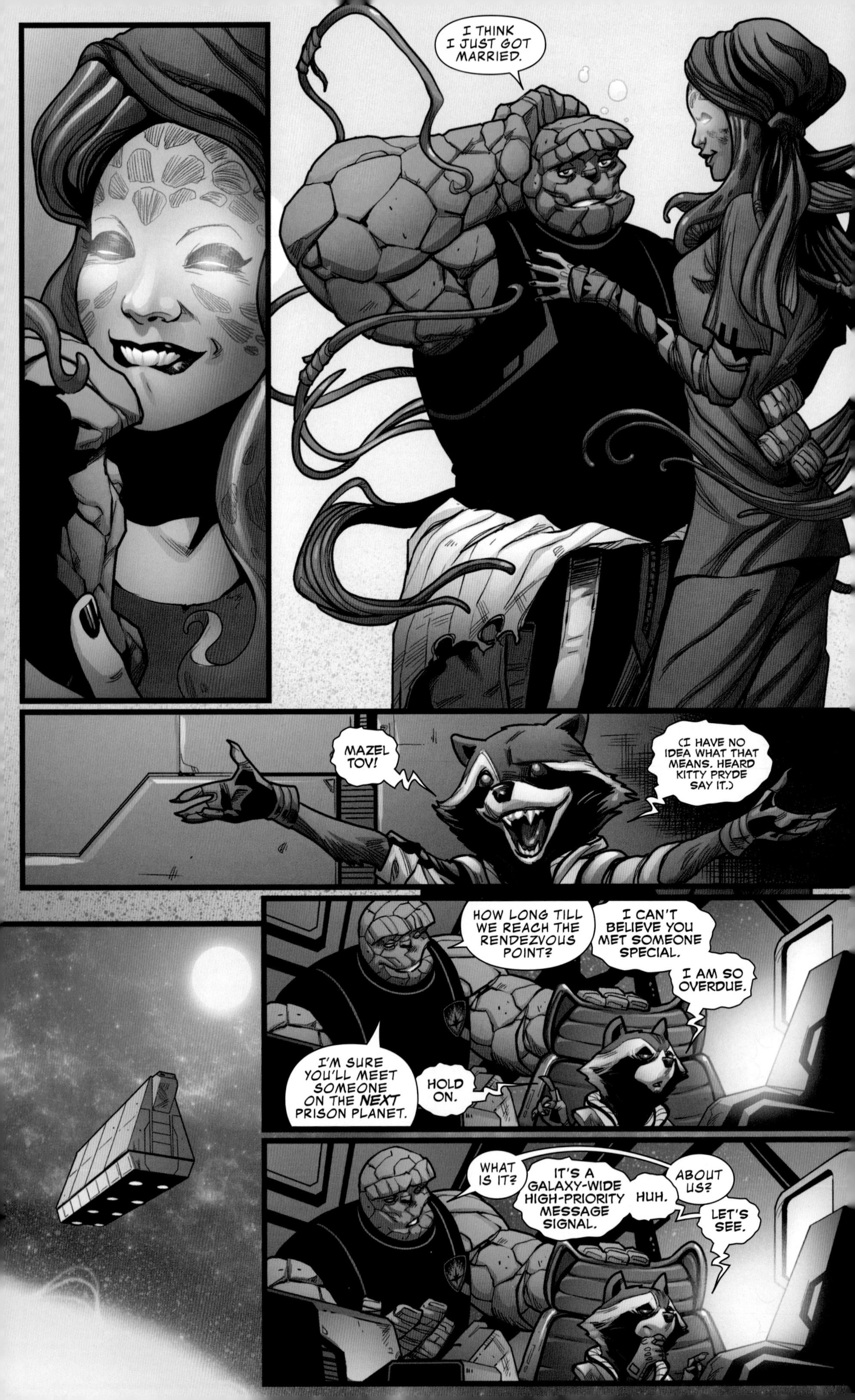

I THINK I JUST GOT MARRIED.
MAZEL TOV!
(I HAVE NO IDEA WHAT THAT MEANS. HEARD KITTY PRYDE SAY IT.)
HOW LONG TILL WE REACH THE RENDEZVOUS POINT?
I CAN'T BELIEVE YOU MET SOMEONE SPECIAL.
I AM SO OVERDUE.
I'M SURE YOU'LL MEET SOMEONE ON THE NEXT PRISON PLANET.
HOLD ON.
WHAT IS IT?
IT'S A GALAXY-WIDE HIGH-PRIORITY MESSAGE SIGNAL.
HUH.
ABOUT US?
LET'S SEE.

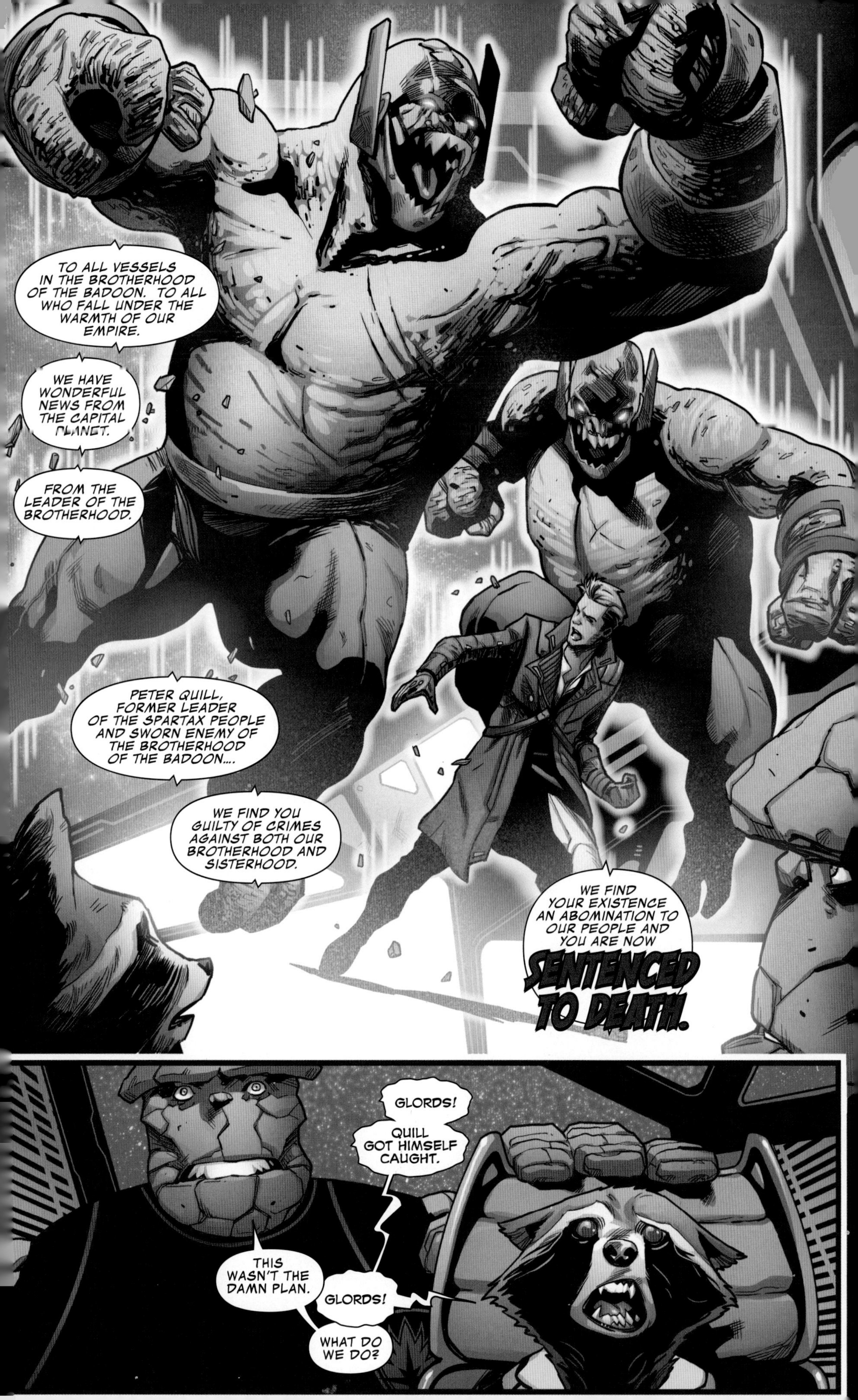
TO ALL VESSELS IN THE BROTHERHOOD OF THE BADOON. TO ALL WHO FALL UNDER THE WARMTH OF OUR EMPIRE.
WE HAVE WONDERFUL NEWS FROM THE CAPITAL PLANET.
FROM THE LEADER OF THE BROTHERHOOD.
PETER QUILL, FORMER LEADER OF THE SPARTAX PEOPLE AND SWORN ENEMY OF THE BROTHERHOOD OF THE BADOON....
WE FIND YOU GUILTY OF CRIMES AGAINST BOTH OUR BROTHERHOOD AND SISTERHOOD.
WE FIND YOUR EXISTENCE AN ABOMINATION TO OUR PEOPLE AND YOU ARE NOW SENTENCED TO DEATH.
GLORDS!
QUILL GOT HIMSELF CAUGHT.
THIS WASN'T THE DAMN PLAN.
GLORDS!
WHAT DO WE DO?

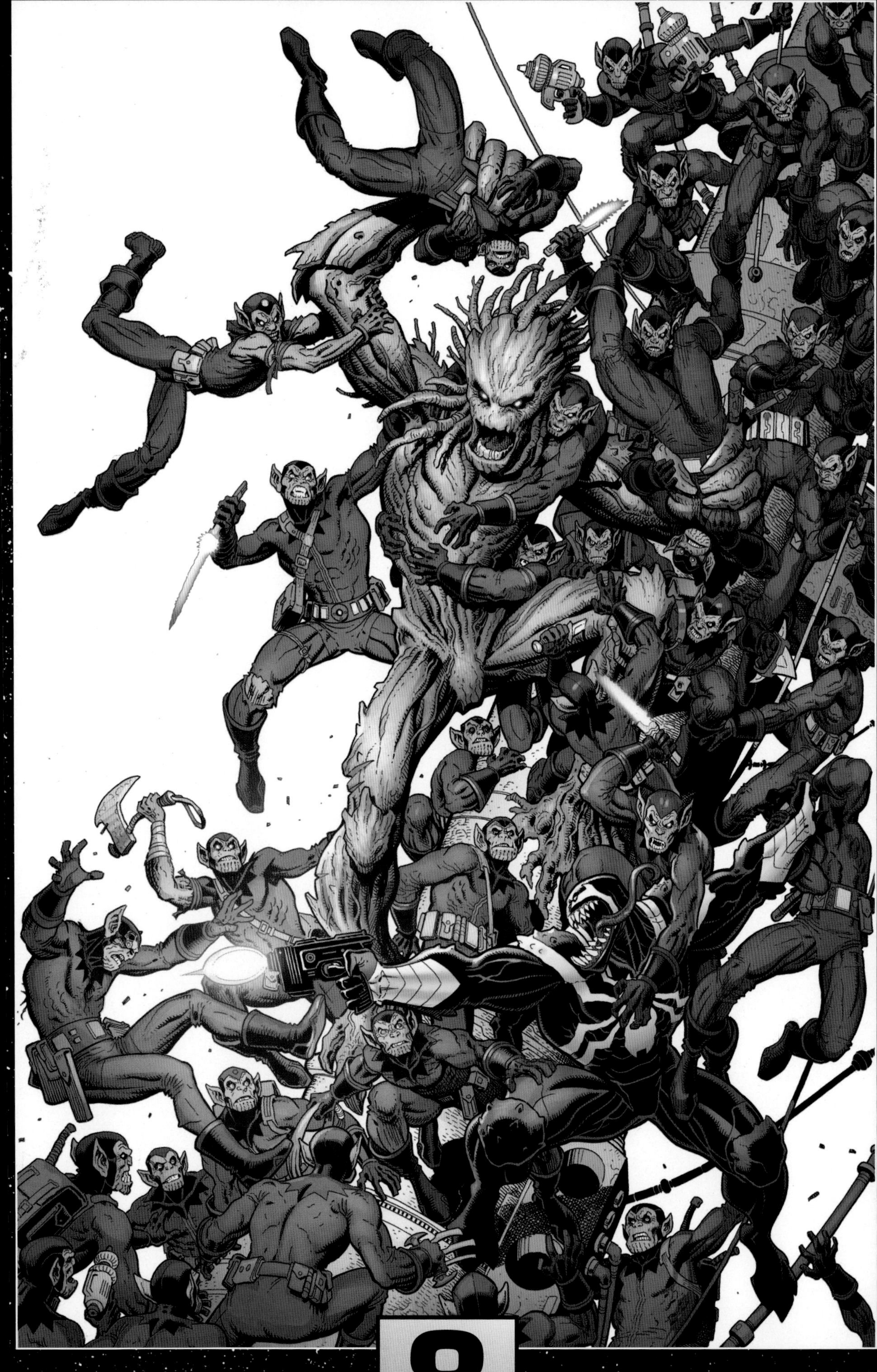

8

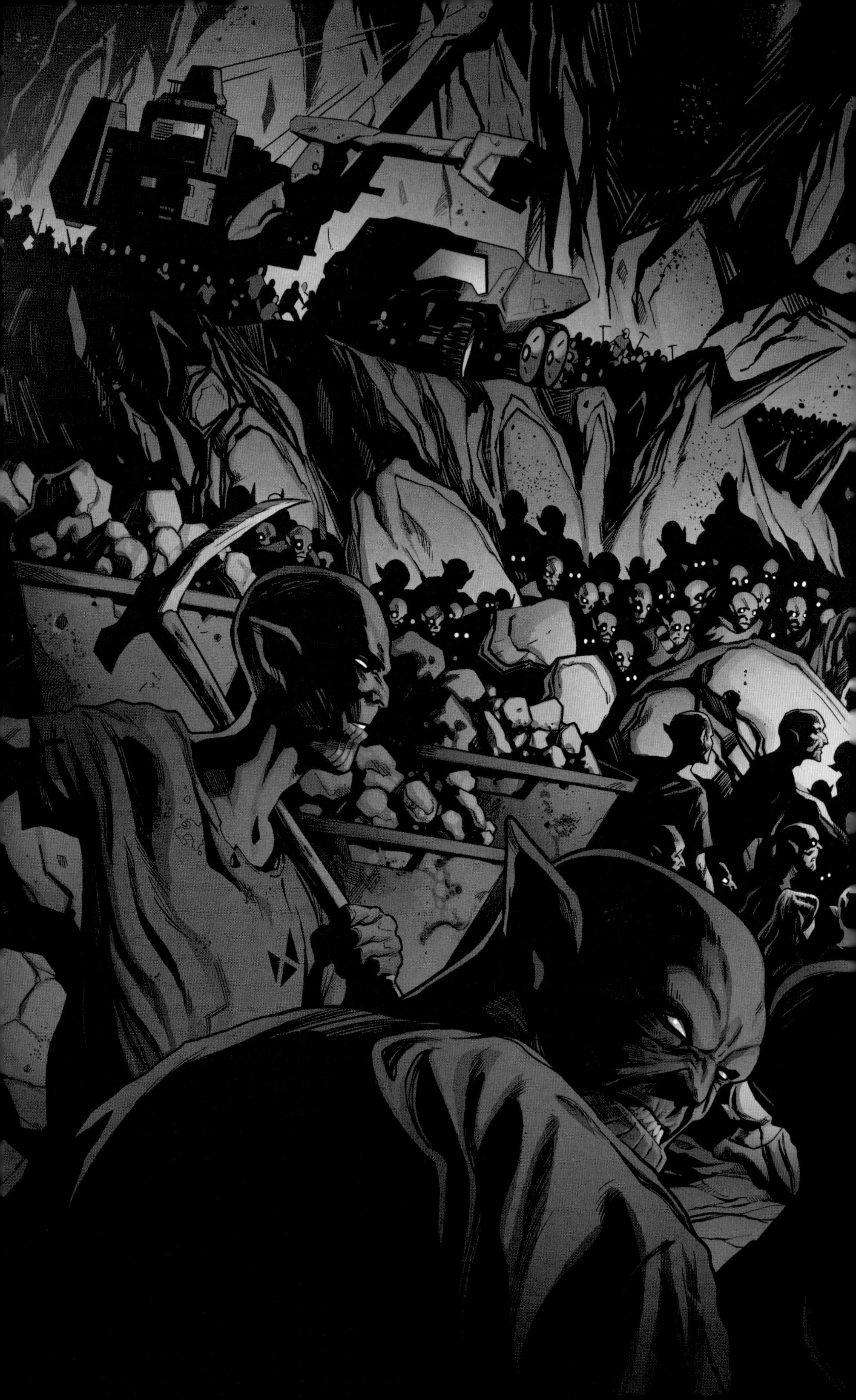

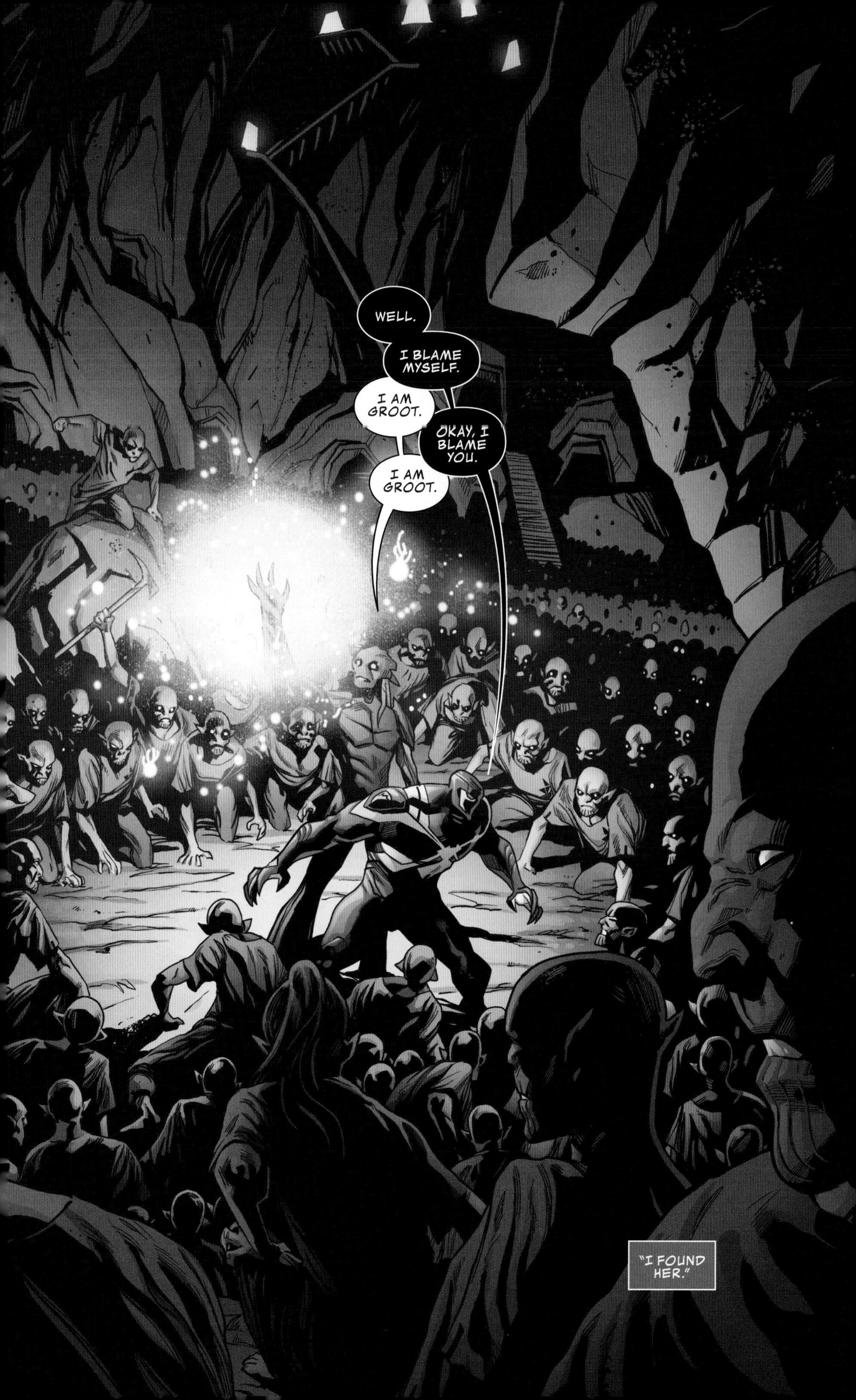
WELL.
I BLAME MYSELF.
I AM GROOT.
OKAY, I BLAME YOU.
I AM GROOT.
"I FOUND HER."

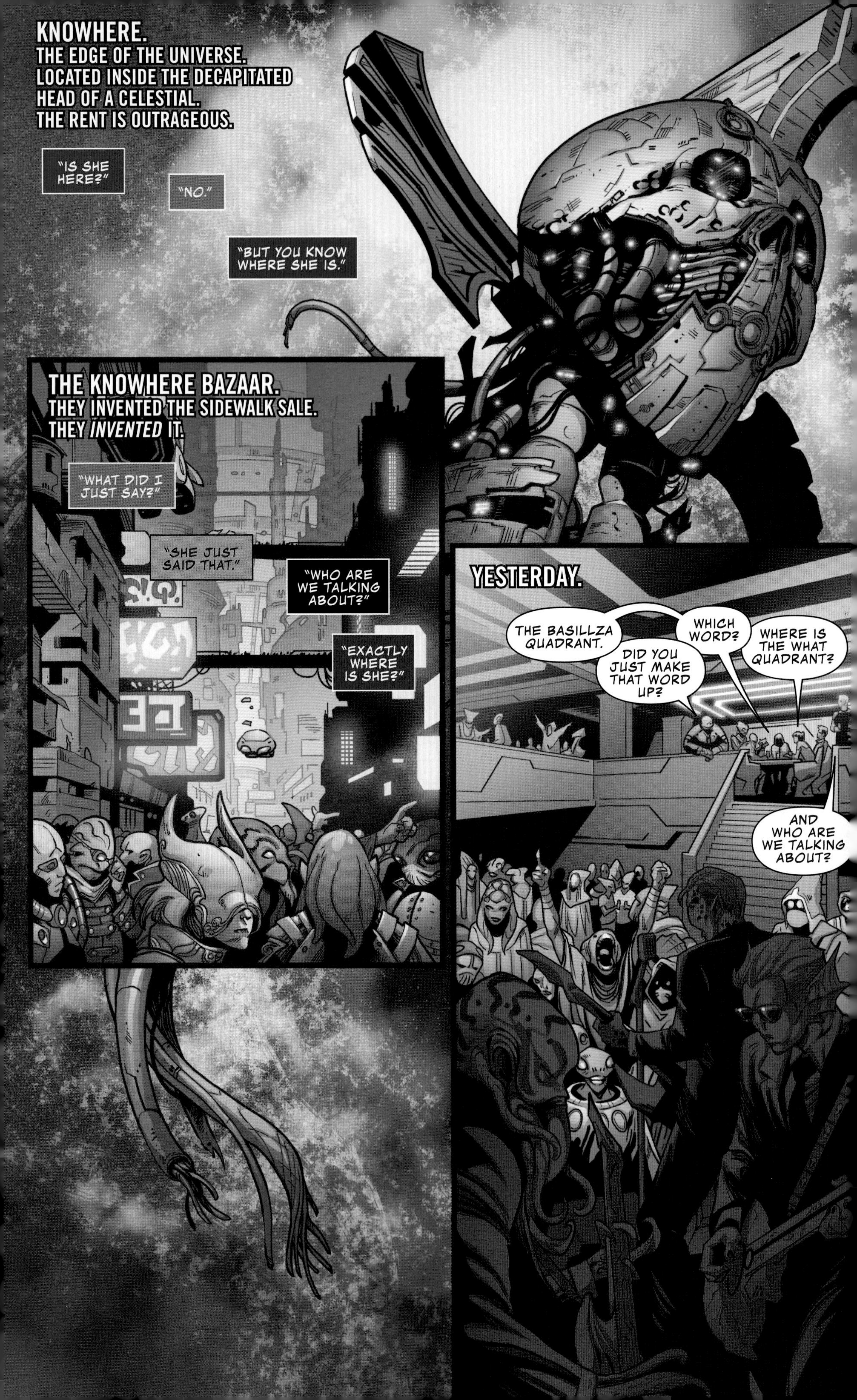
KNOWHERE.
THE EDGE OF THE UNIVERSE.
LOCATED INSIDE THE DECAPITATED HEAD OF A CELESTIAL.
THE RENT IS OUTRAGEOUS.
"IS SHE HERE?"
"NO."
"BUT YOU KNOW WHERE SHE IS."
THE KNOWHERE BAZAAR.
THEY INVENTED THE SIDEWALK SALE.
THEY *INVENTED* IT.
"WHAT DID I JUST SAY?"
"SHE JUST SAID THAT."
"WHO ARE WE TALKING ABOUT?"
"EXACTLY WHERE IS SHE?"
YESTERDAY.
THE BASILLZA QUADRANT.
WHICH WORD?
DID YOU JUST MAKE THAT WORD UP?
WHERE IS THE WHAT QUADRANT?
AND WHO ARE WE TALKING ABOUT?

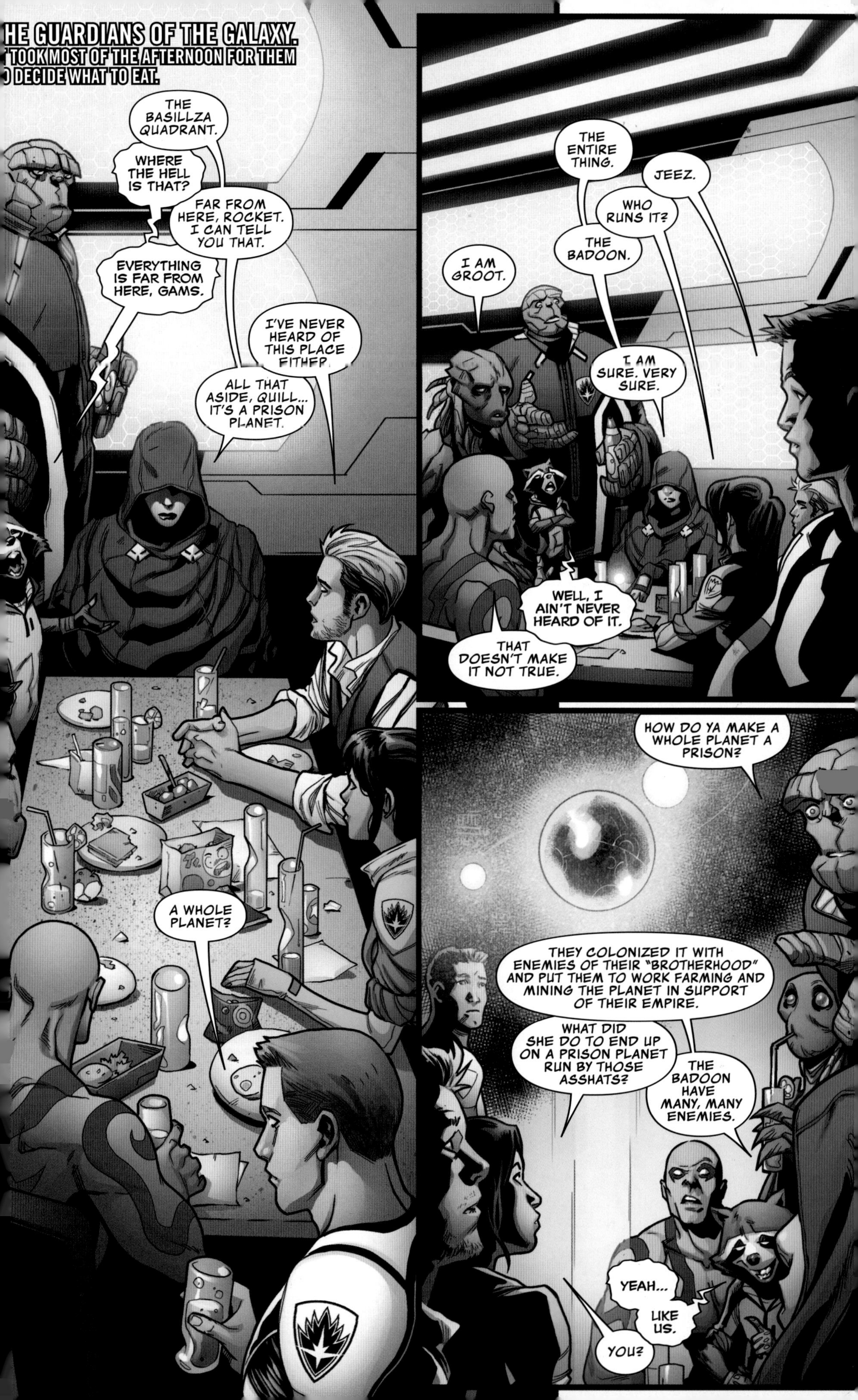
HE GUARDIANS OF THE GALAXY.
TOOK MOST OF THE AFTERNOON FOR THEM
DECIDE WHAT TO EAT.
THE BASILLZA QUADRANT.
WHERE THE HELL IS THAT?
FAR FROM HERE, ROCKET. I CAN TELL YOU THAT.
EVERYTHING IS FAR FROM HERE, GAMS.
I'VE NEVER HEARD OF THIS PLACE EITHER.
ALL THAT ASIDE, QUILL... IT'S A PRISON PLANET.
A WHOLE PLANET?
THE ENTIRE THING.
JEEZ.
WHO RUNS IT?
THE BADOON.
I AM GROOT.
I AM SURE. VERY SURE.
WELL, I AIN'T NEVER HEARD OF IT.
THAT DOESN'T MAKE IT NOT TRUE.
HOW DO YA MAKE A WHOLE PLANET A PRISON?
THEY COLONIZED IT WITH ENEMIES OF THEIR "BROTHERHOOD" AND PUT THEM TO WORK FARMING AND MINING THE PLANET IN SUPPORT OF THEIR EMPIRE.
WHAT DID SHE DO TO END UP ON A PRISON PLANET RUN BY THOSE ASSHATS?
THE BADOON HAVE MANY, MANY ENEMIES.
YEAH...
LIKE US.
YOU?

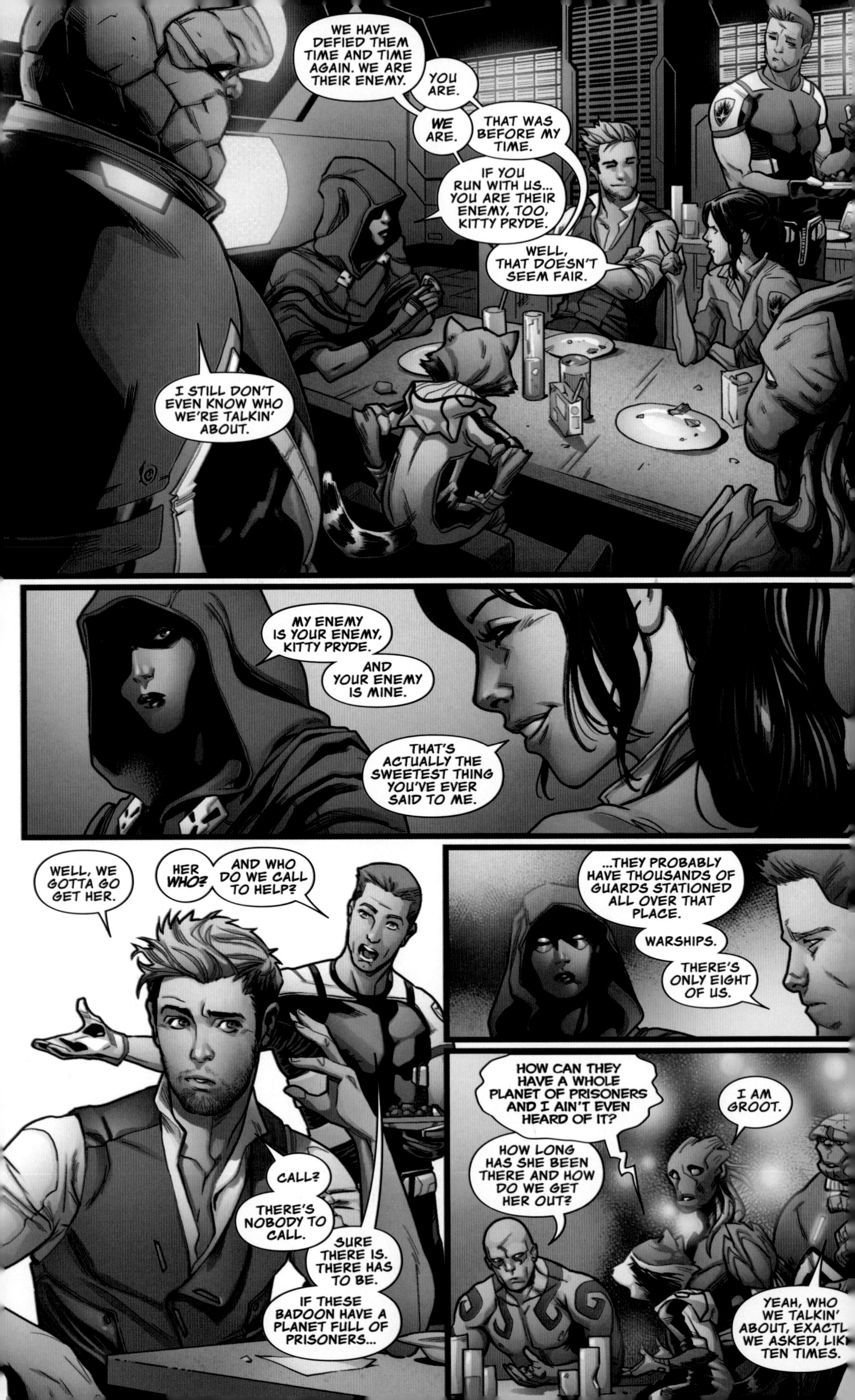
WE HAVE DEFIED THEM TIME AND TIME AGAIN. WE ARE THEIR ENEMY.
YOU ARE.
WE ARE.
THAT WAS BEFORE MY TIME.
IF YOU RUN WITH US... YOU ARE THEIR ENEMY, TOO, KITTY PRYDE.
WELL, THAT DOESN'T SEEM FAIR.
I STILL DON'T EVEN KNOW WHO WE'RE TALKIN' ABOUT.
MY ENEMY IS YOUR ENEMY, KITTY PRYDE.
AND YOUR ENEMY IS MINE.
THAT'S ACTUALLY THE SWEETEST THING YOU'VE EVER SAID TO ME.
WELL, WE GOTTA GO GET HER.
HER WHO?
AND WHO DO WE CALL TO HELP?
CALL?
THERE'S NOBODY TO CALL.
SURE THERE IS. THERE HAS TO BE.
IF THESE BADOON HAVE A PLANET FULL OF PRISONERS...
...THEY PROBABLY HAVE THOUSANDS OF GUARDS STATIONED ALL OVER THAT PLACE.
WARSHIPS.
THERE'S ONLY EIGHT OF US.
HOW CAN THEY HAVE A WHOLE PLANET OF PRISONERS AND I AIN'T EVEN HEARD OF IT?
I AM GROOT.
HOW LONG HAS SHE BEEN THERE AND HOW DO WE GET HER OUT?
YEAH, WHO WE TALKIN' ABOUT, EXACTL WE ASKED, LIK TEN TIMES.

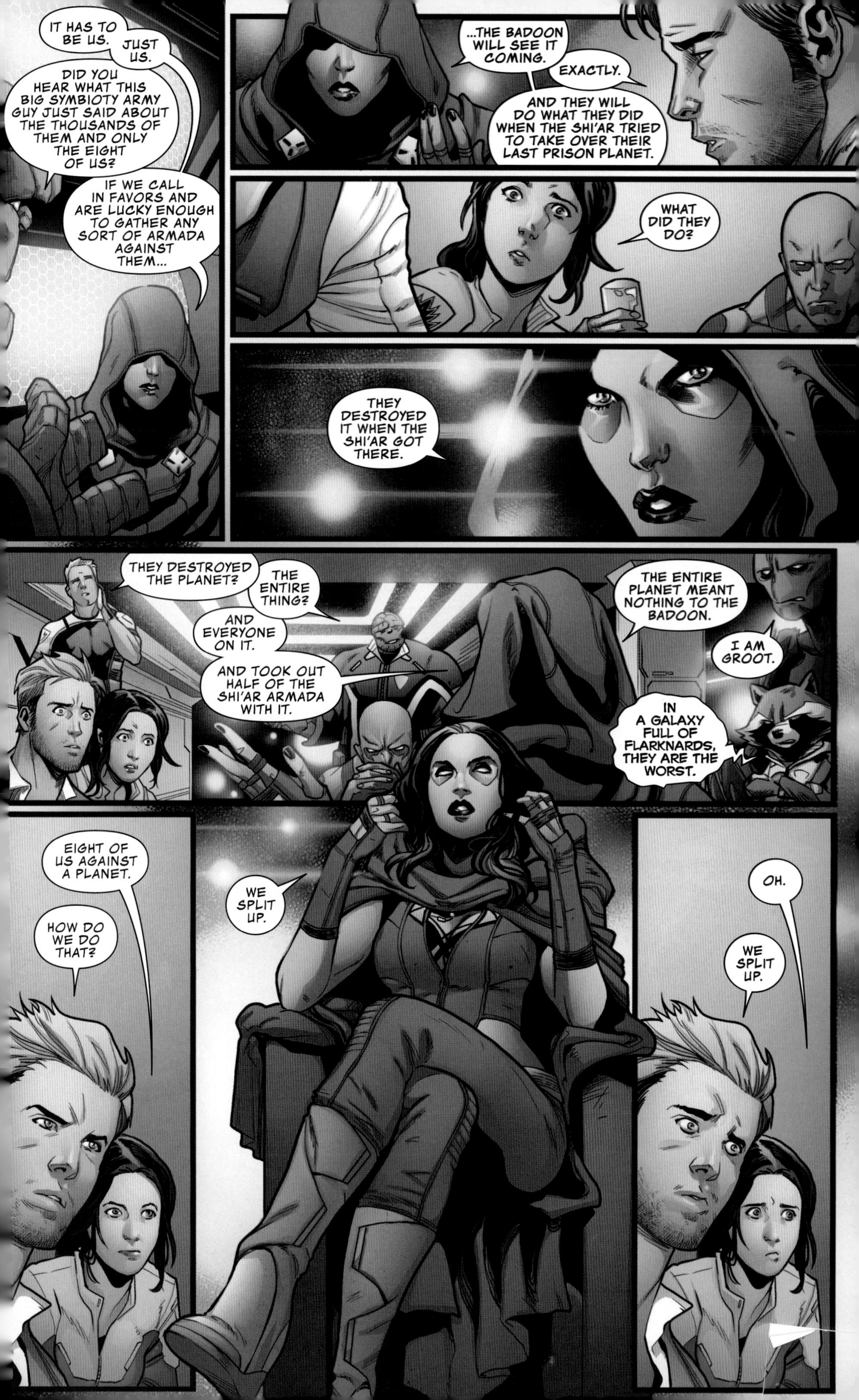

IT HAS TO BE US.
JUST US.
DID YOU HEAR WHAT THIS BIG SYMBIOTY ARMY GUY JUST SAID ABOUT THE THOUSANDS OF THEM AND ONLY THE EIGHT OF US?
IF WE CALL IN FAVORS AND ARE LUCKY ENOUGH TO GATHER ANY SORT OF ARMADA AGAINST THEM...
...THE BADOON WILL SEE IT COMING.
EXACTLY.
AND THEY WILL DO WHAT THEY DID WHEN THE SHI'AR TRIED TO TAKE OVER THEIR LAST PRISON PLANET.
WHAT DID THEY DO?
THEY DESTROYED IT WHEN THE SHI'AR GOT THERE.
THEY DESTROYED THE PLANET?
THE ENTIRE THING?
AND EVERYONE ON IT.
AND TOOK OUT HALF OF THE SHI'AR ARMADA WITH IT.
THE ENTIRE PLANET MEANT NOTHING TO THE BADOON.
I AM GROOT.
IN A GALAXY FULL OF FLARKNARDS, THEY ARE THE WORST.
EIGHT OF US AGAINST A PLANET.
HOW DO WE DO THAT?
WE SPLIT UP.
OH.
WE SPLIT UP.

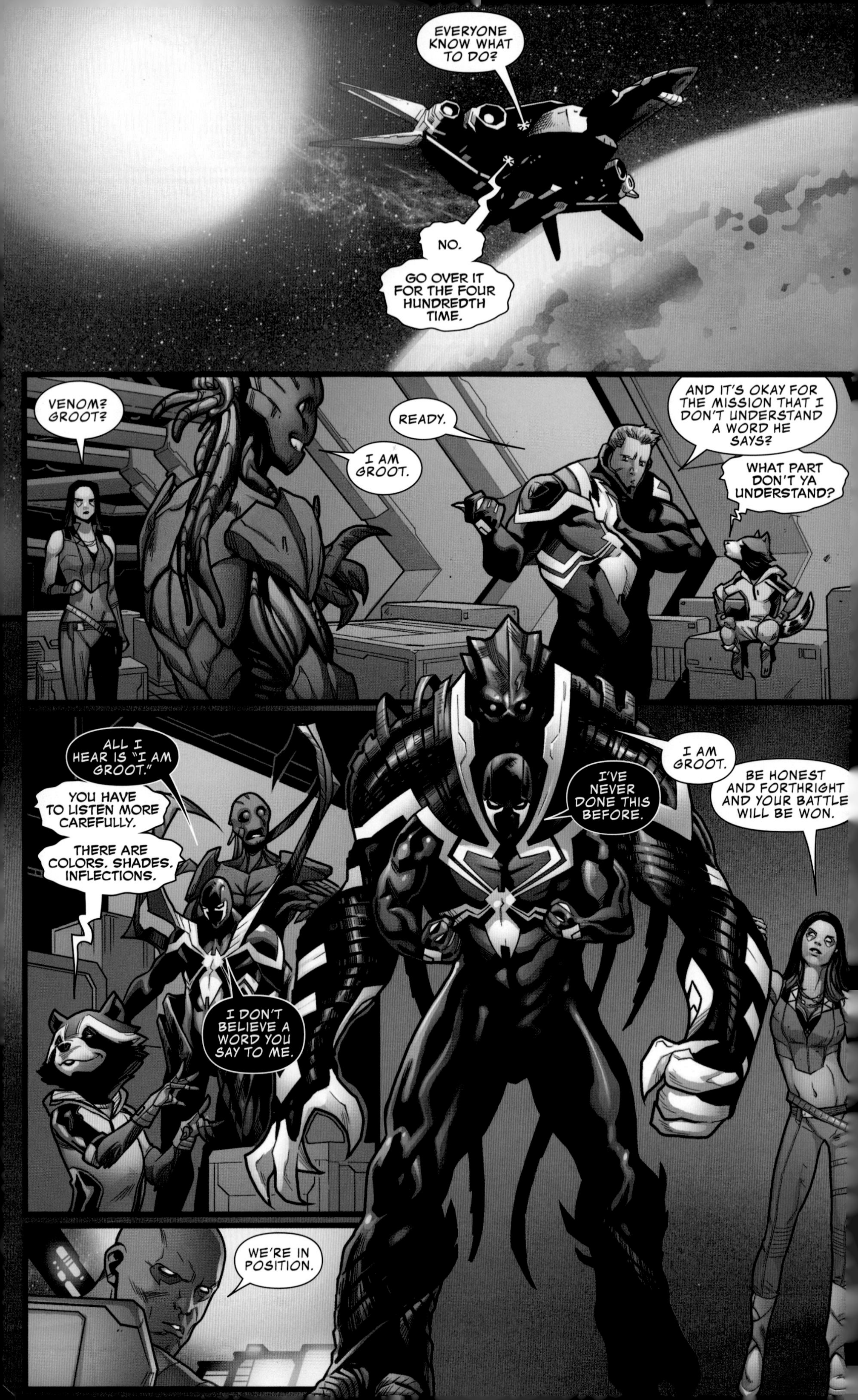
EVERYONE KNOW WHAT TO DO?
NO.
GO OVER IT FOR THE FOUR HUNDREDTH TIME.
VENOM? GROOT?
I AM GROOT.
READY.
AND IT'S OKAY FOR THE MISSION THAT I DON'T UNDERSTAND A WORD HE SAYS?
WHAT PART DON'T YA UNDERSTAND?
ALL I HEAR IS "I AM GROOT."
YOU HAVE TO LISTEN MORE CAREFULLY.
THERE ARE COLORS. SHADES. INFLECTIONS.
I DON'T BELIEVE A WORD YOU SAY TO ME.
I'VE NEVER DONE THIS BEFORE.
I AM GROOT.
BE HONEST AND FORTHRIGHT AND YOUR BATTLE WILL BE WON.
WE'RE IN POSITION.

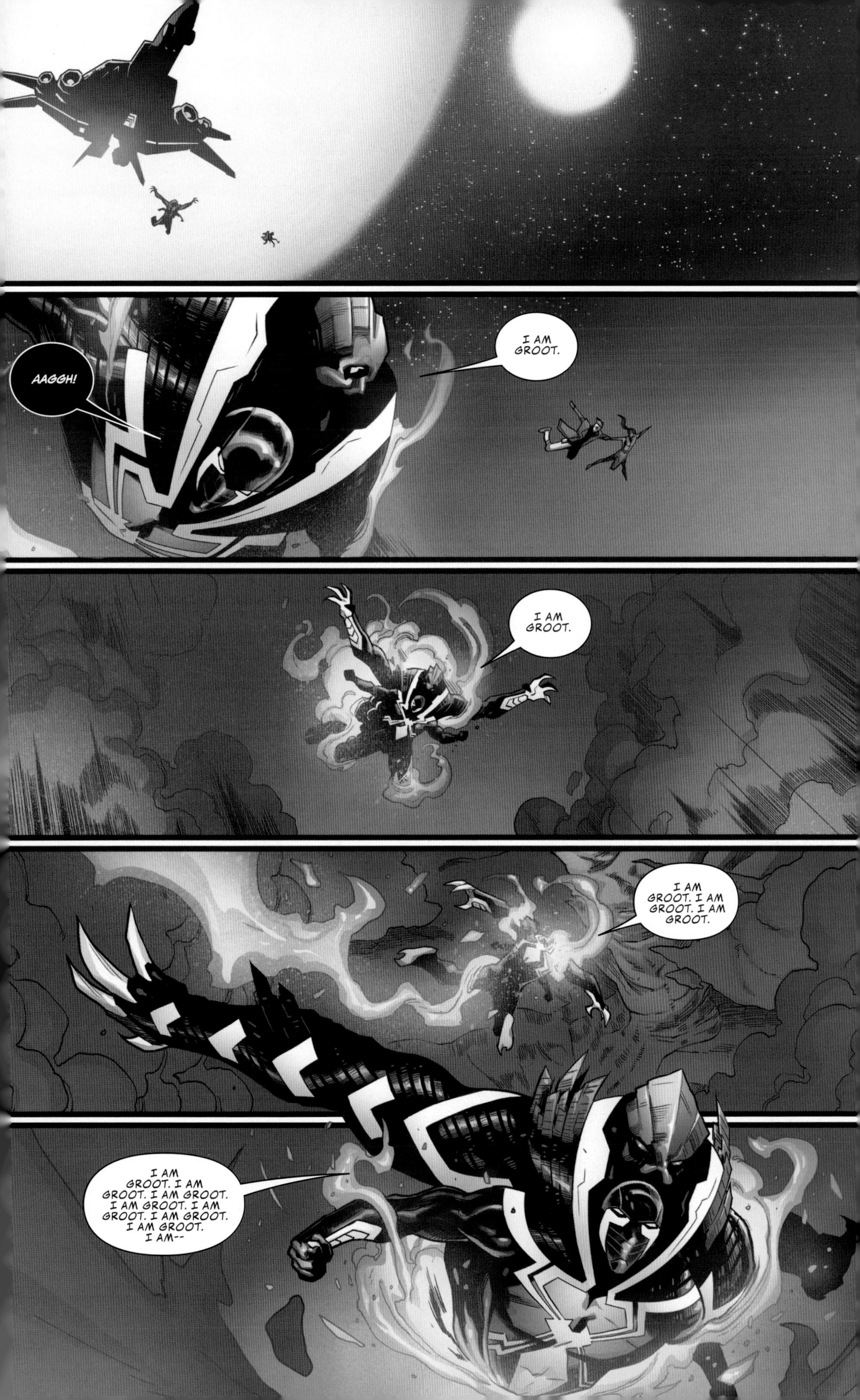
AAGGH!
I AM GROOT.
I AM GROOT.
I AM GROOT. I AM GROOT. I AM GROOT.
I AM GROOT. I AM GROOT. I AM GROOT. I AM GROOT. I AM GROOT. I AM GROOT. I AM GROOT. I AM--

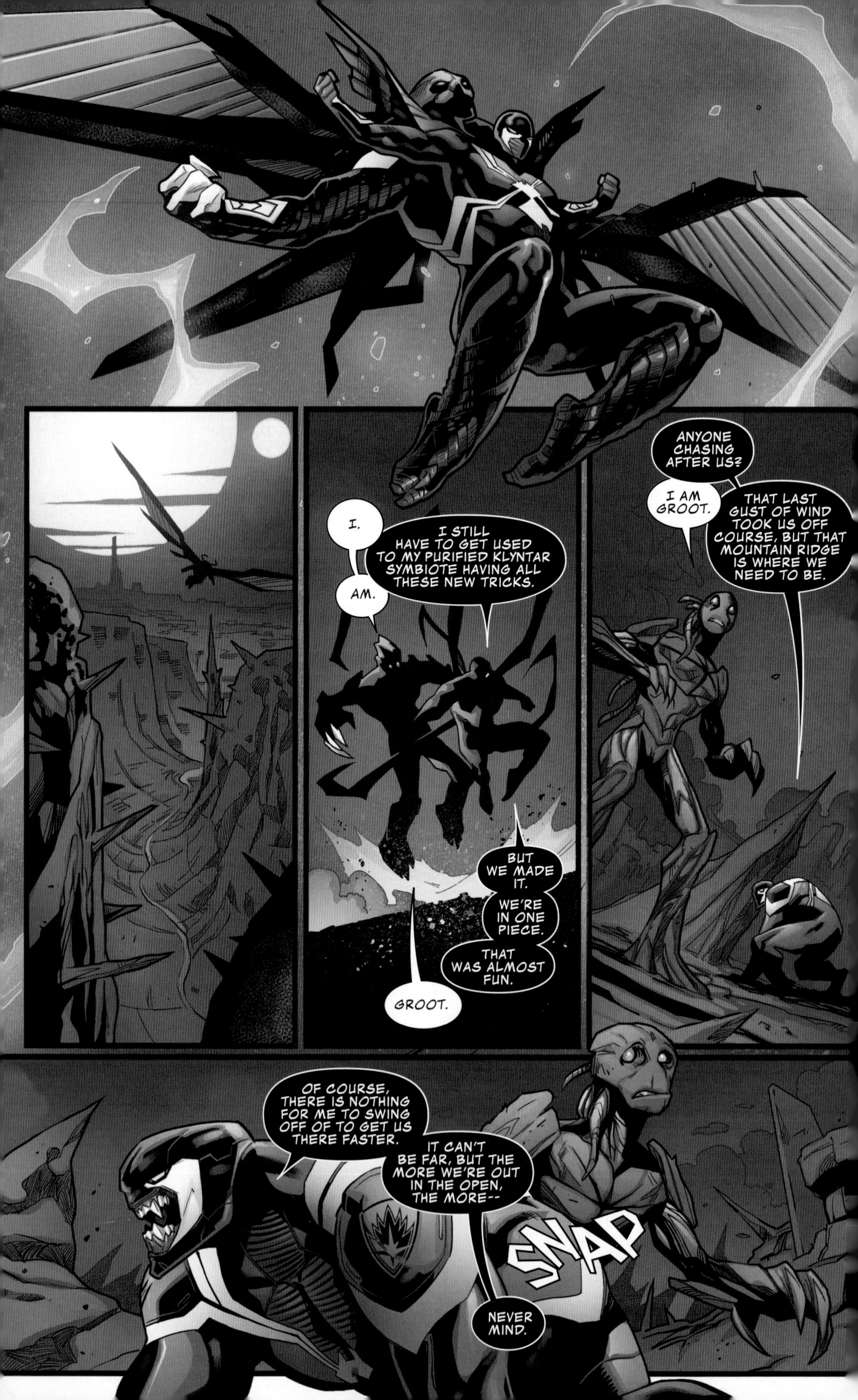

I.
I STILL HAVE TO GET USED TO MY PURIFIED KLYNTAR SYMBIOTE HAVING ALL THESE NEW TRICKS.
AM.
BUT WE MADE IT.
WE'RE IN ONE PIECE.
THAT WAS ALMOST FUN.
GROOT.
ANYONE CHASING AFTER US?
I AM GROOT.
THAT LAST GUST OF WIND TOOK US OFF COURSE, BUT THAT MOUNTAIN RIDGE IS WHERE WE NEED TO BE.
OF COURSE, THERE IS NOTHING FOR ME TO SWING OFF OF TO GET US THERE FASTER.
IT CAN'T BE FAR, BUT THE MORE WE'RE OUT IN THE OPEN, THE MORE--
SNAP
NEVER MIND.

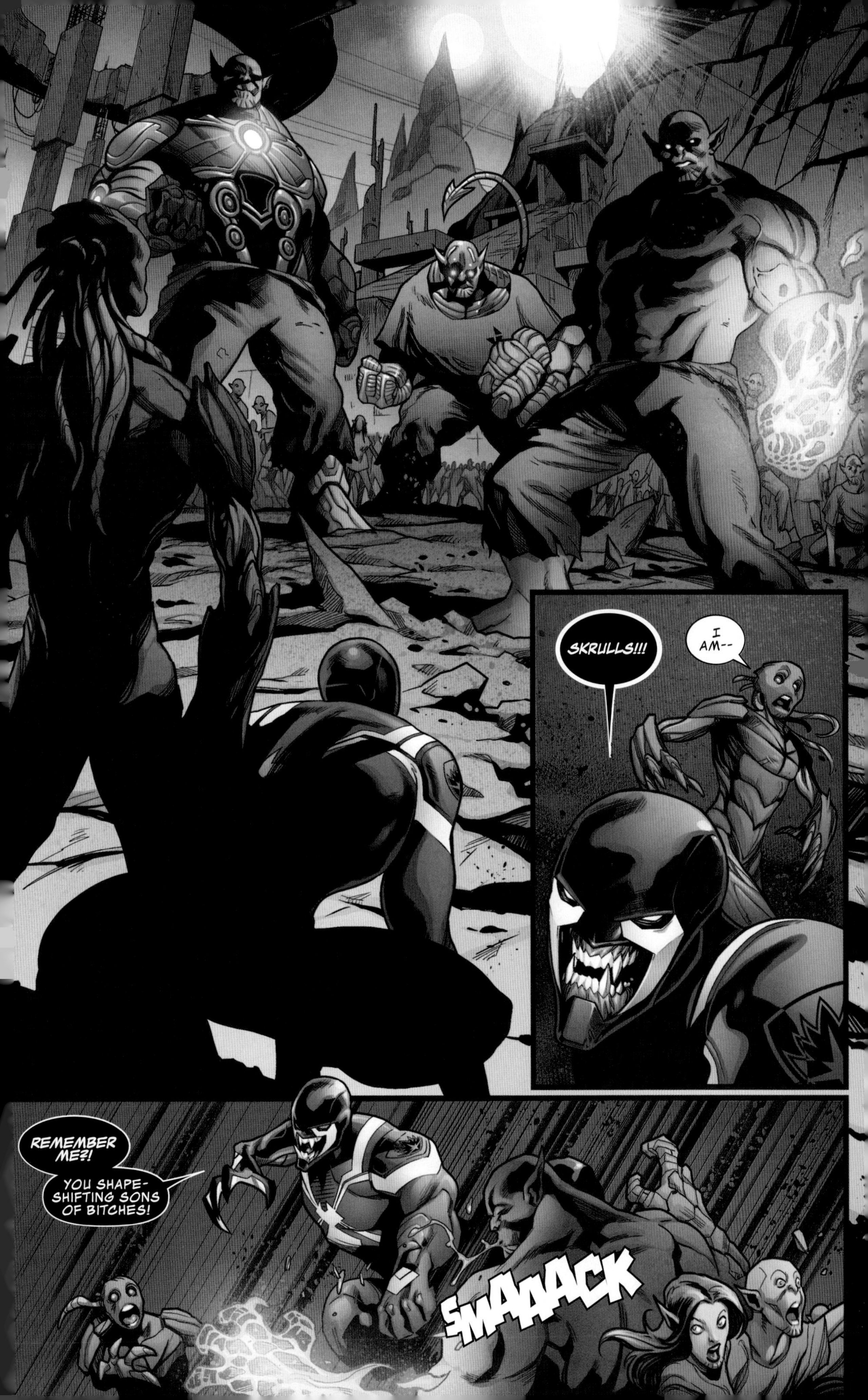
SKRULLS!!!
I AM--
REMEMBER ME?!
YOU SHAPE-SHIFTING SONS OF BITCHES!
SMAAACK

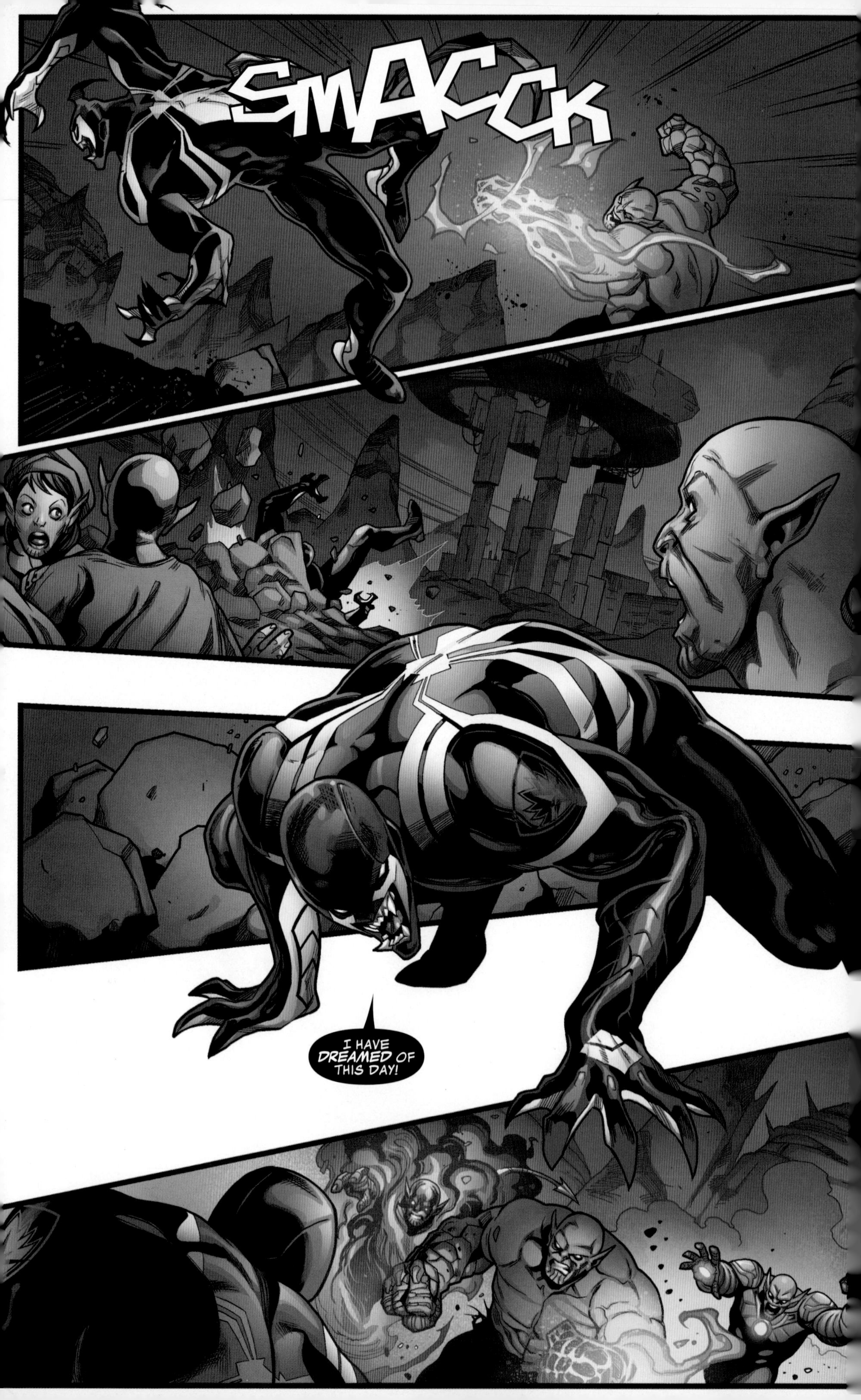
SMACCK
I HAVE DREAMED OF THIS DAY!

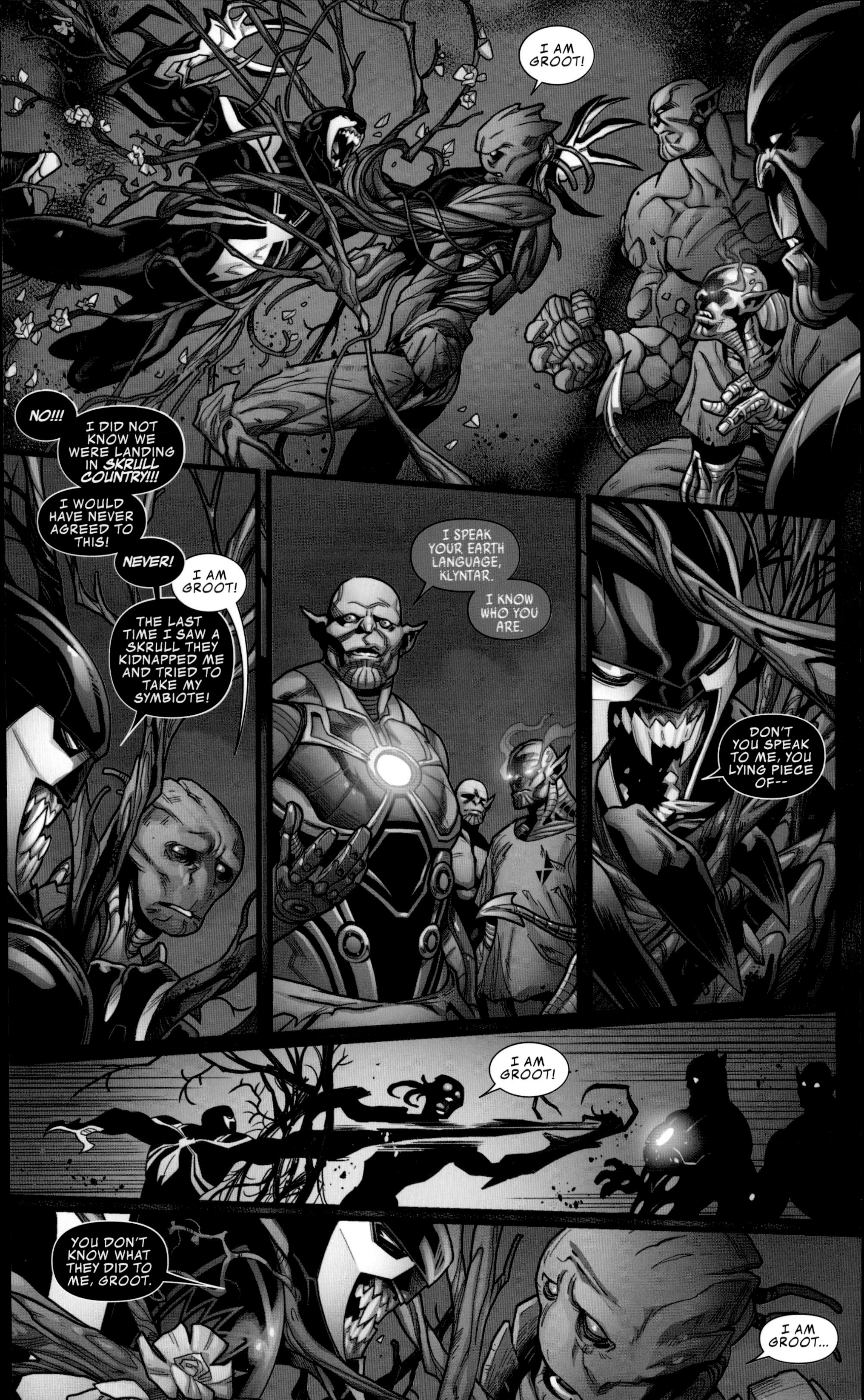
I AM GROOT!
NO!!!
I DID NOT KNOW WE WERE LANDING IN SKRULL COUNTRY!!!
I WOULD HAVE NEVER AGREED TO THIS!
NEVER!
I AM GROOT!
THE LAST TIME I SAW A SKRULL THEY KIDNAPPED ME AND TRIED TO TAKE MY SYMBIOTE!
I SPEAK YOUR EARTH LANGUAGE, KLYNTAR.
I KNOW WHO YOU ARE.
DON'T YOU SPEAK TO ME, YOU LYING PIECE OF--
I AM GROOT!
YOU DON'T KNOW WHAT THEY DID TO ME, GROOT.
I AM GROOT...

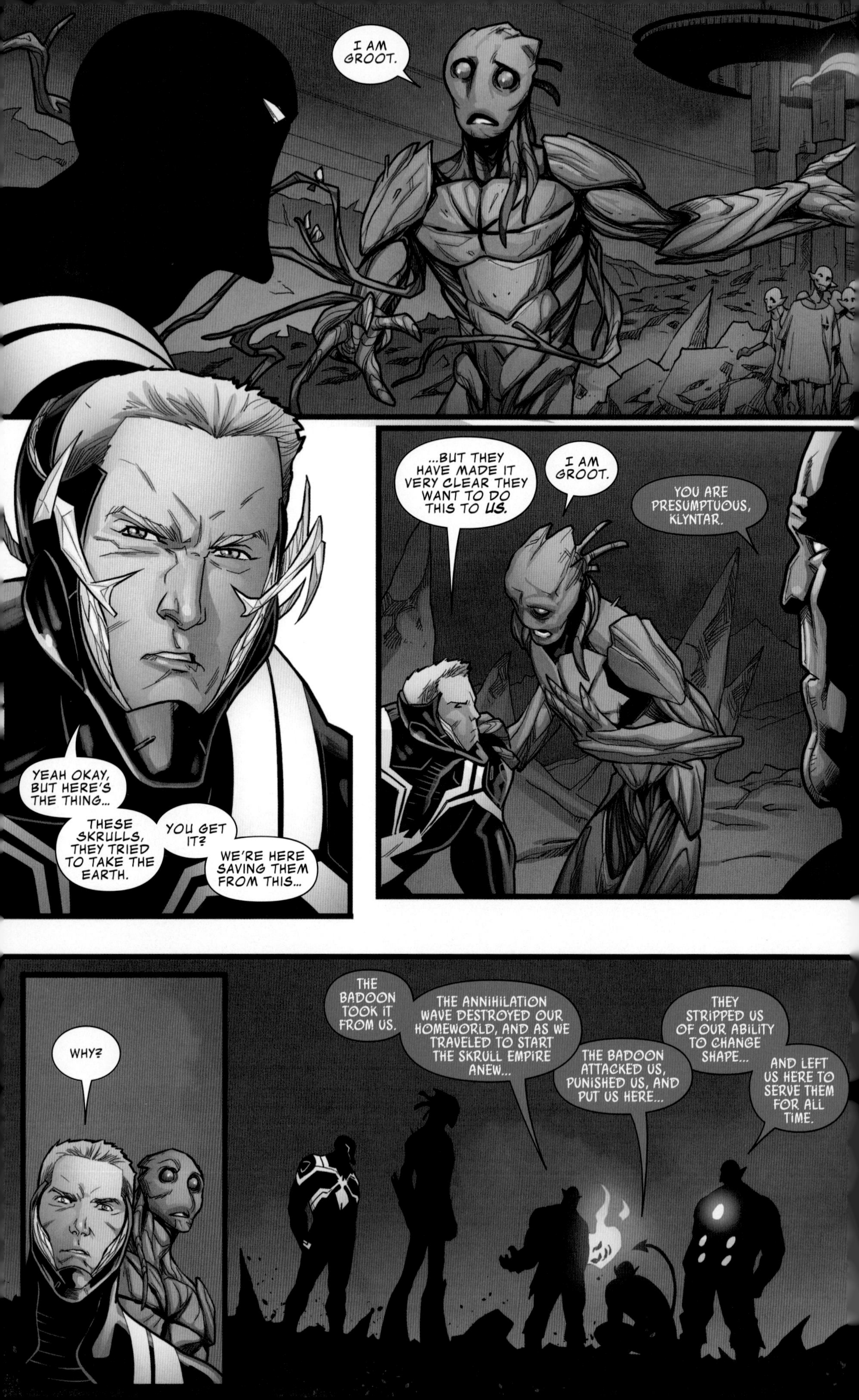

I AM GROOT.
YEAH OKAY, BUT HERE'S THE THING...
THESE SKRULLS, THEY TRIED TO TAKE THE EARTH.
YOU GET IT?
WE'RE HERE SAVING THEM FROM THIS...
...BUT THEY HAVE MADE IT VERY CLEAR THEY WANT TO DO THIS TO US.
I AM GROOT.
YOU ARE PRESUMPTUOUS, KLYNTAR.
WHY?
THE BADOON TOOK IT FROM US.
THE ANNIHILATION WAVE DESTROYED OUR HOMEWORLD, AND AS WE TRAVELED TO START THE SKRULL EMPIRE ANEW...
THE BADOON ATTACKED US, PUNISHED US, AND PUT US HERE...
THEY STRIPPED US OF OUR ABILITY TO CHANGE SHAPE...
AND LEFT US HERE TO SERVE THEM FOR ALL TIME.

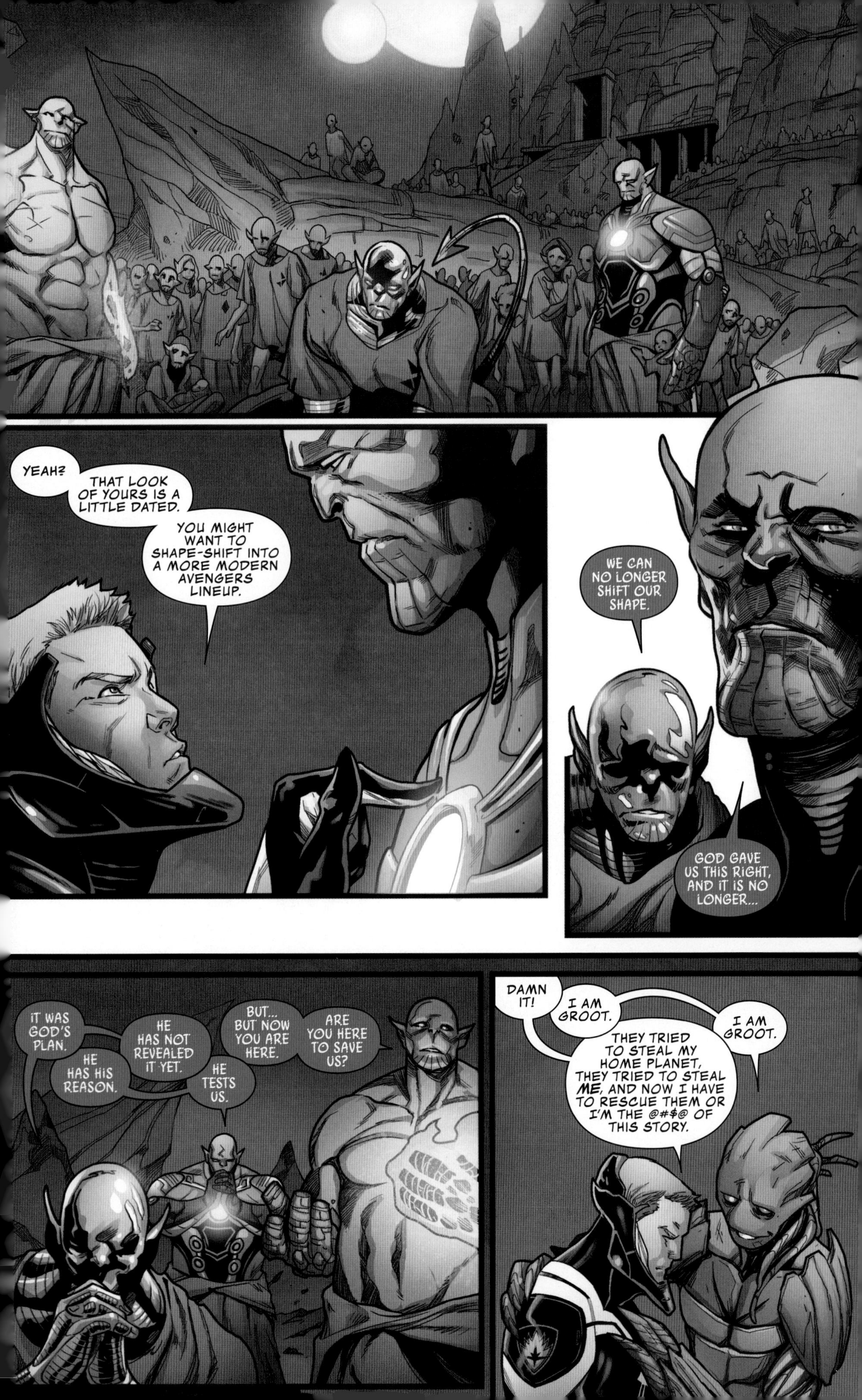
YEAH?
THAT LOOK OF YOURS IS A LITTLE DATED.
YOU MIGHT WANT TO SHAPE-SHIFT INTO A MORE MODERN AVENGERS LINEUP.
WE CAN NO LONGER SHIFT OUR SHAPE.
GOD GAVE US THIS RIGHT, AND IT IS NO LONGER...
IT WAS GOD'S PLAN.
HE HAS HIS REASON.
HE HAS NOT REVEALED IT YET.
HE TESTS US.
BUT... BUT NOW YOU ARE HERE.
ARE YOU HERE TO SAVE US?
DAMN IT!
I AM GROOT.
I AM GROOT.
THEY TRIED TO STEAL MY HOME PLANET, THEY TRIED TO STEAL ME, AND NOW I HAVE TO RESCUE THEM OR I'M THE @#$@ OF THIS STORY.

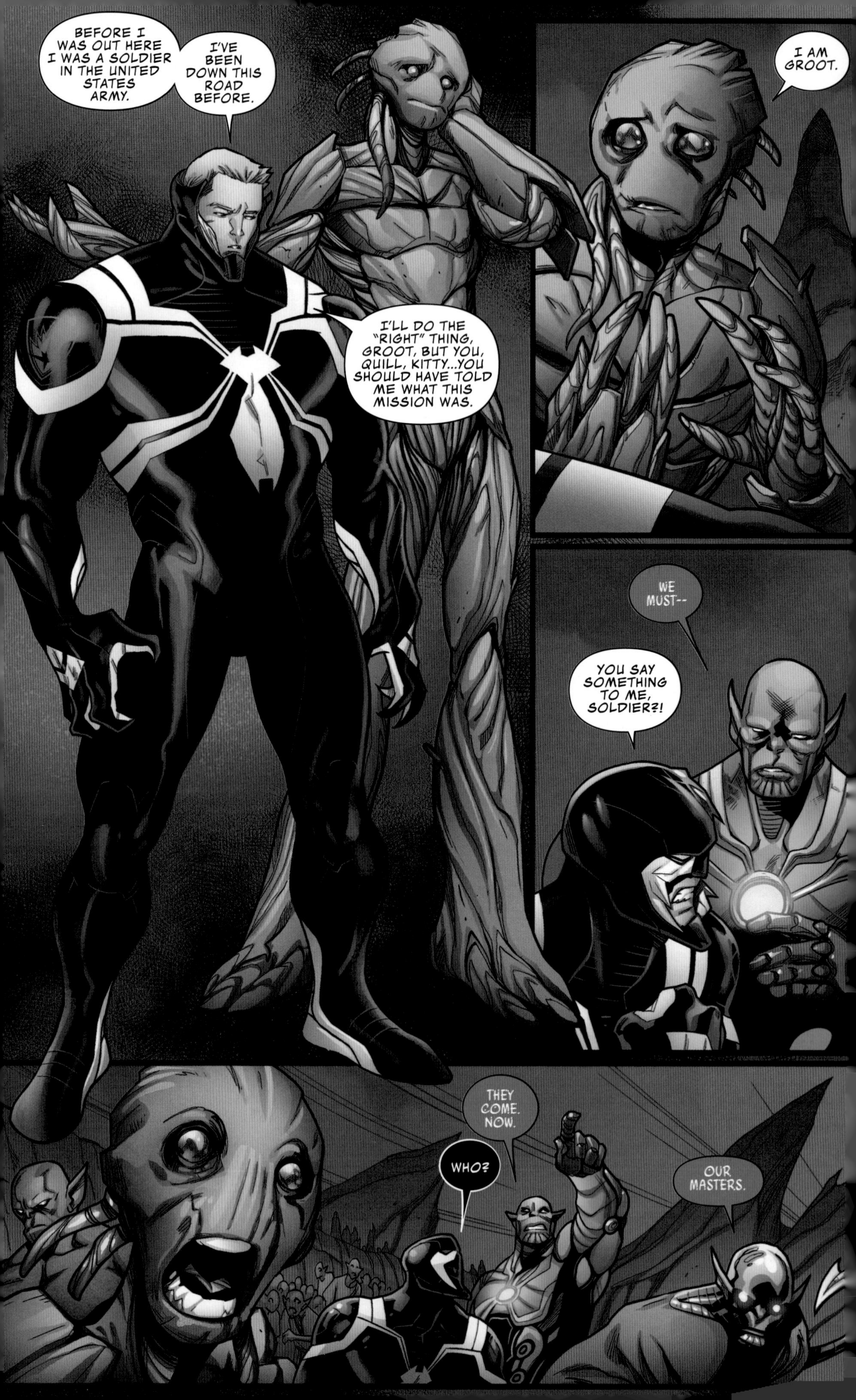
BEFORE I WAS OUT HERE I WAS A SOLDIER IN THE UNITED STATES ARMY.
I'VE BEEN DOWN THIS ROAD BEFORE.
I'LL DO THE "RIGHT" THING, GROOT, BUT YOU, QUILL, KITTY...YOU SHOULD HAVE TOLD ME WHAT THIS MISSION WAS.
I AM GROOT.
WE MUST--
YOU SAY SOMETHING TO ME, SOLDIER?!
THEY COME. NOW.
WHO?
OUR MASTERS.

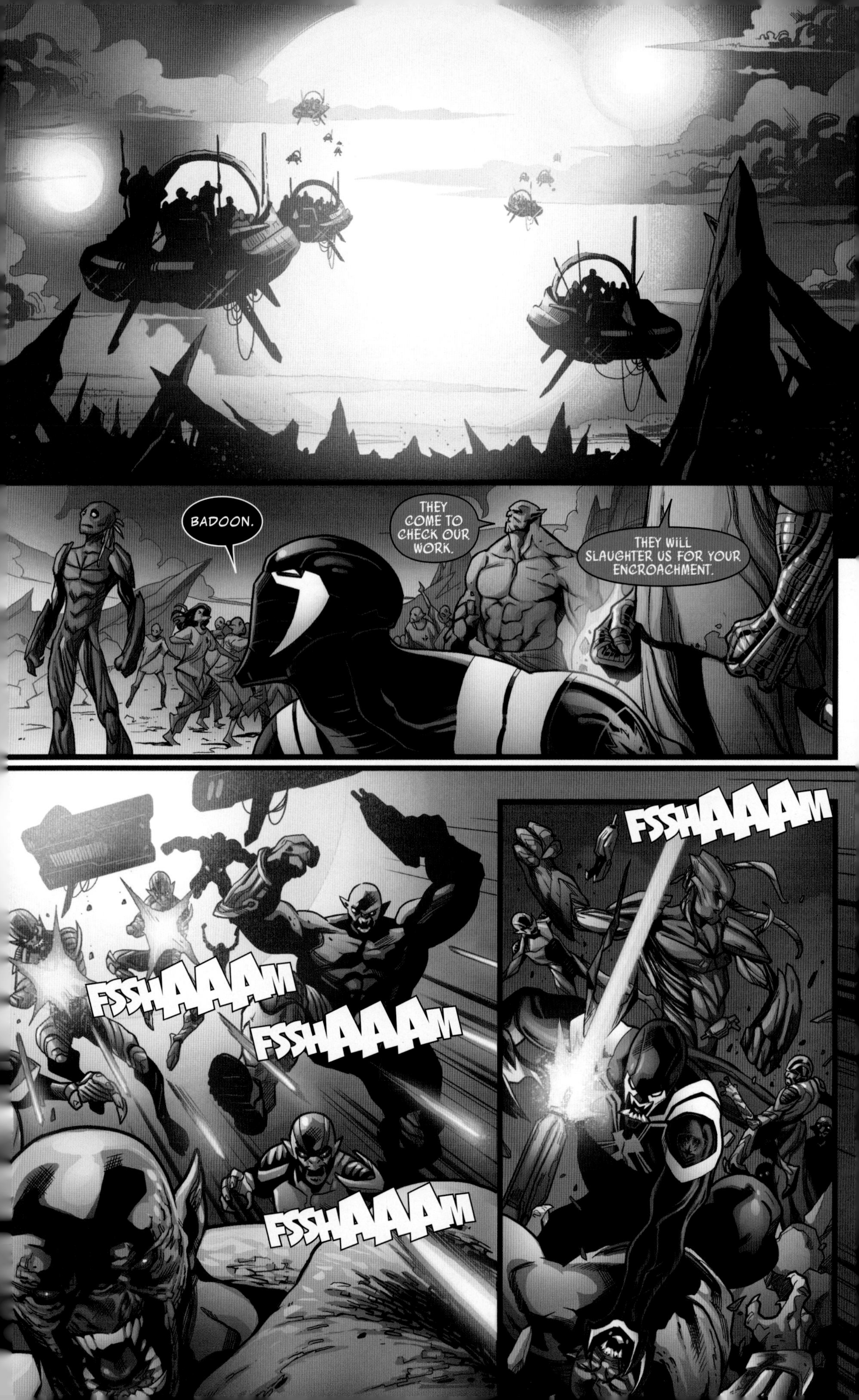
BADOON.
THEY COME TO CHECK OUR WORK.
THEY WILL SLAUGHTER US FOR YOUR ENCROACHMENT.
FSSHAAAM
FSSHAAAM
FSSHAAAM
FSSHAAAM

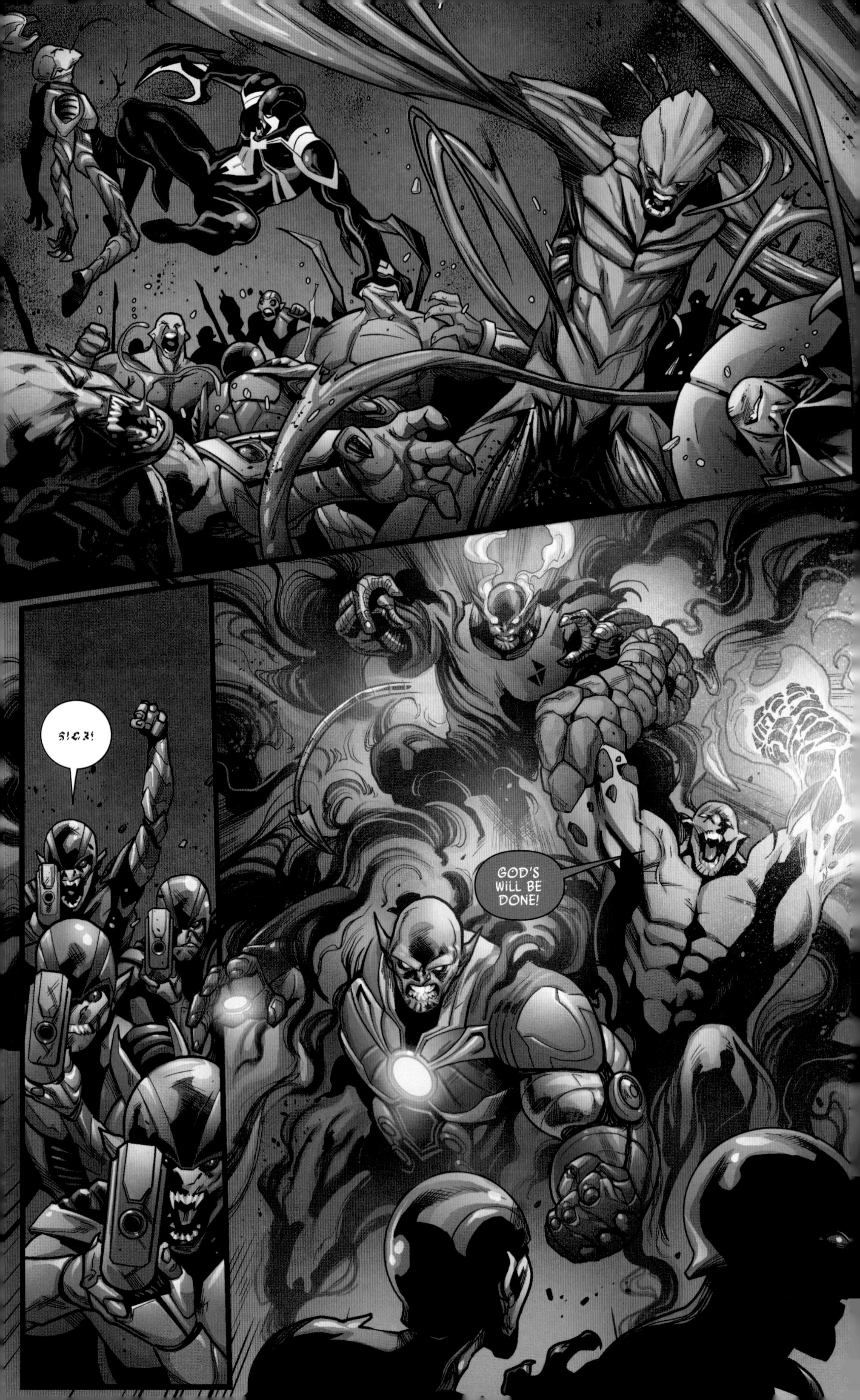
GOD'S WILL BE DONE!

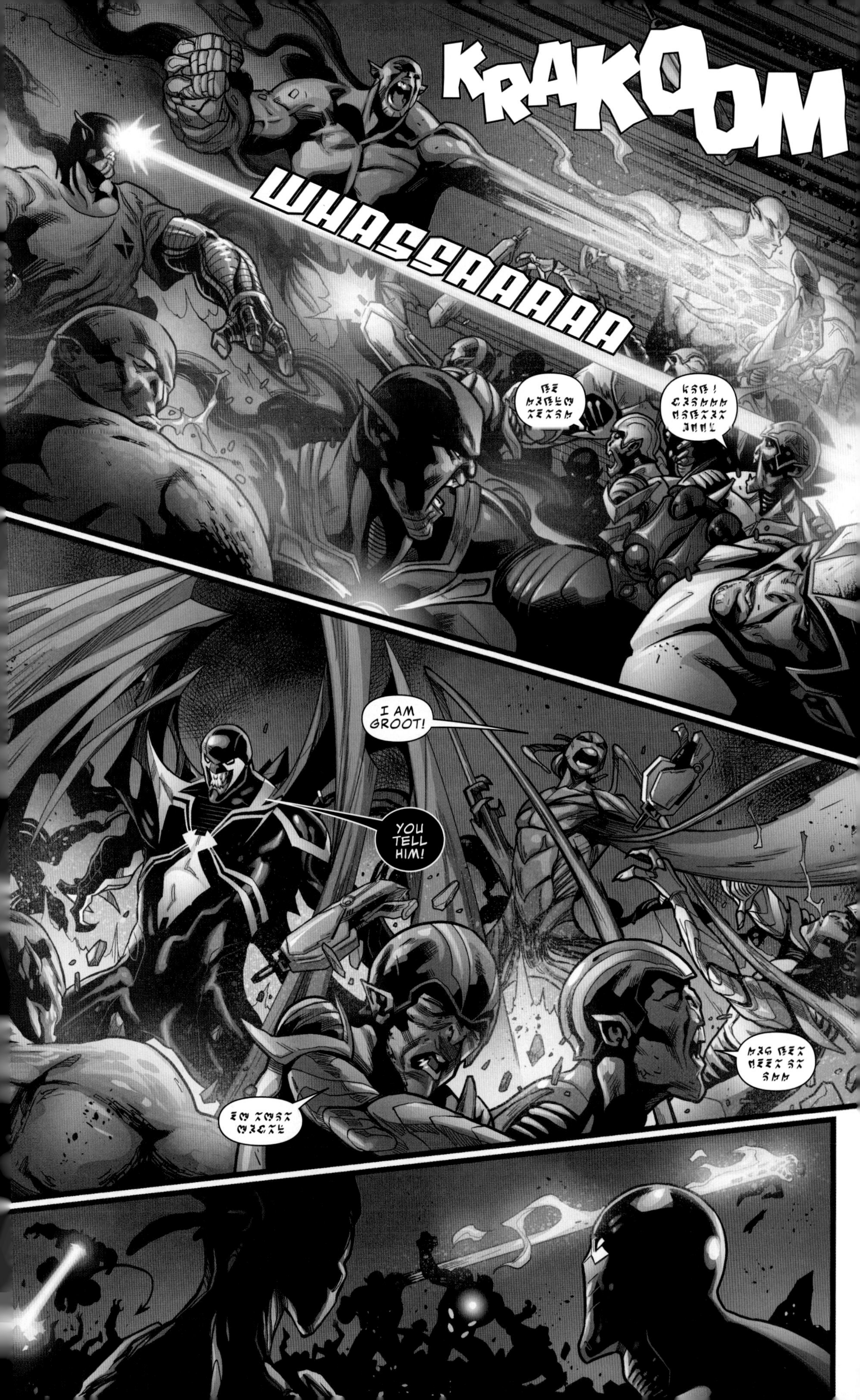
KRAKOOOM
WHASSAAAAAA
I AM GROOT!
YOU TELL HIM!

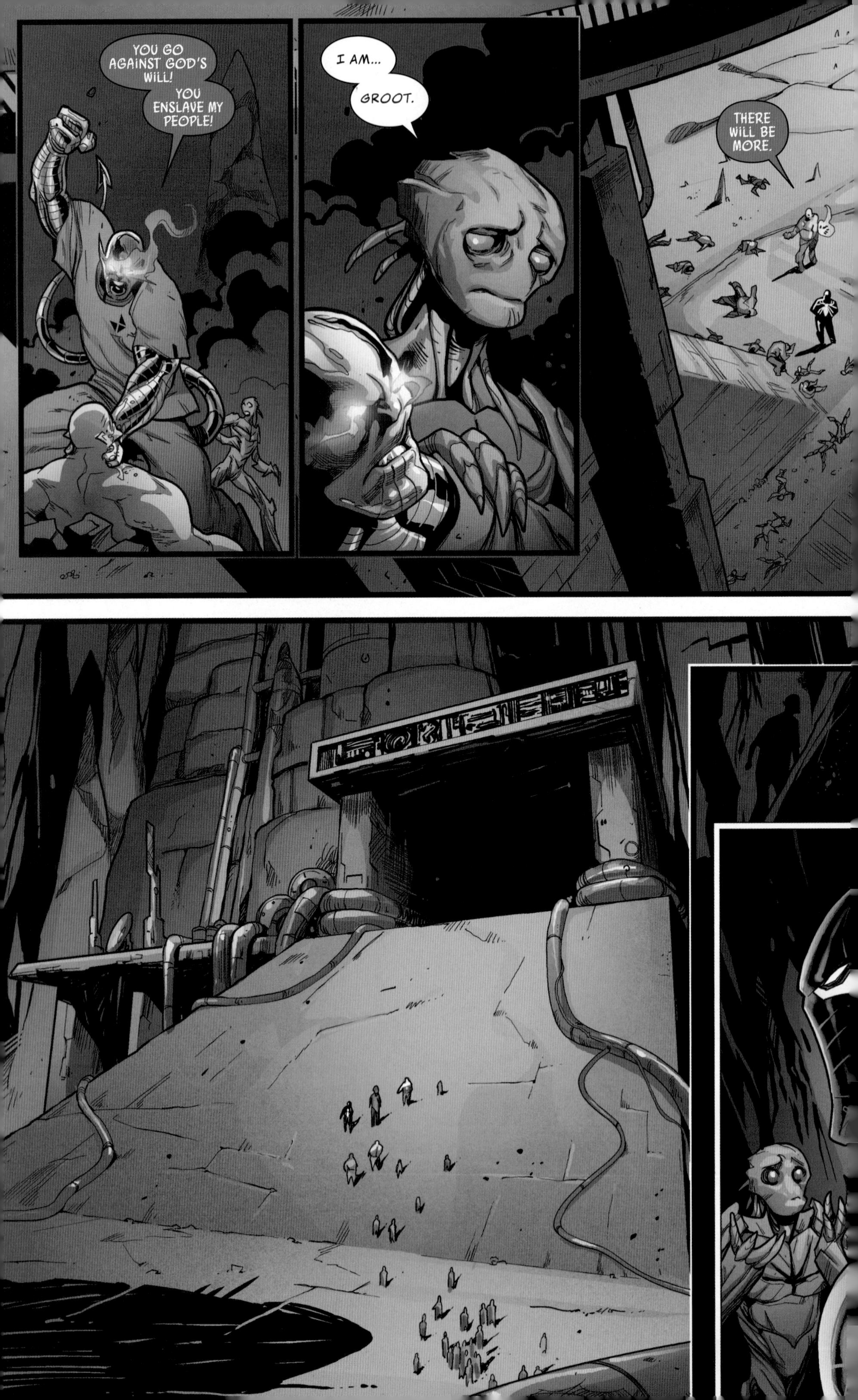
YOU GO AGAINST GOD'S WILL!
YOU ENSLAVE MY PEOPLE!
I AM...
GROOT.
THERE WILL BE MORE.

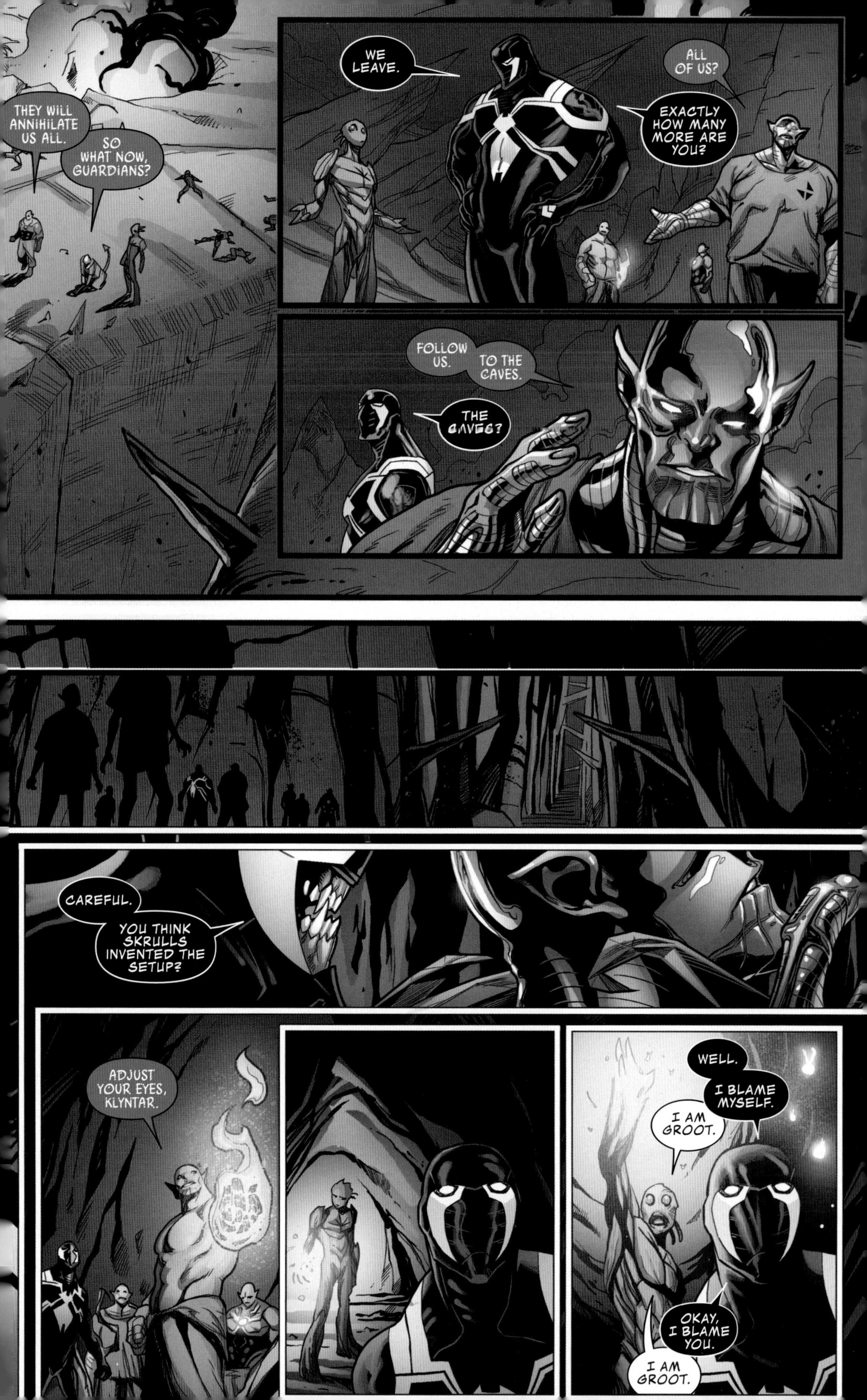
THEY WILL ANNIHILATE US ALL.
SO WHAT NOW, GUARDIANS?
WE LEAVE.
ALL OF US?
EXACTLY HOW MANY MORE ARE YOU?
FOLLOW US.
TO THE CAVES.
THE CAVES?
CAREFUL.
YOU THINK SKRULLS INVENTED THE SETUP?
ADJUST YOUR EYES, KLYNTAR.
WELL.
I BLAME MYSELF.
I AM GROOT.
OKAY, I BLAME YOU.
I AM GROOT.

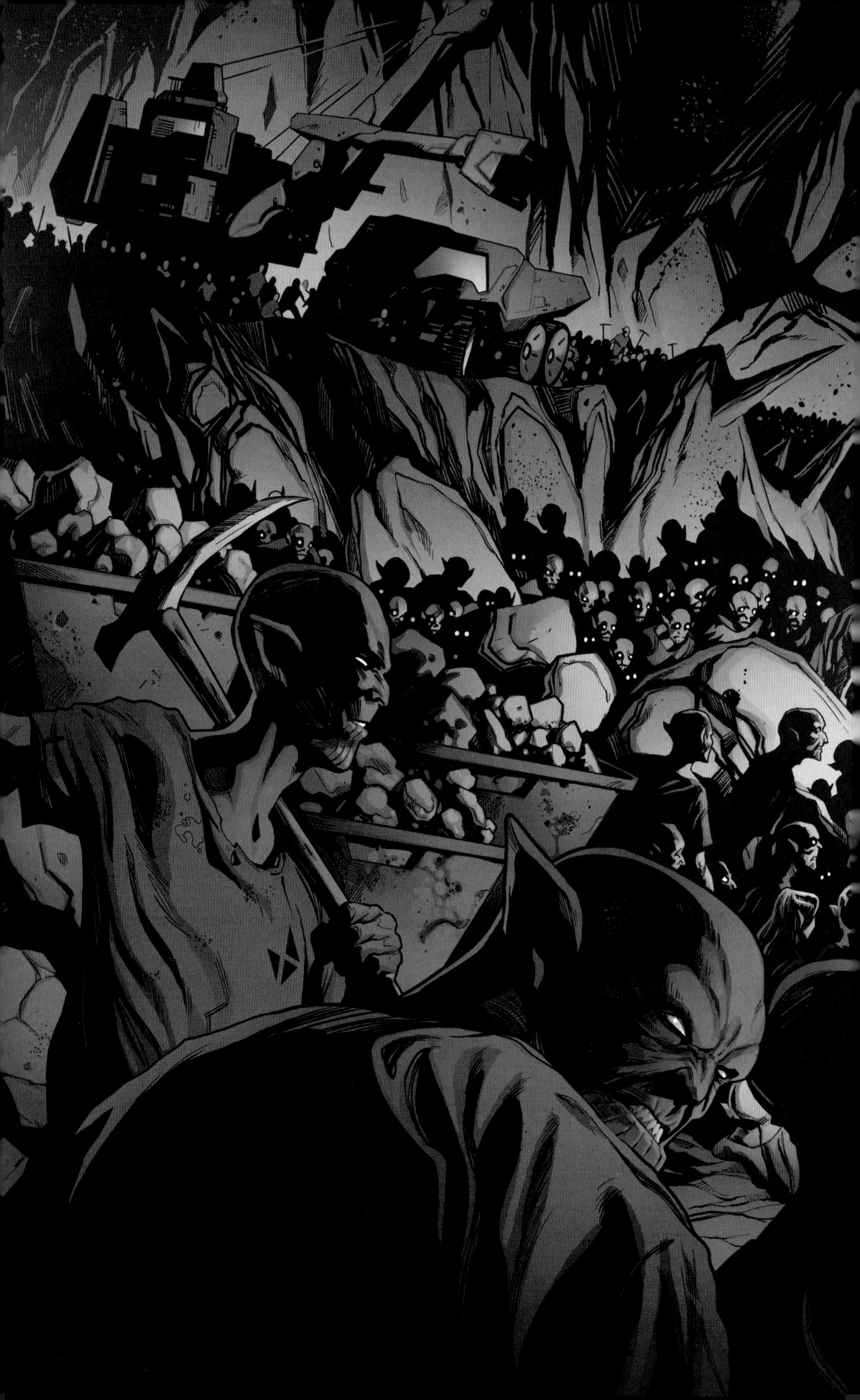

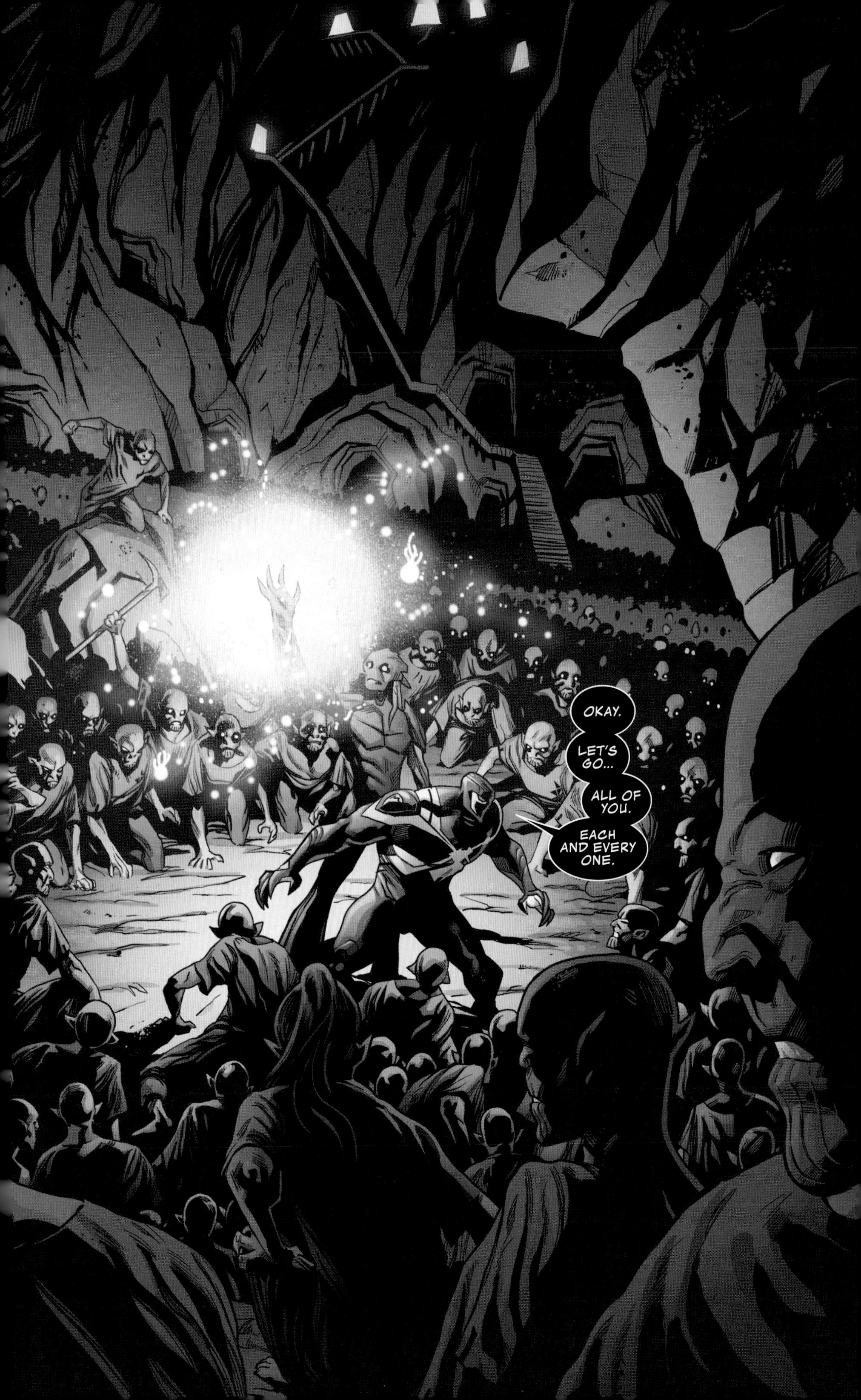
OKAY.
LET'S GO...
ALL OF YOU.
EACH AND EVERY ONE.

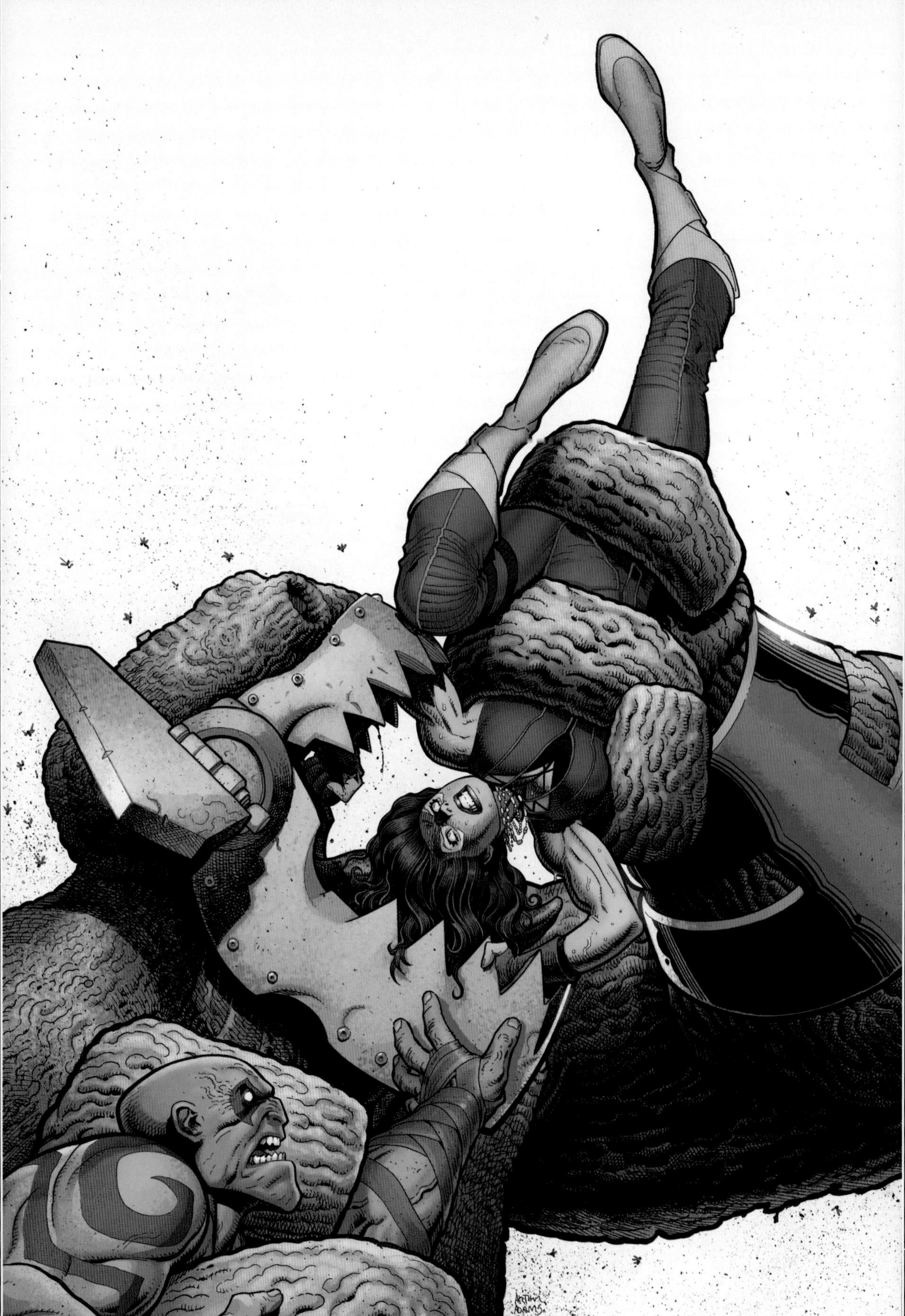

9

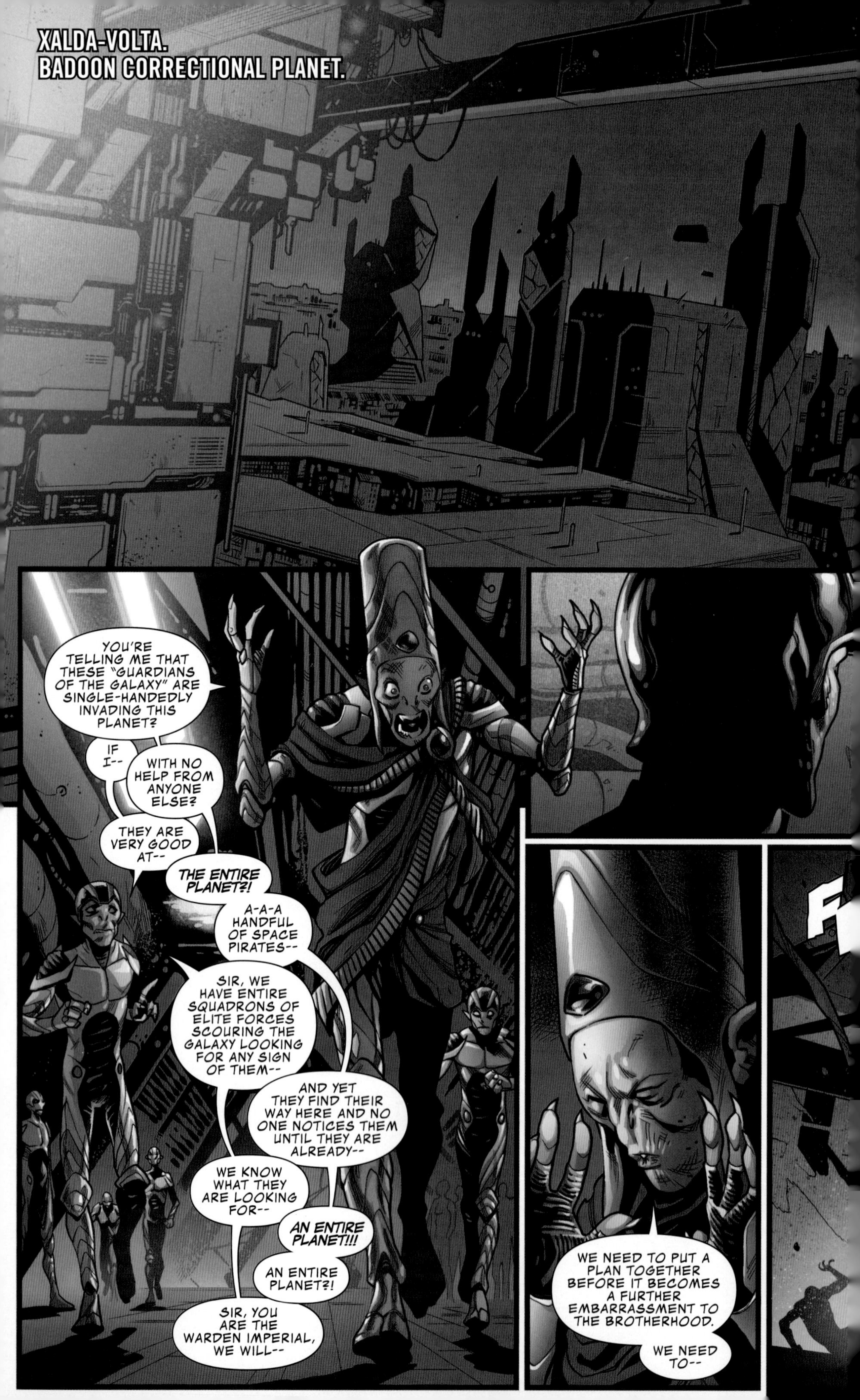
XALDA-VOLTA.
BADOON CORRECTIONAL PLANET.
YOU'RE TELLING ME THAT THESE "GUARDIANS OF THE GALAXY" ARE SINGLE-HANDEDLY INVADING THIS PLANET?
IF I--
WITH NO HELP FROM ANYONE ELSE?
THEY ARE VERY GOOD AT--
THE ENTIRE PLANET?!
A-A-A HANDFUL OF SPACE PIRATES--
SIR, WE HAVE ENTIRE SQUADRONS OF ELITE FORCES SCOURING THE GALAXY LOOKING FOR ANY SIGN OF THEM--
AND YET THEY FIND THEIR WAY HERE AND NO ONE NOTICES THEM UNTIL THEY ARE ALREADY--
WE KNOW WHAT THEY ARE LOOKING FOR--
AN ENTIRE PLANET!!!
AN ENTIRE PLANET?!
SIR, YOU ARE THE WARDEN IMPERIAL, WE WILL--
WE NEED TO PUT A PLAN TOGETHER BEFORE IT BECOMES A FURTHER EMBARRASSMENT TO THE BROTHERHOOD.
WE NEED TO--

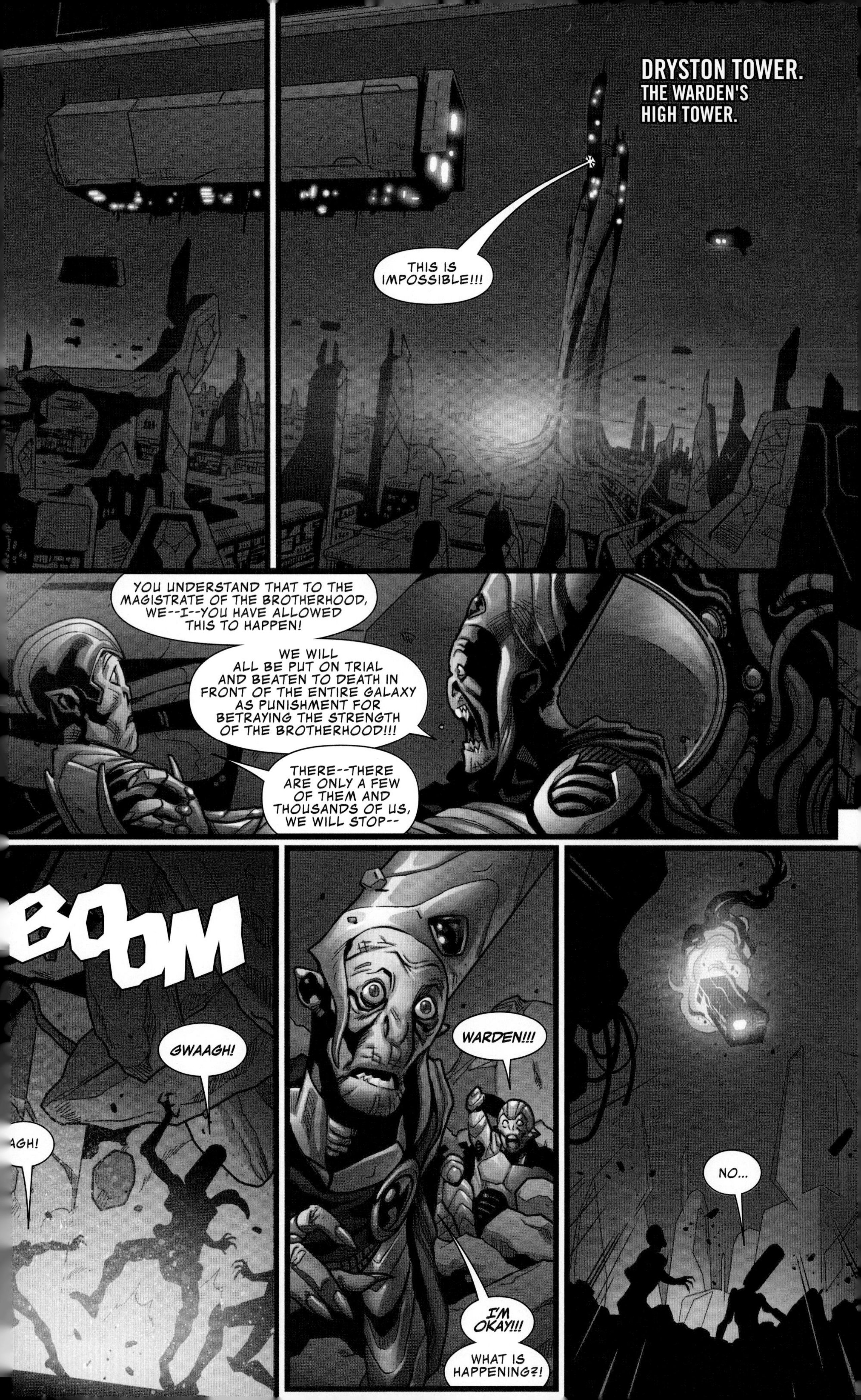
DRYSTON TOWER.
THE WARDEN'S HIGH TOWER.
THIS IS IMPOSSIBLE!!!
YOU UNDERSTAND THAT TO THE MAGISTRATE OF THE BROTHERHOOD, WE--I--YOU HAVE ALLOWED THIS TO HAPPEN!
WE WILL ALL BE PUT ON TRIAL AND BEATEN TO DEATH IN FRONT OF THE ENTIRE GALAXY AS PUNISHMENT FOR BETRAYING THE STRENGTH OF THE BROTHERHOOD!!!
THERE--THERE ARE ONLY A FEW OF THEM AND THOUSANDS OF US, WE WILL STOP--
BOOM
GWAAGH!
AGH!
WARDEN!!!
I'M OKAY!!!
WHAT IS HAPPENING?!
NO...

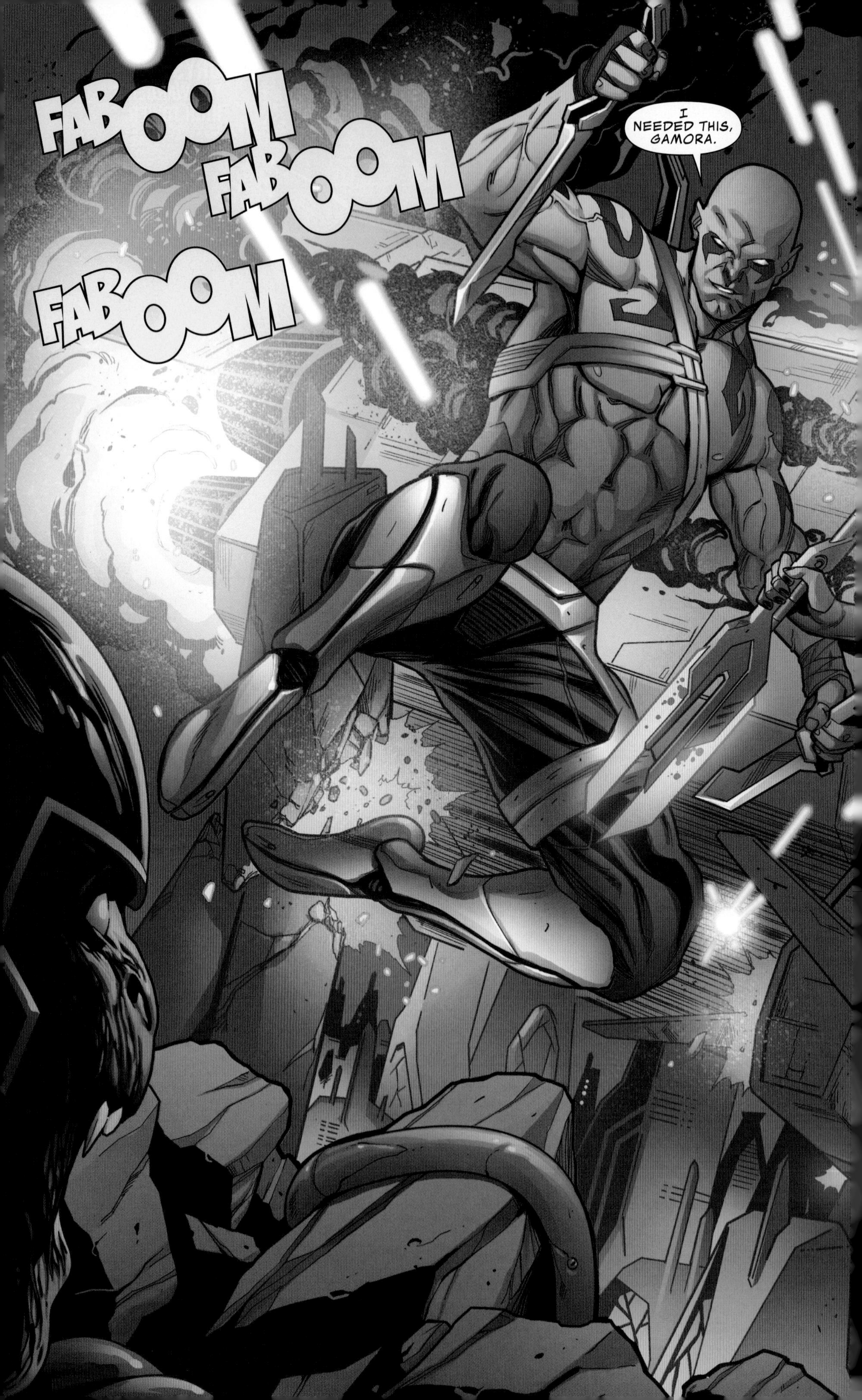
FABOOM
I NEEDED THIS, GAMORA.
FABOOM
FABOOM

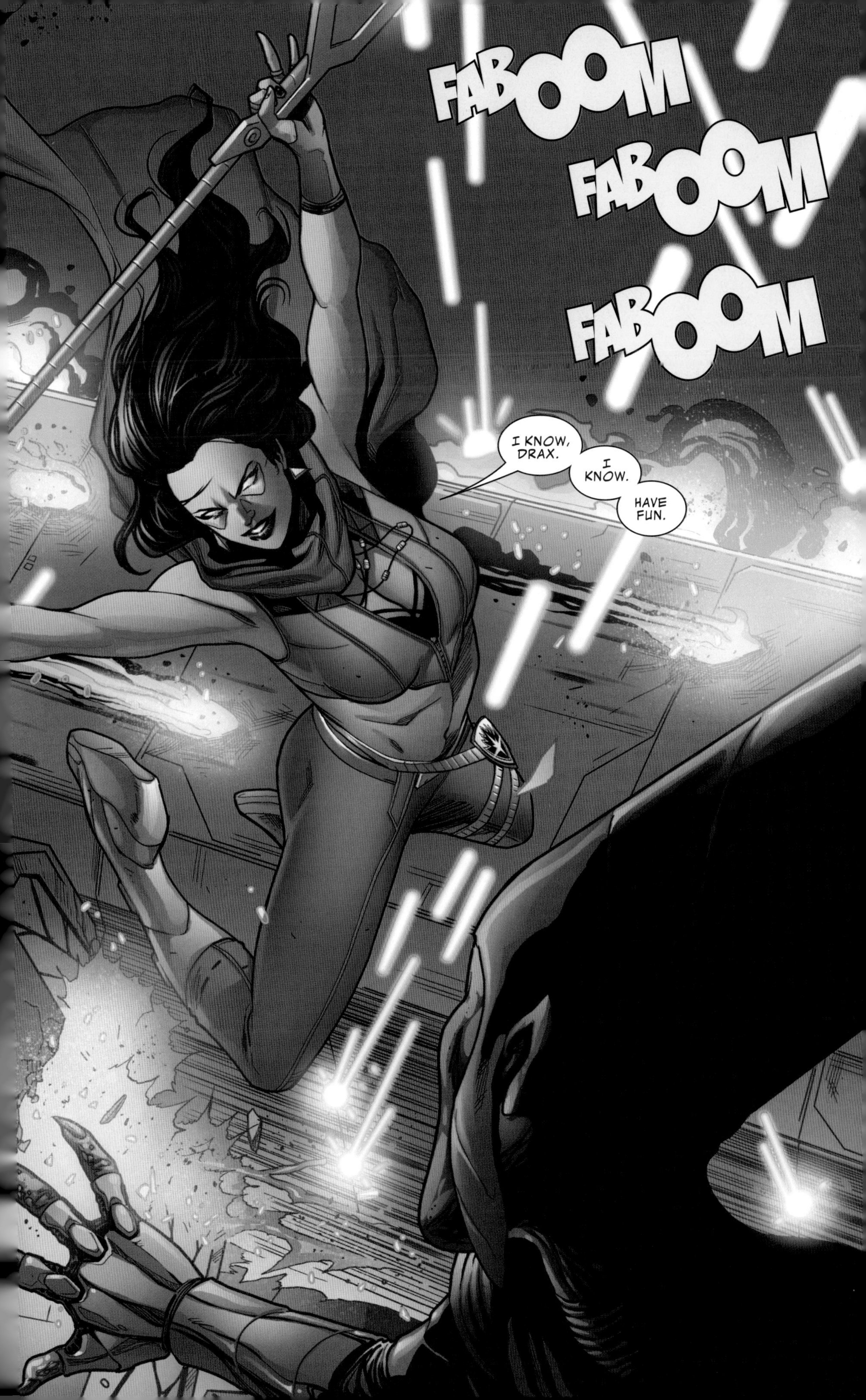
FABOOM
FABOOM
FABOOM
I KNOW, DRAX.
I KNOW.
HAVE FUN.

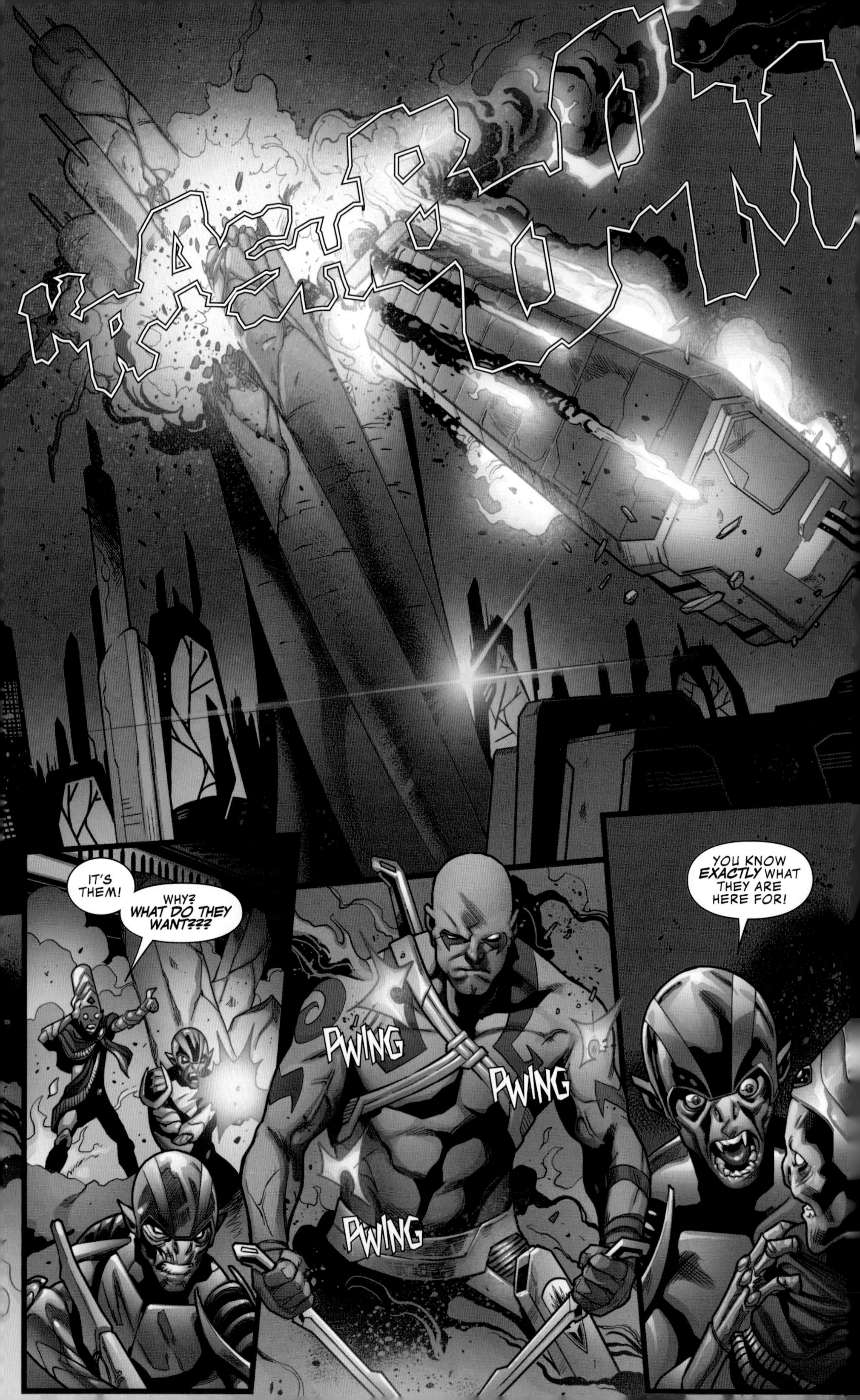
IT'S THEM!
WHY? WHAT DO THEY WANT???
PWING
PWING
PWING
YOU KNOW EXACTLY WHAT THEY ARE HERE FOR!

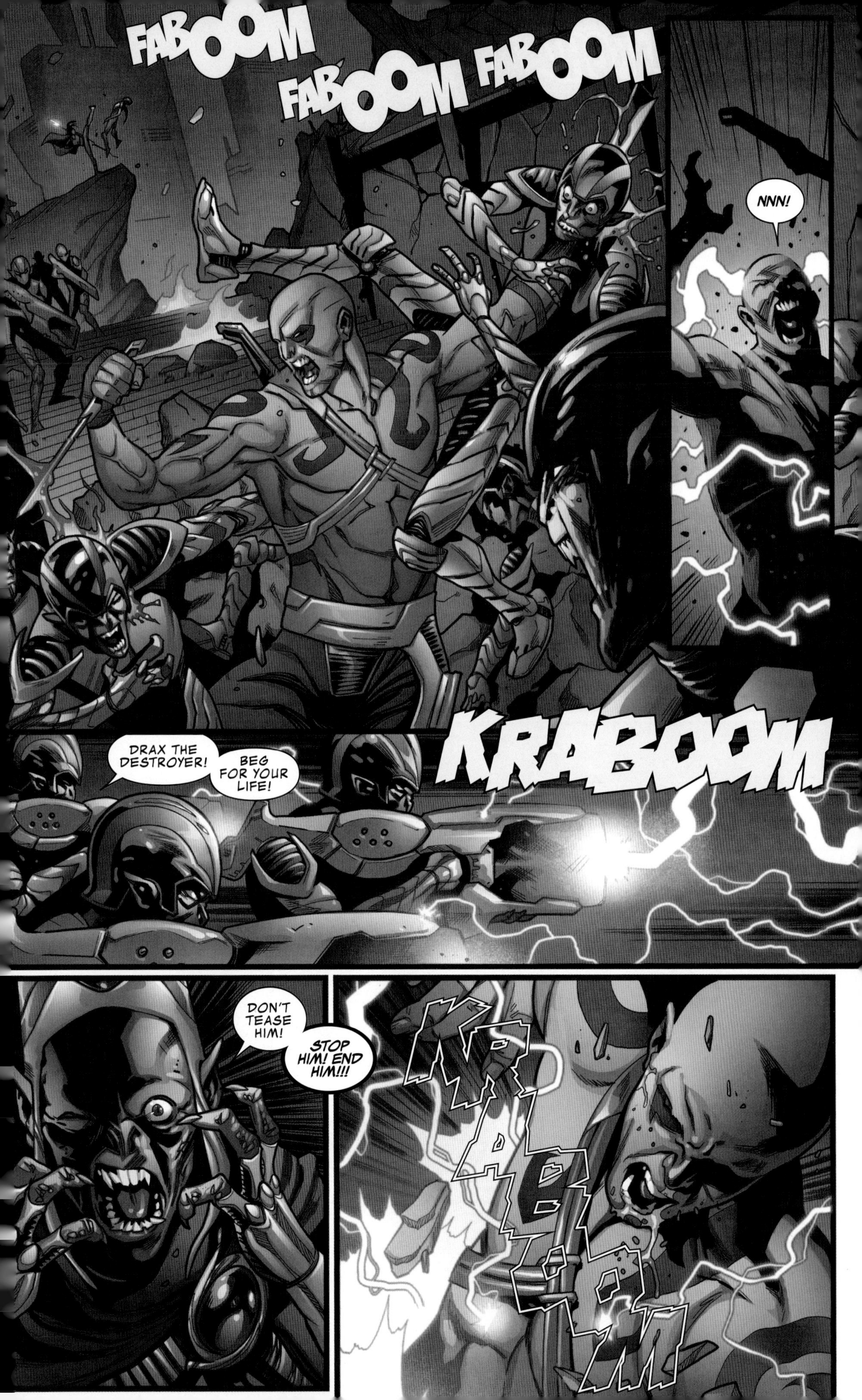
FABOOM
FABOOM FABOOM
NNN!
KRABOOM
DRAX THE DESTROYER!
BEG FOR YOUR LIFE!
DON'T TEASE HIM!
STOP HIM! END HIM!!!
KRABOOM

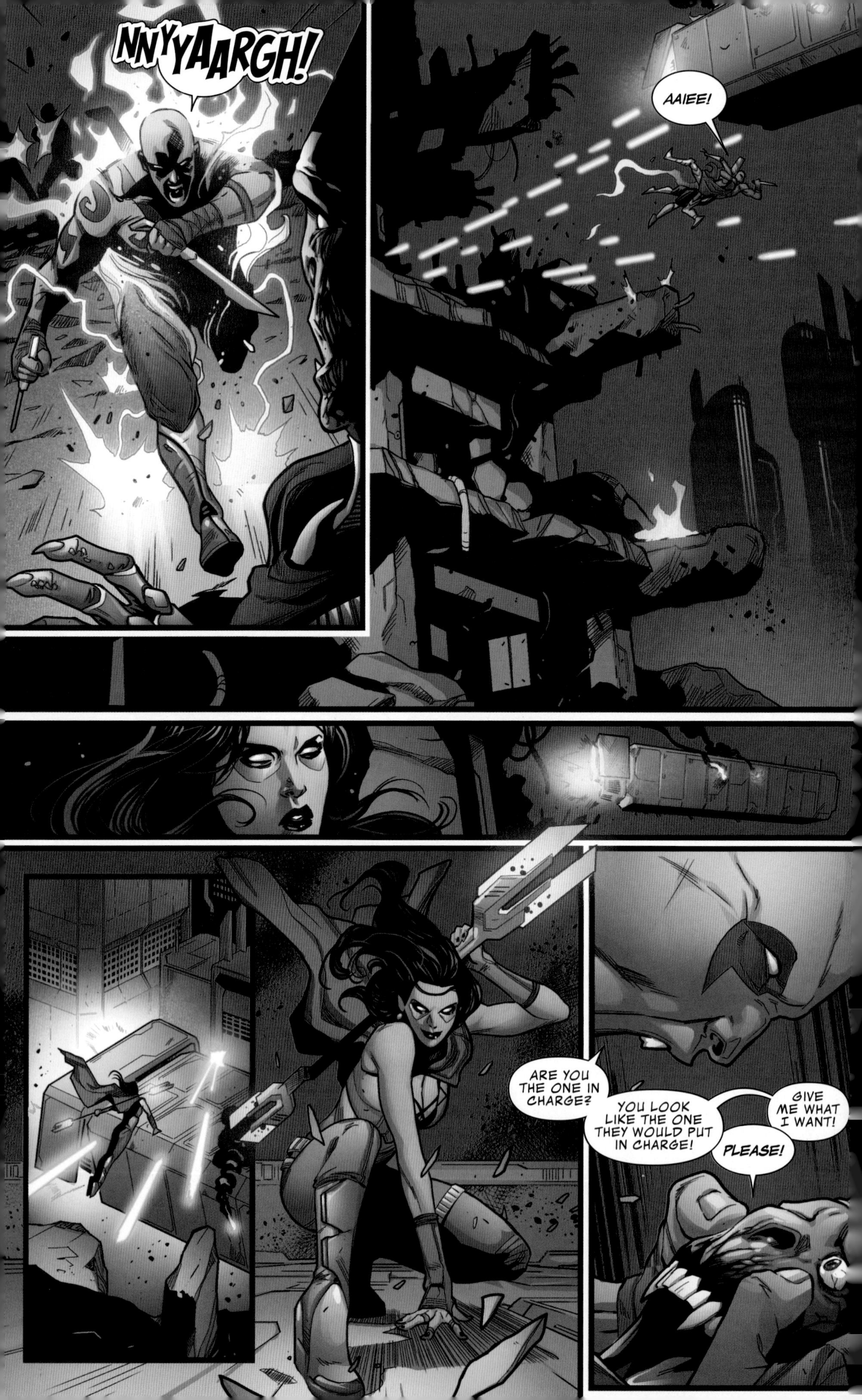
NNYYAARGH!
AAIEE!
ARE YOU THE ONE IN CHARGE?
YOU LOOK LIKE THE ONE THEY WOULD PUT IN CHARGE!
GIVE ME WHAT I WANT!
PLEASE!

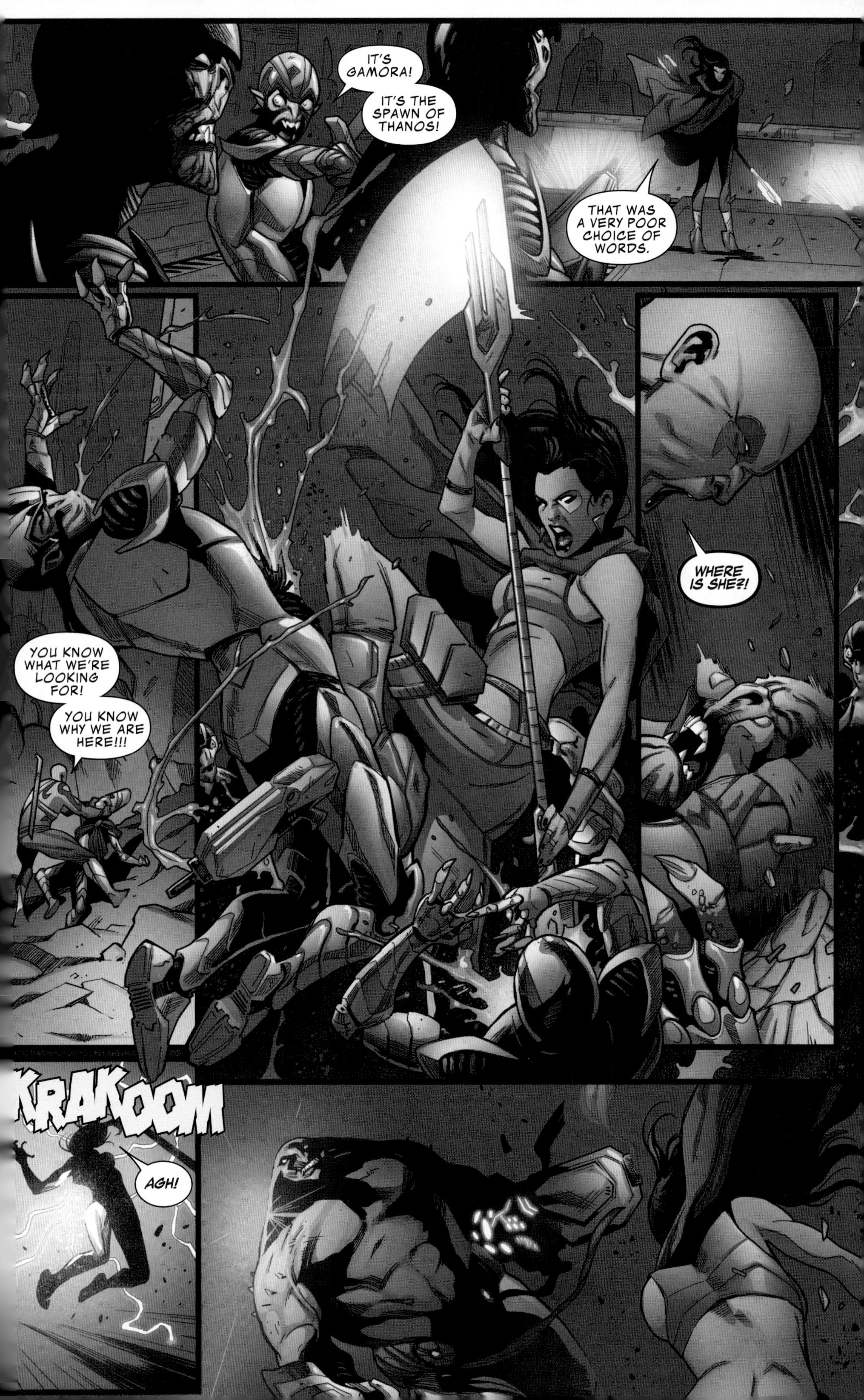
IT'S GAMORA!
IT'S THE SPAWN OF THANOS!
THAT WAS A VERY POOR CHOICE OF WORDS.
WHERE IS SHE?!
YOU KNOW WHAT WE'RE LOOKING FOR!
YOU KNOW WHY WE ARE HERE!!!
KRAKOOM
AGH!

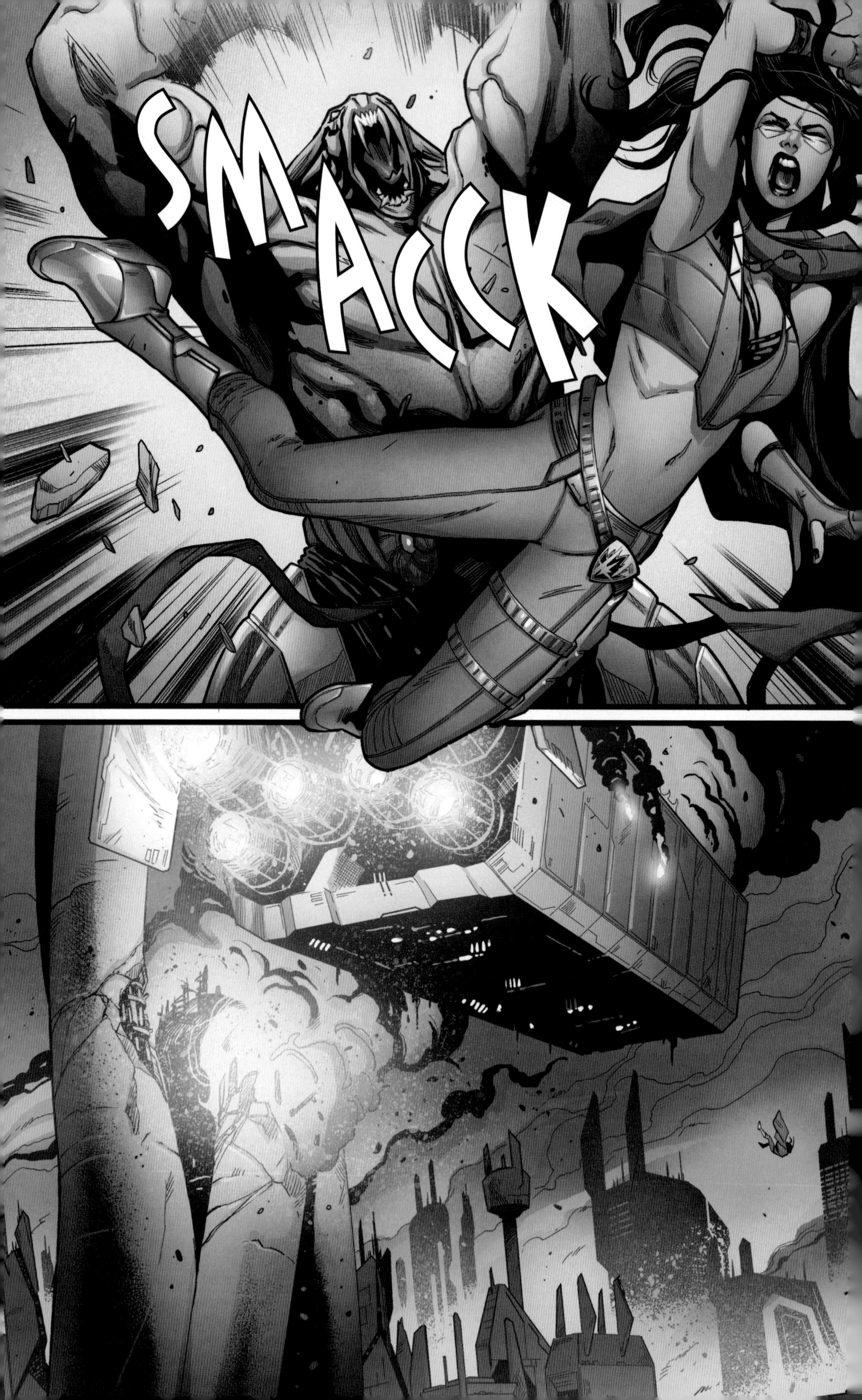
SMACCK

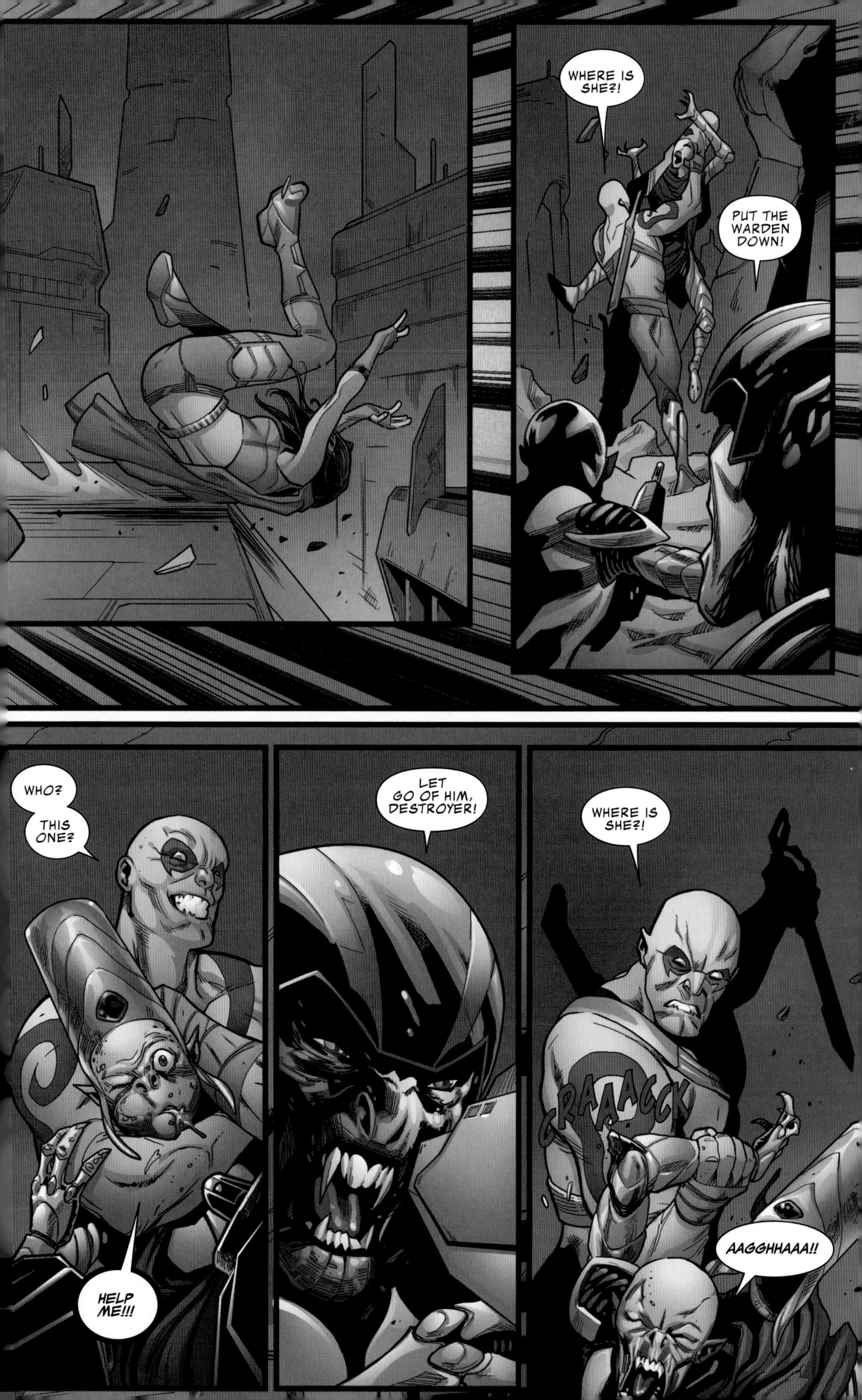
WHERE IS SHE?!
PUT THE WARDEN DOWN!
WHO?
THIS ONE?
HELP ME!!!
LET GO OF HIM, DESTROYER!
WHERE IS SHE?!
CRAAACK
AAGGHHAAA!!

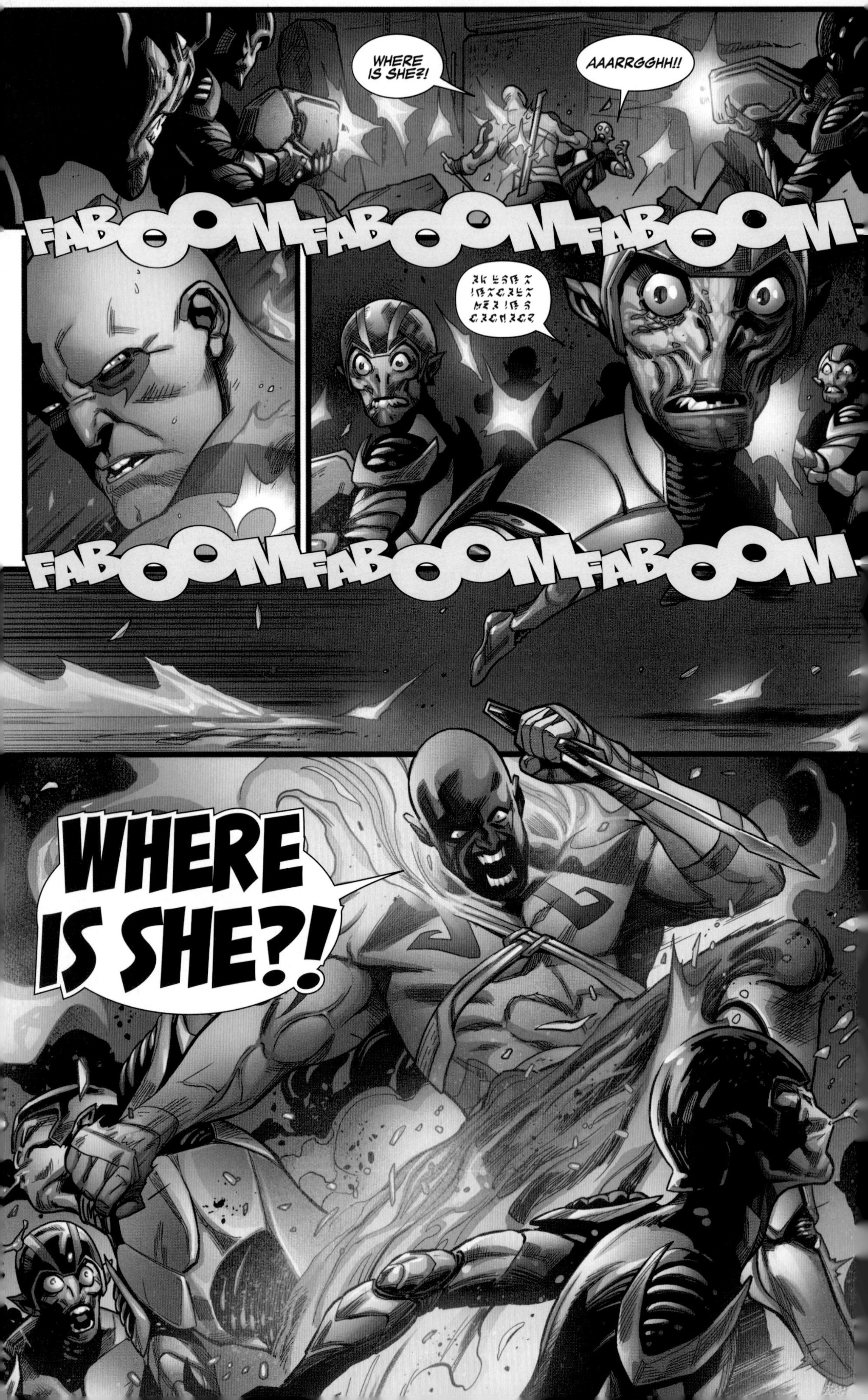
WHERE IS SHE?!
AAARRGGHH!!
FABOOM FABOOM FABOOM
FABOOM FABOOM FABOOM
WHERE IS SHE?!

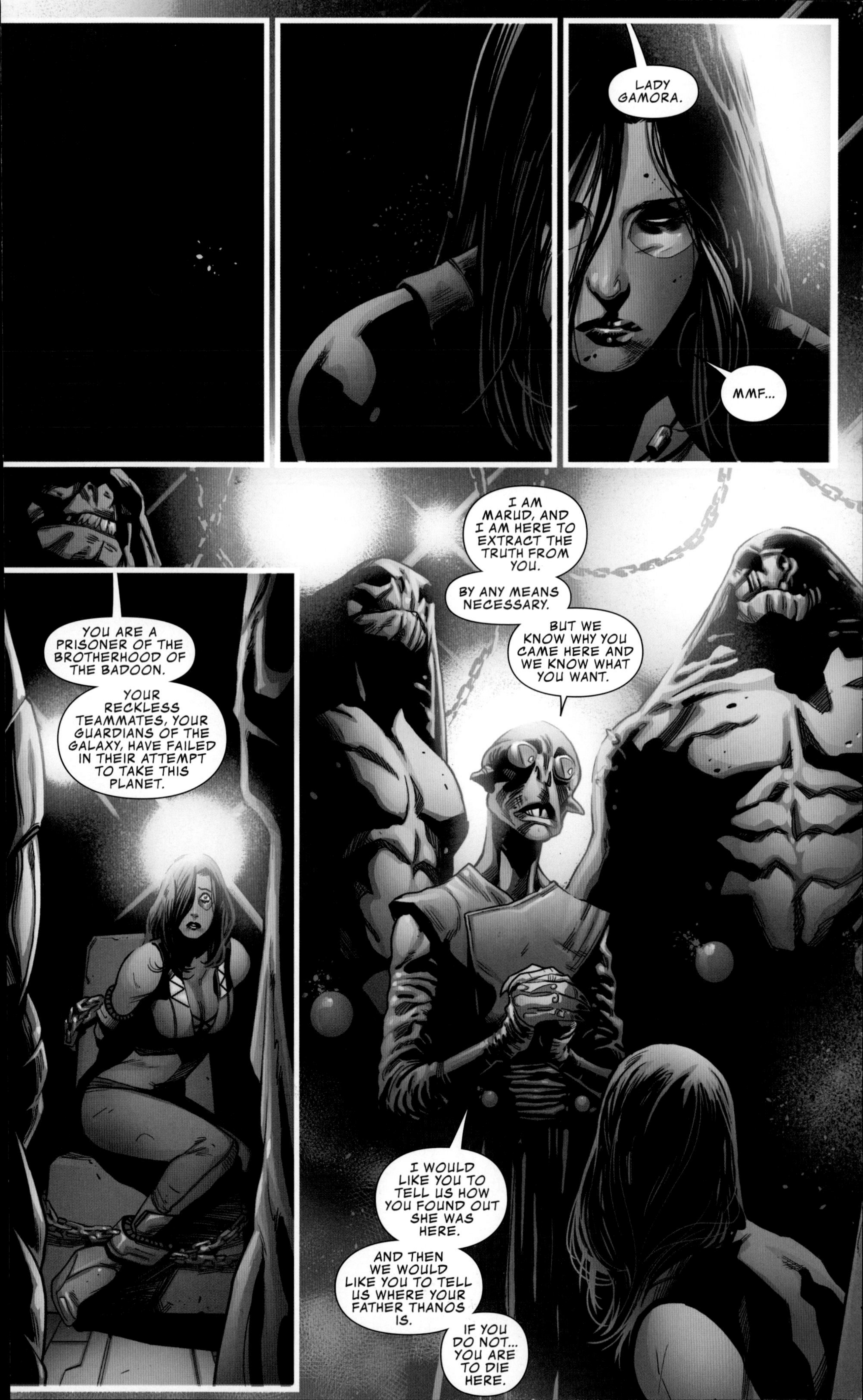
LADY GAMORA.
MMF...
I AM MARUD, AND I AM HERE TO EXTRACT THE TRUTH FROM YOU.
BY ANY MEANS NECESSARY.
YOU ARE A PRISONER OF THE BROTHERHOOD OF THE BADOON.
YOUR RECKLESS TEAMMATES, YOUR GUARDIANS OF THE GALAXY, HAVE FAILED IN THEIR ATTEMPT TO TAKE THIS PLANET.
BUT WE KNOW WHY YOU CAME HERE AND WE KNOW WHAT YOU WANT.
I WOULD LIKE YOU TO TELL US HOW YOU FOUND OUT SHE WAS HERE.
AND THEN WE WOULD LIKE YOU TO TELL US WHERE YOUR FATHER THANOS IS.
IF YOU DO NOT... YOU ARE TO DIE HERE.

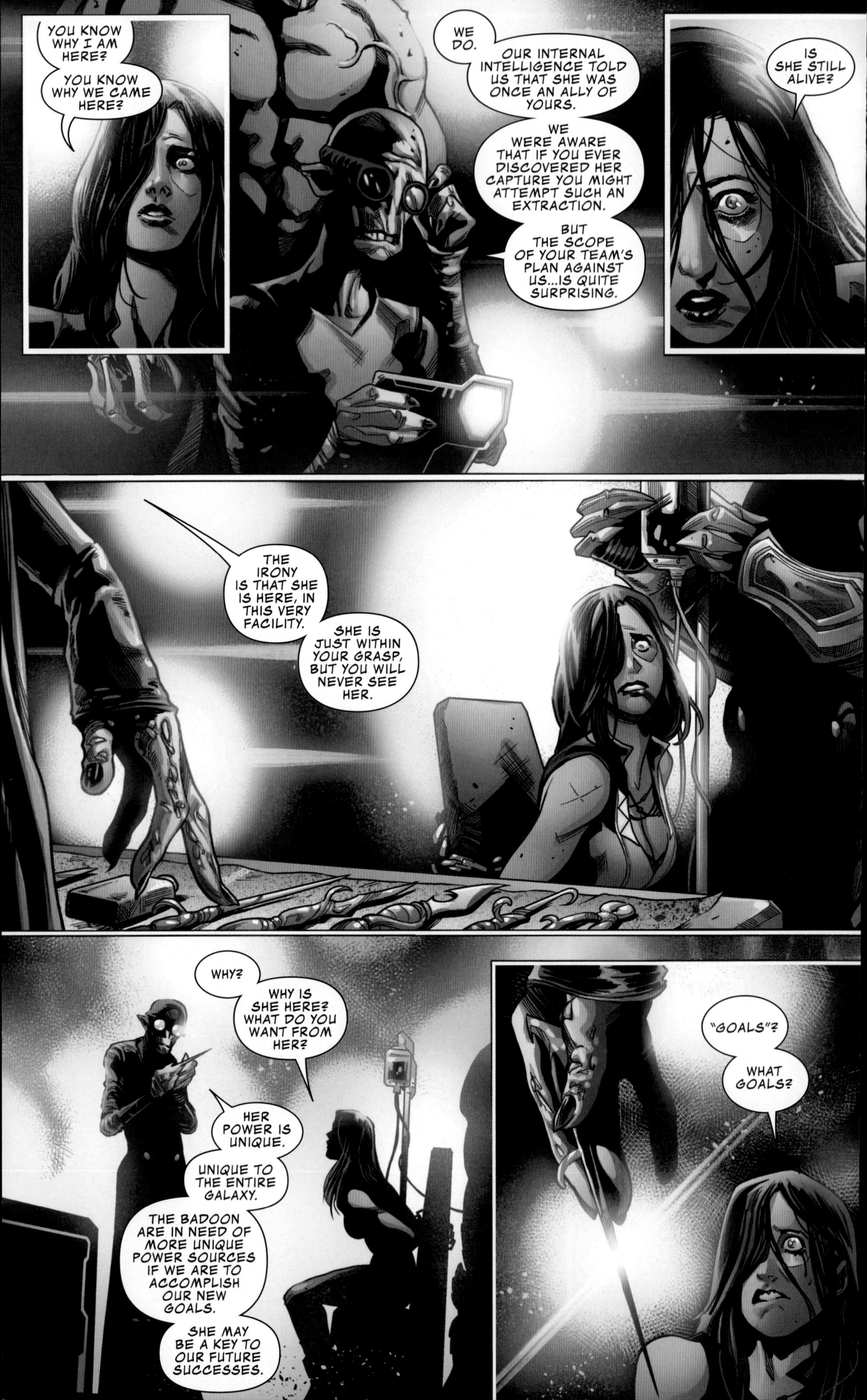

YOU KNOW WHY I AM HERE?
YOU KNOW WHY WE CAME HERE?
WE DO.
OUR INTERNAL INTELLIGENCE TOLD US THAT SHE WAS ONCE AN ALLY OF YOURS.
WE WERE AWARE THAT IF YOU EVER DISCOVERED HER CAPTURE YOU MIGHT ATTEMPT SUCH AN EXTRACTION.
BUT THE SCOPE OF YOUR TEAM'S PLAN AGAINST US...IS QUITE SURPRISING.
IS SHE STILL ALIVE?
THE IRONY IS THAT SHE IS HERE, IN THIS VERY FACILITY.
SHE IS JUST WITHIN YOUR GRASP, BUT YOU WILL NEVER SEE HER.
WHY?
WHY IS SHE HERE? WHAT DO YOU WANT FROM HER?
HER POWER IS UNIQUE.
UNIQUE TO THE ENTIRE GALAXY.
THE BADOON ARE IN NEED OF MORE UNIQUE POWER SOURCES IF WE ARE TO ACCOMPLISH OUR NEW GOALS.
SHE MAY BE A KEY TO OUR FUTURE SUCCESSES.
"GOALS"?
WHAT GOALS?

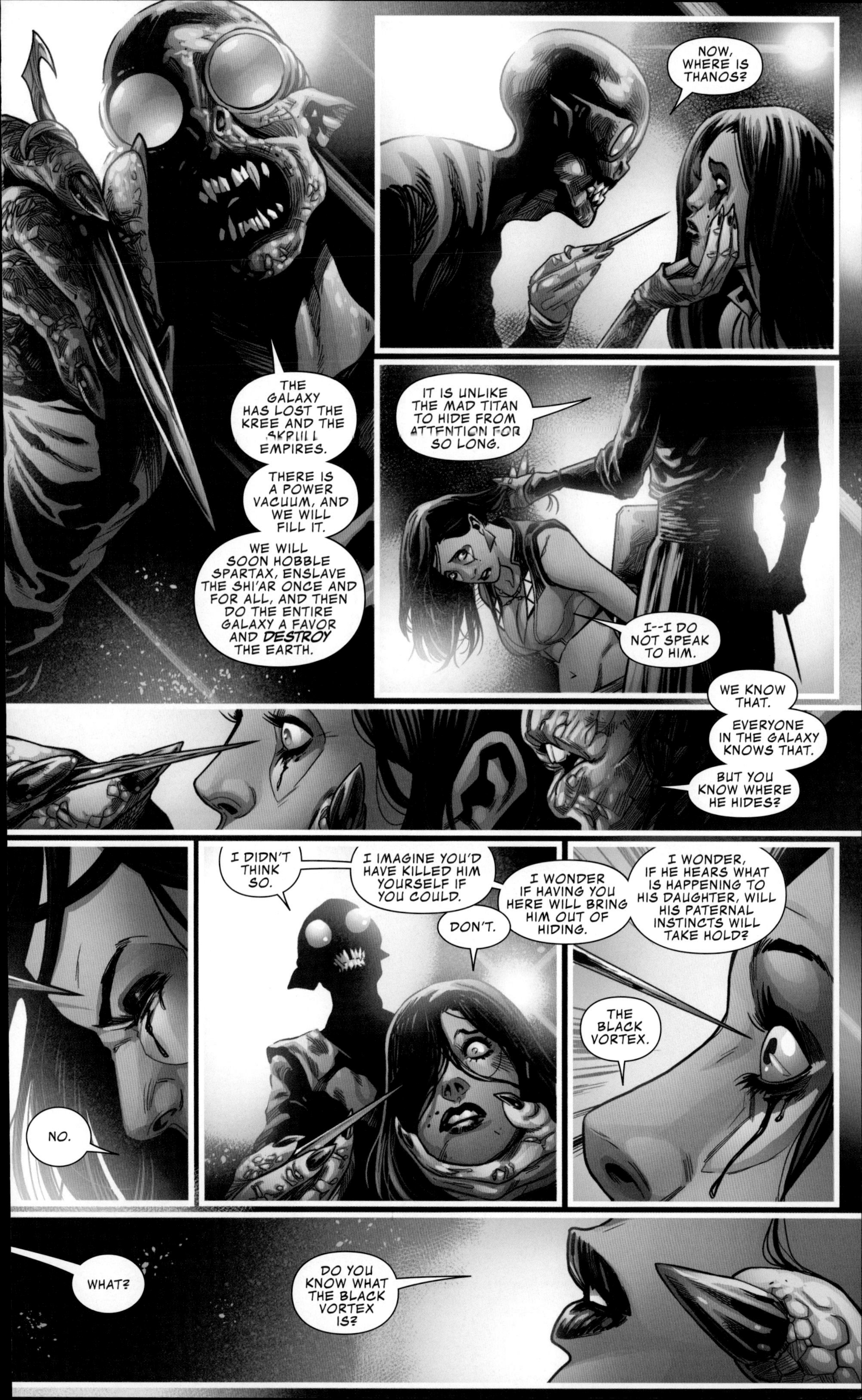
THE GALAXY HAS LOST THE KREE AND THE SKRULL EMPIRES.
THERE IS A POWER VACUUM, AND WE WILL FILL IT.
WE WILL SOON HOBBLE SPARTAX, ENSLAVE THE SHI'AR ONCE AND FOR ALL, AND THEN DO THE ENTIRE GALAXY A FAVOR AND *DESTROY* THE EARTH.
NOW, WHERE IS THANOS?
IT IS UNLIKE THE MAD TITAN TO HIDE FROM ATTENTION FOR SO LONG.
I--I DO NOT SPEAK TO HIM.
WE KNOW THAT.
EVERYONE IN THE GALAXY KNOWS THAT.
BUT YOU KNOW WHERE HE HIDES?
NO.
I DIDN'T THINK SO.
I IMAGINE YOU'D HAVE KILLED HIM YOURSELF IF YOU COULD.
DON'T.
I WONDER IF HAVING YOU HERE WILL BRING HIM OUT OF HIDING.
I WONDER, IF HE HEARS WHAT IS HAPPENING TO HIS DAUGHTER, WILL HIS PATERNAL INSTINCTS WILL TAKE HOLD?
THE BLACK VORTEX.
WHAT?
DO YOU KNOW WHAT THE BLACK VORTEX IS?

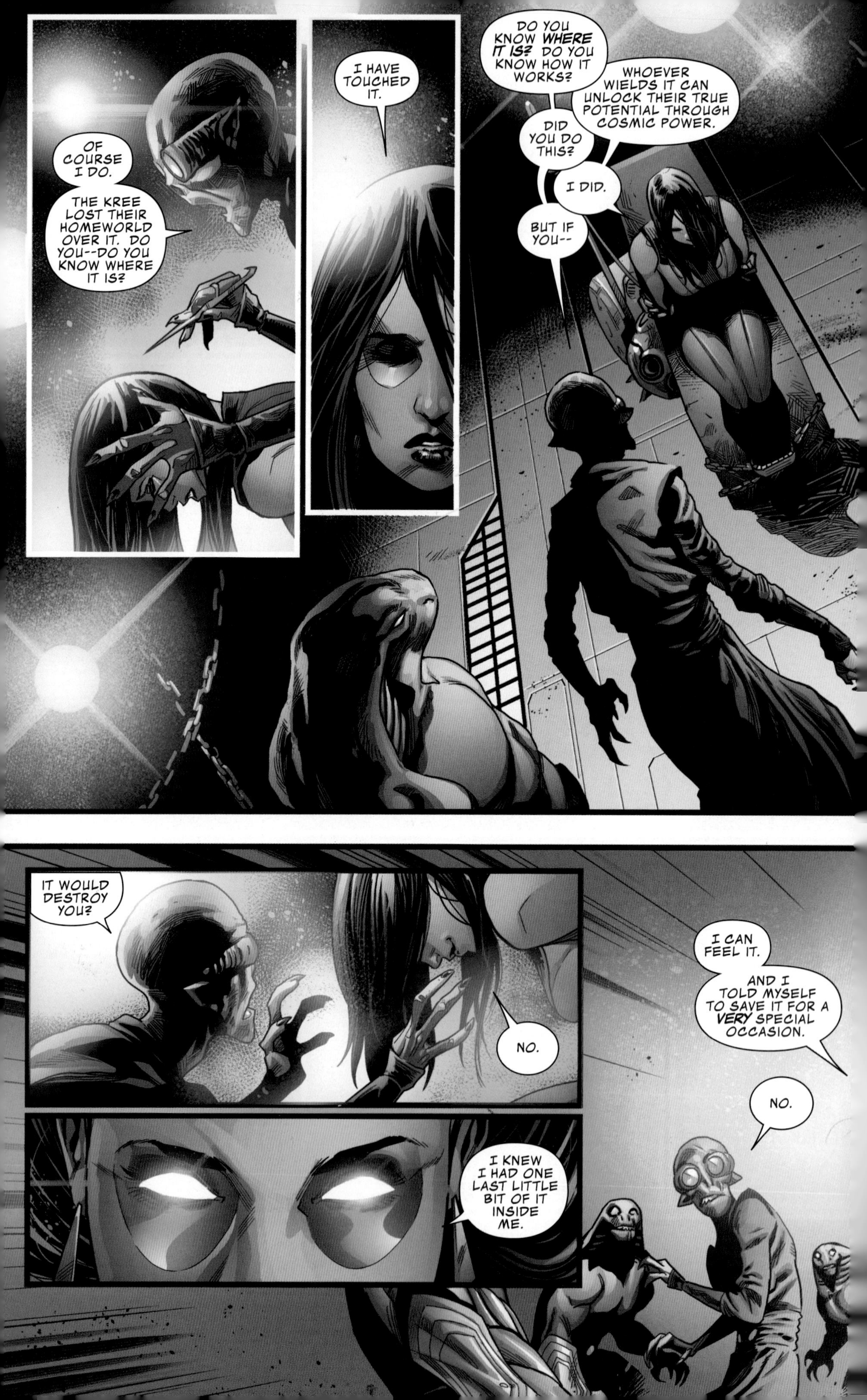

OF COURSE I DO.
THE KREE LOST THEIR HOMEWORLD OVER IT. DO YOU--DO YOU KNOW WHERE IT IS?
I HAVE TOUCHED IT.
DO YOU KNOW WHERE IT IS? DO YOU KNOW HOW IT WORKS?
WHOEVER WIELDS IT CAN UNLOCK THEIR TRUE POTENTIAL THROUGH COSMIC POWER.
DID YOU DO THIS?
I DID.
BUT IF YOU--
IT WOULD DESTROY YOU?
NO.
I KNEW I HAD ONE LAST LITTLE BIT OF IT INSIDE ME.
I CAN FEEL IT.
AND I TOLD MYSELF TO SAVE IT FOR A VERY SPECIAL OCCASION.
NO.

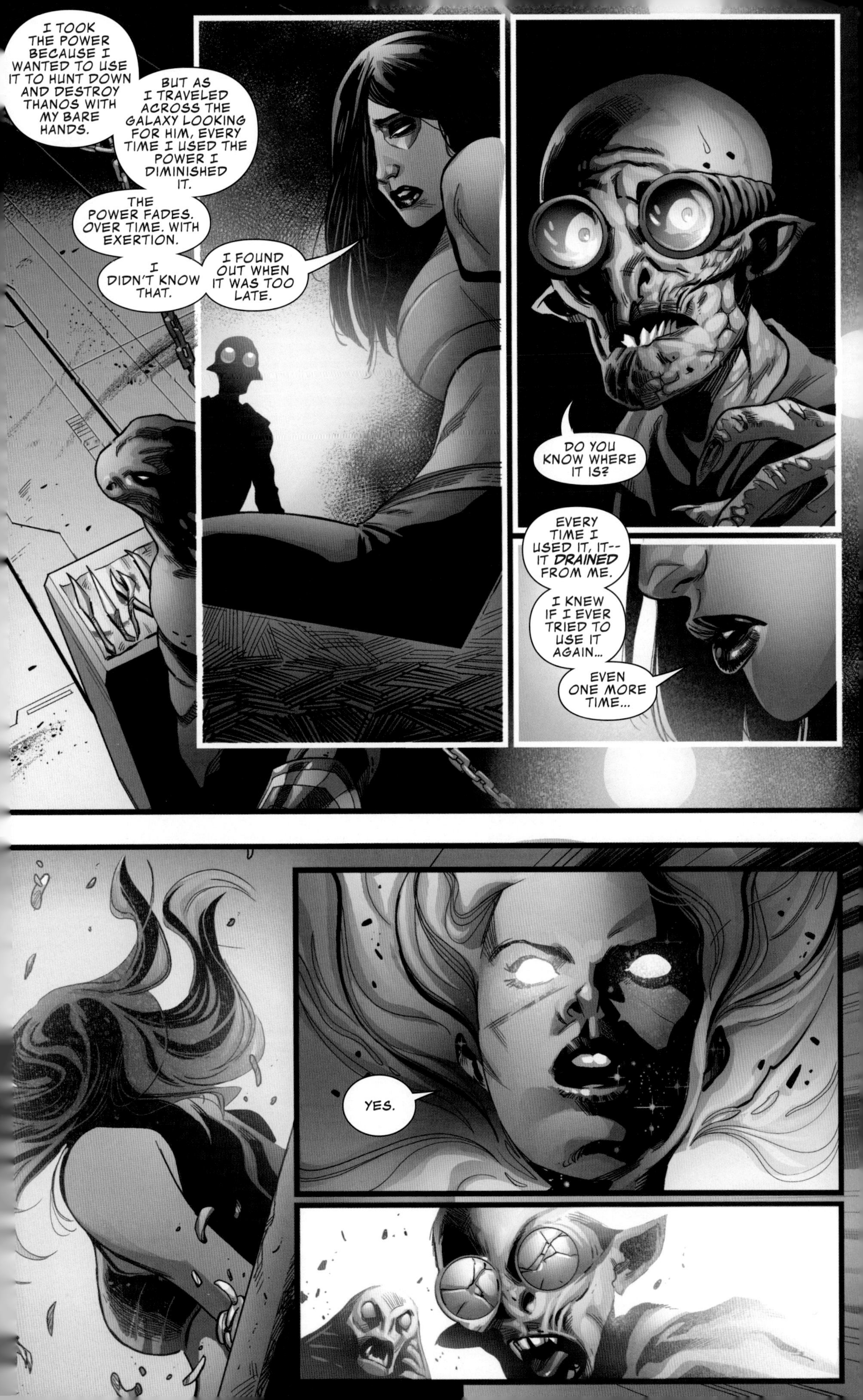
I TOOK THE POWER BECAUSE I WANTED TO USE IT TO HUNT DOWN AND DESTROY THANOS WITH MY BARE HANDS.
BUT AS I TRAVELED ACROSS THE GALAXY LOOKING FOR HIM, EVERY TIME I USED THE POWER I DIMINISHED IT.
THE POWER FADES. OVER TIME. WITH EXERTION.
I DIDN'T KNOW THAT.
I FOUND OUT WHEN IT WAS TOO LATE.
DO YOU KNOW WHERE IT IS?
EVERY TIME I USED IT, IT-- IT *DRAINED* FROM ME.
I KNEW IF I EVER TRIED TO USE IT AGAIN...
EVEN ONE MORE TIME...
YES.

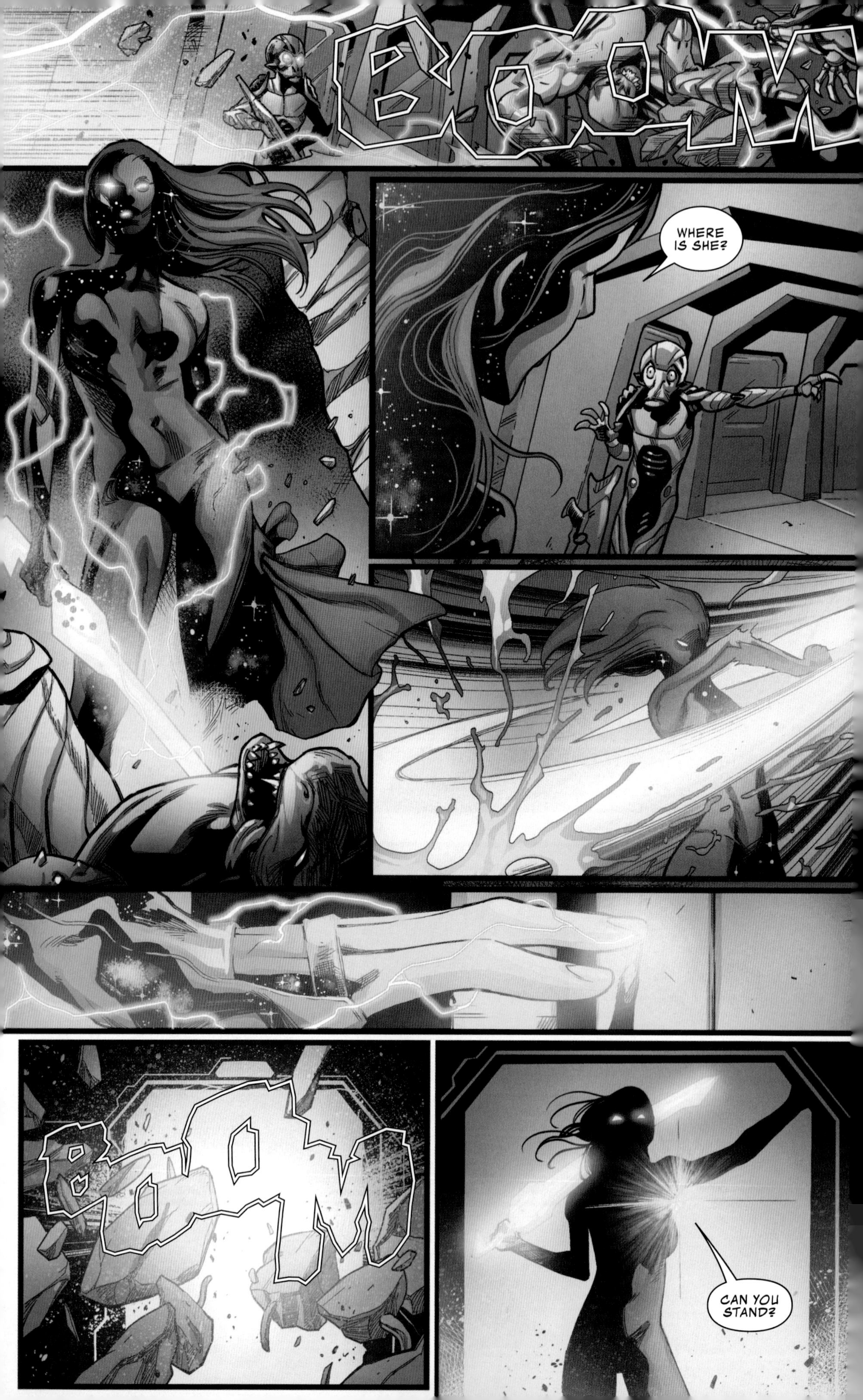

BOOM
WHERE IS SHE?
BOOM
CAN YOU STAND?

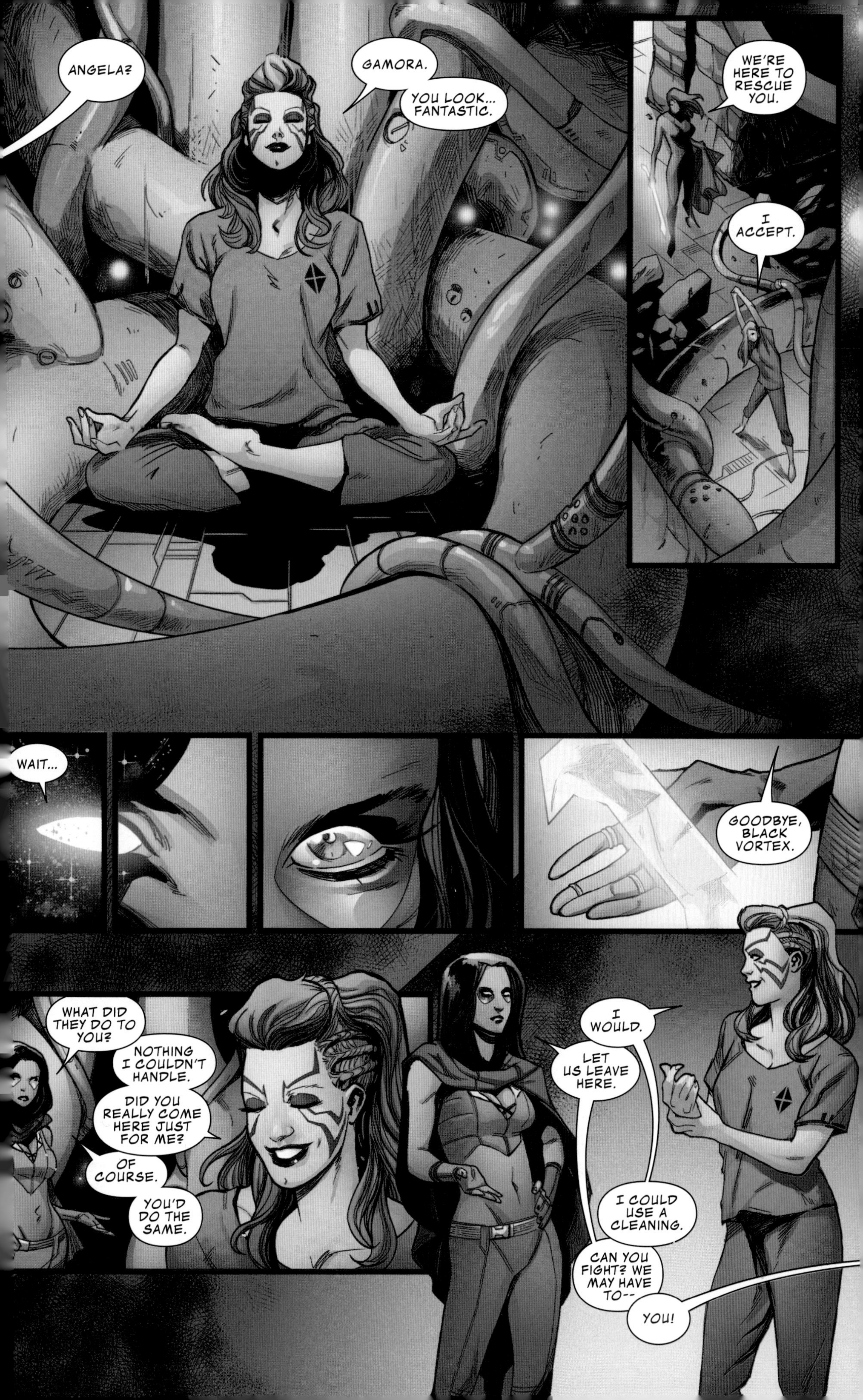
ANGELA?
GAMORA.
YOU LOOK... FANTASTIC.
WE'RE HERE TO RESCUE YOU.
I ACCEPT.
WAIT...
GOODBYE, BLACK VORTEX.
WHAT DID THEY DO TO YOU?
NOTHING I COULDN'T HANDLE.
DID YOU REALLY COME HERE JUST FOR ME?
OF COURSE.
YOU'D DO THE SAME.
I WOULD.
LET US LEAVE HERE.
I COULD USE A CLEANING.
CAN YOU FIGHT? WE MAY HAVE TO--
YOU!

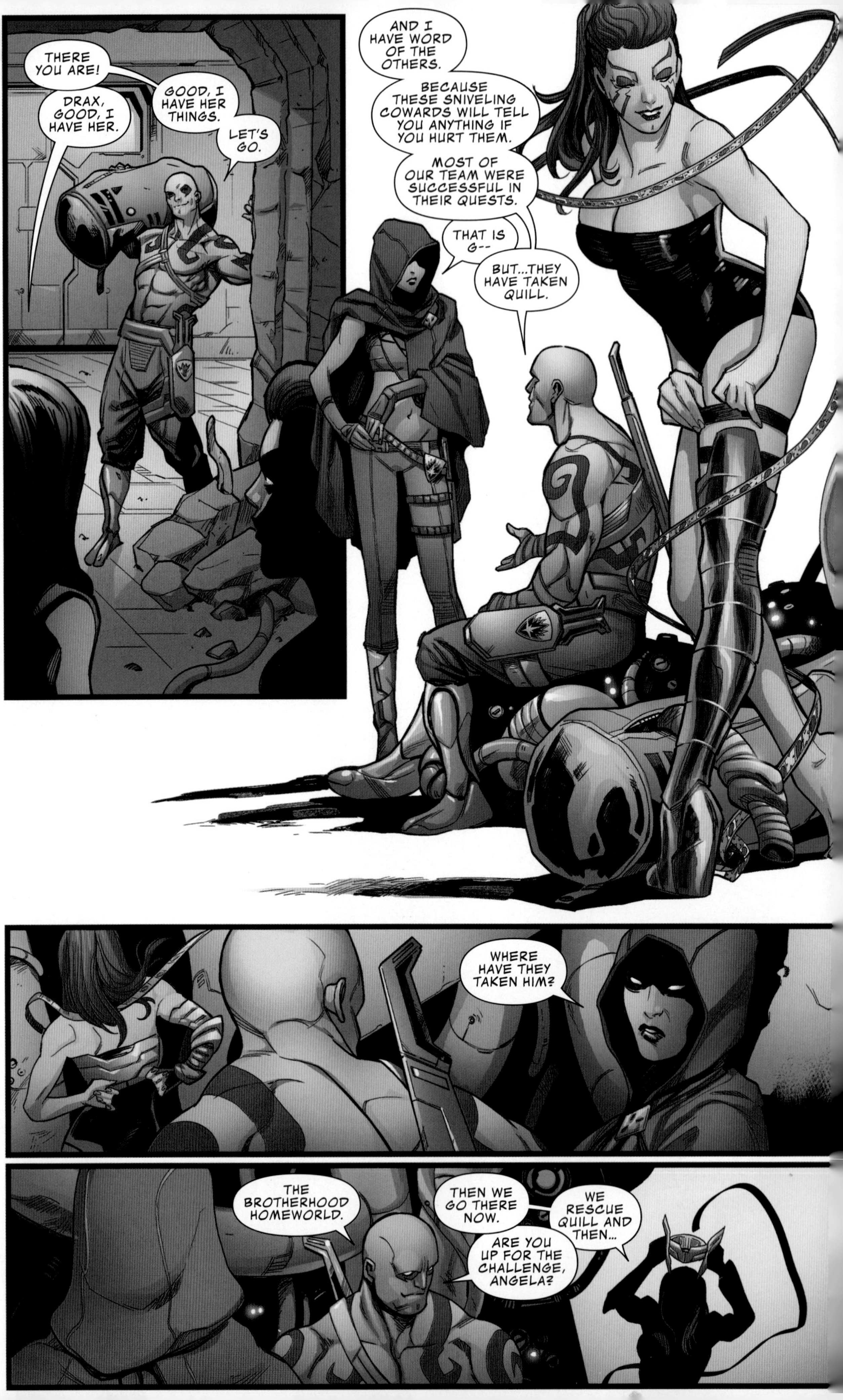
THERE YOU ARE!
DRAX, GOOD, I HAVE HER.
GOOD, I HAVE HER THINGS.
LET'S GO.
AND I HAVE WORD OF THE OTHERS.
BECAUSE THESE SNIVELING COWARDS WILL TELL YOU ANYTHING IF YOU HURT THEM.
MOST OF OUR TEAM WERE SUCCESSFUL IN THEIR QUESTS.
THAT IS G--
BUT...THEY HAVE TAKEN QUILL.
WHERE HAVE THEY TAKEN HIM?
THE BROTHERHOOD HOMEWORLD.
THEN WE GO THERE NOW.
WE RESCUE QUILL AND THEN...
ARE YOU UP FOR THE CHALLENGE, ANGELA?

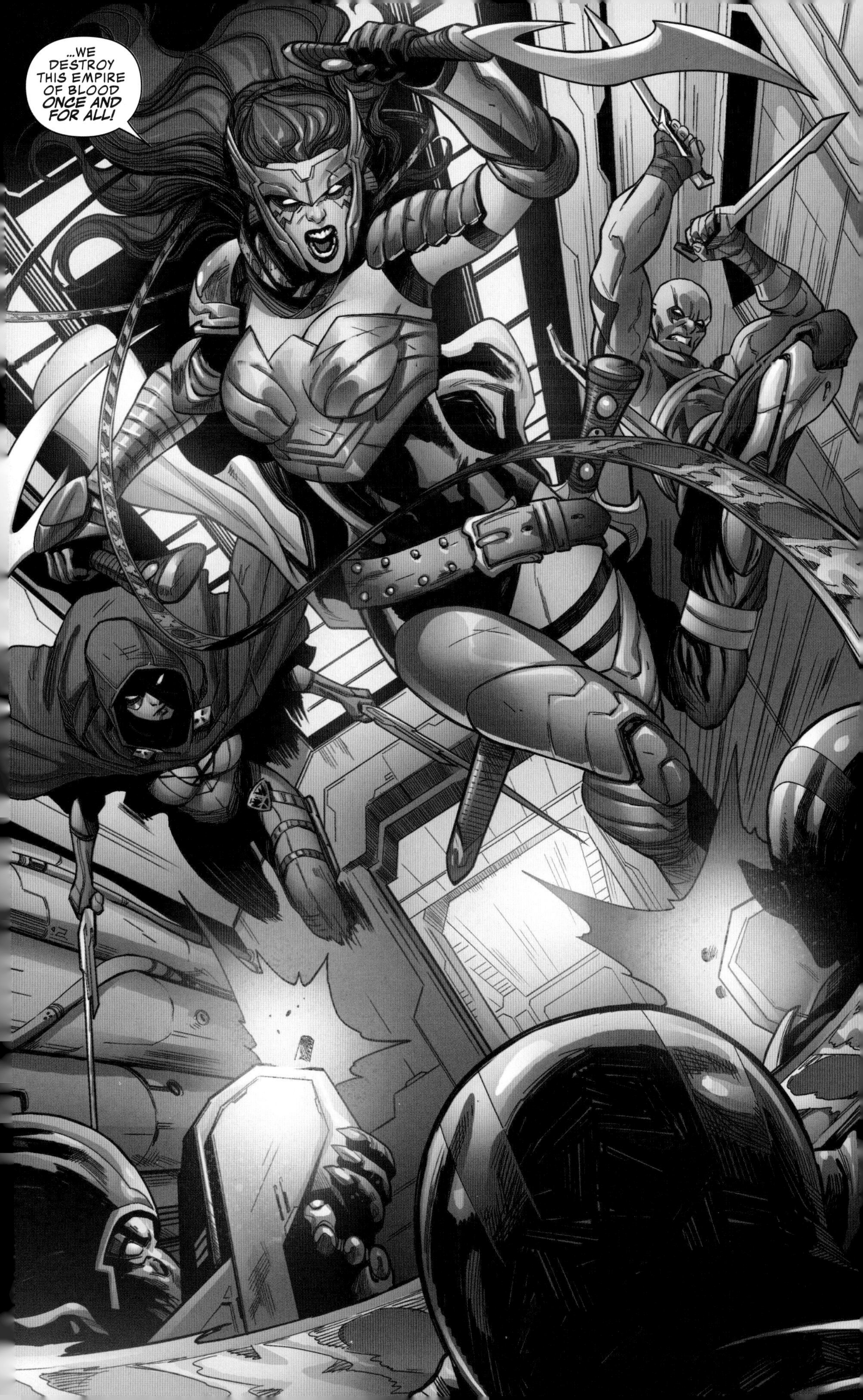
...WE DESTROY THIS EMPIRE OF BLOOD ONCE AND FOR ALL!

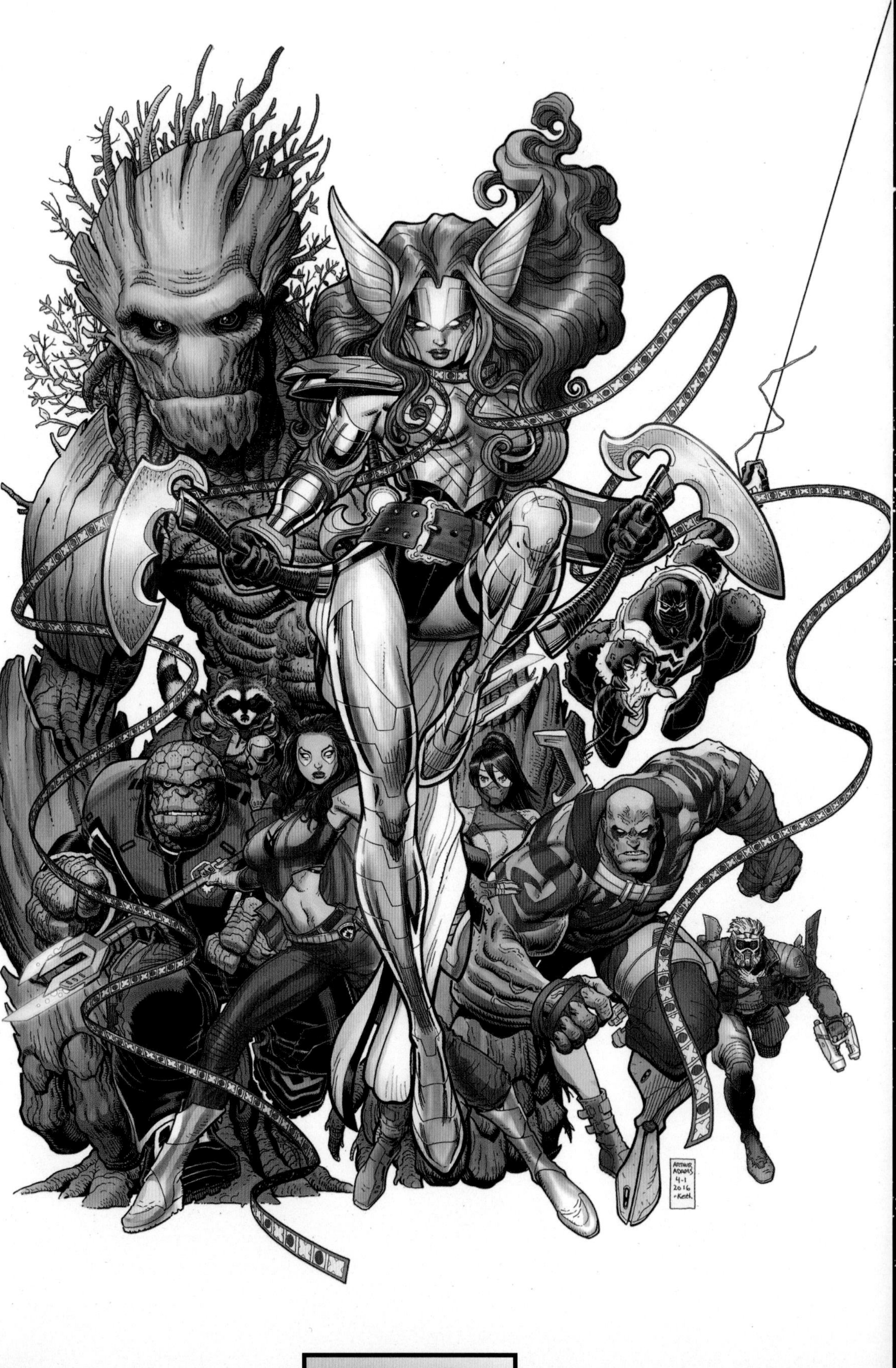
ARTHUR ADAMS 4-1 2016 -Keith

10

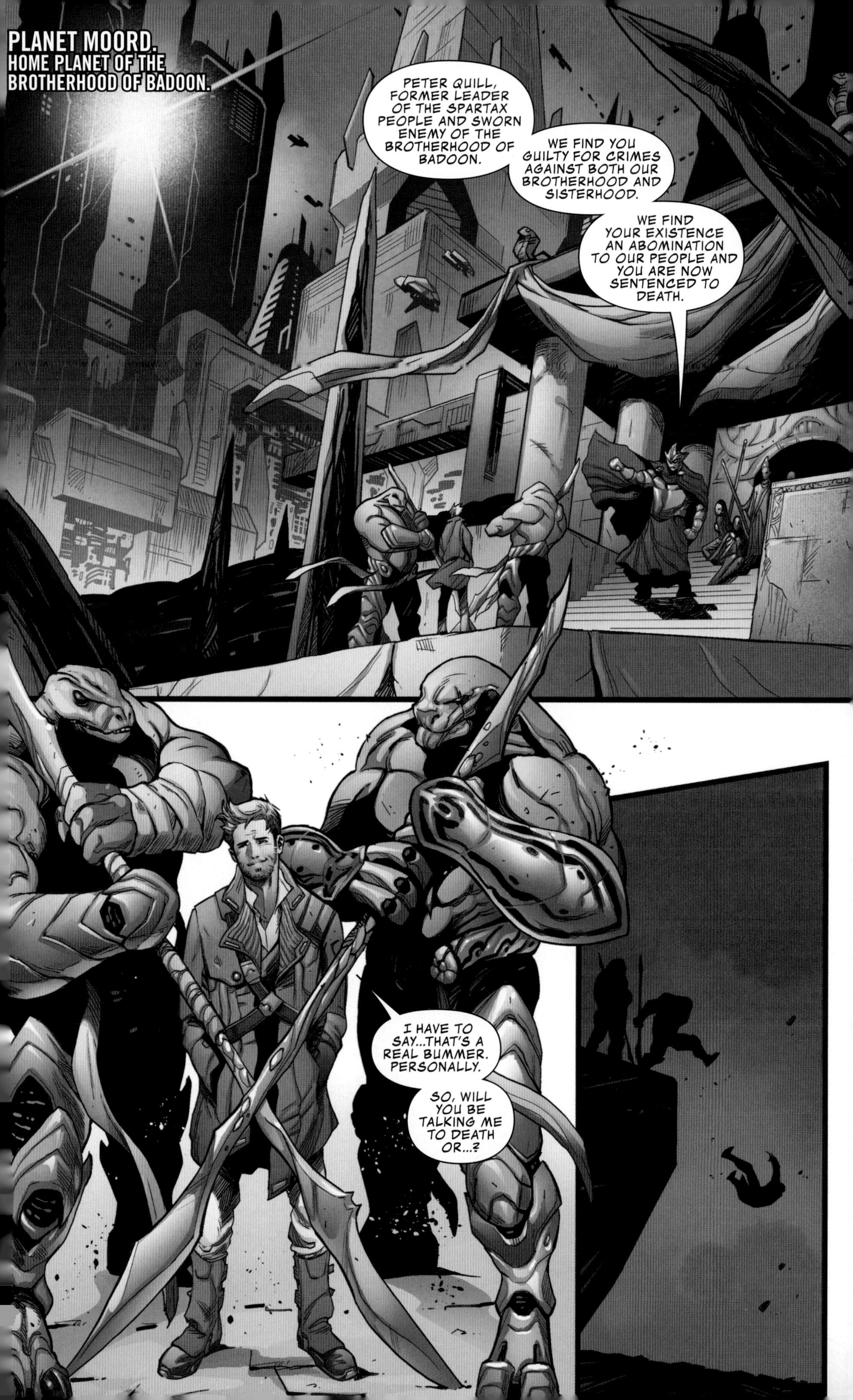
PLANET MOORD.
HOME PLANET OF THE BROTHERHOOD OF BADOON.
PETER QUILL, FORMER LEADER OF THE SPARTAX PEOPLE AND SWORN ENEMY OF THE BROTHERHOOD OF BADOON.
WE FIND YOU GUILTY FOR CRIMES AGAINST BOTH OUR BROTHERHOOD AND SISTERHOOD.
WE FIND YOUR EXISTENCE AN ABOMINATION TO OUR PEOPLE AND YOU ARE NOW SENTENCED TO DEATH.
I HAVE TO SAY...THAT'S A REAL BUMMER. PERSONALLY.
SO, WILL YOU BE TALKING ME TO DEATH OR...?

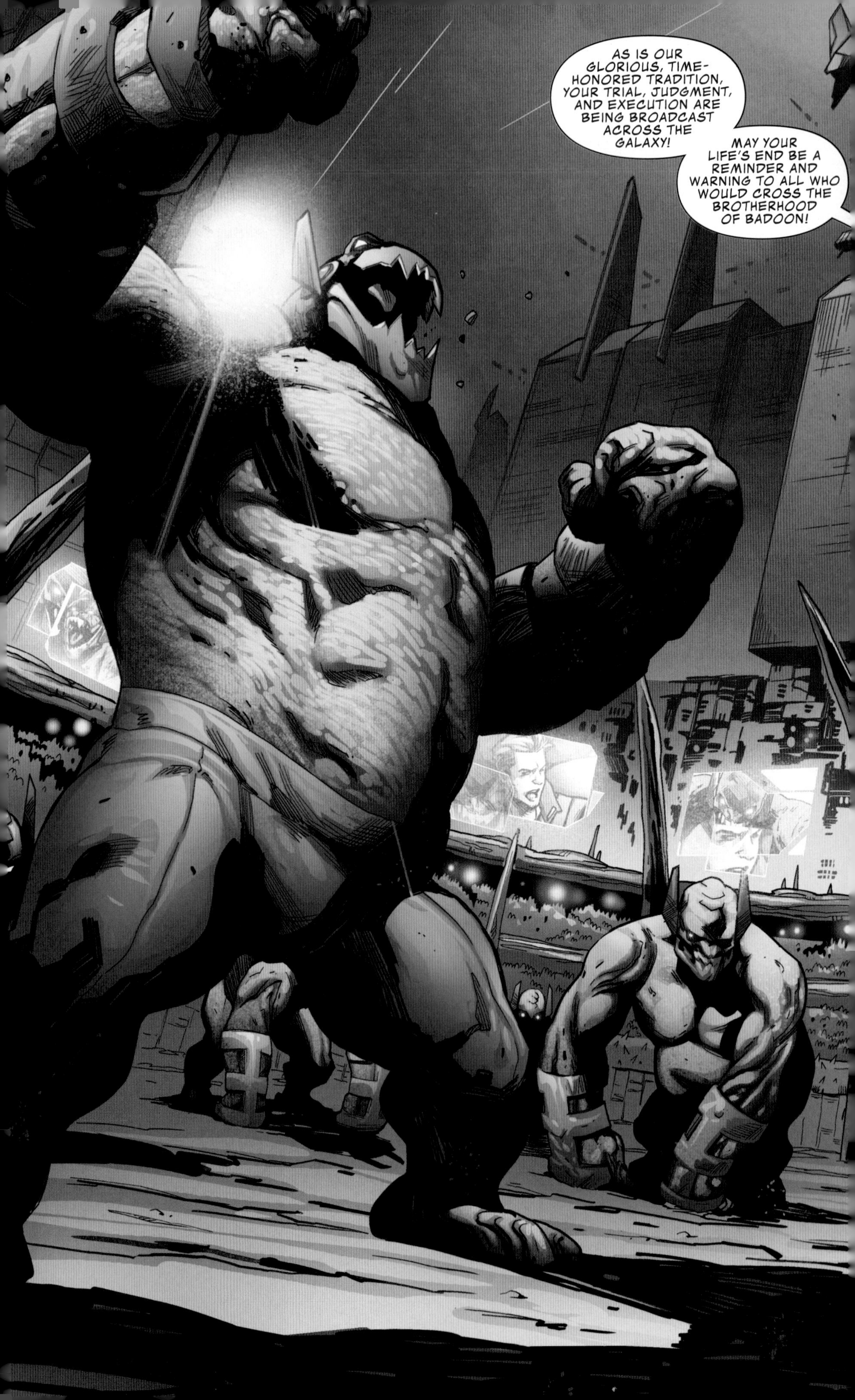
AS IS OUR GLORIOUS, TIME-HONORED TRADITION, YOUR TRIAL, JUDGMENT, AND EXECUTION ARE BEING BROADCAST ACROSS THE GALAXY!
MAY YOUR LIFE'S END BE A REMINDER AND WARNING TO ALL WHO WOULD CROSS THE BROTHERHOOD OF BADOON!

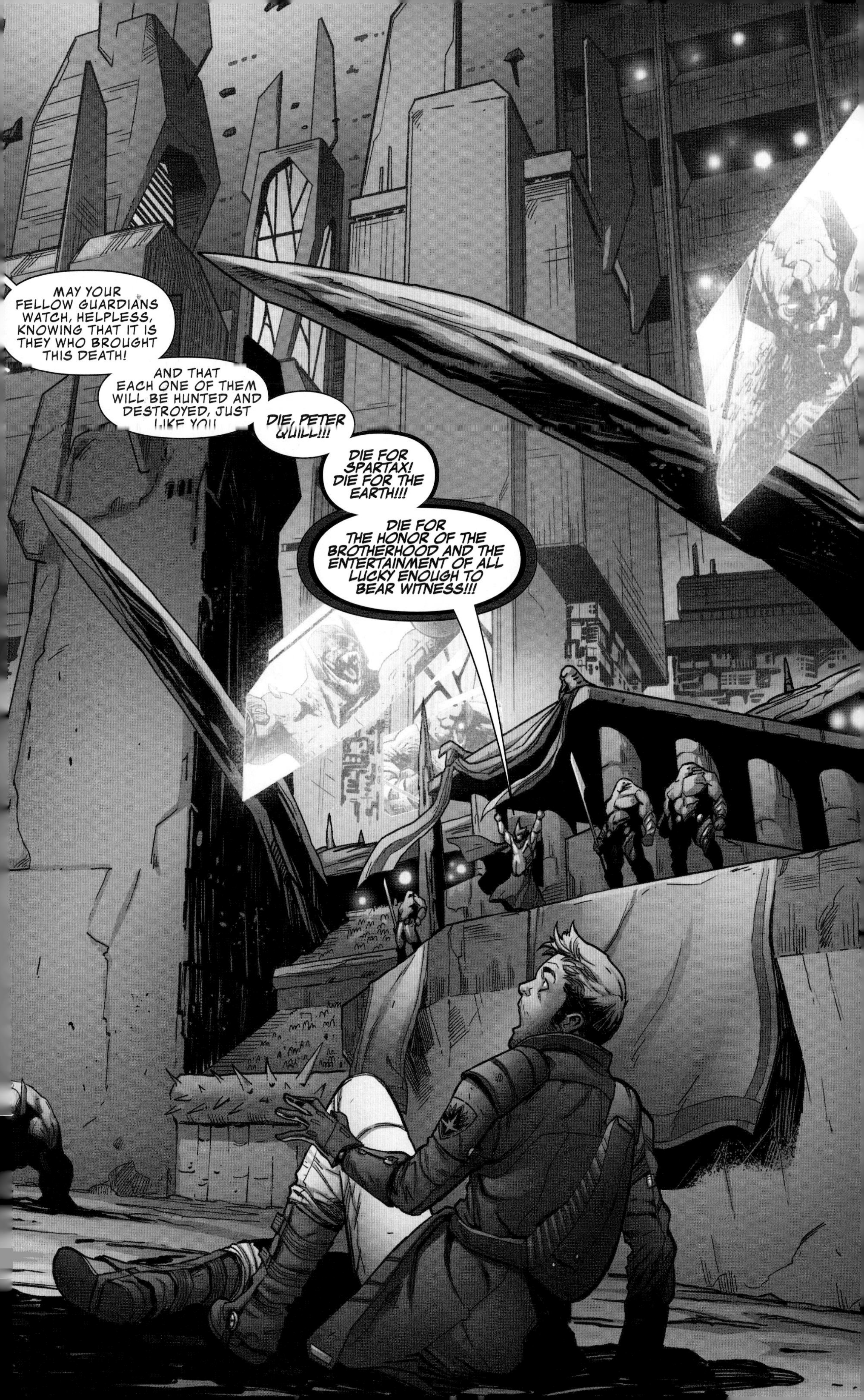
MAY YOUR FELLOW GUARDIANS WATCH, HELPLESS, KNOWING THAT IT IS THEY WHO BROUGHT THIS DEATH!
AND THAT EACH ONE OF THEM WILL BE HUNTED AND DESTROYED, JUST LIKE YOU!
DIE, PETER QUILL!!!
DIE FOR SPARTAX! DIE FOR THE EARTH!!!
DIE FOR THE HONOR OF THE BROTHERHOOD AND THE ENTERTAINMENT OF ALL LUCKY ENOUGH TO BEAR WITNESS!!!

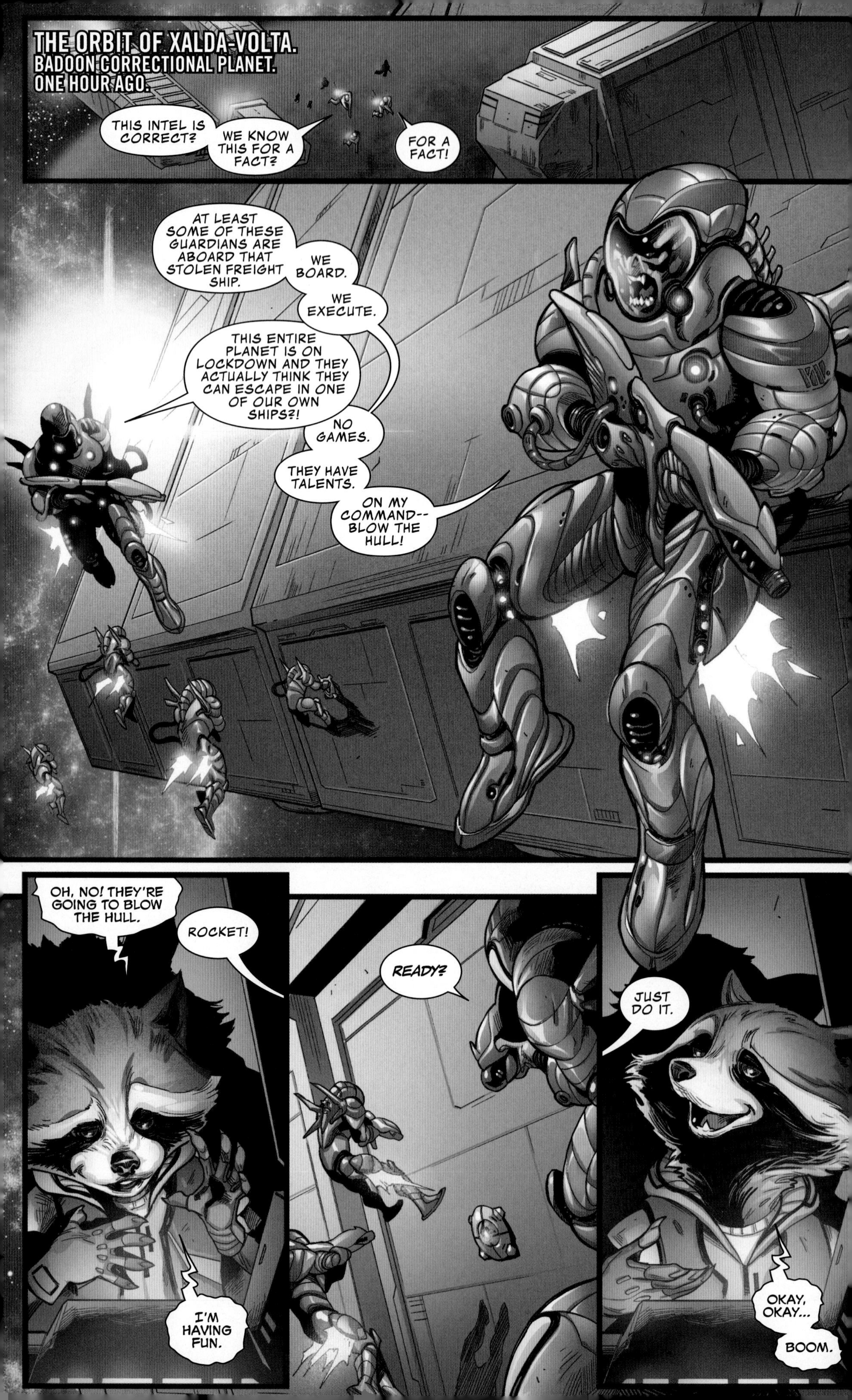
THE ORBIT OF XALDA-VOLTA.
BADOON CORRECTIONAL PLANET.
ONE HOUR AGO.
THIS INTEL IS CORRECT?
WE KNOW THIS FOR A FACT?
FOR A FACT!
AT LEAST SOME OF THESE GUARDIANS ARE ABOARD THAT STOLEN FREIGHT SHIP.
WE BOARD.
WE EXECUTE.
THIS ENTIRE PLANET IS ON LOCKDOWN AND THEY ACTUALLY THINK THEY CAN ESCAPE IN ONE OF OUR OWN SHIPS?!
NO GAMES.
THEY HAVE TALENTS.
ON MY COMMAND-- BLOW THE HULL!
OH, NO! THEY'RE GOING TO BLOW THE HULL.
ROCKET!
I'M HAVING FUN.
READY?
JUST DO IT.
OKAY, OKAY...
BOOM.

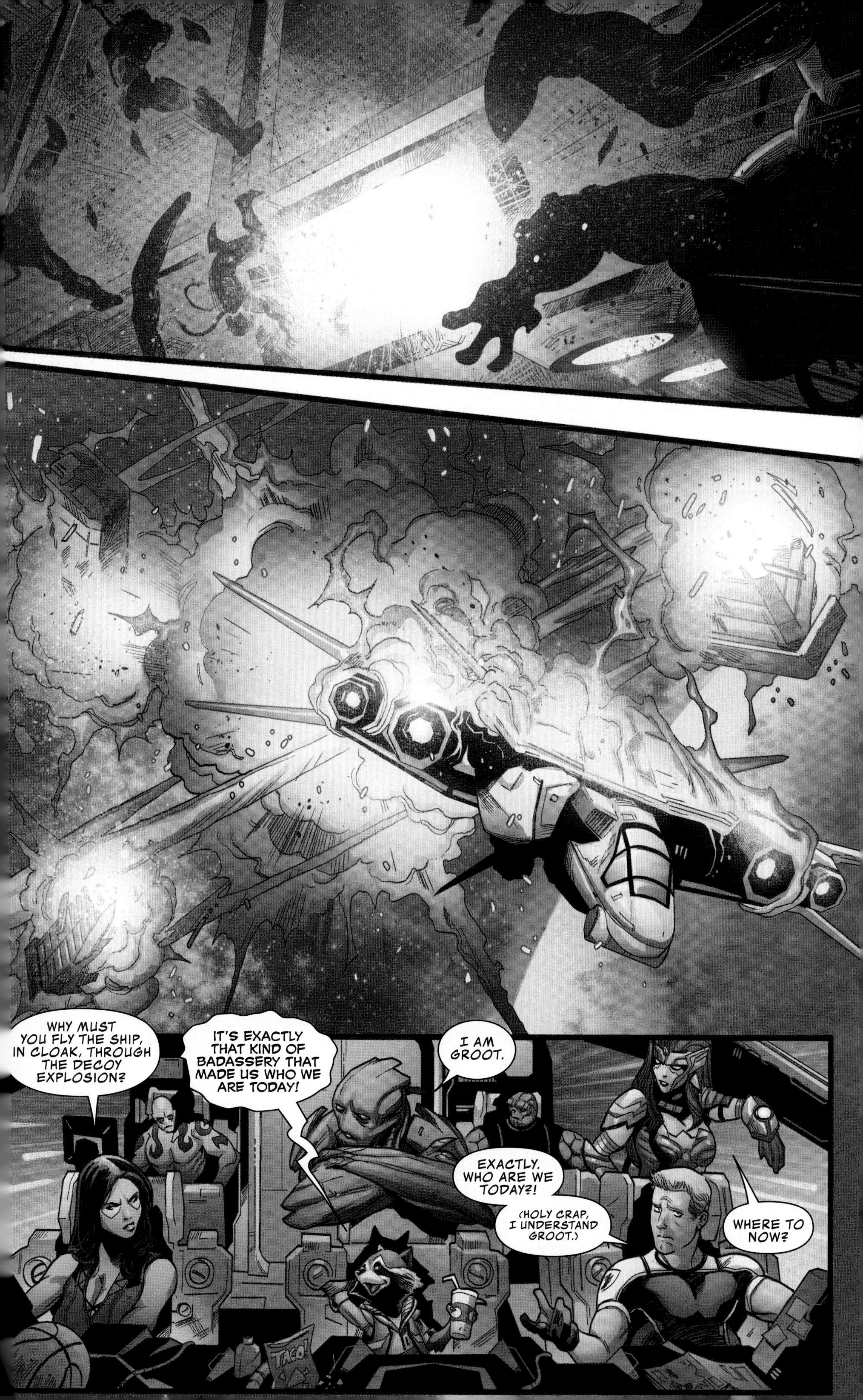
WHY MUST YOU FLY THE SHIP, IN CLOAK, THROUGH THE DECOY EXPLOSION?
IT'S EXACTLY THAT KIND OF BADASSERY THAT MADE US WHO WE ARE TODAY!
I AM GROOT.
EXACTLY. WHO ARE WE TODAY?!
(HOLY CRAP, I UNDERSTAND GROOT.)
WHERE TO NOW?
TACO!

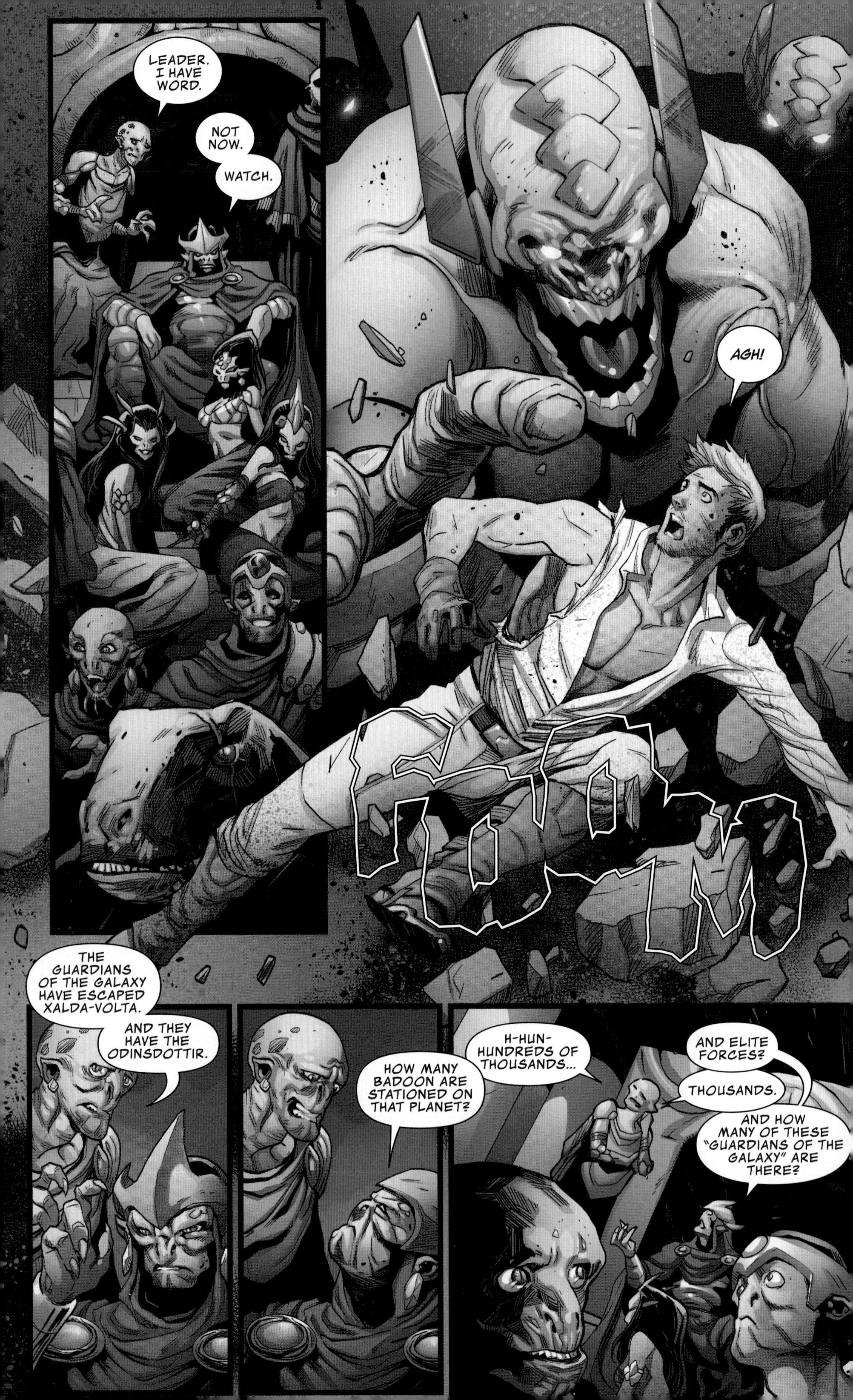
LEADER. I HAVE WORD.
NOT NOW.
WATCH.
AGH!
THE GUARDIANS OF THE GALAXY HAVE ESCAPED XALDA-VOLTA.
AND THEY HAVE THE ODINSDOTTIR.
HOW MANY BADOON ARE STATIONED ON THAT PLANET?
H-HUN-HUNDREDS OF THOUSANDS...
AND ELITE FORCES?
THOUSANDS.
AND HOW MANY OF THESE "GUARDIANS OF THE GALAXY" ARE THERE?

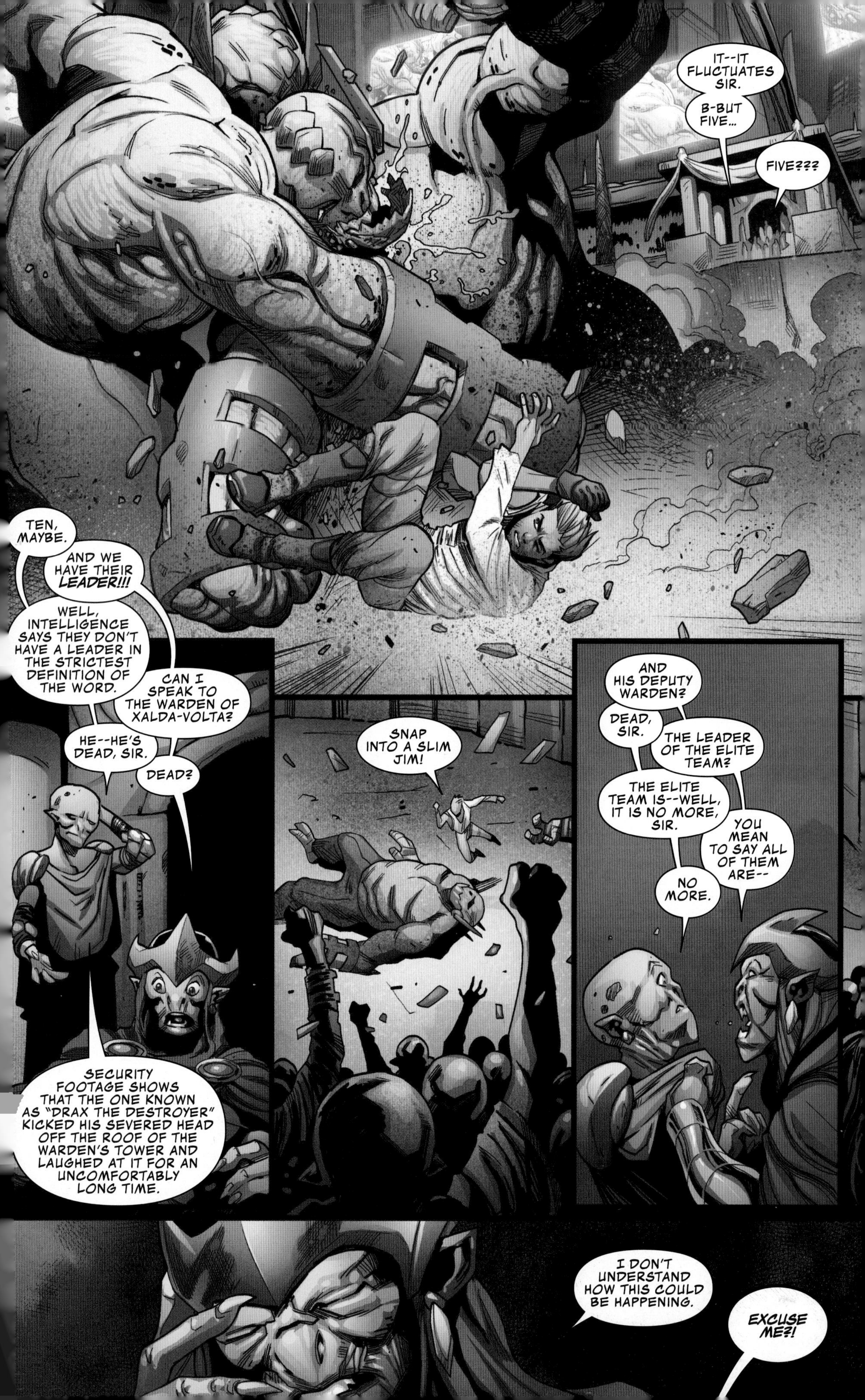
IT--IT FLUCTUATES SIR.
B-BUT FIVE...
FIVE???
TEN, MAYBE.
AND WE HAVE THEIR LEADER!!!
WELL, INTELLIGENCE SAYS THEY DON'T HAVE A LEADER IN THE STRICTEST DEFINITION OF THE WORD.
CAN I SPEAK TO THE WARDEN OF XALDA-VOLTA?
HE--HE'S DEAD, SIR.
DEAD?
SECURITY FOOTAGE SHOWS THAT THE ONE KNOWN AS "DRAX THE DESTROYER" KICKED HIS SEVERED HEAD OFF THE ROOF OF THE WARDEN'S TOWER AND LAUGHED AT IT FOR AN UNCOMFORTABLY LONG TIME.
SNAP INTO A SLIM JIM!
AND HIS DEPUTY WARDEN?
DEAD, SIR.
THE LEADER OF THE ELITE TEAM?
THE ELITE TEAM IS--WELL, IT IS NO MORE, SIR.
YOU MEAN TO SAY ALL OF THEM ARE--
NO MORE.
I DON'T UNDERSTAND HOW THIS COULD BE HAPPENING.
EXCUSE ME?!

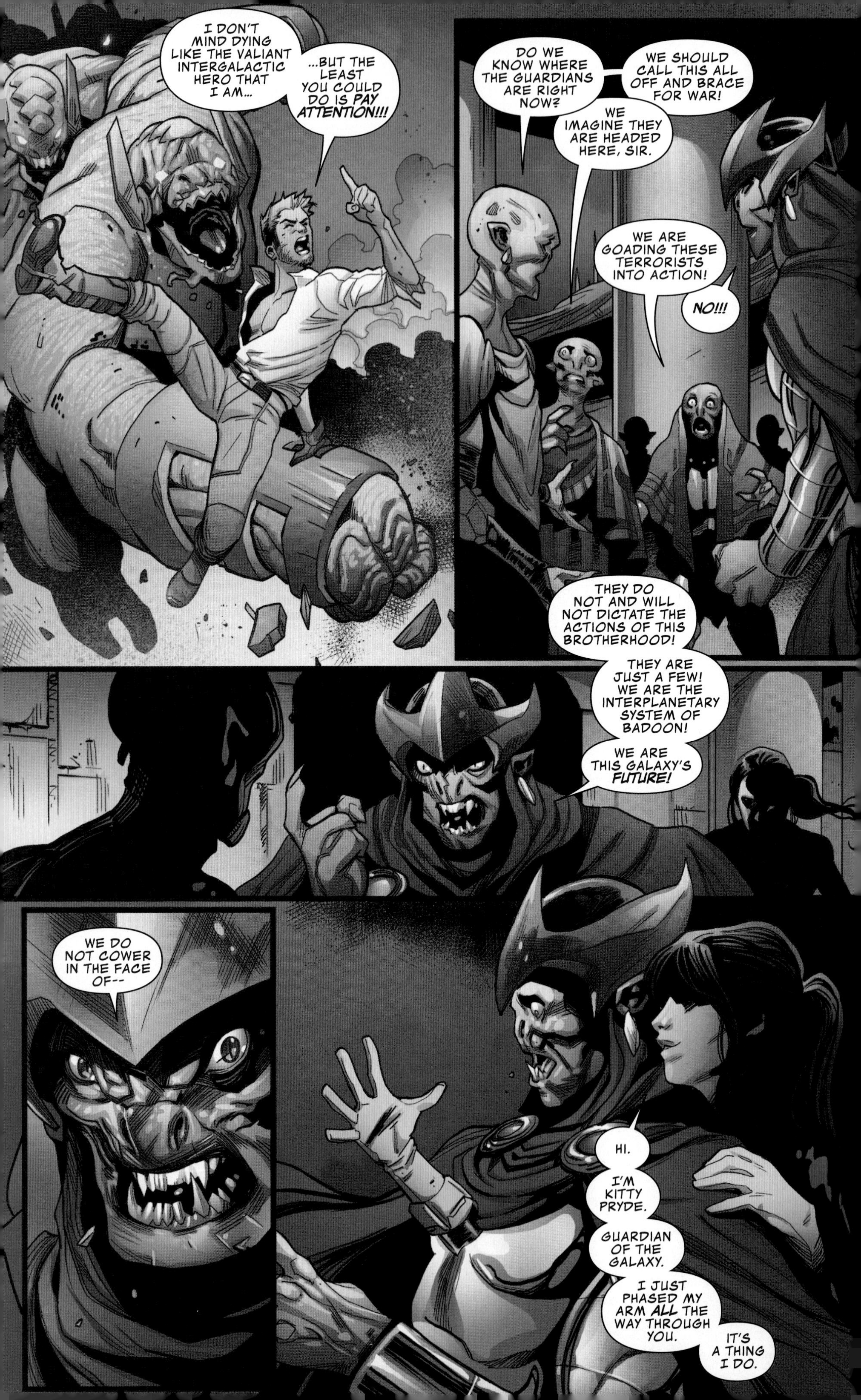

I DON'T MIND DYING LIKE THE VALIANT INTERGALACTIC HERO THAT I AM...
...BUT THE LEAST YOU COULD DO IS PAY ATTENTION!!!
DO WE KNOW WHERE THE GUARDIANS ARE RIGHT NOW?
WE SHOULD CALL THIS ALL OFF AND BRACE FOR WAR!
WE IMAGINE THEY ARE HEADED HERE, SIR.
WE ARE GOADING THESE TERRORISTS INTO ACTION!
NO!!!
THEY DO NOT AND WILL NOT DICTATE THE ACTIONS OF THIS BROTHERHOOD!
THEY ARE JUST A FEW! WE ARE THE INTERPLANETARY SYSTEM OF BADOON!
WE ARE THIS GALAXY'S FUTURE!
WE DO NOT COWER IN THE FACE OF--
HI.
I'M KITTY PRYDE.
GUARDIAN OF THE GALAXY.
I JUST PHASED MY ARM ALL THE WAY THROUGH YOU.
IT'S A THING I DO.

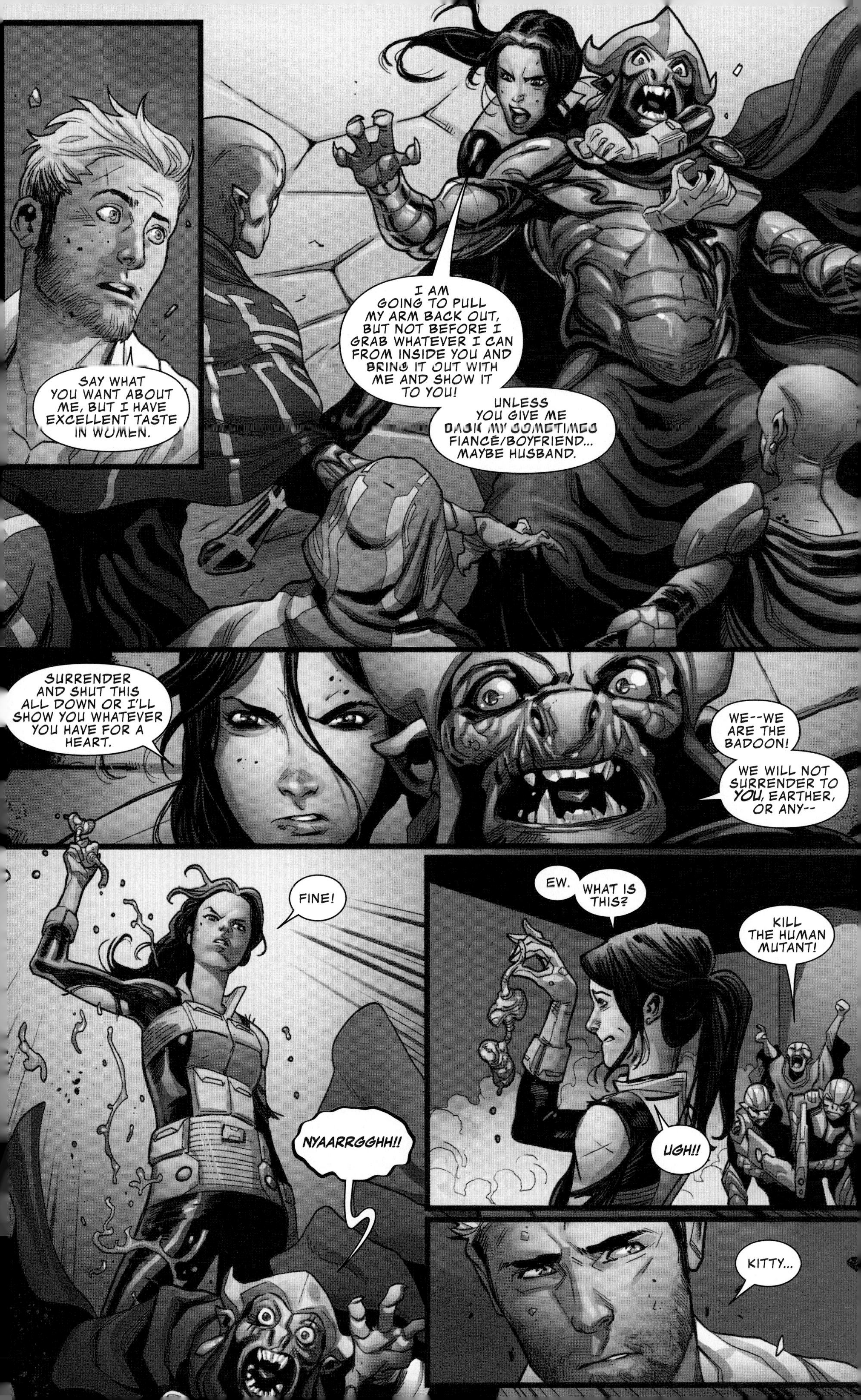
SAY WHAT YOU WANT ABOUT ME, BUT I HAVE EXCELLENT TASTE IN WOMEN.
I AM GOING TO PULL MY ARM BACK OUT, BUT NOT BEFORE I GRAB WHATEVER I CAN FROM INSIDE YOU AND BRING IT OUT WITH ME AND SHOW IT TO YOU!
UNLESS YOU GIVE ME BACK MY SOMETIMES FIANCÉ/BOYFRIEND... MAYBE HUSBAND.
SURRENDER AND SHUT THIS ALL DOWN OR I'LL SHOW YOU WHATEVER YOU HAVE FOR A HEART.
WE--WE ARE THE BADOON!
WE WILL NOT SURRENDER TO YOU, EARTHER, OR ANY--
FINE!
NYAARRGGHH!!
EW.
WHAT IS THIS?
KILL THE HUMAN MUTANT!
UGH!!
KITTY...

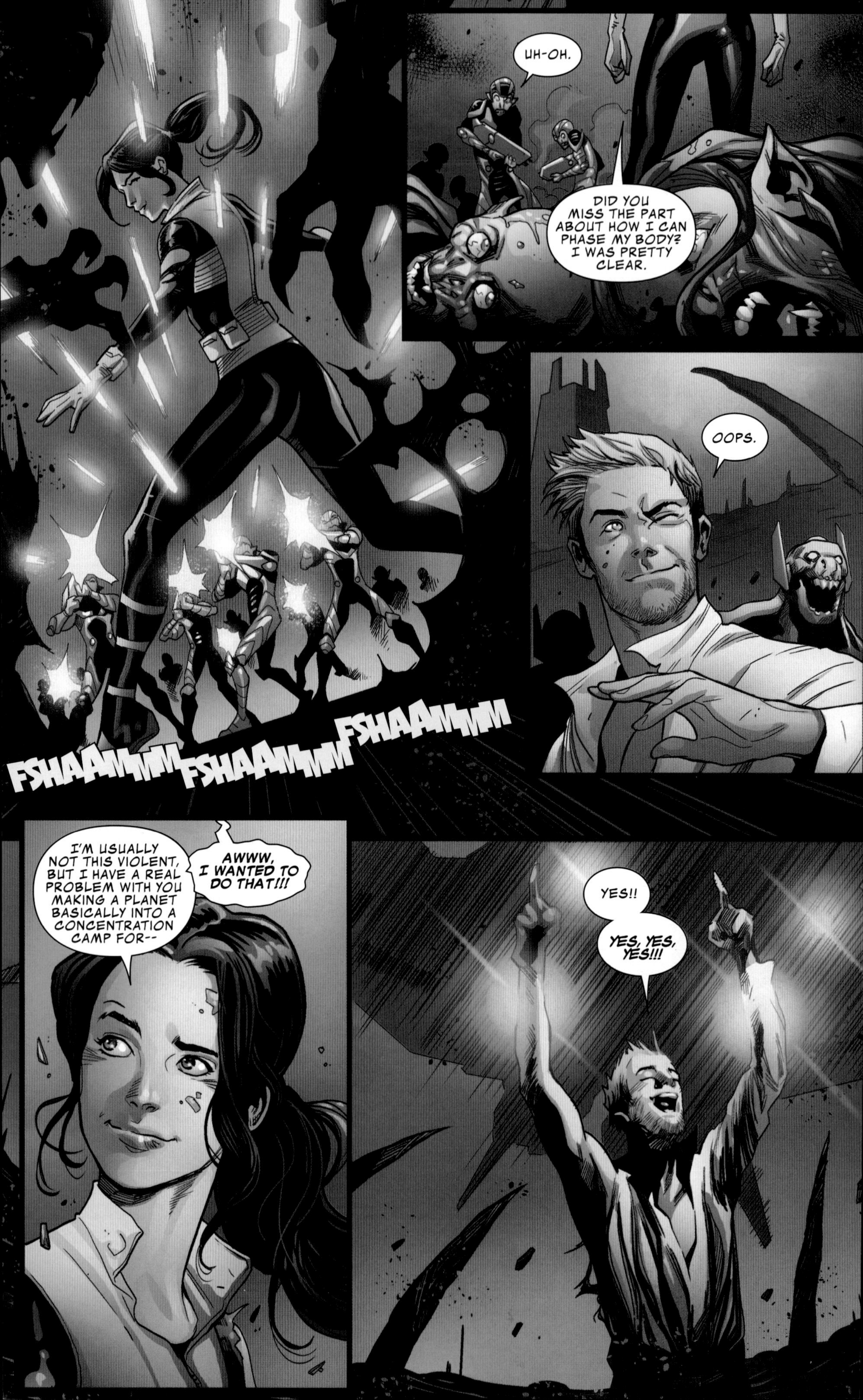
UH-OH.
DID YOU MISS THE PART ABOUT HOW I CAN PHASE MY BODY? I WAS PRETTY CLEAR.
FSHAAMMM FSHAAMMM FSHAAMMM
OOPS.
I'M USUALLY NOT THIS VIOLENT, BUT I HAVE A REAL PROBLEM WITH YOU MAKING A PLANET BASICALLY INTO A CONCENTRATION CAMP FOR--
AWWW, I WANTED TO DO THAT!!!
YES!!
YES, YES, YES!!!

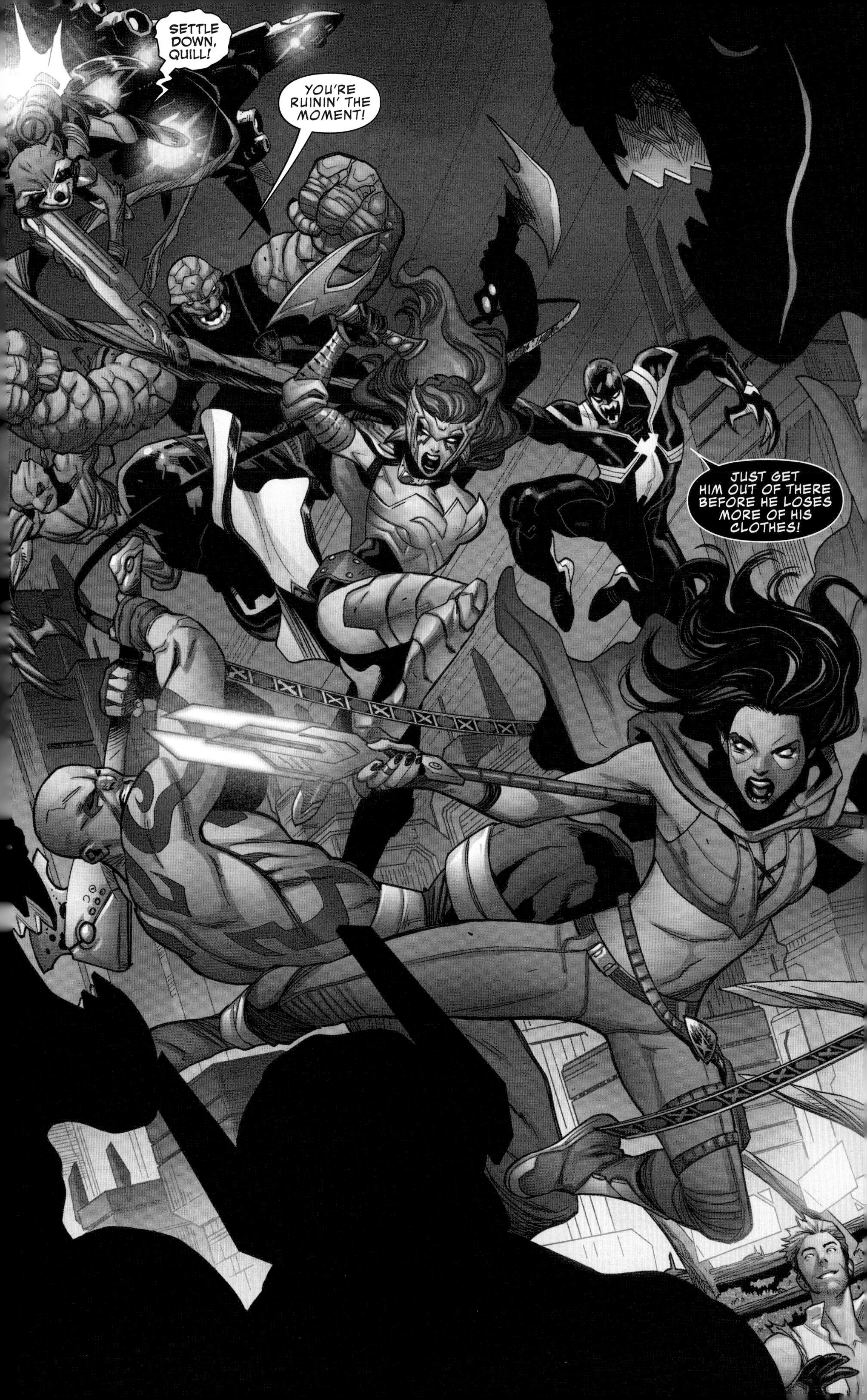
SETTLE DOWN, QUILL!
YOU'RE RUININ' THE MOMENT!
JUST GET HIM OUT OF THERE BEFORE HE LOSES MORE OF HIS CLOTHES!

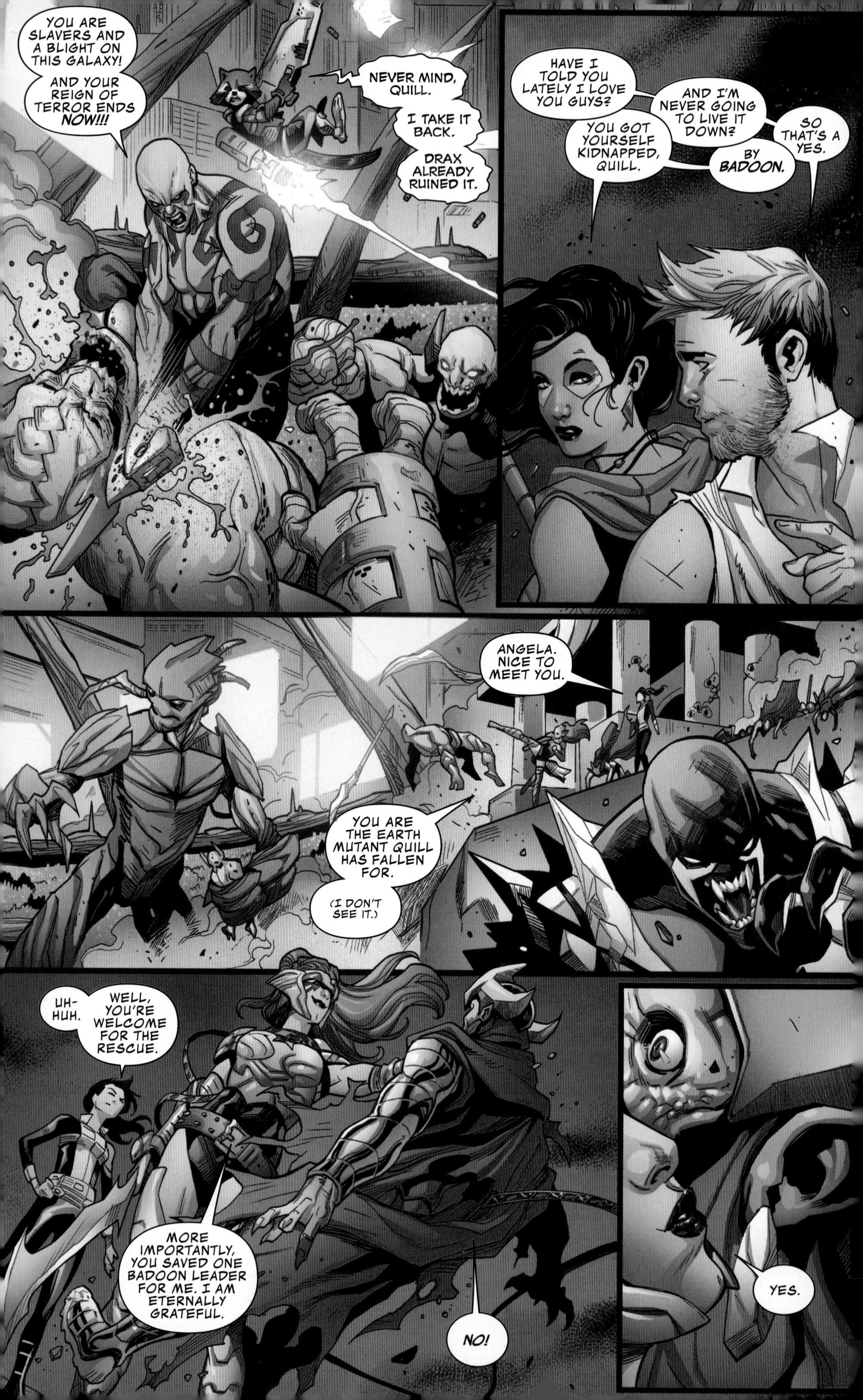
YOU ARE SLAVERS AND A BLIGHT ON THIS GALAXY!
AND YOUR REIGN OF TERROR ENDS NOW!!!
NEVER MIND, QUILL.
I TAKE IT BACK.
DRAX ALREADY RUINED IT.
HAVE I TOLD YOU LATELY I LOVE YOU GUYS?
YOU GOT YOURSELF KIDNAPPED, QUILL.
AND I'M NEVER GOING TO LIVE IT DOWN?
BY BADOON.
SO THAT'S A YES.
ANGELA. NICE TO MEET YOU.
YOU ARE THE EARTH MUTANT QUILL HAS FALLEN FOR.
(I DON'T SEE IT.)
UH-HUH.
WELL, YOU'RE WELCOME FOR THE RESCUE.
MORE IMPORTANTLY, YOU SAVED ONE BADOON LEADER FOR ME. I AM ETERNALLY GRATEFUL.
NO!
YES.

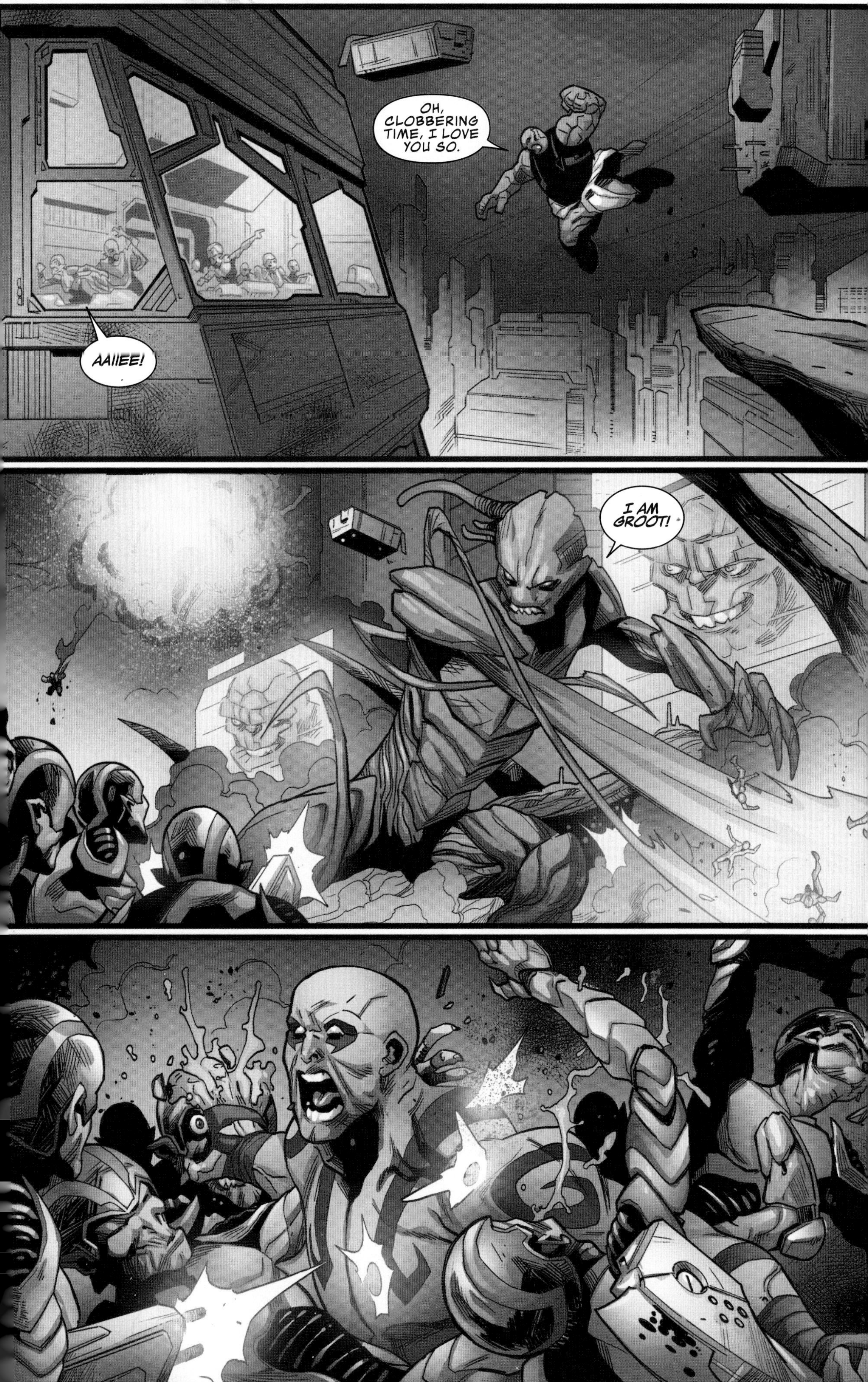
OH, CLOBBERING TIME, I LOVE YOU SO.
AAIIEE!
I AM GROOT!

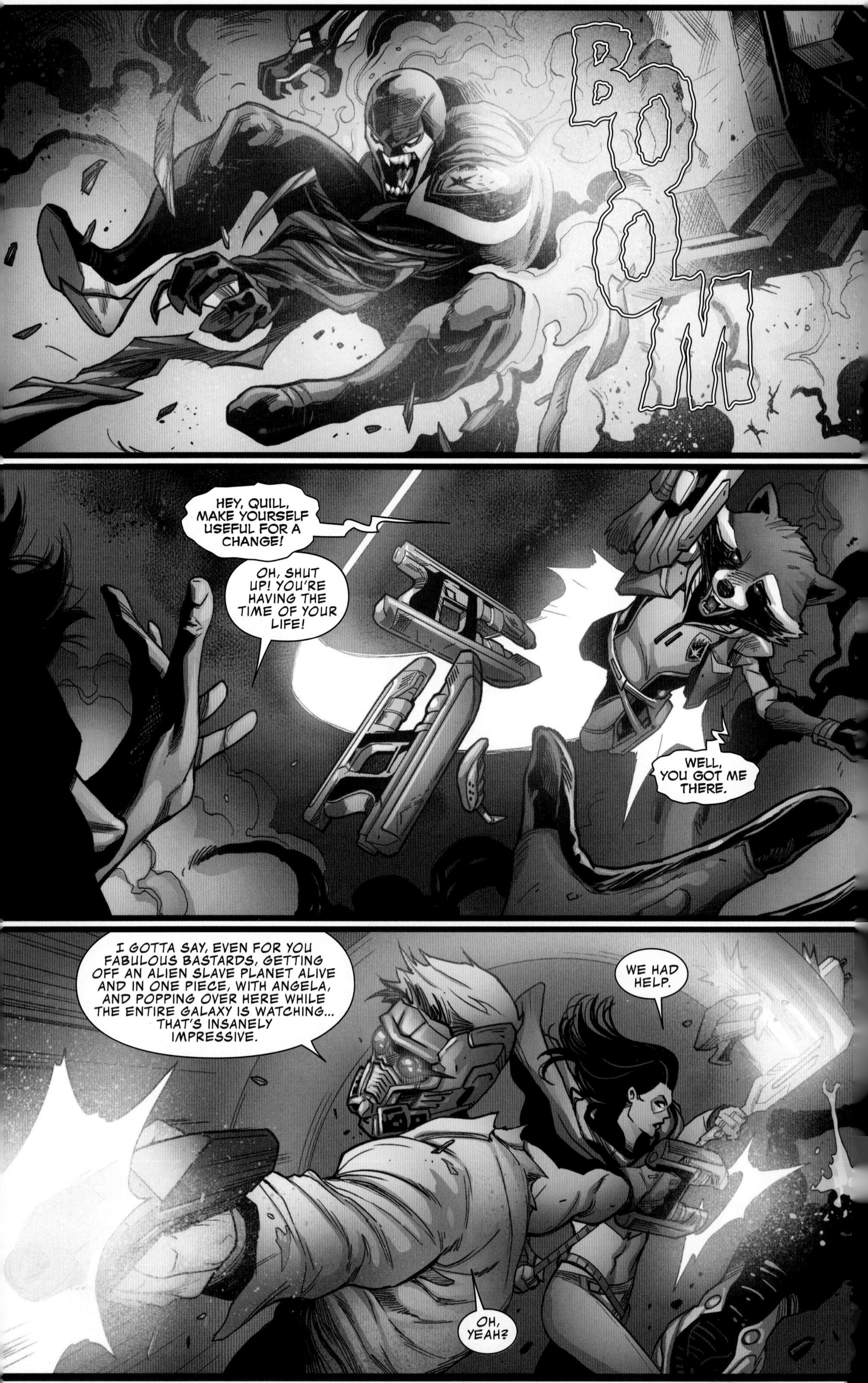
BOOM
HEY, QUILL, MAKE YOURSELF USEFUL FOR A CHANGE!
OH, SHUT UP! YOU'RE HAVING THE TIME OF YOUR LIFE!
WELL, YOU GOT ME THERE.
I GOTTA SAY, EVEN FOR YOU FABULOUS BASTARDS, GETTING OFF AN ALIEN SLAVE PLANET ALIVE AND IN ONE PIECE, WITH ANGELA, AND POPPING OVER HERE WHILE THE ENTIRE GALAXY IS WATCHING... THAT'S INSANELY IMPRESSIVE.
WE HAD HELP.
OH, YEAH?

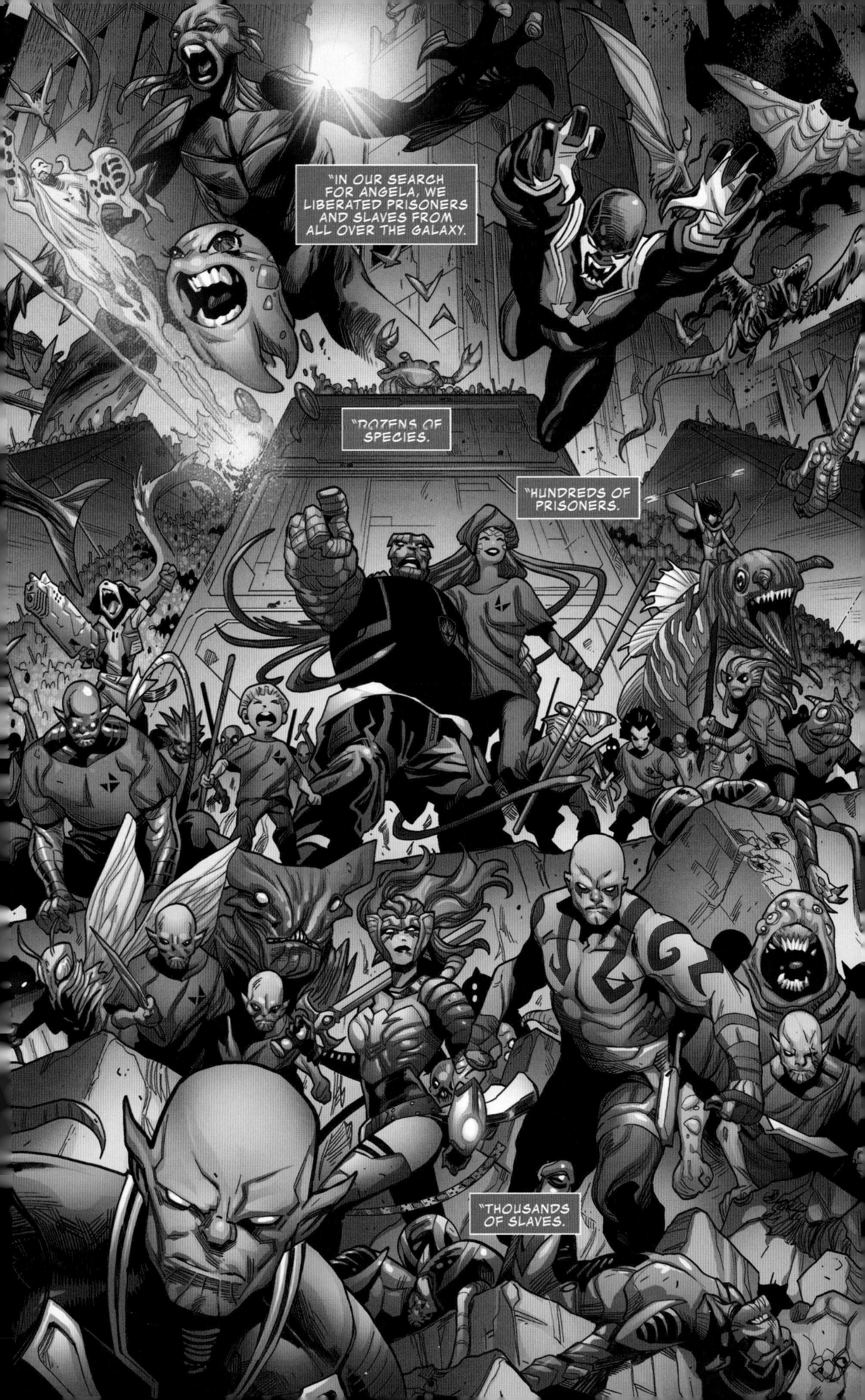
"IN OUR SEARCH FOR ANGELA, WE LIBERATED PRISONERS AND SLAVES FROM ALL OVER THE GALAXY.
"DOZENS OF SPECIES.
"HUNDREDS OF PRISONERS.
"THOUSANDS OF SLAVES.

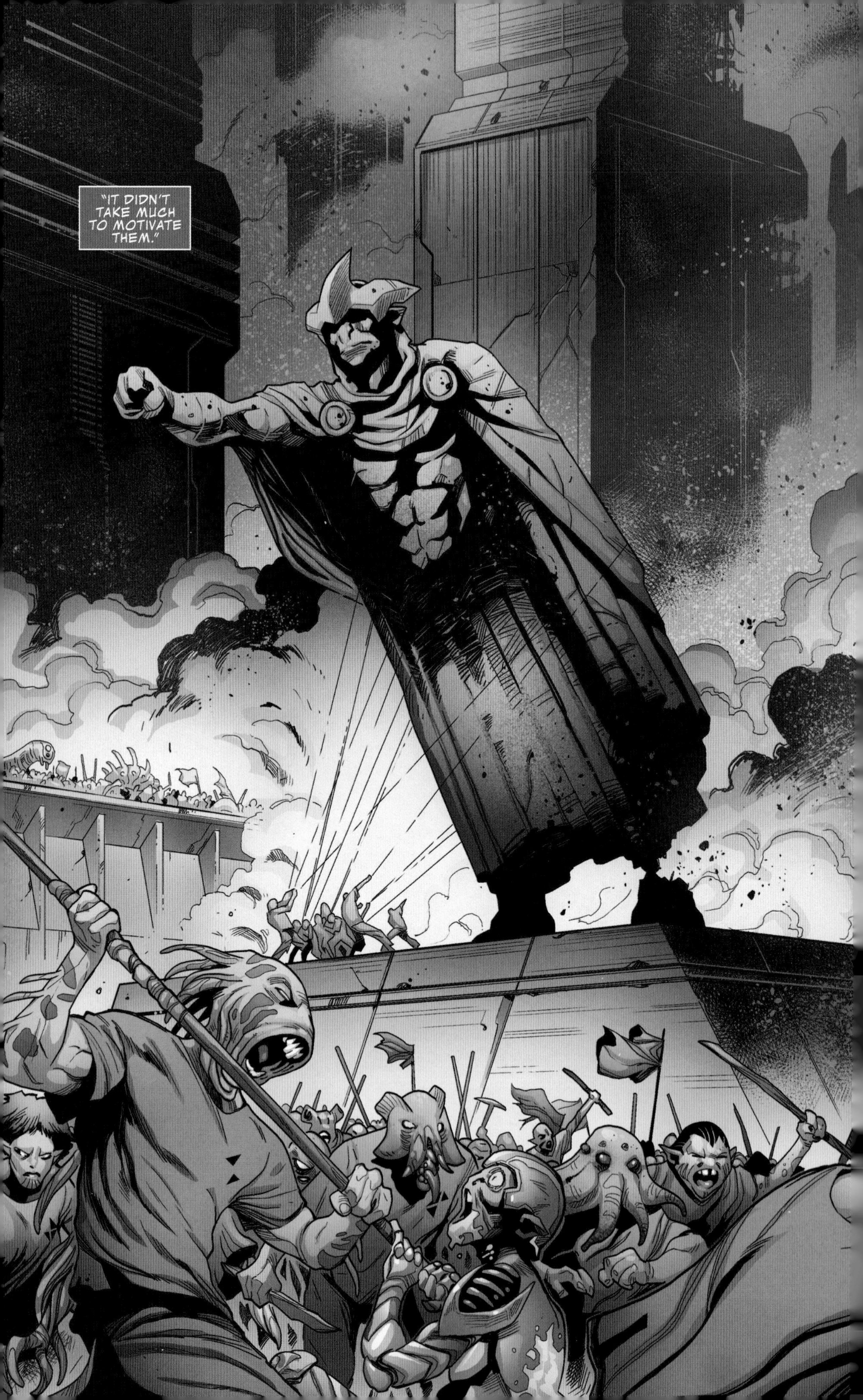
"IT DIDN'T TAKE MUCH TO MOTIVATE THEM."

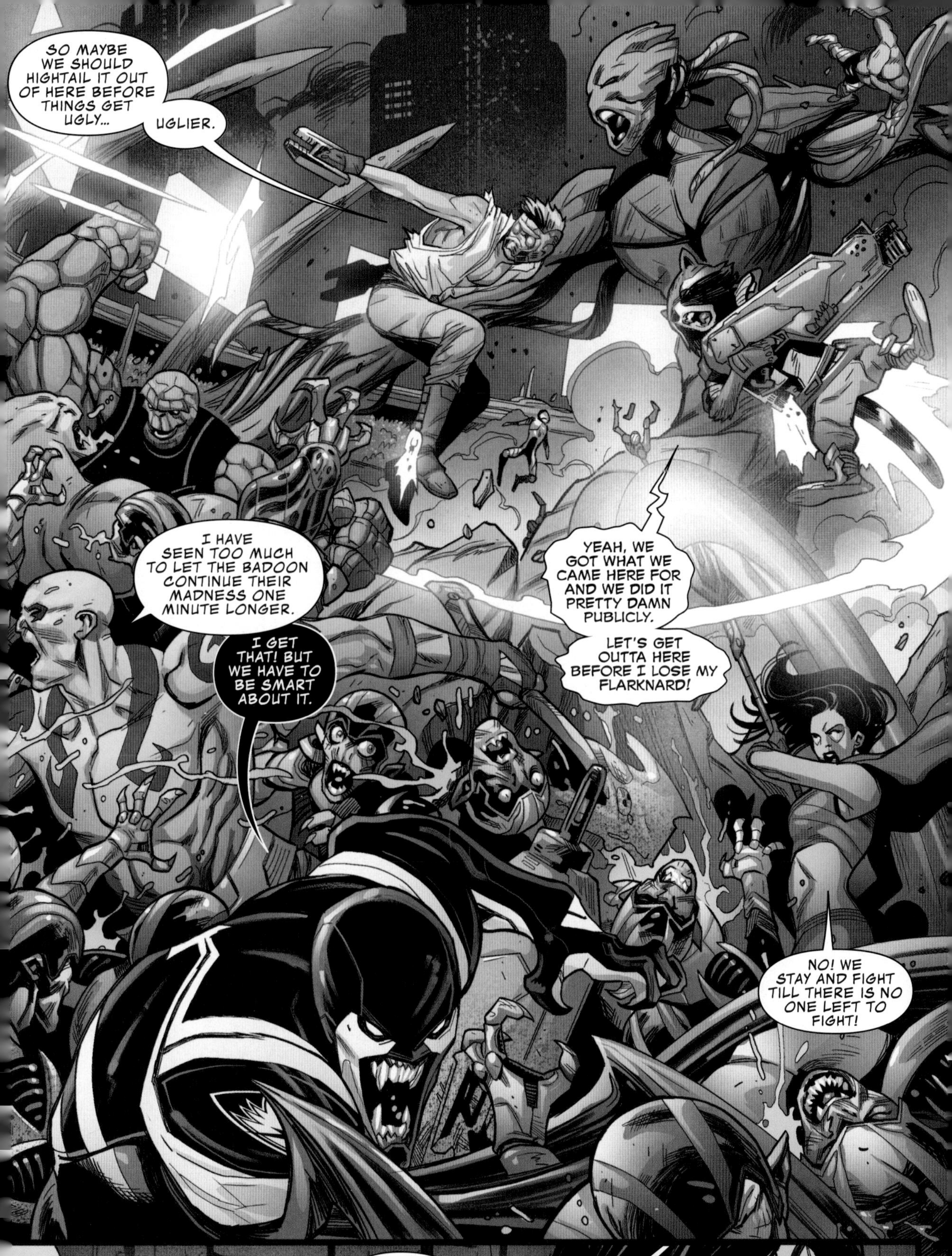
SO MAYBE WE SHOULD HIGHTAIL IT OUT OF HERE BEFORE THINGS GET UGLY...
UGLIER.
I HAVE SEEN TOO MUCH TO LET THE BADOON CONTINUE THEIR MADNESS ONE MINUTE LONGER.
I GET THAT! BUT WE HAVE TO BE SMART ABOUT IT.
YEAH, WE GOT WHAT WE CAME HERE FOR AND WE DID IT PRETTY DAMN PUBLICLY.
LET'S GET OUTTA HERE BEFORE I LOSE MY FLARKNARD!
NO! WE STAY AND FIGHT TILL THERE IS NO ONE LEFT TO FIGHT!

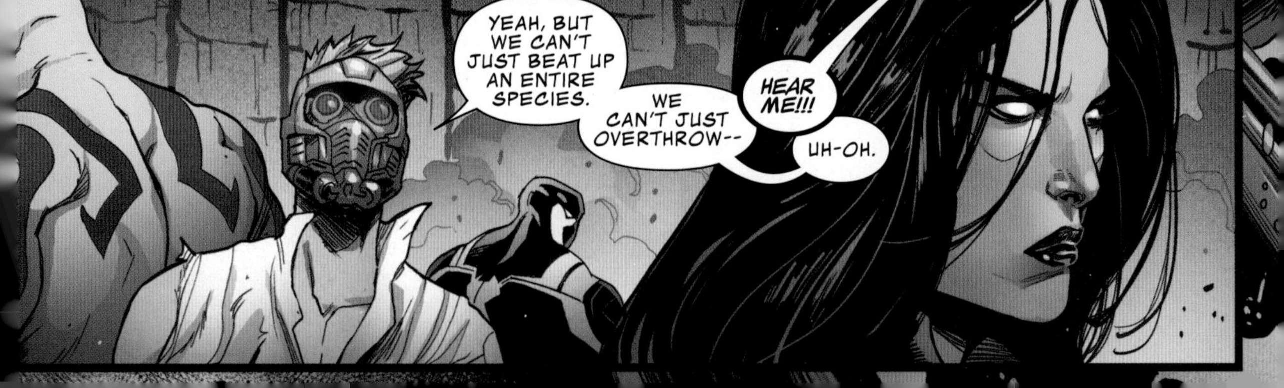
YEAH, BUT WE CAN'T JUST BEAT UP AN ENTIRE SPECIES.
WE CAN'T JUST OVERTHROW--
HEAR ME!!!
UH-OH.

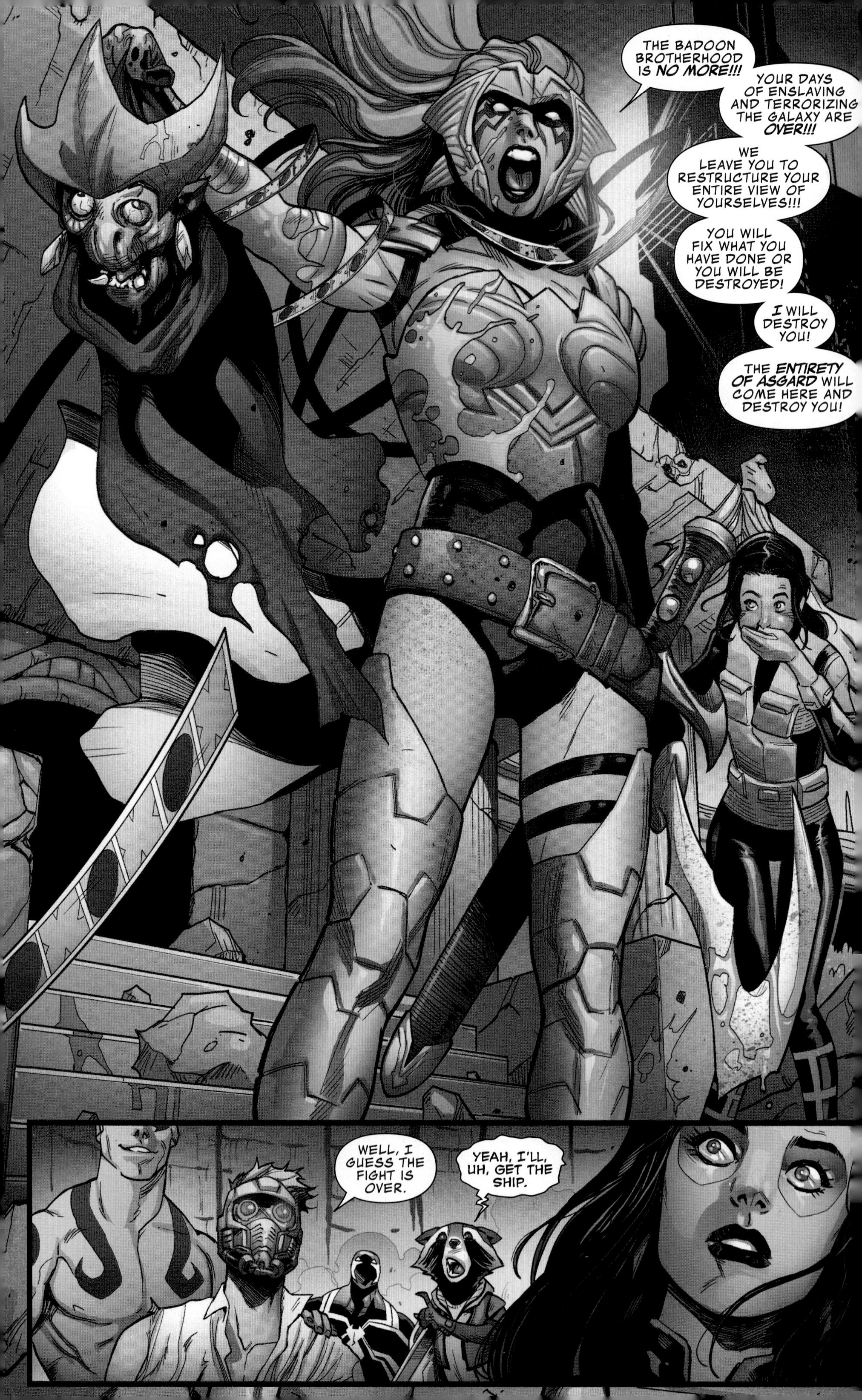
THE BADOON BROTHERHOOD IS NO MORE!!!
YOUR DAYS OF ENSLAVING AND TERRORIZING THE GALAXY ARE OVER!!!
WE LEAVE YOU TO RESTRUCTURE YOUR ENTIRE VIEW OF YOURSELVES!!!
YOU WILL FIX WHAT YOU HAVE DONE OR YOU WILL BE DESTROYED!
I WILL DESTROY YOU!
THE ENTIRETY OF ASGARD WILL COME HERE AND DESTROY YOU!
WELL, I GUESS THE FIGHT IS OVER.
YEAH, I'LL, UH, GET THE SHIP.

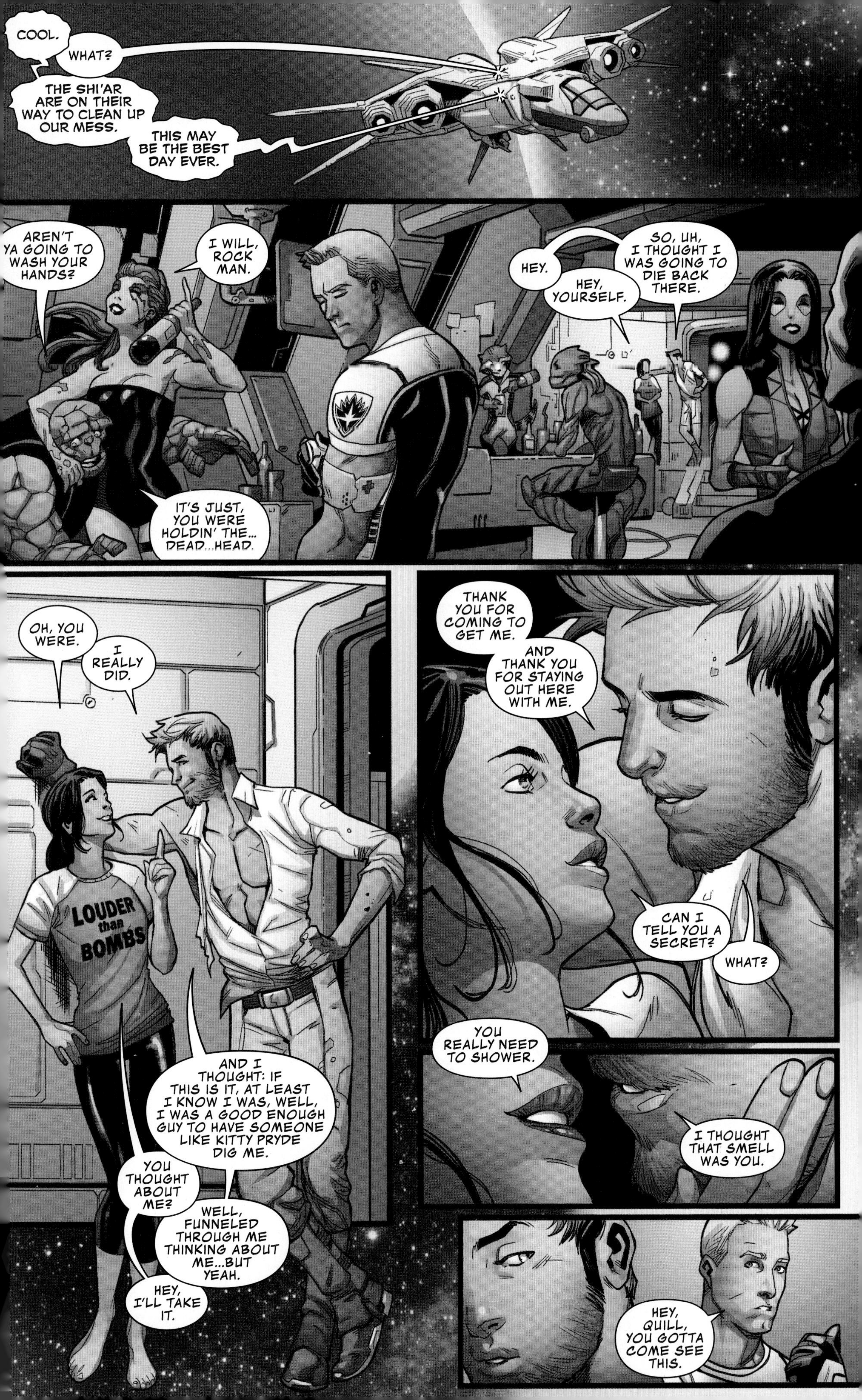
COOL.
WHAT?
THE SHI'AR ARE ON THEIR WAY TO CLEAN UP OUR MESS.
THIS MAY BE THE BEST DAY EVER.
AREN'T YA GOING TO WASH YOUR HANDS?
I WILL, ROCK MAN.
IT'S JUST, YOU WERE HOLDIN' THE... DEAD...HEAD.
HEY.
HEY, YOURSELF.
SO, UH, I THOUGHT I WAS GOING TO DIE BACK THERE.
OH, YOU WERE.
I REALLY DID.
LOUDER than BOMBS
AND I THOUGHT: IF THIS IS IT, AT LEAST I KNOW I WAS, WELL, I WAS A GOOD ENOUGH GUY TO HAVE SOMEONE LIKE KITTY PRYDE DIG ME.
YOU THOUGHT ABOUT ME?
WELL, FUNNELED THROUGH ME THINKING ABOUT ME...BUT YEAH.
HEY, I'LL TAKE IT.
THANK YOU FOR COMING TO GET ME.
AND THANK YOU FOR STAYING OUT HERE WITH ME.
CAN I TELL YOU A SECRET?
WHAT?
YOU REALLY NEED TO SHOWER.
I THOUGHT THAT SMELL WAS YOU.
HEY, QUILL, YOU GOTTA COME SEE THIS.

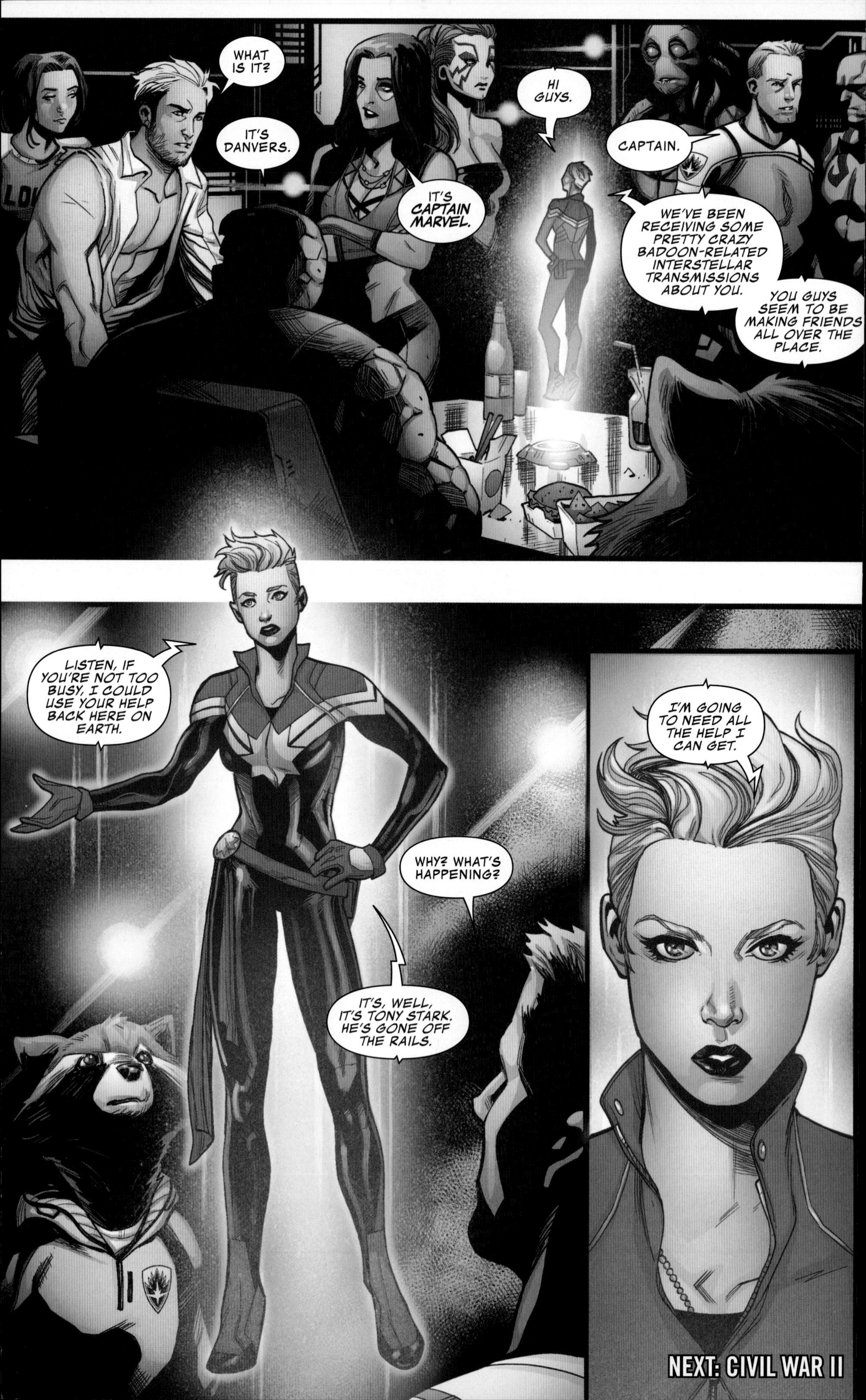
WHAT IS IT?
IT'S DANVERS.
IT'S CAPTAIN MARVEL.
HI GUYS.
CAPTAIN.
WE'VE BEEN RECEIVING SOME PRETTY CRAZY BADOON-RELATED INTERSTELLAR TRANSMISSIONS ABOUT YOU.
YOU GUYS SEEM TO BE MAKING FRIENDS ALL OVER THE PLACE.
LISTEN, IF YOU'RE NOT TOO BUSY, I COULD USE YOUR HELP BACK HERE ON EARTH.
WHY? WHAT'S HAPPENING?
IT'S, WELL, IT'S TONY STARK. HE'S GONE OFF THE RAILS.
I'M GOING TO NEED ALL THE HELP I CAN GET.
NEXT: CIVIL WAR II

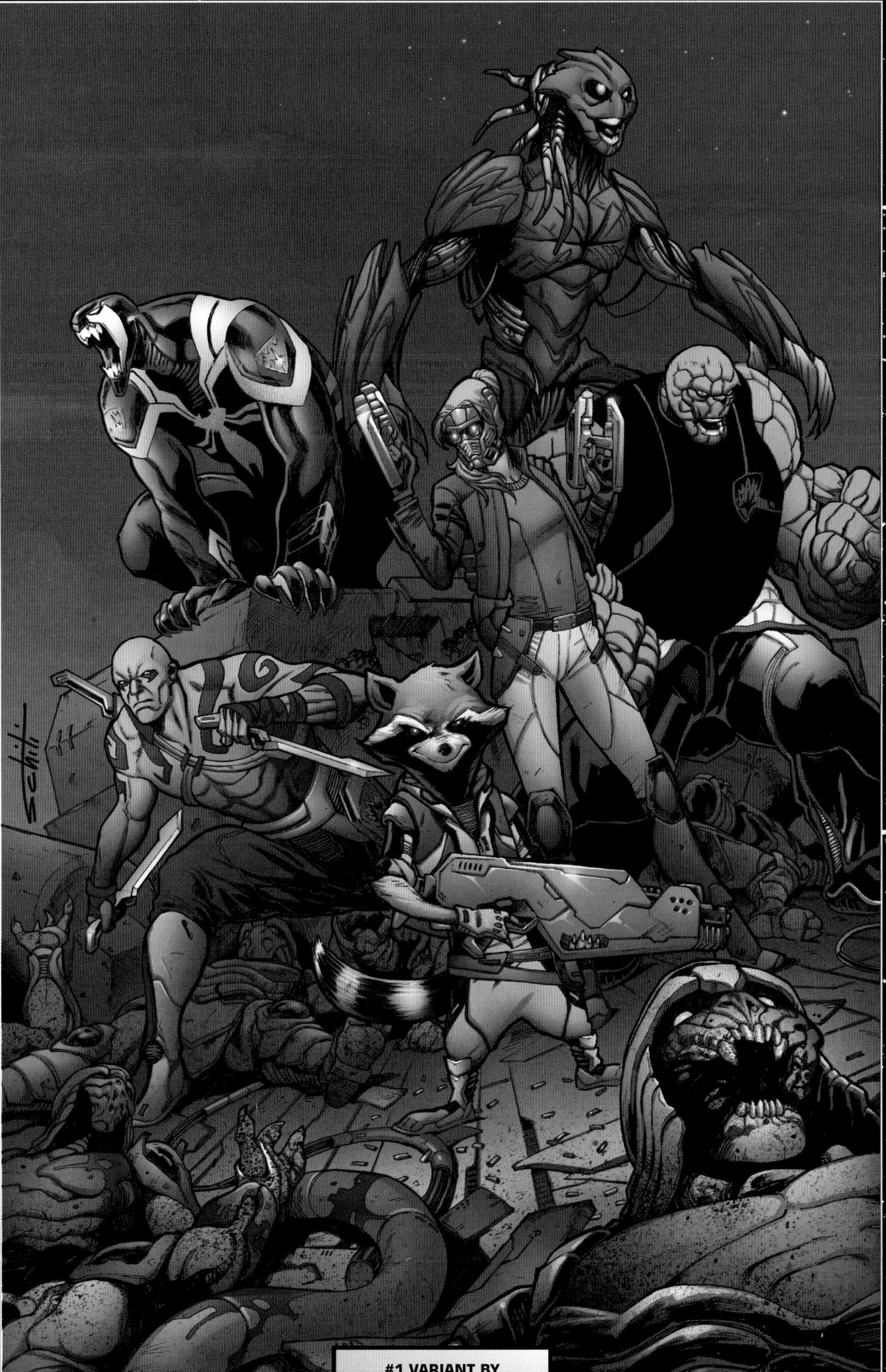

#1 VARIANT BY
VALERIO SCHITI &
RICHARD ISANOVE

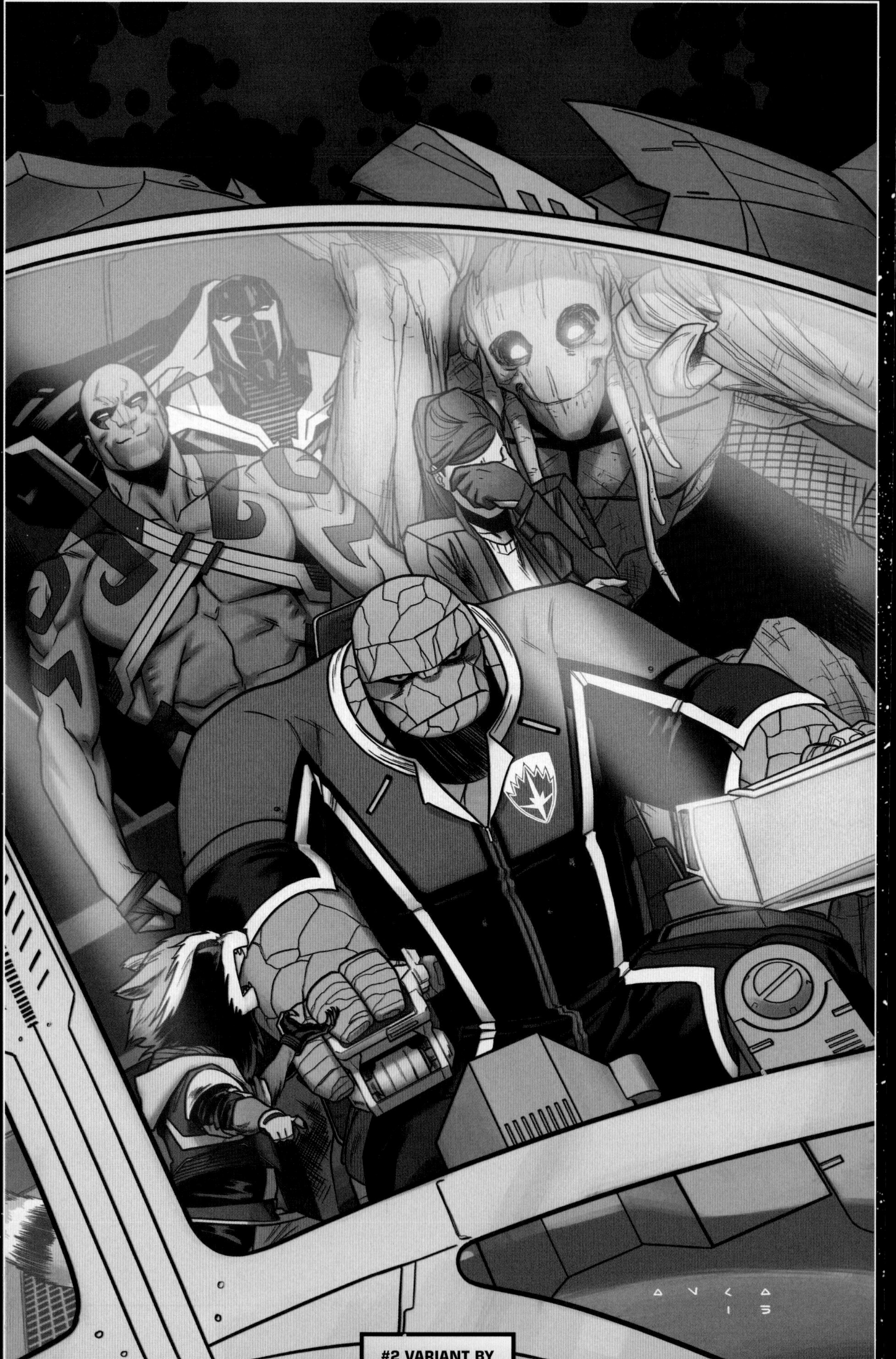

#2 VARIANT BY
KRIS ANKA

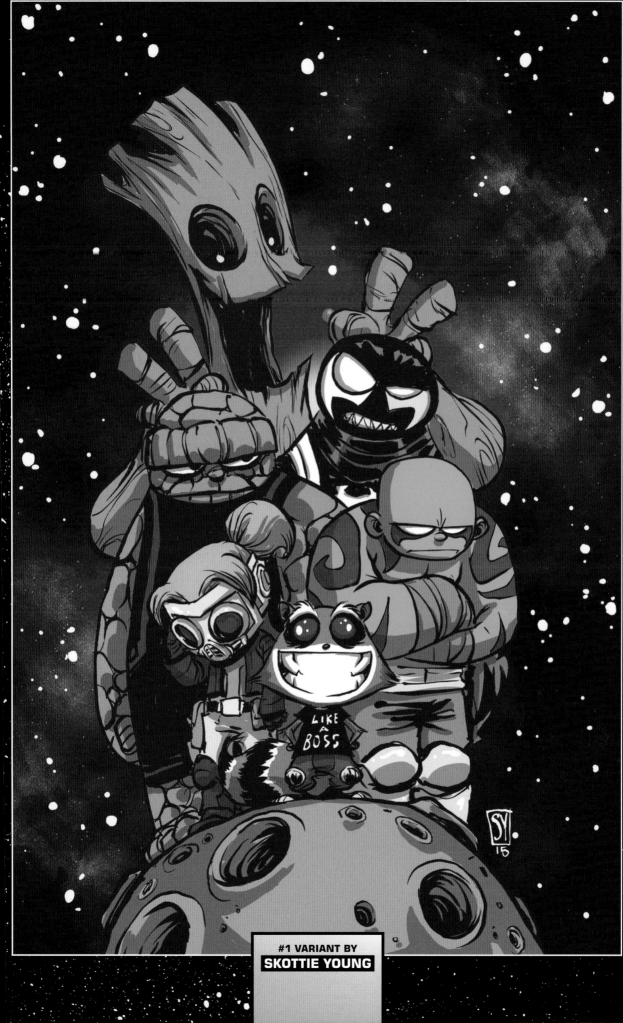

#1 VARIANT BY
SKOTTIE YOUNG

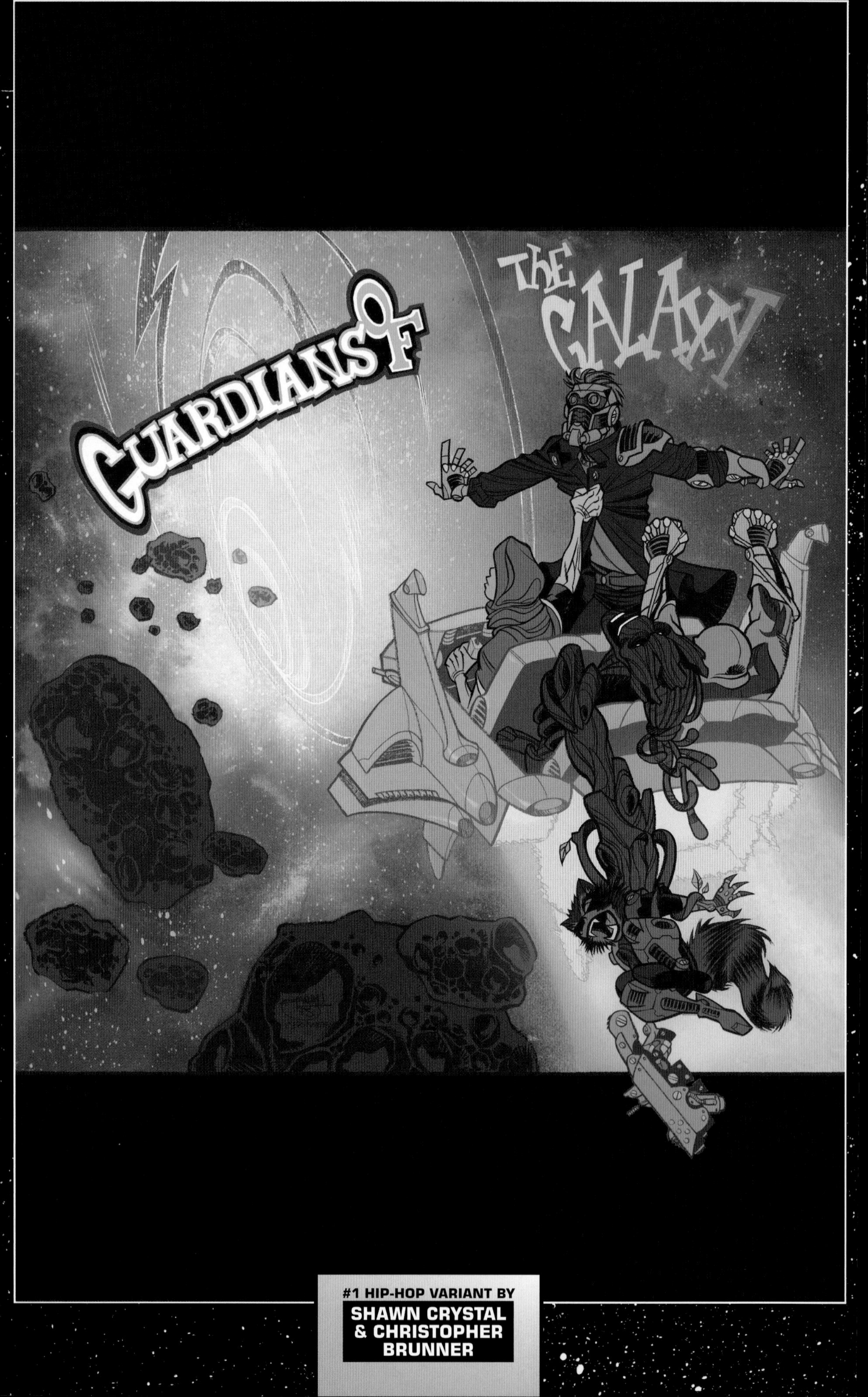
GUARDIANS OF THE GALAXY

#1 HIP-HOP VARIANT BY
SHAWN CRYSTAL
& CHRISTOPHER
BRUNNER

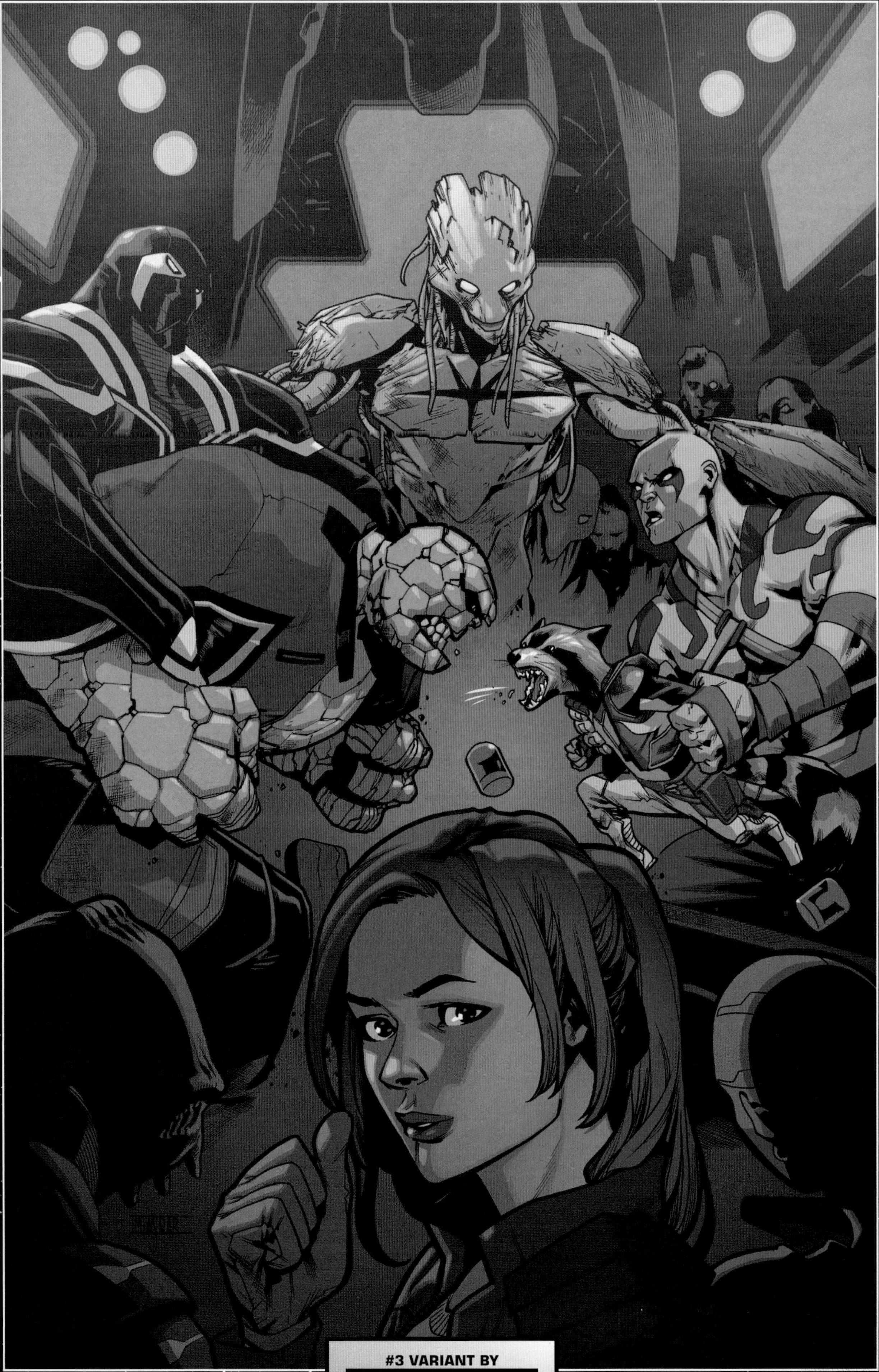

#3 VARIANT BY
MAHMUD ASRAR & DAVE McCAIG

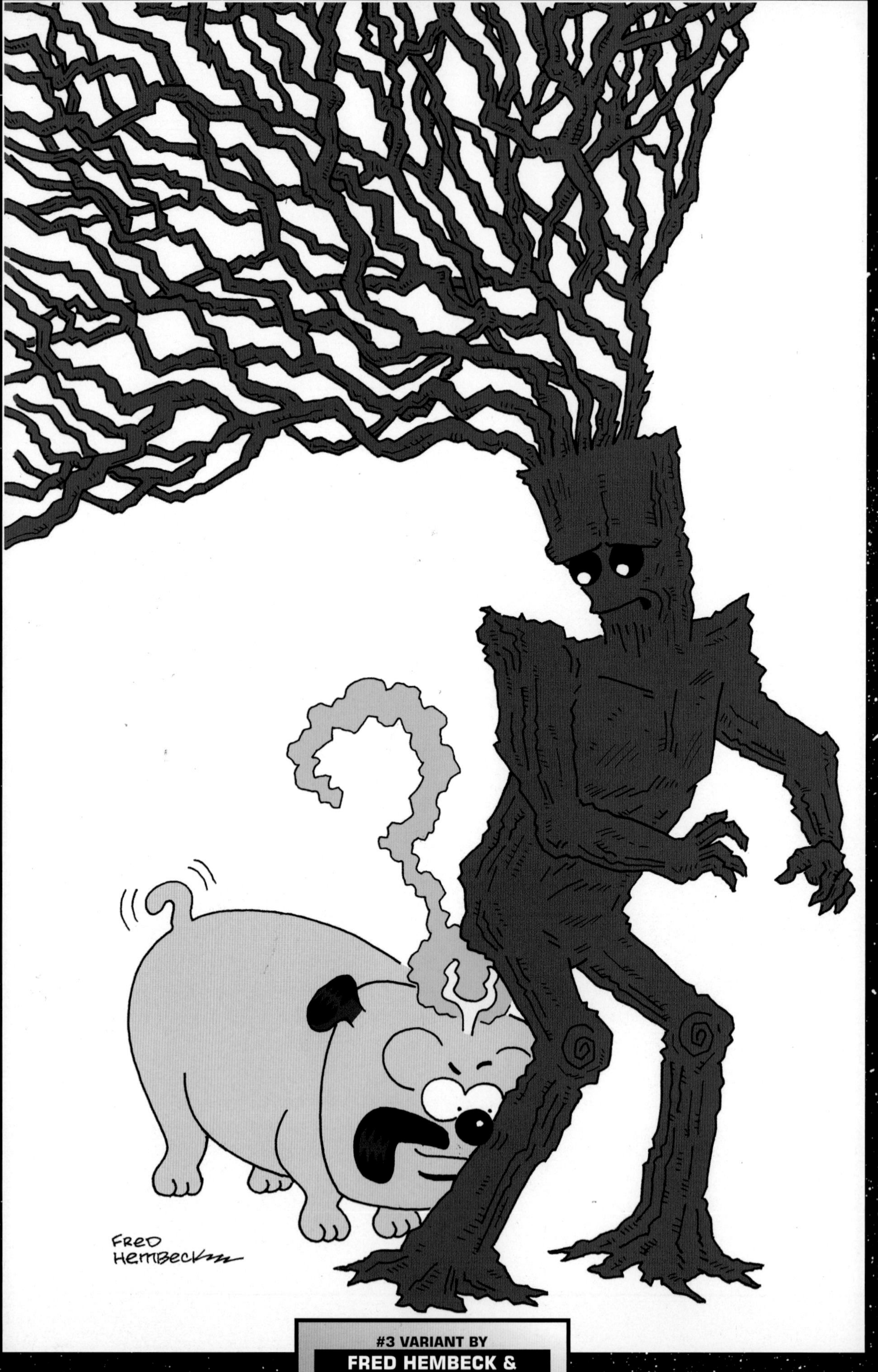
FRED
HEMBECK

#3 VARIANT BY
FRED HEMBECK &
RACHELLE ROSENBERG

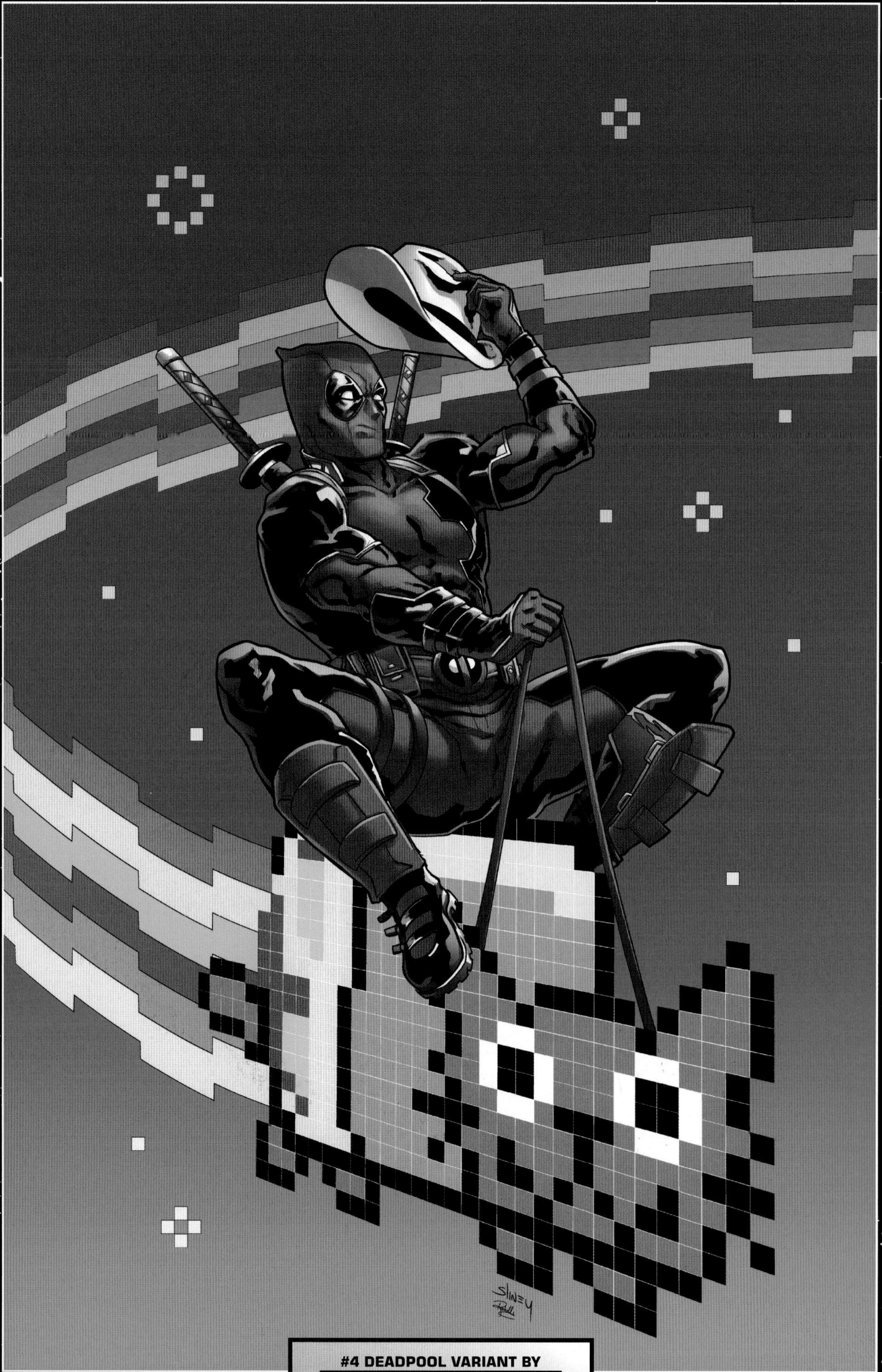
SLINEY
Rachelle

#4 DEADPOOL VARIANT BY

WILL SLINEY & RACHELLE ROSENBERG

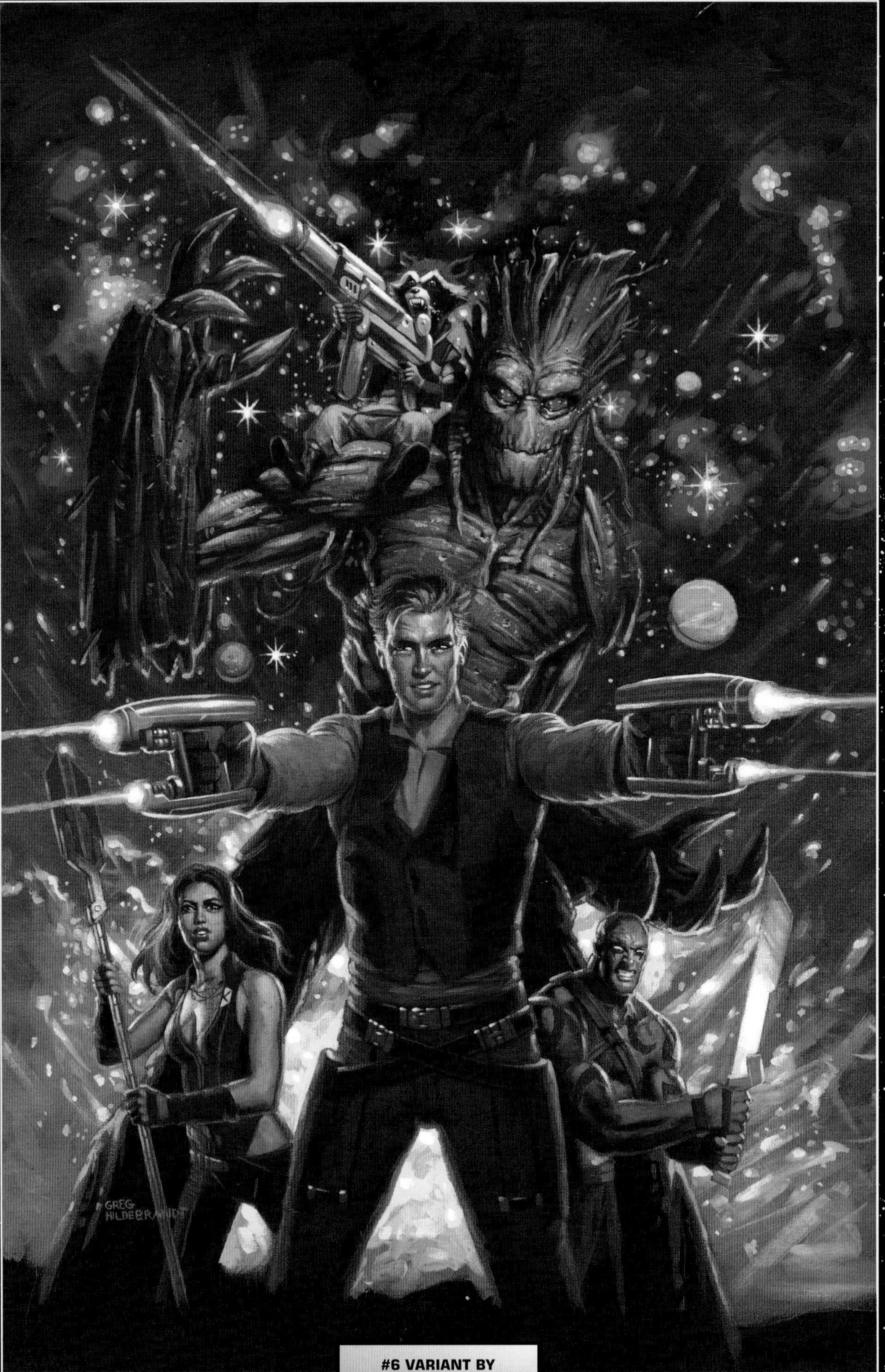
GREG HILDEBRANDT

#6 VARIANT BY
GREG HILDEBRANT

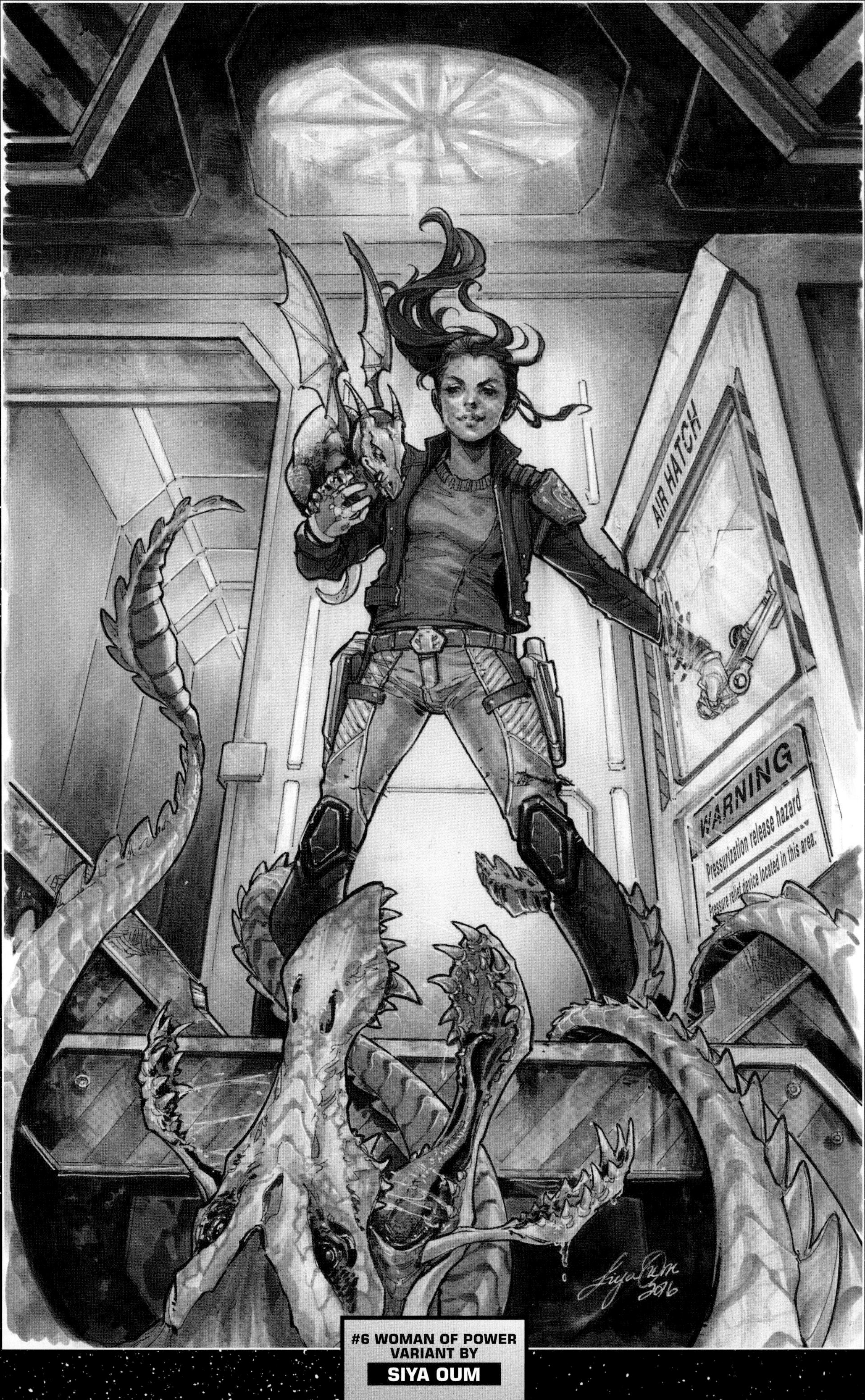
AIR HATCH
WARNING
Pressurization release hazard
Pressure relief device located in this area.

#6 WOMAN OF POWER
VARIANT BY
SIYA OUM

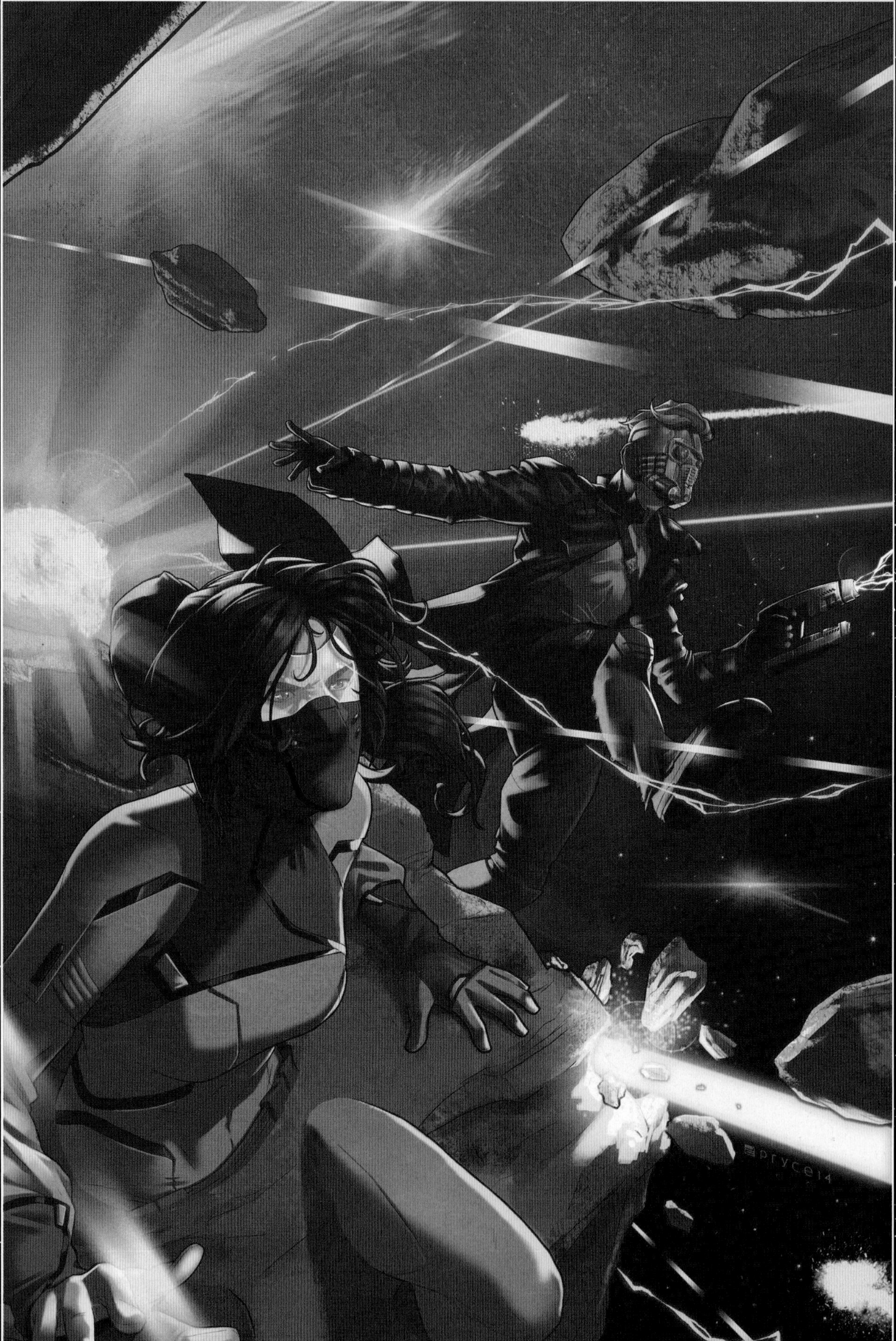
pryce14

#6 VARIANT BY
JAMAL CAMPBELL

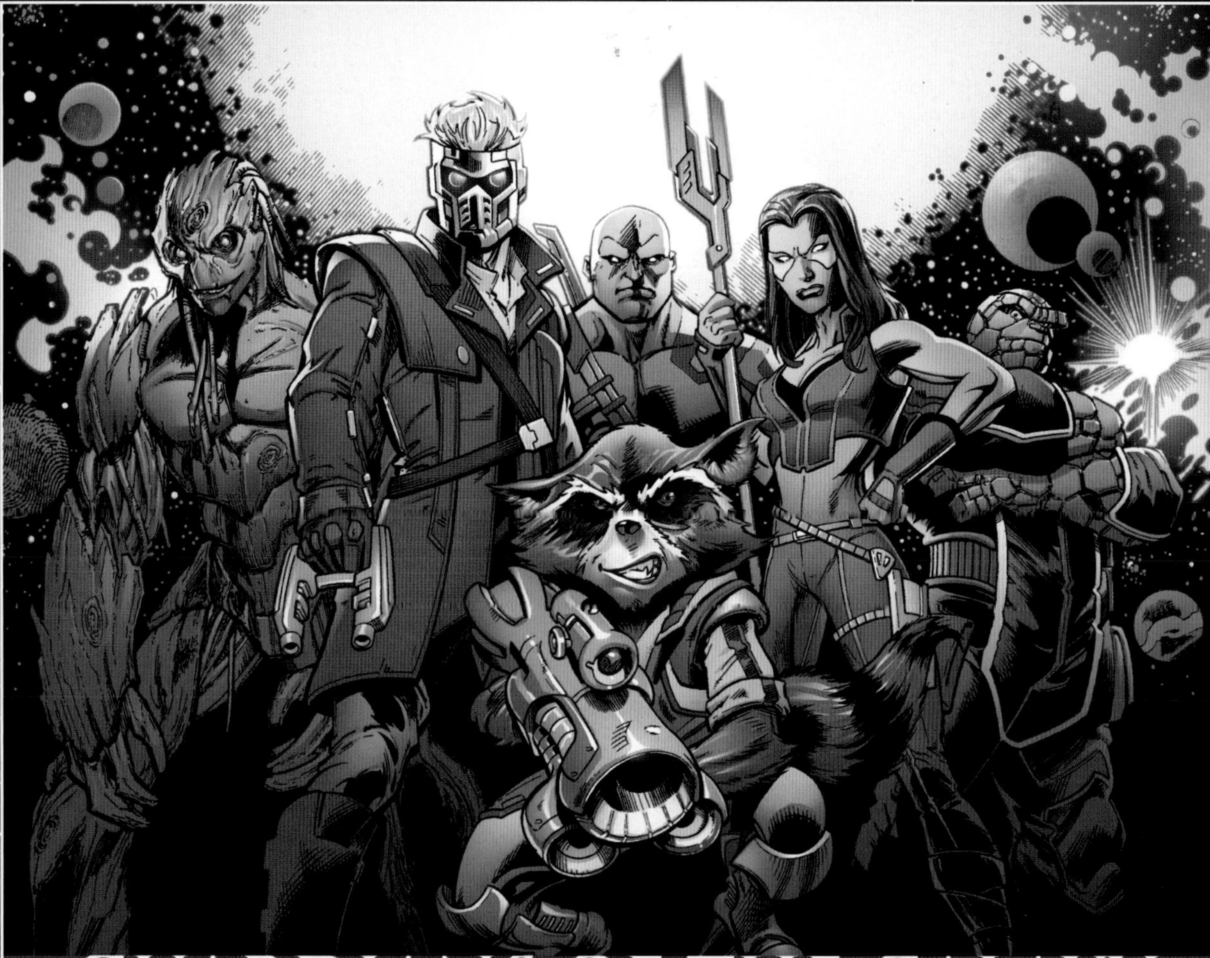

GUARDIANS OF THE GALAXY

A MARVEL COMICS EVENT

CIVIL WAR

#7 CIVIL WAR VARIANT BY

MARK BAGLEY, ANDREW HENNESSY & FRANK D'ARMATA

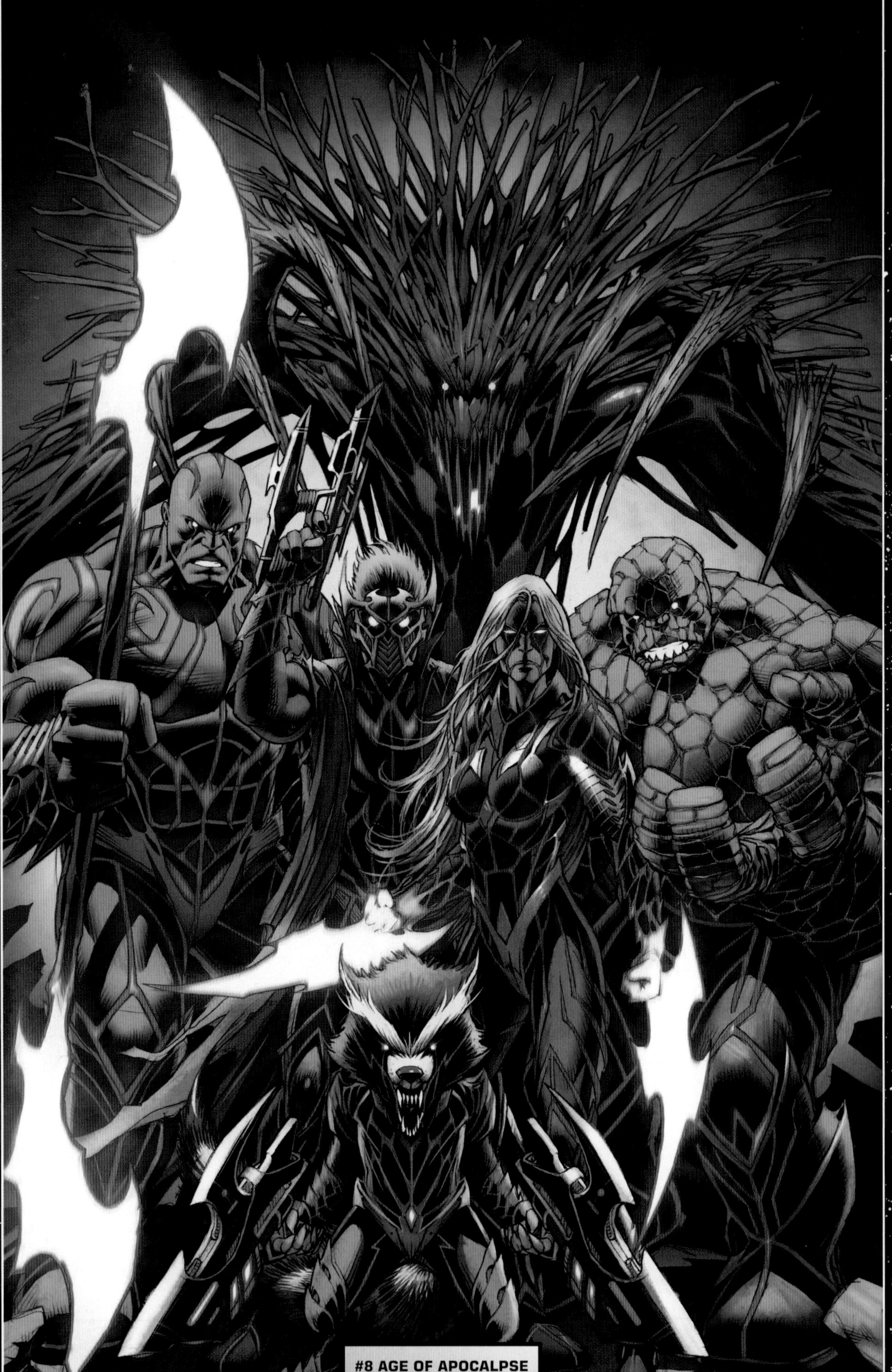

#8 AGE OF APOCALPSE VARIANT BY
DALE KEOWN & JASON KEITH

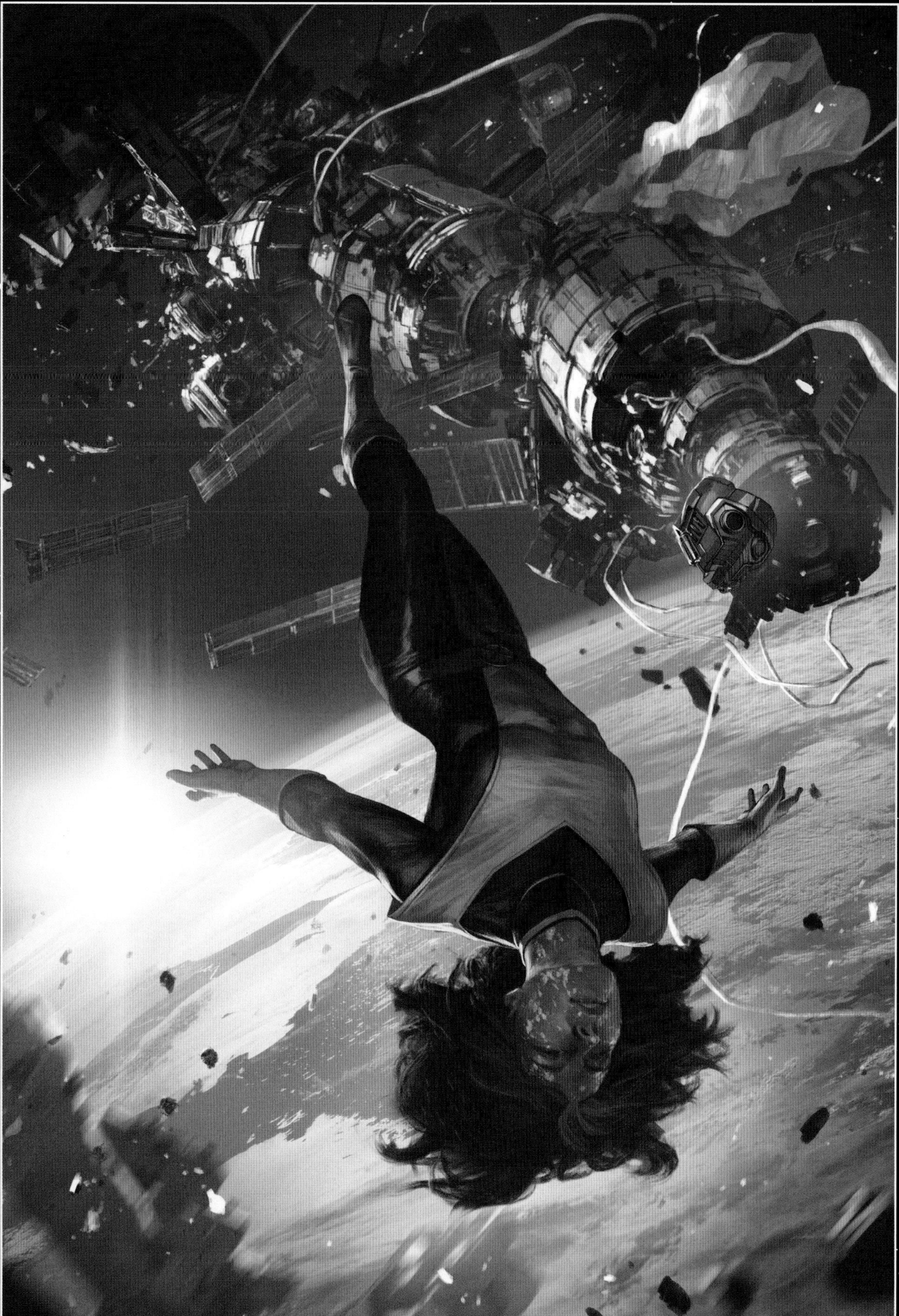

#10 DEATH OF X
VARIANT BY
SKAN

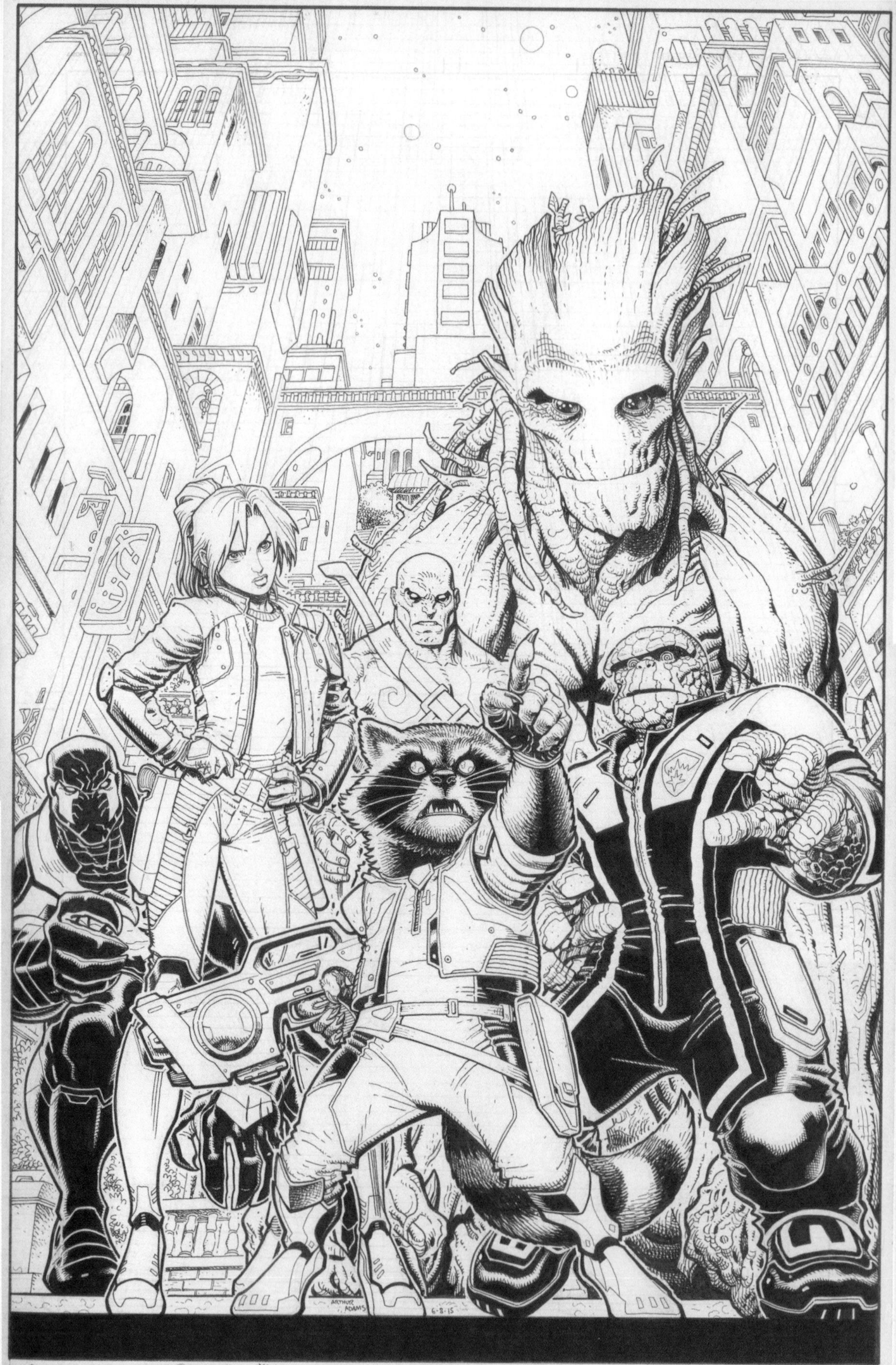
ARTHUR ADAMS
6-8-15
GUARDIANS of the GALAXY #1
ARTHUR ADAMS 6-8-2015

#1 FINAL COVER BY
ART ADAMS

COVER PENCILS BY
ART ADAMS

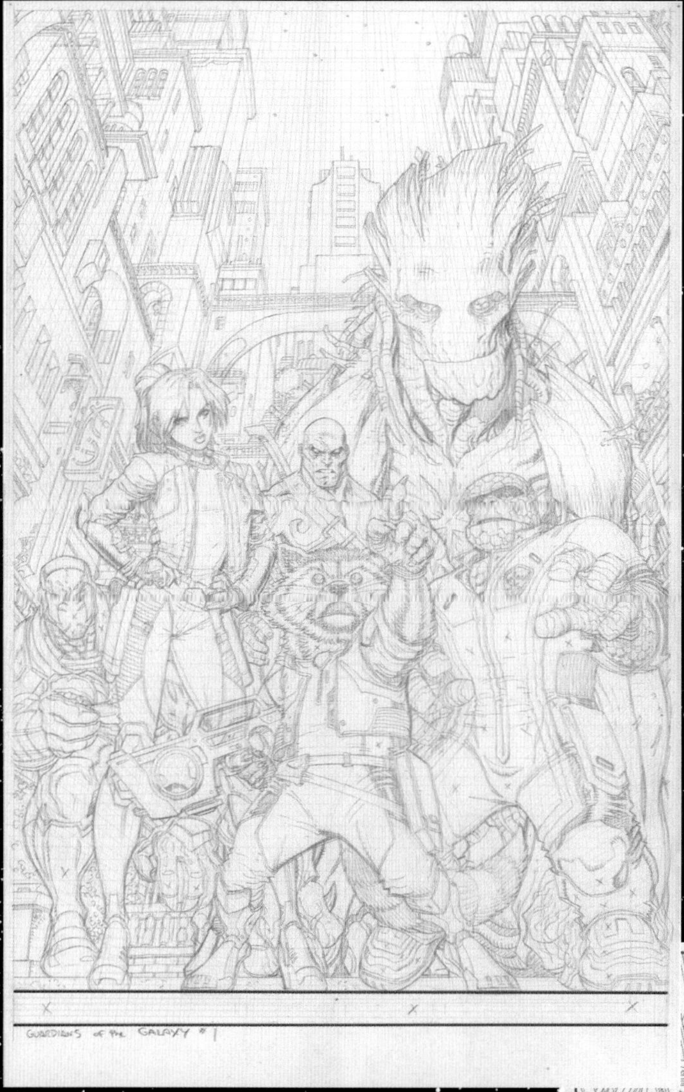
GUARDIANS of the GALAXY #1

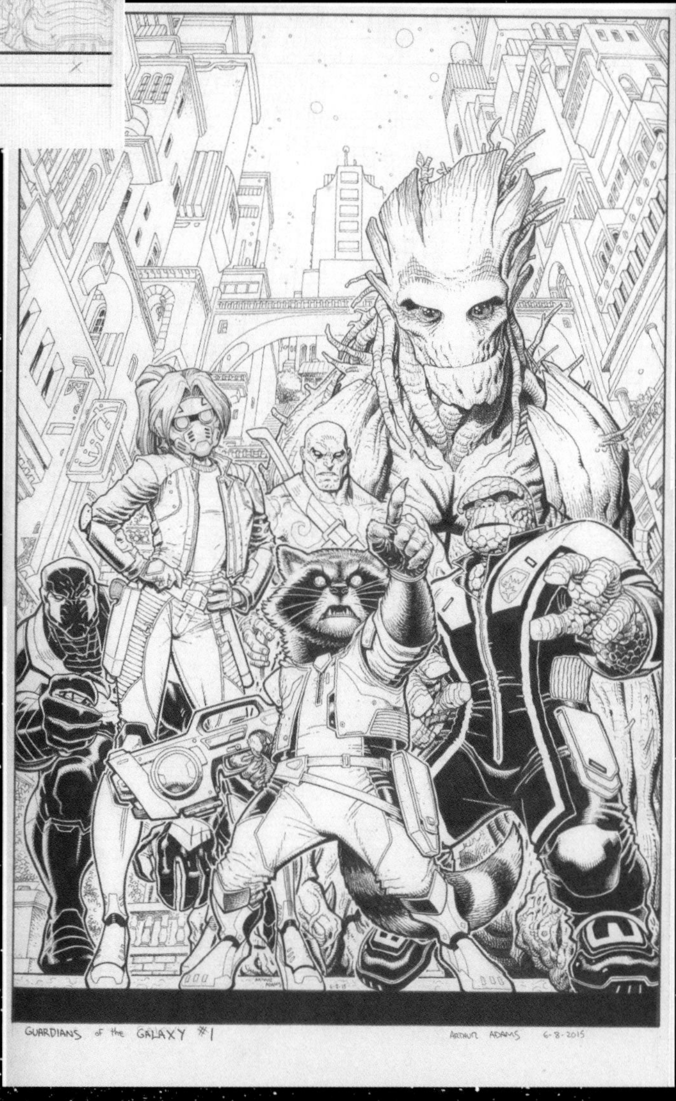
GUARDIANS of the GALAXY #1
ARTHUR ADAMS 6-8-2015

ALTERNATE COVER BY
ART ADAMS

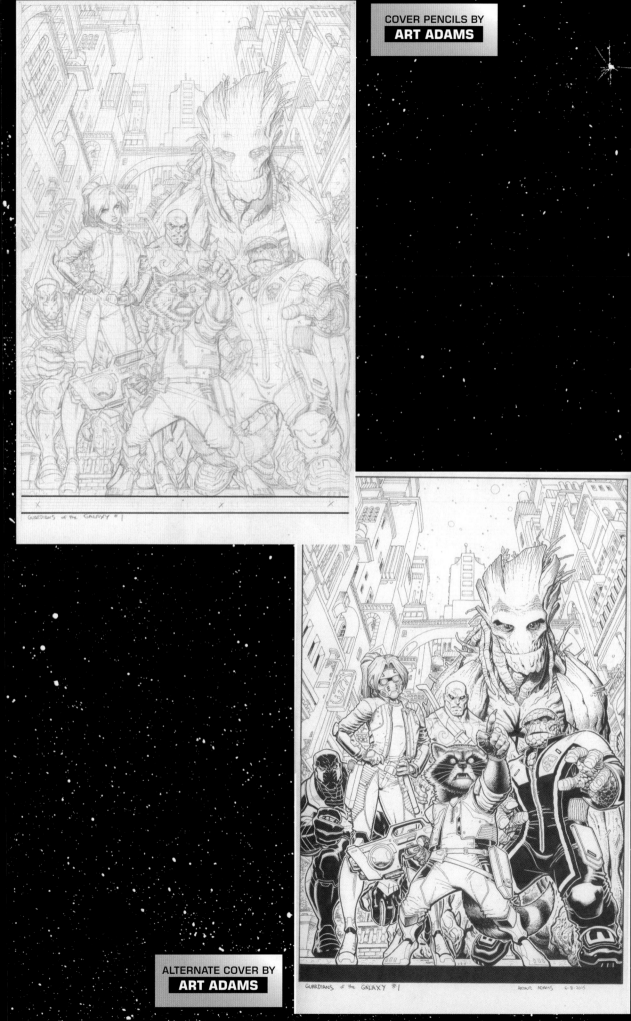

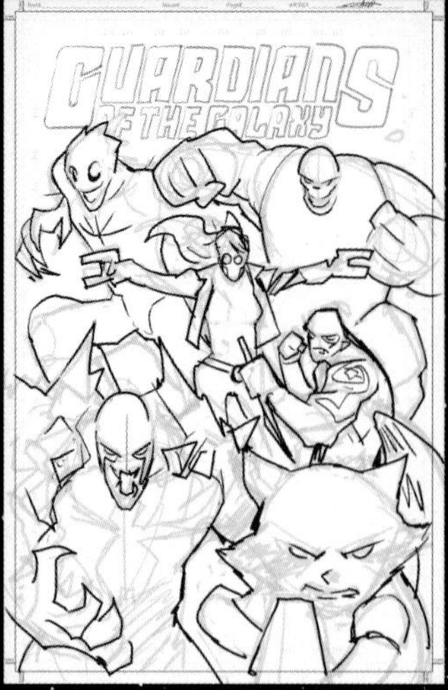
GUARDIANS
OF THE GALAXY

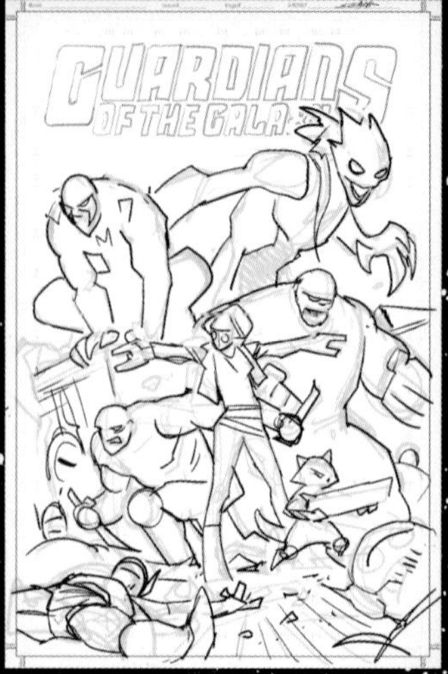
GUARDIANS

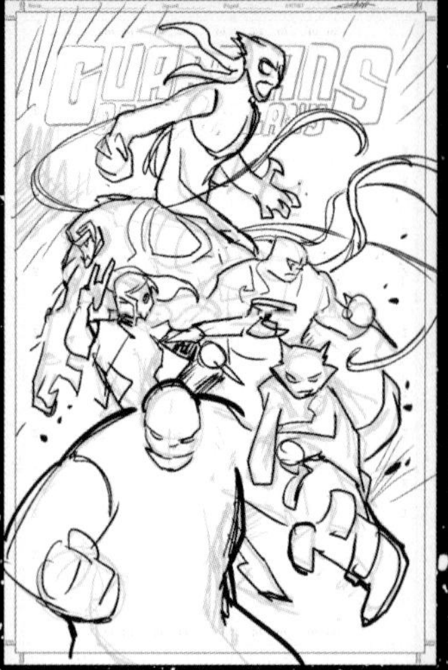

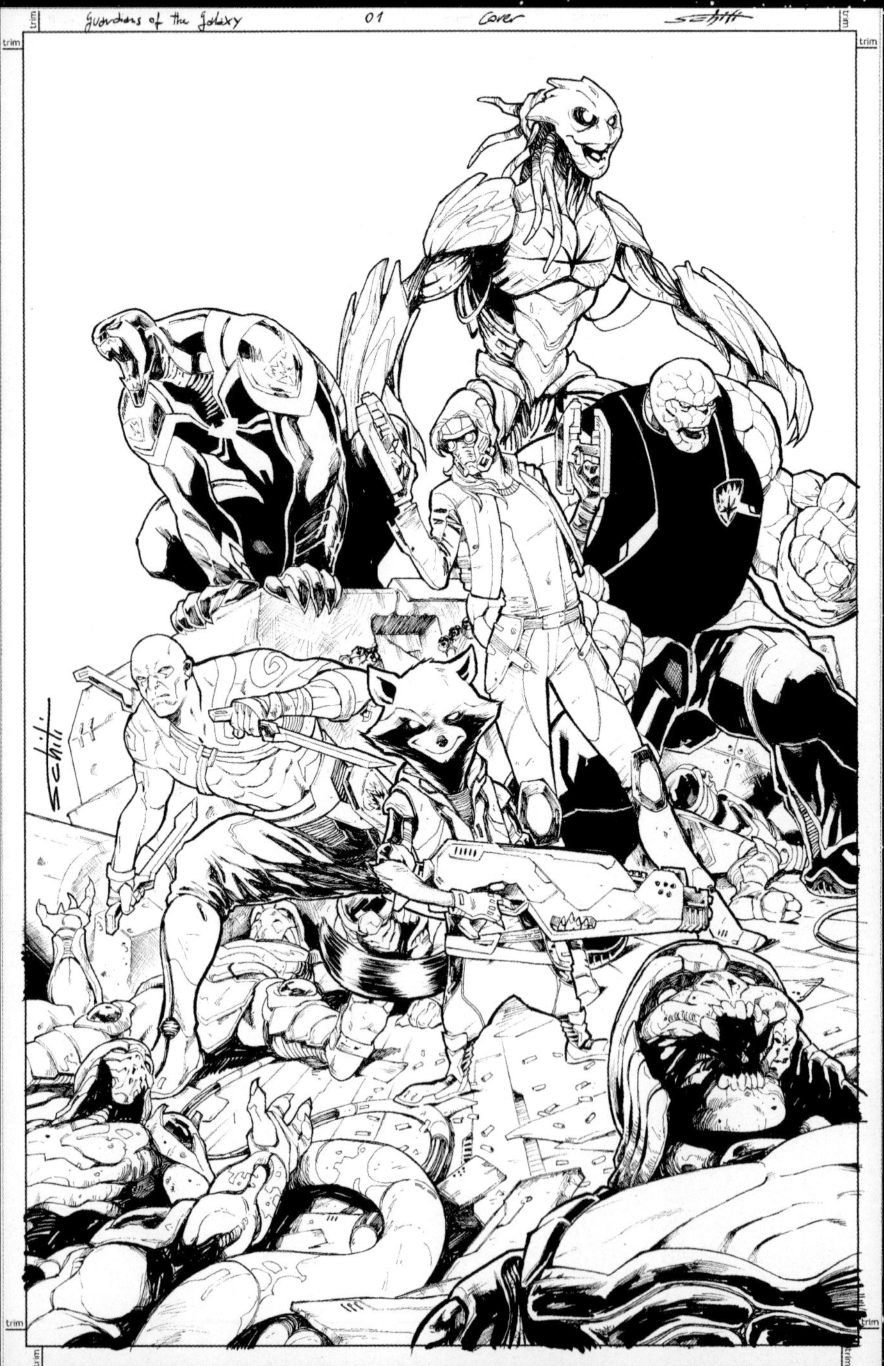
Guardians of the Galaxy
01
Cover
trim

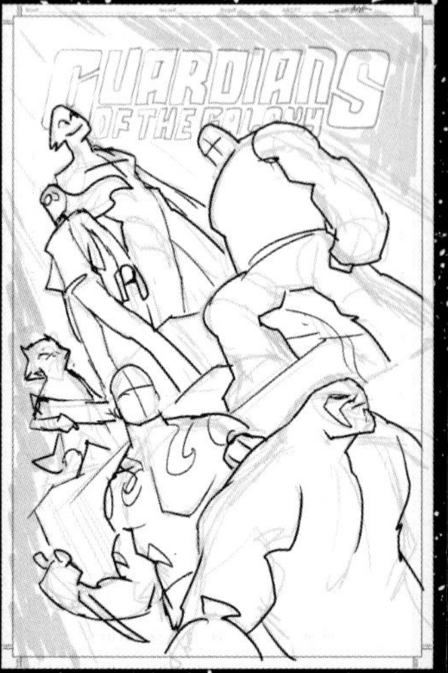
GUARDIANS

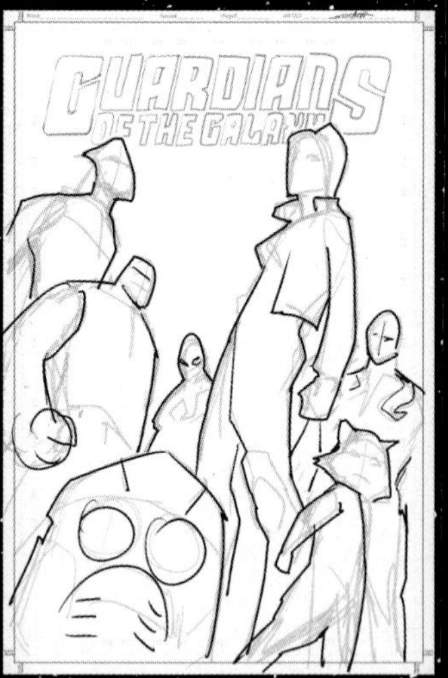
GUARDIANS

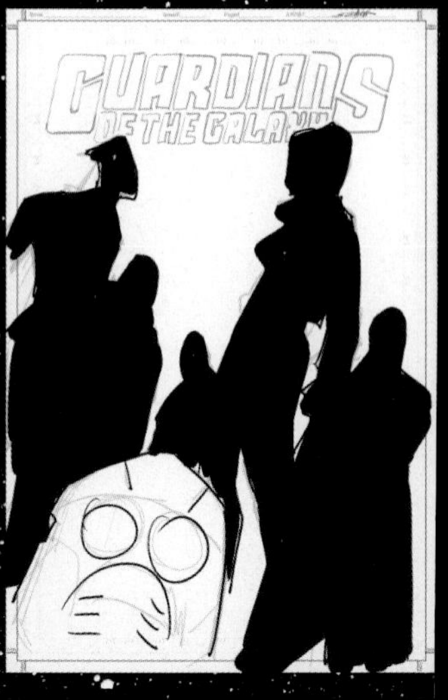
GUARDIANS

#1 VARIANT COVER PROCESS BY **VALERIO SCHITI**

#2 COVER PROCESS BY
ART ADAMS

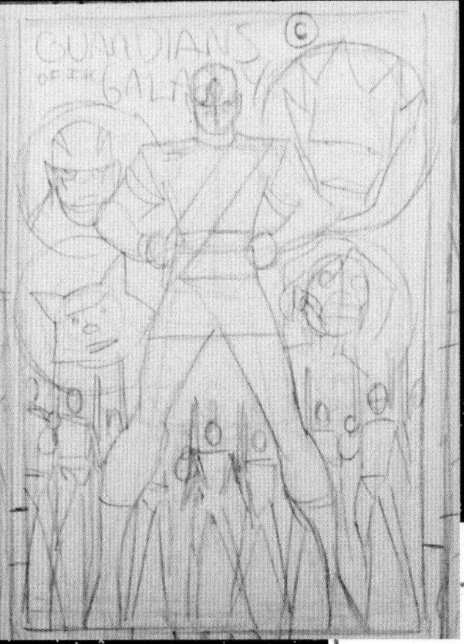
GUARDIANS

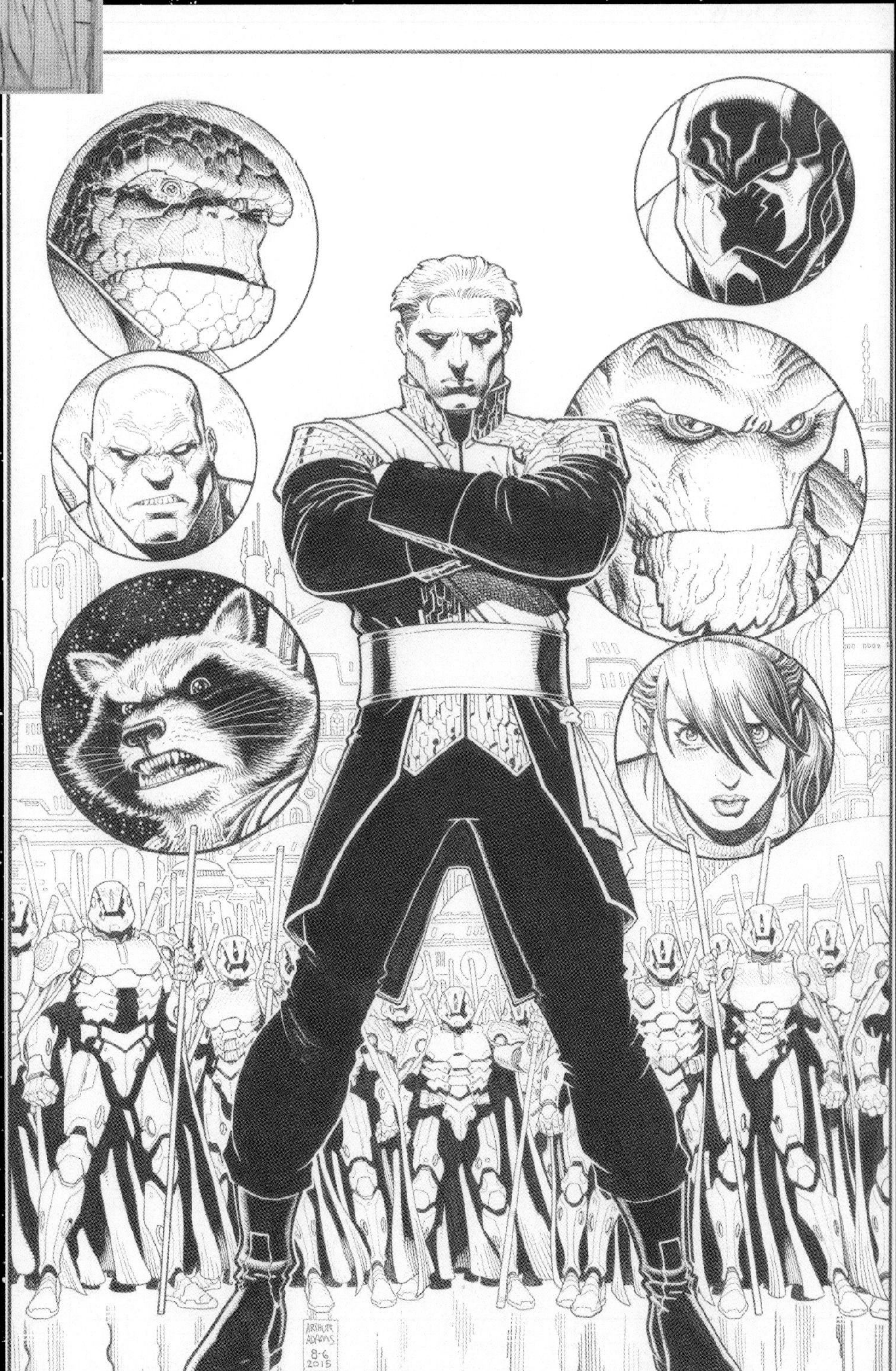
ARTHUR ADAMS 8-6 2015

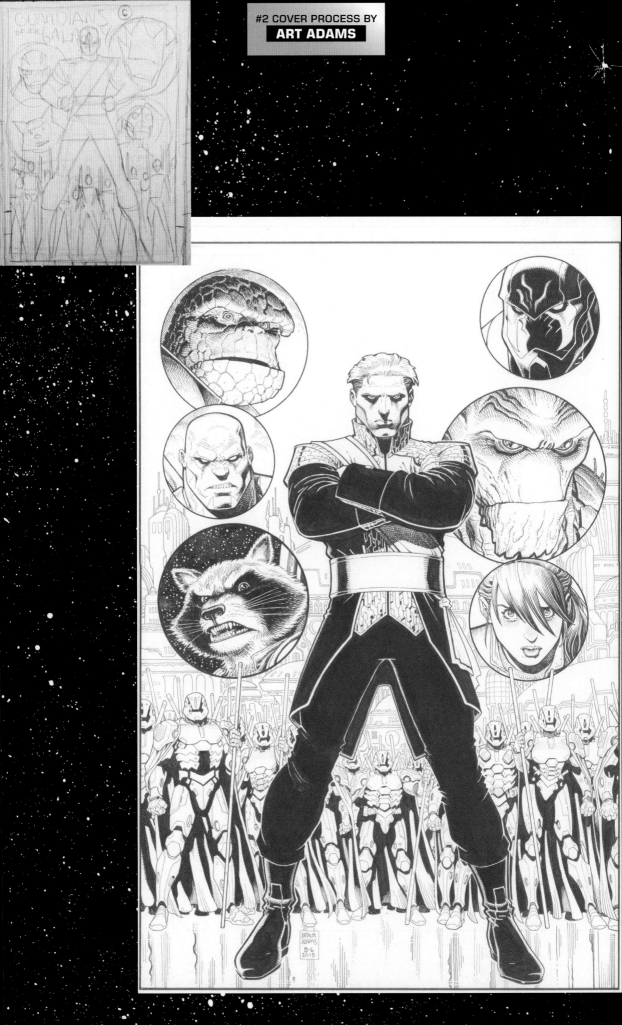

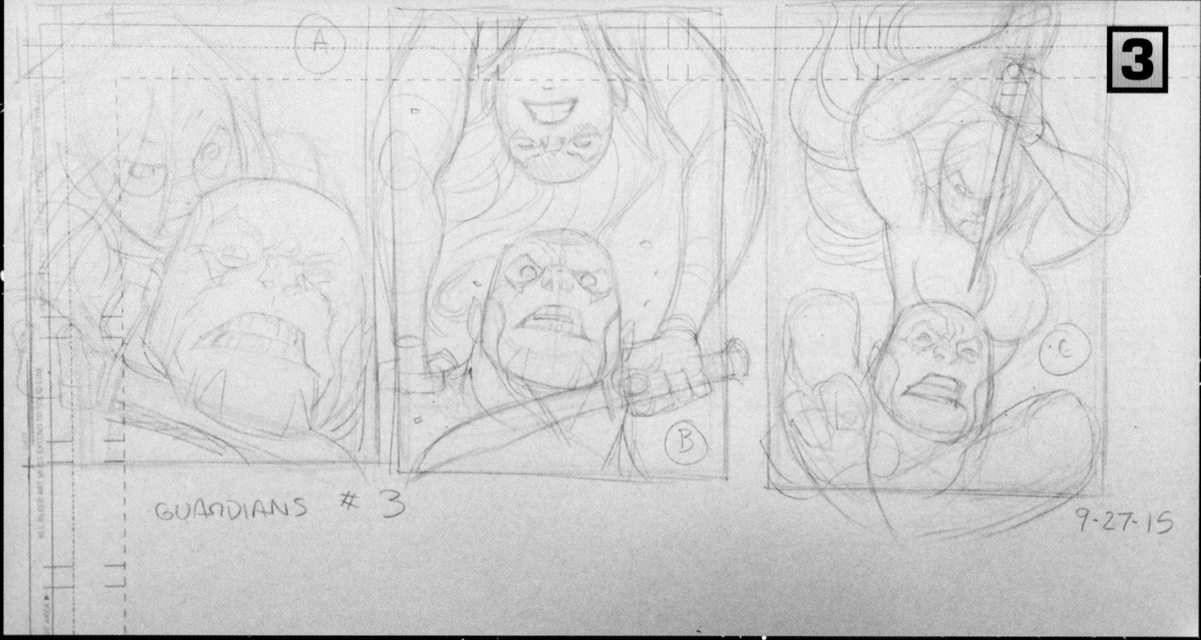
3
A
B
C
GUARDIANS # 3
9-27-15

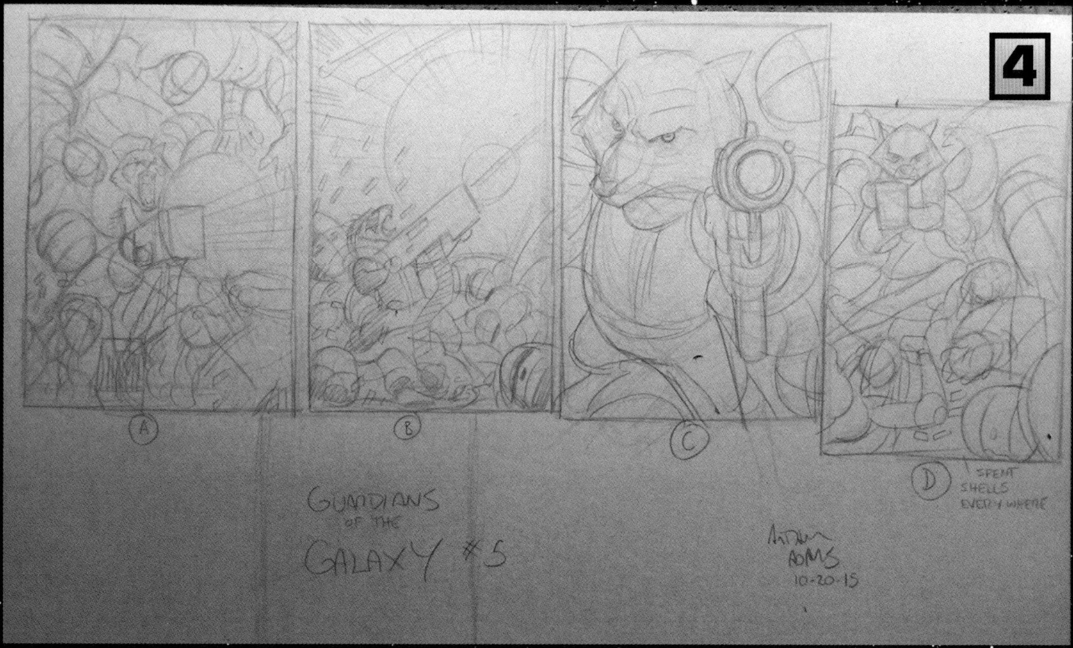
4
A
B
C
D
SPENT SHELLS EVERYWHERE
GUARDIANS OF THE GALAXY #5
ADAMS
10-20-15

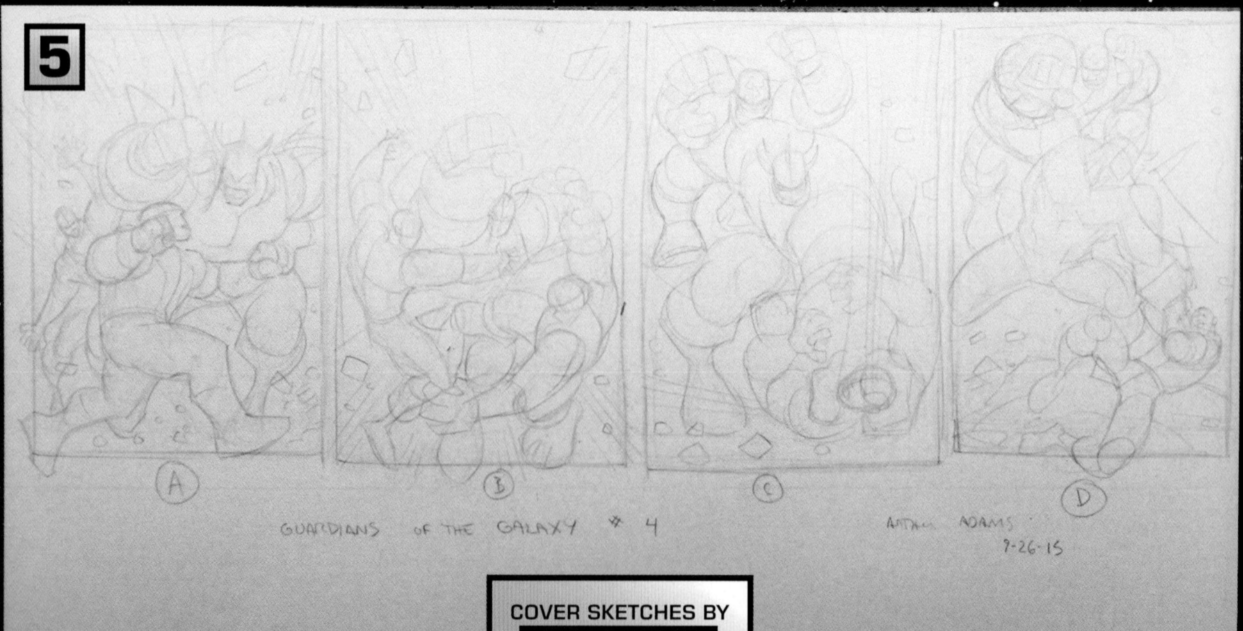
5
A
B
C
D
GUARDIANS OF THE GALAXY # 4
ADAMS
9-26-15

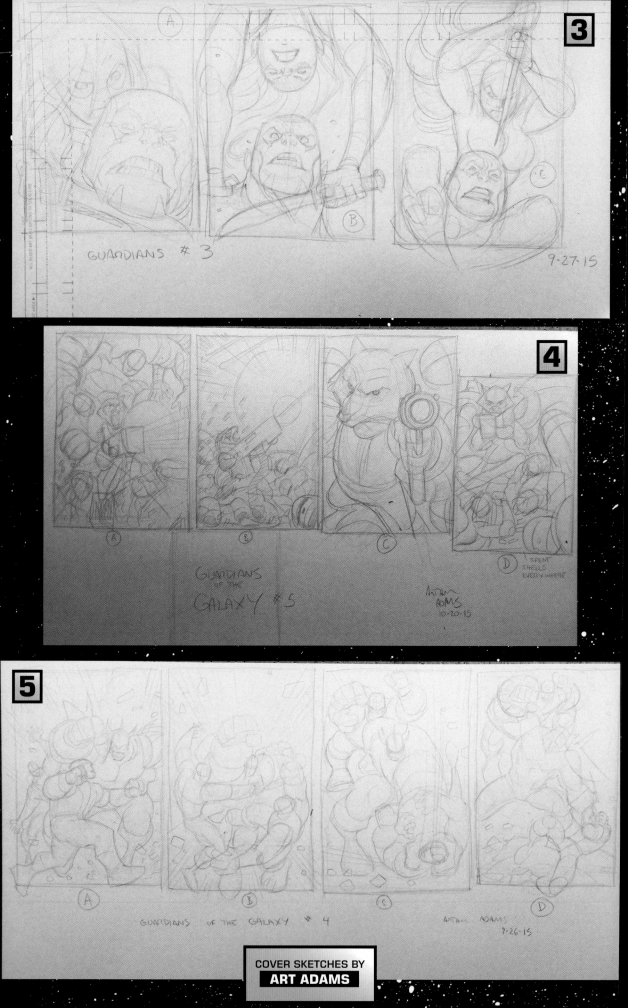

COVER SKETCHES BY
ART ADAMS

4

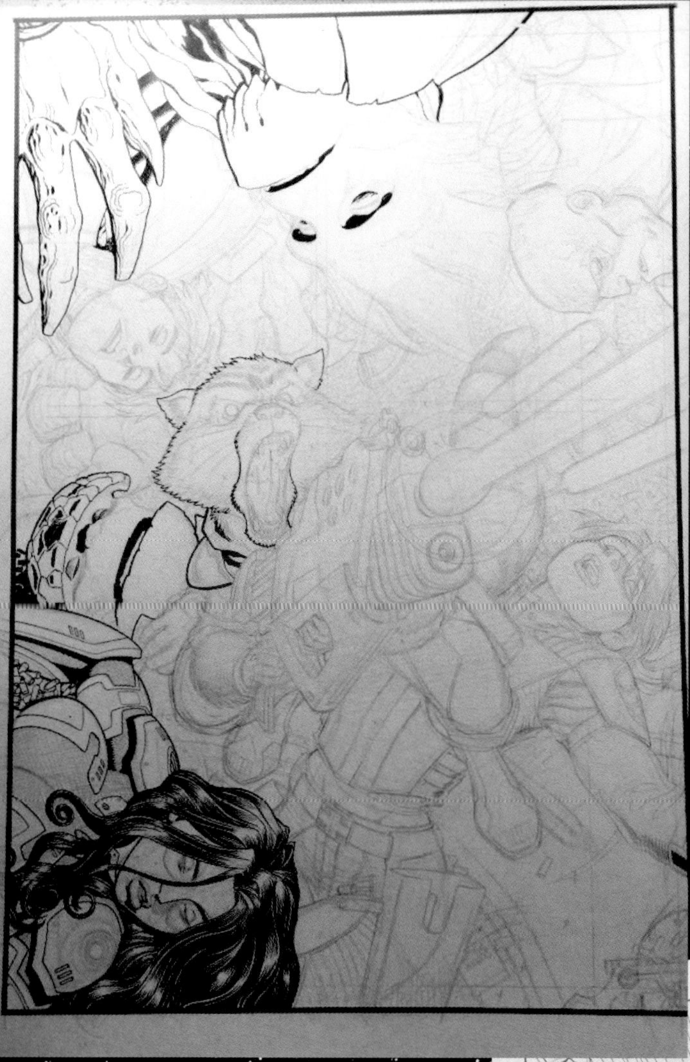

5

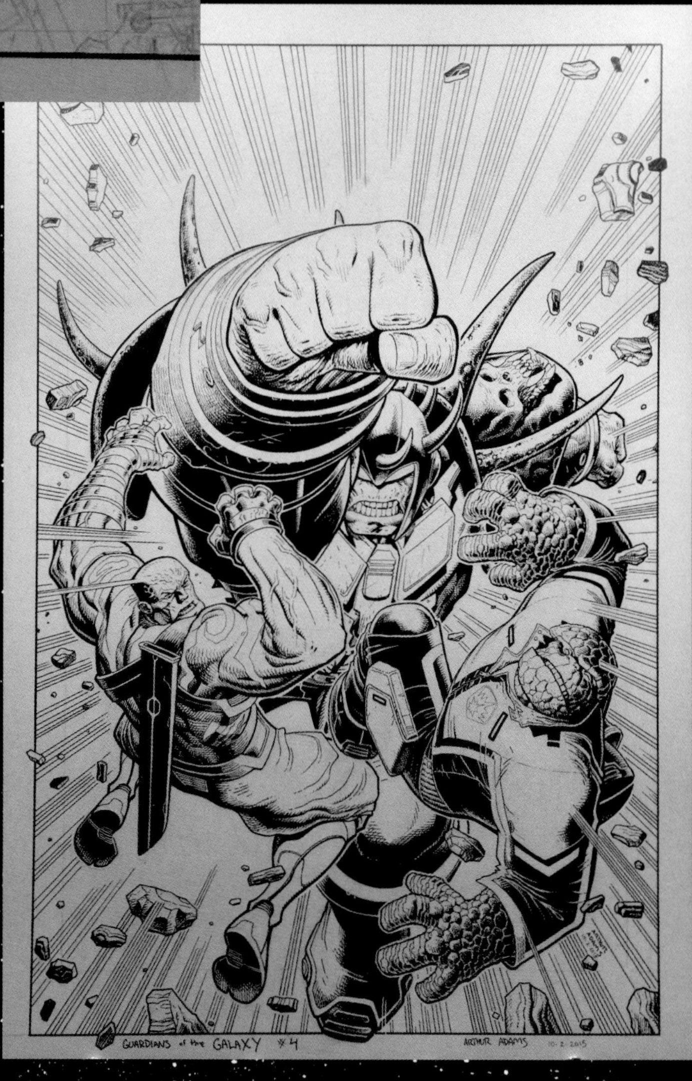
GUARDIANS of the GALAXY #4
ARTHUR ADAMS 10-2-2015

COVER INKS BY
ART ADAMS

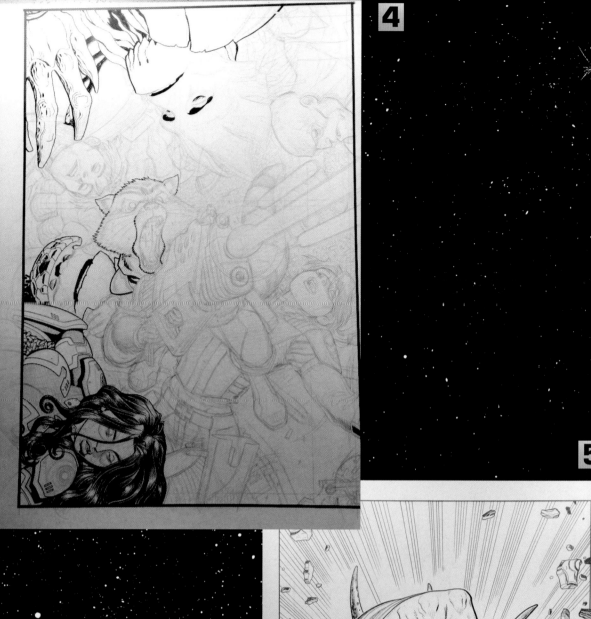

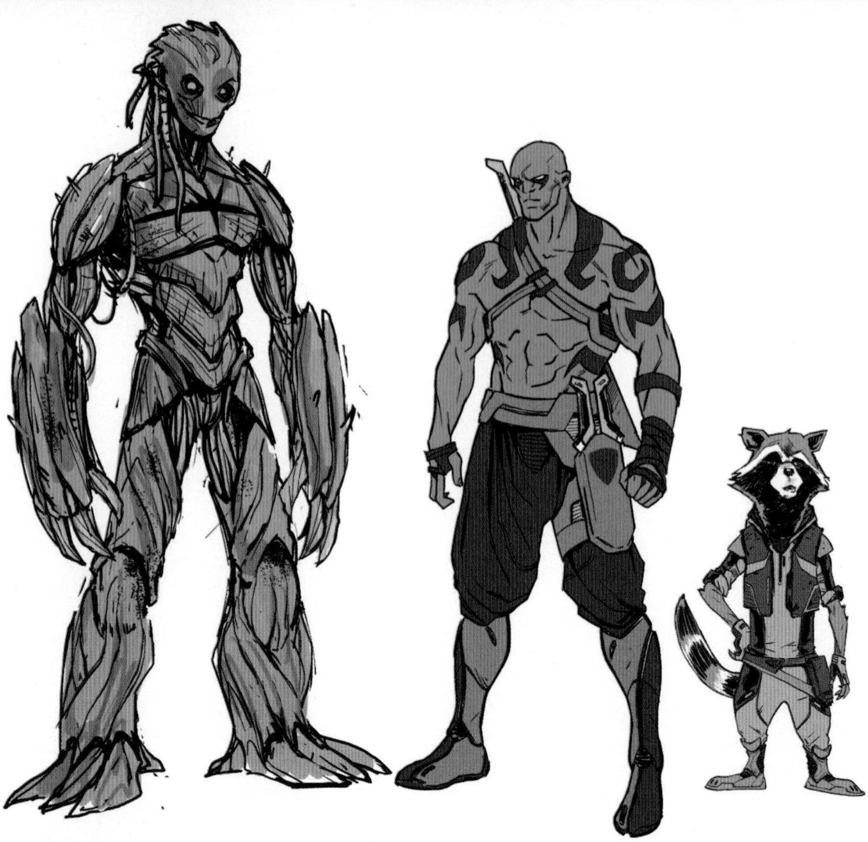

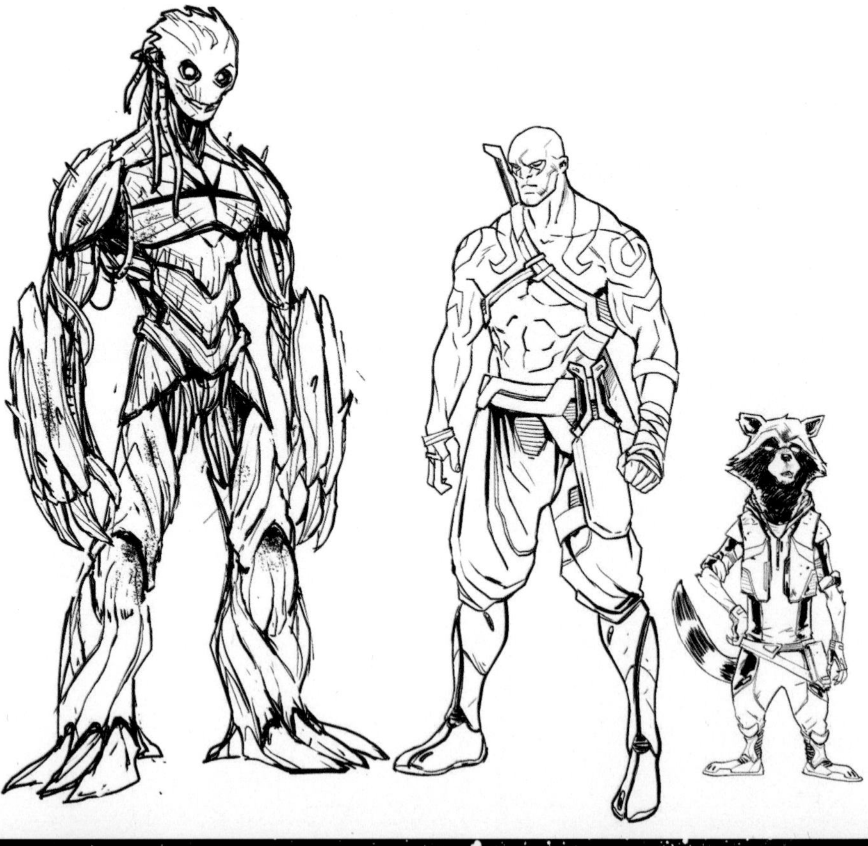

CHARACTER DESIGNS BY
VALERIO SCHITI

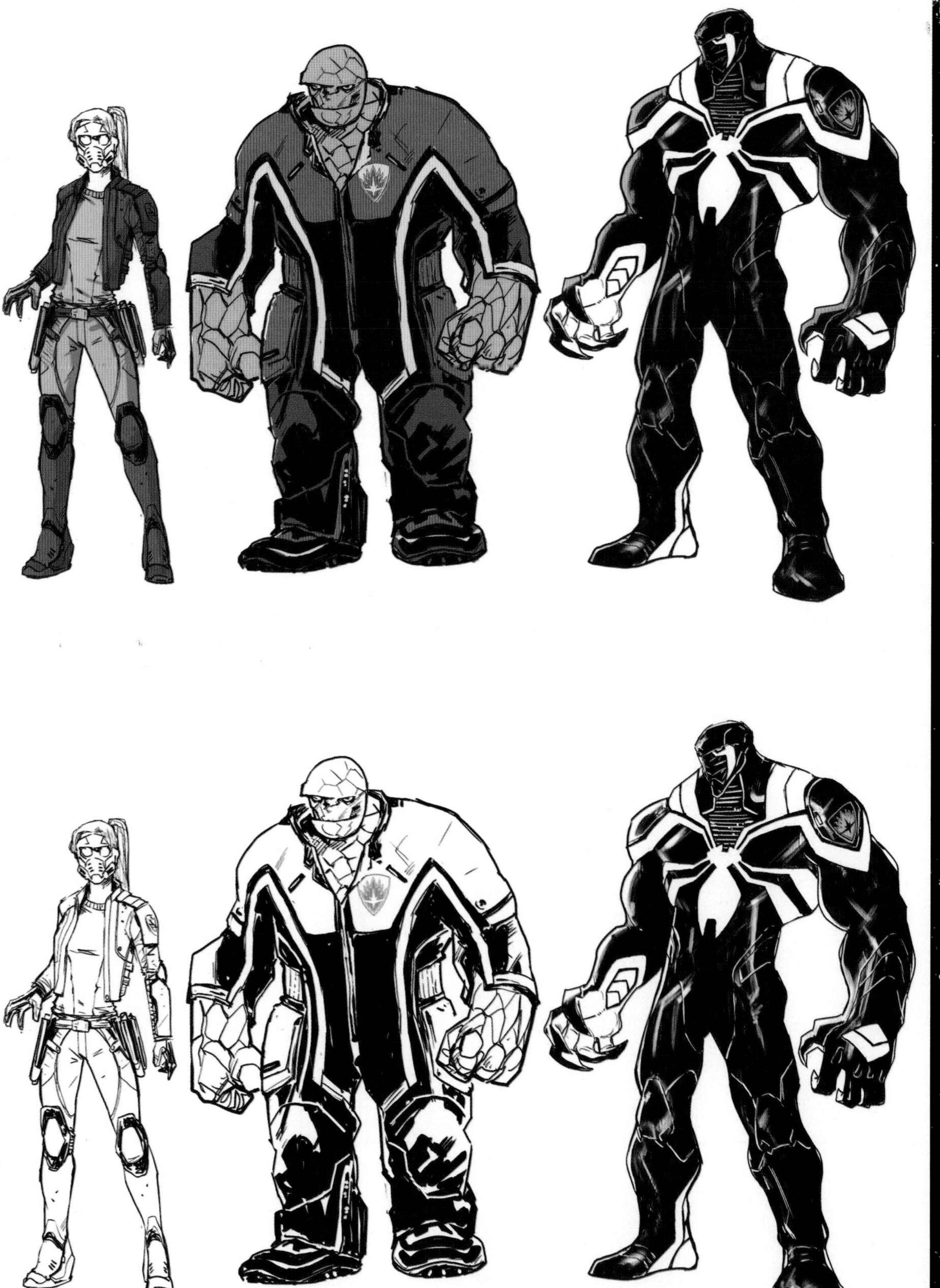

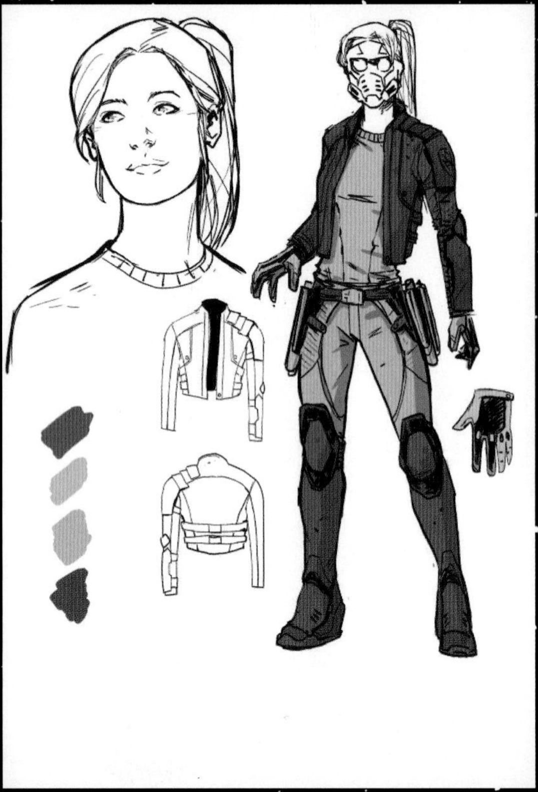

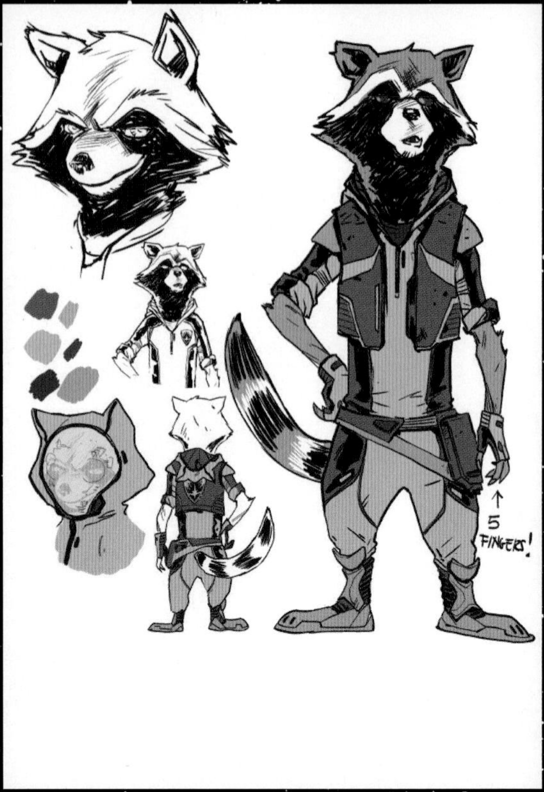
5 FINGERS!

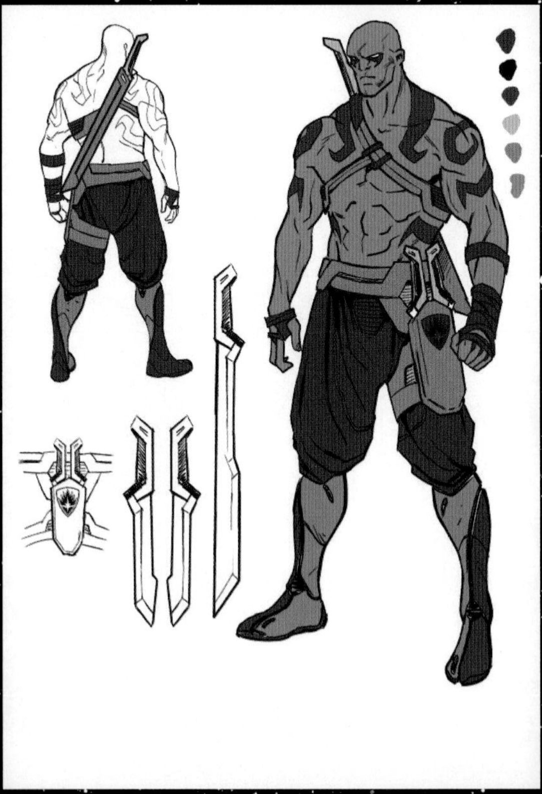

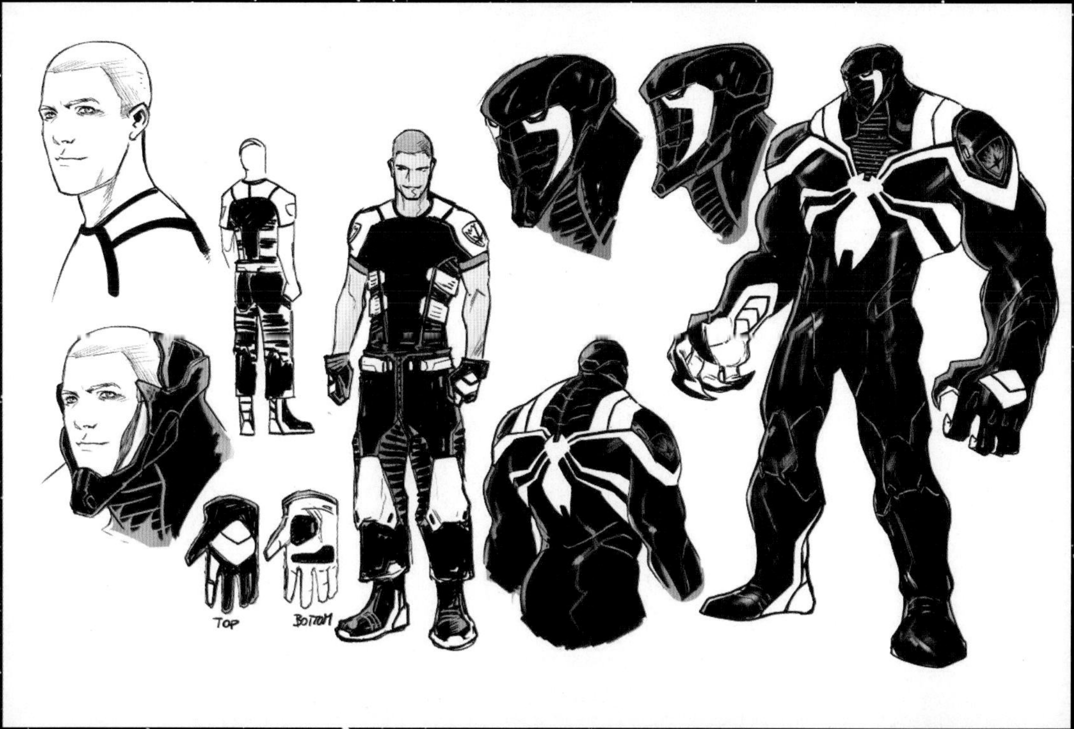
TOP
BOTTOM

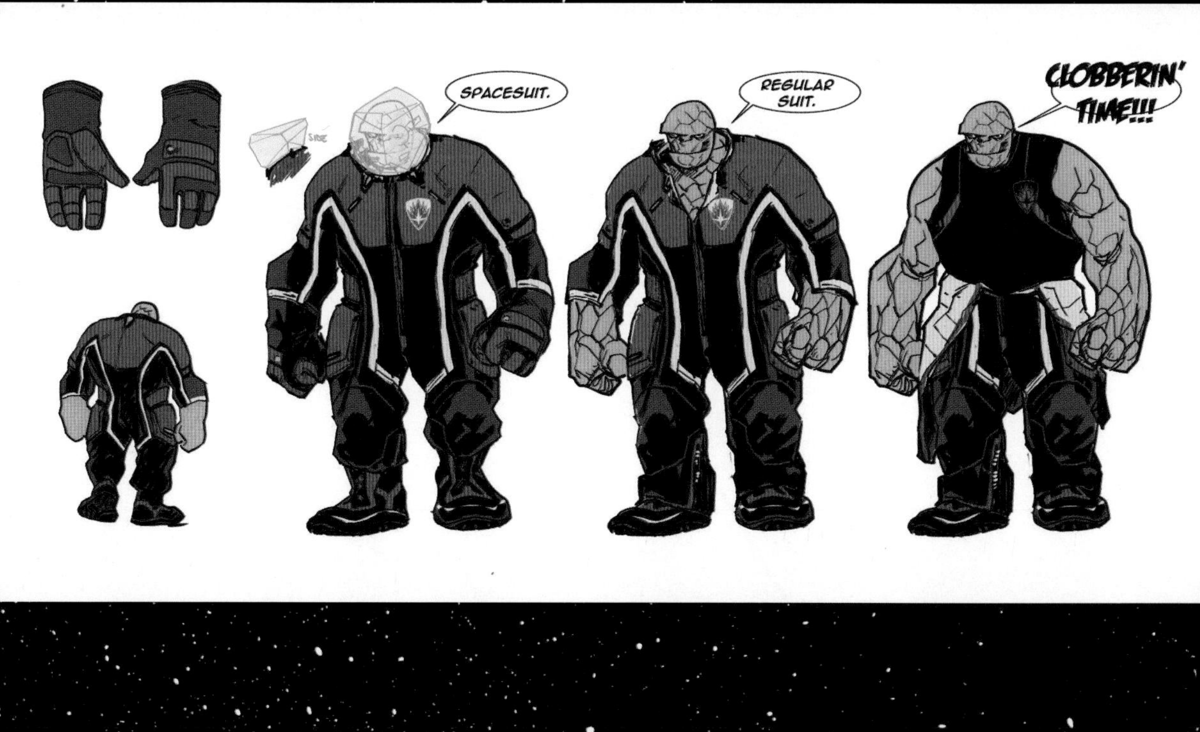
SPACESUIT.
SIDE
REGULAR SUIT.
CLOBBERIN' TIME!!!

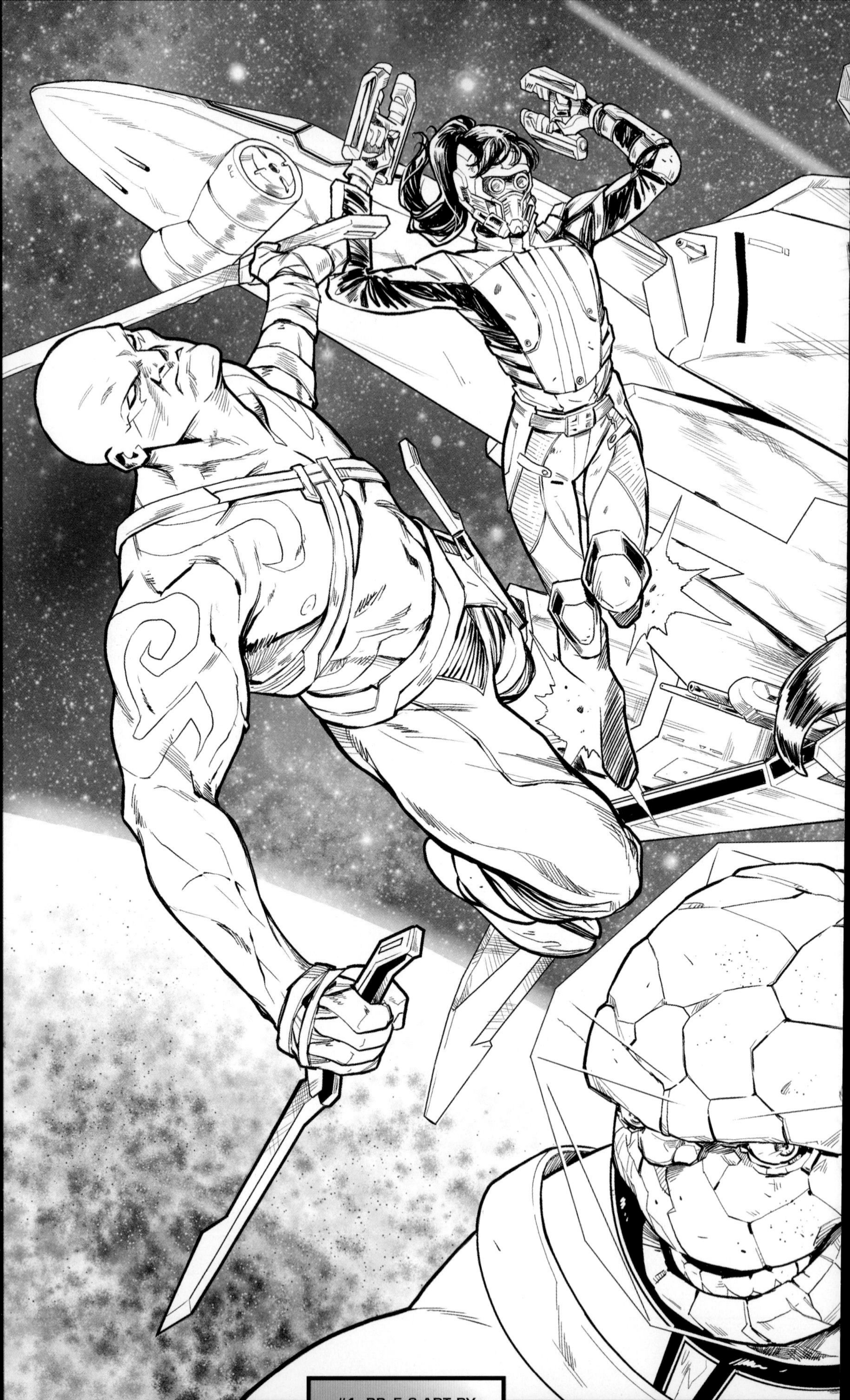

#1, PP. 5-6 ART BY
VALERIO SCHITI

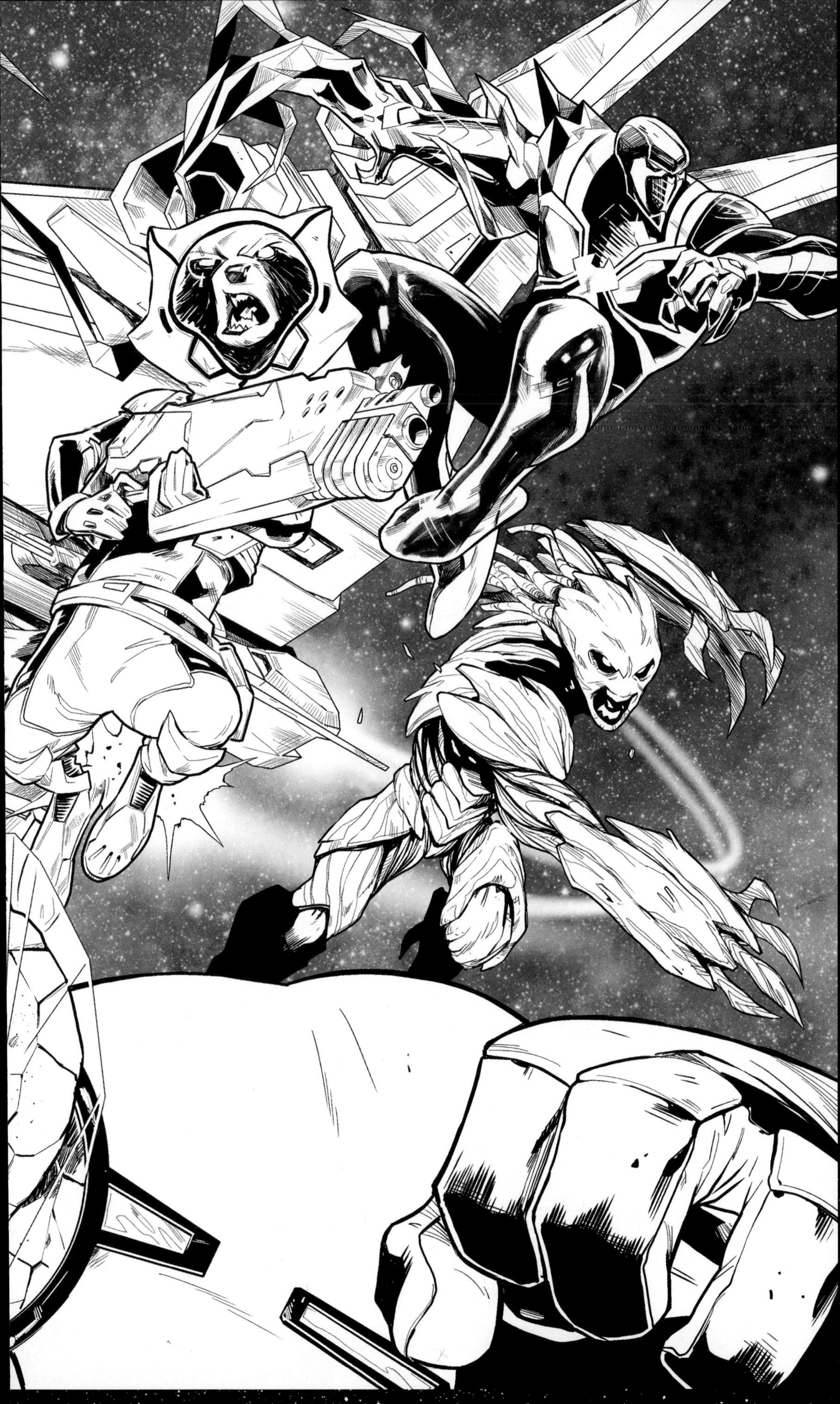

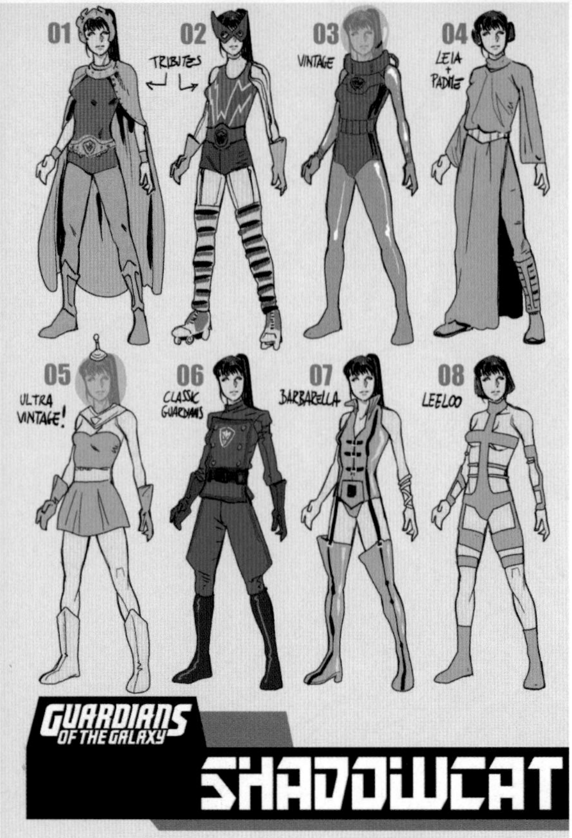
01
02
TRIBUTES
03
VINTAGE
04
LEIA + PADME
05
ULTRA VINTAGE!
06
CLASSIC GUARDIANS
07
BARBARELLA
08
LEELOO
GUARDIANS OF THE GALAXY
SHADOWCAT

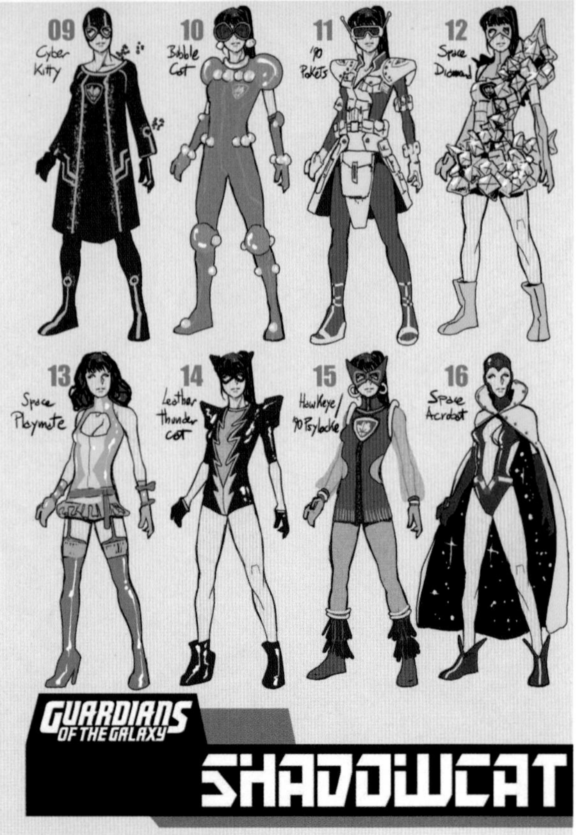
09
Cyber Kitty
10
Bubble Cat
11
'90 Pockets
12
Space Diamond
13
Space Playmate
14
Leather thunder cat
15
HawKeye/ '90 Psylocke
16
Space Acrobat
GUARDIANS OF THE GALAXY
SHADOWCAT

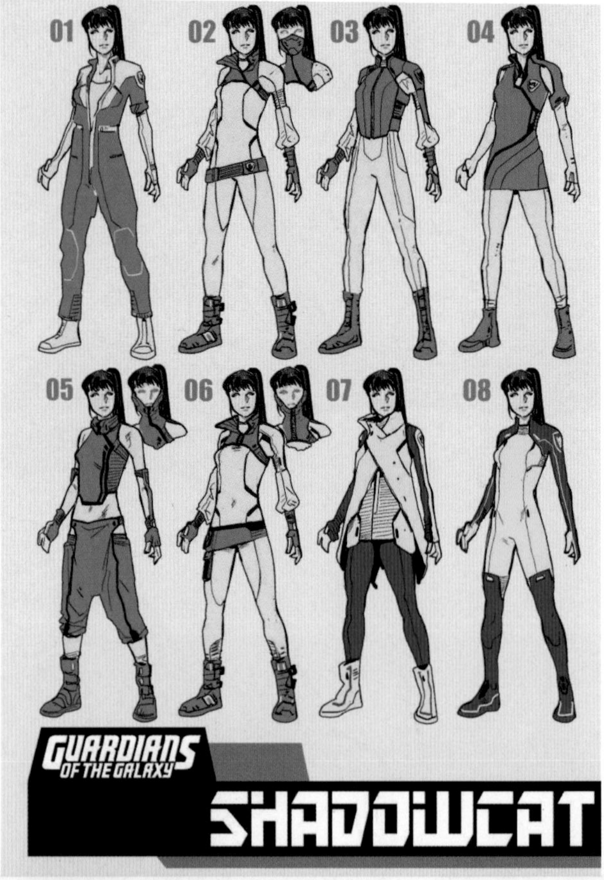
01
02
03
04
05
06
07
08
GUARDIANS OF THE GALAXY
SHADOWCAT

MOCK COSTUME DESIGNS BY
VALERIO SCHITI

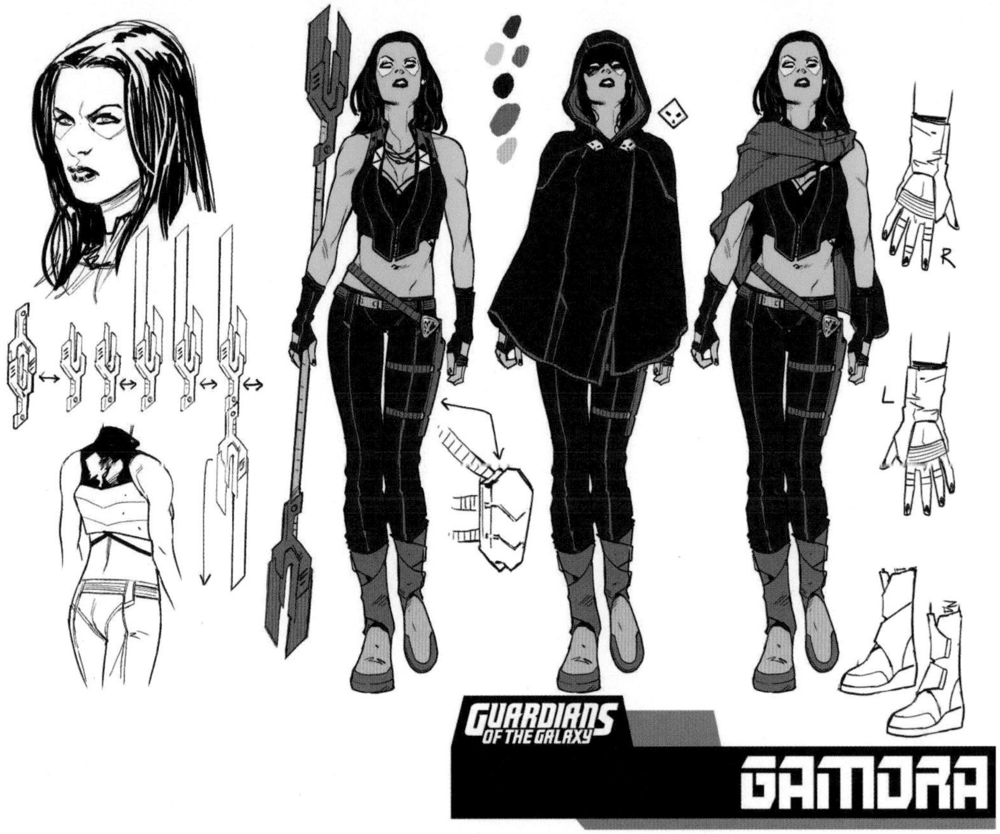
R
L
GUARDIANS OF THE GALAXY
GAMORA

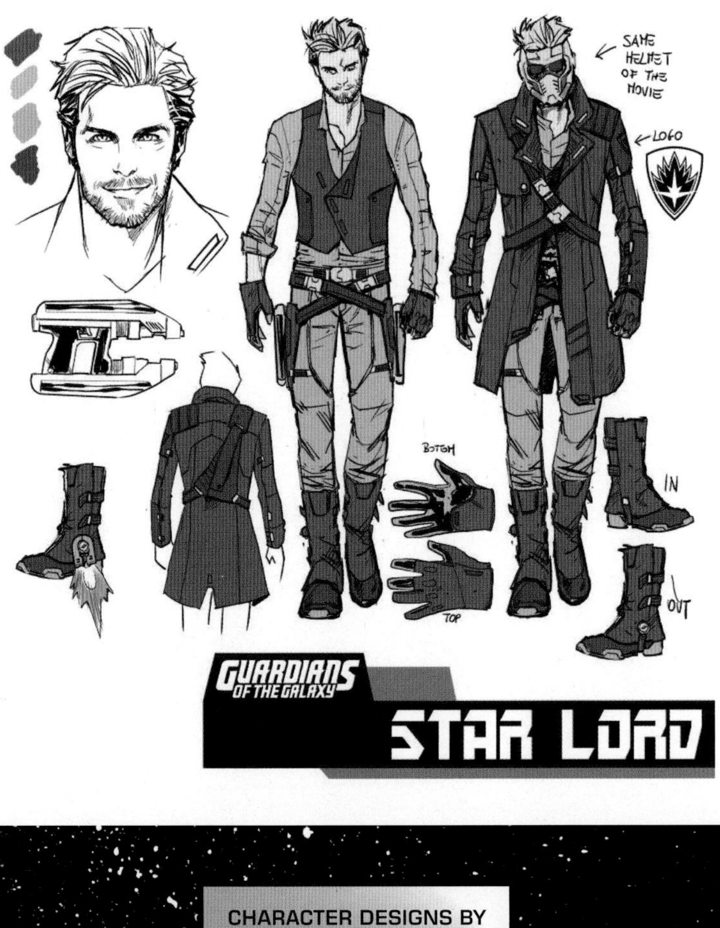
SAME HELMET OF THE MOVIE
LOGO
TOP
IN
OUT
GUARDIANS OF THE GALAXY
STAR LORD

CHARACTER DESIGNS BY
VALERIO SCHITI

FROM THE DESK OF

ARTHUR ADAMS

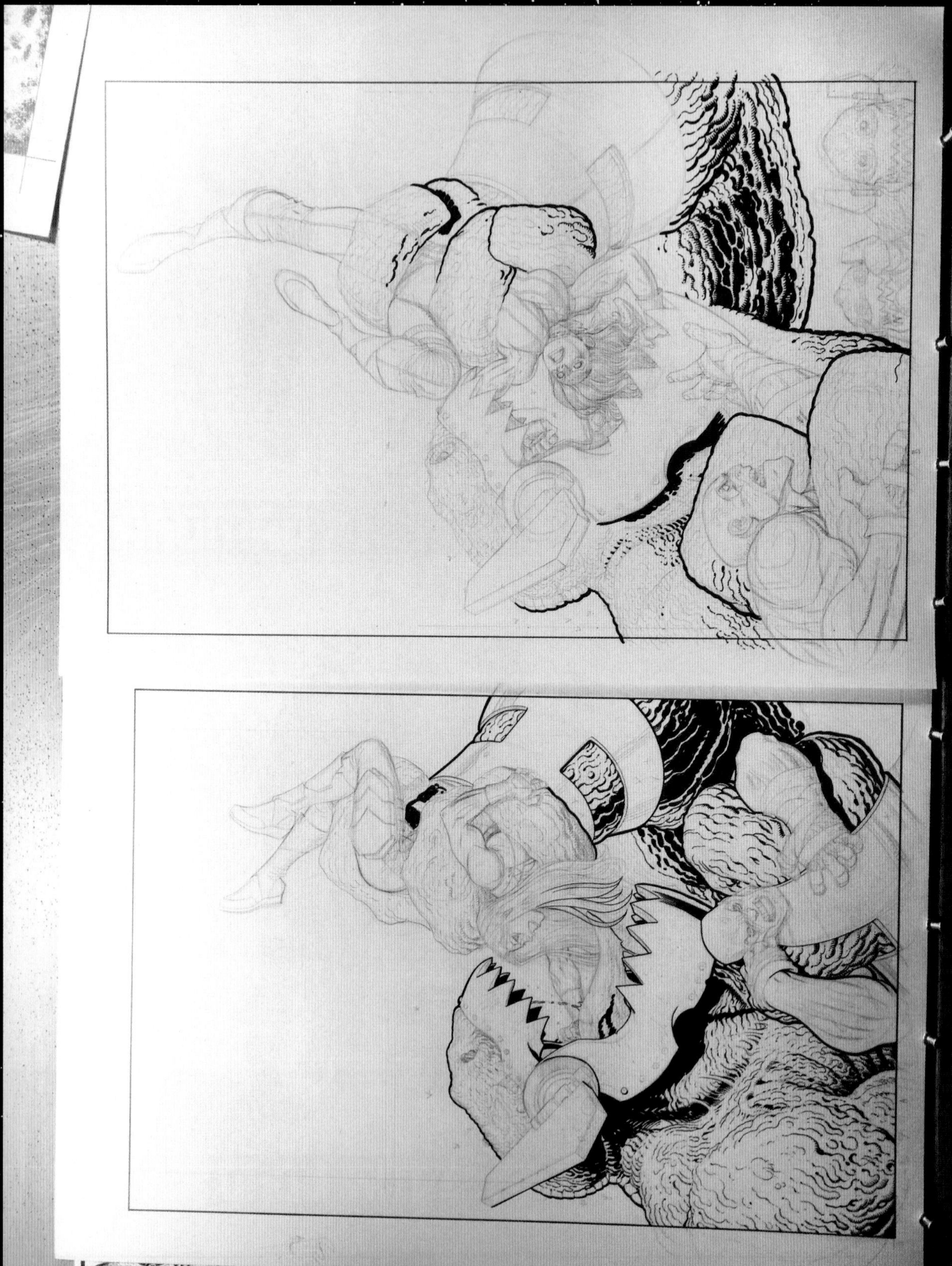

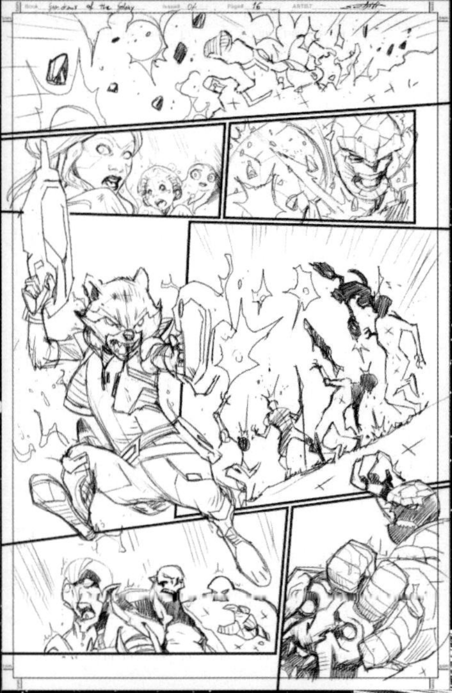

#7, PAGE 15 ART PROCESS BY
VALERIO SCHITI

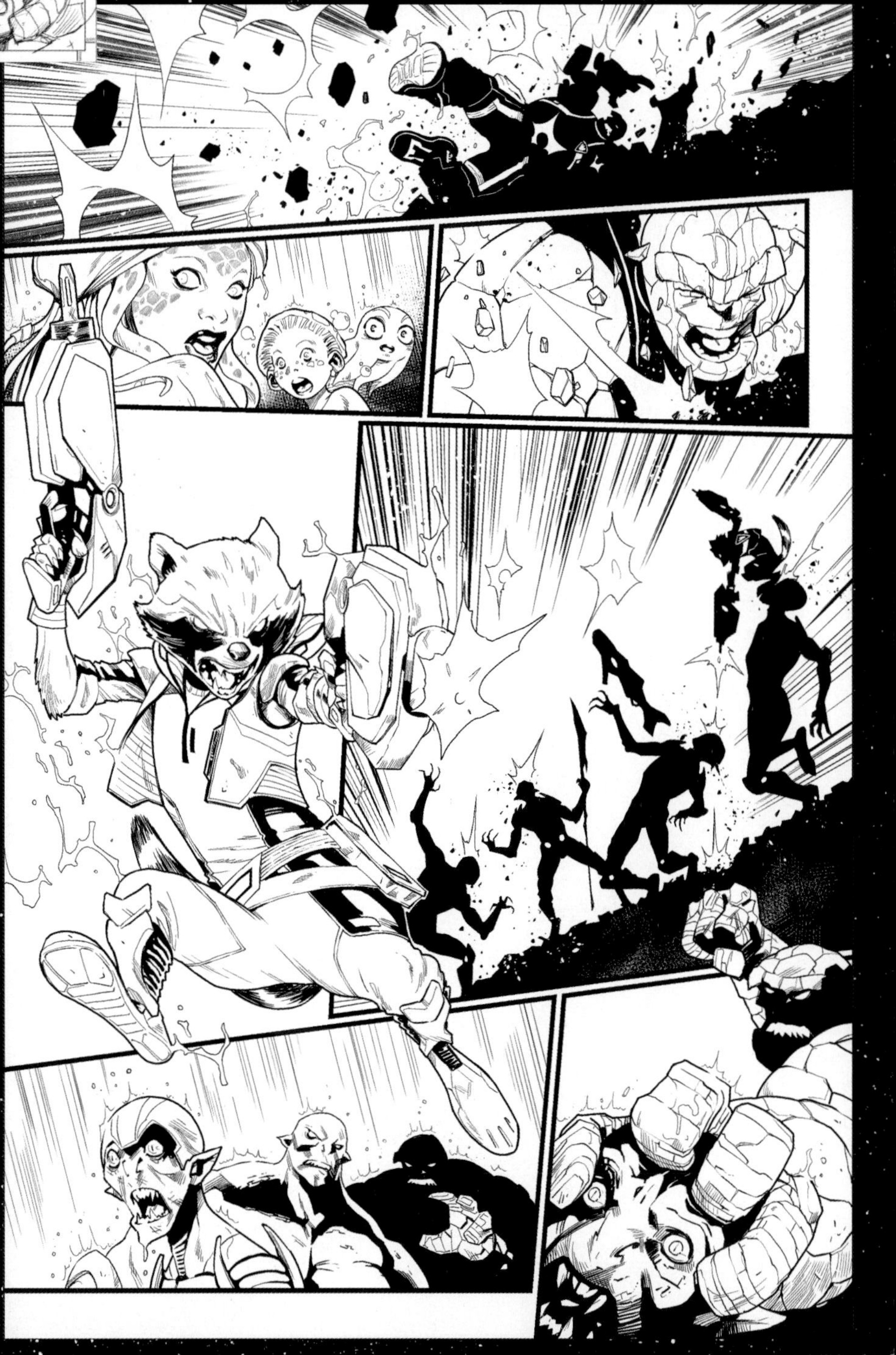

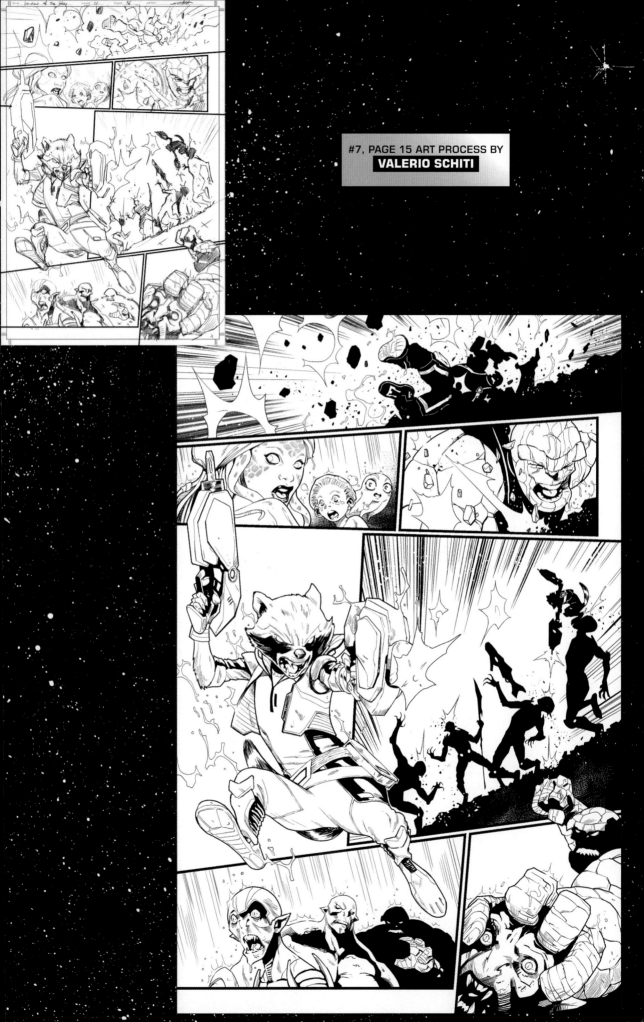

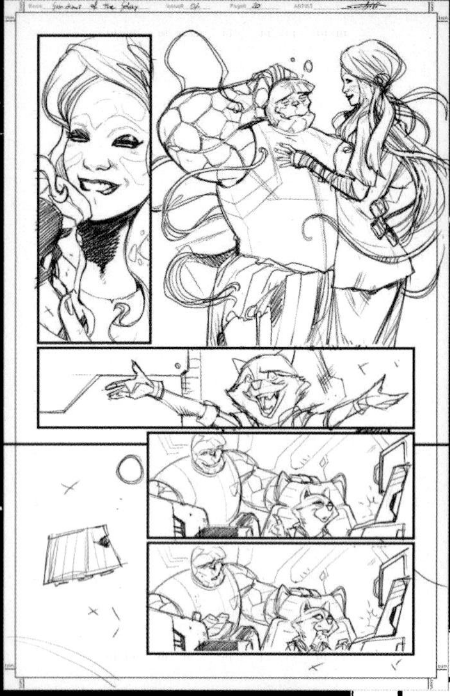

#7, PAGE 19 ART PROCESS BY
VALERIO SCHITI

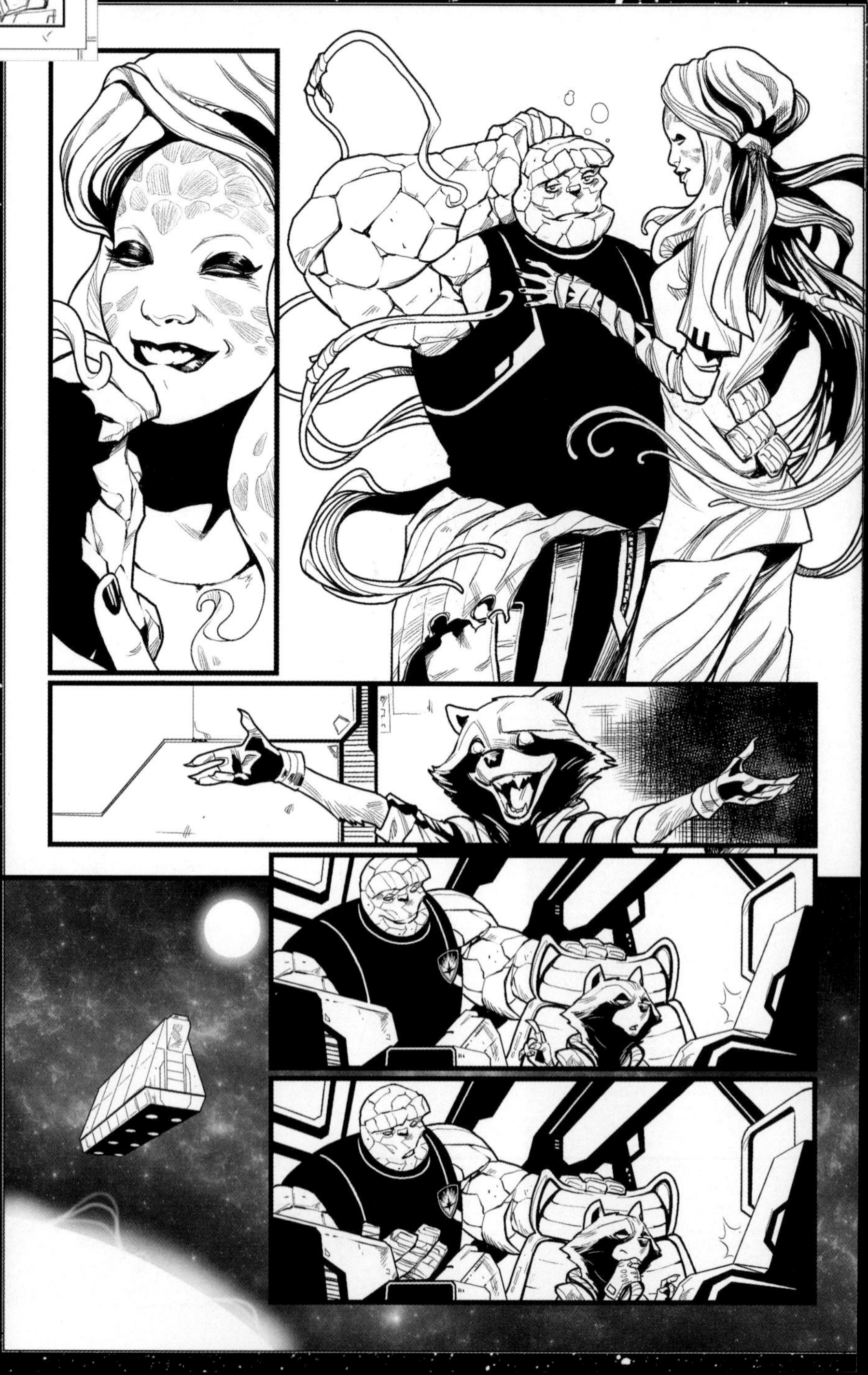

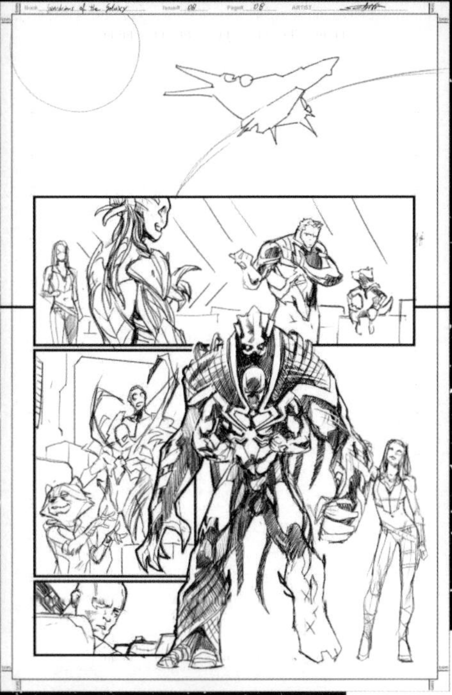

#8, PAGE 7 ART PROCESS BY
VALERIO SCHITI

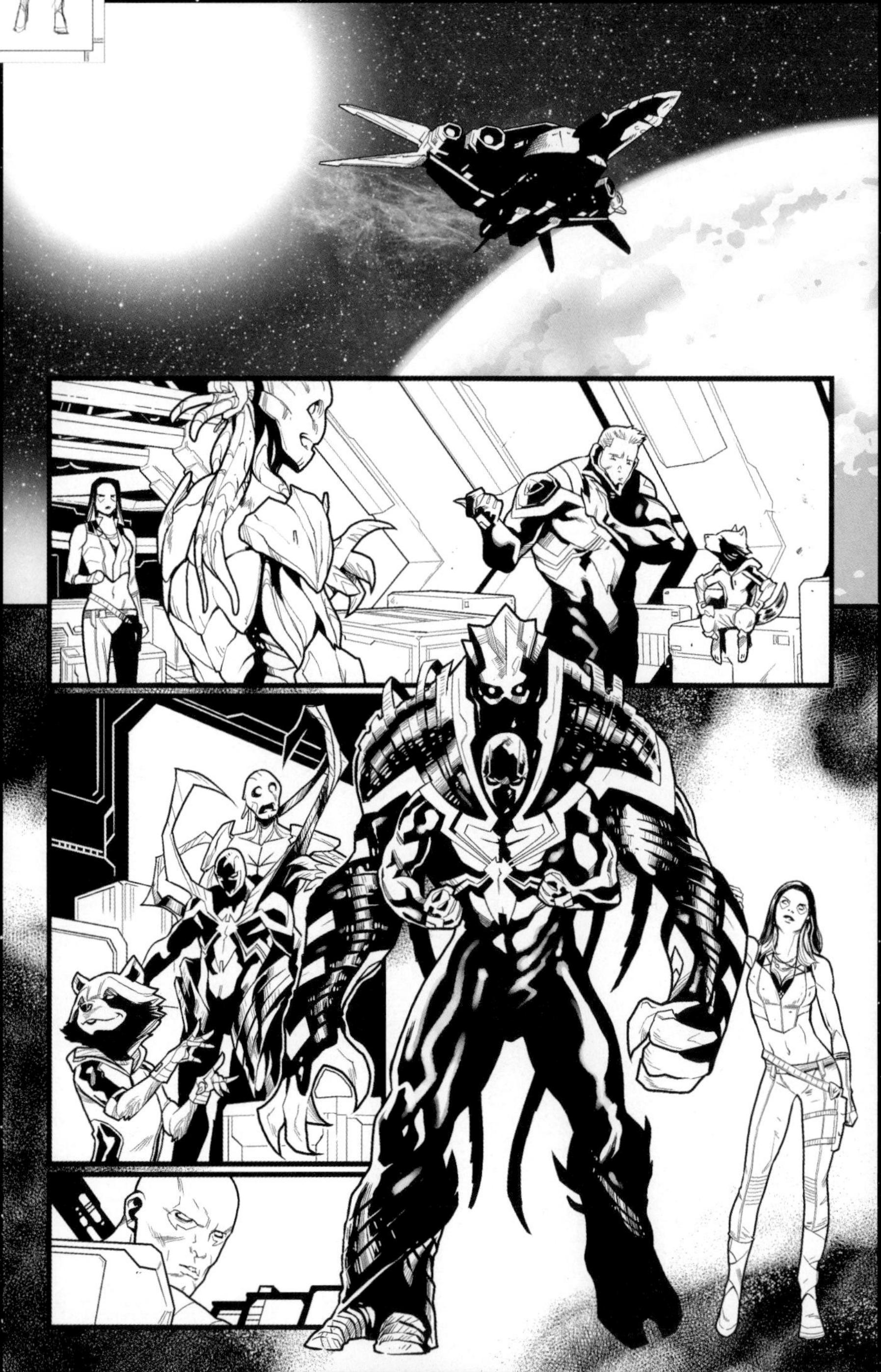

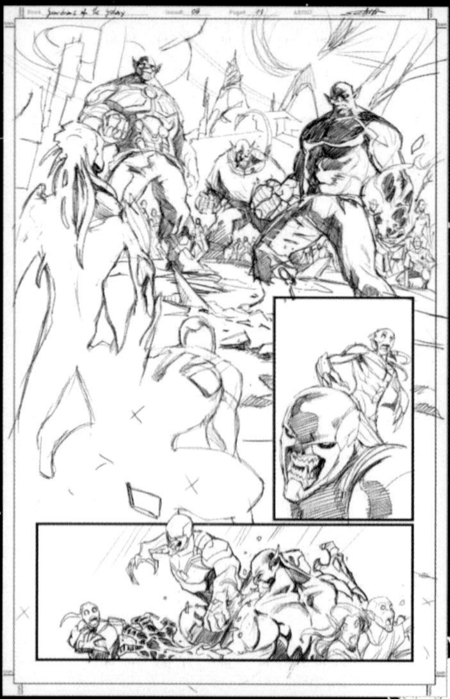

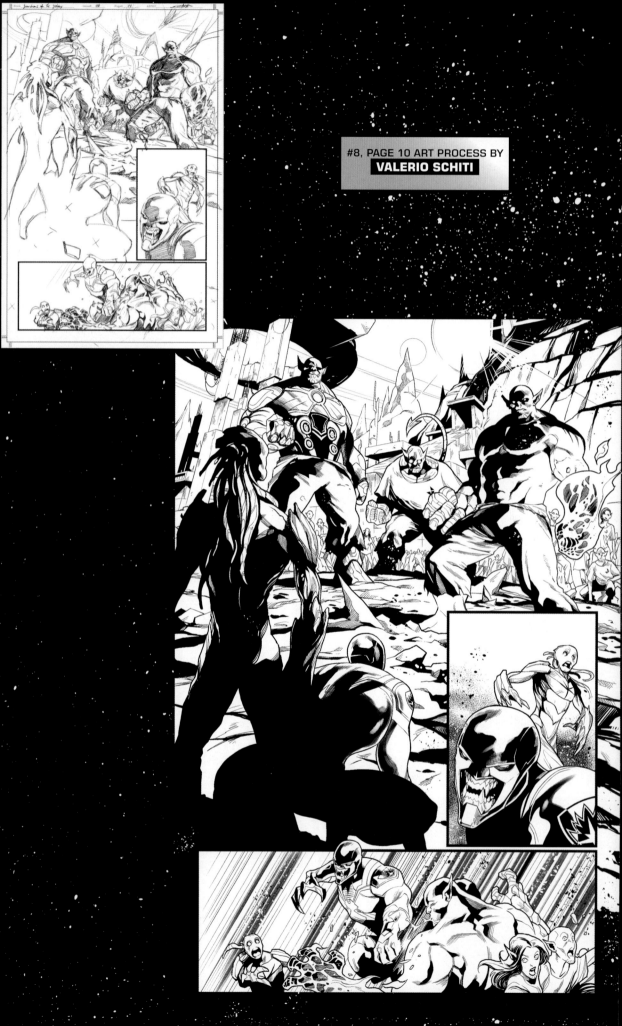

#8, PAGE 10 ART PROCESS BY
VALERIO SCHITI

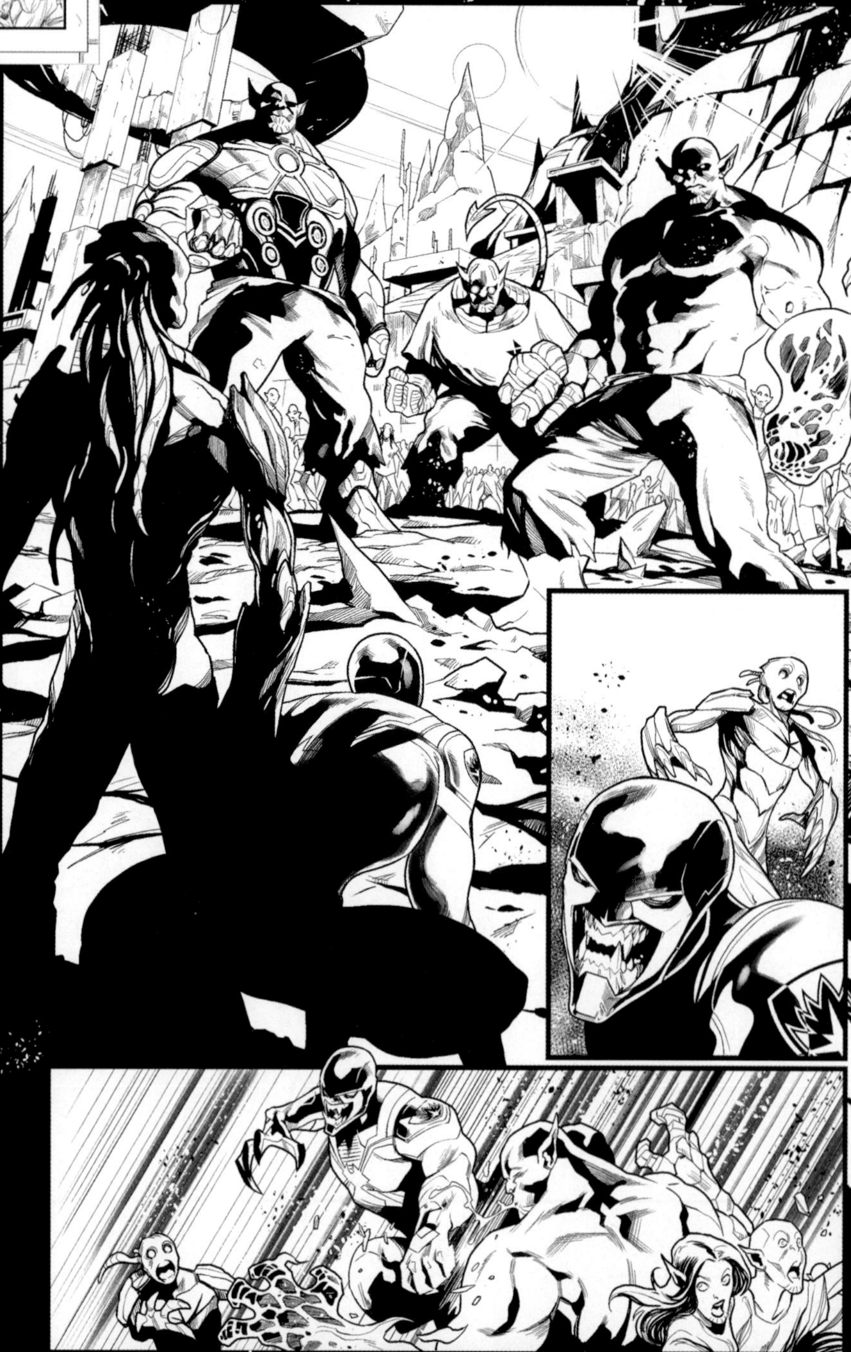

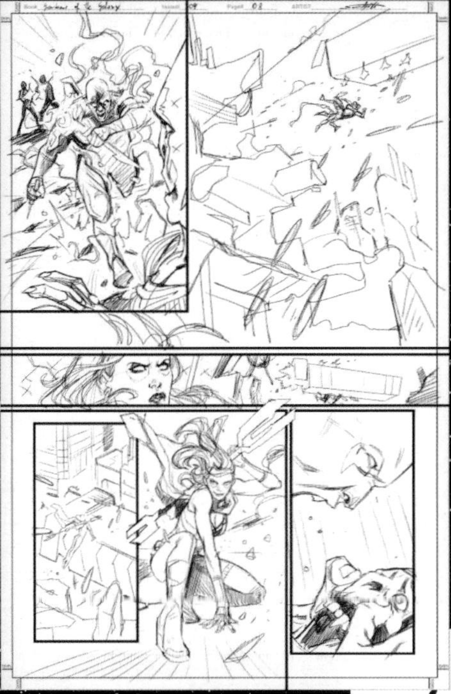

#9, PAGE 7 ART PROCESS BY

VALERIO SCHITI

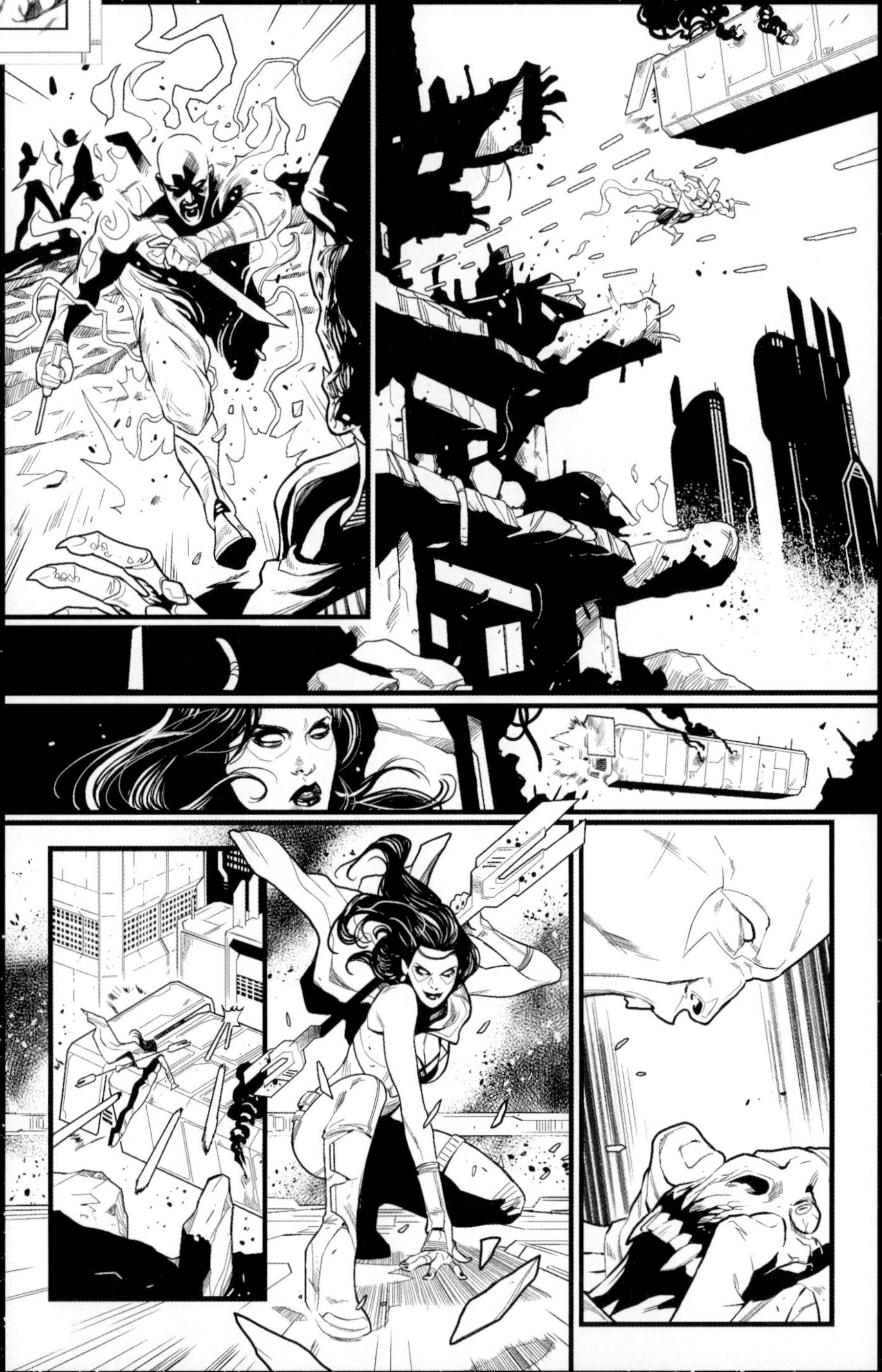

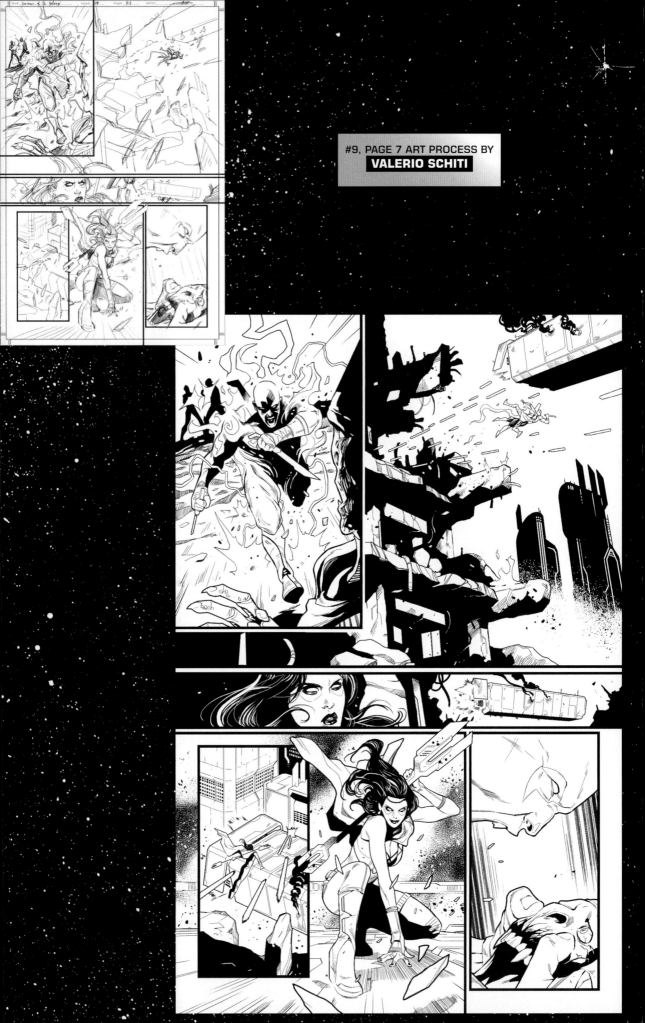

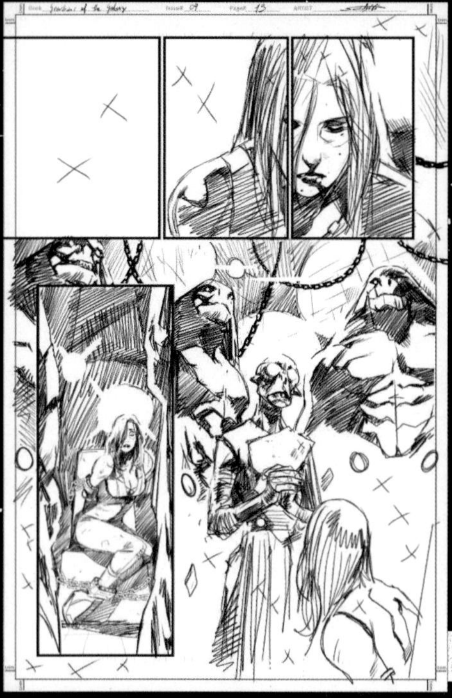

#9, PAGE 12 ART PROCESS BY
VALERIO SCHITI

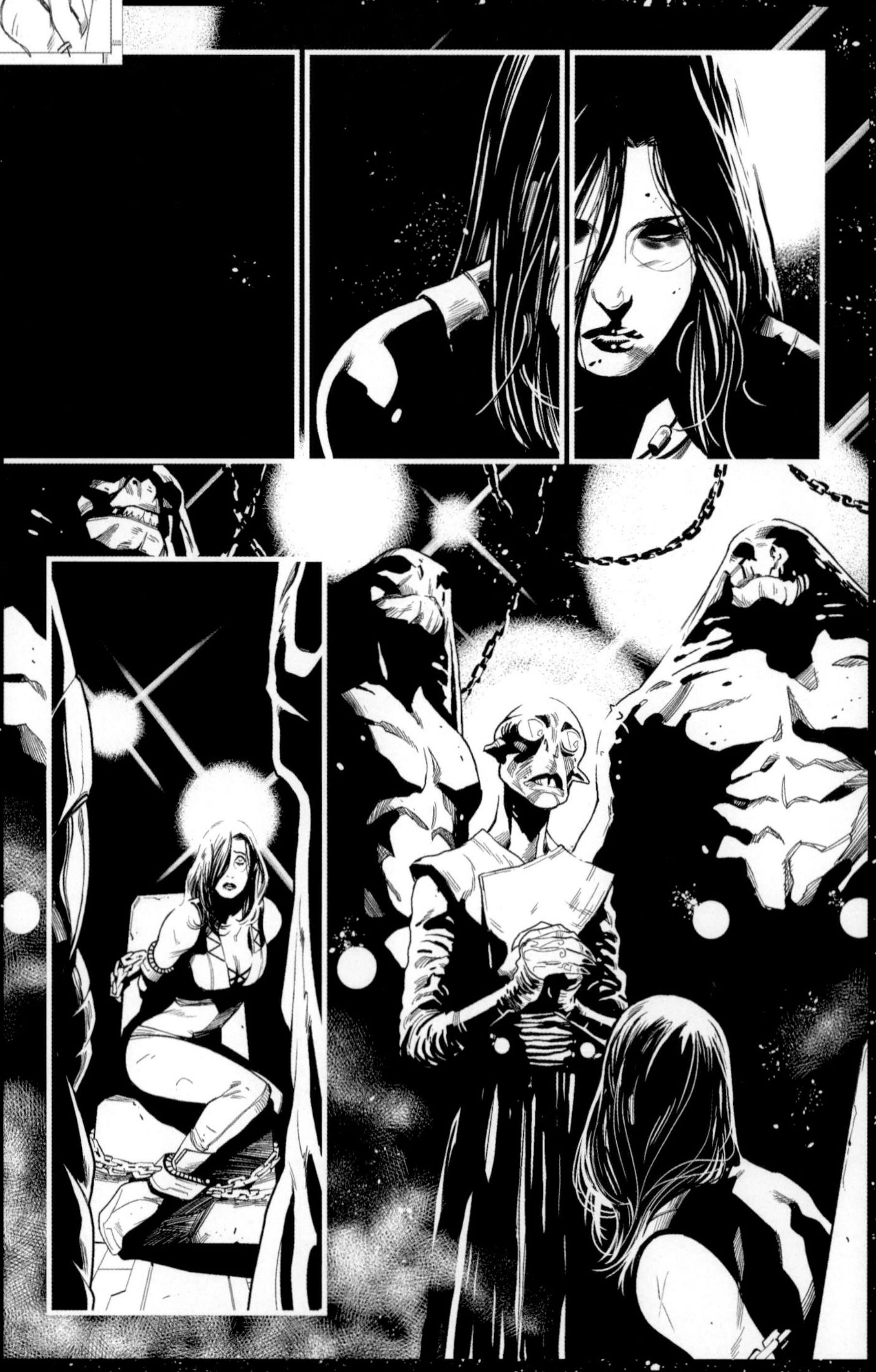

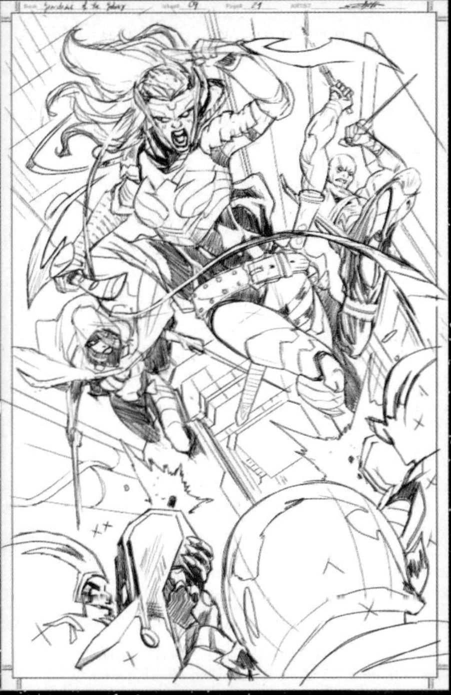

#9, PAGE 20 ART PROCESS BY
VALERIO SCHITI

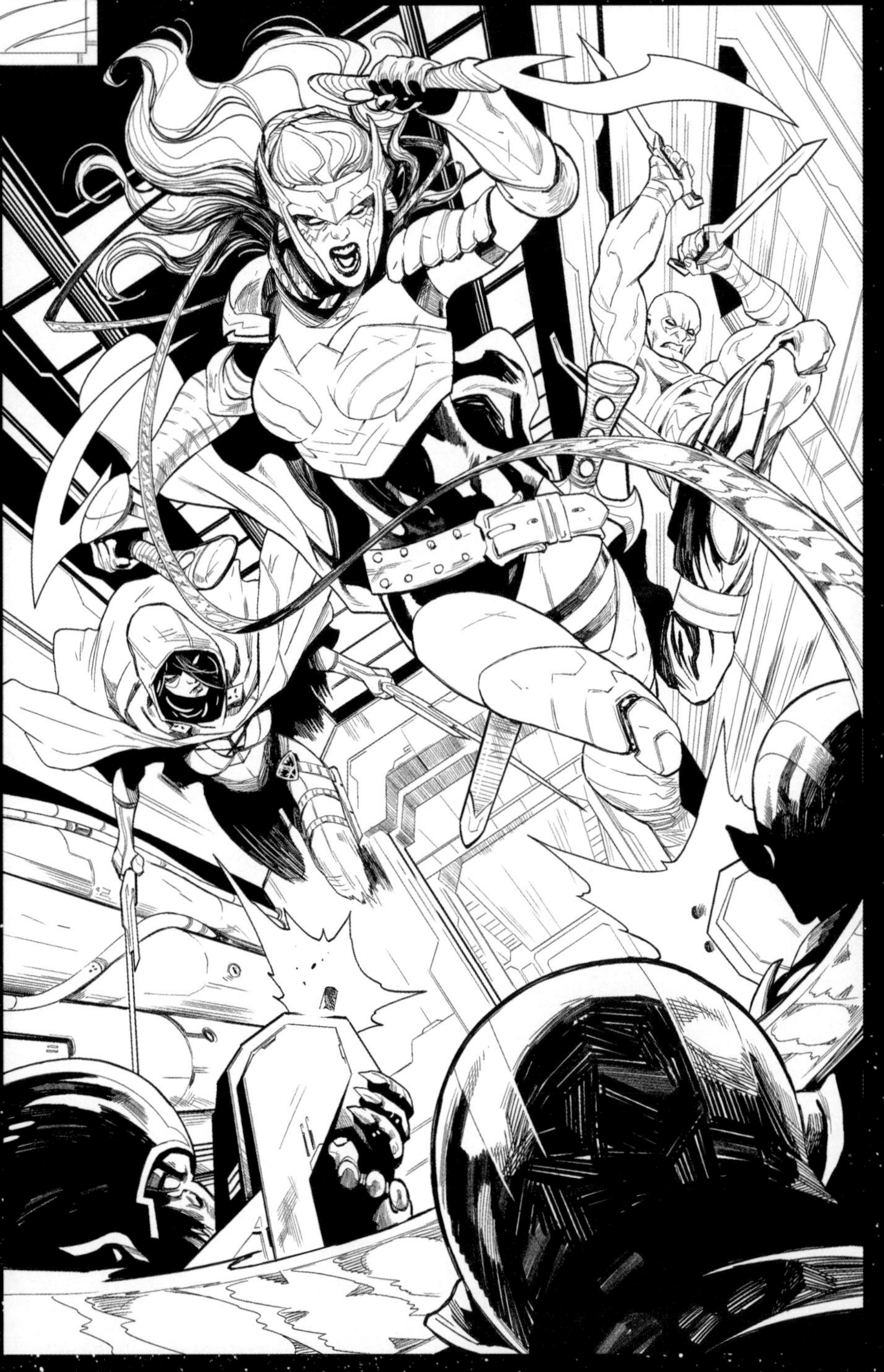

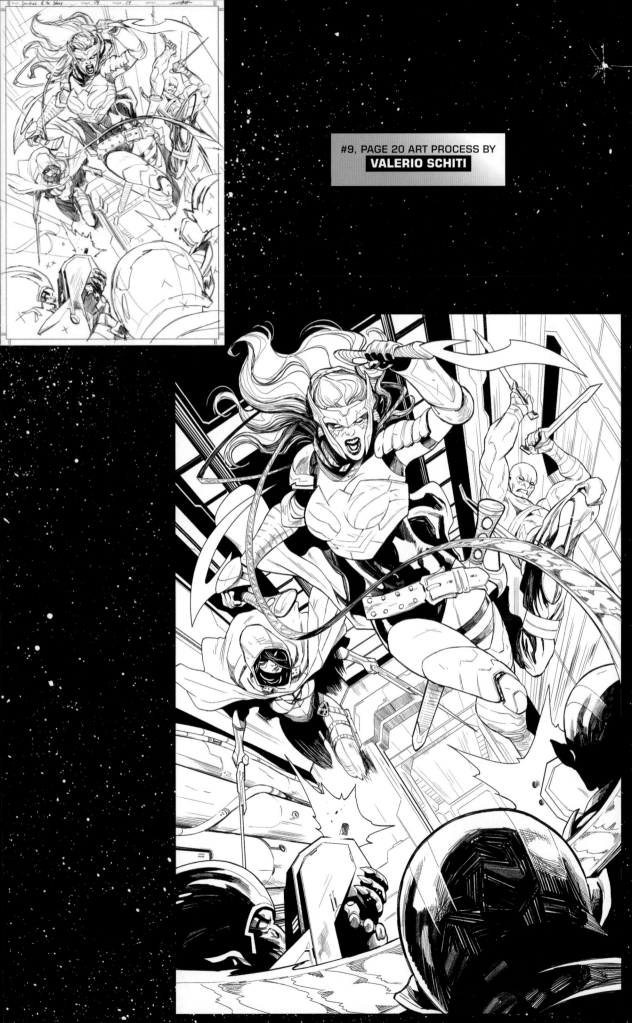

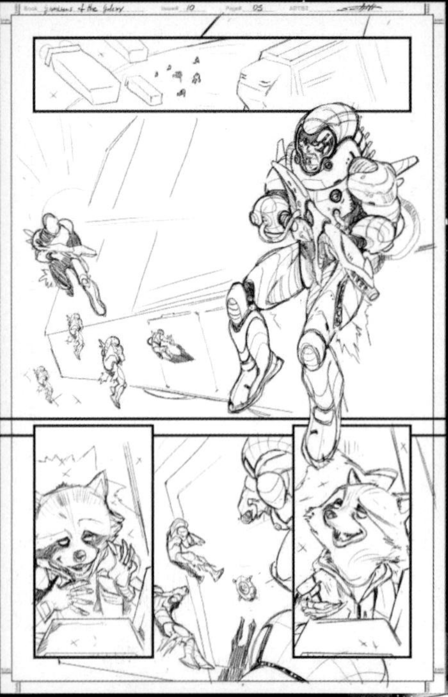

#10, PAGE 4 ART PROCESS BY
VALERIO SCHITI

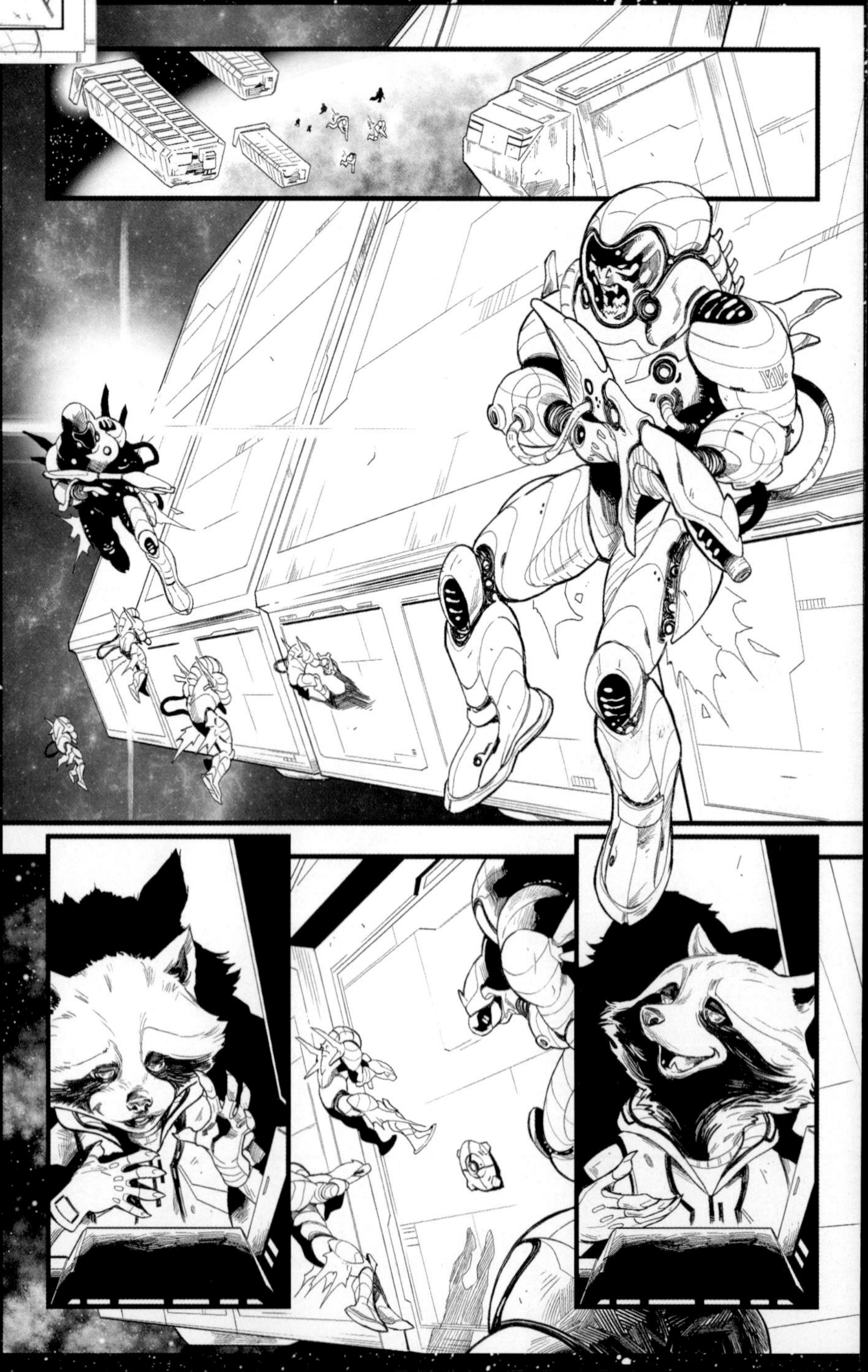

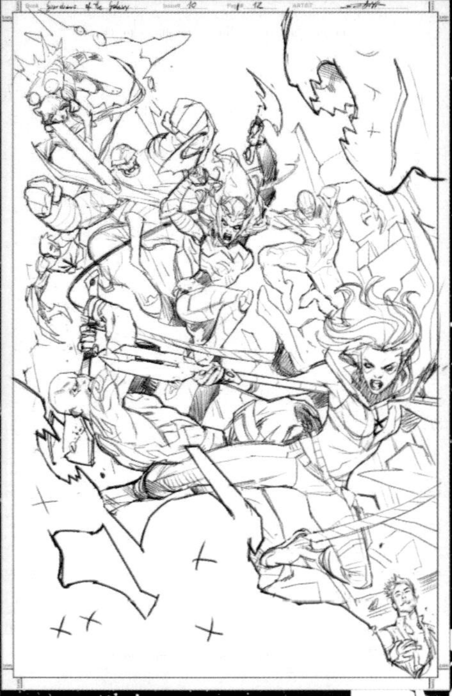

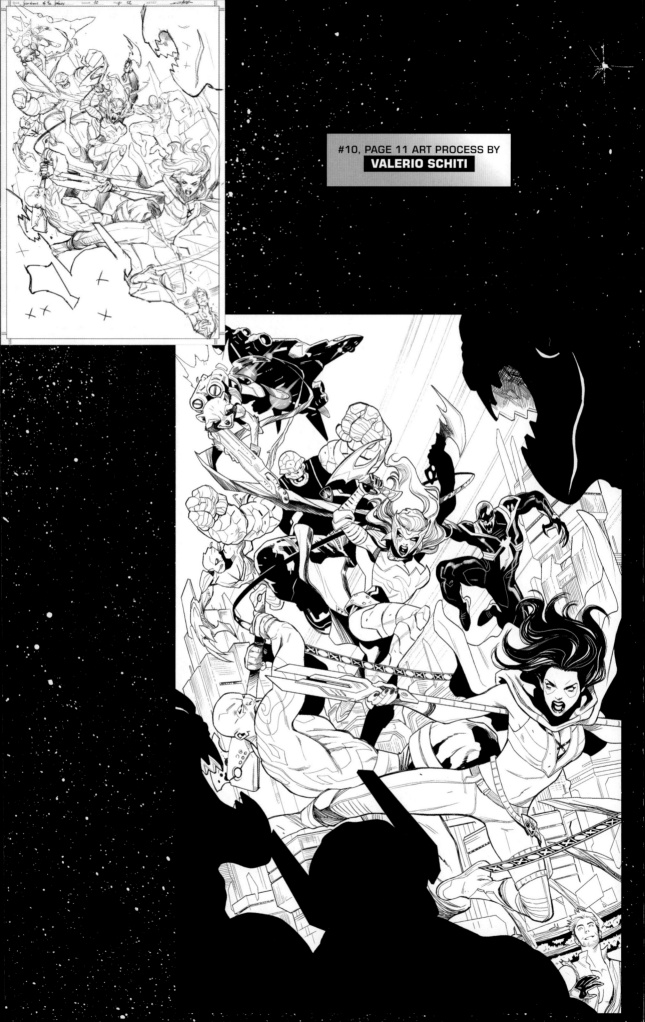

#10, PAGE 11 ART PROCESS BY

VALERIO SCHITI

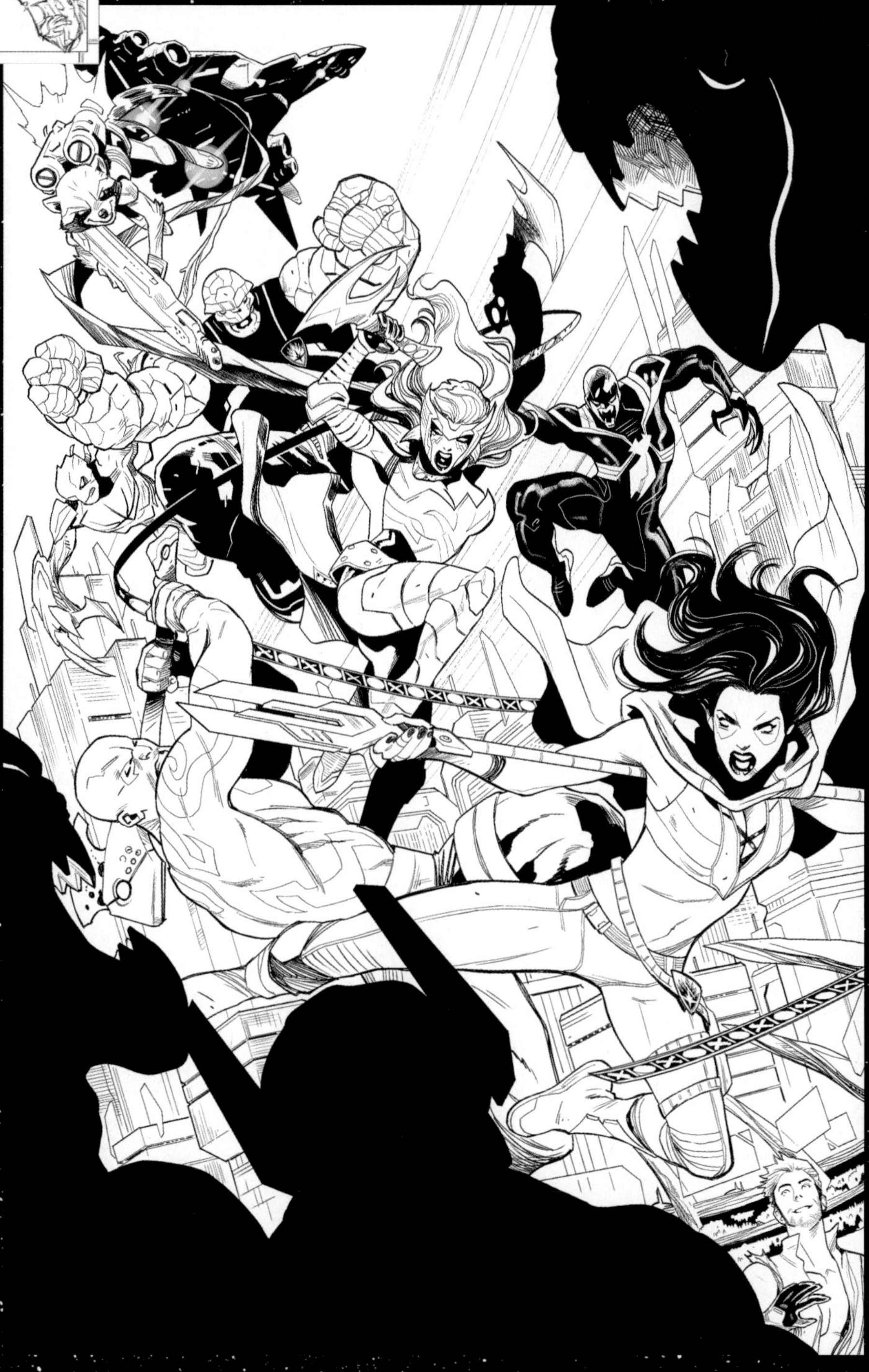

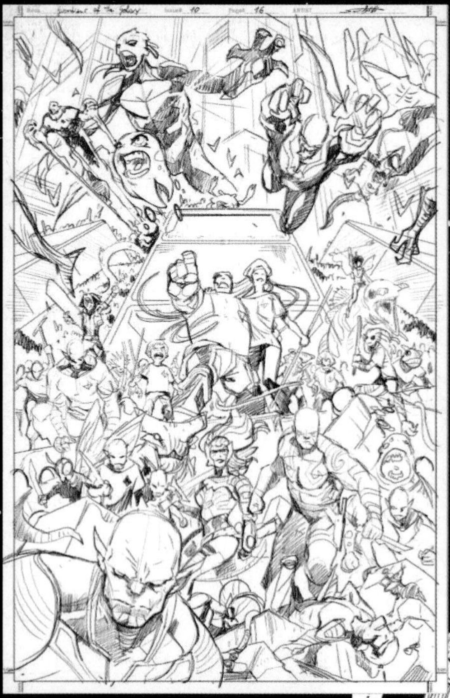

#10, PAGE 15 ART PROCESS BY
VALERIO SCHITI

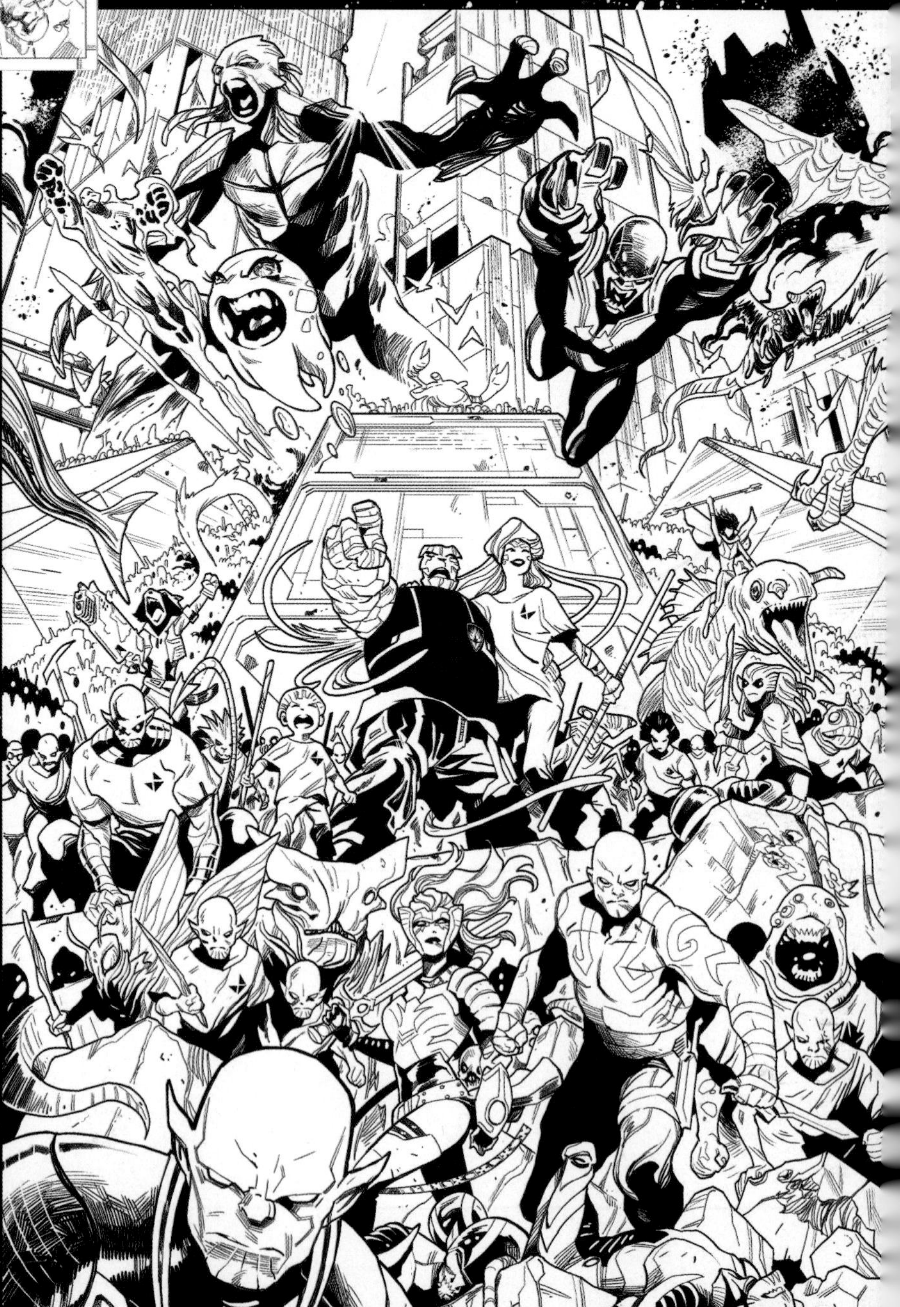

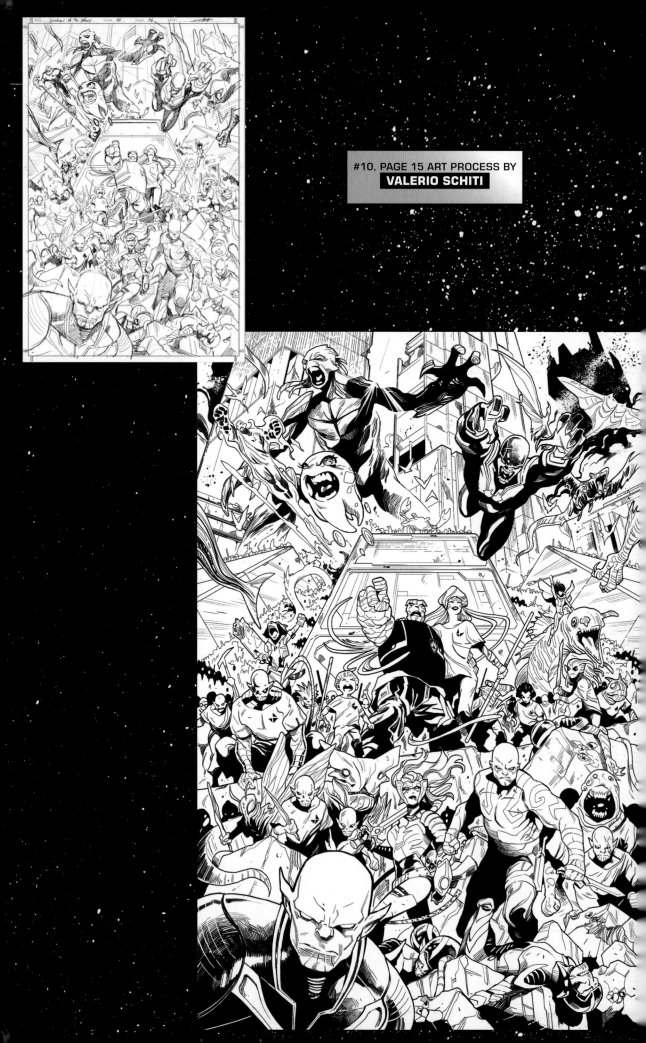

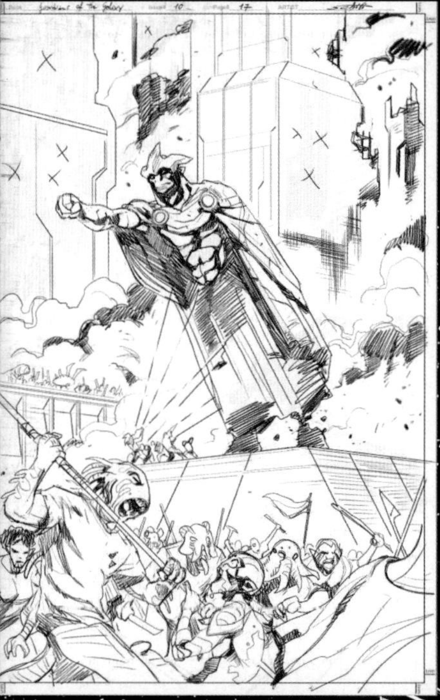

#10, PAGE 16 ART PROCESS BY
VALERIO SCHITI

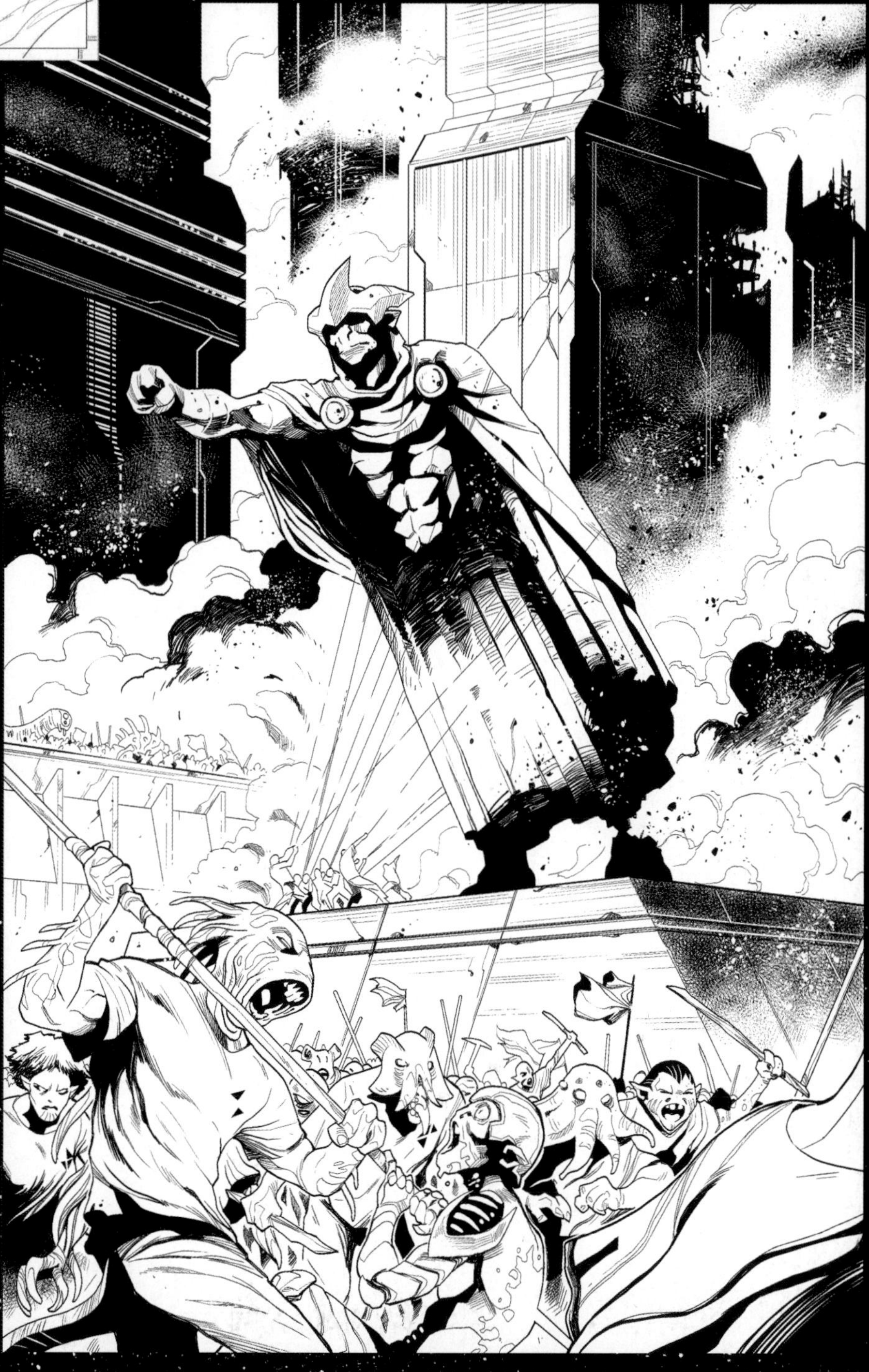

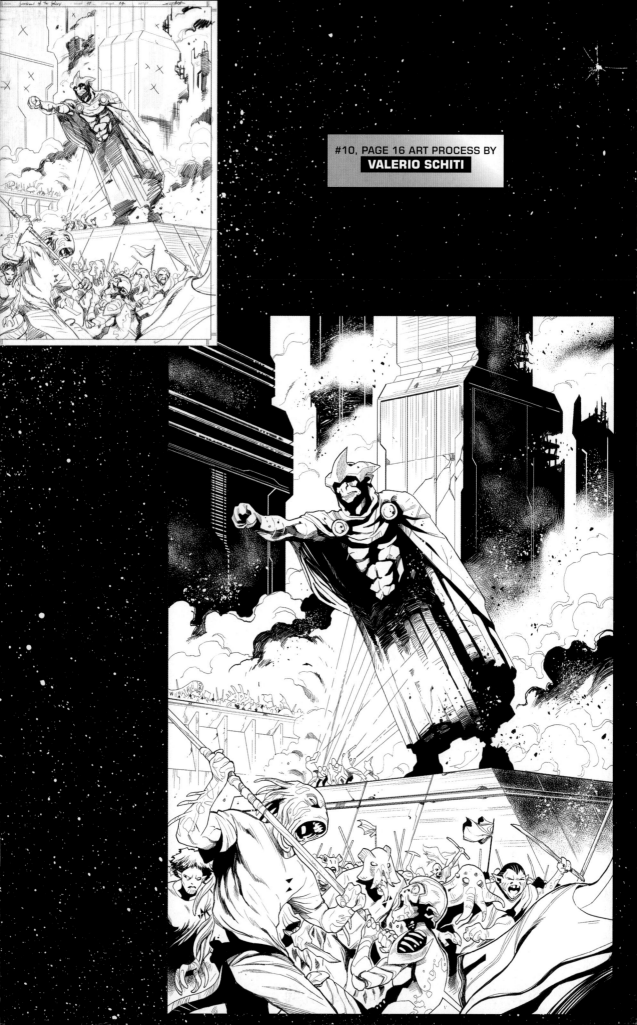

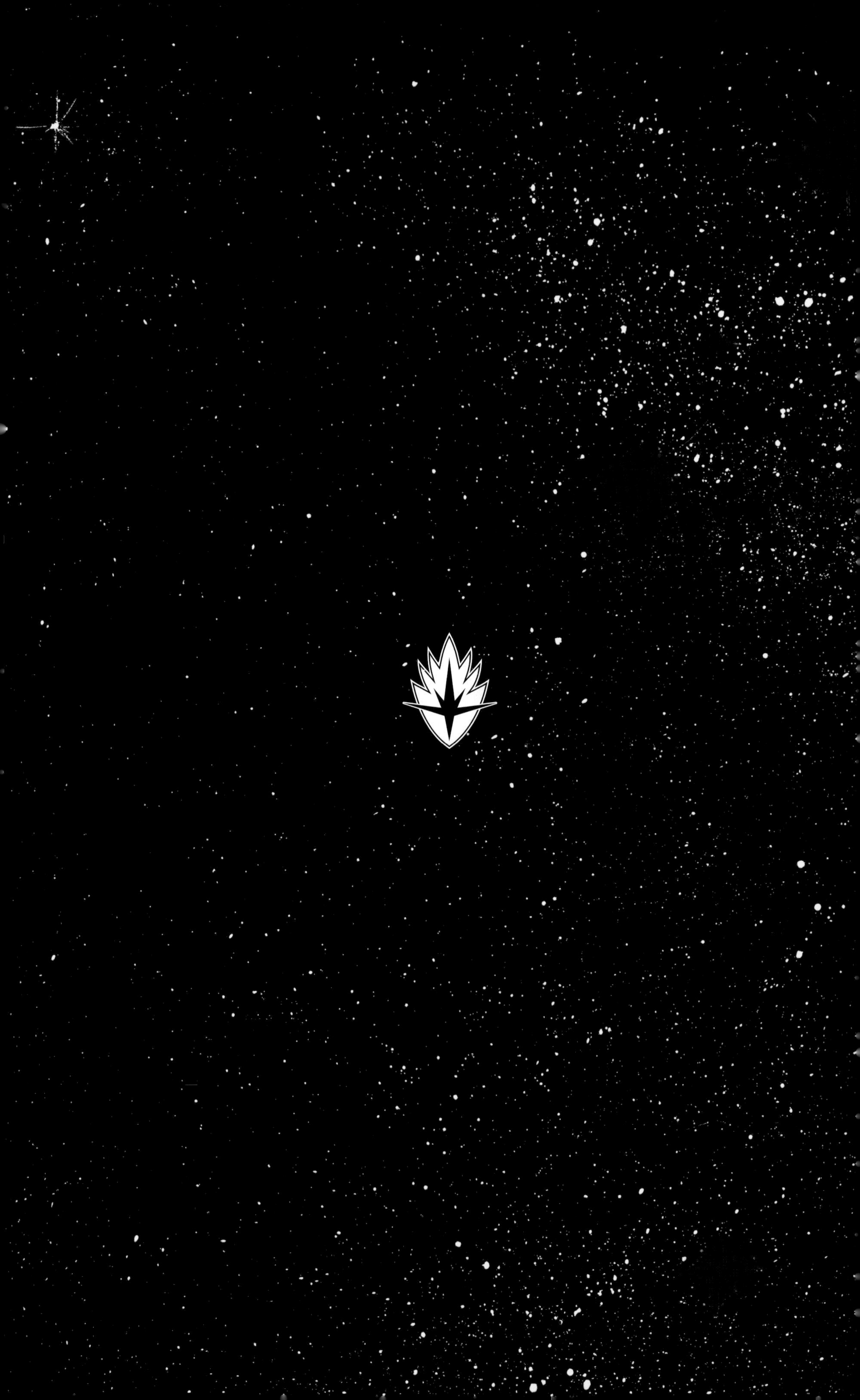